W9-CBQ-418

Encyclopedia of
Children and Childhood
In History and Society

Editorial Board

Encyclopedia of
Children and Childhood
In History and Society

Paula S. Fass, Editor in Chief

Volume 3
S-Z
Primary Sources • Index

THOMSON

★ ™

GALE

Encyclopedia of Children and Childhood: In History and Society
Paula S. Fass, Editor in Chief

For permission to use material from this
product, submit your request via Web at
http://www.gale-edit.com/permissions, or you
may download our Permissions Request form
and submit your request by fax or mail to:

Permissions Department
The Gale Group, Inc.
27500 Drake Road
Farmington Hills, MI 48331-3535
Permissions Hotline:
248-699-8006 or 800-877-4253, ext. 8006
Fax: 248-699-8074 or 800-762-4058

While every effort has been made to
ensure the reliability of the information presented in this publication, The Gale Group,
Inc. does not guarantee the accuracy of the
data contained herein. The Gale Group, Inc.
accepts no payment for listing; and inclusion
in the publication of any organization,
agency, institution, publication, service, or
individual does not imply endorsement of the
editors or publisher.

Errors brought to the attention of the
publisher and verified to the satisfaction of
the publisher will be corrected in future editions.

LIBRARY OF CONGRESS CATALOGING-IN-PUBLICATION DATA

Encyclopedia of children and childhood : in history and society / edited
by Paula S. Fass.
    p. cm.
    Includes bibliographical references and index.
    ISBN 0-02-865714-4 (set hardcover : alk. paper) — ISBN 0-02-865715-2
    (Volume 1) — ISBN 0-02-865716-0 (Volume 2) — ISBN 0-02-865717-9
    (Volume 3)
    1. Children—Encyclopedias. I. Fass, Paula S.

HQ767.84.E53 2003
305.23'03—dc21   2003006666

This title is also available as an e-book.
ISBN 0-02-865915-5

Contact your Gale sales representative for ordering information.

Printed in the United States of America
10 9 8 7 6 5 4 3

S

Salzmann, Christian Gotthilf (1744–1811)

Christian Gotthilf Salzmann, a German theologian, education reformer, and writer, was born in Sömmerda, Germany, in 1744, and died in Schnepfenthal, Germany, in 1811. Salzmann began his pedagogical literary activity while he was still a vicar, but in 1780 went to Dessau to become employed by JOHANN B. BASEDOW in his famous school, the Philanthropinum, and helped develop the school's pedagogy (known as *philanthropinism*). Philanthropinism was characterized by an ideal of a loving relationship of trust between children and adults and by the idea that the education should take place joyfully and playfully, complying with the course of nature in the education of the child (influenced by JEAN-JACQUES ROUSSEAU) and its followers were known as Philanthropinists. In 1784, Salzmann resigned from the Philanthropinum to start his own boarding school in Schnepfenthal. He believed that the school should take the form of a family, and the educator should first and foremost set a good example for his students. Salzmann put much weight on the unfolding of the powers of observation and the abilities of the children to use their intellect as well as the development of their morality. For him it was a fundamental educational principle to start with what was closest to the child, and thus move from the visible to the nonvisible, from things near to things farther away, and from the concrete to the abstract. Finally, PHYSICAL EDUCATION was seen as very important, and Salzmann upheld a focus on health, GYMNASTICS, and manual work (woodwork, gardening, etc.) in his teaching.

Together with Basedow, J. H. Campe, and Fr. E. von Rochow, Salzmann was one of the most important thinkers among the Philanthropinists, and his significance to the pedagogical debate of his day and to the pedagogical practice went far beyond the German-speaking countries. His influence was partly due to his writings, and partly due to his school in Schnepfenthal, which was visited by many teachers and tutors who studied his pedagogy. He also strongly influenced the well-known physical education reformer at Schnepfenthal, JOHANN GUTSMUTHS.

Salzmann's many works in the educational field can be divided into at least two groups: education manuals and pedagogical novels. In his education manuals, Salzmann speaks ironically of the common mistakes in the education of the time which only implants bad qualities in the children, gives instructions on how to provide what he considered a suitable education, and points out the necessity of educating the educator. In his pedagogical novels, Salzmann's pedagogical ideals are couched in lively stories about the way of life and condition of life in the different classes of the old social order. Thus, the novel *Carl von Carlsberg* mainly portrays the conditions of life among the aristocracy and the bourgeoisie, while books like *Conrad Kiefer* describe the sensible or rational education of peasant children. Finally, Salzmann was deeply concerned about the dangers of MASTURBATION which he saw as one of the great diseases of civilization leading to physical as well as MENTAL ILLNESSES.

See also: **Education, Europe.**

SIGNE MELLEMGAARD

Same-Sex Parenting

For as long as people have understood themselves as gay, gay people have parented their children. In the past, however, homosexual parents often shielded themselves and their children from scrutiny by publicly concealing their sexual orientation. By the end of the twentieth century, an estimated six to ten million gay and lesbian parents in the United States were raising six to fourteen million children, often in openly recognized gay families. Most of these children were born to heterosexually married parents, one or both of whom later came out as gay or lesbian. Some were born to single gay men or lesbians. An increasing number, however, were born to same-sex couples living together in long-term partnerships. The sharp rise in same-sex couples having children in the late twentieth century was celebrated as a "gayby boom," yet these couples faced many challenges to creating and protecting their families.

By 1995, studies of children raised in same-sex families were fueled by growing interest in parenting by gays and lesbians, increasing attention to the phenomenon of same-sex parenting in the culture at large, and a burst of custody cases involving gay and lesbian parents. Until the late 1990s, most psychological and sociological research of these children aimed to counteract assumptions made by courts about the unfitness of gay parents. The studies concluded that children raised by gays or lesbians do just as well in school and are as psychologically well-adjusted as children raised in comparable heterosexual families. One study by Charlotte Patterson (1994), however, departed from this trend by identifying two major differences: greater symptoms of stress and a greater sense of well-being among the four- to nine-year-old children of lesbian mothers. Patterson concludes, then, that although children raised from birth by lesbians showed signs of anxiety about their difference from their peers, the substantial support that they received at home buttressed them from outside criticism and shored up their self-esteem more generally. Researchers have noted that data on children raised by gay fathers is especially sparse. Scholars have encouraged, but rarely completed, studies that do more than dispel myths about risks to children and that explore the diversity of gay families themselves.

For many years, social and legal stigma bred shame and fear among same-sex parents and their sons and daughters. Before the rise of the American Gay Liberation Movement in 1969, only six child custody cases involving a gay or lesbian parent dared to challenge the universal assumption that only heterosexuals were fit to raise children. As sociologist Judith Stacey points out, however, the courts' denial of parental rights to these pioneers made their cause visible. In the midst of the vigorously anti-family ideology of the early gay liberation, feminist, and lesbian-feminist movements in the United States, gay and lesbian parents initiated over fifty custody suits in the 1970s. Joined by a growing number of "out" lesbians conceiving outside of marriage, previously married gay and lesbian parents, in the words of Judith Stacey, "level[ed] a public challenge against the reigning cultural presumption that the two terms—gay and parent—are antithetical" (p. 110).

Unfortunately, parents seeking custody of their children were often unsuccessful. In 1995, for example, the Virginia Supreme Court ruled that Sharon Bottoms was an unfit parent because she came out as a lesbian after having a child; as a result, she lost custody of her five-year-old son, Tyler. In 1996, the state appeals court of Florida ruled that John

Ward, a convicted murderer, was a more fit parent than his lesbian ex-wife, Mary. By the early twenty-first century, U.S. courts in most states adopted a "nexus approach" to evaluating parental fitness, requiring that the party suing for custody demonstrate a link between the gay parent's sexual orientation and harm to the child rather than assuming it outright. Nevertheless, child custody and visitation cases involve a great deal of judicial discretion and vary considerably from state to state.

Despite the obstacles, increasing numbers of same-sex couples began bringing children into their lives. Thousands of lesbian women, including several celebrities, around the country, especially in tolerant regions such as the San Francisco Bay Area, have conceived children through donor insemination (DI). Performed at home or by medical professionals, DI is the most common way that lesbian women choose to become mothers. Many women use anonymous sperm from sperm banks (though many doctors and banks still discriminate against unmarried women) for its convenience and/or in order to decrease the chance that the donor will assert himself as the father of his offspring. Other single lesbians and female couples choose to conceive using sperm from a "known donor," avoiding institutional discrimination and/or preferring the opportunity to foster a relationship of some kind between their children and the donor.

At the beginning of the twenty-first century, rising numbers of lesbians and (especially) gay men began pursuing other avenues through which to have children, including SURROGACY, foster parenting, and ADOPTION. Traditional surrogacy, when a woman agrees to bear a child for another person using the father's sperm and her own or a donated egg, allows one member of a gay male couple to form a biological relationship with the resulting child. Similarly, gestational surrogacy, when one woman carries a child conceived using her female partner's egg and donor sperm, links both partners of a female couple to the biology of their son or daughter. In tolerant areas, alternatively, many gays and lesbians create families through foster parenting. Though Florida and New Hampshire prohibited gays and lesbians from adopting children (including their foster children), international adoption became especially common in the 1990s. In addition to "stranger adoption," same-sex parents rely heavily on "second-parent" or "step-parent" adoption, when one member of a couple shares the legal parentage of his or her partner's biological child with the existing legal parent. According to Lambda Legal Defense, as of 1997, courts in twenty-one states had approved second-parent adoptions by same-sex couples. Without access to this process, non-biological parents have no legal right to custody of their children.

Gay and lesbian parental rights in Europe vary by country but usually by 2003 fell short of those afforded in the United States. Only the Netherlands provided same-sex couples all of the protections afforded by civil marriage, including adoption and custody rights. Although Denmark, Norway, Greenland, Sweden, and Iceland created a new marital status for gay and lesbian people in the 1980s and 1990s, Lambda Legal Defense explains that these "registered partnerships" generally do not allow their beneficiaries to adopt either nonrelated or even each other's children. In the early 2000s, other European countries afforded neither marital nor parental rights to their gay and lesbian citizens.

Since the 1980s, gay, lesbian, and bisexual people have created dozens of local and national organizations to support and advocate for same-sex parents and their children. For example, The Sperm Bank of California, founded in 1982 as the nation's only nonprofit sperm bank in order to serve lesbian and bisexual women, reported in 2001 that over one thousand children had been born through their services. California is also home to Maia Midwifery, established in 1994 to facilitate the creation of lesbian families. Other organizations, such as COLAGE (Children of Lesbians and Gays Everywhere), focus on the children of same-sex parents. The National Center for Lesbian Rights has defended lesbian parental rights in court and has educated women about protecting their families from legal assault. Reflecting the emphasis on gay families within the lesbian, gay, bisexual, and transgender civil rights movement, national organizations such as the Equal Rights Campaign added gay-parenting rights to their agendas.

In addition to resources available through organizations, popular books about conception, pregnancy, and child rearing for gay male and (especially) lesbian parents multiplied in the 1990s and early 2000s. On top of practical and legal advice, this literature offers humor, personal reflection, and opinions about topics such as gender-conscious parenting, the role of nonbiological parents, and family formation by transgender people.

See also: **Divorce and Custody; Homosexuality and Sexual Orientation; Parenting.**

BIBLIOGRAPHY

Patterson, Charlotte. 1994. "Children of the Lesbian Baby Boom: Behavioral Adjustment, Self-concepts, and Sex-role Identity." In *Contemporary Perspectives of Gay and Lesbian Psychology: Theory, Research, and Applications,* ed. B. Greene and G. Herek. Beverly Hills, CA: Sage.

Patterson, Charlotte. 1995. "Lesbian Mothers, Gay Fathers and their Children." In *Lesbian, Gay and Bisexual Identities Across the Lifespan: Psychological Perspectives,* ed. A.R. D'Augelli and C. Patterson. New York: Oxford University Press.

Stacey, Judith. 1996. *In the Name of the Family: Rethinking Family Values in the Postmodern Age.* Boston: Beacon Press.

INTERNET RESOURCES

Family Pride Coalition. Available from <www.familypride.org>.

Lambda Legal Defense. 1997. "Lesbian and Gay Parenting: A Fact Sheet." Available from <www.lambdalegal.org>.

National Center for Lesbian Rights. 2003. "NCLR Projects: Family Law." Available at <www.nclrights.org/projects/familylaw.htm>.

AMANDA H. LITTAUER

Sandbox

The precise genesis of sand PLAY and the original rationale for it are not known, but it is a quite natural evolution from the kinds of informal play with earth that children all over the world seem to engage in during early childhood. Sand was a cheap and hygienic solution to early educational theorists' suggestions of the value of free play with materials. The earliest references to children's sand play appear in accounts of playgrounds in mid-nineteenth-century Germany. The educational ideas in this part of the world were greatly influenced by the writings of FRIEDRICH FROEBEL, who introduced the concept of the KINDERGARTEN, or children's garden. His writing stresses the importance of free play and children's contact with nature, and in his plan of a model kindergarten he encouraged the design of a garden. This offered opportunities for children to contact natural materials, including perhaps sand, but he did not specifically include a sand area in his design. The first known use of sand for play provision is the heaps of sand called *sand bergs* piled in the public parks of Berlin in 1850. The kindergarten movement in Germany went on to include sandboxes in their design in the latter half of the century, and in 1889 an issue of the newspaper of the Pestalozzi/Froebel children's houses described how to build a sandbox.

The idea was brought to the United States in 1885 after the physician Marie Elizabeth Zakrzewska saw a sand berg in a Berlin public park. The first "sand gardens," very large sandboxes, were built in Boston. In his 1922 book on the growth of the national playground movement, the sand garden is described by the sociologist Lee Rainwater as the first stage of public playground design. The idea caught on quickly in the United States, and by 1889 there were twenty-one of them in Boston and one in New York City. They were created mostly in poor neighborhoods, often alongside settlement houses for servicing the children of immigrants, and were managed by women. One was built in 1892 in Chicago at the famous community settlement house called Hull-House. The idea of public sand play places grew rapidly in Europe and the United States in the early part of the twentieth century and later spread to the other industrialized countries.

In 1887 G. STANLEY HALL, the pioneer of CHILD STUDY in the United States, wrote *The Story of a Sand-Pile,* wherein he dwelled upon its great values for learning through symbolic and social play. He observed that boys in particular were active in this play and continued to be so until about fifteen years of age. While children today rarely play with this medium after the early childhood years, it does seem to offer opportunities for a wider age range of children than any other material except water, with which it is generally coupled. Authors of early childhood education subsequently wrote consistently about the developmental benefits of sand play, and sandboxes became basic to the design of kindergartens. But sand play provision declined in public spaces in the later twentieth century due to growing concerns over its supposed toxicity due to animal feces and a decreased willingness of municipal agencies to carry out the necessary occasional maintenance.

From the earliest photographs of sandboxes in the United States and Europe we can see that they had wheelbarrows, rakes, buckets and spades, and molds of animal and other shapes. Today implements are usually limited to smaller tools, and these are made of plastic rather than metal.

See also: **Playground Movement; Theories of Play.**

BIBLIOGRAPHY

Frost, J. L. 1989. "Play Environments for Young Children in the USA: 1800–1990." *Children's Environments* 6, no. 4. Also available from <http://cye.colorado.edu>.

Hall, G. Stanley. 1887. *The Story of a Sand-Pile.* New York and Chicago: E. L. Kellogg.

Rainwater, Lee. 1922. *The Playground Movement.*

ROGER A. HART

SAT and College Entrance Exams

The founding of the College Entrance Examination Board (later renamed the College Board) in 1900 culminated two decades of attempts to standardize the college admissions process. CEEB encouraged colleges to accept additional HIGH SCHOOL subjects, and replaced idiosyncratic entrance requirements and exams with uniform ones. But contemporary critics noted these tests measured subject mastery, and did not predict college performance—a need at colleges seeking to limit enrollments after World War I.

In contrast, the psychological or intelligence tests, designed by E. L. Thorndike of Columbia University, and administered to the armed forces during World War I, seemed to predict success in college. After the war, several colleges added these exams to their admissions requirements. The predictive power of intelligence tests, claimed advocates, permitted burgeoning high schools greater curricular latitude to address the needs of the majority of students who would not attend college. Admissions officers at colleges wishing to favor students from "old stock" nationality and ethnic groups seized upon the association between intelligence test scores on one hand and race and ethnicity on the other posited by Princeton's Carl Campbell Brigham in *A Study of American Intelligence* (1923). But Brigham, who be-

came the key designer of the Scholastic Aptitude Test, disavowed this association after CEEB began to offer this psychological exam in 1926. Meritocrats later embraced the SAT as likely to unearth "diamonds in the rough." Initially dominated by verbal questions, the SAT separated math and verbal scores into two separate exams in 1931—the first of several format changes.

Neither CEEB's first subject-based entrance exams nor the SAT took the academic world by storm. Most colleges continued to base admissions decisions on high school transcripts and the principal's recommendation until after World War II. The number of students taking the SAT remained under 10,000 through the 1930s; the proportion of colleges requiring the SAT or equivalent exams for admission increased from less than one percent to 15 percent between 1932 and 1944. CEEB began to offer a Junior (later Preliminary) SAT during the 1930s; it dropped its traditional essay entrance exams in 1942.

The SAT competed with objective achievement examinations administered by the Cooperative Test Service of the American Council on Education, and with exams offered by the Carnegie Foundation for the Advancement of Teaching. In 1947, CEEB, ACE, and the Carnegie Foundation turned all exam-related activities over to the newly founded Educational Testing Service, which offered the SAT and the achievement exams (later called the SAT II, and administered in 23 subject areas by 2003). In 1955, CEEB also assumed responsibility for Advanced Placement exams—developed by the Fund for the Advancement of Education, a Ford Foundation affiliate—that assessed mastery of college-level work completed in high school.

CEEB and ETS had a clear field until 1959, when E. F. Lindquist and Ted McCarrel, both of the University of Iowa, founded the American College Testing Services (later ACT, Inc.). The ACT Assessment—often seen as more aligned with the high school curriculum—examined student knowledge in English, math, reading, and science reasoning. This exam proved especially popular where College Board influence was weak.

Expanded demand for college among the large baby boomer cohort, and a corresponding increase in selectivity at many colleges contributed to the rapid growth of the SAT and ACT, beginning in the 1960s. The University of California adopted the SAT in 1968, thereby nationalizing the exam. In the 2000–2001 school year, 1.3 million high school seniors took the SAT (now SAT I). About one million students took the ACT exam during the 2000–2001 school year, as the test remained popular in the Midwest.

By the 1970s, the SAT and ACT tests often were *the* decisive admissions criteria, despite sponsor insistence that colleges consider multiple factors. The SAT raised several controversial issues for selective colleges. Was the modest predictivity the SAT added to the significant correlation between high school and freshman college grades worth the trouble of preparing for and taking the test? Could the many high schools devoting significant time to SAT preparation make better use of this time? What explained the decline in SAT scores between the 1960s and 1980s? The increased popularity of the SAT, a College Board commission noted in *On Further Examination* (1977), explained some, but not all, of the decline. Could coaching improve SAT scores? The College Board claimed it could not, but a thriving coaching industry disagreed. Was the SAT *biased* against certain racial and cultural groups? Group scores for African Americans, Hispanics, and Native Americans were consistently lower than the scores of whites and Asian Americans. What, precisely, did the SAT measure—intelligence, achievement, or merely membership in the white middle class? Criticism that aptitude remained a synonym for intelligence led the College Board to rename the exam twice in the 1990s: first to Scholastic Assessment Test, then to SAT. The College Board recentered SAT scores in 1995 to account for demographic changes occurring after prior norms were established.

In 2001, University of California president Richard C. Atkinson charged that the SAT I contributed less than the SAT II to predicting freshman grades at his university, adding that any entrance exam should help strengthen the high school curriculum. The College Board satisfied its largest customer by promising a revamped examination in 2005 that replaced the analogy section—antonyms had been eliminated already—with additional critical reading passages. The new SAT would also include a twenty-five-minute essay question. The math section would eliminate quantitative comparisons, and add questions based on Algebra II courses.

The intense debate over the SAT continues. A predictive exam, argue the SAT's supporters, allows talented students to overcome curricular and financial disparities between high schools, while compensating for grade inflation. Critics note the correlation between SAT scores and socioeconomic status, and the stress experienced in preparing for and taking the exam. The 2005 reforms, in any event, moved the SAT I towards assessing subject mastery—the goal CEEB was originally established to address.

See also: **Intelligence Testing; IQ.**

BIBLIOGRAPHY

Brigham, Carl Campbell. 1923. *A Study of American Intelligence.* Princeton, NJ: Princeton University Press.

College Entrance Examination Board. 1977. *On Further Examination: Report of the Advisory Panel on the Scholastic Aptitude Test Score Decline.* Princeton, NJ: College Entrance Examination Board.

Fuess, Claude M. 1950. *The College Board: Its First Fifty Years.* New York: Columbia University Press.

Johanek, Michael C., ed. 2001. *A Faithful Mirror: Reflections on the College Board and Education in America.* New York: The College Board.

Lehmann, Nicholas. 1999. *The Big Test: The Secret History of the American Meritocracy.* New York: Farrar, Straus and Giroux.

Valentine, John A. 1987. *The College Board and the School Curriculum.* New York: College Entrance Examination Board.

Wechsler, Harold S. 1977. *The Qualified Student: A History of Selective College Admission in America, 1870–1970.* New York: Wiley-Interscience.

HAROLD S. WECHSLER

School Buildings and Architecture

EUROPE
Anne-Marie Châtelet

UNITED STATES
Marta Gutman

EUROPE

Public schools in Europe notably increased in the nineteenth century. The establishment of democracy and the right to vote demanded that every citizen know how to read and write. Most of European states therefore devoted a large part of their effort to educating boys, and later girls. This went hand in hand with the secularization of education, with lay teachers replacing religious, placing church and school in a conflict that has left visible traces in some villages, where structures of each type face each other.

The construction of school buildings began mainly in the second half of the nineteenth century, once the educational system was in place and governments could ensure their financing. Until then classes took place in a rectory or in a teacher's home. Discussions about school architecture began early, triggered by the new English educational method known as *mutual education*. Designed to handle the large number of children in growing industrial towns, the method trained more advanced students to become tutors, allowing a single teacher to educate hundreds of children. Mutual education required specific arrangements and furnishings that Joseph Lancaster, one of the promoters of this method, described in his pioneering work *Hints and Directions for Building, Fitting Up, and Arranging School Rooms* (1809). He launched a debate, which quickly spread to France, about the layout of a classroom based on the number of students and arrangement of furniture. Experiences in each country were showcased at the World Fairs which, starting with London's in 1862, devoted an area to the material aspects of teaching. Issues of HYGIENE were prominent, especially in regard to lighting, heating, and classroom furnishing.

Two types of structure were completed. Rural schools, with only one or two classrooms, showed modest and economic architecture, while urban schools, often vast and majestic, were criticized for being "school palaces." The urban schools were typically two or three floors high. Long central hallways featured high ceilinged classrooms on either side, making for buildings with depths greater than twenty meters. These dimensions, along with the jobs to be performed in the schools and the rules of hygiene to be enforced, were all defined by municipal or state laws that were ratified between 1860 and 1880, depending on the country. The schools were an affirmation of both the democratic ideal and the strength of the new institution. The most famous schools were among the last to have been built, and reflect the emergence of Art Nouveau: am Elizabethplatz in Munich (1900–1901, architect Theodor Fischer), the school on the rue Rouelle in Paris (Louis Bonnier, 1908–1911), and Letten in Zurich (Adolf and Heinrich Bram, 1912–1915). The schools were the pride of their towns, which often subsidized them and entrusted their construction to municipal architects. Some of their architects, passionate about the subject, published panoramic surveys of European school building architecture, including Edward Robert Robson (1835–1917), Felix Narjoux (1867–1934), and the Austrian Karl Hintrager (1859–?).

The growing concern with tuberculosis triggered a first wave of criticism. International congresses on school hygiene, the first of which was held in Nuremberg in 1904, exposed the mediocre ventilation and sanitary installations in school buildings, as well as the lack of any medical surveillance. Doctors asked that light and air flow in, embracing the goals of the architects of the modern movement, who, in Le Corbusier's words, were calling for "a new spirit," a house "like a receptacle for light and sun." Windows were enlarged, sometimes to the point of becoming sliding doors, rooftops were converted into terraces for heliotherapy, and concerns about ventilation led to recommendations for diminished thickness of the buildings. The hallways were to have classrooms on only one side. The first pavilion school was built in 1907 in Staffordshire, England. Later, some architects even proposed single-floor buildings, so that every classroom could open to the outdoors, like the Friedrich-Ebert Schule by Ernst May in Frankfurt (1929–1930). This permitted open-air classes, the development of group activities, and the improvement of the students' sense of initiative and autonomy, as advocated by the New Education movement. The general evolution of regulations guaranteed a significant improvement in hygiene in these buildings. The architecture had multiple aspects, evidenced by the schools built by Willem Marinus Dudock in Hilversum, Holland between 1920 and 1931; Fritz Schumacher in Hamburg, Germany between 1909 and 1933; Bohuslav Fuchs in Brno, Czech Republic between 1924 and 1928.

World War II interrupted this evolution of which Alfred Roth, author of noted works on school architecture, published a synthesis in 1950. At the beginning of the fifties, the destruction caused by the war and the emergence of a baby boom led to new construction to meet growing needs. England perfected a system of light-steel school structures that

worked particularly well with single-home development plans, as evidenced by the many schools built in Hertfordshire. Jean Prouve developed similar structures in France (the collapsible school of Villejuif, 1957, for example) but no general system of prefabrication would ever be adopted for all schools. With the exception of some countries where buildings remained dense and elevated, as in France or in Spain, the individual home model dominated, particularly in Germany, Denmark, Holland, and Switzerland. It was interpreted in many different ways: terraced pavilions at the Munkegaard School at Gentoft, Denmark (Arne Jacobsen, 1954–1956), combined pavillions at the Asilo d'Ivrea, Italy (Mario Ridolfi and W. Frankl, 1955–1965), superimposed pavillions at the Riva San Vitale School in Switzerland (Aurelio Galfetti, Flora Ruchat, and Ivo Trumpy, 1962–1964). The desire to provide diverse activities to children and to encourage their autonomy transformed the school into a small village equipped with many communal spaces and rooms, for example Hans Sharoun's 1951 project for Darmstadt, completed at Marl, West Germany, in 1960. These schools were sometimes open to parents and often to the community. There are also cases, as in the small villages of the Grisons region in Switzerland, where the gymnasium is also a communal space, as in Mastrils, by Dieter Jungling and Andreas Hagmann (1991–1995). Monumental school buildings have disappeared practically everywhere, giving way to simplicity and openness. Today, schools are expected to be a living space for the students and a gathering place for the community.

See also: **Children's Spaces; Open Air School Movement.**

BIBLIOGRAPHY

Robson, E. R. 1972 [1874]. *School Architecture.* Leicester, UK: Leicester University Press.

Roth, A. 1957. *The New School.* Zurich, Switzerland: Gisberger.

ANNE-MARIE CHÂTELET

UNITED STATES

Since the beginning of the nineteenth century, children have been educated in a variety of architectural settings in the United States, ranging from church basements and the parlors of private homes to purpose-built school buildings. Historians have considered the design of schools and recognized the importance of spaces to children, teachers, and the state, yet a comprehensive critical history of school buildings in the United States remains to be written. From one-room schools to multistory complexes, educational settings have represented power, order, and democratic aspirations to children and their families; at the same time, resources for education have been distributed unevenly to students throughout the nation's history.

With church-run ACADEMIES in place and HOMESCHOOLING common after the American Revolution, it took several decades for nonsectarian public education to take hold in the new nation, despite the enthusiastic backing of Thomas Jefferson and the gift of land from the Congress to the states for the purpose. As the nation expanded after the turn of the nineteenth century, one-room, ungraded public schools dotted the landscape, usually sited on low-cost plots of land, known colloquially as "waste grounds," at the edges of growing communities. Most often one-room schools were plain, gabled boxes, built of wood, brick, or sod. Layouts recalled the designs of small churches, with rows of benches facing the teacher's desk, which sat on a raised platform. High windows, inserted on the sides of buildings, prevented children from looking outdoors. Although steeple-like clock towers graced the most ornate examples, poor construction, inadequate equipment, and rudimentary sanitary facilities in most schools contributed to calls for reform.

Elsewhere in the new nation, especially in rapidly growing cities along the eastern seaboard, the frugal bankers, businessmen, and politicians who made up public school committees invested in multiroom masonry and wood-frame school buildings during the first decades of the nineteenth century. They expected didactic settings to impart the values of discipline, economy, health, and citizenship to poor children in need of free (or charity) schooling. In the monitorial system of education, worked out by Joseph Lancaster in England, one teacher supervised hundreds of pupils in a large common hall, assisted by older children (the monitors for whom the schools were named). Introduced in New York City in 1806, the system soon structured spaces in schools large and small in the United States, but many students and their families disliked its rigid teaching methods. As interest in a graded system of instruction developed in this period, urban school districts hired ushers to assist master teachers; students recited lessons to these assistants in separate rooms attached to large lecture halls. Frequently, independent masters opened autonomous reading and writing schools inside the same grammar school building, with each school placed on a separate floor.

In the 1830s, when HORACE MANN issued a call for universal education for all American children, he joined Henry Barnard and other reformers to argue that new COMMON SCHOOLS ought to be the building blocks of a democracy. As these critics endorsed centralization and a standard, graded system of instruction, based on Prussian models, they urged taxpayers to replace deteriorating wood-frame buildings with sturdier construction. Architects proposed ideal designs, notably one-room school buildings in the form of octagons (Ithiel Town and Alexander Jackson Davis, 1842) and diamonds (Charles P. Dwyer, 1856), but these proposals were not widely used. In 1847, John D. Philbrick, an eminent New England teacher and school administrator, gave more practical physical substance to demands for improvement with a design for the new Quincy Grammar School in Boston, Massachusetts. The first three floors of the four-

story, centrally heated, masonry block structure held the classrooms (four per floor, opening onto a shared hallway), and a meeting hall filled the top floor. Each classroom of about eight hundred square feet contained a sink and a closet, and all pupils sat in desks that were bolted to the floor in straight lines. With fifty-five students in each room, the design suited drill-and-recite instruction, and school boards embraced the scheme, dubbed the "egg crate plan," due to the rigid pattern of desks, fixed in straight lines within each classroom.

Nonetheless, poverty and prejudice constrained the use of the schools as a tool for building a more democratic nation. Gender divided the space in schools, where boys and girls used separate entries and sat in rows segregated by sex; working-class families could not afford to send children to school; Irish Catholic immigrants resented Protestant influences on pedagogy; and African Americans encountered racial segregation in the North and exclusion in the South. Schools were also plagued by crowded rooms; poor ventilation, heating, lighting, and sanitation; rigid seats; and scarce play space.

As school districts consolidated after the Civil War, imposing, multistory buildings differentiated by student age group set the standard for new construction. In these buildings, later called "cells and bells" schools, students walked down central corridors capped with tall ceilings to reach self-contained, graded classrooms of about the same size as those in the Quincy School. The order in the space complemented the discipline in instruction in primary schools and the new public high schools, which rapidly replaced private academies across the urbanizing nation. Gilded Age architects who specialized in school design used pattern books to endorse eclectic exterior decoration, which turned buildings into emblems of state munificence and local pride as well as instruments of social control. Standardization became the rule of the day, endorsed by architects, state authorities, and schools of education alike. In cities, crenellated massing (the E- and H-shaped plans were typical) brought light and air into big buildings, even on crowded sites. The pattern also accommodated bulky specialized spaces such as the auditorium, library, and gymnasium that became common after 1900. Outside urban areas, one-room schools, many poorly equipped, remained common, with 200,000 such schools in use in 1920.

After the turn of the twentieth century, when state legislatures passed laws restricting CHILD LABOR and compelling education through eighth grade, public schools structured the encounter of most children with the public world. As the philosopher JOHN DEWEY made the case for child-centered education and businessmen demanded educated, skilled workers, social reformers pressed for modern buildings. Influenced by calls for health, hygiene, and orderly city planning, they convinced districts to build OPEN AIR SCHOOLS

(schools with outdoor classrooms and/or classrooms accessible to the open air), vacation schools (the term used in the Progressive Era to describe summer schools), JUNIOR HIGH SCHOOLS, and supervised playgrounds. Some new buildings, for example, the Hillside Home School in Spring Green, Wisconsin, a Progressive boarding school designed by Frank Lloyd Wright in 1901, and the addition to the Corona Avenue Public Elementary School in Los Angeles, California, designed by Richard Neutra in 1935, offered examples of the humanity possible in modern design. However, most new schools looked like factories, as architects (who were often public employees) reacted to building codes, national standards, and demands for efficient, economic solutions. The term *school plant* aptly describes the massive, masonry-clad, steel and concrete frame buildings erected in industrial cities and suburbs. In the South, philanthropists Julius Rosenwald and Pierre S. du Pont subsidized new public schools for AFRICAN-AMERICAN CHILDREN. Usually built of wood and domestic in scale, the schools accommodated programs put in place elsewhere during the Progressive Era: manual training and industrial education were required subjects in Rosenwald schools. Fresh air, natural light, coat closets, and moveable seats were found in the classrooms, and the larger schools contained community rooms, another feature typical of Progressive school architecture.

Prompted by the open-air movement which began in the early twentieth century, California architects experimented in the 1910s and 1920s with low-slung courtyard buildings, seeking to give students light, air, and access to open space from each classroom. In 1940, Lawrence Bradford Perkins and Philip Will, principals of Perkins and Will, together with Eliel and Eero Saarinen, took up the cause in the Crow Island Elementary School in Winnetka, Illinois. The one-story brick structure, divided into administrative and teaching wings, gave life to the concept of child-centered education and became an archetype for informal postwar school design. In 1960, when the same team designed another landmark, the University of Chicago Laboratory High School, they integrated new technologies, building materials, and the open plan into a sleek, urban block. After World War II, one- and two-story schools spread out across the suburbanizing American landscape, sited to encourage development and serve as social centers for new communities. Unfortunately, as the school-age population swelled, many districts elected to replace older structures with mediocre buildings, including sizeable, sprawling HIGH SCHOOLS, and used prefabricated assembly systems to reduce costs.

In the course of the twentieth century, the recognition that separate is inherently unequal opened school doors to African-American students and directly affected building design when the federal government instructed districts to give equal space to girls' athletics and accommodate children with disabilities. In addition, starting in the 1960s and continuing to the early twenty-first century, an interest in cooperative and self-directed learning prompted districts to replace lecture-style seating with tables and workstations, and the desire for smaller schools persuaded some to adopt what historian Jeffrey Lackney calls the *house plan*, which featured clusters of classrooms, offices, and resource spaces. Even so, limited budgets constrained architectural experimentation and building repair as the century drew to a close. Prefabricated classrooms set the standard for new construction in many suburban school yards; the physical decline of older school buildings persisted, most notably in city centers and minority communities; and some middle-class families retreated to private education. At the dawn of a new century, the effects of inequality continued to thread through and differentiate the landscapes of education in the United States as poverty, racial bias, and the reluctance of taxpayers to invest in infrastructure confounded hopes for constructing public architecture, including public schools, suited to and common to all children.

See also: **Children's Spaces; Compulsory School Attendance; Hygiene; Progressive Education; Urban School Systems, The Rise of.**

BIBLIOGRAPHY

Barnard, Henry. 1970 [1848]. *School Architecture*, ed. Jean and Robert McClintock. New York: Teachers College Press.

Cubberley, Ellwood P. 1934. *Public Education in the United States: A Study and Interpretation of American Educational History*, rev. ed. Boston: Houghton Mifflin.

Cutler, William W., III. 1989. "Cathedral of Culture: The Schoolhouse in American Educational Thought and Practice since 1820." *History of Education Quarterly* 29: 1–40.

Duffy, John. 1979. "School Buildings and the Health of American School Children in the Nineteenth Century." In *Healing and History: Essays for George Rosen*, ed. Charles E. Rosenberg. New York: Science History Publications.

Graves, Ben E. 1993. *School Ways: The Planning and Design of America's Schools*. New York: McGraw-Hill.

Gulliford, Andrew. 1984. *America's Country Schools*, Washington, DC: Preservation Press.

Gyure, Dale Allen. 2000. "The Transformation of the Schoolhouse: American Secondary School Architecture and Educational Reform, 1880–1920." Ph.D. diss., University of Virginia.

Hoffschwelle, Mary S. 1998. *Rebuilding the Rural Southern Community: Reformers, Schools, and Homes in Tennessee, 1900–1930*. Knoxville: University of Tennessee Press.

Lackney, Jeffrey A. 2001. "From Home School to House Plan, 1650–2001." *New York Times*, Sunday, August 5, Education Life supplement, p. 23.

Upton, Dell. 1996. "Lancasterian Schools, Republican Citizenship, and the Spatial Imagination in Early Nineteenth-Century America." *Journal of the Society of Architectural Historians* 55: 238–253.

INTERNET RESOURCE

Wojcik, Susan Brizzolara. 2002. *Iron Hill School: An African-American One-Room School*. U.S. National Park Service, National Register of Historic Places. Available from <www.cr.nps.gov/nr/twhp/wwwlps/lessons/58iron/58iron.htm>.

MARTA GUTMAN

School Choice

The phrase *school choice* covers a wide variety of political, policy, and practical student enrollment options available to educators who manage the public school K–12 systems throughout the United States. Traditionally, American elementary and secondary education has been organized along the principle of students attending their local neighborhood public school with the option that students can attend private schools at their family's or their own expense. Public sector school choice developed in the late twentieth century with the advent of MAGNET SCHOOLS, schools with special curricula, schools for children with special needs, and schools requiring entrance examinations.

Criticisms of public education intensified after the 1980s because critics believed that public education failed to provide a rigorous educational environment for too many of students. These critics pointed to the relative poor performance of many American students on standardized tests when their scores are compared to the scores of their international peers. Many argued that public education ought to be deregulated and become more competitive, because competition promotes accountability, standards, and transparency. Deregulation challenges the traditional concept of the COMMON SCHOOL as locally based and as such, is a controversial policy alternative. Those opposing deregulation argued that as a policy option, deregulation was less likely to produce increased student learning than smaller class size, improved curricula and professional development for teachers and principals.

There are basically three types of school choice: intra- and inter-district public school choice; CHARTER SCHOOLS; and SCHOOL VOUCHERS. The first option, intra- and inter-district public school choice, allows students to attend public schools other than their neighborhood schools, either within a school district or across district lines. Public school options are widely available in most states and do not provoke political controversy. The second option, charter schools, involves public schools that are specially chartered by the state or a chartering agency and are freed from many of the regulations that affect regular public schools. There were approximately 2,400 charter schools in the United States by 2003, scattered across thirty-seven states and the District of Columbia. There is wide political support for charter schools, while at the same time, many charter schools struggled because of resource limitations. The third option, voucher, is a mechanism by which public monies are transferred to private schools by giving to parents a voucher that may be redeemed at a private school of their choice. By 2003 publicly funded voucher plans existed in Wisconsin, Ohio, and Florida. Of all the school choice options, vouchers are the most controversial because they transfer public money to private schools and because they can be used to support religious education. However, in 2002, a U.S. Supreme Court decision ruled that it was constitutional for public monies to be spent on private schools even if the schools are religious in nature.

Deregulation of public education, especially in the form of charters and vouchers, raises a number of policy issues. Will school choice plans lead to more equitable access or will school choice plans further stratify education? Is school choice related to improved student learning? What evidence is there that school choice leads to more innovative educational opportunities? How economical are school choice programs, especially in an era of declining resources?

In the early twenty-first century, scholars and researchers studied school choice systematically, but there was little consensus about answering the questions raised above. There has been some evidence that while some students benefit from attending a school of their choice, from a systems perspective; school choice tends to favor the middle class, thus leading to increasing educational stratification. The evidence concerning school choice and student achievement was mixed with little convincing data upon which to draw a firm conclusion. There also has been some evidence that public school choice and charter schools have allowed for educational innovation although these innovations have not yet transformed the traditional nature of public education. The economics of school choice have been hotly debated, but it is clear that many charter schools have failed because of the lack of financial support.

See also: **Education, United States; Private and Independent Schools.**

BIBLIOGRAPHY

Chubb, John E., and Terry M. Moe. 1990. *Politics, Markets, and America's Schools.* Washington, DC: Brookings Institution Press.

Cookson, Peter W., Jr. 1994. *School Choice: The Struggle for the Soul of American Education.* New Haven, CT: Yale University Press.

Henig, J. R. 1994. *Rethinking School Choice: The Limits of the Market Metaphor.* Princeton, NJ: Princeton University Press.

PETER W. COOKSON JR.

School Desegregation

Ever since Benjamin Roberts, an African-American printer, sued the Boston School Committee in the mid-nineteenth century for the unlawful exclusion of his daughter from the city's white elementary schools, the struggle for racial equality in education has been closely bound up with the demand for school desegregation. Not until the post–World War II era, however, when the National Association for the Advancement of Colored People's (NAACP) legal campaign, the growth of black political power, and the rise of the civil rights movement prompted government action to address the demands of those denied equal educational opportunity, did desegregation move from the periphery to the center of educational policy. From the time of the U.S. Supreme Court's 1954 decision outlawing state-mandated segregation in BROWN V. BOARD OF EDUCATION through the 1970s, no other educational issue provoked as much conflict or so preoccupied students, parents, and public officials responsible for making educational policy.

The results of this struggle for desegregated schools have been ambiguous. From one perspective, the fight for desegregated schools accomplished much that it set out to do. At the time the Court handed down its decision in *Brown*, seventeen southern and border states as well as the District of Columbia had laws requiring separate schools for blacks and whites, and segregation was widespread in the North even though several northern states had provisions prohibiting it in local schools. A decade after *Brown*, this system of racial apartheid in the South was still intact, while in the North, increasingly vocal protests had won only minor concessions from school officials who argued that segregation resulted from housing patterns and not their own actions. But, largely because of the Johnson administration's enforcement of strict guidelines prohibiting the distribution of federal funds to segregated schools, the Fifth Circuit Court of Appeals' insistence that school districts comply with these guidelines, and a series of Supreme Court decisions that banned freedom of choice plans and approved busing, southern schools desegregated rapidly between 1964 and 1972, as did many school districts in the North and West. Whereas 64 percent of African Americans nationwide attended schools with 90 to 100 percent minority enrollment in 1968, the percentage had dropped to 33 percent by 1980 and was even lower in the South.

By almost any historical standard, this constituted an extraordinary achievement. But because compliance was left in the hands of local school officials, it typically occurred on terms advantageous to whites. Faced with federal pressure to desegregate, southern school districts complied by closing black schools, demoting African-American principals, and dismissing African-American teachers. At the same time, as African Americans began to go to school with whites, southern school officials sought to assuage white fears that interracial contact would increase and academic standards would deteriorate by disproportionately placing black students in the least desirable academic programs, a practice that was widespread in the North as well. As a result, even though desegregation offered African Americans access to educational resources previously denied them, many began to question its benefits.

Desegregation reached its legal high water mark in 1973 when, in *Keyes v. Denver School Board No. 1*, the Supreme Court extended desegregation requirements to northern and western cities and included Latinos as well as African Americans in desegregation plans. But this victory also turned out to be a partial one. Although the Court's decision ended the

practice whereby cities had sent Mexican-American and African-Americans to school together and called it desegregation, it did little to end urban segregation. Because suburbanization and white flight increasingly left so few white students in most big city school systems, few could accomplish any meaningful desegregation within their own borders.

One way advocates proposed to remedy this was through mandatory metropolitan-wide desgregation. By the early 1970s, however, governmental support for such strong measures had begun to wane. Presidents Nixon, Ford, and Carter all opposed busing, as did a majority of Congress. They passed legislation barring the use of federal funds for busing to overcome racial imbalance and considered an amendment to the U.S. Constitution prohibiting the reassignment of students to schools outside their immediate neighborhood. In 1974 in *Milliken v. Bradley*, a reconstructed Supreme Court with four Nixon appointees began what was to become a long retreat from its demand that violating school districts take aggressive action to overcome segregation and reversed a lower court ruling that ordered urban–suburban desegregation in Detroit. Without compelling evidence that suburban boundaries had been drawn with discriminatory intent, a five to four majority of the Court argued, local autonomy should take precedence over the right of African-American and Latino students to a desegregated education.

Because school districts in many large metropolitan areas in the South are countywide, this decision did not resegregate southern schools. Outside the South, however, especially in the Northeast and Midwest, where school district boundaries correspond to urban/suburban political jurisdictions, *Milliken* effectively excluded white suburbs from the requirements of desegregation. Subsequently, desegregation plans in northern and midwestern cities focused instead on voluntary city–suburban transfers and special magnet programs designed to hold white students in the city or to entice them from the suburbs to attend urban schools. These plans offered some African-American and Latino students an alternative to segregated, inner-city schools, but, since they did not require much of whites, they did little to alter the racial composition of urban schools or of those in surrounding communities.

Despite the limitations of these programs, additional action to promote desegregated schools attracted little support. Instead, beginning in the 1980s, equal opportunity was increasingly redefined to mean greater choice in schooling, and proposals such as SCHOOL VOUCHERS and CHARTER SCHOOLS were promoted as the best way to expand educational opportunities for low income and minority students. In some case, these proposals, which were initiated primarily by white policymakers who favored market-based solutions to social problems, also won support from a growing number of African-American and Latino parents who were disillusioned by the slow pace of desegregation and who viewed SCHOOL CHOICE as a way to escape deteriorating inner-city schools.

In this climate, segregation persisted or got worse between 1980 and 2000, though patterns varied by group and region. For African Americans, the South remained the most desegregated region of the country. But after a series of Supreme Court decisions between 1991 and 1995 that allowed districts to return to neighborhood schools before desegregation requirements had been fully met, the proportion of African Americans in schools with 90 to 100 percent minority enrollment in the South began to rise again, though black segregation remained most intense in big cities in the Northeast and Midwest. Latino segregation was also greatest in urban schools in the Northeast, where the majority of Latinos were from Puerto Rico and the Caribbean. As the migration of Mexican Americans and Mexican immigrants to cities in other regions of the country increased after 1970, however, Latino segregation also intensified in the South and West. In 1996 35 percent of Latino students nationwide were in schools with 90 to 100 percent enrollment, compared to 23 percent of Latino students in 1968.

Some observers at the turn of the twenty-first century seized on this evidence to pronounce desegregation a failure and urge that it be abandoned. But the lesson that history teaches is more complex. In essence, the struggle for desegregated schools sought to make the benefits of education equally available to all citizens. By ending Jim Crow in southern education and winning recognition for the right of Latinos as well as African Americans to a desegregated education, it accomplished a good deal toward the realization of that goal. What was equally clear, however, was that without governmental support for complementary changes in the distribution of power, control, and resources, desegregation based on equality of academic and social status in the classroom would remain an illusory goal.

See also: **African-American Children and Youth; Law, Children and the; Magnet Schools.**

BIBLIOGRAPHY

Arnez, Nancy. 1978. "Implementation of Desegregation as a Discriminatory Process." *Journal of Negro Education* 47: 28–45.

Bell, Derrick, ed. 1980. *Shades of Brown: New Perspectives on School Desegregation.* New York: Teachers College Press.

Cecelski, David S. 1994. *Along Freedom Road: Hyde County, North Carolina, and the Fate of Black Schools in the South.* Chapel Hill: University of North Carolina Press.

Donato, Rubén. 1997. *The Other Struggle for Equal Schools: Mexican Americans During the Civil Rights Era.* Albany: State University of New York Press.

Orfield, Gary. 1978. *Must We Bus? Segregated Schools and National Policy.* Washington, DC: Brookings Institution.

Orfield, Gary, and Susan Eaton. 1996. *Dismantling Desegregation: The Quiet Reversal of Brown v. Board of Education.* New York: Free Press.

Orfield, Gary, Mark Bachmeier, David James, et al. 1997. "Deepening Segregation in American Public Schools: A Special Report from the Harvard Project on School Desegregation." *Equity and Excellence in Education* 30: 5–23.

Patterson, James T. 2001. *Brown v. Board of Education: A Civil Rights Milestone and Its Troubled Legacy.* New York: Oxford University Press.

Rossell, Christine, and Willis D. Hawley, eds. 1983. *The Consequences of School Desegregation.* Philadelphia: Temple University Press.

Wilkinson, J. Harvie. 1979. *From Brown to Bakke: The Supreme Court and School Integration: 1954–1978.* New York: Oxford University Press.

HARVEY KANTOR

School Shootings and School Violence

When Eric Harris and Dylan Klebold walked into Columbine High School in Colorado on April 20, 1999, and killed twelve students and one teacher, the United States reacted with horror and disbelief that such a thing could happen in American schools. The nature of violence in schools seemed to change overnight from isolated acts of disaffected students or gang power struggles to premeditated acts of terrorism. But violence in schools did not emerge as a phenomenon of the late twentieth century. School violence is as old as schools.

From at least the seventeenth century, schoolchildren in Europe were armed. Primarily of the aristocracy and nobility, they routinely wore swords and carried guns to school. In the early eighteenth century, the King of France was forced to dispatch troops to the University of Paris to disarm violent students. In England, there were student mutinies and rebellions throughout the eighteenth century at such well-respected schools as Rugby and Eton, prestigious private schools, where pupils set fire to their books and desks, requiring army troops to disband them. By the late eighteenth century, the most prevalent and popular form of school misrule was *barring out the master*. This practice originated in England when students would demand a holiday or other treat. If the master refused, students would bar him from entering the school, damaging school furniture, barricading windows and doors, and robbing neighbors in marauding sorties to gain provisions to sustain the siege.

In the United States, this practice of misrule was more benign. Taking over the schoolhouse and barring the master from entrance was a time-honored tradition in many nineteenth-century rural schools, but in most cases, barrings-out were confined to symbolic subversion of authority and to symbolic violence. Typical of this symbolic violence was a barring-out in Tennessee, in which students barricaded themselves inside the schoolhouse and denied the master entrance until their demands—for two bushels of apples and five pounds of candy—were met. Presenting no resistance whatsoever, the master ordered two of the smaller boys to run to town and get two bushels of apples and ten pounds of candy. Staying long enough to distribute the candy and apples, he then wished them a Merry Christmas and went home. Real violence was a mistake, an unintended consequence that occurred when the master refused to acquiesce and met resistance with force, as in the 1830s case of a Tennessee school in which the teacher was stabbed and dropped into a well (he lived) and the schoolhouse burned down.

There was nothing symbolic about another common form of nineteenth- and early-twentieth-century school violence in the United States. Attacks on teachers by older male students were a familiar part of nineteenth-century school practice. Teachers in these often rural schools literally fought to prove their right to their positions and often resorted to extreme uses of corporal punishment to maintain them. Unlike the carnivalesque aspects of barrings-out, violent attacks were a direct challenge to the schoolmaster's authority. While the application of physical domination was one way in which male teachers established their clear and unchallenged authority, women teachers also experienced physical and psychological intimidation that required courage and determination to withstand. In many instances, parents did not interfere in the pupils' attempts to run the teacher out of town and did not punish them when they did.

By the early twentieth century, the institutionalization of schools had transformed the autonomous nature of many of these rural and local school districts into a more centralized and bureaucratized structure that made acts of violence against either the master or the schoolhouse ill-advised. Parental sentiment, which in the nineteenth century had condoned and even encouraged such behaviors, had now changed. The disruption of authority was no longer seen as a boisterous acting out of ADOLESCENCE, but as a decidedly illegal activity.

The twentieth century saw both the type and the focus of school violence change. In the eighteenth and nineteenth centuries the master or the school itself was the target of violence, with the students often acting in concert as the perpetrators. By the twentieth century, student-on-student violence had become the norm. Parents began to fear for the safety of their children as violence escalated from sticks and fists in the 1920s to bricks, bats, and chains in the 1940s, knives in the 1960s, and guns in the 1980s and 1990s. The intensification of the means of violence reflected greater social changes. Gang violence rocked schools in the 1960s and 1970s. Schools were considered gang turf and the violence resulted from issues of crime as well as control. Vandalism and schoolboy fights gave way to assault, armed robbery, rape, and murder.

The late 1990s saw another transformation of the nature of school violence. While the majority of earlier incidences took place in urban and inner-city schools, this new wave of violence took place in suburban, largely white, middle-class

neighborhoods. Individual disaffected students sought to purge their particular demons by shooting schoolmates and teachers in calculated acts of violence. Between October 1997 and May 1998 there were five school shootings in which children as young as eleven shot and killed fourteen students and teachers and wounded twenty-nine others. The Columbine shootings in 1999 sparked a flurry of other shootings. From April 1999 through March of 2001, nine additional school shootings occurred. Six people, ranging in age from a six-year-old girl to a thirty-five-year-old teacher, were killed, including one student shooter. Twenty-four were wounded. These incidents have caused the court system in the United States to rethink juvenile crime. Thirteen-year old Nathaniel Brazill, who shot and killed his teacher in May 2000, was tried as an adult, found guilty of second-degree murder, and sentenced to twenty-eight years in prison.

The nature of violence in higher education has also evolved over the years in the United States. During the eighteenth and nineteenth centuries, when college students were primarily the children of wealthy or influential Americans, a common type of violence derived from perceived affronts to individual honor, often resulting in duels. Students periodically rebelled against the authority of their faculty at such diverse schools as Yale, Brown, Dartmouth, and North Carolina. Barrings-out were a "standing frolic" at Princeton, among others, into the 1850s. Misrule in twentieth-century colleges included freshman hazing, which in some cases were brutal physical trials that led to loss of life. Some acts of violence took on a more sexual meaning, ranging from the relatively benign panty-raid to the criminal act of date-rape.

See also: **Charivari; Delinquency; Discipline; Education, Europe; Education, United States; Violence Against Children; Youth Gangs.**

BIBLIOGRAPHY

Ariès, Philippe. 1962. *Centuries of Childhood: A Social History of Family Life.* Trans. Robert Baldick. New York: Vintage Books.

Davis, Natalie Zemon. 1971. "The Reasons of Misrule: Youth Groups and Charivaris in Sixteenth-Century France." *Past and Present* 50 (February): 41–75.

Knox, George W., David L. Laske, and Edward D. Tromanhauser. 1992. *Schools Under Siege.* Dubuque, IA: Kendall/Hunt.

Rudolph, Frederick. 1962. *The American College and University: A History.* New York: Knopf.

Wyatt-Brown, Bertram. 1986. *Honor and Violence in the Old South.* New York: Oxford University Press.

JAN PRICE GREENOUGH

School Vouchers

In the United States a school voucher is a subsidy that grants limited purchasing power to a student to choose among a restricted set of private schools. In the traditional school funding configuration, public funds for public schools flow from national and state governments and local communities, directly to school districts. A family wishing to send its child to a private school must do so with its own funds. A large-scale voucher plan would change that arrangement: in a voucher plan, families that wish to enroll their children in private school could have the tuition partially or completely covered by tax-levied dollars.

The idea of school vouchers is as old as the American Revolution. The American revolutionary Thomas Paine advocated a voucher system because he felt that compulsory education violated individual conscience. He was following the perspective of John Stuart Mill, who believed that state-sponsored education was a contrivance for molding people to be exactly like one another. During the 1960s, educational activists such as Ted Sizer advocated vouchers to enable urban children to escape their local public schools.

In the 1990s, the voucher movement gained new momentum, which led to voucher pilot sites in Wisconsin, Ohio, and Florida. In 2001, the Rand Corporation published a research report by Brian Gill, Michael Timpane, and Dominic I. Brewer evaluating the effects of choice on several outcomes: student achievement, parental satisfaction, access, integration, and civic socialization. The report determined that small, experimental, privately funded vouchers may show modest benefits after a year or two for African-American students but that there is no evidence of benefit for children of other racial groups. Parental satisfaction is high among choice parents, although the number of families involved in the study was quite small.

Some voucher programs targeted specifically at low-income, low-achieving minority students have provided access for some students. In general, however, most choice programs have not extended access opportunities to the poor, and in fact voucher-like tuition tax benefits favor middle- and upper-income families. Likewise in highly segregated communities voucher programs may modestly increase racial integration, but evidence from abroad suggests that most choice programs result in increasing the degree of educational stratification, not decreasing it. In terms of civic socialization, there is little distinction to be made between private and public schools.

To a large degree, the debate over school vouchers has less to do with empirical outcomes than with deep-seated beliefs about liberty, community, and the role of individual preference in creating a good society. The intensity and tone of the debate depends in great part upon the more general spirit of the times; that is, to the degree that market competition is seen as the way to a productive and just society, vouchers will appeal to a substantial minority of citizens. To the degree that government is seen as the protector of democracy, vouchers will appeal to a smaller group of citizens,

many of whom resist government schooling as a matter of principal. Debate over vouchers also involves questions about separation between church and state, since religious schools could become voucher recipients. At the start of the twenty-first century, the debate over school vouchers was refueled by a U.S. Supreme Court decision that lowered the legal wall between church and state.

See also: **Charter Schools; Education, United States; Magnet Schools; Parochial Schools; Private and Independent Schools; School Choice.**

BIBLIOGRAPHY

Gill, Brian, Michael Timpane, and Dominic I. Brewer. 2001. *Rhetoric Versus Reality: What We Know and What We Need to Know about Vouchers and Charter Schools.* Santa Monica, CA: Rand Education.

Greene, Jay D., Paul E. Peterson, and Jiangtao Du. 1996. "Effectiveness of School Choice: The Milwaukee Experiment." John F. Kennedy School of Government. Cambridge, MA: Harvard University.

Hanus, Jerome J., and Peter W. Cookson Jr. 1996. *Choosing Schools: Vouchers and American Education.* Washington, DC: American University Press.

Peterson, Paul E. 2001. "Choice in American Education." In *A Primer on America's Schools,* ed. Terry M. Moe. Stanford, CA: Hoover Institution Press.

Rouse, Cecelia E. 1997. "Schools and Student Achievement: More Evidence from the Milwaukee Parental Choice Program." Working Paper No. 396, Industrial Relations Section. Princeton, NJ: Princeton University Press.

Steuerle, C. Eugene. 1999. "Common Issues for Voucher Programs." In *Vouchers and the Provision of Public Services,* ed. C. Eugene Steuerle et al. Washington, DC: Brookings Institution.

Witte, John F. 1996. "Who Benefits from the Milwaukee Choice Program?" In *Who Chooses? Who Loses? Culture, Institutions, and the Unequal Effects of School Choice,* ed. Bruce Fuller et al. New York: Teachers College Press.

PETER W. COOKSON JR.

Scientific Child Rearing

The origins of scientific child rearing in the United States are diverse and may be traced back as far as the seventeenth century, when poet and mother of seven children Anne Bradstreet theorized: "Diverse children have their different natures; some are like flesh which nothing but salt will keep from putrefaction, some again like tender fruits that are best preserved with sugar. . . . Those parents are wise that can fit their nurture according to their nature." Bradstreet's comparison of the techniques of food preservation to disciplining children was only one of many scientific analogies that would inform thinking about child rearing. Her conception of the mother as a scientist of child nurture would have salience in the centuries to come, even as it vied with the idea that mothers must rely on experts to raise their children.

Seventeenth-century philosopher and physician JOHN LOCKE offered another analogy for child rearing when he conceived of the child's mind as a *tabula rasa*, or blank slate, for parent's to write upon. His influential *Some Thoughts Concerning Education* (1693) articulated his vision of parenting as a systematic and consequential enterprise. In *Émile* (1762), JEAN-JACQUES ROUSSEAU also shed philosophical and scientific light on childhood. Unlike Locke, who was primarily concerned with discerning how best to prepare children for adulthood, Rousseau urged parents and educators to preserve and nurture the "natural" child. In succeeding centuries, scientific child rearing literature would veer between emphases on socialization versus development. However, scientific child rearing has traditionally been the province of middle-class parents, who have had the time, leisure, financial resources, and inclinations to utilize expert advice in parenting.

The idea of child rearing as a scientific enterprise made increasing headway in the nineteenth century. The focus on specialized techniques of child rearing was at least partially a consequence of economic and demographic changes, which contributed to smaller family sizes and intensified nurturing. In 1800, the average family raised seven children to adulthood; by 1900, that number had shrunk to three or four. With fewer children and productive responsibilities in the home, child rearing became a focal point of women's work in the home. In a society where one's fortunes could rise and fall in a lifetime, parents sought to inculcate children with the habits and virtues that would allow them to maintain or improve their economic position and social status. While philosophy and religion initially provided the theoretical rationales for informing parents about the best means of rearing children, science and medicine began to make inroads on this discourse by the close of the century.

The advent of the field of PEDIATRICS in the nineteenth century was central to the evolution of scientific child rearing. Physicians acquired greater influence over family life throughout the century, but it was not until 1887 that the American Pediatric Society was established, and the idea of well baby health care took hold. Pediatricians orchestrated campaigns to alleviate INFANT MORTALITY, initiated regularly scheduled well baby examinations, and pronounced themselves as authorities on INFANT FEEDING. During the World War I era, child health activists sponsored infant welfare clinics, better baby contests, and milk stations. In both rural and urban areas mothers congregated at settlement houses, county fairs, and government offices to have their babies weighed, measured, and receive milk. In these venues, mothers learned that there were scientific rationales for psychological as well as for physical care. Physicians and nurses offered advice about feeding, clothing, and how to respond to a crying infant. However, there was variability in the extent to which mothers accepted scientific authority over their mothering practices. Poor mothers, especially, were often receptive to suggestions concerning sanitation and nutrition,

while remaining skeptical about the idea that science should determine their techniques of nurture and DISCIPLINE.

CHILD PSYCHOLOGY accompanied pediatrics into the twentieth century as both an academic enterprise and source of knowledge for popular consumption. Pioneer psychologist G. STANLEY HALL championed CHILD STUDY as a vital subject of research in the late nineteenth century. He enlisted mothers and teachers to gather data on children's habits and development as a means of reforming education and parenting. Hall's message that children's discipline and education should be normative and shape their educations and upbringing became, he himself claimed "almost like a new gospel."

Hall was practically a patron saint to the National Congress of Mothers, forerunner to the PTA, which was founded in 1897. This national organization of mothers' groups was the most prominent advocate for scientific motherhood. In 1896, African-American women founded the National Association of Colored Women, which similarly promoted the concept of "better motherhood." The National Association of Colored Parents and Teachers was formed in 1926 for African-American segregated school districts. These various women's organizations differed in their definitions of parent education, but all agreed on the centrality of science in improving the conditions of childhood.

In 1909, the first WHITE HOUSE CONFERENCE ON CHILDREN was held, uniting scientists, reformers, and educators to craft public policy on childhood. The conference led to the establishment of the U.S. CHILDREN'S BUREAU (1912), which gathered data on infant and maternal health problems and issued a series of bulletins relating to children's physical and emotional care. The Bureau maintained a voluminous correspondence with mothers from both rural and urban settings about many aspects of childcare and nurture and helped to advance the idea that government should play a role in parenting.

By the 1920s, scientific child rearing had become an obsession for the American middle class. A slew of publications warned that faulty child rearing could lead to criminality and psychological disease. Many argued that the radically transformed conditions of the modern era were such that neither the maternal instinct nor tradition could be relied upon to raise children. In *Psychological Care of Infant and Child* (1928) JOHN BROADUS WATSON portrayed children as human "machines" whose behavior could be programmed by maternal technicians. Watson chided mothers for their indulgence, warned about the dangers of "too much mother love," and prescribed strictly regimented feeding schedules for infants. While influential throughout the 1920s and 1930s, behaviorist ideas of child rearing were eclipsed by more child-centered philosophies of parenting as World War II approached. However, Watson's perception that twentieth-century children were "spoiled" by indulgent parents and required more objective handling would be a recurring refrain as the century progressed.

Child-centered parenting received a boost from the research of pediatrician and psychologist ARNOLD GESELL during the 1930s and 1940s. Gesell produced and popularized developmental norms that detailed the physical, behavioral, and temperamental characteristics of children of different ages. While these norms enabled parents and physicians to identify developmental delays and disorders, they could also be rigidly applied and exacerbate anxiety about children whose walking or talking was slightly behind schedule. In terms of discipline, Gesell's norms advanced child-centered disciplinary strategies, by redefining behaviors such as temper tantrums as normal consequences of the process of development, rather than undesirable habits that needed to be extinguished.

BENJAMIN SPOCK's *Baby and Child Care*, first published in 1946, was heralded as a watershed in advice literature to parents. The paperback was inexpensive, widely distributed to parents at hospitals and doctor's offices, and covered a range of topics from diaper rash to dawdling. The post–World War II era was characterized both by large families and geographical mobility, leaving many mothers far from relatives and friends who could offer timely advice. The book was more often used for midnight medical emergencies than for psychological advice. Yet the idea that an expert such as Spock was a more valid source of information than friends or relatives increasingly permeated the experience of motherhood.

Spock's baby book distilled a number of concepts that would be influential throughout the Cold War era. Whereas earlier scientific child-rearing literature sought to eradicate the notion that motherhood was based on instinct, Spock described motherhood as natural and instinctual. A student of psychoanalysis, he sought to reassure mothers of their competence and alleviate their anxieties, believing that negative emotions could cause psychological damage to children.

Research on war ORPHANS and institutionalized children during the 1940s and 1950s dramatically underscored the significance of the mother-child bond. Scientists ANNA FREUD, Dorothy Burlingham, and JOHN BOWLBY offered compelling evidence that children who were deprived of individual caregivers during the early years suffered emotional and cognitive damage. This research had positive implications for public policy relating to dependent children, but it stigmatized working mothers and women who were discontented with full-time motherhood. Instead of suffering from "too much mother love," children without access to their mothers on a twenty-four hour basis were thought to be victims of maternal neglect and rejection.

By the 1950s, scientific child-rearing advice had come full circle. From a rejection of the maternal instinct in the 1920s to a vindication of motherhood in the 1950s, science did not yield a clear and coherent message to parents in the twentieth century. Fortunately, parents, and mothers in particular, have tended to utilize scientific child-rearing advice selectively, picking and choosing from among the diverse messages being delivered to them. Yet the idea that the science of childhood should influence child rearing continued to influence parenting and public policy throughout the century. Research on attachment, the infant brain, and day care and divorce informed pediatric practices, parent education, and public policy, making science a primary frame of reference for parenthood in the twentieth and twenty-first centuries.

See also: **Child-Rearing Advice Literature; Parenting.**

BIBLIOGRAPHY

Apple, Rima D. 1987. *Mothers and Medicine: A Social History of Infant Feeding, 1890–1950.* Madison: University of Wisconsin Press.

Beatty, Barbara. 1995. *Preschool Education in America: The Culture of Young Children from the Colonial Era to the Present.* New Haven: Yale University Press.

Bowlby, John. 1953. *Child Care and the Growth of Love.* Baltimore: Johns Hopkins University Press.

Bradstreet, Anne. 1981. "In Anne's Hand." In *The Complete Works of Anne Bradstreet,* ed. Joseph R. McElrath, Jr., and Allen P. Robb. Boston: Twayne.

Cravens, Hamilton. 1985. "Child-Saving in the Age of Professionalism." In *American Childhood: A Research Guide and Historical Handbook,* ed. Joseph Hawes and N. Ray Hiner. Westport, CT: Greenwood Press.

Eyer, Diane E. 1992. *Mother-Infant Bonding: A Scientific Fiction.* New Haven: Yale University Press.

Freud, Anna, and Dorothy Burlingham. 1944. *Infants Without Families: The Case for and Against Residential Nurseries.* New York: Medical War Books.

Gesell, Arnold, et al. 1940. *The First Five Years of Life: A Guide to the Study of the Child.* New York: Harper.

Grant, Julia. 1998. *Raising Baby by the Book: The Education of American Mothers.* New Haven, CT: Yale University Press.

Hall, G. Stanley. 1923. *Life and Confessions of a Psychologist.* New York: Appleton.

Ladd-Taylor, Molly. 1994. *Mother-Work: Women, Child Welfare, and the State 1890–1930.* Urbana: University of Illinois Press.

Locke, John. 1922. "Some Thoughts Concerning Education." In *The Educational Writings of John Locke,* ed. John William Adamson. Cambridge, UK: Cambridge University Press.

Meckel, Richard A. 1990. *Save the Babies: American Public Health Reform and the Prevention of Infant Mortality, 1850–1929.* Baltimore: Johns Hopkins University Press.

Ross, Dorothy. 1972. *G. Stanley Hall: The Psychologist as Prophet.* Chicago: University of Chicago Press.

Rousseau, Jean-Jacques. 1979. *Émile: or, On Education.* Trans. Allan Bloom. New York: Basic Books.

Schlossman, Steven L. 1976. "Before Home Start: Notes Toward a History of Parent Education in America, 1897–1929." *Harvard Educational Review* 61: 436–467.

Spock, Benjamin. 1946. *The Commonsense Book of Baby and Child Care.* New York. Pocket Books.

Watson, John Broadus. 1928. *Psychological Care of Infant and Child.* New York: Norton.

JULIA GRANT

Scottsboro Boys

On April 9, 1931, a white judge in northern Alabama summarily sentenced nine black male youths to death after local all-white juries had convicted the young black men of raping two white women on March 25, principally on the women's testimony. In vain the young men insisted upon their innocence. A long-term and ultimately successful struggle to save the youths' lives and, in time, to exonerate them led to one of the most dramatic and revealing civil rights struggles in U.S. history.

A stalwart defense effort led initially by the International Labor Defense (ILD), the legal wing of the Communist Party, combined with international as well as domestic support campaigns to keep the young men's cause alive. On one hand, the word-of-mouth reportage and extensive newspaper coverage played upon the intertwined psychosexual and interracial aspects of the alleged crime. On the other, the youths' defense teams and innumerable supporters consistently emphasized how those very same aspects combined to render a fair trial virtually impossible in the white supremacist social order of the Jim Crow South.

Olen Montgomery, Clarence Norris, Haywood Patterson, Ozie Powell, Willie Roberson, Charley Weems, Eugene Williams, and Andrew Wright found that as black male youths in the Jim Crow South, neither innocence nor adolescence protected them. Leroy Wright, a thirteen year old and a ninth accused youth, was never sentenced to life imprisonment due to his young age. Nevertheless, the inflammatory allegation of having raped white women, especially in such a high-profile case, haunted forever all of their lives.

In the April 1933 retrial of Haywood Patterson, Defense Attorney Samuel Leibowitz demonstrated that Victoria Price and Ruby Bates, the alleged victims, had fabricated the rape charge as a way to avoid being charged with vagrancy and prostitution. At that same retrial, Ruby Bates went so far as to recant her testimony against all the defendants and to speak out on behalf of the innocence of Patterson and the other Scottsboro Boys. White male juries in Alabama, however, refused to accept Bates's retraction and new story, and continued in their legal persecution of the Scottsboro Boys. As a result, a series of defense appeals kept the cause alive. In *Powell v. Alabama* (1932), the Supreme Court ordered new trials for all eight defendants, ruling that in capital cases defendants merited a real, as against a *pro forma*, defense. In *Norris v. Alabama* (1935), the highest court overturned the convictions of Norris and Patterson and demanded that the state court retry the case because of the systematic exclusion of blacks from the juries.

The saga of the Scottsboro Boys demonstrated the deep-seated, racist, white fear of the alleged black male rapist, in this case in the guise of youth. It likewise illustrated the power of this fear to override evidence and reason in the determination of guilt and innocence. Indeed, the issue was neither guilt nor innocence; rather, it was the maintenance of white supremacy and the repression of black freedom. Nevertheless, the concerted and inspiring efforts to undo the wrongs against the Scottsboro Boys contributed significantly to the ongoing African-American Freedom Struggle and the interrelated struggle to defeat Jim Crow.

See also: **African-American Children and Youth; Juvenile Justice; Law, Children and the.**

BIBLIOGRAPHY

Carter, Dan T. 1976. *Scottsboro: A Tragedy of the American South*, 2nd ed. Baton Rouge: Louisiana State University Press.

Goodman, James. 1994. *Stories of Scottsboro: The Rape Case that Shocked 1930's America and Revived the Struggle for Equality.* New York: Pantheon.

WALDO E. MARTIN JR.

Self-Esteem

The roots of the self-esteem movement go back to the later nineteenth century, where they intertwined with larger notions of children's vulnerability and the need for adult protection and support. Most of the psychologists associated with the CHILD STUDY movement specifically discussed the concept of self-esteem as a key component in successful child rearing. Progressive-era educators used the idea as well in seeking a supportive school environment. But it was only in the 1960s that this long-established belief of experts won popular and institutional backing as a way to reconcile academic commitment with parental concerns for childhood frailty and for the special value of their own children.

The 1880s through 1930s

JOHN DEWEY and William James were among the early psychologist proponents of the importance of the self. Dewey discussed "intuition of self" in his seminal 1886 work, *Psychology*, using knowledge of self as the talisman for knowledge gains in general. Selfhood was, in this view, essential to freedom. But it was James who, in 1892, first used the term *self-esteem* with an explicit scientific definition. A key task in socializing children, in James's view, involved helping them gain the capacity to develop "self" and, with it, the capacity to adapt to different social settings with appropriate projections of self. Self-esteem, more specifically, involved the kind of perceptions that, properly honed, were crucial to achievement and success.

The popularization of psychology and the growing notion that children often needed expert help brought concerns about self-esteem to greater attention during the 1920s and 1930s. If children needed a sense of self to operate successfully, but if children were also vulnerable, it was certainly possible that special measures might be necessary to assure that the mechanism (the self) was in working order.

The 1950s to the Present

During the 1950s and 1960s the connection between self-esteem and supportive school programs was fully forged. A clear symptom, as well as a cause of further awareness, was a growing spate of expert studies on the subject. Stanley Coopersmith, in 1967, identified the link between self-esteem and frailty, noting the "indications that in children domination, rejection, and severe punishment result in lowered self-esteem. Under such conditions they have fewer experiences of love and success and tend to become generally more submissive and withdrawn (though occasionally veering to the opposite extreme of aggression and domination)" (p. 45).

While experts debated the precise correlatives of self-esteem—in their eyes, the subject was extremely complicated—three points shone through. First and most obviously, self-esteem was vitally important to a well-adjusted, high-functioning child or adult. This conclusion was amply prepared for by previous generations of scientific writing. Second, self-esteem was crucially affected by what parents did to children. Levels of DISCIPLINE, family affection, and marital stability all registered in a child's emerging concept of self-worth. And finally, self-esteem played a crucial role in school success. As Coopersmith put it, "Ability and academic performance are significantly associated with feelings of personal worth."

The self-esteem movement served as an adjustment between school commitments and worries about overburdening children. It also arose at a time of significant rethinking about the preconditions of adult success, with the rise of service-sector jobs that depended on people skills, that is, the skills needed in salesmanship or in maneuvering in management bureaucracies. In addition, the movement also reflected a reduction in confidence in the middle-class home environment, which was linked to the rising divorce rate, and also very practical problems in dealing with the surge in population due to the baby boom, as children suffered from crowded classrooms.

As early as 1950, enhanced discussions of self-confidence and the need for explicit parental support were becoming standard segments in the childrearing manuals. Thus in 1952, Sidonie Gruenberg wrote, "To value his own good opinion, a child has to feel that he is a worthwhile person. He has to have confidence in himself as an individual. This confidence is hard for children to develop and there are many experiences that may shake it" (p. 192). The approach was in interesting contrast to Gruenberg's voluminous writings in the 1930s, where the subject received little explicit comment. Now, however, she gave extensive attention to the need for parents to display pride in their children, with a particular plea that children be encouraged through the mistakes they made. "We must not let the mistakes and failures shatter our faith in the child. . . . He needs real and lasting self-respect if he is to develop" both integrity and a durable capacity to achieve (p. 193). Self-esteem, clearly, began in the home, and a more flexible approach to discipline was urged on parents.

The application of self-esteem concepts in the schools from the 1960s onward involved a number of specific programs and a more general reorientation. Programs typically focused on the importance of providing children a wide range of activities so that they could gain a sense of achievement or mastery, whatever their strictly academic talents. Thus many schools enhanced standard lessons with new opportunities for self-expression. History or literature courses added often-elaborate role-playing exercises to reading and discussion. By playing a historical character, children might demonstrate skills that would not come to light if they were merely called upon to recite facts about the same character. It was also crucial that most of these additional exercises were not graded, again in the interests of encouraging a sense of competence at all levels. Another set of self-esteem exercises involved a growing emphasis on "service learning." Here, students could directly contribute to the community while also building an opportunity to display an individual capacity to perform. Thus the Challenge Program in California involved high school students in tutoring gradeschoolers, in working in a historical society, or in participating in environmental efforts. The rationale was central to the self-esteem approach: through these nonacademic activities, students would "have a reason to enjoy and a recipe for personal success."

The approach was fascinating in its effort to provide alternatives to academic competence and competitiveness, and even more fascinating in its assumptions that school must be leavened by nonacademic exercises. Proponents argued that when involved students were compared with control groups participation in the self-esteem programs reduced discipline problems in the schools and improved academic performance. It was less clear why overall American academic achievement levels continued to falter (for example, compared to other nations that did not stress self-esteem) despite the growing utilization of self-esteem activities.

Self-esteem arguments also entered into recommendations for teacher behavior. Thus teachers were urged to add positive comments on all student work, in addition to (and perhaps instead of) critical observations. Some education authorities argued essentially that rewarding good behavior was far more useful, given self-esteem needs, than castigating bad. The portfolio movement also included some self-esteem justifications as well, although it had a number of other justifications. Instead of grading students through conventional tests alone, portfolio programs allowed them to offer a collection of different kinds of expression in the subject area, from art to computer graphics, so that various learning styles could be accommodated with equal access to self-esteem. And self-esteem concerns had a further impact on the concept of grading, probably contributing substantially to grade inflation.

Self-esteem notions and activities were often criticized, and movements to develop more rigorous testing procedures in the 1990s represented something of a counterattack. Through most of the final third of the twentieth century, however, self-esteem ideas strongly influenced many teachers, and even some athletic coaches, while helping to reconcile parents to the demands of schooling by providing some buffer between strict academics and the psychological development of their children.

See also: **Child Psychology; Child-Rearing Advice Literature; Emotional Life.**

BIBLIOGRAPHY

Coopersmith, Stanley. 1967. *The Antecedents of Self-Esteem.* San Francisco: W. H. Freeman.

Gruenberg, Sidonie. 1958. *The Parents' Guide to Everyday Problems of Boys and Girls.* New York: Hill and Wang.

Rosenberg, Morris. 1965. *Society and the Adolescent Self-Image.* Princeton, NJ: Princeton University Press.

Stearns, Peter N. 2003. *Anxious Parents: A History of Modern Childrearing in America.* New York: New York University Press.

Wang, Jianjun, Betty Greathose, and V. M. Falcinella. 1996. "An Empirical Assessment of Self-Esteem Enhancement." *Education* 119: 99–105.

PETER N. STEARNS

Sendak, Maurice (b. 1928)

Maurice Sendak, one of the greatest twentieth-century writers and illustrators of children's books, as well as a gifted opera and ballet set and costume designer, was born in "a land called Brooklyn," on June 10, 1928, the son of Polish-Jewish immigrants. After a mediocre high school career and some part-time art training, he took a job in 1948 as a window dresser at the F.A.O. Schwartz toy store. The book buyer there introduced him in 1950 to the children's book editor at Harper and Brothers, a meeting that resulted in eighty books in more than a dozen languages selling more than seven million copies.

Sendak illustrated some fifty books by other authors during the 1950s and early 1960s while also doing storyboards for advertising firms and covers for adult fiction. *Where the Wild Things Are* (1963), the first book he both wrote and illustrated, established his reputation as an artist and writer of extraordinary psychological power. In the story Max's mother exiles him to his bedroom without supper for chasing the family dog. (Dogs are a recurring creature in Sendak's works.) "I'll eat you up," Max responds before encountering and taming the fantasy monsters of his rage—his old country

Jewish relatives Sendak once remarked—and coming to peace with himself. The book stirred enormous controversy because its illustrations were said to be too frightening and its hero's anger too explicit. "It is my involvement with this inescapable fact of childhood—the awful vulnerability of children and their struggle to make themselves King of all Wild Things—that gives my work whatever power and passion it may have" Sendak said in accepting the Caldecott Medal in 1964.

In the Night Kitchen (1970), offensive to some because of the full frontal nudity of its protagonist Mickey, and the last of what might be seen as a trilogy, *Outside Over There* (1981), in which a young girl saves her baby sister from goblins who have stolen her from a peaceful landscape dominated by the figure of Mozart, engage the same "inescapable facts." Sendak's first book after more than ten years, *We Are All in the Dumps with Jack and Guy: Two Nursery Rhymes with Pictures* (1993), is about a band of homeless children. Living in boxes under a bridge in a nightmare city, wrapped in *New York Times* real estate pages, and surrounded by emblems of AIDS, they save a baby from rats. The infant sleeps in Jack's arms. It is the *Where the Wild Things Are* of a rawer age.

Sendak is a passionate music lover—especially of Mozart—who began working in the theater in 1979. His opera projects, most explicitly *Hansel and Gretel* but also *The Magic Flute* and *Idomeneo*, engage in the same themes as his books: children triumphing over danger, fear and love of parents, and food and eating. He also has illustrated adult literature, most notably a 1995 edition of Herman Melville's *Pierre.* Sendak received the National Medal of the Arts from President Bill Clinton in 1996.

See also: **Children's Literature.**

BIBLIOGRAPHY

Lanes, Selma G., and Robert Morton. 1993. *The Art of Maurice Sendak.* New York: Abradale Press/Henry Adams.

INTERNET RESOURCE

"Maurice Sendak (1928–)." Available from <www.northern.edu/hastingw/sendak.htm>.

THOMAS LAQUEUR

Series Books

Series books are considered to be any number of similarly plotted novels involving the same characters, settings, or genre expectations. They are marketed according to the familiarity of recurring titles or authors. Stressing repeatability of action and character type over complex development, they are generally of two types—either the same sort of plot resolves within each title, or a much lengthier plot is carried over a large number of books. Typical of the latter is the development of a single character over several adventures and years, such as Laura Ingalls Wilder's lengthy Little House series (1932–1971). Many critics believe that the first series books arose in the early to mid-1800s, as entertaining fiction for children began to deviate from the gloom of religious primers and as various characters gained popularity. Jacob Abbott's Rollo series, beginning in 1835, is among the first. Early series books starred extremely pious children, such as the syrupy Elsie in Martha Finley's Elsie Dinsmore series (1867–1909), or ORPHANS—morally upright, hard-working protagonists who overcome adversity and are rewarded for their pluck. Horatio Alger's Ragged Dick, serialized between 1868 and 1870, remains among the most famous and influential examples of the latter type.

Dime novels at the turn of the nineteenth century became some of the most popular fiction of the time. Edward Stratemeyer (1862–1930) became an extensive developer of series titles when he founded a publishing syndicate around 1905. Employing a team of ghostwriters working under pseudonyms, Stratemeyer outlined and sometimes authored over a thousand novels, creating nearly seventy different series, from the Rover Boys (1899–1926) to the Bobbsey Twins (1904–1992). From 1900 through the middle of the century, Stratemeyer's fiction dominated the bookshelves, as he produced novels on sports, travel, adventure, Westerns, and especially mysteries. Nancy Drew (1930–) and The Hardy Boys (1927–), thrilling mysteries featuring extremely bright and fortuitous young detectives, remain Stratemeyer's two most successful creations. Books featuring technology—boats, cars, radios, detecting equipment—included the Tom Swift series (1910–1941), which is about a young scientific genius and his fantastic inventions. By World War II, war series became especially popular, painting volunteerism in romantic strokes. The Cherry Aimes books (1943–1968) by Helen Wells, about a young nurse who works in various settings, and Margaret Sutton's terrific Judy Bolton series (1932–1967) also developed the female protagonist in new directions.

After the heyday of World War II, several different genres rose to prominence, overtaking the success of earlier titles. Mysteries flourished through series such as Gertrude Chandler Warner's The Boxcar Children (1942–) and Donald J. Sobol's Encyclopedia Brown books (1963–), which contained logic puzzles, with answers to the mysteries found in the back of the book. The 1980s saw the increasing popularity of high school serials such as Francine Pascal's Sweet Valley High (1983–) and Caroline B. Cooney's Cheerleader series (1985–1987), while the younger market exploded with Anne Martin's prolific Baby-Sitter's Club (1986 –). Similarly popular, and heavily marketed toward younger girls, were a succession of animal series such as Bonnie Bryant's The Saddle Club (1988–). R. L. Stine meanwhile repopularized the horror genre through such series as Goosebumps (1992–) and Fear Street (1989–1991), terror stories in vari-

ous incarnations featuring young protagonists encountering a plethora of horror clichés. Multicultural trends culminated not only in the very popular American Girl books (1986–) by Pleasant Company, marketed with a collectable line of dolls, but also in the historical memoir tradition, with such books as Scholastic's Dear America series (1996–). By the turn of the century, CONSUMER CULTURE and chain bookstores profoundly influenced series books, linking fiction with marketing more directly than at any time before.

Because of marketing demands, most series books attempt to achieve a tone of familiarity and predictability, drawing on readers' expectations by recreating recognizable worlds of codified plot devices. By doing so, series books often employ rigid patterns in order to carefully balance a feeling of easy security with rich excitement. They are sometimes weighed down by the narrative devices necessary for marketing. These include the need to provide exposition for new readers, often found in asides in early chapters, and advertisements for other titles, enticingly placed on the last few pages. But these narrative specificities do not discount the profound value of these books. The body of fiction characterized as series books includes some of the most popular and significant artifacts of literature for young people and remains deeply pleasurable for those who remember reading them.

See also: **Carolyn Keene; Children's Literature; Harry Potter and J. K. Rowling.**

BIBLIOGRAPHY

Billman, Carol. 1986. *The Secret of the Stratemeyer Syndicate: Nancy Drew, The Hardy Boys, and the Million Dollar Fiction Factory.* New York: Ungar.

Johnson, Deidre. 1993. *Edward Stratemeyer and the Stratemeyer Syndicate.* New York: Twayne Publishers.

Kensinger, Faye R. 1987. *Children of the Series and How They Grew.* Bowling Green, OH: Bowling Green State University Popular Press.

Mason, Bobbie Ann. 1975. *The Girl Sleuth.* Athens: University of Georgia Press.

Prager, Arthur. 1971. *Rascals at Large; or, The Clue in the Old Nostalgia.* Garden City, NY: Doubleday.

CHRIS MCGEE

Sex Education

The idea that schools and the state have a responsibility to teach young people about sex is a peculiarly modern one. The rise of sex education to a regular place in the school curriculum in the United States and Western Europe is not, however, simply a story of modern enlightenment breaking through a heritage of repression and ignorance. Rather, the movements for sex education can be understood from several related angles: as part of larger struggles in the modern era over who determines the sexual morality of the coming generation; as part of the persistent tendency to view ADOLESCENCE—especially adolescent SEXUALITY—as uniquely dangerous; and as part of the broader historical tendency for more and more realms of personal life to come under rational control. Sex education has always been shaped by its historical context.

It is worth noting that formal sex education has never held a monopoly on sexual information. Much to the distress of sex educators, young people do not simply memorize their school lessons and apply them perfectly. They have always cobbled together their own understanding of their (and others') bodies out of their personal experiences and an accidental agglomeration of "official" sex education, parental teaching, playground mythology, popular culture, and even pornography.

Early History

Prior to the twentieth century, sex education was even more haphazard. Most Americans and Europeans lived in the countryside, where chance observation of animal behavior provided young people with at least a measure of information about reproductive sexuality. Beyond that, education was mixed. Given the expectation that girls would remain chaste until their wedding night, sex education for them did not seem pressing until the eve of matrimony, when their mothers were supposed to sit them down and explain sex and reproduction; contrary expectations for boys often meant that a young man's male relatives or co-workers would take him to a brothel to initiate him into the mysteries of sex.

In the 1830s, however, various health reformers and ministers in the United States and in England began to publish a flood of pamphlets and books to inform and fortify the young man who left home for school or a job. These works were typically great stews of theological, nutritional, and philosophical information, but all aimed to help readers control their sexual urges until they could be safely expressed in marriage. More particularly, these early sex educators tended to be obsessed with the dangers of MASTURBATION. For example, the health reformer Sylvester Graham's 1834 *Lecture to Young Men* and the Reverend John Todd's 1845 *The Young Man. Hints Addressed to the Young Men of the United States* followed works by the English physician William Acton in warning that the "solitary vice" (i.e., masturbation) could and probably would lead to a physical and mental breakdown—even death. The literature seldom addressed women, as society generally considered them to be at all times under the protection of their parents and then their husbands, while young men were more mobile. In France, the sex education literature that began appearing in the 1880s, was usually addressed to bourgeois mothers, and focused chiefly on their duty to instruct their daughters on the dual need to be chaste until marriage but prepared for sexual contact after matrimony. Despite these small steps toward

education, later reformers complained that a "conspiracy of silence" about sexual matters existed into the early years of the twentieth century.

Origins of a Movement

The formal movement for sex education commenced in the early twentieth century. Oddly, early reformers seldom said anything about needing to compensate for the loss of barnyard knowledge when families grew up in the city rather than on a farm. In other societies undergoing rapid urbanization, such as China at the dawn of the twenty-first century, newspapers regularly reported on young city couples who wanted children for years but never picked up the essential information on animal breeding that would have suggested how to become pregnant. American reformers, like their counterparts in England at roughly the same time, were more focused on the related dangers of medical and moral decline. First, physicians were growing alarmed about the impact of syphilis and gonorrhea—the "venereal diseases"—among all classes of citizens, and among women as well as men. Investigators had come to recognize that these sexually transmitted diseases (STDs) annually caused thousands of cases of pelvic inflammation, sterility, infant blindness, and even insanity. Second, physicians and their allies associated this "epidemic" with what many Americans considered the immorality of life in the city. Native-born Americans in particular believed that a moral crisis loomed in cities such as Chicago and New York as immigrants and migrants from the countryside crowded together in dismal tenements and children grew up without the "ennobling influence" of life on the farm. Equally alarming, in an era in which prostitution was a fairly open secret in the red light districts of most urban areas, doctors became convinced that the majority of STDs were transmitted through men visiting prostitutes. This meshing together of moral and medical concepts was to remain characteristic of American and, to a lesser extent, European sex education.

Sex education became a significant part of the response to these twin anxieties. Founded in 1914 by the New York physician Prince Morrow and the religious crusader Anna Garlin Spencer, the American Social Hygiene Association (ASHA) quickly took the lead in recommending reforms to accomplish the twin goals of medical and moral improvement. After leading police crackdowns on prostitution and presenting a series of sex education lectures to adults, ASHA and related societies proposed a program in "sex instruction" for high-school-age youth. ASHA's leaders hoped they could reach young people with proper "scientific" facts about sex before they were "corrupted" by harmful misinformation, such as the widely held belief that young men suffered from a "medical necessity" to have sex. If citizens only knew the medical dangers of sexual immorality, reformers believed, then they would rationally decide not to experiment with prostitution or promiscuity.

Although the English movement for sex education grew out of similar anxieties, and was led by a similar combination of medical and moral authorities, the French movement differed in certain essential respects. France officially tolerated and regulated prostitution, for example, so it never became a focus of educators' efforts. Instead, French sex educators were more concerned about preparing young middle-class women for the sexual aspects of marriage and reproduction. They generally ignored working-class females, believing they were already immoral by nature. French authorities occasionally supported sex education for men to combat the scourges of STDs, but after the carnage of World War I, French educators also linked sex education to the need for French families to bear more children to repopulate the state.

Moving into the Schools
Sex educators in the United States sometimes experimented with working through parents, churches, and public lectures, but they quickly turned to the public schools. In the early twentieth century, public school attendance was exploding as compulsory education laws and the changing structure of the economy pressured more students into the classroom and kept them there longer. At the same time, observers were becoming more conscious of youth as a period of life separate from adulthood, with its own particular needs and dangers, and this new conception of the adolescent was widely popularized by the publication of G. STANLEY HALL's essential *Adolescence* in 1904. Trapped between the sexual awakening of PUBERTY and the "legitimate" sexual outlet of marriage, adolescents seemed particularly to need careful guidance, and the public schools could step in to give it to them where parents seemed to be failing. Not coincidentally, moving their mission to the classroom promised to give sex educators a captive audience.

Reflecting their own uneasiness with sexuality, the early sex educators constructed a program whose central mission was to quash curiosity about sex. Initially, the sex education program consisted of an outside physician delivering a short series of lectures outlining the fundamentals of the reproductive system, the destructive power of syphilis and gonorrhea, and the moral and medical dangers caused by sex before or outside of marriage. Boys and girls sat in separate classrooms, and their lessons reflected a strong sense of difference between the sexes. Besides hearing the medical warnings about sexually transmitted diseases, boys learned that they had a moral responsibility to their mothers and future wives to remain chaste. Girls were instructed much more deliberately in raw fear—especially in the high likelihood of contracting syphilis from a male. So vivid were the warnings that some instructors in the first decades of the twentieth century actually worried that their female students might never marry. Because they sought to ennoble sexuality by making it synonymous with reproduction, early sex educators seldom dwelled on the threat of TEEN PREGNANCY.

Despite the educators' moralistic tone, sex education met immediate opposition. When Chicago became the first major city to implement sex education for high schools in 1913, the Catholic Church in particular led a powerful attack on the program and helped secure the resignation of its sponsor, Ella Flagg Young, the famous superintendent of schools.

The Chicago controversy, as it was called, laid out the themes that were to characterize the politics of sex education in the United States over the next century. Both supporters and opponents agreed that youthful sexuality was a problem. But where supporters felt that "scientific" knowledge about sexuality (or at least reproduction) would lead young people down the path to moral behavior, opponents argued that any suggestion of sexuality, no matter how well intended, would corrupt students' minds.

The federal government first became involved in sex education during World War I, when the Chamberlain-Kahn Act of 1918 first earmarked money to educate soldiers about syphilis and gonorrhea. Over half a million young men had their first experience with sex instruction in the war. ASHA later took many of the materials its consultants had developed for the military, such as the film *Fit to Fight*, and adapted them for public school use by editing out the segments on prophylaxis. Until the 1950s, the federal government remained involved in sex education, mainly through the U.S. Public Health Service, emphasizing the medical and moral dangers of sexually transmitted diseases.

More than Hygiene
In the Jazz Age of the 1920s, sex education made progress into the curriculum both in the United States and in France. American sex education typically took place in high school biology classes, but leaders in the movement also faced for the first time a clear divergence between adult sexual ideals and society's expectations for youth. Up to the early twentieth century, when sexual fulfillment was not considered a public or respectable ideal even for married adults, it was easy for educators to condemn sex in their lessons. But in the 1920s, as more Americans came to believe that sexual fulfillment was a crucial part of marriage, educators faced the dilemma of recognizing that sex was a positive force in marriage while at the same time needing to condemn its expression among the unmarried. Sex educators responded partly by reemphasizing the health dangers of sex outside of marriage, but also by incorporating the new ideals. Greatly concerned over the sexual freedom of the "new youth" in the 1920s and 1930s, sex educators appealed to psychology and sociology for evidence that sexual experimentation before marriage endangered a youth's chances for a fulfilling wedded life.

After the discovery of penicillin's uses in World War II lessened the danger of syphilis, ASHA and its allies focused more directly on the social aspects of sexuality and married life. Known by a variety of names, the new "family life education" represented an expansion of the educators' mission. Instead of teaching mostly about sexual prohibitions, family life educators attempted to instruct students in the positive satisfactions to be gained from a properly ordered family life. Lessons on child rearing, money management, wedding planning, DATING, and a wide variety of other daily tasks were intended to bring a new generation of American youth into conformity with white, middle-class norms.

In response particularly to the "sexual revolution" of the 1960s and 1970s, in which rates of premarital sexual activity, pregnancy, and sexually transmitted diseases climbed steeply, sex educators developed what they called "sexuality education," to distinguish their approach from the overt moralizing and narrow heterosexual focus of its predecessors. The leaders in sexuality education, such as the Sexuality Information Education Council of the United States (SIECUS, founded in 1964), believed that teaching about sexuality in a value-neutral manner would allow students to reach their own conclusions about sexual behavior and sexual morality. Sexuality education was intended to include information on BIRTH CONTROL methods, teenage pregnancy, masturbation, gender relations, and, eventually, HOMOSEXUALITY. Although value-neutral sexuality education generally avoided the overt moralizing of its predecessors, it nevertheless stacked the deck in favor of traditional morality—abstinence until heterosexual marriage.

Despite its generally traditional message, sexuality education quickly aroused a firestorm of opposition. Beginning in 1968, conservative groups and previously apolitical religious activists mobilized to attack what one pamphlet called "raw sex" in the schoolhouse. Opponents were offended not only by sexuality education's greater explicitness, but by its refusal to drill students in "proper" sexual morality. Sexuality education seemed to represent a wide variety of liberal attitudes that were beginning to appear in American society, and the struggles over sexuality education helped motivate a new generation of religious conservatives to enter American politics in the 1970s. It was at this point that the American experience began to diverge from the European approach, which had aroused occasional Catholic disapproval but never faced a highly political campaign of opposition.

HIV/AIDS Crisis

In the United States, the debate between opponents and supporters continued to follow the same lines until the pandemic of Human Immunodeficiency Virus/Acquired Immunodeficiency Syndrome (HIV/AIDS) began in the 1980s. As the magnitude and deadliness of this sexually transmitted illness became known (and as the public became aware that heterosexuals as well as homosexuals were at risk), sex educators found their position bolstered. By the mid-1990s almost every western European nation sponsored fairly explicit educational programs in "safe sex"; in the United States, every state had passed mandates for AIDS education, sometimes combined with sexuality education, sometimes as a stand-

alone program. AIDS provided crucial justification for the more liberal sexuality educators' inclusion of information on contraception, homosexuality, and premarital sex. At universities and many high schools, students also started "peer-education" groups to offer students a sex education message that was even less hierarchical and judgmental (and sometimes much more explicit). Despite a renewed conservative attack on these programs, sexuality education's place seemed to have become secure.

As conservative opponents in the United States came to recognize that some form of sex education was going to be almost inevitable, they launched their own movement to replace sexuality education with "abstinence education." Religious conservatives, in particular, helped add provisions for abstinence education to the 1996 WELFARE REFORM ACT, and the federal government for the first time began to direct tens of millions of dollars to abstinence education programs, most of which were tied to religious groups rather than the more traditional public health organizations. Unlike sexuality education's value neutrality, abstinence education was directly moralistic and explicitly supported traditional gender and sexual relations. Abstinence education also harked back to the early years of sex education in its strong emphasis on the dangers of sexual activity. Many curricula intentionally omitted or distorted information about protective measures such as condoms or birth-control pills. Again, this contrasted with the European experience, in which sexuality education was firmly under the control of secular medical authorities and faced little religious or political challenge.

International Context

Outside of Western Europe and the United States, sex education remained largely informal until concerns over a population explosion and the AIDS crisis prompted international organizations such as the United Nations to become involved in educating residents in Africa and South Asia particularly about contraception and prophylaxis. Although the religious opposition there has been muted, educators have often met with resistance from governments unwilling to admit that their populations were experiencing problems with AIDS, and from male traditionalists reluctant to allow women greater control over their own sexuality. Political battles in the United States, too, have affected the shape of sex education in the less-developed regions of the world, as American conservatives at the dawn of the twenty-first century attempted to use U.S. funding to shift the content of international sex education programs away from contraception and towards abstinence and a more moralistic approach to sexual relations.

Conclusion

The response to the AIDS crisis once again underlined the general tendency to justify sex education as disaster prevention in response to diseases or other "epidemics," such as teenage pregnancy. Throughout the history of sex education, adults in the West have generally treated adolescent sexuality as existing in a different world from its grown-up version, blaming hormones or the youth culture for recurring crises in adolescent sexual behavior. But youthful sexual behavior has almost always been closely tied to adult patterns of behavior: rising rates of extramarital intercourse among adolescents, for example, only followed the same phenomenon among adults; the same held true for the "epidemic" of pregnancy outside of marriage in the 1970s, as pregnant teenage females followed their adult counterparts in having more children outside of wedlock.

Although it has undoubtedly dispelled much ignorance and anxiety among students, sex education in the United States, at least, has generally failed to deliver on its promise to change adolescent sexual behavior. Sexual behavior is a complex phenomenon, and hours in the classroom have seldom managed to counteract the influence of class, race, family, region, and popular culture. Nevertheless, the history of sex education reveals a great deal about modern conceptions of sexuality, adolescence, and authority.

See also: **AIDS; Hygiene; Venereal Disease.**

BIBLIOGRAPHY

Bigelow, Maurice A. 1916. *Sex-Education: A Series of Lectures Concerning Sex in Its Relation to Human Life*. New York: Macmillan.

Chen, Constance M. 1996. *"The Sex Side of Life": Mary Ware Dennett's Pioneering Battle for Birth Control and Sex Education*. New York: Free Press.

Hall, G. Stanley. 1904. *Adolescence: Its Psychology and its Relations to Physiology, Anthropology, Sociology, Sex, Crime, Religion, and Education*. New York: D. Appleton.

Irvine, Janice. 2002. *Talk About Sex: The Battles Over Sex Education in the United States*. Berkeley: University of California Press.

Moran, Jeffrey P. 2000. *Teaching Sex: The Shaping of Adolescence in the Twentieth Century*. Cambridge, MA: Harvard University Press.

Smith, Ken. 1999. *Mental Hygiene: Classroom Films 1945–1970*. New York: Blast Books.

Stewart, Mary Lynn. 1997. "'Science is Always Chaste': Sex Education and Sexual Initiation in France, 1880s–1930s." *Journal of Contemporary History* 32: 381–395.

JEFFREY P. MORAN

Cupid as Link Boy (1774), Sir Joshua Reynolds (English, 1723–1792). Not all societies have felt the need to protect children from adult sexuality. In eighteenth-century London streets, link boys held torches that lit the routes of travelers at night; they were also exploited as aids to, and victims of, sexual liaisons. (Oil on canvas; unframed: 30 x 25" [76.2 x 63.5 cm]; Seymour H. Knox Fund, through special gifts to the fund by Mrs. Marjorie Knox Campbell, Mrs. Dorothy Knox Rogers, and Mr. Seymour H. Knox Jr., 1945).

Sexuality

Childhood, in most modern cultures, is defined in large part by its separation from adult sexuality. While many contemporary cultures recognize aspects of sexuality in children, such as the development of sexual curiosity or MASTURBATION practices common among young children, they draw a clear line between such forms of childhood sexuality and children's exposure to adult sexuality and sexual experience. Prepubescent children, in most modern cultures, are not legitimate objects of adult sexual desire or behavior. Paradoxi-

cally, it is this very separation of childhood and adult sexuality that so closely links childhood to sexuality in modern cultures. Societies attempt to enforce that separation through elaborate systems of laws, institutions, and ideologies. Public debates about the proper role of sex and sexual images in the mass media and public culture often turn on notions of childhood innocence. A whole constellation of social practices have been created because modern societies attempt to protect children from sex and adult sexuality.

PUBERTY, the biological process of maturation into sexual and reproductive maturity, commonly marks the end of childhood. It does not, however, always mark the entry into adulthood or adult sexuality. Most modern societies see the years following puberty as directly linked to sex, but in many ways that direct relationship is more problematic than childhood's oblique one. While childhood is defined as a period deserving—demanding—protection from adult sexuality, the proper relationship between ADOLESCENCE and sexuality is less clear. Adolescents are clearly sexual, but not clearly adult. Biological and social maturity are not always considered equivalent. How, then, should the sexuality of youth be

Théodore Géricault's *Louise Vernet* (c. before 1816) confronts the viewer directly with her all-too-worldly gaze. Suggestions of the child's sexual power are reinforced by the dress sliding off her shoulder and the cat she holds on her lap. This image would be at variance with the ideal of girlhood as innocent and passionless that would develop throughout the nineteenth century. Louvre, Paris, France/Giraudon-Bridgeman Art Library.

regulated or controlled? These are not new problems in human history. Human societies have grappled with the common problems of biological and social maturation for thousands of years. But just as the meaning and experience of childhood has differed dramatically across cultures and through time, so have the social definitions of childhood, youth, and sexuality.

Ancient and Premodern Societies

Writing about the history of sexuality is always a complicated task, as it is difficult to find direct evidence about the meaning and practice of sex in history. We come to knowledge of sex indirectly, through debates about sex, regulations governing sex, representations of sex, prohibitions against sex, or demographic data (which may, for example, reveal something of the frequency of conception outside marriage but little about the acts of sexual intercourse that produced it or the meaning of such acts). The problem of access to historical information about sex and its meaning is compounded when dealing with children, who have largely been defined outside the licit realm of sex and sexuality. This problem is compounded further when writing about societies in the distant past or about premodern, nonliterate so-

cieties. Much of our knowledge, especially of ancient cultures, is drawn from codes of law, especially those concerned with INHERITANCE OF PROPERTY. In the case of nonliterate tribal cultures, it is difficult to know how accurately the practices documented by travelers and, later, anthropologists, reflect actual practices and whether those practices are long-standing traditions or relatively recent developments. However, the works of classicists, historians, and anthropologists offer some insight into the distant past. Most strikingly, they reveal something of the enormous variety of cultural definitions of childhood, and of the relation of children and youth to sex and sexuality, that have existed in human cultures.

A survey of a single continent, AFRICA, offers some sense of the great diversity of cultural practices surrounding childhood, youth, and sexuality in premodern cultures (the discussion in this section is particularly indebted to the informative synthesis provided in A. R. Colón's *A History of Children*). According to documentation from the late nineteenth century, about five thousand distinct tribes remained in sub-Saharan Africa at that time. The meaning and experience of childhood differed from tribe to tribe, and so did traditional attitudes toward youth and sexuality and the practices that regulated them. In many sub-Saharan tribes, though children learned gender-appropriate tasks from an early age, puberty marked a new stage of life and was marked by some sort of initiation ceremony, which might last days or even years. Here, recognition of sexual maturity often combined with entry into adult responsibilities and status. The Kpelle, a tribe in what is present-day Liberia, secluded boys for four years in a period of initiation and instruction, including ritual CIRCUMCISION. Among the Pygmy, a boy was not considered ready for marriage until he had killed an antelope or buffalo. Among the Ngoni, boys celebrated puberty with a cleansing ceremony in the river after the first nocturnal emission. The nomadic Fulani gave boys charge of cattle at age ten, at which time ritual circumcisions were performed. Bedouin boys were also ritually circumcised and, in order to gain the endurance of a camel, were expected to eat a piece of bread that had been smeared with camel dung. The Ganda, who considered children property and rarely raised their own children, did not mark puberty in any way and had no rituals for passage into sexual or social adulthood.

For girls, puberty rites were frequently tied to MENARCHE, or the onset of menstruation. Among the Ngoni in central Africa, as in many other African tribes, girls were placed in isolation huts during menstruation. After her first menstrual flow ended, a girl underwent a cleansing ceremony. With her father's sisters and other women from the village, she was led in a procession from the isolation hut to the river, where she was undressed and placed in the water, facing southeast. Afterwards, she was taken to the dwelling of her aunt and given instruction on proper behavior for her new stage of life. This new status included bimonthly vaginal examinations by elder women from the village who were charged with verifying and so maintaining the girl's virginity. Other tribes sought to guarantee girls' virginity through genital surgery. Female circumcision was a common initiation rite at puberty, though the procedure sometimes took place in infancy or during childhood. The sunna circumcision, performed by central Ethiopian tribes on infant girls, removed only the prepuce from the clitoris. Pharaonic circumcision was a major operation in which the girl's clitoris, labia minor, and parts of her labia majora were removed. The remaining portion of the labia majora were sewn together, or infibulated, and her legs bound together for up to forty days until her vulva fused closed. Infections of the urinary tract and vagina were common, as were difficulties in menstruation, and the fused vulva created pain during sexual intercourse and complicated eventual childbirth. Pharaonic circumcision or simple infibulation was practiced throughout Africa, though not by all peoples, and continues to this day in approximately twenty-six (or more than half of the total) African nations. About 90 percent of girls in the Sudan still undergo pharaonic circumcision.

As ISLAM and Christianity spread through Africa, these particular religious traditions merged with local tribal customs and influenced understandings of sexuality, childhood, and family. For example, tribes with traditional matrilineal patterns of inheritance switched to patrilineal models, thus shifting the control of property to men and increasing the importance of marriage for women's economic security and protection. Especially in areas influenced by Islam, by the eighteenth century marriages were contracted and performed at increasingly early ages, ranging from age seven in the San region to ten in Madagascar and twelve or fourteen in the Sudan and southeast Africa. Premodern Pacific Island cultures also illustrate the great range that existed in the social regulation of sexuality. Among the Tiwi, for example, girls were married before puberty while boys underwent a ten-year-long period of initiation, beginning at puberty, before they could marry. On Vanatianai, in Melanesia, sexual activity was seen as an appropriate and pleasurable activity for both boys and girls once they entered puberty at about the age of fourteen.

Through most of human history—and still today in many places—children and youth have been exposed to sex very directly. The vast majority of people lived in small dwellings. Privacy was scarce, and concepts of privacy were different from those of contemporary American and western European cultures. Children commonly slept in the same room with their parents; in many places, especially in cold climates, the entire family might share a single bed or its equivalent. In such conditions, children commonly heard and saw adults having sex. And it was not only people who lived closely together in small spaces. Animals were often a source of sexual knowledge. In rural areas and towns alike, children—often responsible for animal care—learned about sex from watching animals copulate and give birth. Just as people in pre-

industrial and premodern societies were more directly exposed to the processes of birth and death, they were more directly exposed to knowledge of sex. Children shared that knowledge. They were not protected from exposure to sex. However, simply because children had knowledge of sex does not mean that they were not protected from adult sexuality and sexual contact. That protection did exist in many cultures. However, while the notion that "childhood" is an invention of modern times has been strongly refuted by many scholars, it is nonetheless important to note that children were not universally seen as deserving of society's protection, whether in the realm of sex or elsewhere, nor was there steady progress toward a protected status. Some ancient societies wrote the protection of children into law (though protections did not necessarily cover all children), while in others ABANDONMENT, infanticide, child slavery, and CHILD PROSTITUTION were common.

Early written records of human civilization, reaching back to the Sumerians, specify to some extent the proper treatment of children. For example, the eighteenth-century B.C.E. Code of Hammurabi forbids men to commit INCEST with their daughters or to "defile" their sons' betrothed. The Egyptian *Book of the Dead* gives some sense of the restrictions governing sex with children, including "sexual relations with a boy" in its list of acts that would prevent a man from entering into the next life. The ancient Hebrews also prohibited sodomy with children, considering it a form of idolatry related to the worship of the body. Sodomy with a boy under the age of nine was punished by flagellation, and by stoning if the boy were older than nine years. While these restrictions may have aimed less at the protection of children than the prohibition of certain sexual acts, they stand in significant contrast to other cultures in which children found little or no protection. Along the Mediterranean coast, the Phoenicians, who were active in the first millennium B.C.E., were known for their cruelty to children. Infant and child sacrifice, in which babies and small children were burned alive, was common, and the Phoenicians maintained official "temple boys" or "sacred" prostitutes, who were sodomized by adult men.

Roman child-rearing practices combined signs of great affection for children with a striking lack of protection for them. Abandonment of children was common, and the abandoned child—if it survived—was likely to be enslaved or sold into prostitution. Abandoned male infants intended for prostitution were sometimes castrated in order to prolong their androgynous, boyish appearance. Such practices were prohibited by the emperor Nerva during his brief reign from 96 to 98 C.E. Subsequent emperors Trajan and Hadrian built upon these reforms, with Hadrian enforcing the law against castration of boys and prohibiting the sale of children for sexual purposes. Significantly, he extended these protections to slave children as well as to the freeborn. Regulations of sexuality for children and youth also developed around the issue of property. Commonly, elite families with inheritable property were much more concerned with controlling the sexual behaviors of their children. Legally recognized marriages and the production of legitimate heirs were proportionally more important to families with property, and such concerns fostered emphasis on the virginity of daughters before marriage. In ancient China, while among the lower classes young people commonly mated around the age of fifteen, the sexual experiences of elite youth were closely monitored, indicating the greater significance of marriage to those with property. In ancient Persia, girls of elite families commonly entered into polygamous marriages at the age of fifteen. Familial control over sexuality and property here was extreme, as incest was not a taboo, and men could marry their own daughters.

In ancient Greece, a girl's virginity was closely linked to family honor, and unmarried girls were counseled to sleep on a bed of withy, or long, flexible twigs, as a way of preventing sexual desire. Marriage marked the passage to adulthood for girls; only through marriage did a girl become an adult woman. Boys, on the other hand, celebrated passage into manhood and citizenship at the age of eighteen or nineteen—a moment marked not by biological sexual maturation but by their relationship to the state. In medieval and early modern western Europe, the regulation and control of youthful sexuality was structured by the demands of economic subsistence and by the increasing power of religious authority. The highest priority, in what were primarily subsistence agricultural societies, was survival. Limiting reproduction (and thus the number of mouths to feed and the number of children among whom to divide resources) was critical, and families and communities regulated sexuality in order to limit fertility. Biology helped; puberty came relatively late, usually between fourteen and sixteen years of age for girls, because of poor nutrition. Combined with short life-spans (life expectancy in early modern England was thirty-five to forty years) and early menopause, women had a much shorter period of potential childbearing than is common today. However, young people did not commonly mate or marry at puberty. The average age at marriage in early modern western Europe was later than in most contemporary societies: approximately twenty-six years old for women and twenty-seven to twenty-nine years old for men.

While children began work at early ages, and were often sent away from home to serve as apprentices in their midteens, they did not move directly from childhood to adulthood at puberty or at the beginning of their work lives. Instead, the period of "youth" lasted until the young man and woman were able to marry and set up their own household. Thus, most were in the dependent category of youth for almost half of their lives. It was in part a question of resources—the labor of the young was needed to sustain the family, and it was often only upon the death of the older generation that youth inherited sufficient resources to set up

their own households. However, even among affluent, elite families in which there were ample resources, sexual maturity was not the only criterion for marriage. Marriages did occur at earlier ages among the wealthy, but, for example, when the son of the Countess of Warwick was married at nineteen to a young bride, his mother sent him abroad while his wife remained with her; she felt they were too young and inexperienced to live together. And young men who completed their APPRENTICESHIPS with sufficient means to marry sometimes delayed, for marriage and the responsibility for a household was understood not to be simply a matter of means, but of maturity. Certainly, among the poorest, such controls did not always obtain. But in much of medieval and early modern Europe, the family and the community attempted to control the behaviors of these sexually mature but not "adult" young people.

In that respect, they worked in concert with the church. Christian thought, from the High Middle Ages forward, clearly posed adolescence as a time of sexual danger, requiring spiritual control. As Guibert de Nogent wrote in his autobiography from the beginning of the twelfth century, "Thus, while my young body grew little by little, my soul was also aroused by worldly life, titillated in its own right by sexual desires and lust." Adolescence was a time of temptation for "still-naive" souls, and while theologians focused on human beings' propensity for sin, they saw the period of youth as particularly susceptible to the temptations of the flesh. The church, also, placed increasing emphasis on the virginity of girls and young women, praising virginity as a connection to the Virgin Mary, Christ's mother. Thus, religious tenets, the economic needs of communities and the related intensity of community supervision of young people, and cultural definitions of maturity combined to limit the sexual explorations of youth. Specific customs like BUNDLING, where courting couples lay together fully clad, regulated courtship sexuality, usually—although not always—successfully. Nonetheless, for poorer, rural families without dowries and significant property, premarital virginity was less important, premarital sex more common, and marriage often more an informal but long-term pairing (*animus matrimonii*) than the legal marriage that was important to elite families with property. Poorer rural communities accepted premarital sex with the understanding that pregnancy would yield marriage. In sixteenth- and seventeenth-century England, as many as one-fifth of brides were pregnant when they wed, but only about 3 percent of babies were born outside wedlock.

However, as towns and cities grew and more and more young people left rural areas to serve as apprentices or servants in the growing towns, community control weakened. Young women, especially, were increasingly vulnerable to sexual exploitation, often by their masters or other members of the master's household. It was not simply exploitation, however, for young men and young women alike—many of them "youth" in their early twenties—took advantage of the greater freedom they found in cities, and apprentices' masters often allowed a good deal of freedom, sexual and otherwise, to their older apprentices and servants. This freedom had its dangers. If a young woman or girl became pregnant and the man could not or would not marry her, she was likely to be dismissed from her position and prosecuted in court. Livelihood for herself and her baby was uncertain at best. Nevertheless, illegitimacy rates increased in Europe, mainly among young people, in the sixteenth century, and particularly in the eighteenth to early nineteenth centuries. With the growth of towns and cities, the varying customs of different social classes became more obvious and the church, along with members of the growing bourgeoisie who sought clearly defined marriage and familial relations to facilitate the transfer of property, pushed to foster a single standard of behavior. Premarital virginity for women was increasingly stressed, and the church no longer recognized the informal pairing typical of poor rural populations as a form of marriage.

Court records from western European cities during the High Middle Ages and Renaissance also show the prevalence of sexual "vice" and exploitation. Between about 1300 and 1700 C.E., men commonly participated in an age-structured system of sexual relations in which "beardless youths" between puberty and full sexual maturity (aged fifteen to twenty-two or so) were anally penetrated by men in their mid- to late twenties. Constrained from marrying until quite late because of economic factors, and in cultures that emphasized the virginity of girls from respectable families, men commonly had sexual relationships with boys and also with female prostitutes or with lower-class girls and young women who were vulnerable to exploitation or rape. The homosexual pairings between older and younger males were not permanent sexual relationships or roles. Once the youth's beard came in fully, he took the "active" sexual role with a younger boy, while his older partner came of age to marry and left behind the practice of sodomy with men. (Some men, of course, continued to practice sodomy beyond the appropriate age, but that was considered something quite different from the age-regulated system of sexual relations.) This age-based system was illegal and not condoned by the Church, but was seemingly very common. In mid-fifteenth-century Florence at least fifteen thousand men were accused of sodomy in the courts, and—demonstrating tolerance for the practice—penalties were not severe: simply a fine, which was often not paid. This age-based system of relations between men and youths disappeared as common practice in northwestern Europe around 1700, but it persisted in other parts of Europe and the Middle East into the early twentieth century.

Industrializing Societies

The growth of industrial societies and the concomitant development of a larger middle class or bourgeoisie shaped the sexual lives of children and youth in almost diametrically opposite directions. The rise of factories and migration of the rural poor to urban areas led to enormous exploitation and suffering of children and youth. In western Europe, children as young as three years old were put to work in factories. Few protections existed for such children, who worked long and difficult hours and often lacked sufficient food, clothing, or shelter. These children and youths were increasingly vulnerable to forms of sexual abuse and exploitation. With large numbers of children living on the streets, many turned to prostitution or other forms of sexual activity for survival. In the United States, where slavery was not ended until 1865, enslaved African-American girls and women frequently were sexually exploited or raped.

At the same time, middle-class children in North America and western Europe were treasured and protected in new ways. Nineteenth-century religious beliefs and social philosophy defined childhood as a time of innocence, and art and literature from the time portrays children with great sentimentality, often as symbols of purity, innocence, and unspoiled religious sentiment. As children became more of an economic liability than an asset, families intentionally had fewer children. The FERTILITY RATE dropped by almost half during the nineteenth century in the United States. The change was most dramatic in urban middle-class and professional families, who devoted more attention to nurturing and educating each individual child. Children were also seen as malleable in their innocence, and mothers increasingly were held responsible for shaping the moral development of their children. In these new urban-industrial societies, that meant fostering self-control, DISCIPLINE, and education as means to economic success—or at least stability. Girls were also inculcated with the virtues of self-control and industry, but with great emphasis on moral purity, which was seen as fundamental to their future roles as wives and mothers. Expectations about sexual behavior, however, differed by race, class, and region. Premarital sex, and even "outside" children that resulted, were much more acceptable to the rural southern poor, both black and white.

Middle-class notions of purity and self-control, not surprisingly, often centered upon sexuality. A growing advice literature combined medical and moral messages to warn about the dangers of masturbation. While such concerns may be traced back to a series of publications in the eighteenth century, including the anonymous *Onania* and S. A. Tissot's *Onanism*, middle-class North Americans and western Europeans encountered a flood of writing on the subject. This secret vice, it was claimed, could lead to sterility, insanity, idiocy, or a range of lesser effects. Health reformers such as Sylvester Graham offered dietary regimens designed to inhibit masturbation and nocturnal emissions, while others developed mechanical devices. One such device, intended to discourage sexual arousal in young men, encircled the penis with a ring of spikes; another restrained the hands and covered the genital area with a girdle of cold, wet cloths. Fears about masturbatory practices focused on boys and young men. A smaller and more discreet literature was devoted to girls. Mothers were warned to watch for evidence of masturbation, especially lassitude, in their daughters. But compared to their male peers, young women and girls largely escaped this form of sexual surveillance, in part because girls and women were not believed to be as sexual by nature as were men: purity and passionlessness were held up as female ideals. However, young women were much more closely chaperoned and supervised than young men of the same social class, for sexual virtue and a reputation for sexual modesty was critically important to the marriageability of young middle-class and elite women, and for working-class women of many U.S. immigrant groups who held to their traditional cultures. Paradoxically, assumptions that women were less fully sexual than men would allow for greater sexual freedom in one sphere: relations between women or girls. "Romantic friendships" between young women were relatively common and quite acceptable into the early years of the twentieth century. Crushes, or "smashing," as it was sometimes called, were a major part of social life at WOMEN'S COLLEGES into the early twentieth century. The sexual content of such relationships varied, but young women did find relative freedom to pursue same-sex relationships during this era.

Nineteenth century middle-class ideology emphasized the difference between male and female, not only in adult roles but in prescriptions for childhood activities as well. Nineteenth-century understandings of puberty drew the line between male and female very clearly. By the nineteenth century, Western medical science portrayed menstruation as a debilitating monthly event, suggesting that it posed such a physical crisis, especially during puberty, that any strenuous physical or intellectual activity might ruin a girl's health, possibly rendering her a sterile, sexless being. Thus puberty led to the curtailing of girls' freedom of activity. This happened, on the whole, ever earlier. In the nineteenth century, the average age at first menstruation had dropped to fourteen years for European-American girls and eleven for African-American. While it is important to understand how the medicalization of normal menstruation worked to limit girls' lives, it is also worth pointing out that the process of menstruation was poorly understood, and doctors lacked the ability to accurately diagnose and treat painful disorders such as endometriosis or ovarian cysts. Ideology played the greatest role in limiting women's activities because of the "frailty" of their bodies, but modern medicine and products such as disposable sanitary napkins and tampons also helped to free women from limits imposed by menstruation itself.

Limitation of girls' activities at menarche was not confined to industrial, Western societies. In China, also, the onset of menstruation was treated as a sign of female weakness and of uncleanliness. Classical writings on health remained influential in the nineteenth century, including those of sixteenth-century medical writer Li Shizhen, who wrote of the menstruating woman: "Her evil juices are full of stench and filth, hence the gentleman should keep his distance; as they are not clean, they will harm his male essence and invite disease." Puberty, in late imperial China, was defined more broadly than in Western cultures. It was not simply the biological process that signaled physical reproductive maturity, but rather activation of the "true qi of heaven bestowed at conception" by the individual's parents. While the period of adolescence was not defined through specific rituals, classical works such as the *Book of Ritual* did provide for a period of youth, prescribing the appropriate age of marriage as twenty years for women and thirty years for men. These prescriptions for delayed marriage correspond with the belief that it took many years for the yin and yang of the young people to become "replete." However, age at marriage or mating varied greatly by social class and social circumstance; poor young men might experience greatly prolonged bachelorhood because they lacked resources to marry or maintain a family, while such families also might arrange the marriage of a prepubescent boy in order to gain a daughter-in-law needed for household work.

In Western societies, the problem posed by sexually mature but not "adult" youths was exacerbated by industrialization and urbanization. While middle-class Americans and western Europeans attempted to foster the development of self-control in their own sons, they feared the unsupervised and uncontrolled sexual energies of working-class youth in the growing cities, many of whom lived apart from family or effective community supervision. Some scholars have suggested that the actual physical growth of adolescents—in North America, on average, young men had gained two inches in height and fifteen pounds in weight between 1880 and 1920, due to better nutrition—made them more intimidating. No matter the cause, a great deal of effort was devoted to controlling the sexual energies and impulses of youth, especially of young working-class men. And as rates of premarital pregnancy in the United States rose from about 10 percent in the mid-nineteenth century to 23 percent between about 1880 and 1910, reformers sought to protect young working women from sexual exploitation. Building upon a campaign begun in England with an expose of child prostitution, America's largest women's organization, the Woman's Christian Temperance Union (WCTU), launched a drive to raise the AGE OF CONSENT, the age at which girls could legally consent to sexual intercourse. Reformers meant to offer girls and young women legal protection against seduction and sexual exploitation: age of consent laws rendered underage girls legally innocent, no matter their behavior, and placed responsibility for illegitimate sexual conduct on men. Under such laws, a man or boy who had sexual intercourse with an underage girl was guilty of rape, whether or not she had freely participated and whether or not he used force or threats.

In the mid-1880s, the median legal age of consent in the United States was ten. Over the following decade, the median legal age of consent rose to fourteen; by 1885 it was sixteen or older in twenty-two states. Resistance to raising the age of consent was strongest in the South, where opponents argued that such laws might "enable negro girls to sue white men" and sought to exempt girls who were not of "previously chaste character," with the understanding that few black women or girls would be presumed "previously chaste" by white male juries. Georgia did not raise the age of consent from ten to fourteen until 1918. The federal government, on the other hand, in 1899 raised the age of consent in places of federal jurisdiction to twenty-one. The age of consent campaign had mixed consequences. These laws did offer protection to young girls. But the laws were not limited to children. The WCTU waged the campaign in a language of childhood innocence, calling for the protection of "baby girls," "girl children," and "infants," but reformers sought to raise the age of consent to the late teens. By legislating "innocence," states denied young women (even up to the age of eighteen or twenty-one) the *right* of consent. Court records reveal that some parents used these laws to constrain rebellious daughters by charging their boyfriends with statutory rape in court.

Twentieth Century

The twentieth century was a period of dramatic and rapid change in North American and western European social definitions and experiences of childhood, youth, and sexuality. Fundamental to changing understandings of childhood and sexuality in the twentieth century were SIGMUND FREUD's writings on infant and childhood sexuality. Published first in 1905 as *Three Contributions to the Sexual Theory*, Freud's theoretical models were sometimes changed beyond recognition as they passed into public circulation, but were enormously influential. Freud argued that sexuality did not first appear at puberty, but instead defined the stages of development from infancy to the age of six, at which point the child passed into a period of latency that lasted until puberty. According to Freud, the ways in which the child passed through the childhood stages of sexuality (oral, anal, and phallic) would determine in large part their experiences as adults. Acceptance of Freudian theories of child and INFANT SEXUALITY did not undermine the widespread belief that young children should be protected from adult sexuality. Instead, well into the 1960s, explanations for sexual and personal problems in adulthood were sought in the family dynamics of early childhood, and well-educated parents often paid great attention to managing familial relations and childhood sexual development because they understood it to have great consequences for their child's life course and future sexual adjustment.

The early years of the twentieth century were a time of struggle over youth and sexuality, especially in the United States. Increasingly, young people claimed the right to sexuality, if not to sex itself. Working-class girls and young men enjoyed the new commercial amusements of the city—dance halls, amusement parks, nickelodeons. Often without money to pay their own way, "charity girls" traded their favors (ranging from flirting to sexual intercourse) for entertainment. By the 1920s, appearances reflected a new sexualized culture. The FLAPPERS of the 1920s shed yards of fabric from their clothing, including most of the undergarments worn by their mothers' generation. With rouge and lipstick, rolled stockings and bobbed hair, they were frankly sexual. College men copied the sexualized image of movie star Rudolph Valentino. Popular music and dance styles were also more frankly sexual. U.S. college students were mad for jazz, which the *Ladies Home Journal* condemned for its "voodoo rhythms." In cities throughout the nation, young whites adopted (and adapted) physically expressive dances from working-class black culture, such as the shimmy and the turkey trot.

Over the course of the twentieth century, children and youth in the United States and western Europe spent more time together in age-segregated peer cultures. By the early 1940s in the United States, four out of five boys and five out of six girls attended HIGH SCHOOL. In the peer-oriented confines of high schools and colleges, young people developed elaborate social and sexual practices. DATING emerged as the new style of courtship in that era, especially in the United States, and young people "went out" on dates, thus partially escaping the supervision of parents and community. "Necking" and "petting" (which one mid-twentieth century sociologist described as "includ[ing] literally every caress known to married couples but . . . [not] complete sexual intercourse") became expected parts of dating, one of the ways in which young people demonstrated their belonging in an emerging YOUTH CULTURE. Not all young women found such freedom: Mexican-American girls, for example, were often closely chaperoned by parents to whom these new "American" customs were unacceptable.

In the years following World War II, the average age at marriage in the United States dropped dramatically. By 1959, fully 47 percent of all brides married before they turned nineteen, and the percentage of girls between the ages of fourteen and seventeen who were married increased one-third between 1940 and 1959. TEENAGERS were having babies: 27 percent of first births were to married teenage girls in 1950; by 1965, that figure had risen to 39 percent. (In 1960, only 16 percent of births to teens were outside marriage; in 1996, 76 percent of births to teens were nonmarital.) As American teens married in large numbers, their younger siblings moved toward marriage more quickly. Dating, by the late 1940s, had evolved into a system of "going steady," monogamous and frequently intense (though usually short term) relationships that almost mimicked the marriages of the steadies' slightly older peers. Pressure to enter the world of heterosexual dating intensified, as eleven year olds commonly went steady and thirteen year olds who were not yet paired off might be described as developmentally slow, or "late-daters." Not unreasonably, parents and other adults charged with monitoring the sexual behavior of youth worried that going steady increased the desire and opportunity for sexual exploration. Girls, especially, found themselves in a difficult position: "reputations" were easily lost, but necking and petting were an expected part of going steady.

The "sexual revolution" of the 1960s and 1970s brought about major changes in the sexual behaviors of young people in North America and western Europe. In France, for example, the average age at first intercourse dropped five years for women and six years for men between 1968 and 1989; by 1989, 90 percent of French teenage girls had sexual intercourse by the age of eighteen. Average age at marriage also increased sharply, so that few married during their teenage years. In the United States one trend is toward a "single standard" for sexual experience: in 1995, almost equivalent percentages of male and female high school seniors reported having had sexual intercourse (67 percent for males; 66 percent for females). Racial differences in sexual experience remained pronounced, however: in 1995, black high school students were more likely to have had sexual intercourse (73 percent) than their Hispanic (58 percent) or non-Hispanic white peers (49 percent). Teen pregnancy rates decreased 17 percent during the 1990s in the United States, but remained at least four times that of France or Japan.

Gay and lesbian youth also found greater acceptance at the end of the twentieth century, compared to the years before 1973 when homosexuality was classified as a mental illness by the American Psychiatric Association. Many schools and colleges have active lesbian-gay-bisexual-transgendered-queer organizations. However, some studies suggest that gay and lesbian teenagers are at relatively high risk for SUICIDE (representing almost 30 percent of teen suicides), and the 1998 murder of twenty-one-year-old college student Matthew Shepard in Laramie, Wyoming, is an example of the homophobic violence gay and lesbian teens may confront.

Concerns about the control and regulation of adolescent sexuality in North America and western Europe continue, despite greater acceptance of adolescent sexual experience. Abstinence campaigns have been highly visible in the United States since the 1980s Reagan administration, and conservative groups have argued for premarital chastity on moral grounds. However, concern about the spread of sexually transmitted disease, high rates of unintentional pregnancy, and the social and economic costs of unwed teenage parenthood also motivates debates among governmental agencies, scholars, parents, and social critics.

The liberalizing trajectory of change in North American and western Europe should not obscure the continuing differences among cultures. Arranged marriages remain common in India, and to a lesser extent in Japan. In Nepal, 7 percent of girls are married before the age of ten, and 40 percent by the age of fifteen. Premarital sex and homosexuality are strictly outlawed by Islamic law. In 2000, a teenage girl in Nigeria was sentenced to 180 lashes for having premarital sex (one hundred lashes were administered); and into the 1990s in Turkey, young women were legally subject to forcible "virginity control" exams. The average age at first sexual intercourse for boys in Jamaica is 12.7, while fewer than 12 percent of female Chinese college students surveyed in 1990 admitted that they had had sexual intercourse. Such differences, often embedded in strong religious or cultural traditions, pose both practical and philosophical difficulties for child advocacy and human rights groups who seek to improve the conditions for young people worldwide.

In the early twenty-first century, the belief that children deserve protection from adult sexuality, and from sexual exploitation and violence, is widespread if not universal. Article 34 of the UN CONVENTION ON THE RIGHTS OF THE CHILD calls upon all nations to protect children from sexual exploitation and abuse. In a globalizing world, social definitions of childhood have become more homogenous, as has the experience of youth. However, enormous variety remains in the sexual experiences of youth, and in understandings of the proper relationship between children and youth and sexuality.

See also: **Child Abuse; Female Genital Mutilation; Gendering; Homosexuality and Sexual Orientation; Infant Sexuality; Pedophilia; Teen Pregnancy; Theories of Childhood.**

BIBLIOGRAPHY

Alexandre-Bidon, Danièle, and Didier Lett. 1999. *Children in the Middle Ages: Fifth–Fifteenth Centuries.* Trans. Jody Gladding. Notre Dame, IN: University of Notre Dame Press.

Bailey, Beth. 1988. *From Front Porch to Back Seat: Courtship in Twentieth-Century America.* Baltimore, MD: Johns Hopkins University Press.

Bearman, Peter S., and Hannah Bruckner. 2001. "Promising the Future: Virginity Pledges and First Intercourse." *American Journal of Sociology* 106, no. 4 (January); 859–913.

Beisel, Nicola. 1997. *Imperiled Innocents: Anthony Comstock and Family Reproduction in Victorian America.* Princeton, NJ: Princeton University Press.

Ben-Amos, Ilana Krasuman. 1994. *Adolescence and Youth in Early Modern England.* New Haven, CT: Yale University Press.

Bolin, Anne, and Patricia Whelehan. 1999. *Perspectives on Human Sexuality.* Albany: State University of New York Press.

Chauncey, George. 1994. *Gay New York: Gender, Urban Culture, and the Makings of the Gay Male World, 1890–1940.* New York: Basic Books.

Cleverley, John, and Denis C. Phillips. 1986. *Visions of Childhood: Influential Models from Locke to Spock*, rev. ed. New York: Teachers College Press.

Colón, A. R. 2001. *A History of Children: A Socio-Cultural Survey across Millennia.* Westport, CT: Greenwood Press.

Cox, Roger. 1996. *Shaping Childhood: Themes of Uncertainty in the History of Adult–Child Relationships.* London: Routledge.

Darroch, Jacqueline E., et al. 2001. "Differences in Teenage Pregnancy Rates among Five Developed Countries: The Roles of Sexual Activity and Contraceptive Use." *Family Planning Perspectives* 33, no. 6: 244–251.

Devlin, Rachel. 1998. "Female Juvenile Delinquency and the Problem of Sexual Authority in America, 1945–1965." In *Delinquents and Debutantes: Twentieth-Century American Girls' Cultures,* ed. Sherrie A. Inness. New York: New York University Press.

Douglas, Susan J. 1994. *Where the Girls Are.* New York: Random House.

Dunlap, Leslie K. 1999. "The Reform of Rape Law and the Problem of White Men: Age of Consent Campaigns in the South, 1885–1910." In *Sex, Love, Race: Crossing Boundaries in North American History,* ed. Martha Hodes. New York: New York University Press.

Esquibel, Catrióna Rueda. "Memories of Girlhood: Chicana Lesbian Fictions." *Signs* 23, no. 3: 645–682.

Evans, Harriet. 1997. *Women and Sexuality in China: Female Sexuality and Gender Since 1949.* New York: Continuum.

Fass, Paula. 1979. *The Damned and the Beautiful: American Youth in the 1920s.* New York: Oxford University Press.

Furth, Charlotte. 1995. "From Birth to Birth: the Growing Body in Chinese Medicine." In *Chinese Views of Childhood,* ed. Anne Behnke Kinney. Honolulu: University of Hawai'i Press.

Gittins, Diana. 1998. *The Child in Question.* New York: St. Martin's Press.

Hall, Lesley A. 1992. "Forbidden by God, Despised by Men: Masturbation, Medical Warnings, Moral Panic, and Manhood in Great Britain, 1850–1950." *Journal of the History of Sexuality* 2, no. 3: 365–387.

Herdt, Gilbert, and Stephen C. Leavitt, eds. 1998. *Adolescence in Pacific Island Societies.* Pittsburgh, PA: University of Pittsburgh Press.

Kent, Kathryn R. "'No Trespassing': Girl Scout Camp and the Limits of the Counterpublic Sphere." *Women and Performance: A Journal of Feminist Theory* 8, no. 2: 185–203.

Killias, Martin. 2000. "The Emergence of a New Taboo: The Desexualisation of Youth in Western Societies since 1800." *European Journal on Criminal Policy and Research* 8, no. 4: 459–477.

Lesko, Nancy. 2001. *Act Your Age! A Cultural Construction of Adolescence.* New York: Routledge Falmer.

Modell, John. 1989. *Into One's Own: From Youth to Adulthood in the United States 1920–1975.* Berkeley and Los Angeles: University of California Press.

Moran, Jeffrey. 2000. *Teaching Sex: The Shaping of Adolescence in the Twentieth Century.* Cambridge, MA: Harvard University Press.

Murray, Stephen O., and Will Roscoe. 1997. *Islamic Homosexualities: Culture, History, and Literature.* New York: New York University Press.

Nathanson, Constance A. 1991. *Dangerous Passage: The Social Control of Sexuality in Women's Adolescence.* Philadelphia: Temple University Press.

Odem, Mary E. 1995. *Delinquent Daughters: Protecting and Policing Adolescent Female Sexuality in the United States, 1885–1920.* Chapel Hill: University of North Carolina Press.

Ruggiero, Guido. 1985. *The Boundaries of Eros: Sex Crime and Sexuality in Renaissance Venice.* New York: Oxford University Press.

Ruiz, Vicki L. 1998. "The Flapper and the Chaperone: Cultural Constructions of Identity and Heterosexual Politics among Adolescent Mexican American Women, 1920–1950." In *Delinquents and Debutantes: Twentieth-Century American Girls' Cultures,* ed. Sherrie A. Inness. New York: New York University Press.

Sahli, Nancy. 1979. "Smashing: Women's Relationships before the Fall." *Chrysalis* 8: 17–27.

Schneider, Dona. 1995. *American Childhood: Risks and Realities.* New Brunswick, NJ: Rutgers University Press.

Singh, Susheela Wulf, et al. 2000. "Gender Difference in Timing of First Intercourse: Data from Fourteen Countries." *International Family Planning Perspectives* 26, no. 1: 21–28.

Solinger, Rickie. 1992. *Wake Up Little Susie: Single Pregnancy and Race before Roe v. Wade.* New York: Routledge.

Sonobol, Amira al-Azhhhary. 1995. "Adoption in Islamic Society: A Historical Survey." In *Children in the Muslim Middle East,* ed. Elizabeth Warnock Fernea. Austin: University of Texas Press.

West, Mark I. 1988. *Children, Culture, and Controversy.* Hamden, CT: Archon Books.

INTERNET RESOURCE

Office of the Assistant Secretary for Planning and Evaluation, U.S. Department of Health and Human Services. 1997. *Trends in the Well-Being of America's Children and Youth.* Available from <http://aspe.hhs.gov/hsp/01trends>.

BETH BAILEY

Sexual Orientation. *See* Homosexuality and Sexual Orientation.

Shame. *See* Guilt and Shame.

Sheppard-Towner Maternity and Infancy Act

The Sheppard-Towner Maternity and Infancy Protection Act, signed by President Warren G. Harding on November 23, 1921, was the first federal social welfare program created explicitly for women and children. It was a bridge between pre–World War I Progressive reform, especially that which organized women's groups championed, and postwar welfare ideas, as expressed by the "welfare capitalism" of the 1920s, and in later social programs, such as the New Deal. It was also the first major political dividend of the recent success of the woman suffrage movement. Women's organizations protected it as long as they could.

The U.S. CHILDREN'S BUREAU, founded in 1912, conducted major studies that showed that the United States had very high rates of infant and maternal mortality. In 1918 the United States was eleventh in INFANT MORTALITY, and seventeenth in maternal deaths, among industrialized nations. Eighty percent of all pregnant women received no prenatal advice or trained care. Bureau researchers also discovered that poverty and death were closely related. Bureau chief Julia Lathrop championed maternal and infant protection, and, in altered form, Democratic Senator Morris Sheppard of Texas and Republican Congressman Horace Towner of Iowa reintroduced her bill in the sixty-sixth Congress. In the 1920 elections, with full suffrage for women, the National League of Women Voters pressured the Democratic, Socialist, Prohibition, and Farmer-Labor parties to endorse the measure in their platforms; only the Republican Party's platform ignored it, although its presidential candidate, Warren G. Harding, endorsed the bill. It passed the U.S. Senate by a 63–7 margin in July, and the House, after considerable GOP foot dragging and scattered cries of a Communist conspiracy, by a 279–39 margin. Major opponents were the American Medical Association, such antisuffragist organizations as the Woman Patriots, and politicos in either major party resentful of woman suffrage and of feminism.

In a decade in which the United States Bureau of Public Roads spent two billion dollars a year on highways, the Sheppard-Towner Act hardly seemed extravagant. It authorized $1,480,000 for fiscal 1921–1922 and $1,240,000 for the next five years, ending June 30, 1927. Of these sums, $5000 went to each state without exception, and double that amount went to states offering matching funds. The Children's Bureau distributed the remainder according to population. Administrative expenses were limited. Participating states enacted enabling legislation and implementation plans. The law provided for maternal and infant hygienic information through nurses, centers, conferences, and mass pamphlets. Forty-one states joined in 1922. Only three never did. In 1929 Congressional opponents torpedoed the bill, and President Hoover let it lapse with wan endorsements.

Between 1922 and 1929, the Children's Bureau conducted 183,252 conferences, established 2,978 prenatal care units, visiting nurses made 3,131,996 home visits, and 22,020,489 pamphlets had been passed out. America's infant and maternal death rates fell by 16 percent and 12 percent, respectively, but these were still twice what New Zealand and Great Britain experienced in the same years.

See also: **Aid to Dependent Children (AFDC); Social Welfare.**

BIBLIOGRAPHY

Lemons, J. Stanley. 1969. "The Sheppard-Towner Act: Progressivism in the 1920s." *The Journal of American History* 55 (March): 776–786.

HAMILTON CRAVENS

Shyness

Attitudes toward children's shyness have varied over time. These changes frequently reflect cultural shifts in child-rearing goals, interpersonal relationships, or perspectives on femininity and masculinity. In the United States, from the middle of the nineteenth century to the early part of the twentieth century, shyness was regarded as an ideal characteristic for white middle- and upper-class girls, one that ultimately protected their chastity and limited their participation in the public sphere. Domestic fiction written for these girls celebrated the virtues of silence and meekness, while pundits warned them against displays of wit or learning. Some girls seem to have taken these lessons to heart, for a number of foreign visitors complained that it was nearly impossible to engage them in conversation; however, other travelers' disparaging remarks about American girls' decidedly unfeminine self-confidence and outspokenness suggest that not all girls embraced the shy ideal.

White middle- and upper-class boys had a different relationship to shyness. While some degree of timidity may have been acceptable in the home, shyness was a liability among other boys. Nineteenth-century boy culture valued boldness, self-assertion, aggression, and conflict, all qualities at odds with shyness. In his interactions with his peers, a boy engaged in games, dares, and pastimes that left little room for fear of others, and instead taught him to impose his will on other boys.

Adults did not display a great deal of concern about boys' shyness until the last two decades of the nineteenth century, when fears about the feminization of American society focused attention on the apparent lack of manhood among white middle- and upper-class boys. A new term, *sissy*, was created to label insufficiently manly boys and men, and shyness and timidity were identified as two of his prominent characteristics. To reclaim their masculinity, shy, retiring boys were urged to fight with other boys, join all-male organizations like the BOY SCOUTS, or toughen up their bodies at the YMCA.

Changing Attitudes

By the 1920s, shyness was no longer a valued quality for white middle- and upper-class girls, either. In his influential study *Psychological Care of Infant and Child* (1928), psychologist JOHN B. WATSON argued that the ideal child—girl or boy—was free of shyness and able to meet and play with other children easily and openly. This change in attitude toward girls' shyness was due, in part, to the newly emerging culture of personality. Spurred by a growth in leisure activities and consumerism, the previous century's culture of character, with its emphasis on adult self-control, self-sacrifice, and discipline, was replaced by a culture of personality, the key ingredients of which were the ability to appeal to others and to be noticed for one's appearance, poise, charm, and manners. Personality formation became a new goal of child rearing, and a good personality for white middle- and upper-class girls and boys was considered by child-rearing experts to be one devoid of shyness. By the late 1940s, parents were largely in agreement with experts: interviews revealed that parents considered shyness in all of its shadings, including self-effacement, quietness, and insufficient gregariousness, to be an undesirable personality trait in boys and girls.

In the 1950s, child-rearing professionals writing for a white, middle-class audience continued to sound the alarm about shyness. They warned of dire consequences if children's shyness was left unchecked, including school failure, alcoholism, institutionalization, and suicide. Despite this inflammatory rhetoric, parents were given relatively little advice regarding what to do about their children's shyness. At most, mothers (as the assumed primary caregivers) were counseled to encourage greater independence on the part of their shy children and to provide opportunities for them to be with other children. The rest was up to the child—she or he had to learn to face the fear of other children and to get along with them. Getting along well with other children was particularly important during the 1950s, a period in which sociologist David Riesman characterized Americans as increasingly other directed, that is, concerned with securing others' approval and liking. Shy children risked being rejected by their peer group as too submissive; the ideal personality struck a balance between reserve and sociability.

The 1970s saw the introduction of several new ideas about children's shyness, as well as a slight softening of tone regarding the implications of shyness for white middle-class boys and girls. A number of authors of child-rearing manuals argued that shyness was a phase that many young boys and girls went through, related to anxiety over the new and unfamiliar. As a temporary phase of a child's development, parents had much less to fear from shyness. The experts did not mean, however, that parents could ignore it completely: child-rearing experts continued to offer advice to parents on how to help shy children overcome what they still regarded as a decided interpersonal disadvantage. This advice was more complex than it had been in the 1950s, introducing ideas from behavioral psychology like positive reinforcement and systematic desensitization. Rather than simply provide playmates for their shy children, parents were now required to take a more proactive role in managing their children's shyness.

An Inherited Handicap

Beginning in the mid-1980s and continuing into the mid-1990s, many child-rearing professionals began to argue that shyness, previously considered a learned condition, was, in fact, an inherited trait. Some responded to this new perspective on shyness by emphasizing previously unreported positive aspects of shyness—such as good listening skills and empathy—and encouraging parents to simply accept shy children as they were. Most, however, argued that despite the inborn nature of shyness, shy children could be taught to be more outgoing. The key to this training was for parents not to push shy children to change too quickly, and above all, never to label them as shy, for to do so would encourage the child to accept the label, and all it implied, as fact. This aversion to the shy label suggested that, despite the experts' general tone of acceptance toward what was now, after all, assumed to be a characteristic, like eye color, inherited from one's parents, children's shyness remained highly stigmatized, a handicap to be overcome with patient effort on the parents' and child's part.

See also: **Child-Rearing Advice Literature; Emotional Life; Gendering; Parenting.**

BIBLIOGRAPHY

Cable, Mary. 1972. *The Little Darlings: A History of Child Rearing in America.* New York: Charles Scribner's Sons.

Jersild, Arthur J., Ella S. Woodyard, and Charlotte del Solar. 1949. *Joys and Problems of Child Rearing.* New York: Columbia University Teacher's College Bureau of Publications.

Kimmel, Michael. 1996. *Manhood in America: A Cultural History.* New York: The Free Press.

Murray, Gail Schmunk. 1998. *American Children's Literature and the Construction of Childhood.* New York: Twayne Publishers.

Riesman, David. 1950. *The Lonely Crowd: A Study of the Changing American Character.* New Haven, CT: Yale University Press.

Rotundo, E. Anthony. 1993. *American Manhood: Transformations in Masculinity from the Revolution to the Modern Era.* New York: Basic Books.

Susman, Warren I. 1984. *Culture as History: The Transformation of American Society in the Twentieth Century.* New York: Pantheon Books.

Watson, John B. 1928. *Psychological Care of Infant and Child.* New York: W. W. Norton.

Welter, Barbara. 1966. "The Cult of True Womanhood: 1820–1860." *American Quarterly* 18: 151–174.

PATRICIA A. McDANIEL

Siblings

In Western society, relationships among siblings usually comprise the longest relationships experienced by individuals across the life span. An ascribed as opposed to a voluntary status, siblingship is conferred either by birth or by law (as in the case of step- or adopted siblings). Factors that structure the sibling experience include family size, BIRTH ORDER, and age spacing, as well as class, ethnic and cultural traditions, as well as special circumstances. For example, variations in Native American kinship and lineage systems and the separation of African-American families under SLAVERY influenced the character of sibling relationships. Twinship, which occupies a special place in all known societies, also determines the nature of sibling relationships. With twins or MULTIPLE BIRTHS, the differentiation of siblings by age is blurred, and individual autonomy may be reduced by the social identification of the children as one unit.

Gender shapes individuals' family experiences across cultures too, but it does not necessarily represent the dominant influence in sibling relationships, which are often relatively egalitarian rather than hierarchical. While power or status differences may exist, these are not necessarily defined by gender. In childhood, siblings typically experience intimate

The Artist's Daughters Chasing a Butterfly (c. 1756), Thomas Gainsborough. Evidence suggests that in the eighteenth century, sibling relationships became closer and less competitive than they had been in previous ages. Brothers and sisters came to rely on each other for emotional support and companionship throughout their lives. © National Gallery Collection; By kind permission of the trustees of the National Gallery, London/CORBIS.

daily contact. This changes in adulthood, but a growing body of evidence indicates that their relationships endure over time and distance, and that sibling influence continues to old age. Various studies of sibling interactions in western, industrialized societies in the second half of the twentieth century suggest that these relationships are powerful and significant, whether they are characterized by harmony or by tension. Cross-cultural data from other societies document the universal importance of sibling relationships in human lives.

Social scientific research has yielded a range of insights about the nature and significance of sibling ties since the middle of the twentieth century, but relatively few scholars have examined this aspect of family life systematically from a social historical perspective. Some of the earliest discussions of sibling themes in Western culture appear in the Old Testament and in classical mythology. These suggest an early cultural recognition of the significance of sibling relationships and of the inherent potential for both harmony and conflict. As with other aspects of the history of childhood, it is difficult to document children's direct experiences of sibling interactions. Moreover the available evidence reflects an almost exclusively elite or middle-class perspective. Some historians suggest that in the context of high child mortality rates, premodern children learned not to invest emotionally in relationships with siblings, but very little direct evidence exists about this aspect of childhood prior to the eighteenth century.

Eighteenth-Century Siblings

Traditional INHERITANCE practices and marriage customs appear to have fostered sibling rivalry and conflict in early modern Western society. Primogeniture and the reliance on birth order as the principal criterion for permitting daughters to marry discouraged closeness and generated sibling competition based on gender and age. Although historians are just beginning to examine this area, some research suggests that the decline of these practices in eighteenth-century America, and eventually across the Atlantic, shaped a new climate of cooperation and relative equality in which sisters and brothers played central roles in one another's emotional and social lives throughout the life span.

For example, Lorri Glover argues that siblings in eighteenth-century elite families in South Carolina exercised profound influence over one another. Their relationships differed significantly from the hierarchical relationships in both the patriarchal household and the larger social order of colonial America. During the early colonial period, when high mortality rates and migration patterns frequently disrupted relationships between parents and children in South Carolina, siblings often turned to each other as the most reliable and enduring elements of the family. As demographic instability diminished, the utilitarian relationships gave way to more egalitarian ties based in mutuality. In large families, children saw themselves as close companions; they often knew one another better than they knew their parents. Over the course of the eighteenth century, sisters and brothers grew increasingly interdependent, providing vital practical and emotional support from childhood to old age.

Certainly siblings in South Carolina, and in other regions as well, experienced conflict and discord, but such problems stemmed less from any rivalry based on birth order or gender than from other factors. For example, age gaps sometimes created sibling relationships that resembled those of parents and children rather than those of peers. As in contemporary society, differences in education, life stage, or personality, along with the intrinsic complexity of interactions in blended families, could also create difficulties. Generally, however, eighteenth-century culture and society supported the development of strong and lasting sibling ties. Sisters and brothers constructed relationships that bypassed many, although not all, of the patriarchal norms that governed eighteenth-century households. As children and as adults, women deferred to fathers and husbands, but they related to brothers as equals and partners in family life.

While the bonds between sisters and brothers challenged the prevailing gender norms, those between sisters anchored eighteenth-century female culture, and often represented the central relationships in women's lives. Adult women were frequently called upon to care for or educate younger sisters. Sisters close in age cherished lifelong intimacy as "best" friends, and young women found separation from a beloved sister painful and distressing, even when such separation resulted from ostensibly happy events such as courtship and marriage.

Nineteenth-Century Siblings

Nineteenth-century sibling relationships in middle-class families reflect the influence of a family culture that stressed the spiritual nature of LOVE; the importance of loving relationships in family life, particularly between mothers and children; and the importance of harmony, cooperation, and affection between siblings. Middle-class Victorian parents emphasized family continuity; they urged children to be loyal to their siblings and to look after younger sisters and brothers in the event of parental death. Thus, although the economic fortunes of individuals were no longer directly linked to their sibling status, the psychological importance of sibling unity increased. In this context, middle-class childhood experience often involved deep love for siblings. JEALOUSY certainly existed, but neither parents nor child-rearing literature described it or defined it as an issue of concern until the end of the century.

Intimate, lifelong relationships with sisters continued to play major roles in the lives of individual women, and in the nineteenth-century female world more generally. Young women frequently experienced severe emotional anguish when courtship and marriage displaced sibling bonds. Like their eighteenth-century counterparts, older children often took charge of younger siblings, and older sisters became surrogate mothers to younger sisters or stepsisters. In families where children received most of their early education at home, siblings served as the primary intellectual and emotional outlets for one another.

The prescriptive literature of this period portrayed the tie between sisters and brothers as a model of pure, Christian love between men and women. However, the brother-sister relationship provided more than a cultural ideal. As the first peer relationship with the opposite sex for most children, it offered a natural and comfortable context in which boys and girls socialized more easily than they did at school. In this sense, sibling relationships bridged the gap between the nineteenth-century male and female worlds. Parents communicated specific expectations for these interactions: young boys were required to protect and defend their sisters; young girls were required to perform household services for their brothers. These obligations fostered reciprocity and closeness, but they also promoted inequality and gender separation. Nevertheless, issues of power did not preclude genuine love and affection, and like their predecessors, nineteenth-century sisters and brothers played significant roles for each other throughout their lives.

For enslaved AFRICAN-AMERICAN CHILDREN, separation from siblings often precluded the sort of intimacy experienced by their white peers. Nevertheless evidence of affective ties between slave and former slave adult siblings can be discerned, as in the frequent practice of naming a child for a parent's sibling who had been sold away from his or her family.

Twentieth-Century Siblings

The turn of the twentieth century ushered in a new period in the history of sibling relationships. Although the birthrate in America had been declining since the first decade of the nineteenth century, small sibling sets of two or three only became common in the middle class around 1890, while rural and working class families tended to remain larger. Smaller family size, along with the Victorian emphasis on maternal-child love, fostered an increase in the intensity of middle-class mothering. In this context, children competed for maternal affection and the arrival of a new baby was much more disruptive than in earlier middle-class families. Moreover, extended high school experiences for twentieth-century adolescents and closer child spacing meant that older siblings had fewer opportunities for involvement in child rearing. These conditions fostered an increase in sibling rivalry and jealousy.

Parents and child-rearing manuals now defined sibling rivalry as a serious issue. It was portrayed as an inevitable occurrence, a threat to children's safety, and an experience that could lead to problems in adulthood. In the past, sibling jealousy over inheritance or marriage prerogatives had created tension between young adults, but now such rivalry was identified with young children. Although adult concern over this issue exaggerated the dimensions of the problem, twentieth-century family conditions did encourage an increase in sibling rivalry.

Family culture from the 1920s through the 1980s discussed sibling relationships more in terms of peaceful coexistence than deep love. Less emphasis on sharing and more emphasis on separate rooms and separate toys fostered a sense of separateness that extended to adulthood. Starting in

the 1960s as more mothers began to work outside the home and children spent time with babysitters, day care providers, and even fathers, intense cultural anxiety over sibling rivalry declined. The growing influence of peer culture at a younger age and more involvement with age peers provided an antidote to sibling jealousy. As the birthrate continued to decline, more single-child families and more space between children also helped to mitigate the problem. Furthermore, by the 1950s it was no longer common for children to assist in caring for younger siblings. Yet new conditions—more blended families and half-siblings, for example—could be conducive to sibling rivalry.

The sense of change in sibling experiences is clear, but some continuities link the twentieth century with earlier periods. Thus, for example, research in the 1950s revealed that adults who grew up in families of six or more children remembered a self-sufficient childhood world of play, a group spirit, and older siblings who disciplined their younger brothers and sisters. These respondents consistently referred to the importance of siblings in adolescence and reported closeness throughout adulthood. They mentioned rivalry less frequently than subjects from small families.

See also: **Emotional Life; Family Patterns.**

BIBLIOGRAPHY

Atkins, Annette. 2001. *We Grew Up Together: Brothers and Sisters in Nineteenth-Century America.* Urbana: University of Illinois Press.

Cicirelli, Victor G. 1995. *Sibling Relationships Across the Lifespan.* New York: Plenum Press.

Crispell, Diane. 1996 "The Sibling Syndrome." *American Demographics* 18: 24–30.

Dunn, Judy. 1985. *Sisters and Brothers.* Cambridge, MA: Harvard University Press.

Glover, Lorri. 2000. *All Our Relations: Blood Ties and Emotional Bonds among the Early South Carolina Gentry.* Baltimore: Johns Hopkins University Press.

Gutman, Herbert G. 1976. *The Black Family in Slavery and Freedom 1750–1925.* New York: Vintage Books.

Mintz, Steven. 1983. *A Prison of Expectations: The Family in Victorian Culture.* New York: New York University Press.

Stearns, Peter N. 1988. "The Rise of Sibling Jealousy in the Twentieth Century." In *Emotion and Social Change: Toward a New Psychohistory,* ed. Carol Z. Stearns and Peter N. Stearns. New York: Holmes and Meier.

Stearns, Peter N. 1989. *Jealousy: The Evolution of an Emotion in American History.* New York: New York University Press.

Stewart, Elizabeth A. 2000. *Exploring Twins: Towards a Social Analysis of Twinship.* New York: St. Martin's Press.

Stowe, Steven M. 1987. *Intimacy and Power in the Old South: Ritual in the Lives of the Planters.* Baltimore: Johns Hopkins University Press.

LINDA W. ROSENZWEIG

SIDS. *See* Sudden Infant Death Syndrome.

Slavery, United States

The enslaved population in the United States increased significantly from the initial arrival in 1619 of twenty Africans until 1808, when the transatlantic slave trade was legally ended in the United States. For nearly two hundred years the direct importation of Africans fueled the slave population's growth; however, once the direct trade ended reproduction accounted for the continued increase. As a result, in 1860 there were 3,953,760 slaves in the United States. By December 1865, when Congress ratified the Thirteenth Amendment to the Constitution, the numbers had escalated to more than four million. More than one-half of the slaves emancipated were under twenty years of age.

Published and unpublished accounts by young Middle Passage survivors often mention their childhood prior to being kidnapped. One child remembered her chores, primarily guarding poultry from hawks. Others wrote about playing with peers when traders raided their villages and captured them. They protested, but it was of no consequence for the traders who hurried the children along to the seacoast where they boarded ships that transported them across the Atlantic to the New World.

Their accounts of the capture, overland trek from the interior to the coast, and voyage from AFRICA to America via the Middle Passage is akin to one rendered by Olaudah Equiano. He was eleven years old in 1756 when kidnappers stole him and his sister from their village in Nigeria. The girl's fate remains unknown, but the intruders sold the boy to overseas traders. They were unable to sell him to sugar planters in Barbados, who perhaps believed he was too young to perform arduous work in the cane fields, so the traders carried the child to Virginia, where a tobacco planter bought him. Olaudah Equiano and Florence Hall were among the more than eleven million Africans of all ages spirited away from their homeland between 1518 and 1850 and brought to the Americas, where they toiled as agricultural laborers, skilled mechanics, miners, or domestic servants. Less than 10 percent of the Africans reached continental North America where their initial legal status was uncertain.

Some Africans in the British colonies of North America were indentured for a specified period, usually four to seven years of service. As a result, the possibilities of gaining freedom were greater than would be the case years later. Between 1630 and 1660, perpetual servitude for blacks became an accepted practice, and the law soon followed suit. In 1662 the Virginia Assembly passed an act declaring that all children born in the colony were "bond or free only according to the condition of the mother." Whether in Virginia or elsewhere in English-speaking North America, free women

bore free children; however, the mulatto offspring of unmarried white women were considered black and subjected to bound apprenticeships until adulthood. Afterwards, they were indeed free. By contrast, the legislation relegated the children of enslaved women, regardless of color, to a life of bondage for generations to come. Among the perpetually bound were "quasi-slaves," people who lived, worked, and behaved as if they were emancipated. "We were free," declared the biracial Cornelia Smith, who came of age in the home of her grandfather, a North Carolina planter, while her mother and half-brother lived across the yard in the slave quarters. "We were just born in slavery, that's all," she explained (Murray, p. 49). For a variety of reasons, Smith, along with an untold number of other slaves in similar circumstances, enjoyed a form of liberty and suffered little or no interference from owners. Only legal documents made them chattel.

Enslaved parents often linked their offspring to kinship circles by NAMING them in honor of real and fictive kin. More often than not girls received a grandmother's name, while a firstborn son frequently carried his father's name. Traditional African day-names, which named children based on the day of their birth, are present in early records, but disappear in the nineteenth century as a reflection of the actual birth day. Instead, day-names became kin names passed from one generation to another as signs of respect for cherished members of immediate and extended families.

If slave children survived long enough to receive a name, the most critical period of their existence followed, when health challenges snuffed out the lives of children up to four years of age at rates more than double that of white children in the major slaveholding states. Aside from nutritional deficiencies, complications from teething and illness from lockjaw and tetanus were among the life-threatening maladies that endangered slave children. Records of slaveholders include "suffocation" as a cause of death, but contemporary scholars believe SUDDEN INFANT DEATH SYNDROME (SIDS) was responsible, contradicting earlier theories of exhausted mothers accidentally smothering the children who slept alongside of them.

Both parents and planters lamented the deaths of enslaved children, for they were valuable. Parents were vested in their welfare for sentimental reasons, but their owners' investments were economic. Healthy children represented capital assets while sickly ones signaled forbidding pecuniary losses. As a result, it was not unusual for owners to worry about their youthful chattel, especially after the closing of the overseas slave trade in 1808. Comments from slaveowners reflect their concern as those made by Andrew Flinn who wrote, "The children must be particularly attended to for rearing them is not only a duty, but also the most profitable part of plantation business" (Kiple and King, p. 96). In Thomas Jefferson's opinion, "a child raised every 2 years is of more profit than the crop of the best laboring man" (Cohen, p. 518). Enslaved children were worth little economically at birth but increased in value as they matured enough to enter the work place, where they were subjected to arduous labor and arbitrary power.

There was no set age or season at which slave children began work in fields, homes, or shops, since the needs of owners determined when and where the youngsters worked and what chores they performed. According to Frederick Douglass, who spent his formative years on a Maryland plantation, slaves toiled in all weather. "It was never too hot, or too cold; it could never rain, blow, snow, or hail too hard for us to work in the field" (Douglass, p. 124). Whether laboring inside or outside girls and boys who were too young to assume full work responsibilities assisted adults and performed simple chores. They carried water, swept yards, churned milk, gathered kindling, chased birds away from crops, and attended to children younger than themselves.

Thomas Jefferson gave specific orders for "children till 10 years old to serve as nurses," meaning child care providers, without gender distinction. "From 10 to 16," wrote Jefferson, "the boys [were to] make nails, the girls spin" (quoted in Betts, p. 7). According to gender conventions only boys learned the trades of coopers, cobblers, wrights, smiths, and other artisans, while girls were relegated to skills concerned with domesticity. Differences in opportunities meant selected boys had more chances of earning extra money to purchase necessities, luxuries, or freedom than girls. Such gender distinctions in the work place were common, but some owners ignored them. One former slave told Works Progress Administration interviewers in the 1930s that she "split rails like a man," and another reported that her "Mama plowed wid three horses." She asked, "Ain't dat somp'n?" and appeared more intrigued by the number of draft animals used than by the fact that her mother "worked like a man." The ex-slave commented, "Thought women was 'sposed to work' long wid men, I did" (Perdue et al., p. 292). Indeed, many enslaved males and females worked together and shared a mean sort of equality. Both were exploited.

Although Frederick Douglass said "Work, work, work, was scarcely more the order of the day than of the night" (p. 124), and Booker T. Washington claimed he had no recreation, enslaved children had some leisure time and participated in ring, rope, and ball games. Furthermore, there were opportunities for play that reflected events in everyday life, and spontaneous play after work, on Sundays and holidays, or after the lay-by and harvest. Slaves did not spend all of their leisure in play, however, since some managed to carve out enough time for sacred and secular lessons to restore the mind and spirit. It was also on their own time that children learned life lessons from folktales and stories told by their elders at nightfall. But no amount of leisure was sufficient to shield the children from the abuses associated with bondage, including arduous labor, corporal punishment, sexual exploitation, and family separations. There was little if any direct action children could take that would change their situations unless slavery was abolished. Until that time, parents and others taught children how to work satisfactorily, handle injustices, and pay deference to whites while maintaining their self-respect. This was vital to their well-being. As the children matured and had children of their own, they passed the lessons from one generation to another to ensure that they all survived.

See also: **African-American Children and Youth; Work and Poverty.**

BIBLIOGRAPHY

Betts, Edwin Morris, ed. 1953. *Thomas Jefferson's Farm Book: With Commentary and Relevant Extracts from Other Writings.* Charlottesville: University Press of Virginia.

Cohen, William. 1969. "Thomas Jefferson and the Problem of Slavery." *Journal of American History* 56 (December): 503–526.

Douglass, Frederick. 1962. *Life and Times of Frederick Douglass.* New York: Collier Books.

Equiano, Olaudah. 1995. *The Interesting Narrative of the Life of Olaudah Equiano, Written by Himself.* Ed. Robert J. Allison. Boston: Bedford/St. Martin's.

Handler, Jerome S. 2002. "Survivors of the Middle Passage: Life Histories of Enslaved Africans in British America." *Slavery and Abolition* 23 (April): 23–56.

Hening, William W. 1923. *The Statutes at Large: Being a Collection of all the Laws of Virginia.* New York: Bartow.

King, Wilma. 1995. *Stolen Childhood: Slave Youth in Nineteenth-Century America.* Bloomington: Indiana University Press.

King, Wilma. 1997. "Within the Professional Household: Slave Children in the Antebellum South." *The Historian* 59 (spring): 523–540.

Kiple, Kenneth F., and Virginia Himmelsteib King. 1981. *Another Dimension to the Black Diaspora: Diet, Disease, and Racism.* Cambridge, UK: Cambridge University Press.

Leslie, Kent Anderson. 1992. "Amanda America Dickson: An Elite Mulatto Lady in Nineteenth-Century Georgia." In *Southern Women: Histories and Identities,* ed. Virginia Bernhard, Betty Brandon, Elizabeth Fox-Genovese, et al. Columbia: University of Missouri Press.

Leslie, Kent Anderson. 1995. *Woman of Color, Daughter of Privilege.* Athens: University of Georgia Press.

Meyer, Leland Winfield. 1932. *The Life and Times of Colonel Richard M. Johnson of Kentucky.* New York: Columbia University Press.

Murray, Pauli. 1987. *Proud Shoes: The Story of an American Family.* New York: Harper and Row.

Perdue, Charles L., Jr., Thomas E. Barden, and Robert K. Phillips, eds. 1980. *Weevils in the Wheat: Interviews with Virginia Ex-Slaves.* Bloomington: Indiana University Press.

WILMA KING

Sleep

Sleep is a difficult topic to grapple with historically, and at present the most interesting historical episode involves relatively recent change. Child-rearing manuals in nineteenth-century America did not deal with sleep as a problem, despite or perhaps because of extensive health advice in other categories. Surely, individual parents faced children with unusual sleep difficulties, but a sense of a larger category of issues did not emerge. Snippets of advice, for example in American women's magazines, suggested that relatively short periods of formal sleep were required of children—six to eight hours were often mentioned, which confirms the impression that sleep was not viewed as a source of problems.

Analyzing a lack of concern is a challenging task historically. Several factors help explain why nineteenth-century adults (and probably their counterparts in earlier periods as well) did not pay much attention to children's sleep in general. First, naps were common, for many adults as well as children. Historians have noted how adult sleep patterns before modern times were less rigidly defined than they are now, and children's sleep benefited from a similarly relaxed definition. Where sleep was an issue, for individual children, many parents undoubtedly used opiates or alcohol to help. The absence of much artificial light reduced nighttime stimulation and facilitated getting children off to bed.

Concern about adult sleep began to increase toward the end of the nineteenth century, as part of the attack on stress disorders such as the then-popular disease, neurasthenia, and the general tensions seen in modern life. Growing use of electric lights and the popularization of caffeine drinks added to the emergence of sleep as a problem. Some discussions began to spill over into the treatment of children, but it was not until the 1920s that child-rearing manuals picked up the question of children's sleep as a standard topic. From that point onward, sections of all the major manuals, plus publications like PARENTS MAGAZINE, were devoted to sleep. Pediatricians also dispensed sleep advice, and doctors took the lead in recommending increasing amounts of sleep, from infancy onward. Getting children to bed became a major daily ritual for parents and children alike, a regular opportunity for contests between freedom and authority. For their part, child experts, headed by the behaviorists, urged that set bedtimes were a vital part of the socialization of children, as well as the protection for their health. New rituals such as daily bathing, story reading, mass-produced toys like the new TEDDY BEARS, or night lights were variously employed.

Why did sleep standards escalate, and why did sleep become a more significant issue? Experts were clearly eager to promote a variety of problems to which they had solutions, and the inclusion of sleep obviously qualified as yet another area where well-meaning parents needed outside help. Growing psychological interest in dreams, and research on the troubled dreams of children, provided an additional scientific basis for sleep concerns. New distractions, such as the radio, plus the noise of modern urban life may have made sleep, in fact, more difficult to achieve than before. School-

ing requirements reduced the opportunity for naps except for the very young. Most children, like most adults, now had to be taught to sleep intensively for a period of time, rather than indulging more on the spur of the moment.

It was also true that children's sleep arrangements had been changing in the United States, from the late nineteenth century onward. Babies were increasingly placed in cribs at a fairly young age, rather than rocked in cradles as their parents worked or relaxed. Learning to sleep alone was an important modern discipline, and cribs allowed parents to put infants in a separate space. As adults had new recreations in the evening, they looked for ways to free themselves from on-the-spot care of sleeping children. Older children graduated from cribs to beds and were not as likely to sleep with other siblings. Birth rate reductions meant that there were fewer siblings, and experts urged that children were better off with their own, separate rooms. These specific changes in sleeping arrangements, aimed at a new level of individuation, may well have created the kinds of new sleep problems to which the child-rearing literature responded.

Specific recommendations about getting children to sleep oscillated during the twentieth century. The strict regimen of the behaviorist approach in the 1920s was modified in the mid-twentieth century by more permissive experts such as DR. BENJAMIN SPOCK. But adult concern about children's sleep persisted at a fairly high level. Many children who learned of sleep as a problem in their own early years may have been encouraged to worry about sleep in new ways even as they grew to adulthood. The implications of the twentieth-century change in approach to children's sleep, at least in the United States, remain a fascinating area of study.

See also: **Child-Rearing Advice Literature; Children's Spaces.**

BIBLIOGRAPHY

Ekirch, A. Roger. 2001. "Sleep We Have Lost: Pre-Industrial Slumber in the British Isles." *The American Historical Review* 106, no. 2: 343.

Fishbein, Morris. 1926. "The Tired Child." *Hygeia*: 406–407

Stearns, Peter N., Perrin Rowland, and Lori Giarnella. 1996. "Children's Sleep: Sketching Historical Change." *Journal of Social History* 30: 345–366

PETER N. STEARNS

Smallpox. *See* Contagious Diseases; Epidemics; Vaccination.

Smith, Jessie Willcox (1863–1935)

During her lifetime, illustrator Jessie Willcox Smith's representations of children made her one of the best-known artists in the United States. From 1917 until 1933, Smith provided the cover illustration for every issue of *Good Housekeeping* magazine. She was known to her friends as "The Mint" because of the huge sums she commanded in the flourishing field of commercial illustration. Smith's original oil paintings and sketches were also widely exhibited.

Smith was born in Philadelphia in 1863 and did not take up art until she was in her twenties. She had originally trained as a KINDERGARTEN teacher, but in 1885 she enrolled at the Pennsylvania Academy of the Fine Arts. After graduation, Smith went to work in the production department of the *Ladies Home Journal*, making advertising illustrations. In 1894, when the illustrator Howard Pyle began teaching at the Drexel Institute, Smith enrolled in his course. It was here that Smith met her lifelong friends and collaborators Elizabeth Shippen Green and Violet Oakley. These three women would live and work together for the next fifteen years. Collectively, they became known as the Ladies of the Red Rose.

Smith, Green, and Oakley were encouraged to produce scenes of childhood and maternity, which appealed to the increasingly powerful female consumer. Smith, in particular, was influenced by the tradition of the English illustrator KATE GREENAWAY, who depicted innocent children in nostalgic settings. Smith's first real success came with the publication of the *Book of the Child* (1903), which was a compilation of calendar illustrations by Smith and Elizabeth Shippen Green. That same year, Smith was selected to illustrate Robert Lewis Stevenson's *A Child's Garden of Verses* (1905). Smith produced more than seven hundred illustrations during her career, and illustrated about sixty books. The most famous is *The Jessie Willcox Smith Mother Goose*, first published in 1914 and still in print in the early twenty-first century. Smith's favorite works were her illustrations for Charles Kingsley's *The Water Babies* (1916), which confirmed Smith's vision of childhood as a time of magic and fantasy.

See also: **Gutmann, Bessie Pease; Images of Childhood; Victorian Art.**

BIBLIOGRAPHY

Carter, Alice A. 2000. *The Red Rose Girls: An Uncommon Story of Art and Love.* New York: Harry N. Abrams.

Higonnet, Anne. 1998. *Pictures of Innocence: The History and Crisis of Ideal Childhood.* London: Thames and Hudson.

Nudelman, Edward D. 1989. *Jessie Willcox Smith: A Bibliography.* Gretna, LA: Pelican Publishing.

Stryker, Catherine Connell. 1976. *The Studios at Cogslea.* Wilmington: Delaware Art Museum.

A. CASSANDRA ALBINSON

Smoking

Tobacco use and cultivation originated in South America and spread northward through the Americas, reaching the upper Mississippi Valley by 160 C.E. An important part of the Columbian exchange, tobacco took root in western Europe in the late sixteenth century, and then in Africa and the Asian mainland in the seventeenth century. Though Europeans first regarded tobacco as a medicinal herb, they discovered that the real demand was of a recreational nature. By the mid-1600s tobacco had joined alcohol and caffeine as one of the world's three great social DRUGS and had become an important source of revenue for colonial planters, merchants, and tax collectors.

Early Modern and Modern Tobacco Use

Early modern tobacco rituals varied by geography, class, and local custom. Some users preferred pipes, others chewing tobacco, others snuff. Though governments imposed different regulations and levels of taxation, a few generalizations hold across nations and cultures. Men used tobacco more often than women. Tobacco use typically began in childhood or ADOLESCENCE. The more abundant the local supply, the larger the crop of neophytes and the sooner they started. Children as young as seven smoked in Britain's Chesapeake colonies, where tobacco pipes were nearly as ubiquitous as tobacco plants.

Tobacco initiation was a social process. It signified coming of age, that a boy was taking on the attributes of a man. Tobacco enhanced standing among male peers. It provided an occasion for relaxation and conviviality. Only later, as tobacco users became dependent on nicotine and suffered withdrawal symptoms in its absence, did the motive for consuming tobacco change. This reversal of effects is the single most consistent pattern running through the history of smoking. Children and adolescents began smoking for social reasons. They continued to smoke, often after they wished they could quit, because they had become addicted.

Knowing that youthful indulgence in tobacco led to a lifelong habit, and knowing that the habit was dirty, dangerous, and unhealthful, many parents, especially those of middle-class standing or pious temperament, discouraged children from using tobacco. Girls' use was considered particularly unseemly, though boys courted a whipping as well. The writer Samuel Clemens (1835–1910), better known as MARK TWAIN, admitted to smoking at age nine—privately at first, then in public only after his father died two years later. To acquire a supply, he and his friends traded old newspapers to the local tobacconist for cheap cigars.

That Clemens smoked, rather than chewed or sniffed, tobacco symbolized a broader nineteenth-century trend. Oral use remained popular in a few places, such as Iceland or Sweden, but elsewhere children's initiation into tobacco use increasingly meant initiation into smoking. Cigarette smoking was especially dangerous and addictive, because smoke could be inhaled into the lungs, where it delivered a powerful dose of nicotine directly to the bloodstream. At first store-bought cigarettes, hand-rolled specialty products aimed at the carriage trade, were too expensive for most children to afford. Then, in the 1880s, James B. Duke (1856–1925) transformed the industry with machine-production techniques. Prices dropped and use expanded. The United States, where per capita cigarette consumption increased tenfold between 1900 and 1917, was the epicenter of the first global cigarette revolution.

City boys were among the most avid consumers of Duke's products, and their insouciant smoking proved a powerful affront to bourgeois morality. Evangelical and progressive reformers attacked cigarettes on moral and health grounds, blaming "the little white slaver" for ruining children's health, encouraging intemperance, and poisoning the race. But such legislative barriers as they managed to erect (fifteen states outlawed some aspect of cigarette manufacture, distribution, or promotion) were soon swept aside. Widespread military use during World War I, Hollywood valorization, and mass advertising, including a successful campaign to recruit female smokers—the fastest growing segment of the market during the 1920s, 1930s, and 1940s—all helped legitimate cigarettes. Smoking's ordinariness became its best defense. Laws banning sale to minors persisted, though vending machines and mothers' purses provided easy means of circumvention. Youthful smoking became unremarkable, even de rigueur. Those who didn't smoke, the writer John Updike remembered, got nowhere in the Pennsylvania high-school society of the late 1940s. Updike's Irish contemporary and fellow writer Frank McCourt recalled his friends asking him, incredulously, how he could possibly go out with girls if he didn't smoke.

The accumulation of evidence that smoking caused cancer and other deadly diseases, which reached a critical mass in the early 1950s, threatened the prosperity of cigarette companies. They tried to defuse the crisis through public relations, suggesting that the jury was still out on the health question. This was, at best, a delaying tactic. The growing medical data eventually led to declining adult domestic consumption, heavier taxation, and increased regulation—the broad pattern in Western societies during the last third of the twentieth century.

Confronted with decreasing demand in North America and Europe, multinational companies like Philip Morris and British-American Tobacco adopted a two-pronged strategy. First, they recruited teenage smokers to replace the adults who died or quit, using advertising to suggest that smokers were independent, sexually potent, and disdainful of authority—in a word, cool. A social fact, that cigarettes served as accessories of teenage identity (and, for girls, of thinness), became a means of recruiting those who would ultimately come to depend on cigarettes as nicotine-delivery vehicles. Where advertisements were banned, companies devised alternative promotions, such as colorful logo tee shirts, or company-sponsored sporting events aimed at getting brand names and package colors before a youthful audience.

In 1997, the Federal Trade Commission charged R. J. Reynolds with unfair practice, stating that the company was using its Joe Camel ads to market cigarettes directly to children. The Advertising Archive Ltd.

Smoking in the Developing World

Overseas expansion was the second means of acquiring new customers. In the 1970s, cigarette companies began to move more aggressively into developing nations. By the decade's end, smoking was up 33 percent in Africa, 24 percent in Latin American, and 23 percent in Asia. By 2001, of the approximately 1.1 billion people who smoked worldwide, 80 percent lived in the developing world. As in the industrialized nations, these smokers had started young. Most were male, although in a few cultures, such as the Maori—relative newcomers to cigarettes—women outnumbered men among smokers under the age of twenty-four. In China, where smoking remained a largely male pastime, advertisers targeted young women, hoping to enlarge the market, just as their predecessors had in the United States after World War I.

Western cigarettes also displaced traditional means of tobacco consumption. During the 1970s, Bangladeshi smokers put aside their *hookahs* and *bidis* (cheap, hand-rolled cigarettes) for manufactured brands. The change was particularly noticeable among young people, who saw cigarettes as a way to differentiate themselves from older generations. Advertisers encouraged the impulse, pitching brands like Diplomat (Ghana) or High Society (Nigeria) that connoted worldly success and Western values. Brand consciousness developed at an early age. By century's end 29 percent of South African five-year-olds could recognize specific brands of cigarettes. In Jordan 25 percent of adolescent children aged thirteen to fifteen said company representatives had offered them free cigarettes.

The result was a growing public-health crisis. According to the World Bank, by 1996 developing nations were losing $66 billion a year to smoking-related illnesses. Because the most serious effects of cigarettes did not begin to appear until twenty years or thirty years later, epidemiologists forecast worse to come. The World Health Organization (WHO) predicted 10 million tobacco-related deaths annually by 2030. Fully 50 percent of those in developing countries who began smoking would die of smoking-related diseases. Half again of that 50 percent would die in middle age, losing years of productive life and wasting the social resources that had been invested in their upbringing and education. In essence, tobacco companies' globalized drive for profit and survival had lured another, even larger generation into the pulmonary minefield. In 2001 alone, between 64,000 and 84,000 young people in the developing world began smoking every day.

Despite the health threat and economic consequences, governments in developing nations did little to challenge the cigarette's spread, typically imposing fewer restrictions on advertising and marketing than did their Western equivalents. As of 2001, forty nations required no warnings on cigarettes. Others permitted warnings in English, rather than the native language. Restrictions on advertising, where enacted, were often indifferently enforced. Few regulations governed the levels of tar in cigarettes, which were often higher than those sold in Western nations.

Alarm over this regulatory vacuum and the lethal, mounting consequences of smoking in developing nations has provoked an increasingly vocal public health response, a situation reminiscent of attempts to negotiate controls on the international narcotic traffic in the early twentieth century (a historical parallel that the industry's critics have not been shy about developing). Several international organizations, including the WHO, have proposed global treaties aimed at curtailing, or at least slowing, sales of cigarettes and other tobacco products. The highest profile effort has been the Framework Convention on Tobacco Control (FCTC), a comprehensive regulatory scheme that includes such provisions as restrictions on tobacco advertising, promotion, and sponsorship that target minors. In May 2003 the World Health Assembly adopted the FCTC; at this writing the treaty awaits ratification by member nations.

BIBLIOGRAPHY

Courtwright, David T. 2001. *Forces of Habit: Drugs and the Making of the Modern World.* Cambridge, MA: Harvard University Press.

Kiernan, V. G. 1991. *Tobacco: A History.* London: Hutchinson Radius.

Nath, Uma R. 1986. *Smoking: Third World Alert.* Oxford, UK: Oxford University Press.

Tate, Cassandra. 1999. *Cigarette Wars: The Triumph of "The Little White Slaver."* Oxford, UK: Oxford University Press.

Winter, Joseph C., ed. 2000. *Tobacco Use by Native North Americans: Sacred Smoke and Silent Killer.* Norman: University of Oklahoma Press.

INTERNET RESOURCES

Action on Smoking and Health. 2001. "Tobacco in the Developing World." Available at <www.ash.org.uk/html/factsheets/html/fact21.html#_edn18>.

World Bank. 2002. "Economics of Tobacco Control." Available at <www1.worldbank.org/tobacco/about.asp>.

World Health Organization. 2002. "Tobacco Free Initiative." Available at <www5.who.int/tobacco/>.

DAVID T. COURTWRIGHT
ANDREW M. COURTWRIGHT

Social Settlements

Social settlements, or settlement houses, are centers for neighborhood social services and social reform activities typically located in densely populated urban areas. During the Progressive Era (1890–1920), educated reformers established settlement houses in low-income communities with the goals of bridging the widening gap between social classes, providing essential neighborhood services, and solving pressing urban social problems. The settlement movement grew in scope and political influence until World War I. Despite waning popularity in the conservative postwar era, the social settlements themselves, and the institutions and policies they built, continue to advocate for children and families well into the twenty-first century.

The social settlement movement began with the 1884 founding of Toynbee Hall in London's East End slums by parish priest Samuel Barnett and his wife, Henrietta. Toynbee Hall established opportunities for British intellectuals to reside in and study the urban problems of London's impoverished Jewish and Irish neighborhoods. Shortly after its founding, American reformers Stanton Coit and Jane Addams went to visit Toynbee Hall. They returned with the mission of bringing the social settlement movement to the United States. Coit proceeded to establish the Neighborhood Guild in 1886 on the Lower East Side of New York City. Addams and her friend Ellen Gates Starr purchased the famed Hull-House on Chicago's West Side in 1889. The settlement movement quickly spread throughout urban centers of the country; by 1910, there were roughly four hundred social settlements nationwide.

The settlement movement was responding to an array of urban social problems stemming from massive immigration and overcrowding, unrestrained capitalism, and the severe economic depression of 1893. Social settlement residents, who were primarily wealthy, white, well-educated women, strove to fulfill a "neighborhood ideal." They believed that their living in the heart of impoverished immigrant communities would help to solve many of the problems that plagued modern industrial cities, such as disease, alcoholism, prostitution, overcrowding, and harsh working conditions. Many settlement workers were guided by a religious call to service and a quest to fulfill their professional ambitions in an era of restricted choices for women. Settlement workers were optimistic that a blend of residence, research, and reform would offset the major social ills of the modern age.

As part of the era's CHILD-SAVING movement, social settlement workers appealed to public sympathies by raising concerns about the care and the protection of children. Their responses to the perceived needs of immigrant children and youth ranged from direct neighborhood services to national policy reforms. A typical social settlement provided an array of direct services for young people, such as nurseries, day care, after-school clubs, creative activities, and educational programs. The settlements organized neighborhood activities that emphasized culture and socialization for immigrant youth. Some historians, such as Elizabeth Lasch-Quinn and Anthony Platt, characterize the settlements as seeking to assimilate immigrant youths; others, such as Allen Davis and William Trattner, suggest that the settlements tried to respect and preserve the traditions of immigrant cultures.

The settlement workers had great faith in the promise of fashionable social science techniques. They learned sociological methods such as survey research and carefully crafted numerous studies of urban social problems. Armed with an array of facts and information, they used their data to advocate for progressive policy reforms, such as protective labor legislation for women and children. In some cases their reform efforts led to local improvements; in others, to state and federal workplace legislation.

In addition to advocating for protective child labor legislation, settlement workers regarded public education for all children as the key to social and human progress. They orchestrated several important and long-lasting education initiatives that enriched and expanded the role of public schools in the lives of children and families. These reforms included playgrounds, kindergartens, nursery schools, and school public health and social work services. They also strove to pass compulsory education laws in several U.S. states.

Settlement workers are also well known for their work in JUVENILE COURTS and probation services. Hull-House pioneers Julia Lathrop, JANE ADDAMS, and Grace Abbott helped to establish the first juvenile court in Cook County, Illinois,

in 1899. By 1928, all but two states had institutionalized separate judicial systems to contend with cases of juvenile DELINQUENCY and dependency. Juvenile courts suspended jury trials for children, created separate facilities for incarcerated youth, and developed juvenile probation systems. Although rife with inconsistencies and flaws, the establishment of a separate justice system for children was considered great social progress compared to prior treatment of delinquency and dependency.

Several social settlement women, mainly from Chicago's Hull-House, rose to prominent national leadership positions dealing with public policy issues concerning children and families. Florence Kelly, who resided at both Addams's Hull-House and Lillian Wald's Henry Street Settlement, was appointed secretary of the National Consumers' League and organized the NATIONAL CHILD LABOR COMMITTEE in 1904. Kelly, along with Julia Lathrop and Grace Abbott, all Hull-House residents, organized the first WHITE HOUSE CONFERENCE ON CHILDREN in 1909. In 1912, President Taft appointed Lathrop as the first chief of the U.S. CHILDREN'S BUREAU. Among other major accomplishments, the Children's Bureau played a key role in crafting sweeping national public welfare reforms for children and families such as Mothers' Pensions and the SHEPPARD-TOWNER MATERNITY AND INFANCY ACT.

While the settlement movement unequivocally pushed a progressive children's agenda, its legacy concerning race is less obvious. Some of the settlement leaders were involved in civil rights groups and even helped to found the National Association for the Advancement of Colored People (NAACP). However, historians such as Lasch-Quinn argue that the settlements largely ignored the poverty and race discrimination that haunted African Americans. They did not serve African-American families, nor did they work in concert with African-American reformers, who more often than not organized separate settlement houses. Social reformers such as Janie Porter Barrett and Birdye Henrietta Haynes founded settlements that focused on direct services, "moral uplift," and civil rights work. For African Americans, civil rights were intertwined with solving the problems of the poor.

Many current social welfare policies and services for children and youth can be traced back to the ideas and activities of the social settlements. Several settlement house buildings still exist in the form of neighborhood or family resource centers. These centers continue to provide after-school and other neighborhood activities for children, youth, and families. Moreover, the framework for the late-twentieth- and early-twenty-first-century U.S. child welfare system is based on the premise of "best interest of the child," an idea that emerged from this movement. Finally, the social settlements movement left enduring notions of children as a protected class of citizens and of a public responsibility to provide children with education, separate institutions, and the promise of quality life opportunities.

See also: **Child Labor in the West; Education, United States; Law, Children and the; Social Welfare; Work and Poverty.**

BIBLIOGRAPHY

Addams, Jane. 1910. *Twenty Years at Hull-House: With Autobiographical Notes.* New York: Macmillan.

Davis, Allen. 1973. *Spearheads for Reform: The Social Settlements and the Progressive Movement, 1890–1914.* New York: Oxford University Press.

Katz, Michael B. 1986. *In the Shadow of the Poorhouse: A Social History of Welfare in America.* New York: Basic Books.

Lasch-Quinn, Elizabeth. 1993. *Black Neighbors: Race and the Limits of Reform in the American Settlement House Movement, 1890–1945.* Chapel Hill: University of North Carolina Press.

Muncy, Robin. 1991. *Creating a Female Dominion of American Reform.* New York: Oxford University Press.

Platt, Anthony. 1977. *The Child Savers: The Invention of Delinquency.* Chicago: University of Chicago Press.

Salem, Dorothy. 1990. *Black Women in Organized Reform, 1890–1920.* New York: Carlson Publishing.

Trattner, William. 1996. *A History of Social Welfare in America,* 6th ed. New York: Free Press.

Trolander, Judith A. 1987. *Professionalism and Social Change: From the Settlement House Movement to Neighborhood Centers, 1886 to the Present.* New York: Columbia University Press.

LAURA S. ABRAMS

Social Welfare

HISTORY
  Hamilton Cravens

COMPARATIVE TWENTIETH-CENTURY DEVELOPMENTS
  Ning de Coninck-Smith
  Bengt Sandin

HISTORY

Modern social welfare and social welfare institutions have undergone three distinct periods of historical development. In the early and mid-nineteenth century, in North America and in western and central Europe, reformers tinkered with a variety of social insurance schemes, mainly pensions for the aged and certain voluntary or market-based remedies. They also organized various institutions designed to care for the mentally ill, promote public health, ward off EPIDEMICS, expand public education, and improve the lot of entrepreneurs, artisans, mechanics, and the poor. These programs influenced only fractions of any nation's population. This was an age of liberal and democratic idealism, and these efforts reflected the spirit of that age. Between the 1870s and the 1920s, in the second period, the United States, together with Great Britain, Imperial Germany, Sweden, Denmark, Austria, and France, had various social insurance schemes that

embraced some groups in their polities, thus reflecting commonly embraced notions of efficiency and hierarchy. The third phase began with the GREAT DEPRESSION of the 1930s, especially with the United States and its broad Social Security program and with most of western and central Europe, which adopted something like an all-embracing social welfare state in the wake of World War II (1939–1945). In the 1990s and early 2000s opponents in Europe and the United States made some politically effective criticisms of the welfare state, thus suggesting that yet another phase of modern social welfare's history may be about to begin, or even that the social welfare experiment may be terminated.

Social Welfare and Nineteenth Century Liberalism

In the early to mid-nineteenth century, three nations—Great Britain, the German-speaking states that Otto von Bismarck unified under Prussian hegemony in 1871, and the United States—did the most with social welfare. These three nations had vigorous public and political histories, large middle classes, considerable industrial development, and laissez-faire market capitalism.

Great Britain. In Great Britain, the Elizabethan Poor Law since the seventeenth century had mandated that each of the kingdom's fifteen thousand parishes was responsible for maintaining the poor, leading to the creation of workhouses where the poor learned to support themselves. The law neither alleviated nor solved the problem. In the early 1800s and into the 1830s, a radical individualistic laissez-faire ideology reigned in Britain, stalling any collective or governmental efforts at regulation and reform. By the early 1830s circumstances had changed. For one thing, laissez-faire ideology now contemplated the competition of interest groups in the economy, in the context of which government could do more. And, leading from this ideological shift, the new entrepreneurs of the early Industrial Revolution wanted the realm's labor force to be mobile, following capital investment wherever it established factories, shops, and stores. Hence Parliament enacted the Poor Law Amendment Act of 1834. The new law freed labor to move about for jobs in a rapidly industrializing economy and dramatically reduced the expense of poor relief.

A major midcentury issue was public health, which encompassed cleanliness, disease, and related issues. As more people worked in factories, health conditions often deteriorated, and voluntary or individualistic solutions were proven ineffectual. Within a few years Edwin Chadwick, who had worked for the enactment of the Poor Law Amendment, took the lead in advocating sanitary surveys in Britain's urban places of work and of residence, insisting that filth, crowding, and disease were all related and that sanitation was good business as well as humane and pleasant. In 1842 came the famous report on the sanitary condition of the working population. Filled with hard-won, reasonably accurate facts and figures, the report argued that filth, the degradation of the population, and the potential destruction of the economy were related. Creation of a national permanent board of health was politically and ideologically infeasible, but the board of health Parliament created, with Chadwick serving as commissioner, generated much information and knowledge in its five years of operations (1848–1854). Sanitation was now an important factor in economic and political public policy, and in maintaining and advancing the population's vigor, energy, vitality, and even fecundity. It remained important into the next century, when the germ theory of disease redirected public health and sanitary science efforts.

Protection of women and children flowed from the original Poor Law as had protection and liberation of male adult workers. In 1802 the Health and Morals of Apprentices Act, an outgrowth of the Crown's responsibilities under the Poor Law for all apprentices, women and children alike, forbade certain gross working conditions, such as poor sanitation, danger from machines, and night work, but only in cotton mills. Not until passage of the Factory Act of 1833 was there effective enforcement of such stipulations. The broader struggle over factory regulation was part of the larger conflict between the nation's two elites, the landowners and the manufacturers. But factory workers also organized themselves to fight for better conditions.

The Factory Act of 1833 protected only children and applied to all textile factories (except lace). But the inspectors appointed under the act were charged with noting the welfare of their charges in all senses. The movement spread to inspection and regulation of working conditions in the mines, where conditions were even worse than in the textile factories. As the reports came out, Victorian Britain was shocked at the potential for disease, accidents, and even immorality between the sexes in the coal mines, leading to the Mines and Collieries Act of 1842, which forbade the employment underground of females and of boys under age thirteen. The political momentum created by this measure helped the movement for the ten-hour day, enacted in 1847, which limited the workweek to fifty-eight hours for all females and for boys thirteen to eighteen years of age; and for another measure, passed in 1850, that stipulated specific working hours and meal times. By the 1870s Great Britain had several more laws that provided more regulations to protect industrial and domestic workers. As yet there was no legislation to prevent occupational diseases, nor was there much in the way of any schemes for social insurance for anyone. All had been accomplished as governmental regulation, meaning inspection of conditions, recommendations to Parliament for action, and precedents for forbidding the worst circumstances of work insofar as the public and its representatives were concerned. In all this, the image of the working child had great symbolic value, as writers such as Charles Dickens knew.

The German states. The German-speaking states in the nineteenth century were also developing the economy and

outlook that led to welfare state actions. It took the German states some time to recover from the wars of the French Revolution and Napoleon of the late eighteenth and early nineteenth centuries, and much longer to become politically unified. Enlightened absolutism ruled these states at the eighteenth century's end, and the German physician Johann Peter Frank's (1745–1821) system of "medical police," in which inspectors of the prince or the king ferreted out unsanitary conditions believed to be unhealthy, held sway into the early nineteenth century, reinforcing legendary German cleanliness—liberal applications of hot water, soap, and lye. The new liberal Germans of the early nineteenth century, however, sought to break away from absolutism, enlightened or not, taking ENLIGHTENMENT rationalism and applying it to the marketplace, while at the same time having to put up with older forms of mercantilism and absolutism in matters of political economy.

There were certain conditions that made a social welfare state conceivable in Germany. From German feudalism came the intertwined notions that the state was obliged to promote social welfare and to exercise social control, ideas that all groups in Germany accepted according to their interests. Even liberal thinkers combined the new ideas of a state based on law with these older notions of the state. Pioneers of German social science insisted that an active state must intervene in industrial society to promote the commonweal. The higher civil service and the professions supported the new liberalism, whereas the commercial classes and industrial bourgeoisie did not, fearing unbridled economic growth and a resulting revolutionary proletariat. Before the 1830s, German liberals championed self-help societies for the workers, thus embracing a laissez-faire individualism paralleled in Britain, but such views later turned into adaptations of social welfare to the new industrial conditions in the cities. The tool of state intervention was powerful, authoritarian German bureaucracy. After the Revolution of 1848, the German states seized the initiative and laid down certain benefit and regulation schemes as palliatives for their enhanced state authority. Most important was Prussia's 1854 law turning poor relief into a modern contributory welfare program, which became the original blueprint for the later Bismarckian welfare state.

As factories grew in Germany, and as German science and technology rivaled that of England, Prussia led the other German states to regulate child labor, to enact protective conditions for women, and to provide for certain basic decent conditions of labor for the working classes. At midcentury and later the public sanitation movement swept through the German-speaking lands. Liberalism had penetrated German society and culture to its limit as Bismarck, chancellor to the Prussian king, unified the German states as the German Empire, under Prussian leadership, in 1871.

The United States. Nineteenth-century political and economic liberalism held sway even more powerfully in America than in Europe. The federal constitution adopted in 1789 made possible an internal customs union within all the states, thus achieving laissez-faire economic liberalism in one dramatic step. This ideal state would permit rational, civilized individuals to pursue commerce and trade with a minimum of interference. Within a generation the American Revolution had swept away mercantilism's remnants, thus bringing about a new individualistic democracy centered on civilized, rational individuals who would pursue the republican virtues with minimal governmental interference. Either volunteers or for-profit private firms took responsibility for most municipal and county public services. When the public health was threatened—as it was by cholera epidemics in 1832—a temporary board of health would be appointed to attend to the emergency, enforcing quarantines, burying bodies, and the like, and would disband once the danger was gone. The federal government could do, and did do, even less, attending to the public lands, to matters of war and diplomacy, to the delivery of the mails, and to advancing the interests of economic groups represented in the federal political system. From the 1830s to the 1870s American assistance to the needy was largely charitable rather than government sponsored. For those needing care and supervision, so-called moral reformers devised many institutions as remedies, such as ORPHANAGES for children without parents, houses of refuge for juvenile offenders, and organizations like the NEW YORK CHILDREN'S AID SOCIETY and the SOCIETIES FOR THE PREVENTION OF CRUELTY TO CHILDREN that sought to protect those who they believed were abused or neglected. All were usually drawn from among the urban poor. But the state governments, at least in the North, did develop mass education schemes. By the 1880s and 1890s, however, there were signs of a shift toward a new model of society and thus of social welfare.

Social Welfare in an Age of Hierarchy, Efficiency, and System

Between the 1870s and the 1920s, the Western world was dominated by a new set of ideas about how to organize human experience. It was an age of science, of expertise, of hierarchy, of orderly systems of nature and of society, of efficiency. How to make society work at peak efficiency was the underlying issue to many Europeans and Americans. Such notions embraced social welfare and its institutions as well. Many of these changes came from new political situations as well as new worldviews. In Scandinavia, for example, it was farmers, not the progressive middle classes or the socialist left, that led the fight for tax-supported universal pensions—in Denmark in 1891 and in Sweden in 1913, after protracted political struggles. In Imperial Germany, it was the "Iron Chancellor," Bismarck, who pushed for workers' pensions on a contributory, not a tax-based, scheme, hoping to dampen workers' enthusiasm for socialism and revolution and to make them beholden to the conservative Junker class and the Prussian state. This social insurance scheme covered industrial accidents, illness, invalidism, and old age. Its enactment

resulted from many compromises; workers, employers, and the state all contributed to the fund. And the scheme, in various reincarnations, has survived into the twenty-first century and has been widely imitated, in Hungary (1891), Austria (1889), Switzerland (1911), and even France (1928). The German states, like many industrialized polities on the continent, had already enacted legislation regulating the labor of children, on the grounds that a healthy adult population was impossible without such measures. In the early twentieth century, societies for infant welfare in such cities as Berlin and Düsseldorf took the lead in educating mothers about child health, functions that local governments later appropriated. From 1873 on there was a national public health bureau, and in the 1900s the public HYGIENE movement spread throughout the Second Reich.

If Bismarck inaugurated a welfare program to counter revolution, the British in the early twentieth century did so in the face of mass poverty brought about by the nation's industrial decline as compared with the United States and Imperial Germany. In the early 1900s, certain British politicians noted the greater efficiency of the German welfare system and its effectiveness in promoting the Reich's economic competitiveness. David Lloyd George and Winston Churchill, in particular, led the campaign for what became the National Insurance Act of 1911, which brought unemployment compensation, health and disability insurance, hospital insurance, and even maternity allowances in its wake. In turn these programs upgraded the health prospects of the poor and helped unify the nation politically. Eventually the British system was more generous than the German one, although those who lived under the German system found it very satisfactory. Europe, then, by the early twentieth century, had created a variety of nationally administered and financed welfare schemes to cover unemployment, illness, disability, and old age. In these five decades many of the European nations also imitated the United States in adopting mass public education and mass adult male suffrage.

In this age of system, America did innovate in social welfare. And its differences with its European sister national cultures seemed to derive from the same factors that made the European states different from one another: largely questions of politics, the state, and temporal context. Americans rebuilt the shattered states of the Confederacy and created mass public education, promoted public health and sanitation through the establishment of the U.S. Public Health Service, regulated foods and drugs, and established a large and eventually generous pension program for Civil War veterans (including some Confederate veterans) and their dependents, meaning widows and ORPHANS. This federal program, which conveniently discharged the huge surpluses generated by high protective tariffs, was self-liquidating: when the last veteran died, it did too. But it represented the idea of social insurance of the age: that a group could insure itself against the vagaries of life. It differed in no important respect from contemporary European schemes. America made an important contribution to welfare ideas thanks to its tradition of middle-class women participating in politics with an agenda for child welfare, education, and morality, just as American men concerned themselves with the welfare of adult male workers. It was the child welfare movement of the period from 1900 to 1920 that advanced social welfare and its institutions in America and, by example, in the Western world. A maternalistic welfare state, still largely rooted in the states and the cities, not the federal government, almost perfectly balanced the British-German patriarchic welfare programs. The American child welfare movement emphasized child health and protection, and new institutions such as the JUVENILE COURT, FOSTER CARE, the children's bureau, and mother's pensions were all defined as ways to increase social efficiency while they also expressed a new consciousness of care. Many of these also reflected deep-seated white prejudice against persons of color and the "new" immigrants from southern and eastern Europe.

The Welfare State in Depression and World War

In the years between the 1920s and the 1950s, notions that government and the private sector could work together were the watchwords of the age. While the Scandinavian countries had already established fairly comprehensive social welfare states, the United States took steps toward the modern, all-embracing welfare state with the adoption of social security through the Social Security Act of 1935. A large difference between the American and European systems had to do with the lack in the former of a national health scheme, whether national health insurance or nationalized medicine. The reason for this was the rising power and prestige of American doctors in the twentieth century based on their identification with experimental science. Social Security made possible old-age pensions on a tax basis, as a supplement to private pension schemes. Through AID TO DEPENDENT CHILDREN, later Aid to Families with Dependent Children, child welfare became part of the new federal program of welfare, just as unemployment insurance, disability insurance, and other programs came to constitute the American welfare state. In the 1960s the American welfare state began to expand dramatically in the numbers of its client populations.

During this time, much of the European continent was ravaged by war, and the Marshall Plan, to rebuild Europe, laid the groundwork for political reform and provided the requisite energy and creativity for a much expanded welfare state. The British Labour Party, which gained control of Parliament and the government in the immediate postwar period, enacted legislation that extended the welfare state by nationalizing certain industries and creating the National Health Service (1948), which put most doctors in state employ, and cautiously began to extend public education as well. Following its creation in 1949, the Federal Republic of Germany (or West Germany) soon revived and extended the

Bismarckian welfare state, now with generous pension schemes; first-rate medical care combined with a sophisticated national health scheme; expanded public health, sanitation, and other welfare provisions; and even *Kindergeld* (money for children) to encourage families to have more children and rebuild the national population. Other European nations extended the national welfare state in the post–World War II era, many such as France and Sweden by providing each family with specific allowances to ensure that children not grow up in poverty. In addition, they provided nursery schools, day-care centers, paid vacations, and free higher education.

Wither the Welfare State?

In the closing decades of the twentieth century, there were signs of a revolt against the welfare state, an expensive luxury for the underdeveloped or Third World nations and a costly investment for many of the developed nations. As the populations of the developed nations grew older and less able to contribute to the maintenance of a national welfare state, perhaps the end of the welfare state was in view. In any event, it would appear that modern social welfare and its institutions have always risen and fallen in tandem with the trends in national politics—politics being the art and science of what is possible at any given time.

See also: **Child Labor in the West; Child Saving; Social Welfare: Comparative Twentieth-Century Developments; Work and Poverty.**

BIBLIOGRAPHY

Baldwin, Peter. 1990. *The Politics of Social Solidarity: Class Bases of the European Welfare State, 1875–1975.* Cambridge, UK: Cambridge University Press.

Cravens, Hamilton. 1993. *Before Head Start: The Iowa Station and America's Children.* Chapel Hill: University of North Carolina Press.

Mazower, Mark. 1999. *Dark Continent: Europe's Twentieth Century.* New York: Knopf.

Ritter, Gerhard A. 1986. *Social Welfare in Germany and Britain: Origins and Development.* Trans. Kim Traynor. New York: Berg.

Rosen, George. 1993. *A History of Public Health,* expanded ed. Baltimore, MD: Johns Hopkins University Press.

Skocpol, Theda. 1995. *Social Policy in the United States: Future Possibilities in Historical Perspective.* Princeton, NJ: Princeton University Press.

Tiffin, Susan. 1982. *In Whose Best Interest? Child Welfare Reform in the Progressive Era.* Westport, CT: Greenwood.

HAMILTON CRAVENS

COMPARATIVE TWENTIETH-CENTURY DEVELOPMENTS

The welfare state in the twentieth century emphasized publicly sponsored care, in contrast to earlier state forms, which left care to the family, the local community, professional associations such as guilds, or in the nineteenth century, if no other form of help was available, philanthropic societies. Welfare states are, however, not identical. Scandinavian systems, with their predominantly universal benefits and extended involvement in the security and well-being of their citizens, can be said to represent one model. Other models are the liberalist, or Anglo-Saxon, model, which helps only the weakest members of society, and the continental European model, which links social benefits to conditions of work and pay.

This system of classification is not, however, universally accepted. Some researchers have pointed out that these models do not exist in unadulterated forms and that the differences between them produce disparate results if they are compared according to social sector rather than according to whether universal benefits apply. If we look, for instance, at how welfare states care for younger and older members of society, France with its special family allowances and public preschool provision (*écoles maternelles*) resembles Scandinavia more than it does Germany or Holland. In these two countries consideration for motherhood has played an important role in the formation of social and labor policy during the twentieth century. There is, therefore, a relative shortage of day-care institutions but provision for lengthy maternity leave. This illustrates how the construction of welfare states is influenced by and also helps form existing views of childhood and parenthood.

This is also illustrated by studies made by the political scientist Göran Therborn of how welfare states handle CHILDREN'S RIGHTS. He concludes that Scandinavian countries should be regarded as being in the vanguard here, since even at the outbreak of World War I the aim of legislation relating to the family was to protect the interests of the child, including ensuring equal rights for legitimate and illegitimate children. A logical result of this was the extension of the child's legal status, which ensued in the 1970s and 1980s. This involved laws against hitting children and the obligation to take children wishes into consideration in cases of separation and child custody disputes. These developments have ensured a central place for Scandinavian countries in international human rights work and in the forming of the 1989 UN CONVENTION ON THE RIGHTS OF THE CHILD. To explain this development, Therborn cites the presence of a weaker patriarchal system, a weaker church, and a more individually oriented welfare model in Scandinavia than was the case in the remainder of Europe.

Despite often being linked to the growth of social democracy, the welfare state in Europe has had broad political backing throughout the twentieth century, even from conservative political regimes. The organization of welfare corresponds, then, as much to the underlying features of a country's political culture as to political ideology. Behind the first experimental schemes for single mothers, children, and the poor at the end of the nineteenth century lay a combination of consideration for the population's size and quality—noticeable particularly in Germany, but also in France—and a desire to take preventative measures against social unrest at a time when immigration to the large urban centers threatened to topple the social order. The welfare state has also been linked to the development of bourgeois democracies, in that participation in decision-making and the right to vote both presuppose some degree of education and of homogenization of social and cultural differences. The belief that welfare would create greater equality was widespread, and the welfare state and democracy have provided political legitimacy for each other. The interaction between democracy and social welfare has also resulted in the establishment of new methods for the control of the population. Thereby the Janus face of the welfare state—social assistance on one side and control on the other—became visible. As a result, in the building of the welfare state the citizen has changed in status from being the passive object of state care to being a partner to the many experts of the welfare state in everything from health to child rearing, and in this way has acquired increased visibility as an empowered individual. This applies to adults and children alike.

There has also been debate about the extent to which the welfare state was an extension of the philanthropic commitment that developed in the nineteenth century, especially to the poor city dwellers, or whether it was, in fact, a break with the past. In fact, the collaboration between public and private initiatives, especially in areas relating to family and children, played an important part well into the twentieth century. In Catholic countries this involvement, particularly in ecclesiastical circles, has been maintained to this day, as evidenced by concerns for the single mother, child nutrition, and children's homes. As an extension of philanthropic work and founded in the developing commitment by the welfare state to the life of the citizen from the cradle to the grave, a series of new professions arose, including health visitors, preschool teachers, and doctors, dentists, and psychologists specializing in child health. An important aspect of this professionalization was its mutual international inspiration. American health care schemes, for instance, were incorporated into Danish and Finnish reality in the 1940s and 1950s; in the same way Scandinavian countries borrowed heavily from each other, for instance in the 1930s, when declining population was an issue.

The Welfare State and Parenthood

In considering the change in parenthood during the epoch of the welfare state, certain features draw immediate attention. The social content of parenthood has changed due to demographic, social, and cultural changes, and also as a result of changes in the scientific understanding of the relationship between children and parents.

In northern Europe it is no longer a disgrace to be a single mother, or for a child to be born out of wedlock. Equally, parents wishing to adopt receive the same support as other parents, and artificial insemination is free for heterosexual couples; 40 percent to 50 percent of all children in northern Europe are born to couples who are not married, and 90 percent of all women now have children, while 25 percent were childless 100 years ago. The reasons for this increase in motherhood are that 100 years ago many women were unmarried and that motherhood was not compatible with the professions a woman could work in outside the home, such as teaching and nursing. It may also have been caused by involuntary sterility due to infection. Women at the turn of the twentieth century had an average of four children, compared to two at the start of the twenty-first century, but they became mothers at roughly the same age, between twenty-five and thirty-five. It was only in the 1950s and 1960s—the years when the family headed by a male breadwinner was at its height—that birthing age was lower. The late birthing age at the beginning and end of the twentieth century has two different explanations. Firstly, in agricultural societies starting a family required a degree of financial stability. Secondly, in welfare societies many young women wish to complete their education before starting a family. Together with the increasing number of separations—which affect about 50 percent of all marriages—this reflects the individualization of parenthood. Parenthood is nowadays a project of individual importance to men and women and a right which the state has taken upon itself to guarantee.

In southern Europe, too, changes are on the way. Birth rates changed during the final thirty years of the twentieth century, from being the highest in Europe to being the lowest. In countries such as Italy, Spain, or Greece, 40 percent of all women give birth to no children or to just one child. Those children born, however, are generally born to married couples and face less likelihood of experiencing parental separation compared with children in northern Europe.

The making of parenthood into a science is to a large extent due to the intervention of the welfare state. While philanthropists might previously have regarded mothers as incompetent and fathers as social problems, the broadening of state involvement to include all citizens meant that parents gradually acquired the status of partners in a common project of child rearing based on the newest scientific insights into children and their development. The first step down this road involved child welfare and maternity services, which arose as a result of concern in the period between the wars against INFANT MORTALITY and the falling birthrate. In the sphere of education and day care, a similar development could be seen.

If in the nineteenth century medical science determined what a good childhood was, its role was supplemented by psychology in the twentieth. A modern pattern of child rearing emphasizing the child as a self-sufficient individual has gradually replaced an older, more authoritarian view

founded on a regard for quietness, regularity, and cleanliness. Just as parents were expected to participate with the welfare-state professionals as partners in a common child-rearing project, a similar development took place for children—especially in Scandinavian countries—around 1980. Children were regarded as being competent and as having rights—to physical and psychological integrity among other things. This development has been sanctioned through the statutory prohibition of physical castigation of children (in Sweden first, in 1979), the establishment of the first child ombudsman (in Norway first, in 1981) and the ratification of the UN Convention on the Rights of the Child in 1989.

The Welfare State and Childhood

If changes in childhood are seen in context of the development of the welfare state during the twentieth century, three features stand out. Childhood has become institutionalized, professionalized, and more homogeneous in the sense that the formerly middle-class concept of childhood as an independent life of PLAY and learning has become the norm, transcending divisions of gender, culture, and social class. The differences between the north and the remainder of Europe, which have been noted in relation to parenthood, are also clearly discernible here.

The universalization of elementary schooling after the 1870s involved marked changes to children's lives. Gradually work took second place to school. The development was supported by legislation against child labor, even though this legislation was primarily directed at factory work and so affected neither children working in agriculture and in various non-factory forms of urban work nor girls' unpaid help in cleaning or minding smaller siblings. At the same time a series of new initiatives focusing on the child's physical and mental health were linked to schooling: school meals, school baths, school medical inspections, holiday camps, school gardens and playgrounds. In this way children from the broad social spectrum gradually came to have a share in a childhood which had previously been the preserve of middle-class children. Children's work has, however, not entirely disappeared; in the poorer areas of southern Europe, the child's economic contribution to the family is still important, while in northern Europe children work to line their own pockets.

In other areas, too, the child's life changed. Infant mortality was markedly reduced after 1900, just as mortality among older children fell. The causes for this were improved living conditions, penicillin, and vaccination. Prolonged life spans enabled parents and grandparents to live for a longer portion of their children's and grandchildren's lives, and toward the turn of the twenty-first century children once again began to have a greater number of siblings, this time in the form of half-sisters and -brothers in the wake of increased divorce and separation.

It was, however, not only the spread of schooling and the gradual disappearance of children's work that altered children's lives. Just as important was the increasing tendency since the 1960s for mothers to work outside the home. Where many had previously combined family life with a part-time job—assisting on the farm or in the shop or washing or cleaning in the neighborhood— they were increasingly away from home by day. The child's life became institutionalized, a process that took place in two different ways. In Scandinavia a combination gradually developed comprising relatively short maternity leave, short working hours, and an extended system of day care and KINDERGARTEN for children one year and above. In the rest of Europe, maternity leave generally covers the child's first three years, after which the child begins to go to school for half the day. It is, therefore, hardly surprising that 80 percent of mothers of small children in Sweden and Denmark have full-time jobs, while in southern and mid-Europe they are mainly housewives or have part-time jobs. For single mothers in countries such as Portugal, Italy, and Spain, full-time work is the rule with less comprehensive public care for single-parent families.

Institutionalization allows the ordinary young child and his or her abilities to be visible to the eyes of the professional. While conceptions of the good childhood adopted around 1900 had arisen through studies of poor and sick children, the new, scientifically based norm of the good life for the child was increasingly based on studies of ordinary children. The institutionalizing and professionalizing of childhood resulted, therefore, in new standards, but also in a harmonizing of children's lives across gender, class, and cultural difference as public child-minding gradually became part of daily life for more and more children through the 1980s.

This move toward regimenting childhood has also been supported by a huge investment in training, with a resulting democratization of the system of higher education, which gave children from the countryside, and not least girls, the chance to acquire further education. RADIO, TELEVISION, and most recently the Internet have also contributed to the establishment of a common set of references among children and young people, primarily nationally but also increasingly internationally.

Harmonization is, however, far from synonymous with all children having the same living standards. Data from the European Union show that 9 percent of children and young people live in families that have difficulties making ends meet. Marginalization has a particularly severe impact on children of single parents or children from immigrant families. The worst scenario is in England, where 23 percent of all children live in poor families. England, together with Greece and Ireland, has the highest rate of infant mortality in Europe. Finally it should be mentioned that in the Scandinavian countries children and young people today struggle with problems relating to lifestyle—weight problems, smoking, alcohol, and stress.

Conclusion

The dream of the good childhood has characterized the welfare states of the twentieth century, but the dream has undergone marked alterations. The picture of the child has changed; once an incompetent being with a right to state care and protection, the child is now seen as a competent fellow citizen. This altered understanding of childhood has led to fresh perceptions of parenthood, primarily a broadening of the role to include not just the mother but also the father. Parental competencies should be developed in a dialogue with science and its experts. Ambitions on behalf of parenthood and childhood could scarcely have been higher than at the beginning of the twenty-first century.

It is, however, important to stress that there are considerable differences between the lives of children across the European welfare community. The two decisive but interconnected differences consist of the degree to which the public sector takes the individual or the family as its point of departure and the degree to which childhood is seen as a phase of life in its own right or as a preparation for adult life. The former is the case in the north, while the latter applies to southern and mid-Europe.

See also: **Child Care: Institutional Forms; Social Welfare: History.**

BIBLIOGRAPHY

European Commission / Eurostat. 2002. *European Social Statistics: Demography*. Luxembourg: Office for Official Publications of the European Communities.

Lewis, J. 2002. "Gender and Welfare State Change." *European Societies* 4, no. 4: 331–357.

Michel, Sonya, and Rianne Mahon, eds. 2002. *Child Care Policy at the Crossroads: Gender and Welfare State Restructuring*. New York: Routledge.

Mitchell, Brian R., ed. 1998. *International Historical Statistics: Europe 1750–1993*, 4th ed. London: Macmillan Reference.

Pedersen, Susan. 1993. *Family, Dependence, and the Origins of the Welfare State: Britain and France 1914–1945*. Cambridge, UK: Cambridge University Press.

Sainsbury, Diane, ed. 1994. *Gendering Welfare States*. Thousand Oaks, CA: Sage.

Therborn, Göran. 1993. "The Politics of Childhood: The Rights of Children in Modern Times." In *Families of Nations: Patterns of Public Policy in Western Democracies*, ed. Francis G. Castles. Aldershot, UK: Dartmouth.

Trägårdh, L. 1997. "State Individualism: On the Culturality of the Nordic." In *The Cultural Construction of Norden*, ed. Øystein Sørensen and Bo Stråth. Oslo: Scandinavian University Press.

NING DE CONINCK-SMITH
BENGT SANDIN

Societies for the Prevention of Cruelty to Children

Attorney and patrician Elbridge Gerry founded the first Society for the Prevention of Cruelty to Children (SPCC) in

New York City in December 1874. The NYSPCC sparked a movement. Within twenty-five years, over 150 organizations across the nation joined the effort to protect children from abuse. Gerry's involvement in the rescue of an eight-year-old girl, Mary Ellen, from her physically abusive guardians had persuaded him of the need to organize a society to protect children. What made the idea so contagious?

Since the mid-eighteenth century, many Americans had become increasingly sensitive to the pain of others, a development evidenced by their establishment of innumerable volunteer societies to ameliorate suffering. Most famously, these new "humanitarians" struggled for the abolition of slavery. The establishment of SPCCs came very late in the humanitarian revolution, even after the movement to protect animals from abuse. Before the Mary Ellen case, Elbridge Gerry worked as a lawyer for Henry Bergh, founder of the New York Society for the Prevention of Cruelty to Animals. Only after repeated criticisms of his seeming indifference to the plight of children did Bergh instruct Gerry to help a concerned charity worker named Etta Wheeler rescue Mary Ellen.

Humanitarian reformers had expressed concern for children before the 1870s, organizing efforts to end the corporal punishment of school children, creating institutions to care for ORPHANS, and even sending orphans by train to foster families in the West. But reformers were reluctant to interfere in families, which had a recognized right to privacy. By the 1870s, the relative weights of the concern for children and the concern for family privacy had shifted. Mary Ellen's residence with foster parents (her biological parents were dead) may have eased her protectors' willingness to cross that boundary. Differences in class and culture also facilitated the creation of the SPCCs. The organizations were directed by wealthy, conservative, Protestant white men, whereas their clientele were mostly poor, Catholic immigrant families or poor black families. These were powerful distinctions during the late nineteenth century.

Their founders conceived of the SPCCs as law enforcement agencies. Agents were to find abused children—on the street or through tips made by concerned neighbors, relatives, and even the abused children themselves—investigate their families, and prosecute abusers. Many states gave the societies police powers, such as the right to issue warrants, or allowed the police to aid them. Most importantly, "the cruelty" (as SPCC agents were sometimes known in poor neighborhoods) could remove children from their homes.

In the early twentieth century the SPCCs made a radical shift from policing to welfare work. In 1903 the Massachusetts Society for the Prevention of Cruelty to Children elected Grafton Cushing to be the agency's new president. Cushing believed that SPCCs had to prevent abuse by fixing the social problems that underlay it. He hired C. C. Carstens, who had a background in charity work, to lead the MSPCC along its new path. Carstens shifted the agency's focus from physical abuse to neglect, which he believed stemmed from bad social conditions. Instead of investigating and prosecuting families, his agents were to prevent family breakdown. Many other SPCCs followed Carstens's lead.

The new approach redressed a serious deficiency in the earlier model, but it also created new problems. The social problems identified by agents were sometimes better reflections of their own prejudices than of the objective problems poor families suffered. The agents often confused poverty with malfeasance, or blamed victims for their traumas. Many criticized mothers who worked as neglectful, even if the family depended on her income. Girls who had been molested or raped were labeled sexual delinquents. Women who separated from abusive husbands were faulted for desertion. Carstens himself believed that hereditary "mental feebleness" was the primary source of neglect, and supported the sterilization of people with "mental defects." These judgments carried more than moral weight; they figured into the agents' calculations about who would receive financial aid.

The shift to welfare work also deflected the public's attention from the problem of physical abuse. Many of the welfare functions of the SPCCs were taken over by the federal government during the New Deal. For example, Title IV of the Social Security Act (1935) established the AID TO DEPENDENT CHILDREN Program, which distributed benefits to female-headed families. Case workers also scrutinized the moral "suitability" of recipient families, much as SPCC agents had done. However the effort to stop physical abuse was forgotten. The brutal treatment of children did not become an important issue again until the 1960s, when the widespread use of x-ray technology revealed to doctors the histories of trauma underlying many childhood injuries.

See also: **Brace, Charles Loring; Child Abuse; Child Saving; Law, Children and the; New York Children's Aid Society; Orphan Trains; Police, Children and the.**

BIBLIOGRAPHY

Antler, Joyce, and Stephen Antler. 1979. "From Child Rescue to Family Protection." *Children and Youth Services Review* 1: 177–204.

Costin, Lela B. 1996. *The Politics of Child Abuse in America.* New York: Oxford University Press.

Gordon, Linda. 1988. *Heroes of Their Own Lives: The Politics and History of Family Violence.* New York: Viking.

Pleck, Elizabeth. 1987. *Domestic Tyranny: The Making of Social Policy Against Family Violence from Colonial Times to the Present.* New York: Oxford University Press.

RACHEL HOPE CLEVES

Sociology and Anthropology of Childhood

Prior to the 1980s children were on the margins of sociology (an academic discipline that focuses on social relations and

FIGURE 1

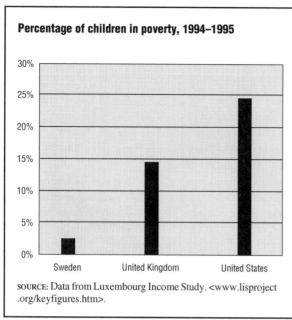

Percentage of children in poverty, 1994–1995

SOURCE: Data from Luxembourg Income Study. <www.lisproject .org/keyfigures.htm>.

institutions) and anthropology (a neighboring field that emphasizes the study of culture). When children did come into the view of anthropologists, they were primarily studied as learners being inducted into the social and cultural worlds of adults. In the 1930s the anthropologist MARGARET MEAD wrote about cross-cultural variation in child-rearing practices, which, she argued, shape cultural differences in adult personalities. Over the next four decades anthropologists continued this line of inquiry in places as diverse as JAPAN, Samoa, New Guinea, Bali, AFRICA, Russia, and the United States.

Sociologists also have a long tradition of studying children as learners or as adults-in-the-making, using the concept of socialization. Talcott Parsons, an influential sociologist of the 1950s and 1960s, theorized social systems as smoothly functioning wholes. When children are born, he wrote, they are like pebbles thrown into a social pond. First the family and then schools and other institutions shape the growing child, who comes to internalize the values and rules of adult society. Sociologists in this time period focused on children not only as learners but also as threats (research on juvenile DELINQUENCY emerged in the 1950s) and as victims of adults (child physical abuse became a topic in the 1960s, and child sexual abuse in the 1970s).

The New Social Studies of Childhood

In the 1980s, a growing number of European and American scholars called attention to the relative absence of children in the knowledge of the social sciences. They argued that children should be studied in their own right, as full social actors, rather than being framed primarily as adults-in-training or as problems for the adult social order. In an early critique, Enid Schildkrout observed that children rarely entered descriptions of social systems and proposed that they should be understood as children rather than as the next generation of adults. Reversing the familiar equation of children with dependence, Schildkrout asked, "What would happen to the adult world (other than its extinction) if there were no children?" and "In what ways are adults dependent upon children?" Drawing upon fieldwork among the Hausa, a Muslim society in Nigeria, Schildkrout described children's contributions to sustaining the religious institution of purdah, which involves the spatial seclusion of women. Among the Hausa, married men earned income away from their households as butchers and artisans; women earned money by cooking food and embroidering hats and trousers to sell at the local market. Confined to their households by purdah, income-earning women depended on children to purchase materials and to deliver and sell the final products at the market. Up until PUBERTY, both girls and boys were free to move between households and the market. These arrangements—with spatially mobile children actively contributing to economic and religious institutions—reverse late-twentieth-century Western assumptions about children's place, highlighting varied constructions of both childhood and adulthood.

The "new social studies of childhood," as scholars began to call the movement to pay closer attention to children as social actors with varied lives and experiences, gained momentum in the 1980s and 1990s. This critical approach to adult-centered frameworks was enhanced by increasing criticisms of knowledge organized around the outlooks and interests of the powerful. Scholarly attention to women and people of color helped inspire calls for research that would bring children more fully into knowledge. Critical examination of age relations, childhood, and categories such as *child* and *adult* was also spurred by a theoretical approach called *social constructionism*, which involves digging beneath categories that are taken for granted to examine the varied ways in which they have been organized and given meaning. A unitary category like *the child* is especially ripe for examination because it encompasses a wide range of ages and capacities, with an ambiguous and often disputed upper boundary.

Sociologists of childhood often credit the French historian PHILIPPE ARIÈS with opening conceptions of age, the child, and childhood for social and historical analysis, beginning in the early 1960s. Viviana Zelizer, a historical sociologist, also highlighted changing views of children and childhood in an influential 1985 book on the transition in late-nineteenth- and early-twentieth-century America from the "economically useful child" to the ideal of an "economically useless, but emotionally priceless" child, removed from paid labor and located in the protected spaces of families and schools. Historians of childhood have helped other social scientists gain critical perspective on contemporary Western assumptions about children's place, including the definition of children by processes of learning and development.

International political and economic changes of the late twentieth century also heightened awareness of the varied lives and circumstances of children. Global economic restructuring strengthened ties among geographically distant nations, with increasing circulation of commodities, labor, information, and images. In many parts of the world, these changes forced children into new conditions of poverty and increased their numbers among refugees and among those who work in highly exploitative conditions. Televised images of children living in situations of war, violence, poverty, and famine have undermined the assumption that children are an innocent and protected group, safely ensconced in families and schools. In the late twentieth century, the global cultural politics of childhood became an area of contention as well as a focus of anthropological and sociological research.

The Cultural Politics of Childhood

The United Nations highlighted the varied, sometimes devastating, circumstances of the world's children when the General Assembly declared 1979 the Year of the Child, followed, in 1989, by the adoption of the UN CONVENTION ON THE RIGHTS OF THE CHILD. By 2003 the Convention had been ratified by every country except Somalia and the United States. This document was developed by representatives of forty-three nations, who wrestled with cultural and political differences as they sought to articulate worldwide moral standards for the treatment of children. The convention is organized around four core principles: nondiscrimination, the best interests of the child, the rights to survival and development, and attention to the views of the child (a principle that recognizes children as somewhat independent of adults). Critics, including many anthropologists, have argued that the UN Convention assumes and imposes Western ideas about childhood, family, and individual rights, and that it is insensitive to other cultural understandings of children and morality. Defenders have responded to these criticisms by noting the widespread effects of global economic and political change and by arguing that ethical action should be forged between the two extremes of universal claims about individual rights and the refusal to judge other cultures (cultural relativism).

A growing body of research on children living in contexts of extreme poverty, forced migration, and war has extended the study of childhoods far beyond the worlds of families, neighborhoods, and schools, situating children within processes of political and economic change. For example, scholars have studied children who live and work on the streets in cities in LATIN AMERICA, Asia, Africa, and EASTERN EUROPE. The term *street children* is often used to describe these children, but researchers and activists have argued that the term is misleading since the circumstances and social relations of these children vary a great deal and many of them continue to sustain ties with their families. Scholars such as Tobias Hecht have charted the economic, social, and political forces that draw or push children into living and working on the streets; their social networks and varied relationships with urban environments, including both the opportunities and risks that street life poses for survival; and governmental and other efforts to control and reform this stigmatized group. Some activist researchers have sought access to the perspectives of street children themselves, working with them to change the conditions of their lives. Others have examined the hypervisibility of street children, whose lives have become fodder for journalists, researchers, and even a Michael Jackson video about a *favela*, or slum, in Rio de Janeiro. They have argued that the sensationalizing of extreme poverty obscures the situations of the chronically poor—a large proportion of children and adults in countries like BRAZIL.

The many types of research on street children illustrate three central theoretical approaches in the new social studies of childhood: (1) comparative analysis of the political economy and social structuring of particular childhoods; (2) the study of symbolic or discursive constructions of children and childhoods; and (3) attention to children as social actors and as creators and interpreters of culture. Although these approaches overlap, each draws upon a distinctive set of theoretical tools and research methods.

Comparative Research on the Structuring of Children's Lives

In the late 1980s and early 1990s, Jens Qvortrup, a Danish sociologist, coordinated an ambitious comparative study of the living conditions of children in thirteen European countries plus Israel, Canada, and the United States. The researchers relied, in part, on the techniques of demography—that is, the use of statistical methods to study the size, structure, and distribution of particular populations. Defining children as a category spanning the ages of birth through fourteen, the research team compared the age structuring of national populations. They found, for example, that from 1950 to 1990 the proportion of children declined in all sixteen industrialized countries, with the greatest decline in Finland and the least in ISRAEL. They also analyzed comparative information about the size and composition of the households in which children resided, patterns in the employment of children and in children's daily duties at home, the amount of time children spent in school and in organized activities outside of school, the legal and health status of children, and the proportion of social resources, such as income and housing, that were allocated to children in each national economy. Guided by a view of childhood as a position in social structure, this comparative study emphasized relations among legal, political, economic, health, educational, family, and other institutions.

Qvortrup and his colleagues found that available statistical information about children was highly uneven, since parents or households, rather than children themselves, have often been the categories used in the gathering of statistical information. When demographic information is gathered with children at the center, the picture shifts, sometimes dramatically. For example, Donald Hernandez found that in 1988, 18 percent of U.S. adult parents but 27 percent of children lived in poverty. Thus the distribution of children's economic status differs from that of the parents.

What accounts for national variation in the proportion of children who live in poverty? To shed light on this question, sociologists have examined relationships among families, states, and markets. States assign responsibilities to parents, limit their power, and define the ages at which children can legally engage in wage labor. States also provide resources for children, but to varying degrees. Scandinavian countries, such as Sweden, which assume that the state will cooperate with and support families, have traditions of generous and universal state provisioning for children through paid parental leaves and state-funded child and health care. The United States is at the other end of the continuum, with a privatized family system, which assumes that parents will purchase services such as health and CHILD CARE and that the state will step in only when the family and the market are deemed to have failed, as in federal child-care subsidies to very low-income families. In the United Kingdom, which is in the middle of this continuum, there is movement from a welfare state toward a privatized family system. These different institutional arrangements help account for variation in rates of child poverty.

The Symbolic or Discursive Construction of Childhoods

Research on the social construction of childhood has focused not only on the institutional arrangements that shape children's lives but also on beliefs about the nature of children or particular groups of children, such as infants or girls entering PUBERTY. Anthropologists and sociologists often use the term *discourse* to refer to ideas and images that convey a particular view of the world or, in this case, a particular view of children and childhood. For example, street children in Brazil have been portrayed as threats to the social order (a discourse the police have used to justify arrests), as victims (the discourse of social welfare agencies), and through a discourse of CHILDREN'S RIGHTS used by activists who argue that children should participate in changing the conditions of their lives.

Social scientists who study discursive constructions of children and childhoods have analyzed not only the ways in which meanings are made but also their effects in the world. For example, sociologists and anthropologists often puzzle about the gap between the stated goal of public education in industrialized countries—to open equal opportunity for all children—and the reality that schools, by and large, reproduce social class and racial inequalities. Although teachers may try to use even-handed practices and to focus on children as individuals, assumptions about social class and race are embedded in processes of sorting and tracking. In the United States, for example, some schools provide special resources for children deemed to be gifted, a discourse that appears to represent an objective and natural difference but that embeds social class and racial assumptions. Ann Ferguson studied the consequential use of another discourse—"bad boys"—in the daily world of a multiracial middle school in California. Assuming that low-income African-American boys were especially prone toward misbehavior, teachers monitored them more closely than other students. To sustain a sense of dignity in the face of this negative control, the boys sometimes engaged in acts that the adults saw as defiance. The spiral of labeling, conflict, and discipline reproduced patterns of inequality.

Children are discursively constructed not only by experts and by the media, but also by corporations that design and sell goods to an expanding child market. Marketing campaigns target groups that are narrowly defined by age and gender, promoting particular conceptions of childhood. For example, in the 1990s corporations began to sell distinctive styles of clothing, such as platform shoes and rock music by groups like Hansen, to a new market segment they called tweens—eight to thirteen year olds ("ten going on sixteen," as they were often described). Market-driven ideas about the pace of growing up enter into negotiations between children, parents, and teachers over issues such as what clothing can be worn to school. Ann Solberg, a Norwegian sociologist, coined the term *social age* to refer to negotiated conceptions of being older or younger, a more flexible construction than chronological age.

Children as Social Actors

The fields of anthropology and sociology share a theoretical interest in the relationship between structure and agency. Karl Marx framed the issue in 1852 when he observed that people make their own history, but under circumstances shaped and transmitted from the past. Structural theories emphasize the external circumstances—economic forces, institutional arrangements, systems of belief—that have shaped the lives of children in particular times and places. These approaches, like the traditional socialization framework, imply that children are relatively passive, and that their lives are molded from the outside. Seeking to modify this image, the new social studies of childhood emphasize children's agency, that is, their capacity to help shape the circumstances in which they live.

The concept of children's agency has been used in varied ways. A flourishing body of research on children's everyday lives emphasizes their capacities as experiencing subjects who are capable of autonomous action and cultural creation. (Researchers who observe or interview children wrestle with questions about the capacity of children to consent to being studied, and about adult power as a barrier to access and understanding.)

William Corsaro has observed preschools in the United States and in Italy, documenting children's use of ideas from the adult world as they created distinctive peer cultures. He coined the term *interpretive reproduction* to emphasize children's participation in cultural production and change. Marjorie Harness Goodwin, an anthropological linguist, tape-recorded and analyzed the conversations of a mixed-age group of AFRICAN-AMERICAN CHILDREN in an urban U.S. neighborhood, showing how they used talk to constitute and disrupt social bonds and to mark social hierarchies. Barrie Thorne did fieldwork with children in U.S. elementary schools, highlighting their marking and negotiation of gender divisions, for example in playground games where boys chase the girls.

Social scientists have also interviewed children about their experiences of and perspectives on varied subjects, such as consumption, daily activities, divorce, and childhood itself. Solberg found that ten-year-old Norwegian children and their employed mothers had quite different perspectives on children taking care of themselves at home after school. The mothers worried that their children came home to an "empty house," but some of the children spoke instead of coming home to a "welcoming house," with independent access to food, television, and the telephone.

There is no doubt that children have agency in the sense of the capacity to experience, interact, and make meaning. But when Marx wrote that people make their own history, he used *agency* in a stronger sense, referring to collective efforts to change existing power arrangements—for example, by challenging patterns of exploitation. Do children exercise this kind of political agency? It partly depends on one's definition of children. In the 1970s and 1980s children as young as twelve were arrested for their participation in the struggle against apartheid in South Africa. But infants and three-year-olds are clearly not capable of this kind of action.

The division between children and adults or teens is somewhat arbitrary and continually negotiated. But is it wholly misguided to study children, especially younger children, with a different set of frameworks than one uses in studying adults? The quest to rescue children from a conceptual double standard and to include them in frameworks, such as theories of agency, that emphasize autonomous social action may have been overdrawn. Issues of dependence, interdependence, vulnerability, need, and development should also be in focus. And not just in the study of children, since these are also strands in the experiences of adults.

See also: **Comparative History of Childhood; History of Childhood.**

BIBLIOGRAPHY

Ariès, Philippe. 1962. *Centuries of Childhood.* Trans. Robert Baldick. New York: Knopf.

Chin, Elizabeth. 2001. *Purchasing Power: Black Kids and American Consumer Culture.* Minneapolis: University of Minnesota Press.

Christensen, Pia, and Allison James, eds. 2000. *Research with Children: Perspectives and Practices.* London: Falmer Press.

Corsaro, William A. 1997. *The Sociology of Childhood.* Thousand Oaks, CA: Pine Forge Press.

Ferguson, Ann Arnett. 2000. *Bad Boys: Public Schools in the Making of Black Masculinity.* Ann Arbor: University of Michigan Press.

Goodwin, Marjorie Harness. 1990. *He-Said-She-Said: Talk as Social Organization Among Black Children.* Bloomington: Indiana University Press.

Hecht, Tobias. 1998. *At Home in the Street: Street Children of Northeast Brazil.* Cambridge, UK: Cambridge University Press.

Hernandez, Donald. 1993. *America's Children: Resources from Family, Government, and the Economy.* New York: Russell Sage Foundation.

James, Allison, and Alan Prout, eds. 1990. *Constructing and Reconstructing Childhood.* London: Falmer Press.

Jenks, Chris, ed. 1982. *The Sociology of Childhood: Essential Readings.* London: Batsford Academic and Educational.

Kehily, Mary, ed. 2003. *Children's Cultural Worlds.* New York: Wiley.

Kenny, Mary Lorena. 2002. "Orators and Outcasts, Wanderers and Workers: Street Children in Brazil." In *Symbolic Childhood*, ed. Daniel T. Cook. New York: Peter Lang.

Margolin, Leslie. 1994. *Goodness Personified: The Emergence of Gifted Children.* Hawthorne, NY: Aldine de Gruyter.

Marx, Karl. 1963 [1852]. *The Eighteenth Brumaire of Louis Bonaparte.* New York: International.

Mayall, Berry. 2002. *Towards a Sociology for Childhood.* Buckingham, UK: Open University Press.

Mead, Margaret. 1930. *Growing Up in New Guinea.* New York: Morrow.

Parsons, Talcott, and Robert F. Bales. 1955. *Family, Socialization, and Interaction Process.* New York: The Free Press.

Qvortrup Jens, et al., ed. 1994. *Childhood Matters: Social Theory, Practice, and Politics.* Aldershot, UK: Avebury.

Reynolds, Pamela. 1995. "Youth and the Politics of Culture in South Africa." In *Children and the Politics of Culture*, ed. Sharon Stephens. Princeton, NJ: Princeton University Press.

Scheper-Hughes, Nancy, and Carolyn Sargent, eds. 1998. *Small Wars: The Cultural Politics of Childhood.* Berkeley: University of California Press.

Schildkrout, Enid. 1978. "Age and Gender in Hausa Society: Socio-Economic Roles of Children in Urban Kano." In *Age and Sex as Principles of Social Differentiation*, ed. Jean S. LaFontaine. London: Academic Press.

Smart, Carol, Bren Neale, and Amanda Wade. 2001. *The Changing Experience of Childhood: Families and Divorce.* Cambridge, UK: Polity Press.

Solberg, Anne. 1995. "Negotiating Childhood: Changing Constructions of Age for Norwegian Children." In *Constructing and Reconstructing Childhood*, ed. Allison James and Alan Prout. London: Falmer.

Stephens, Sharon, ed. 1995. *Children and the Politics of Culture.* Princeton, NJ: Princeton University Press.

Thorne, Barrie. 1993. *Gender Play: Girls and Boys in School.* New Brunswick, NJ: Rutgers University Press.

Vleminckx, Koen, and Timothy M. Smeeding. 2001. *Child Well-Being, Child Poverty, and Child Policy in Modern Nations.* Toronto: University of Toronto Press.

Zelizer, Viviana. 1985. *Pricing the Priceless Child: The Changing Social Value of Children.* New York: Basic Books.

INTERNET RESOURCES

Bandelij, Nina, Viviana A. Zelizer, and Ann Morning. 2001. "Materials for the Study of Childhood." Available from <www.princeton.edu/~children>.

Child Trends Data Bank. 2003. Available from <www.childtrendsdatabank.org>.

UNICEF. 2002. "The State of the World's Children." Available from <www.unicef.org/sowc02/>.

UNICEF. 2003. "Convention on the Rights of the Child." Available from <www.unicef.org/crc/crc.htm>.

University of Amsterdam. 2003. "Annotated List of Web-Links on Children and Youth." 2003. Available from <www.pscw.uva.nl/sociosite/topics/familychild.html#CHILD>.

BARRIE THORNE

Soldier Children: Global Human Rights Issues

As long as wars have been fought, children have been victims and participants. They have been among the civilians whose percentage of total casualties rose throughout the twentieth century. According to statistics compiled by the United Nations, civilians comprised 10 percent of all casualties in World War I, 45 percent during World War II, and perhaps 90 percent in the 1980s and 1990s. In the last decade of the twentieth century alone, an estimated 1.5 million children were killed and another four million were injured by warfare, while twelve million became refugees.

Only a fraction of those child casualties were combatants, but the issue of underage soldiers had become an international issue by the end of the twentieth century. An unfortunate truth behind the military use of children is that they make good soldiers. Political scientists have shown that small children, especially, accept war and violence as solutions to conflict more easily than adults or older children. Moreover, they can easily handle lightweight modern weapons; they are easily motivated and natural "joiners," willing to take risks; and they can often infiltrate enemy positions and territory because most adult soldiers are reluctant to fire on children. At the turn of the twenty-first century, an estimated three hundred thousand boys and girls under the age of eighteen were fighting on behalf of governments, opposition forces, or both in Afghanistan, Angola, Burma, Columbia, Iraq, Lebanon, Liberia, Mali, Sierra Leone, Somalia, Sri Lanka, Sudan, the former Yugoslavia, and perhaps two dozen other countries.

Children as Volunteer Soldiers

A few children have always gone to war willingly, out of patriotism, a sense of adventure, or religious conviction. French and German children mounted the Children's Crusade in 1212, which ended in disaster but created a legend that inspired faithful Christians. Children of French soldiers in the Napoleonic era were educated and trained by the national government, often accompanying their fathers on campaign and into the army. Thousands of Northern and Southern children, like ten-year-old John Clem, ran away from home to be drummer boys for American Civil War armies; many ended up carrying guns rather than drums. In countless other countries and colonies boys and girls became men and women before their time to fight invaders, colonists, and oppressors. Late-twentieth-century Burmese children, for instance, were raised on stories of heroes like General Aung San, who helped to liberate the country from Britain and Japan, and of the famous warriors of the nation's diverse ethnic groups. There, and in many other societies, becoming a soldier is a sign of manhood, accompanied by prestige and honor. In the West, a similar romanticization of drummer boys and other underage soldiers and the frequent use of children as patriotic symbols in wartime has for centuries encouraged governments to allow children to enlist.

These "pull" effects are often complemented by an equally strong "push." The grinding poverty in many developing—and war-prone—regions force children to work long, hard hours in fields or shops. Some are ORPHANS with no family to support them; others are refugees with no hope for a stable source of income. They join government or rebel forces because they see their service as a way to improve their lives. For these children, entering the military is not necessarily a matter of leaving behind childhood, but of exchanging different modes of premature adulthood.

Ideology is an important element of voluntary service by underage soldiers. Children, eager to be part of political or social movements in which their parents participate, often gravitate toward popular uprisings, especially if those uprisings offer a chance to exact revenge on enemies. The murders of family members, the ethnic cleansing of cultural groups, and long-time political and economic discrimination all fuel the hatred that can provide important motivations for young soldiers (as they do adult soldiers). Brought up in an environment in which politics, religion, and economic distress are interrelated, thousands of Palestinians in their teens and younger took part in the massive revolt against Israeli occupation that began late in 2000. Scores died and hundreds more were injured in clashes with Israeli forces; some became suicide bombers. While not, strictly speaking, soldiers, these boys and a few girls certainly considered themselves patriots and warriors for their cause. The remarkable story of Johnny and Luther Htoo, the thirteen-year-old twins who between 1999 and 2001 led a band of Karen rebels called God's Army against the government of Myanmar, shows how children can become willing participants in armed conflict. According to the legend that quickly grew around them, the brothers demonstrated mystical powers when they led a successful counterattack during a government raid on their village.

Death of Joseph Bara (1794), Jacques-Louis David. Children have frequently been used as romanticized patriotic symbols in wartime. In 1793, thirteen-year-old Joseph Bara, a soldier in the French revolutionary army, was lauded as a martyr after his death at the hands of royalist troops. He was killed reportedly for refusing to shout "Long live the King!" Musée Calvet, Avignon, France/Peter Willi/Bridgeman Art Library.

Children Forced into Military Service

Children increasingly became unwilling warriors in the twentieth century, especially in the brutal revolutionary and ethnic struggles that plagued developing countries. Some were conscripted formally into established armies; the Iranian army, for example, drafted tens of thousands of teenaged boys during the bloody Iran–Iraq war of the 1980s. Others were captured and forced into service when their villages were attacked by irregular units fighting inconclusive wars against existing governments. The Lord's Liberation Army, for example, a rebel organization fighting against the Ugandan government, kidnapped over eight thousand children and forced them to be soldiers, menial laborers, and in some cases, sex slaves. Some of the children who "volunteered" for military service had no choice; they joined because recruiters—especially from irregular forces conducting popular rebellions against established governments—threatened their families or threatened to kill the children themselves if they did not join up.

Effects of Military Service on Children

Over and above the dangers of actual combat, the effects on children of military service can be devastating. The rigors of hard marching with heavy packs can deform young spines, the uncertain availability of rations can lead to malnutrition, exposure to all kinds of weather can cause skin diseases and respiratory infections, and taking part in forced or consensual sex with other, often much older, soldiers can lead to pregnancy and sexually transmitted diseases. The brutal discipline and disregard for human life that characterized many of the rebel units operating outside of formal military channels also took a heavy toll; if a child was unable to continue a march or refused to obey orders, he or she was simply shot on the spot.

The psychological consequences of these experiences can be profound. Child soldiers and victims frequently draw pictures and tell stories haunted by images of death, destruction, and violence. These youngsters, especially those forced into military service, are a kind of "lost generation." Most rebel and other irregular armies in the developing world tend to be rather disorganized forces concerned more with profit and violence than with actually trying to establish governments or defend homelands. Child-development experts believe that among the worst effects of the use of child soldiers are the brutality that they internalize and the disdain for political and moral authorities that they learn. Because they are normally seized and indoctrinated before their moral values are fully formed, children often become thoughtless killers. Ironically, some of the worst atrocities carried out against children are committed by children.

Child Soldiers as a Political and Diplomatic Issue

The use of child soldiers has not gone unchallenged; indeed, much of the media's coverage of children and war confronts the practice directly. It has also become a political issue, with the public outcry against the use of child soldiers led by the United Nations Children's Fund (UNICEF), Human Rights Watch, Rädda Barnen (a Swedish organization), the Coalition to Stop the Use of Child Soldiers, and a number of other CHILDREN'S RIGHTS and humanitarian groups. The current standard of fifteen as the minimum age for military service was established by the 1989 UN CONVENTION ON THE RIGHTS OF THE CHILD. Since then, activists have sought to bring the military service provision into step with the other conditions in the Convention, which recognize as a child anyone under the age of eighteen. Some progress occurred in the late 1990s. The United Nations established a policy refusing to allow soldiers under the age of eighteen to serve in peacekeeping forces, a number of governments raised their minimum age to eighteen, and a more strongly worded document (the "Optional Protocol to the Convention on the Rights of the Child on Involvement of Children in Armed Conflict") was developed by the UN. The protocol forbade the use of children under the age of eighteen in nongovernmental armed groups, required states to demobilize child soldiers and reintegrate them into society, and forbade the voluntary recruitment of children under the age of sixteen.

But the basic issue of child soldiers remained unresolved. The wording of the "Optional Protocol" only asks governments to take "all feasible measures" to ensure that children under the age of eighteen are not exposed to combat. The chief opponent of a worldwide minimum age of eighteen is the United States, which allows seventeen year olds to volunteer for its armed forces but promises not to send them into battle. Another ambiguity is the protocol's banning of underage soldiers from "direct participation" in combat—a nearly meaningless condition, since in a typical war of the late twentieth and early twenty-first centuries the front line and the home front are not clearly distinguished.

See also: **Juvenile Justice: International; Violence Against Children; War in the Twentieth Century.**

BIBLIOGRAPHY

Brown, Ian. 1990. *Khomeini's Forgotten Sons: The Story of Iran's Boy Soldiers.* London: Grey Seal.

Dodge, Cole P., and Magne Raundalen. 1991. *Reaching Children in War: Sudan, Uganda, and Mozambique.* Bergen, Norway: Sigma Forlag.

Images Asia. 1997. *No Childhood at All: A Report about Child Soldiers in Burma.* Chiangmai, Thailand: Images Asia.

Marten, James, ed. 2002. *Children and War: A Historical Anthology.* New York: New York University Press.

McManimon, Shannon. 2000. "Protecting Children from War: What the New International Agreement Really Means." *Peacework* 27: 14–16.

Rosenblatt, Roger. 1983. *Children of War.* Garden City, NY: Anchor Press/Doubleday.

Skinner, Elliott P. 1999. "Child Soldiers in Africa: A Disaster for Future Families." *International Journal on World Peace* 16: 7–17.

Susman, Tina, and Geoffrey Mohan. 1998. "A Generation Lost to War." *Newsday* October 10: A6–A7, A54–A57, A60.

United Nations. 1996. *Promotion and Protection of the Rights of Children: Impact of Armed Conflict on Children.* New York: United Nations.

JAMES MARTEN

Sonography

Medical sonography, in which very high-frequency sound waves are bounced off internal organs to gather information about their shape and density, was first used to create images of a fetus *in utero* in 1955, using machinery built to detect flaws in industrial metal. Often called *ultrasound*, it has been incorporated into the routine practice of obstetrics and widely used as a noninvasive diagnostic and monitoring technology in pregnancy since the 1970s. Physicians have used sonography to assess fetal development and determine either the birth due date or the appropriate method for abortion; to detect gross anatomical abnormalities, usually untreatable; to establish and tighten definitions of "normality" in fetuses; and by the 1990s, to provide visualization for invasive monitoring and therapies such as amniocentesis and fetal surgery. In the United States by the late 1990s, many physicians also claimed that sonography provided the psychological benefits of reassuring parents that the fetus was healthy and providing an opportunity for "bonding" with the fetus. In some countries, such as India and China, in which it is financially or legally unfeasible to raise many children and boys are valued strongly over girls, ultrasound has frequently been used to identify female fetuses, which are then aborted.

Ultrasound safety has not been confirmed through large-scale medical trials; it has been assumed to be safe because there has been no evidence of harm after widespread use. However, a 1993 study also concluded that the use of ultrasound in routine pregnancies did not improve outcomes. Despite these results, the use of ultrasound during pregnancy is almost universal at the beginning of the twenty-first century in most of North American and Western Europe, and quite common in other places as well.

Some feminists have raised concerns about sonography's role in medicalizing reproduction, pointing out that evidence based on women's experiences of pregnancy (such as a woman's sense of her fetus's health and growth as indicated by its movements) is usually dismissed by doctors in favor of ultrasound images, and that ultrasound is yet another mode of surveillance of women's bodies by those in positions of power. Feminists have also noted that in the United States, ultrasound images have been popularized by anti-abortion activists, who manipulate, interpret, and publicize the images to promote the idea that fetuses really are just like babies, and should be protected as such. On the other hand, anthropologists have observed that in the United States and Canada, pregnant women and their partners often enjoy viewing ultrasound images, sharing them with family and friends as prebirth "baby pictures," and appreciate what they perceive to be the psychological benefits of visualizing their fetuses. In the United States, images of fetuses are viewed by the general public as well, in advertising that promotes consumption in the name of fetal safety and comfort.

Ultrasound carries very different meanings depending on the cultural context in which it is being used. In contrast to the United States and Canada, in Greece, where ultrasound is used even more heavily, women, their partners, and their doctors see it as part of a package of technologies and practices necessary to having a desirable "modern" pregnancy. The uses and meanings of ultrasound have been culturally shaped in many different ways; but in every place where it is widely used, it has offered the possibility of altering understandings of pregnancy, the fetus, and the role of physicians and technology in reproduction.

See also: **Conception and Birth; Obstetrics and Midwifery; Pediatrics.**

BIBLIOGRAPHY

Duden, Barbara. 1993. *Disembodying Women: Perspectives on Pregnancy and the Unborn.* Cambridge, MA: Harvard University Press.

Farquhar, Dion. 1996. *The Other Machine: Discourse and Reproductive Technologies.* New York: Routledge.

Saetnan, Ann Rudinow, Nelly Oudshoorn, and Marta Stefania Maria Kirejczyk. 2000. *Bodies of Technology : Women's Involvement with Reproductive Medicine.* Columbus: Ohio State University Press.

Taylor, Janelle S. 1998. "Image of Contradiction: Obstetrical Ultrasound in American Culture." In *Reproducing Reproduction: Kinship, Power, and Technological Innovation,* ed. Sarah Franklin and Helena Ragoné. Philadelphia: University of Pennsylvania Press.

LARA FREIDENFELDS

Spears, Britney (b. 1981)

"Pop Princess," "Teen Queen," and "Video Vixen" are all terms that have been used to describe Britney Spears since she burst onto the music scene at the age of seventeen in 1998's "Hit Me Baby One More Time" video. Not since Madonna in the 1980s had a young female artist been as scrutinized for her appearance as for her music. Unlike Madonna, however, the only vote Britney Spears was old enough to cast at the time of her debut was for a video to appear on MTV's *Total Request Live,* a show on which viewer requests determined video airplay.

Britney Spears made her first foray into the entertainment industry at the ripe age of eight, when she applied for DISNEY's *The Mickey Mouse Club* and was rejected on account of her age. This would be the first of many times Spears's youth would be more of a concern than her music. Though at eleven she finally became a Mouseketeer, it was not long before mouse ears gave way to Spears's "wardrobe" staple, the bare midriff.

Some found it difficult to see Britney Spears, with her songwriters, stylists, and choreographers as anything but a pawn of the entertainment industry. She was a young girl performing songs written largely by men (though she co-wrote five songs on her third album) for boys under the pretext of being the voice of girls everywhere. By 2003 Spears had sold more than thirty-seven million albums. She had also appeared on countless magazine covers, won numerous awards and endorsements, written two autobiographies, and starred in the 2002 film *Crossroads.* Spears garnered a wide fan base, with old and young alike having responded to something in her image, if not her music.

The teen idol, his/her fans, and their disapproving parents date back to Elvis Presley, with his censored hip-swinging. The same element of a teen idol's persona to which the young look up is that which parents criticize—their SEXUALITY. Britney Spears, herself, attested that her over-the-top sexuality as expressed in her clothing (or lack thereof) and dance moves was just a performance, that she was really an innocent young woman whose virginity would be staunchly upheld until marriage. In so doing, her sexuality was debased to a marketing ploy, which brought on even more criticism.

Her commercial success prompted the music industry to crank out numerous Britney Spears derivatives according to the same formula of the sexy young girl next door. With TELEVISION rather than RADIO as the dominant source for music, image rather than talent dictated success.

Born in 1981 in Kentwood, Louisiana, Britney Spears made a career of entertaining the listener rather than engaging him or her, which proved successful in the wake of the brooding, hard-edged form of ROCK AND ROLL known as grunge that had been popular in the early 1990s.

See also: **Teenagers; Youth Culture.**

INTERNET RESOURCE

Official Britney Spears Website. Available from <www.britneyspears.com>.

NIKA ELDER

Special Education

In the twenty-first century, schooling for children with disabilities is a public responsibility. In the United States, the Education of All Handicapped Children Act of 1975, reauthorized as the Individuals with Disabilities Education Act (IDEA) of 1990, mandated a Free Appropriate Public Education (FAPE) for all children and youth, ages three to twenty-one, with disabilities. The law mandates that no child can be excluded from schooling because of a physical, mental, or emotional disability, no matter how severe. It also mandates individualized educational and related services based on an Individual Education Program (IEP) and implemented in the Least Restrictive Environment (LRE), the setting providing maximum appropriate opportunity to learn together with peers who do not have disabilities. IDEA thus constituted the legal basis for the inclusion movement.

This dramatic public policy development culminated historic trends beginning with the establishment of residential schools in the nineteenth century, largely supplanted in the United States and Europe in the twentieth century by day classes that permitted children to live at home with their families. No longer a philanthropic enterprise, specialized schooling in the United States had come to be recognized as a responsibility of the COMMON SCHOOLS. The history of children with disabilities is often described as steadily increasing educational integration leading, in adulthood, to societal integration and independence. Given this general historical trend, however, each form of disability has a unique and complex history.

Deafness, the oldest special educational challenge, was the first to be addressed through formal schooling. Modeled after Paris's famed National Institute for the Deaf, the Connecticut Asylum for the Education of Deaf and Dumb Persons (later renamed the American School for the Deaf) opened in Hartford on April 15, 1817. Under the leadership of Thomas Hopkins Gallaudet and Laurent Clerc, a deaf teacher Gallaudet had recruited from the Paris School, the school featured academic instruction, as well as training useful in a trade, incorporating an Americanized version of the French system of manual signing. In time, American Sign Language (ASL) would be recognized as the fully legitimate language of the Deaf communities of the United States and Canada.

A conflicting tradition arose from the centuries-old quest to teach deaf persons to speak, predicated on the belief that speech was essential, not only for integration in the majority society but for reason itself. Through the strong advocacy of (hearing) leaders, notably Alexander Graham Bell, the inventor of the telephone, an international, late-nineteenth-century movement culminated in official adoption of oralism in teaching the deaf, favoring day classes rather than residential schools. Parents, in most instances not themselves deaf, and hearing professionals considered the communication models provided in children's own homes and public schools preferable to the exclusive company of other deaf students. Beginning with Ohio in 1898, successive states mandated funding for day classes, a development facilitated by the new capability to transport students with this relatively low-incidence disability to centralized, yet community-based school sites. However, since Deaf cultural identity issues have parallels among other minorities, conflicts concerning both instructional setting and instructional mode remain unresolved.

Samuel Gridley Howe, a leading nineteenth century reformer, founded Massachusetts' famed Perkins School for the Blind in 1832, then successfully lobbied various state legislatures to establish residential schools for persons (adults, as well as children) who were blind. Yet he, together with his strong ally HORACE MANN, came to oppose such "institutions," increasingly envisioning the day when blind children could attend the common schools. That new era began when in 1900 the Chicago schools formed classes for the blind, intended to foster social integration with sighted classmates. While this Chicago Plan was followed in cities in Ohio and Massachusetts, a major shift from congregate, residential schools to day classes and itinerant specialists (in Braille and orientation and mobility training) did not occur until the 1970s, with the aid of parents' advocacy efforts and a general deinstitutionalization movement.

While efforts to integrate deaf and blind children in regular schools were certainly motivated by concerns for their well-being, another force early in the twentieth century was a growing EUGENICS movement. Some leaders believed educational integration essential to reduce the likelihood of marriage within these communities and thus hereditary transmission of such "defects." In the case of mental RETARDATION (and also epilepsy) eugenics-related fears, erroneously linking various social evils with the condition led to state sterilization laws and more widespread institutional confinement less for the purpose of schooling than to protect society. In the meantime, with general adoption in schools of psychometric testing, by the 1930s states and individual districts were enacting policies to exclude children believed incapable of benefiting from education.

Paralleling the newly established day classes for deaf and for blind students, by 1900 the first special classes had been formed for children who were then referred to as "backward" or "feeble-minded." They were characterized by smaller class size, emphasis on practical life skills, and an individualized approach recognizing differences in readiness, motivation, and pacing. Contributing to this trend was the increasing adoption, especially in large, urban school districts, of psychoeducational clinics, modeled after the clinic Lightner Witner had established in 1896 at the University of Pennsylvania. While school-based clinics played a major role in assessing pupils' eligibility for special class placement (or for school exclusion), Witner's individualized, diagnostic approach would later be influential in education of students with orthopedic or health impairment, social-emotional problems, and specific learning disabilities.

As special classes became more numerous, however, concerns grew that placement was often arbitrary and discriminatory, and by the 1960s, influenced by the civil rights movement, that minority students were inordinately likely to be labeled as "slow" and placed accordingly, or as "disruptive" and placed in the far less numerous classes for students with emotional or behavioral disorders. These concerns, together with growing advocacy by parents of many other children not served by special education, yet not succeeding in school and needing individually appropriate instruction led to IDEA and the era of inclusion.

See also: **Education, United States; IQ.**

BIBLIOGRAPHY

Lane, Harlan. 1992. *The Mask of Benevolence: Disabling the Deaf Community.* New York: Knopf.

Meyen, Edward L., and Thomas M. Skrtic. 1995. *Special Education and Student Disability: An Introduction: Traditional, Emerging, and Alternative Perspectives,* 4th ed. Denver, CO: Love Publishing.

Safford, Philip L., and Elizabeth J. Safford. 1996. *A History of Childhood and Disability.* New York: Teachers College Press.

Safford, Philip L., and Elizabeth J. Safford. 1998. "Visions of the Special Class." *Remedial and Special Education* 19, no. 4: 229–238.

Scheerenberger, Richard C. 1983. *A History of Mental Retardation.* Baltimore: Paul H. Brookes.

Turnbull, Ann P., Rud Turnbull, Marilyn Shank, and Dorothy Leal. 1995. *Exceptional Lives: Special Education in Today's Schools,* 2nd ed. Upper Saddle River, NJ: Merrill/Prentice-Hall.

Turnbull, Ann P., and H. Rutherford Turnbull. 1997. *Families, Professionals, and Exceptionality: A Special Partnership,* 3rd ed. Upper Saddle River, NJ: Merrill/Prentice-Hall.

Winzer, Margret A. 1993. *The History of Special Education: From Isolation to Integration.* Washington, DC: Gallaudet University Press.

PHILIP LANE SAFFORD

Spock, Benjamin (1903–1998)

Benjamin Spock was the most influential author of child-rearing advice of the twentieth century. His principal work,

Baby and Child Care, went through seven editions, was translated into thirty-eight languages, and sold more than fifty million copies around the world. Aside from the Bible, it was the best-selling book of the century.

Spock was born in New Haven, Connecticut, the son of a successful corporate lawyer. He graduated from Yale, where he rowed on a varsity crew that won a gold medal in the 1924 Olympics, and from the medical school at Columbia. He studied at the New York Psychoanalytic Institute and was the first psychoanalytically trained pediatrician in New York, where he maintained a private practice from 1933 to 1943.

His Park Avenue practice brought him overtures from publishers, who pressed him to write a book setting forth his distinctive combination of PEDIATRICS and CHILD PSYCHOLOGY. In 1946, he did. The first edition of *Baby and Child Care* began, as all the subsequent editions did, "Trust yourself. You know more than you think you do." It invited mothers to indulge their own impulses and their children's, assuring them on the basis of the latest scientific studies that it was safe to do so. In the process, it overturned the consensus of the previous generation of experts and authorized mothers to express their "natural" feelings toward their children. Spock's book was an immediate success both inside and outside of the United States.

Earlier advice, embodied in the convergence of JOHN WATSON's best-selling book and the U.S. government's *Infant Care* pamphlets, warned against parental deviation from rigid disciplinary schedules and undue display of fondness or physical affection. Spock urged spontaneity, warmth, and a fair measure of fun for parents and children alike. He pressed mothers to recognize that each child had to be treated differently.

Conservative critics later complained that Spock promoted what they called permissive child rearing. In one of the earliest expressions of the "culture wars" that marked the last quarter of the twentieth century, they held him responsible for the counterculture and the collapse of conventional morality. On their face, such charges were difficult to sustain. Spock never counseled permissiveness, and after the first edition he explicitly advised against it. But he did become progressive in his politics in the 1960s and after.

Even before the war in Vietnam, Spock warned against the dangers of nuclear testing and served as co-chairman of the National Committee for a Sane Nuclear Policy. He was a vocal opponent of the Vietnam War, helped lead the march on the Pentagon in 1967, and was convicted and sentenced to jail for conspiracy to aid draft resisters in 1968. (His conviction was reversed on appeal.) He ran for president in 1972 as the candidate of the People's Party and continued his activism thereafter. Long after the age of seventy, he was arrested for protesting against a nuclear power plant in New

Hampshire, against budget cuts at the White House, and against nuclear weapons at the Pentagon. Past the age of eighty, he still gave as many as a hundred talks a year on the nuclear arms race, as well as on pediatrics.

Spock's child-rearing advice changed as his political views and American family life evolved. In successive editions, he made a place for fathers as well as mothers in childcare, allowed new gender roles for boys and girls, acknowledged divorce and single PARENTING, and explicitly urged his readers toward a vegetarian lifestyle.

But the essentials of Spock's advice never changed. He always meant to write a guide for living more than a medical reference book. He challenged conventional notions of normality and sought to alleviate anxiety, in parents and children alike. He always offered reassurance, in the down-to-earth manner in which he set forth his advice. He had a genius for popularization. No one ever explained Freud better in everyday language. No one ever wrote more gender-neutral prose.

Even as he set himself in militant opposition to the status quo in politics, he endeavored to help parents accommodate their children to it in the society and economy they would encounter. However inadvertently, he pushed mothers and fathers to prepare children for the corporate bureaucracies in which they would make their careers. He emphasized the cooperativeness and congeniality that organizational life demands. He held that parents "owe it to the child to make him likeable" and that they had to make him be like others to be likeable. He never reconciled his dissident politics and his conformist approach to child rearing.

See also: **Child-Rearing Advice Literature.**

BIBLIOGRAPHY

Bloom, Lynn. 1972. *Doctor Spock: Biography of a Conservative Radical.* Indianapolis: Bobbs-Merrill.

Hulbert, Ann. 2003. *Raising America: Experts, Parents, and a Century of Advice about Children.* New York: Alfred A. Knopf.

Mitford, Jessica. 1969. *The Trial of Dr. Spock, the Rev. William Sloane Coffin, Jr., Michael Ferber, Mitchell Goodman, and Marcus Raskin.* New York: Alfred A. Knopf.

Spock, Benjamin, and Mary Morgan. 1989. *Spock on Spock: A Memoir of Growing Up with the Century.* New York: Pantheon.

Zuckerman, Michael. 1993. "Doctor Spock: The Confidence Man." In *Almost Chosen People: Oblique Biographies in the American Grain.* Berkeley and Los Angeles: University of California Press.

MICHAEL ZUCKERMAN

Sports

Children's PLAY and children's games have always been an important part of a culture. The role and social significance of that play, however, varied according to its historical con-text. Often the games and play were just that—"play" for the purpose of pleasure, entertainment, and diversion. When given unstructured time or even during their daily chores, children likely throughout history have created games that involved footraces and throwing contests or that otherwise mimicked the adult activity around them, all of which could be considered sport.

Youth Sport in the Ancient World and Medieval Europe

Sometimes games were designed to teach socially approved gender roles, to indicate maturation, and to teach skills necessary for future survival of the individual and the culture. Some African tribes encouraged pubescent girls to wrestle each other as part of the ritual initiation into adulthood. The Diola of Gambia promoted physical strength by encouraging the male and female wrestling champions to marry. Boys in ancient Greece were encouraged to attend the Olympic Games, and races for the younger boys were sometimes organized separately. Girls of the time had their own games: they participated in the female version of the Olympics, the Hera Games. Spartan children were encouraged to compete in track-and-field and to participate in mock battle events to become stronger and more competent adults. Boys in the Roman civilization were similarly expected to begin their training as youngsters, competing in games and individual sports.

The Christians of medieval European society, however, cared less for sport than their predecessors in imperial Rome and ancient Greece. As a result, games and play in the Middle Ages were more childish diversions than socially promoted means of teaching appropriate behavior. But children and adults did play games, despite the concern of the church that sports created a dangerous focus on the physical body that might distract the individual from the importance of the salvation of the soul. For example, large games of medieval folk football involved many adults and children of the town. Girls and milkmaids also played a game called stoolball, a variation of the sports that would later evolve into BASEBALL and cricket. The European ambivalence towards such activities continued for centuries despite King James I of England's Declaration of Sports (also called the Book of Sports). This proclamation encouraged lawful recreation among children and adults and was opposed by the religious Puritans.

Early North American Sports

When the Puritans arrived in the New World of North America, they continued their tradition of intolerance of games and sports. Their encounters with the indigenous Native Americans, who attached religious significance to their organized sports and limited participation to adults, served to harden the Puritans' conviction that sport, even among children, would endanger the immortal soul. The lack of organized or team sports for children among both Native Americans and Puritans in North America did not mean that children there did not engage in play. However, the adults

A 1913 Brooklyn, NY, girls' high school basketball team. Basketball was adopted for girls' physical education programs soon after the invention of the game in 1891. © Bettman/CORBIS.

did not provide structured sports in the ways that had been common in the Old World and that would become widespread beginning in the 1800s.

Although few organized sports existed in the seventeenth and eighteenth centuries in the northern colonies of America, the southern regions had a greater emphasis on outdoor activity and less of a Puritan focus on the soul. Almost all southern boys and many southern girls were taught to ride horses and to hunt wild game, both as a means of survival and as a kind of sport in races and competitions. While northerners in the late eighteenth century had developed harness racing as an organized sport, signifying their appreciation of equestrian events, the role of boys in this sport was generally limited to that of exercisers and grooms.

Clubs and the Turner Movement

Organized sports and team sports for adults seem to have evolved throughout America in the early- and mid-nineteenth century. Private athletic clubs were formed around sports like fishing, archery, and rowing. In 1860 men and boys formed cricket clubs in about 100 different cities

in the United States. Many of these clubs were intended for the wealthy, but later athletic clubs would be organized around ethnic lines, as a place for immigrants to preserve their culture and language as well as their sports.

In the early nineteenth century, social reformers noticed that young men and boys who worked in factories and lived in the cities lacked the physical health and stamina of their rural counterparts. Accordingly, they founded private gymnasiums and promoted the Turner movement. A key figure in this undertaking was Friedrich Jahn, a Prussian who combined German culture with GYMNASTICS (the word *Turner* derives from the German term that means to perform gymnastics). In 1842, Jahn's Turner exercises were incorporated into German education for boys, but beginning as early as the 1830s in America, Jahn's transplanted students taught gymnastics in private gyms for boys and college-age youth.

In that same era, collegiate sports began on an informal level in the United States, and after the Civil War's conclusion, professional leagues for baseball were established. Although organized youth sports had not yet appeared, club sports and professional sports provided a model for youngsters, both native-born and immigrants, and they played these games in their own space and their own manner. Sporting experiences differed among the different cultures, based in part on race, class, and nationality.

Muscular Christianity

The evolution of youth sports stemmed in part from the rise of "Muscular Christianity." Victorian leaders in both England and America feared that boys, in particular, were too physically frail to become effective and powerful leaders. Thomas Arnold, the headmaster at the Rugby School in England from 1828 to 1842, organized team sports for his male students in order to build strong physical bodies. The activities also served to keep the boys occupied, tired, and away from the temptations of alcohol and prostitutes, which Arnold feared would corrupt their souls and their ability to effectively lead. The Rugby headmaster was the first modern educator to actively link physical education with the education of the mind. Arnold's model was lauded and ultimately subscribed to by leading American social reformers.

The YMCA and YWCA

The Young Men's Christian Association (YMCA) was founded in England in 1844 and appeared in the United States in 1851. The YMCA was initially intended to provide a refuge for boys and young men, particularly those of lower-class or immigrant status, who were seen as being at risk from the non-Christian temptations that were common in large cities. Within twenty-five years, over 260 YMCA gyms were established across America, encouraging young men to play baseball and football, lift weights, row, swim, and otherwise build healthy bodies. By 1895 the YMCA had adopted as an emblem an inverted triangle to emphasize the three parts of a fully developed man: mind, body, and spirit. Although a Young Women's Christian Association (YWCA) would appear in the late 1870s, the YWCA did not have the same emphasis on athletics, offering only a few gymnastics programs based on German and Swedish models.

The YMCA organization would create several new American sports. In 1891 young James Naismith, an instructor at the YMCA training school in Springfield, Massachusetts, was asked to create a game that could be played indoors during the winter, and he invented BASKETBALL. Naismith did not specify that the game would be for males only, and female physical educators quickly adopted the game but modified it to a less strenuous six-on-six version that minimized exertion. William Morgan, another YMCA physical director in Massachusetts, created volleyball, and the game was quickly incorporated into PHYSICAL EDUCATION programs across the country.

Playground Movement

Linked to Muscular Christianity was the PLAYGROUND MOVEMENT, based on the belief of many reformers that youth sports could be used as a way to Americanize immigrant youth, to lower crime rates, and to exert social control over the working classes and the poor. Many philanthropists had worried that poor urban children without supervision, fresh air, and a place to play would turn to crime. As a result, beginning in the late 1890s a number of urban parks and playgrounds were founded through private land donations in conjunction with public rezoning. Originally, playgrounds were supervised by volunteers, but around the turn of the twentieth century, educators began to recognize the value of sports as a control mechanism, and many communities began to hire adults to organize games and activities for the children. The Boston School Committee, for example, began supervising playgrounds because they considered it an appropriate function of the public schools.

Collegiate Sports and Physical Education

Collegiate sports began informally in the mid 1800s. Students at Yale and Harvard began rowing against each other in the 1840s, and in 1859, about ten years after the appearance of baseball, two other New England colleges formed club teams and played against the other with some regularity. These events would lay the groundwork for the vibrant collegiate sports scene that continues today. Collegiate athletics first gained widespread popularity in the United States at the end of the nineteenth century, when more and more teams began to participate in a variety of sports. President Theodore Roosevelt served as a link between Muscular Christianity and collegiate sports. Roosevelt was himself an avid outdoorsman and the product of rigorous physical training as a boy. He strongly supported youth and collegiate sports, believing that every boy should participate in athletics to build strength of body and of character. His leadership would be critical in 1905, when collegiate football was most at risk. The popular American sport had evolved in part from rugby and, in its early form, was extremely rough and dangerous. After a number of deaths, collegiate leaders were encouraged by Roosevelt to meet in order to decide if the game should be banned, but instead they were able to agree upon a number of rule changes to better protect the players. In 1910 the National Collegiate Athletic Association (NCAA) was formed to oversee the growing number of college athletic conferences. Aside from brief declines during the two world wars, participation in college athletics grew throughout the twentieth century and became culturally significant not just on college campuses but across the country, especially in its popularity among spectators.

Women's collegiate sports originally grew out of physical education departments. Early teachers in the programs were concerned about the risks to young women from overstrenuous activities and the dangers of excessive competition. As a result, college women often played variations of the games played by the men. Teachers also promoted gymnastics and calisthenics rather than sports and encouraged intramural games rather than intervarsity competitions.

Female college students enjoyed sports, however, and African-American women, in particular, were encouraged to compete in track-and-field events at several schools. Throughout the mid 1900s, the United States national women's track-and-field team was dominated by African-American collegians. The rise of the women's rights movement and the enactment of TITLE IX in 1972 had a profound affect on women's collegiate sports. As a result of the law, female college athletes received better facilities, coaches, and greater access to sports, and the result has been an unprecedented rate of female participation in college athletics. Like their male counterparts, female athletes are part of the business of college sports, which is based on public spectatorship through television and in-person attendance.

School-Age Physical Education

Physical education in the schools began in the 1830s with the appointment of Dr. Charles Beck, a student of the Turner movement, to the faculty of the Round Hill School in Massachusetts—the first physical-education teacher in America. In addition to gymnastics, Beck also taught his students to swim, skate, wrestle, and dance. His work was a model for other schools that chose to teach calisthenics and gymnastics to both their boys and girls in order to build their health. Often the exercises were led in the classroom by the classroom teacher rather than by a specialized physical education instructor. However, as more colleges embraced physical education in the early twentieth century, they began training young people who then employed in the schools specifically to teach sporting and recreational activities.

After World War I, when many American leaders had been concerned by the physical inadequacies of the early troops, several states passed laws requiring that physical education be taught in the schools. Although most of these laws focused only on boys, a few states required that girls also receive similar instruction. Some of these programs were dropped during the GREAT DEPRESSION. As a result, there were renewed concerns about the fitness of American troops during World War II, and increased attention was paid to physical education thereafter.

Moreover, the growth of suburban areas in America after World War II resulted in a shift from the traditional focus on physical education in an urban school setting and instead placed new emphasis on suburbia. In both urban and suburban schools physical education included not just calisthenics but games and sports.

School Athletic Organizations

When boys in the 1890s began playing sports, they simply organized their own high school teams, much like their collegiate counterparts had, and the teams began first in urban areas. LUTHER HALSEY GULICK Jr., formerly the director of the YMCA Training School, became the director of physical training for the New York City public schools in 1903. A great believer in the need for physical development to match moral development, Gulick understood that organized sport could be more beneficial for boys than gymnastics and calisthenics alone. He formed the Public Schools Athletic League (PSAL), which promoted interscholastic competition in sports such as rifle shooting. A girls' division was later created, but it did not allow interscholastic competition.

Adult supervision of high school team sports began at roughly the same time. Some football programs at the turn of the twentieth century were facing the same problems as the collegiate programs of the time—a large number of injuries and instances of preferential treatment for athletes and the use of "ringers" (skilled outsiders added to teams to improve performance). In 1902 high school educators across the country met to increase their authority over INTERSCHOLASTIC ATHLETICS, and by 1923 all but three states had established statewide interscholastic athletic associations. Like most reformist movements, organized high school sports were intended to control the energized mass of students and focus their attention on academics rather than sex and hooliganism. High school sports also formed a bond among students, both athletes and spectators, and helped give the local community an identity. Further, as educators in the 1970s began to impose academic minimums for athletic participation, sports became a motivator for better performance in the classrooms.

Sports opportunities for high school girls were limited in the beginning. A few states had widespread participation in certain high school sports. Oklahoma and Iowa, for example, had extensive and very popular high school girls' basketball programs, but the girls still played six-on-six ball until the 1980s. However, Title IX and the women's rights movement greatly increased the opportunities for high school girls, just as they had for collegiate women, and their participation rates grew dramatically beginning in the 1970s.

Youth Sports Leagues

In the twentieth century more and more private organizations began organizing and sponsoring youth sport leagues for children—boys, in particular. One of the first was established in 1930 with the foundation of the Catholic Youth Organization. Immediately it launched basketball and BOXING tournaments for Catholic boys in order to combine religious and physical instruction. Throughout the remainder of the twentieth century, other church leagues were formed, and there were also a growing number of publicly funded community leagues. Organized sports were available for children as young as age four and five in many areas of the country.

Little League Baseball, Inc., the largest youth sports program, was founded in 1939. Throughout its history, Little League Baseball has had an extensive participation rate around the world and an organizational structure modeled so closely after professional baseball that the season culminates in a Little League World Series. In its first few decades, Little League Baseball drew boys of all ages, but girls were usually excluded. In 1974, after a series of lawsuits had been filed against Little League Baseball and other similar youth baseball leagues, Little League Baseball officially opened the dugout to girls. At the same time, however, Little League Softball came into being, and girls were often encouraged to join that league instead. Today, some girls play on Little League Baseball teams but more play Little League Softball. A few boys, in turn, have played on the Little League Softball teams. Parental involvement in Little League has also been extensive and, to a degree, notorious. In the 1960s and 1970s some Little League parents (especially fathers) earned the reputation of being loud, abusive types who pushed their children too hard and threatened coaches, umpires, and opposing players.

Little League Baseball was a model for other youth sports organizations that were founded after World War II and expanded over the next thirty years. These included Pee-Wee and Pop Warner Football, Pee-Wee and Midget Hockey, and Biddy Basketball. Until the 1970s, when the courts ordered the leagues opened to girls, most of these programs were for boys only. The Amateur Athletic Union (AAU) offered programs in track-and-field, wrestling, skiing, and swimming, which were divided by age group. Again, many of these were initially aimed at boys more than girls, but the swimming program was always coeducational. The hockey programs popular in large, northern cities, limited by a lack of ice time, have been criticized for having practice times for four- and five-year-olds that take place too late at night and too early in the morning. Many of these programs have also suffered adversely from excessive parental involvement. Parents have been convicted of assault, battery, and manslaughter for their behavior at the sporting events of their children.

In the 1960s the American Youth Soccer Organization (AYSO) was founded and marketed partly as an alternative to Little League Baseball and that organization's sometimes overinvolved parents. Soccer was a relatively new sport to the United States, and fathers did not have the same emotional attachment to the game as they did to baseball and football. As a result, girls were encouraged to play from the very beginning of the AYSO. The league marketed itself as being kinder and gentler than Little League Baseball, emphasizing the lack of parental involvement and the active participation of all children on the team. "Every player's a quarterback" was the unofficial AYSO slogan. The popularity of youth soccer has grown dramatically since its inception, though it too has experienced some of the same problems with overenthusiastic parents that were previously identified with other sports. Nonetheless, parental involvement— sometimes supportive and constructive, sometimes excessive and negative—remains a large factor in youth sports.

See also: **GutsMuths, J. C. F.; Organized Recreation and Youth Groups; YWCA and YMCA.**

BIBLIOGRAPHY

Berryman, Jack W. 1996. "The Rise of Boys' Sports in the United States, 1900 to 1970." In *Children and Youth in Sport: A Biopsychosocial Perspective*, ed. Frank L. Smoll and Ronald E. Smith. Madison, WI: Brown and Benchmark Publishers.

Cozens, Frederick W., and Florence S. Stumpf. 1953. *Sports in American Life.* Chicago: University of Chicago Press.

Dunning, Eric, and Kenneth Sheard. 1979. *Barbarians, Gentlemen, and Players.* Oxford: Oxford University Press.

Fields, Sarah K. 2000. "Female Gladiators: Gender, Law, and Contact Sport in America." Ph.D. diss., University of Iowa.

Garnham, Neal. 2001. "Both Praying and Playing: 'Muscular Christianity' and the YMCA in North-East County Durham." *Journal of Social History* 35: 397–409.

Gorn, Elliott, and Warren Goldstein. 1993. *A Brief History of American Sports.* New York: Hill and Wang.

Guttmann, Allen. 1988. *A Whole New Ball Game: An Interpretation of American Sports.* Chapel Hill: University of North Carolina Press.

Guttmann, Allen. 1991. *Women's Sport: A History.* New York: Columbia University Press.

Kerrigan, Colm. 2000. "'Thoroughly Good Football': Teachers and the Origins of Elementary School Football." *History of Education* 29: 517–542.

Rader, Benjamin G. 1999. *American Sports: From the Age of Folk Games to the Age of Televised Sports*, 4th ed. New Jersey: Prentice Hall.

Swanson, Richard A., and Betty Spears. 1995. *History of Sport and Physical Education in the United States*, 4th ed. Dubuque, IA: Brown and Benchmark Publishers.

Wiggins, David K. 1996. "A History of Highly Competitive Sport for American Children." In *Children and Youth in Sport: A Biopsychosocial Perspective*, ed. Frank L. Smoll and Ronald E. Smith. Madison, WI: Brown and Benchmark Publishers.

SARAH K. FIELDS

Steiner, Rudolf (1861–1925)

Austrian philosopher Rudolf Steiner was born in Kraljevic, Austria-Hungary, in 1861. He was educated in Wiener Neustadt and graduated from the Technical University in Vienna in 1884. Rudolf Steiner's view of life is called *anthroposophy*: wisdom of men. It stresses the unity of body, mind, and soul, in the sense not of a personal but of a cosmic unity. According to this philosophy, there are three worlds, the physical, the soulish, and the spiritual. Humans are part of all three worlds through the seven forms of their whole existence on earth. They are "rooted" in the physical world with their physical, ethereal, and soulish bodies, and "blossomed" into the spiritual world with their spiritual selves, their spirit of life and spiritual existence.

Anthroposophy is intended to be a counterproject to Western scientific culture, one that includes the doctrines of cosmic fate and reincarnation. When this purely occult philosophy is applied to education, the child is considered to be the "human in being" whose "substance" is known only when the "hidden" or "secret" nature of man is revealed. Education then is part of the *Geheimwissenschaft*: that is not publicly known but revealed only to its believers. This view is in opposition to all that constitutes modern education since the ENLIGHTENMENT.

For Steiner and his followers, the basis of education is neither teaching nor learning, but development. Development, however, refers not to nature, as Rousseau had stated, nor to mind, as JEAN PIAGET proposed. Steiner spoke of the "three births of men" that succeeded one after the other in a sequence of seven years. Up to the age of seven the child is woven within the ethereal and astral cover. After the child's second dentition, the ethereal body is born; at the age of fourteen the astral body, or the body of sensation, is revealed; and at the age of twenty-one the "body of I" is set into spiritual life. The means of education during the first period are imitation and modelling, during the second period succession and authority, and in the third period the road to the "higher soul of men" is opened.

Teaching in the first periods, Steiner believed, should not take place in an "abstract" manner, but in a concrete way, with "lively, vivid pictures" representing true spirituality for the understanding of the child. The educator should be "sensitive, warm and imbued with empathy" as a result of his or her studies of the sources of spiritual science. In the end the educator should represent the "true knowing of spirtual science" and this would be at the heart of all true education. Until the child reaches sexual maturity, teaching relates to the memory of the child, Steiner argued, and after that it relates to reason. Working with concepts is necessary only after sexual maturity. Teaching has one central principle, namely that memory comes first and only then comes comprehension. The better the memory, the better the understanding will be, so all first schooling should be based upon memorizing.

In February 1919, Steiner delivered four public lectures in Zurich. These lectures were published soon after as "the key points of the social question." Steiner developed his later famous principles of the "trinominal organization of society," namely economy, law, and spiritual life. Education and schooling are part of the spiritual life, or the *geistige Kultur*, which can only work when it is completely free. Thus schooling should be completely free, too. The Waldorf Schools, following this principle, are nonstate enterprises and call themselves Free Schools because they operate independently from the curricula of the state.

The grounding principle of the schools is "rhythm," not lecturing: the rhythm of the day, of the week, and of the year. The curriculum is constructed around a seven-year cycle, with special forms of teaching, such as epoch-instruction or the learning of eurythmics. The schools are nonselective and use neither grades nor rankings. The pupils are not divided into classes but remain together as a group with one teacher as long as one cycle lasts. The schools are coeducational and have an independent administration and a close connection between teachers and parents. They attempt to avoid putting pressure on children and allow them to work according to their own personal potential.

See also: **Child Development, History of the Concept of; Child Psychology; Neill, A. S.; Progressive Education.**

BIBLIOGRAPHY

Lindenberg, C. 1997 *Rudolf Steiner. Eine Biographie.* Stuttgart, Germany: Verlag Freies Geistesieben.

Steiner, Rudolf. 1919. *Die Kernpunkte der Sozialen Frage in den Lebensnotwendigkeiten der Gegenwart und Zukunft.* Stuttgart, Germany: Greiffer and Pfeiffer.

Steiner, Rudolf. 1948 [1907]. *Die Erziehung des Kindes vom Gesichtspunkte der Geisteswissenschaft.* Stuttgart, Germany: Verlag Freies Geistesleben.

Steiner, Rudolf. 1982 [1925]. *Mein Lebensgang. Eine nicht vollendete Autobiographie.* Ed. M. von Sievers. Dornach, Switzerland: Rudolf Steiner Verlag.

Steiner, Rudolf. 1994 [1904]. *Theosophy: An Introduction to the Supersensible Knowledge of the World and the Destination of Man.* London: Rudolf Steiner Press, 1973.

Wilkinson, Roy, ed. 1993. *Rudolf Steiner on Education: A Compendium.* Stroud, UK: Hawthorn.

JÜRGEN OELKERS

Stepparents in the United States

Stepparents in America have experienced at best a grudging acceptance, and at worst a negative and suspicious reception throughout American history. Overall, their role has been poorly defined by law, public policy, and social custom. Still, stepparents have always had an important role to play in raising children. In early colonial times because of high mortality rates and more recently because of divorce, the common occurrence of remarriage has meant a substantial proportion of American children are raised in stepfamilies.

Stepfathers

Widowhood was a common phenomenon in colonial America. Although many widows with children remarried, the role of stepfathers is prominent yet unclear in colonial America. Under seventeenth-century English common law, as indeed under modern American family law, the stepfather stood in an uncertain position with regard to his stepchild. Under common law, the mere relationship of stepfather and stepchild conferred no rights and imposed no duties. If, however, the stepfather voluntarily received the child into the home and treated it as a member of the family, the reciprocal rights and duties of the parent–child relationship were established and continued so long as the relationship lasted. If a man died without a will his stepchildren would not inherit from him. Beyond that the law is mostly silent.

We do have historical evidence that as heads of households, stepparents took on virtually all the responsibilities of natural fathers even if they were not officially recognized as such. Certainly all the colonial laws requiring fathers, parents, and masters to maintain, educate, and train children and servants in their households applied to stepfathers, who may well have had natural children in the household as well. There are also many references to stepfathers apprenticing their stepchildren to others, a role normally reserved for fathers. The mother of the children, as *femme couverte* (without a legal status separate from her husband) in remarriage, had no ability to make indenture contracts in her own right.

Stepfathers, however, were limited in their obligation to support their stepchildren. As heads of households, they were obliged to support the child they had accepted into the household, but not if the natural father was available. If the child was born out of wedlock, the natural father still had to pay maintenance for the child, which he gave directly to the stepfather. In one such case the biological father was forced to make payments for his sexual transgressions both to the stepfather and to his wife's natural father. A Massachusetts County Court decided

> Joseph Hall of Lyn, charged by Elizabeth wife of Nathll Eastman of Salisbury, as being the father of her child before her marriage, and the charge having been proved true, was ordered to pay 121i.[pounds] toward the child's maintenance to the husband of Elizabeth, in provisions within two years. Hall was also to pay 51i.[pounds] according to the law to Johathan Hudson, father of Elizabeth, for enticing her and frequenting her company contrary to her father's warning. (Records and Files of the Quarterly Courts of Essex County, Massachusetts, Vol. V:1672–1674, p. 103)

If the stepchild's mother died, the rights of the stepfather were greatly weakened. ADOPTION was not available until the nineteenth century, so stepfathers had no legal right to retain their stepchildren. The courts determined the placement of children in these circumstances based mainly on practical considerations. Labor was scarce and healthy children were an important asset, a fact not ignored by the courts. Petitions on behalf of the stepfather before the Maryland Orphan's Court arguing for custody of the child as against the claims of the grandparents did not mention the best interests of the child, but rather stressed the investment that the stepfather had already made in the maintenance of the children and his need for their services.

In practice, most children remained with their stepfather if he chose to keep them, but the community continued to keep a close watch on stepfathers. Court records are filled with accusations about stepfathers squandering children's estates or mistreating them. Under guardianship law, minors could appoint their own guardians for their estates at age fourteen. At that age, Aaron Prother asked the Maryland court for permission to choose his own guardian since "he has had the mishap sometime since to fall under the lash of an unfortunate father in law [stepfather]" (quoted in Wall, p. 90). Neighbors and town officials also monitored the behavior of stepfathers, as they did of fathers, but courts appeared more willing to remove a child from a stepfather than from a father for what was frequently referred to as "evil usage" or "hard usage" of their stepchildren.

Stepmothers

Since widowers remarried just as did widows, stepmothers constituted a large class in colonial America. There is very little to say about the legal status of stepmothers, however, because like natural mothers they were *femme couverte* and had a legal existence only in the shadow of their husbands. Like biological mothers, their only claim was to "love and respect." Upon the death of her husband, a stepmother had a weaker claim to the custody of her stepchildren than would a stepfather, since her economic and marital future was uncertain. Only if the father had made a will appointing the stepmother as the guardian of his children could a stepmother have a strong claim.

In some cases, the court chose a blood relative over a stepmother. In Connecticut, the stepdaughter of Edward Clark's widow was bound out to her aunt against the widow's objection. Since adoption was not yet a legal concept, binding out by contract, or apprenticing, was as close as one could come to adoption. It gave the relative a firm legal hold on the child until the child reached majority. This decision could mean that, in the court's judgment, the stepmother was unable to maintain the girl and the nearest relative offered to do so. It could also mean that the court chose the aunt because she was a blood relative and the stepmother was not.

These contradictory decisions indicate both the lack of clear legal principles regarding stepparents' rights and also the practical strategy followed by the courts in placing the children where they could provide critical labor. The nineteenth century changed the status of stepparents somewhat both through the new option of adoption and the elimination of APPRENTICESHIPS or "binding out" as a way of dealing with children whose fathers had died. The "best interest of the child" replaced the labor value of the child in determining the relationships with nonbiological parents. Still, adoption did not suit all stepparent situations, particularly where there were children from a previous marriage. The act of adoption gave the child inheritance rights that were often resented by children of the first family. Therefore most stepchildren and stepparents continued to coexist in an ambiguous relationship.

Modern Stepfamilies

A great shift in stepfamily demographics occurred in the twentieth century as divorce replaced death as the most common reason for remarriage. The modern stepfamily is different and more complex than the colonial stepfamily in several important ways. With divorce rather than death as a background event it is the remarriage of the custodial mother that usually forms the stepfamily. Some 86 percent of stepchildren live primarily with a custodial mother in their stepfamily. In most cases the noncustodial parent is still alive, creating the phenomenon of children with more than two parents. This fact precludes the option of adoption for many stepfathers. In addition to divorce, 28 percent of children are born to unwed mothers, many of whom eventually marry someone who is not the father of their child. In a study including all children, not just children of divorce, it was estimated that one-fourth of the children born in the United States in the early 1980s will live with a stepparent before they reach adulthood.

Still the role of stepparents continues to be ignored as a social or legal concept. While the rights and obligations of biological parents, particularly unwed fathers, have been greatly expanded in recent years, stepparents have received almost no attention from policy makers. Stepparents in most states have no obligation during the marriage to support their stepchildren, nor do they enjoy any right of custody or control. Consistent with this pattern, if the marriage terminates through divorce or death, they usually have no rights to custody or even visitation, however long-standing their relationship with their stepchildren. Conversely, stepparents have no obligation to pay child support following divorce, even if their stepchildren have depended on their income for many years. And stepchildren have no right of inheritance in the event of the stepparent's death.

Some social scientists believe that stepparent–stepchildren relationships are not as strong or nurturing as those in biologically related families, and that stepchildren do not do as well in school and in other outside settings. Other studies show that when single or divorced mothers marry their household income increases more than threefold, rising to the same level as nuclear families. In many cases this lifts the mother and children out of poverty. Studies also show us that residential stepparents perform many of the same caregiving functions as biological parents: helping with homework, driving the children to school, and so on. And in many stepfamilies the affectionate bond between stepparent and child is warm and strong. Stepfamilies are likely to remain an important family configuration. There is little indication, however, that they will soon receive the recognition and acknowledgement they deserve.

See also: **Divorce and Custody; Parenting; Same-Sex Parenting.**

BIBLIOGRAPHY

Mason, Mary Ann, et al. 2002. "Stepparents: De Facto Parents, Legal Strangers." *Journal of Family Issues* 23, no. 4.

Mason, Mary Ann, Arlene Skolnick, and Stephen Sugarman. 2002. *All Our Families: New Policies for a New Century*, 2nd ed. New York: Oxford University Press.

Vernier, Chester G. 1971 [1931–1938]. *American Family Laws: Vol. 4. Parent and Child*. Westport, CT: Greenwood Press.

Wall, Helena M. 1990. *Fierce Communion: Family and Community in Early America.* Cambridge, MA: Harvard University Press.

MARY ANN MASON

Street Arabs and Street Urchins

An alarming 1849 report by New York City police chief George Matsell raised the specter of over ten thousand "vagrant, idle and vicious children of both sexes" roaming the city streets, begging, stealing, or making their way as prostitutes. That same year, British journalist and social critic Henry Mayhew lamented the "licentious and vagabond propensities" of the thousands of children "flung" into London's streets through neglect and destitution. While Mayhew and other social observers illuminated the hardships and squalor that characterized the lives of street arabs and street urchins—the legions of raggedly dressed children, girls as well as boys, who worked, played, and sometimes lived in the streets of urban slums—their view of street children was framed as much by their own middle-class attitudes toward the poor as by the actual conditions of the children. Urban dwellers throughout the United States and Western Europe faced a bewildering array of social changes during the Victorian era that gave rise to fears of social chaos and violent class confrontation. Considering poor children to be "endangered and dangerous youth," urban reformers came to see these children as both the symbol of social disintegration and the key to social stability.

During the nineteenth century, urban centers such as New York City received a steady stream of foreign immigrants, unskilled native-born workers, and free blacks who, by economic necessity, settled in the poorest, most densely populated wards of the city. Although social reformers and the press publicized only the most sensational stories of children who ran away from or toiled to support alcoholic, abusive parents, the vast majority of children worked to supplement their families' meager incomes. Children scavenged for coal and scrap wood to burn, ran errands, and gathered scrap metal, glass, and rags to sell to junk dealers. Boys blacked boots and sold newspapers and matches. Girls peddled corn or flowers on street corners. The growth of street trades also led to an increase in the amount of petty crime committed by juveniles. Many children became adept at pilfering salable objects, though pickpocketing was the preserve of a small cadre of young professionals.

Police cited vagrancy, however, as the principal "crime" committed by the young, though most had homes and jobs that required their presence in the streets. The emphasis on children's "vagrancy" reflects middle-class biases about what constituted a home. In the eyes of many middle-class observ-

In Victorian England, race, class, and hygiene were often conflated, as can be seen in the figure of the dark-skinned girl in a tattered dress standing in a gutter in the foreground of Ford Madox Brown's *Work* (1852–1865). (Oil on canvas. 53 15/16 x 77 11/16 in. © Manchester Art Gallery).

ers, the poor had no homes, merely dark, filthy hovels. In fact, the term *street arab*, first used in the mid-nineteenth century, alludes to the nomadic lifestyle of some Arabic peoples. More than any other issue, the presence of children in the streets symbolized the disorder of lower-class family life to social reformers. In poor families, home life spilled out of the crowded tenement rooms into the bustling streets below. By contrast, domesticity defined the experience of bourgeois families. Instead of keeping children within the domestic sphere to protect them from the perceived evils of urban life, lower-class parents allowed their offspring to work and play in the city streets.

Fueled by these beliefs, organizations for the moral reform of destitute and delinquent youth emerged on both sides of the Atlantic: Rauhe Haus in Germany, Colonie Agricole in France, Kingswood and Tower Hill in England, and the Houses of Refuge in the United States. These reformatories sought to remold children's characters through discipline and hard work. Other organizations, notably the Children's Aid Society and the SOCIETY FOR THE PREVENTION OF CRUELTY TO CHILDREN, took a different tack, interven-

ing in the home life of the poor. They rescued children not only from the streets, but, when they deemed it necessary, from their parents as well. Modern conceptions of foster care and children's services evolved directly from these programs.

See also: **Child Saving; Delinquency; Homeless Children and Runaways in the United States; New York Children's Aid Society; Work and Poverty.**

BIBLIOGRAPHY

Ansbinder, Tyler. 2001. *Five Points*. New York: Free Press.

Brace, Charles Loring. 1872 [1973]. *The Dangerous Classes of New York and Twenty Years' Work among Them*. Washington, DC: National Association of Social Workers.

Gish, Calasha. 1995. "The Petit Proletariat: Youth, Class, and Reform, 1853–1890." Ph.D. diss., New York University.

Gordon, Linda. 1988. *Heroes of Their Own Lives: The Politics and History of Family Violence*. New York: Penguin Books.

Mayhew, Henry. 1861. *London Labour and the London Poor*, vol. 1. London: Griffin, Bohn.

CLAY GISH

Street Games

The outdoor PLAY of girls and boys has exhibited remarkable persistence over time—and considerable similarity throughout the world. Evidence of games of tag, hide-and-seek, hopping, jumping, marbles, and the competitive throwing of balls, sticks, and other objects is found in the earliest historical records of virtually every culture. Whether these activities originated as amusements and recreation or were part of adult rituals that were imitated by children is uncertain. Origins, however, are less relevant to understanding the importance of children's outdoor play and street games than the cultural contexts in which the games are played. In most cultures, childhood is a time of life when girls and boys engage in games and play. Through these games, in addition to having fun and getting exercise, they learn leadership and cooperation, rules (and rule evasion), physical skills, and social roles.

Street *play* may be defined as any pleasurable activity engaged in by children outside their homes, schools, and supervised playgrounds. Street *games* are those kinds of play that have names and rules, persist over time, and are recorded by adults. Popular games in the United States include: *red rover, jump rope, king of the mountain, kick the can, hide-and-seek, stickball, marbles,* and *hopscotch* (there is regional variation in many names). Jacks, board games, cards, and similar games may be played outside as well as indoors.

History of Games

Pieter Brueghel's 1560 painting *Children's Games* is a record of Dutch children engaged in more than ninety activities, most of them in streets and courtyards. The painting has been the subject of extensive scholarship and debate about its meanings. Whatever allegorical interpretations may be made, it provides a useful baseline from which to measure the survival or loss of children's games over 400 years. Prominent in Brueghel's assemblage are jacks (knucklebones), DOLLS, dollhouses, popguns, blindman's buff, leapfrog, marbles, various kinds of tag, ball, and pretend games, fighting, and fire-making—in short, games remarkably similar to those played today throughout the world.

For example, the knucklebones used in a game by two young women in the painting are clearly tali, or ankle bones, probably of sheep. These bones have four distinct sides and in Mongolia, for example, they are labeled "goat," "sheep," "camel," and "horse." In some games the ancient Greeks named only two sides, "dog" and "Venus." The bones can be used to play various games that have obvious kinship with both dice and marbles. They may be thrown on the ground with points assigned to each side of the talus; they may be flicked with a finger to strike and capture another bone; or they may be tossed in the air and caught on the back of the hand—a variation of this game using small stones was known as *jackstones* or *fivestones* in the United States. The manufac-

New York (c. 1942), Helen Levitt. Children in the increasingly crowded cities of twentieth-century America incorporated the features of the cities themselves into their games. Courtesy Fraenkel Gallery, San Francisco.

ture in the nineteenth century of six-pointed metal jacks and small rubber balls allowed the game to evolve into its present form.

William Wells Newell, in his book *Games and Songs of American Children,* published in 1883, described almost 200 kinds of children's play as observed or remembered by Newell and his friends. Like Brueghel's painting, Newell's work provides another baseline from which to measure persistence and change in children's play. Newell lists half-a-dozen variations of jackstones played by boys and girls in New England, including *otadama* or *Japanese jacks.* This game was played with seven little bags of rice and involved complex patterns of arrangement, throwing, and catching, similar to games played with bones, stones, and pieces of iron.

In parts of the United States, jackstones was also known as *dibs,* linking it with slang terms for money and claims on property. In NEW ZEALAND, as in Mongolia, children hunted for the remains of dead sheep, removed the anklebones, cleaned them, dyed them, carried them in specially made bags, and traded them. Before the arrival of Europeans and their livestock, Maori children played their version of jacks with stones. A few years after Newell's book, Stewart Culin, a curator who worked for the Smithsonian Institution and later the Brooklyn Museum, described how bison ankle-bones were used by Papago Indians in yet another variation of jacks. Folklorists in late-twentieth-century New York City found children in Chinatown playing jacks with buttons.

Jacks is presented in both memoirs and ethnographies as a game of hand-eye coordination and friendly competition—unlike marbles, which often involves playing "for keeps." Marble games are also of great antiquity. Made of clay, bone, fruit pits, shells, stone, glass, metal, or other material, games with these small round objects usually consist in "shooting" one marble into another by flicking it with a thumb or finger, with the intent of capturing the other marble. A variation involves shooting a marble from hole to hole to win all the marbles in the final hole. Marbles are also valued according to their material, style, and personal tastes of their owner. The distinction between playing for "keepsies" as opposed to "funsies," marks marbles, also called *taws*, as a gambling game. Played outdoors on uneven ground, marbles adds an element of luck to a game of skill. Historical sources suggest that marbles were played for reasons beyond amusement, acquisitiveness, or greed. A slave in Louisiana exploited his skill to accumulate marbles that he then used to pay a white boy to teach him to read. Culin notes that the Philippine game of *pungitan*, which involves shooting a shell at another shell in a ring, was played for money, food, and cigarettes.

Games of tag have been analyzed for what they suggest about power relationships. Folklorists and psychologists see elements of personal power in the "it" role in chase, tag, and capture games such as *Black Tom* (also known as *black man*, *wall-to-wall*, and *pom pom pull away*). This power confers prestige and self-esteem on the child who is "it," even if he or she is not the fastest runner or most skilled player. This is because the "it" person exercises control over the other players by positioning himself or herself before calling out the words that require the others to run between bases. Conversely, low power "it" roles in dodge the skunk (like Black Tom, but without the call to start the game) and pickle-in-the-middle (a version of keepaway), in which the chosen player cannot control the movement of the other players, convey little prestige and often result in a sense of failure leading to arguments, fights, and abandonment of the game.

Variation in Games

Examples of children's games with worldwide occurrence can be extended indefinitely. As important as the similarities may be, the subtle variations brought about by different cultural styles and social conditions are also meaningful. In the singing game *Sally Waters*, African-American children in St. Louis added lyrics that changed the rhythm and gestures of

the game from "Turn to the east/Turn to the west/Turn to the one that you love best," to "Put your hand on you hip/Let your backbone slip/Shake it to the east/O baby/Shake it to the west/Shake it to the one you love the best." In one version of the traditional southern game *chickamy, chickamy, craney crow* (also known as *fox and chickens*), in which a hawk or a witch tries to pull a player from a line of "chickens" behind a "mother," an overseer was substituted for the witch. By substituting a dreaded historical figure for a witch, the children preserved the memory of slavery, and in a slight way transformed the meaning of the game. IONA AND PETER OPIE cite versions of this game throughout Europe, Asia, and the Caribbean. A Mexican version, *A que te robo un alma*, has a devil stealing a soul, then punishing the soul by putting it to work at some disagreeable task. In another example of name change that illustrates children's humor, boys in the state of Jalisco play a version of Johnny-on-the-pony called *chinche lagua* (bed bug), in which boys climb on the back of a boy braced against a wall until the pile of boys collapses.

These are a few of the dozens of street and outdoor games played by American children from the seventeenth century to the present. The increasing density and congestion of cities in the twentieth century has changed the nature of street play. Stewart Culin was one of the first to notice distinctly urban forms of traditional games. Some were minor variations of old chase-and-capture games. Relievo, a "prisoner's base" type of game common in Scotland, Wales, and Northern England, became, in Brooklyn, *ring relievo* (or *ringoleavio*), a rough and tumble game in which the prisons for captured players were marked in chalk on the sidewalk and pursuit went around a city block instead of across open fields. An observer in 1902 reported that city boys had substituted chalk marks on walls for the colored paper used by the hares in the chase game of hare and hounds. Architectural features of cities were incorporated into games. Walls and the steps leading up to the doors of apartment houses became courts for handball and stoopball. Manhole covers and fire hydrants were used as bases in stickball. *Pictures* was a gambling game in which boys tossed or flipped picture cards from cigarette packs toward a wall about twelve feet away. The boy whose card landed nearest the wall won all the other cards that had fallen picture side up.

Games in U.S. Cities

Reformers and advocates of supervised playgrounds were dismayed by what they saw on the streets of America's major cities in the early twentieth century. In New York City, one observer found the ten most popular games from October through May of 1904 were: playing with fire, craps, marbles, hopscotch, leapfrog, jump rope, BASEBALL, cat (hitting and catching a stick), picture-card flipping, and tops. A survey in Cleveland, Ohio, on June 23, 1913, concluded that almost half the children were "doing nothing," which consisted of breaking windows, destroying property, setting fires, chalking suggestive words on buildings, standing around, fighting, gambling, and stealing. Those who were "playing" in streets, alleys, yards, vacant lots, and playgrounds were engaged in baseball, kite flying, digging in sand piles, or playing tag and jackstones.

Cleveland, which had an active playground association that provided SANDBOXES, swings, and other apparatus, had a higher percentage of children "playing" than many cities. In the early 1930s, Richmond, Virginia, reported that 65 percent of the city's children spent their time "idling." Ipswich, Massachusetts, and Eveleth, Minnesota, had even higher percentages of children bereft of play. Other surveys suggest that the reformers may have defined play and games too narrowly, perhaps or missed some activities.

Weather conditions and changing seasons often determine the choice of games. Newell and others noted that marbles was a game of late winter and early spring, as were kites and tops. In Georgia the season for popguns was when the chinaberries ripened on the trees. In 1898 an observer in Chicago noted that the first appearance of marbles, jacks, and jump rope was on March 6, when the weather turned mild, as well as their virtual disappearance by the end of April, when they were replaced by ball games in the day and chase and tag in the evening. Some activities, of course, are almost completely dependent on weather, such as swimming in the summer and sledding and snowball fighting in the winter.

The Twentieth Century

In the 1950s, Brian Sutton-Smith and B. G. Rosenberg collected information on almost 200 games played by 2,689 children between the ages of nine and fifteen in northwestern Ohio and compared them to collections from the 1890s, 1920s, and 1940s. Ball games, tag, marbles, bicycle riding, and make-believe games such as cops and robbers were among the favorites of boys for over 60 years. Jump rope, tag, hopscotch, and dolls continued to rank high among girls, but by the 1950s girls showed an increasing preference for traditional boys' activities such as swimming, marbles, and kite flying. More highly organized games with inflexible rules, such as BASKETBALL and football, rose in popularity among boys as a result of the expansion of physical education programs. Although many changes in game preferences may be attributed to the differences in methods and places of the surveys, Sutton-Smith and Rosenberg concluded that there had been a significant shift away from singing and dialogue games, such as Sally Waters and chickamy, and some shift away from traditional chase-and-capture games that involved choosing leaders and establishing group relations. Instead, games of individual skill became more prominent. The range of play for boys was narrowing and the games of both sexes involved smaller numbers of players.

The impact of school recreation programs, suburbanization, TELEVISION, and electronic games have further altered children's play since the mid-twentieth century. Although the memoirs of men and women who grew up in the 1950s and 1960s still contain references to regional styles of informal ball games, tag, jump rope, hopscotch, and dolls, there are increasing references to the influence of electronic media and commercial amusements. From the Davy Crockett fad of the 1950s to television shows and movies marketing specific TOYS, children's play has increasingly become a target for the manufacturers and retailers of clothing, electronic games, sports apparatus, and other paraphernalia.

Nevertheless, there is evidence that children do not passively accept the blandishments of adult culture. A 1992 study of almost 1,000 children, mostly three to seven years old, in twenty-two schools and day-care centers in the Philadelphia area, provides a fascinating glimpse of the impact, or lack thereof, of television and electronic games. Although Nintendo topped the list of favorite games and toys, Monopoly and hide-and-seek were close behind, while BARBIE dolls and baseball outranked generic video games. Watching TV and playing video games dominated indoor activities, although drawing and reading made the top ten, while for outside activities biking, swimming, baseball, soccer, and playing in playgrounds and yards topped the list. Responding to questions about what they liked best about where they lived, children listed friends, house, yard, park, bike, playmates, and their rooms—and while these rooms may contain video games, this seems to indicate that from a child's perspective it is the opportunity to play, not any particular activity, that is the prerequisite for perpetuation of children's games.

Even more remarkable was the number of different activities named by the children in the survey. Over 500 distinct activities, most named only once, were recorded, from "fixing things" to "playing spooky in the dark," to "playing with bugs." Many traditional tag, chase, and jumping games were mentioned, but the evidence suggests somewhat more solitary play for contemporary children than that experienced by earlier generations.

Paradoxically, children have lost some of their autonomy. This is the conclusion of a study of three generations of children who grew up in a neighborhood on the northern tip of Manhattan. From 1910 to 1980, the age at which children were first allowed to go out of their yards alone rose from five-and-a-half to seven-and-a-half. Moreover, the number of places children recall visiting away from home declined for both young children and teenagers. Most dramatic was the increase in the number of professionally supervised activities for children. For those growing up in the 1920s and 1930s the only supervised play was a summer sports program in a schoolyard. By the 1950s, however, Little League, Boy and Girl Scouts, the Police Athletic League, youth centers, and public libraries were offering a wide variety of organized recreation.

Street games have become a topic of nostalgia, with newspapers and the media regularly reporting on the survival of stickball, handball, and double-dutch jump rope in organized leagues and competitions. Picture books and websites on street play appeal to adults who have happy memories of childhood. Currently, streets are being reclaimed for play by boys and girls on roller blades and skateboards, and efforts to ban these activities recall earlier contests over control of play spaces. Street play is, in the final analysis, a public performance by children of games and rituals that both mock and confirm the larger social order.

See also: **Boyhood; Girlhood; Indoor Games; Playground Movement; Theories of Play.**

BIBLIOGRAPHY

Culin, Stewart. 1891. "Street Games of Boys in Brooklyn, N.Y." *Journal of American Folklore* 4 (September–October): 221–237.

Culin, Stewart. 1900. "Philippine Games." *American Anthropologist* 2 (October–December): 643–656.

Culin, Stewart. 1992 [1907]. *Games of the North American Indians.* Lincoln: University of Nebraska Press.

Dargan, Amanda, and Steven Zeitlin. 1990. *City Play.* New Brunswick, NJ: Rutgers University Press.

Ferretti, Fred. 1975. *The Great American Book of Sidewalk, Stoop, Dirt, Curb, and Alley Games.* New York: Workman.

Gaster, Sanford. 1991. "Urban Children's Access to the Neighborhoods: Changes Over Three Generations." *Environment and Behavior* 23, no. 1 (January): 70–85.

Grover, Kathryn, ed. 1992. *Hard at Play: Leisure in America, 1840–1940.* Amherst: University of Massachusetts Press.

Hindman, Sandra. 1981. "Pieter Bruegel's Children's Games, Folly, and Chance." *Art Bulletin* 63, no. 3 (September): 447–475.

Howard, Dorothy Mills. 1977. *Dorothy's World: Childhood in Sabine Bottom.* Englewood Cliffs, NJ: Prentice Hall.

Howard, Dorothy. 1989. *Pedro of Tonalá.* Roswell, NM: Hall-Poorbaugh.

Kabzinska-Stawarz, Iwona. 1991. *Games of Mongolian Shepherds.* Warsaw: Institute of the History of Material Culture, Polish Academy of Sciences.

Knapp, Mary, and Knapp, Herbert. 1976. *One Potato, Two Potato: The Secret Education of American Children.* New York: Norton.

Mergen, Bernard. 1982. *Play and Playthings: A Reference Guide.* Westport, CT: Greenwood Press.

Newell, William Wells. 1963 [1883]. *Games and Songs of American Children.* New York: Dover.

Rosenberg, B. G., and Sutton-Smith, Brian. 1961. "Sixty Years of Historical Change in the Game Preferences of American Children." *Journal of American Folklore* 74 (January–March): 17–46.

Sutton-Smith, Brian, ed. 1972. *The Folkgames of Children.* Austin: University of Texas Press.

Sutton-Smith, Brian, et al., eds. 1999. *Children's Folklore: A Source Book.* Ogden: Utah State University Press.

Ward, Colin. 1978. *The Child in the City.* New York: Pantheon.

INTERNET RESOURCE

Streetplay. 2002. Available from <www.streetplay.com>.

BERNARD MERGEN

Student Government

The American belief that education transmits democratic ideals to a new generation is as old as the republic. Throughout the nineteenth century examples in secondary schools and colleges can be found of students taking on responsibilities for the functioning of their institutions. The widespread expansion of student government began at the end of the nineteenth and the beginning of the twentieth century.

In colleges the impulse came from students' beliefs that they should be involved in the aspects of college life which most affected them. Advocates of Progressive-era political and educational reform, meanwhile, saw training young people in the practicalities of democratic citizenship as an answer to a political system they feared was dominated by "bosses." The school, as an increasingly universal experience, seemed the logical site for such instruction.

Adult proponents saw student government as an extension of the progressive educational concept of learning by doing. They assailed authoritarian school systems and argued that only if students experienced democracy in their school life would they become effective adult citizens. Experiments in student participation modeled on existing structures of city and federal governments were tried in many secondary schools during the first decades of the twentieth century, gaining media attention and support from political and educational leaders. Opponents, however, charged the schemes would simply reproduce the corruptions of the existing political system rather than offer a model of democratic behavior. Despite successes, programs that established a "school city" or "school republic" faded in the years after World War I.

By the 1920s, fraternities and sororities had become the center of college society and these social organizations dominated many student governments. The first national organization of student government leaders, the National Student Federation (founded in 1925), supported reforms of education and restrictions on student behavior.

A focus by administrators on school as the center of young people's lives made student government an important component of HIGH SCHOOL culture during the 1920s and in subsequent years. New initiatives were based on life *within* the school and became a means to promote "school spirit." Student government stood at the head of an array of clubs that operated outside the standard curriculum. Many student councils and their teacher advisers had responsibility for promoting social activities, monitoring halls, lunchrooms, and organizing assembly programs. During World War II, councils turned to drives for war bonds in addition to their management of social life.

While participation had once been limited to club officers and those who met certain academic requirements, by mid-century councils were increasingly elected at large and in homerooms and qualifications for participation were removed. The Progressive-era focus on modeling adult structures had been replaced by an emphasis on students learning "responsibility" and "cooperation." Student government was a special kind of "delegated authority" in which students stood at the bottom of a long chain of command.

Promoted by the National Association of Secondary School Principals, student government entered the postwar years as a predictable aspect of any high school life. The high school became the appropriate focus for students' patriotism and student government the principal's cooperative partner in managing the school.

College student government hit a high-water mark during the 1950s as a larger and demographically diverse student population poured onto campuses. Student government was almost universal in colleges of all sizes. Although leaders complained about apathy, most students voted in campus elections. Student government leaders, represented nationally by the National Student Association (founded in 1947), felt student government should have greater responsibility and involvement not only in student social affairs but also in the educational matters facing their institutions. When they called for academic freedom, an end to racial discrimination, and reform of in loco parentis authority over students, leaders imagined such changes would occur within a college's existing power structure.

While students played significant roles in the civil rights and antiwar movements during the 1960s, student government declined in its importance during this period. Although many activists were or had been student government leaders, student governments themselves waded into the fray only tentatively. Campus protests against the unequal distribution of power in college students' lives and demands for greater involvement in campus decision-making that resulted in significant upheaval often made the student government appear to be a "sandbox" for make-believe politics. The National Student Association's reputation was damaged significantly when it was revealed in 1967 that the Central Intelligence Agency had been providing substantial funding for its international student exchange programs and had exerted unofficial influence on its policies since the early 1950s.

The transformation of educational governance policies in the early 1970s prompted by student unrest seemed to presage a renaissance for student government. In secondary schools, a robust student council that focused on dropouts and drugs as much as, or more than, improving lunchroom behavior and the participation of student representatives on local school boards were deemed the best way to promote democracy and avoid future strife. Colleges and universities transformed many of their governing bodies to involve students in decisions regarding student life and educational policy. As the years went on, however, the feeling of urgency re-

garding student involvement in governance began to fade. Studies found declining sentiment for student involvement in governance and participation in college elections. High school involvement declined even more and experts' proposals for increased student participation were often precisely the same ones described as accomplishments of a dynamic student council in the 1940s.

By the end of the twentieth century, high school students involved in government balanced the demands of multiple extracurricular activities; school councils made announcements and coordinated clubs and social events but even that level of responsibility was declining. On college campuses, student government leaders often sat on university committees, managed a considerable student activities budget funded by activities fees, provided other services to students, and worked with an expanding staff of "student affairs" professionals. While the belief that a new generation must learn the skills of democracy remained, the role of student government in that quest is less clear than it was to its progressive advocates.

See also: **Youth Activism.**

BIBLIOGRAPHY

Altbach, Philip G. 1974. *Student Politics in America: A Historical Analysis.* New York: McGraw-Hill.

Drewry, Raymond G. 1928. *Pupil Participation in High School Control.* New York: Harcourt, Brace and Company.

Falvey, Frances E. 1952. *Student Participation in College Administration.* New York: Teachers College, Columbia University.

Fass, Paula S. 1977. *The Damned and the Beautiful: American Youth in the 1920s.* New York: Oxford University Press.

Freidson, Eliot, ed. 1955. *Student Government, Student Leaders and the American College.* Philadelphia: United States National Student Association.

Smith, Joe. 1951. *Student Councils For Our Times.* New York: Teachers College, Columbia University.

Terrell, Melvin C., and Michael J. Cuyjet, eds. 1994. *Developing Student Government Leadership.* San Francisco: Jossey-Bass Publishers.

GLENN WALLACH

Sudden Infant Death Syndrome

Sudden infant death syndrome (SIDS, also known as crib death) is the unexpected death of an infant for which postmortem examination fails to find adequate cause. It has a long history and has been explained, at various times, as infanticide, overlaying (accidental suffocation in a family bed), and thymus death, or *status lymphaticus.* The reasons why infants died suddenly were often obscure. In 1855 Thomas Wakley, the founder and editor of the *Lancet,* wrote about "infants found dead in bed," and there has been a stream of publications on the subject ever since. During the nineteenth century, the frequency of infanticide was a matter of growing concern. In the mid-1860s over 80 percent of all coroners' reports of murder in England and Wales involved infants. Disraeli said that infanticide was "hardly less prevalent in England than on the banks of the Ganges." The subject excited considerable interest in British newspapers and medical journals from the 1860s onwards. Death from overlaying was also common, perhaps because of overcrowding and the prevalence of drunkenness.

The unexpected death of an infant without obvious cause was long thought to be due to an enlarged thymus. This was a misunderstanding, but it lasted until modern times. Normal infants have large thymus glands, but most infant deaths occurred after prolonged illness had depleted the thymus so that postmortem examinations revealed small thymuses. A child who died suddenly was likely to have a normal, large thymus, and this was taken to be the cause of death. A disease, *status lymphaticus*, was invented to legitimize it. During the early twentieth century this disease caused considerable interest and anxiety. It was later questioned and eventually shown to be nonexistent.

Yet infants continued to die unexpectedly. During the 1940s the concept of crib death (also called *cot death*) became prominent and gradually the label changed to sudden infant death syndrome. Most experts in the field agree that it has many possible causes. These include infection (often sudden pneumonia), hyperthermia (overheating due to too hot a room or too many bedcoverings), murder, and unintentional poisoning (perhaps from cigarette smoke or chemicals, possibly arsenic, phosphorus, and antimony in crib mattresses, perhaps from obscure fungi that grow in old mattresses). The possible involvement of mattresses has led to accusations of cover-ups by governments and manufacturers. Increasing publicity has promoted the adoption of baby monitors, which record a baby's breathing and sound an alarm if the infant ceases to breathe.

The current consensus of opinion is that crib death appears to be an abnormal response to everyday challenges and stresses that do not affect most babies. After (or coincidental with) new regulations about crib mattresses and public advice to put babies into their cribs on their backs rather than on their stomachs, the incidence of SIDS fell by two-thirds, but it is still the largest single killer of babies under one year and the subject is of considerable interest to both pediatricians and the public. The Foundation for the Study of Infant Deaths initiates research and also campaigns for greater compassion to be shown by health professionals to bereaved parents.

See also: **Infant Mortality; Pediatrics.**

BIBLIOGRAPHY

Bergman, Abraham B., J. Bruce Beckwith, and C. George Ray, eds. 1970. *Sudden Infant Death Syndrome: Proceedings.* Seattle: University of Washington Press.

Byard, Roger, and Stephen D. Cohle. 1994. *Sudden Death in Infancy, Childhood and Adolescence.* New York: Cambridge University Press.

Golding, J. 1989. "The Epidemiology and Sociology of the Sudden Infant Death Syndrome." In *Paediatric Forensic Medicine and Pathology*, ed. J. K. Mason. London: Chapman and Hall Medical.

ANN DALLY

Suicide

Suicide rarely occurs before age ten, and although suicide rates for ten to fourteen year olds and adolescents greatly increased in the United States between the mid-1970s and the mid-1980s, suicide rates for children and adolescents are lower than for other age groups. Nevertheless, by the end of the twentieth century, suicide was the second greatest cause of death in adolescents, after (mainly automobile-related) accidents. In children age ten to fourteen suicide is the third leading cause of death, following unintentional injuries and malignant neoplasms. In the United States, males age ten to fourteen die by suicide three times more than females, and males age fifteen to nineteen have five times more suicides than females. The difference between male and female suicide rates may be explained by males being more vulnerable, or it may be due to their preferences for more lethal methods, particularly firearms: gunshot wounds are the leading cause of suicide deaths in the United States for all age groups. For each person who dies by suicide (a "completed suicide") there are an estimated 50 to 100 suicide attempts. When people under age eighteen are asked if they have ever seriously attempted suicide, at least one out of twenty say that they have.

The Historical Problem

The contemporary concern about adolescent suicide raises a complex historical problem. First, how new is the pattern? We know that adolescents and very young adults committed suicide in the past. In Germany in the late 1700s, the publication of *Die Leiden des jungen Werthers* (*The Sorrows of Werter*), a novel by Johann Wolfgang von Goethe, presumably spurred some suicides in young men who were attracted to death by the prevailing romantic culture. Studies of suicide in England in the late nineteenth century also reveal some adolescent suicides. It is unclear how much the current patterns reflect new developments, as opposed to new levels of attention and concern.

To the extent that there is change, the question then arises: what might the causes be? A culture permeated with images of violence, but in which children rarely experience death directly, is sometimes held accountable. New tensions at school and in peer groups may be involved, sometimes complemented by drug use. Suicide is closely linked, of course, to psychological depression, which also seems to be on the rise among young people.

Children's Understanding of Suicide

Although young children (less than ten to twelve years) rarely die by suicide, contemporary children develop an understanding of suicide at an early age, and their conceptions of suicide may influence their behaviors later in life, when they experience the vulnerabilities of ADOLESCENCE.

Research indicates that by age seven or eight most children understand the concept of suicide, can use the word *suicide*, and can name several common methods of committing suicide. Young children, as young as age five and six, can understand and talk about killing themselves, even if they do not understand the word *suicide*. Children by age seven or eight report that they have talked about suicide with other children, and most have seen at least one fictional suicide on television. These suicides usually occur in cartoons in which the villain takes his or her own life when he or she has lost an important battle and has no way to escape. Children also experience suicide attempts and threats in adult television programs, including soap operas and the news. Despite children's knowledge of and exposure to the subject, they receive little guidance about it from adults.

Children age five to twelve generally have quite negative attitudes toward suicide; they consider suicide something that one should not do and generally feel that people do not have a right to kill themselves. When there is a suicide in the family or in the family of their friends, children usually know about the suicide, despite parents' attempts to hide the facts by avoiding talking about it or explaining that the death was an accident. For example, in studies conducted in Quebec, Canada, by Brian L. Mishara, 8 percent of children said that they knew someone who committed suicide, but none of the children said that they were told about the suicide by an adult. Surveys of parents found that 4 percent of children have threatened to kill themselves at some time but these threats are rarely taken seriously or discussed.

Children at a young age are curious about understanding death, and although they know that one can commit suicide, their view of what occurs when someone dies may be very different from an adult's understanding of death. However, children learn fairly early (generally by age seven or eight) that death is final—that someone who dies may not come back to life. Younger children often believe that people who have died are able to see, hear, feel, and be aware of what living people are doing.

Suicidal Behavior in Children and Adolescents

Suicide is a relatively rare event that results from a combination of risk factors, usually a precipitating event combined with access to a means of committing suicide and a lack of appropriate help. Suicide is generally understood to be the result of complex interactions between developmental, individual, environmental, and biological circumstances. Despite the complexity of factors that may result in suicidal behavior, it is possible to identify children at risk.

Depression is a major risk factor for suicide, although depression symptoms in children may be difficult to recognize and diagnose. In prepubescent children, symptoms may include long-lasting sadness, frequent crying for no apparent reason or, conversely, inexpressive and unemotional behavior, including speaking in a monotone voice. Other signs include difficulty concentrating on schoolwork, lack of energy, social withdrawal, and isolation. Children and adolescents who threaten suicide or become interested in the means of killing themselves, such as tying nooses or playing suicide games or trying to acquire a firearm, should be considered as potential suicide risks.

The best way to verify the risk of suicide is to ask direct questions of the child. They might include the following: "Are you thinking of killing yourself?"; "have you thought about how you would kill yourself?"; "do you think you might really commit suicide?" Many adults hesitate to ask such questions because they are afraid they might "put ideas" in a child's head. However, decades of experience indicate that talking about suicide cannot suggest suicidal behavior to children and can only help children express their concerns to an adult.

It is also important to ask suicidal children what they think will happen when a person dies. If the child indicates that they think someone can return from the dead or that being dead is like being alive, it may be useful to correct that impression and describe with some details what it means to die.

Children who have symptoms of depression or threaten suicide may benefit from help from a mental-health professional. It is also important to talk with a child or adolescent when there is a suicide in the family or in the school environment. Most children already have a good understanding of what occurred and do not feel that this is appropriate behavior. However, in the event that the child glorifies or trivializes a death by suicide or feels that the suicide victim is "better off" after dying, it is important to clarify what occurred and, if necessary, seek counseling or professional help. It is also important to help children express their feelings about a loss by suicide, even if they include "unacceptable" feelings such as being angry at the suicide victim for having abandoned them. It is important to communicate that suicide is a tragic event that is usually generally avoidable and certainly is not beneficial for anyone.

See also: **Drugs; Emotional Life; Mental Illness.**

BIBLIOGRAPHY

Bailey, Victor. 1998. *This Rash Act: Suicide across the Life Cycle in the Victorian City.* Stanford, CA: Stanford University Press.

Kushner, Howard I. 1989. *Self-Destruction in the Promised Land: A Psychocultural Biology of American Suicide.* New Brunswick, NJ: Rutgers University Press.

Maris, Ronald W., Alan L. Berman, and Morton M. Silverman, eds. 2000. *Contemporary Textbook of Suicidology.* New York: Guilford Press.

Mishara, Brian L. 1999. "Conceptions of Death and Suicide: Empirical Investigations and Implications for Suicide Prevention." *Suicide and Life-Threatening Behavior* 29, no. 2: 105–108.

World Health Organization. 2001. *Preventing Suicide: A Resource for Primary Health Care Workers.* Geneva: World Health Organization.

BRIAN L. MISHARA

Summer Camps

Summer camps—overnight camps attended by children without their parents—were first established in the 1880s in North America, fueled by Victorian convictions about nature's moral and physical benefits, as well as newer concerns about degeneracy and falling birth rates. In the twentieth century, the summer camp idea became an international phenomenon, supported by organizations with varied social, political, religious, and pedagogical agendas. In short, summer camps have become an increasingly important means for socializing modern children.

The earliest camps were small, private camps for older boys, developed in response to growing concerns about the emasculating tendencies of what was called overcivilization. Catering to the sons of elite families, many of these camps were located in the woods of northern New England, far from the temptations of city life and the refinements of the "feminized" home. Among the earliest were Chocorua (in operation between 1881 and 1889), Asquam (founded as Camp Harvard in 1885 and renamed in 1887), and Pasquaney (established in 1895), all located on or near Squam Lake in New Hampshire. Although the physical character of these camps was highly rustic (with unhewn timbers used liberally in the construction of their permanent buildings), camp life was rougher in some camps than in others; at Chocorua, for instance, campers did all the cooking and cleaning, and ate off tin plates, while at Pasquaney, a professional cook served meals on china.

A camp building boom in the 1890s brought camping to a wider audience, including the urban poor (who attended camps organized by religious organizations, SOCIAL SETTLEMENTS, and other social welfare agencies) and middle-class boys served by the YMCA (which established its first boys' camp, later known as Camp Dudley, in 1885). By 1901, the YMCA estimated that it served five thousand boys each summer, a number that grew to 23,300 by 1916. Unlike elite camps, these early YMCA camps tended to mimic military encampments with sleeping tents pitched around a square parade ground where campers enacted reveille, morning inspection, calisthenics, and taps. While these military trappings allowed boys to experience an all-male environment that contrasted sharply with the feminized home, they also insured that these camps sat lightly on their natural sites. Tents could be taken down at the end of each season, a par-

ticular advantage for camps held on land borrowed from supporters eager to promote the cause of camping for boys. In the early twentieth century, Native American motifs, which had appeared in some camps from the beginning, became even more popular, thanks in part to the Woodcraft Indians, a precursor to the BOY SCOUTS of America, another organization that encouraged summer camping for boys after 1910.

Camps for girls were established in the early twentieth century to foster a new, more self-reliant generation of young women. Among the earliest were private camps (like Camp Kehonka in New Hampshire and the Wyonegonic Camps in Bridgton, Maine, all founded in 1902), although the Camp Fire Girls (established in 1911) and GIRL SCOUTS of the U.S.A. (established in 1912) soon started camps for middle-class girls. By 1925, there were some three hundred Girl Scout camps in the United States.

Whether serving boys or girls, camps offered a range of activities: campcraft (i.e., skills needed to survive in the wild), nature study, manual training (later called arts and crafts), calisthenics, swimming, and a range of the other SPORTS (although early camp organizers frowned on BASEBALL and BASKETBALL as too "urban" for camp). Popular camp games included Rover, All Come Over and Indian and White Man, in which campers designated as Indians try to capture other campers representing "white people travelling over the prairie" (Gibson, p. 217). The evening campfire was the setting for theatrical entertainments, songs, and storytelling, as well as special rituals to mark the opening and closing of camp. Calling upon a long-standing conviction that a natural setting enhances religious feeling (something already practiced at camp meetings attended by adults and family groups), many camps featured a spiritual component as well. On Sundays, the regular routine was suspended, while white-clad campers attended services in a forest chapel fitted out with rustic furniture and a wood or stone altar, framed by a lake view.

By the 1920s, this sense of nature's spiritual associations prompted many religious groups to move beyond their early charitable camping endeavors into religious-based camping for the children of middle-class and elite families. In addition to Catholic camps and Protestant Bible camps, Jewish camps enjoyed a surge of popularity between the 1920s and the 1950s, as they sought to maintain ethnic practices threatened by modernization and assimilation. The approach to Jewish identity varied widely at such summer camps, some of which (like Camp Ramah in Wisconsin) were explicitly religious in orientation, others (like Massad Hebrew Camps) were also Zionist, and still others (like Cejwin Camps at Port Jervis, New York) emphasized secular Jewish cultural practices.

In other parts of the world, turn-of-the-century experiments with charitable camps gave way to a wider range of camping endeavors in the 1920s. In NEW ZEALAND, camps were closely associated with rebuilding the health of delicate children. Established in 1919, the first health camp used Army surplus tents provided at a nominal rate by the Defence Department. By the 1930s, nine health camp associations had instituted camps, including Canterbury's Sunlight League, which emphasized sunbathing as prescribed by the new science of heliotherapy. In the late 1930s, health camps came under government regulation, resulting in a new emphasis on permanent, year-round facilities. By the 1950s, increasingly stringent government standards forced many summer-only camps to close.

In other settings, the 1920s and 1930s saw the rise of summer camps of a political bent, including a range of left-wing camps in the United States (there were twenty-seven Communist camps in New York state by 1956), Communist camps in France, Germany, and Austria, Fascist *colonie* in Italy, and camps to sustain Polish culture on the contested border between Poland and Germany. Unlike radical camps in the United States, which differed little in physical form from other North American camps, French *colonies de vacances* established by Communist-governed municipalities (like Ivry-sur-Seine) were instituted in part to secure party loyalty and thus served large audiences. The *colonie* at Les Mathes opened in 1929 near Royan on nineteen hectares of pine woodlands; supplementing old farm buildings were five new dormitories (each with a capacity of one hundred children) and a refectory/kitchen serving eight hundred. Notable, too, was the practice of children's self-government; decisions about daily life at Les Mathes were taken collectively, under the guidance of a municipal council of colons elected each summer by universal childhood suffrage, with half the seats reserved for girls. Equally massive were the *colonie* established in Fascist Italy to aid in the cause of political indoctrination; they housed children in large, austere, modern buildings adjoining vast, unplanted terraces for mass sunbathing and calisthenics.

Just before World War II, North American camp-planning practices were transformed as professional experts lent their advice to camp directors (themselves newly professionalized since the formation of the American Camping Association in 1935). The findings of child psychologists prompted the introduction of the unit plan (which divided the camp landscape into age-based living units), and the construction of elaborate sleeping quarters (including socializing space to facilitate closer camper-counselor interaction). Water safety experts at the American Red Cross suggested improved waterfront designs with lifeguard towers, checkboards, and carefully demarcated areas for non-swimmers, beginners, and swimmers. Camp planning experts (many of whom had worked for the National Park Service under the aegis of the New Deal designing camps in thirty-four federal Recreation Demonstration Areas) advocated both master planning (to control the development of the camp landscape)

and picturesque planning principles (to disguise the extent of that control).

Codified in camp planning manuals published in the 1940s by the YMCA, the Girl Scouts, and the Camp Fire Girls, this professional advice guided the postwar camp-building boom that paralleled the BABY BOOM. Not only were there more camps to choose from in this period, but these camps served larger populations of younger campers. Camp counselors were younger, too. Even at sixteen (the median camper age in the late nineteenth century), many postwar teenagers considered themselves too old for summer camp, prompting many camp organizers to establish Counselor-in-Training (CIT) programs to keep these youngsters coming to camp.

In the postwar period, camps for children with disabilities became increasingly common, as did skill-based camps teaching foreign languages, music, and computer programming. At the end of the twentieth century, however, the traditional, rustic, character-building summer camp enjoyed renewed popularity.

Summer camps, then, are among the first institutions designed to educate the whole child, providing twenty-four-hour care that fostered physical health, social development, and spiritual development in generations of children in North America, Europe, and Australasia. Yet, if the general goals of summer camps have remained unchanged since the 1880s, the particular ways that camps achieved those goals have varied, as camp organizers grappled with changing ideas of what is best for children.

See also: **Children's Spaces; Communist Youth; Fascist Youth; Organized Recreation and Youth Groups; Vacations; YWCA and YMCA.**

BIBLIOGRAPHY

de Martino, Stephano and Alex Wall, ed. 1988. *Cities of Childhood: Italian Colonie of the 1930s.* London: Architectural Association.

Downs, Laura Lee. 2002. *Childhood in the Promised Land: Working-Class Movements and the Colonies de Vacances in France, 1880–1960.* Durham, NC: Duke University Press.

Gibson, Henry W. 1911. *Camping for Boys.* New York: Association Press.

Joselit, Jenna Weissman, and Karen Mittelman, eds. 1993. *A Worthy Use of Summer: Jewish Summer Camping in America.* Philadelphia: National Museum of American Jewish History.

Macleod, David I. 1983. *Building Character in the American Boy: The Boy Scouts, YMCA, and Their Forerunners, 1870–1920.* Madison: University of Wisconsin Press.

Maynard, W. Barksdale. 1999. "'An Ideal Life in the Woods for Boys': Architecture and Culture in the Earliest Summer Camps." *Winterthur Portfolio* 34: 3–29.

Mechling, Jay. 2001. *On My Honor: Boy Scouts and the Making of American Youth.* Chicago: University of Chicago Press.

Mishler, Paul C. 1999. *Raising Reds: The Young Pioneers, Radical Summer Camps, and Communist Political Culture in the United States.* New York: Columbia University Press.

Tennant, Margaret. 1996. "Children's Health Camps in New Zealand: The Making of a Movement, 1919–1940." *Social History of Medicine* 9: 69–87.

Van Slyck, Abigail A. 2002. "Housing the Happy Camper." *Minnesota History* 58: 68–83.

Van Slyck, Abigail A. 2002. "Kitchen Technologies and Mealtime Rituals: Interpreting the Food Axis at American Summer Camps, 1890–1950." *Technology and Culture* 43: 668–692.

ABIGAIL A. VAN SLYCK

Sunday

For centuries Sunday has had a distinct set of boundaries and meanings for children growing up in Catholic and Protestant households and nations. As styles of religious practice changed over time, so did proscriptions for Sunday observances. Broadly speaking, before the PROTESTANT REFORMATION there was little difference between Sundays and other days, but afterward both Catholics and Protestants engaged in a reformation of the calendar that resulted in a regular rhythm of six days work and one day's rest (Sunday). Children's activities did not escape from this new emphasis on Sunday as a day strictly reserved for religious observance and instruction, thus giving rise to the oft-heard youthful lament about the tedium of Sundays.

Throughout the eighteenth century children were expected to observe Sunday in the same manner as adults, that is, to refrain from all but religious thoughts and actions; but in the early nineteenth century, shifting attitudes toward religion, family relations, and child rearing resulted in the development of new understandings about the Sundays of children. These new attitudes emphasized the belief that children had different religious and recreational needs than adults. In the United States, the resulting schematic applied most directly to the children of the middle classes, however many children of factory workers, African Americans, and of other marginalized Americans experienced Sundays that were distinct from the other days of the week, whether in attending services or gathering with family and friends or donning an outfit reserved for Sundays and special occasions.

In terms of religion, the most important and lasting development in the United States was the SUNDAY SCHOOL. At first devoted to teaching the children of the urban poor to read and write, by the 1820s Sunday schools assumed a position as one of the central Protestant institutions devoted to inculcating religious literacy in children. Rising in large part out of the ferment of the Second Great Awakening, a nationwide religious revival that gave primacy to the centrality of personal conversion, the Sunday school movement at first aimed to foment religious awakening in the nation's youth. Soon, however, it settled into a complacent form of mostly nondenominational religious education, one that continues to inform American religious experience into the twenty-

first century. Despite the recognition that children had special religious needs, it was still expected that they sit attentively through services (an expectation that only diminished in the second half of the twentieth century). Parents continued to take part in their children's religious-oriented education, overseeing family prayer and bible study at home. During the 1820s and 1830s, they were encouraged to let their children play on Sunday (which was in great contrast to their own childhood Sundays), but to sanctify this play with religiously oriented reading, games, and TOYS. By mid-century, Bible picture puzzles, inexpensive Bible books, Sunday reading, Christian-oriented games and toys (such as the Noah's Ark) were available through mail-order houses. Observant households witnessed children putting their everyday books and toys away Saturday night in preparation for a Sunday of special experiences, books, and playthings. As such, the theory went, children would learn to love Sunday, and consequently become committed Christians.

During the decades after the Civil War the emphasis on religious education and play dilated into a widespread acceptance of certain kinds of Sunday recreation, especially family-oriented recreation. As more and more men engaged in paid labor outside of the home, Sunday became "Daddy's Day with Baby" (as went the refrain of one popular song). As such, many began to emphasize family togetherness and recreation, often at the expense of religious observances. After midcentury, the Sunday dinner became a fixture in many households, while excursions of many varieties, including the uncomplicated Sunday drive, provided much desired and needed change for adults and children alike. Entrepreneurs met the demand for Sunday entertainment, especially that which was child-centered. Picnic grounds, beach resorts, and amusement parks all catered to the special needs of children with merry-go-rounds, pony rides, and such. Trolleys, railroads, steamships, and other forms of mass transportation did vigorous business on Sundays, often due to the patronage of large family groups. Publishers of the Sunday newspaper, whose widespread introduction in the 1880s elicited scorn and condemnation, also recognized the special needs of children, first with children's sections, and then, beginning in the 1900s, with the comics insert. In the twentieth century RADIO and TELEVISION producers fashioned special shows for children's Sunday afternoons, such as *The Wide World of Disney* and *Mutual of Omaha's Wild Kingdom*. The church, the family, and the market, then, have recognized Sunday as an unique space of time in the lives of children, and have sought in various ways to cater to their needs.

See also: **Birthday; Halloween; Parades; Vacations; Zoos.**

BIBLIOGRAPHY

Boylan, Anne. 1988. *Sunday School.* New Haven, CT: Yale University Press.

McCrossen, Alexis. 2000. *Holy Day, Holiday: The American Sunday.* Ithaca, NY: Cornell University Press.

McDannell, Colleen. 1986. *The Christian Home in Victorian America, 1840–1900.* Bloomington: Indiana University Press.

Taves, Ann. 1986. *The Household of Faith.* Notre Dame, IN: University of Notre Dame Press.

ALEXIS MCCROSSEN

Sunday School

Since the 1870s, the Sunday school in Protestant churches has been called the nursery of the church. It has been a primary means of growing children into church members. Estimates from the 1890s in mainline denominations in the United States (i.e., Baptist, Congregational, Methodist, and Presbyterian) were that over 80 percent of all new members were nurtured through the Sunday school. Today the Sunday school continues to encourage membership and denominational formation. Throughout the twentieth century, approximately 60 to 70 percent of church members in mainline denominations were nurtured through the Sunday school; in evangelical denominations (like the Assemblies of God and Southern Baptist), the percentage was even higher.

Begun in the latter half of the 1700s, Robert Raikes, an English prison reformer, is credited with inventing the Sunday school. Raikes and other philanthropists sought to provide basic education, particularly in reading and religion, for children of the working poor. The hope was that education on Sunday, often extending to morning and afternoon sessions, would provide the children who worked in factories with the basic skills and character to become contributing members of society. This same vision of character reform and basic education fueled the Sunday school in industrial American cities and on the American frontier.

By the 1830s, this social outreach purpose was expanded to include the children of church members. Therefore, through the nineteenth century, Sunday schools were sponsored by both churches and philanthropic agencies for two purposes: (1) mission, the character building and evangelization of unschooled children, and (2) congregational education, the denominational formation of the children of church members. Most Sunday schools in the United States used a uniform lesson curriculum (cooperatively approved in 1872 at a meeting of denominational leaders, the National Sunday School Convention) that consisted of a seven-year pattern of biblical study studying each week the same lesson across age groups. Because the uniform lesson was also used in worldwide church missions, many proclaimed that the same text was studied throughout the world each Sunday.

In the early twentieth century, the educational tasks of the Sunday school were enhanced. Renamed *the church school*, significant teacher training, increased pedagogical sensitivity, additional educational programs for youth and adults, and curricular resources emphasizing religious development were added. Sunday church school instruction grew uniformly throughout Protestant education into the 1920s until a division of churches occurred resulting from conflict over methods of historical biblical scholarship (the fundamentalist/modernist controversy). Two major forms resulted: mainline denominations emphasized a school teaching theology and biblical scholarship while evangelical denominations focused on appropriating the witness of the biblical story.

In the twenty-first century, complemented by family education, youth and children's ministries, NURSERY SCHOOLS, music ministry, and intensive biblical and theological studies of the issues of faith and living, the Sunday school continued as a primary setting of congregational education. Curricula were diverse, produced by denominational and interdenominational publishing houses, ranging from Bible study (including lectionary studies complementing the biblical texts defined for worship) to sophisticated studies addressing ethical issues. Sunday schools provided their members education and spiritual growth, personal support and community, and evangelism and social outreach.

See also: **Youth Ministries.**

BIBLIOGRAPHY

Seymour, Jack L. 1982. *From Sunday School to Church School: Continuities in Protestant Church Education, 1860–1929.* Lanham, MD: University Press of America.

Seymour, Jack L., Robert T. O'Gorman, and Charles R. Foster. 1984. *The Church and the Education of the Public: Refocusing the Task of Religious Education.* Nashville, TN: Abingdon Press.

Wyckoff, D. Campbell, ed. 1986. *Renewing the Sunday School and CCD.* Birmingham, AL: Religious Education Press.

JACK L. SEYMOUR

Surrogacy

Surrogacy involves the gestating of a fetus by one woman, the surrogate mother, with the understanding that the baby she bears will be raised by another person or couple, usually including the man who contributed the sperm. In what is known as traditional surrogacy, the surrogate mother is artificially inseminated, contributing her own egg to the fetus. In gestational surrogacy, the embryo is produced through IN VITRO FERTILIZATION (IVF) and implanted in the surrogate mother.

Surrogacy, while resembling practices familiar to many times and cultures (for example, the practice in traditional Chinese families of a concubine's sons becoming the ritual and legal children of the primary wife in cases where the primary wife did not bear sons), was first legally and socially recognized in the United States in 1980. It has received a great deal of critical attention and debate in the United

States and Europe, especially in cases where surrogacy has been commercialized through payment to the surrogate mother or to a for-profit surrogacy agency. By 2000, commercialized surrogacy had been banned in most of Europe and North America.

Social and religious conservatives have opposed surrogacy because it separates sex, reproduction, and family creation, thereby challenging the "natural" basis for the heterosexual nuclear family. Some feminists have supported surrogacy for the same reason, but debates over surrogacy have made clear fundamental differences among feminist philosophies regarding reproduction. Some feminists have compared surrogacy to slavery and prostitution, arguing that surrogacy is likely to become a means of exploiting poor women's sexual and reproductive capacities by wealthier women and men. Others, emphasizing reproductive choice for women and the right of a woman to control her own body, have argued that just as people are allowed to choose dangerous jobs such as fire fighting, they should be allowed to take on the physical and psychological risks of surrogate mothering, with the caveat that surrogate mothers should retain legal control over their bodies during the pregnancy, and that they should be significantly better paid than they are currently.

Contested surrogacy agreements, debated in court, have served as a focus for contemporary public discussion. In the late 1980s, public attention was riveted on the case of Baby M, in which a "traditional" surrogate mother tried to break her contract and keep the baby she had birthed. Notably, the arguments on both sides of the case, as well as the judges' decisions, were made in terms of upholding the "traditional family." William Stern, the biological father, argued that surrogacy was a legitimate mode of infertility treatment to provide the traditional family he and his wife desperately wanted. Mary Beth Whitehead, the surrogate mother, argued that she had grown unexpectedly attached to Baby M as a natural part of gestating a fetus, and that this natural connection between baby and mother should not be broken. On appeal, the New Jersey Supreme Court ruled that the commercial surrogacy contract was illegal under New Jersey laws prohibiting baby-selling, and treated the case as a custody battle between two parents, Stern and Whitehead. Critics pointed out that Stern received custody based on criteria, such as financial stability, which favored the higher-income party, and that these criteria will almost always be biased against the surrogate mother. Surrogacy is likely to remain controversial as long as biology is regarded as the "natural" basis for social parenting; two-parent, heterosexual, nuclear families are considered the norm and the ideal; and economic and social inequities leave some women particularly vulnerable to exploitation.

See also: **Adoption; Artificial Insemination; Conception and Birth; Egg Donation; Fertility Drugs; Obstetrics and Midwifery.**

BIBLIOGRAPHY

Cohen, Sherrill, and Nadine Taub. 1989. *Reproductive Laws for the 1990s.* Clifton, NJ: Humana Press.

Dolgin, Janet L. 1997. *Defining the Family: Law, Technology, and Reproduction in an Uneasy Age.* New York: New York University Press.

Farquhar, Dion. 1996. *The Other Machine: Discourse and Reproductive Technologies.* New York: Routledge.

Hartouni, Valerie. 1997. *Cultural Conceptions: On Reproductive Technologies and the Remaking of Life.* Minneapolis: University of Minnesota Press.

Holmes, Helen B. 1992. *Issues in Reproductive Technology I: An Anthology.* New York: Garland Publishing.

LARA FREIDENFELDS

Swaddling

The swaddling of infants is a child-care practice that has been known for centuries over most of Europe, Asia, South and North America. The technique is not commonly practiced in tropical areas. In the twenty-first century swaddling is still practiced by various population groups.

Swaddling means to wrap pieces of cloth around an infant's body, before covering the child with bands, called *swaddling bands*, that are swathed over and round the baby's clothes. The swaddled infant may be firmly tied to a cradle board for stiff support or be placed in a type of carry-cot. Among Native American peoples infants normally slept in a vertical position. European swaddled infants slept horizontally.

Several reasons were given for swaddling infants. The babies were kept warm and at the same time the swaddling band gave support to the child's body. All types of swaddling methods more or less constrain the child from moving. One of the most common assumptions was that the baby's limbs were loose-jointed and that sudden movements of the baby could be harmful.

In Europe, the tightly swathed circular method and the apparently looser crisscross method were the two main techniques of swaddling. The physician Soranus from the second century C.E. wrote about the swaddling practice, recommending that infants be tightly swaddled from shoulders to feet. His recommendations were later printed in medical and midwifery books, throughout Europe from the late fifteenth century.

The ENLIGHTENMENT brought a change to swaddling practices in Europe. For example, in 1762 the philosopher JEAN-JACQUES ROUSSEAU argued in *Émile* for the liberation of babies from restrictive swaddling clothing. However, Rousseau's recommendations were followed only by the most wealthy upper class, and more than a century passed before his ideas won general acceptance.

Throughout the nineteenth century, the medical profession recommended a less constraining form of swaddling. In this type of swaddling, often practiced by the middle classes, the infant was able to move its legs and the arms were kept free from restraints, although mothers were still advised to keep the swaddling band to support the baby's back. Baby clothing also became more comfortable.

In the late 1800s several doctors claimed that the swaddling band was unnecessary and in fact was harmful to the child because it inhibited the mobility of the body. Nevertheless, the practice of using swaddling bands around babies' stomachs and backs did not quickly disappear. Most women learned how to take care of babies from their mothers and so traditional ideas and practices were kept among women of the family with little influence from society. In some areas of Europe swaddling bands were used until the early 1930s.

In the twenty-first century, after a long period of resistance against restraining children's natural movements, new thinking has begun to consider possible benefits from swaddling. Swaddling has proved to be comforting, for example, to restless babies need of physical contact.

BIBLIOGRAPHY

Rose, Clare. 1989. *Children's Clothes Since 1750.* New York: Drama Book Publishers.

Rousseau, Jean-Jacques. 1979 [1762]. *Émile, or On Education*, introduction, translation, and notes by Allan Bloom. New York: Basic Books.

KIRSTEN LINDE

T

Tattoos and Piercing

Since the mid- to late 1980s, body modification has moved from the margins of society to the mainstream, especially among adolescents, for whom the three most common forms are piercing, tattooing, and scarification. All three can be found in various cultures, ancient and modern, worldwide. Piercing is the most widespread form of body modification. Historically, tattooing has been more prevalent among peoples with lighter skin and scarification has been more prevalent among peoples with darker skin; however, among adolescents in contemporary American culture, such generalizations cannot be made.

With the exception of piercing female earlobes, these modifications have historically been interpreted as marginal or taboo activities in Western culture, but they were hardly unknown. As Europeans encountered new peoples during the era of colonialism, they brought back practices that had been part of ancient European cultures, but had been dormant for centuries. Piercing was among them, but tracing the history of piercing is difficult, since the European men who were involved in colonialism or foreign travel were more likely to have their glans penis pierced than more visible parts. Tattooing, which was introduced to Europe from Polynesia and Japan, was also a private pleasure among those who wished to remain part of polite society. Scarification, also known as branding, was generally not adopted into Western culture, except as a means of marking slaves and criminals.

Piercing and tattooing remained private vices of the upper classes or were considered public vices of sailors and criminals until the mid-twentieth century. During the 1960s, when American youth were being exposed to free expression and cultural differences via the hippie movement, rock-and-roll, and the Peace Corps, tattooing and piercing moved from private or forced acts and expressions to acts of self-expression and identity, although they were still signs of marginalization. The associations of tattooing and piercing with criminality and SEXUALITY and the Christian notions that the body is a temple and should not be altered were enough to prevent either tattooing or piercing from becoming part of the mainstream during the 1960s and 1970s.

During the 1980s, two things happened that changed the evolution of body modification in Western society: Music Television (MTV) and the AIDS virus. MTV was able to bring the countercultural expressions of rock musicians to younger audiences (especially since many children were unsupervised when they watched television) and to far greater numbers than ever could have attended concerts. The video audience was also able to see the musicians up close, so body modifications were more visible. However, these children were also being told that needles could spread AIDS. This delayed the advent of tattooing and piercing among young MTV viewers. By the late 1980s and early 1990s, however, as AIDS was better understood and tattooing and piercing establishments began advertising the sterility of their equipment, many college-age and teenage individuals began getting tattoos. Within a few years, tattooing became common at high schools and colleges. In "Tattoos and Tattooing, Part I," Kris Sperry estimated that as many as 25 percent of fifteen to twenty-five year olds had tattoos.

Once tattooing became this common, it no longer represented individuality or rebellion, and by the mid to late 1990s was replaced by piercing as the body modification of choice for adolescents. The most prevalent and generally the first piercing is the earlobe. For most of the twentieth century, only girls had their ears pierced. Some parents have their daughters' ears pierced only months after birth. Before the 1980s, pierced ears for men and boys were considered the domain of criminals or homosexuals. However, during the 1980s, there was a radical shift in the sexual connotation of pierced ears for boys; it was considered cool for boys to get their ears pierced, and many did and still do, with their parents' consent or encouragement, at ages as early as five or six

Since the 1980s tattooing—once considered suitable only for sailors and criminals—has moved into the mainstream as a form of body art. Jeff White © 2003.

years. By the 1990s, with so many girls and boys having their ears pierced, one had to pierce other parts of the body in order to set oneself off as different, to gain attention, or to rebel. Body parts that are frequently pierced include the nose, eyebrow, lip, tongue, navel, nipple, penis, and labia.

According to Myrna Armstrong and Cathy McConnell, adolescents often get their first tattoo around age fourteen, although some started as early as ten. Since many states prohibit the tattooing of minors without a parent's consent, and most who get tattoos at this age do so without a parent's knowledge, almost half of adolescent tattooing is done with straight pins or sewing needles and ink, or pens and pencils. Since the 1980s, professional tattooing has shifted in the eyes of many from the sign of a social outsider to a form of body art. The technology and artistry has improved, and the color and definition last much longer. Many who get tattooed state their reasons for doing so as aesthetics, individuality or community, sexuality, or to commemorate a person or event (this is much more common with women).

Scarification is the broad term that describes the deliberate scarring of the body by burning and/or cutting. With scarification, intent is important: if one burns or cuts oneself with the intent to do bodily harm, then it is considered self-mutilation; however, if the motive is aesthetics, commemoration, individuality, rebellion, sexuality, or attention, then it is body modification. The great majority of scarification is self-inflicted, although there are scarification artists who use surgical tools and chemicals. Those who cut or burn themselves generally begin earlier than those who tattoo—all one needs is a razor blade or a cigarette lighter—but many who begin earlier are considered self-mutilators. The visibility or location of the body modification can also signify meaning and intent. Visible modifications can suggest acts of rebellion or cries for attention or help. Body modifications that are covered by clothing tend to be more personal or sexual; they also indicate that the individual is conscious of the social or familial ramifications of such behavior.

See also: **Fashion.**

BIBLIOGRAPHY

Armstrong, Myrna. 1998. "A Clinical Look at Body Piercing." *RN* 61, no. 9: 26–30.

Armstrong, Myrna, and Paul R. Fell. 2000. "Body Art: Regulatory Issues and the NEHA Body Art Model Code." *Journal of Environmental Health* 62, no. 9: 25–30.

Armstrong, Myrna, and Cathy McConnell. 1994. "Tattooing in Adolescents, More Common Than You Think: The Phenomenon and Risks." *Journal of School Nursing* 10, no. 1: 22–29.

Camphausen, Rufus C. 1997. *Return of the Tribal: A Celebration of Body Adornment: Piercing, Tattooing, Scarification, Body Painting.* Rochester, VT: Park Street Press.

Ferguson, Henry. 1999. "Body Piercing." *British Medical Journal* 319: 1627–1629.

Greif, Judith, and Walter Hewitt. 1999. "Tattooing and Body Piercing: Body Art Practices among College Students." *Clinical Nursing Research* 8, no. 4: 368–385.

Hardin, Michael. 1999. "Mar(k)ing the Objected Body: A Reading of Contemporary Female Tattooing." *Fashion Theory: The Journal of Dress, Body, and Culture* 3, no. 1: 81–108.

Houghton, Stephen, and Kevin Durkin. 1995. "Children's and Adolescents' Awareness of the Physical and Mental Health Risks Associated with Tattooing: A Focus Group Study." *Adolescence* 30: 971–988.

Sperry, Kris. 1991. "Tattoos and Tattooing, Part I: History and Methodology." *American Journal of Forensic Medicine and Pathology* 12, no. 4: 313–319.

Waldron, Theresa. 1998. "Tattoos, Body Piercing Are Linked to Psychiatric Disorders in Youth." *Brown University Child and Adolescent Behavior Letter* 14, no. 7: 1–3.

Michael Hardin

Teddy Bear

Teddy bears became popular at the very beginning of the twentieth century. Prior to their introduction, most soft

TOYS for children were rag DOLLS, usually given to both boys and girls to encourage nurturing instincts. The first stuffed animal toys were made in Germany in the latter part of the nineteenth century, generally consisting of felt-covered animals mounted on wheels. As rigid pull toys rather than soft, huggable playthings, this type of stuffed toy virtually disappeared as the teddy bear craze took hold.

The first teddy bears appeared in 1902. According to popular history, American president Theodore Roosevelt went on a hunting trip in Mississippi in November 1902 as a break from his ongoing efforts to resolve a border dispute between that state and Louisiana. Most versions of the story agree that "Teddy" refused to shoot a bear that was captured for him. Roosevelt had already achieved fame as both an enthusiastic sportsman and conservationist. The episode inspired a cartoon by Clifford Berryman, entitled "Drawing the Line at Mississippi," published in the *Washington Post.* Berryman continued to draw the scene (with different versions of the trapped bear) for several years after.

Shortly after the publication of the first cartoon, Russian immigrant Morris Michtom displayed a plush bear sewn by his wife Rose in the window of their Brooklyn novelty and stationery store with the label "Teddy's Bear." The couple wrote to President Roosevelt asking for permission to use his name, which was readily granted. The toy was immediately successful, leading to the establishment of the Ideal Novelty and Toy Company by the Michtoms in 1903.

At the same time, a German company was also developing designs for a string-jointed bear. Margarete Steiff first began making stuffed felt toy animals in 1880, expanding her business in 1893. In 1902 her nephew Richard Steiff, who was an artist, began working on a plush bear prototype. Steiff based his designs on drawings made at the local zoo. The final design was successfully distributed through wholesalers George Borgfeldt and Company of New York in early 1903.

In 1906 the American toy trade journal *Playthings* shortened "Teddy's Bear" to "teddy bear," and the phrase was quickly adopted by manufacturers. By 1913, several American companies were producing teddy bears, competing with German manufacturers. During World War I, German imports to Great Britain were banned, leading to the creation of the British stuffed toy industry, spurred on by the success of the teddy bear. France entered the market immediately following the war.

The teddy bear became one of the most popular children's toys, as well as the center of a thriving collectibles market fueled primarily by adults. Companies such as the American Vermont Teddy Bear Company or Margarete Steiff GmbH (still in business at the beginning of the twenty-first century) began creating character bears specifically aimed at adult collectors. In addition, stuffed toys in general became enormously popular with both children and adults, as confirmed by the Beanie Baby craze in the 1990s.

Teddy bears form part of the collections of the Bethnal Green Museum of Childhood, in London, England, and the Margaret Woodbury Strong Museum in Rochester, New York, the finest publicly held collections of toys in the world.

See also: **Indoor Games; Play.**

BIBLIOGRAPHY

Cockrill, Pauline. 1993. *The Teddy Bear Encyclopedia.* London: Dorling Kindersley.

SHIRA SILVERMAN

Teenage Mothers in the United States

It is difficult to define exactly what constitutes teenage motherhood because of inconsistencies in defining its age limits, but studies focusing on the causes and consequences of teen motherhood typically include young women fifteen to nineteen years old. Although births occur among adolescents younger than fifteen, they are often included only in aggregate national statistics. Childbearing among children under age fifteen is considered socially problematic in almost all industrial cultures. Studies describing the trends, patterns, and prevalence of teen motherhood continue to show that the United States has the highest teen birthrates of all industrialized countries and that these patterns have fluctuated over time, declined in the 1960s and 1970s, rose rapidly between the mid-1980s and early 1990s, and decreased substantially in 1999–2000, reflecting the lowest rate observed since 1987 for those fifteen to nineteen years old, and the lowest in three decades for those ten to fourteen years old. Despite these trends, approximately four in ten U.S. girls get pregnant at least once in their teens, 20 percent of teen births are repeated pregnancies, and approximately 18 percent of African Americans, 14 percent of Hispanics, and 7 percent of whites are teen mothers (as Susie Hoffman and Velma M. Murry have pointed out, not all pregnancies result in parenthood).

Risk factors for teen pregnancy include living in southern rural areas, having low educational expectations and school performance, and having a lack of optimism about the future. Additional risk factors include living in a state with high poverty and male incarceration rates or with a gender ratio imbalance, residing in a single-parent family and in a disorganized or dangerous neighborhood, having a lower family income and lower levels of parental education. Other issues include a desire for and a romanticization of motherhood, adolescent mental health (depression and low self-esteem), and poor family relationships that increase reliance on boyfriends and peers for emotional support. Other contributing factors include having older sexually active siblings, having pregnant or parenting teenage sisters, associating with friends who have children, being intimately involved with older males, and sexual victimization. Biological factors, such as androgen hormone levels, the timing of PUBERTY, and the age of MENARCHE among mothers, daughters, and sisters, have been associated with elevated pregnancy risk. Risk factors for repeated pregnancies include depressive symptoms, low self-esteem, poor school performance, and impaired parenting practices.

Teenage motherhood places both the young mother and her child at risk for various problems, including low educational attainment, high unemployment, greater dependency on welfare, and lower levels of psychological functioning for mothers. Family social support and educational attainment differentiate teen mothers who fare well from those who do not. Infants born to teenage parents have greater incidences of low birth weight and learning problems. The desire to be good mothers is compromised by poor parenting skills, fewer positive verbal and emotional interactions with the child, and unrealistic expectations. Conversely, teen parents' parenting behavior is enhanced by the presence of a grandmother in the home when the mother–grandmother relationship is supportive and affectionate. Poor birth outcomes are also moderated by the mother's age: children born to adolescents fifteen years old and younger are at greater risk than those whose mothers are sixteen to nineteen years old. Children's development is also enhanced when mothers have more education, stable employment status, fewer additional children in the household, live in a more advantaged community, and reside with an additional adult, including a male partner.

Stanley Henshaw reports that 22 percent of all teen pregnancies and 44 percent of births among fifteen to nineteen year olds were intended. Factors that encourage adolescents to become mothers are as complex as those that influence adult women's decisions to have a child. Most adolescents who "want" a child lack close fulfilling personal relationships and report that they desire a child for stability, as a way of setting a life course, and to gain maturity. According to Patricia East and Marianne Felice, adolescents who plan pregnancies are different from those whose pregnancies are unplanned. Among those reporting planned pregnancies, 28 percent of black teens, 45 percent of white teens, and 63 percent of Hispanic teens were older (average 17.4 years), more likely to have an ongoing relationship with their child's father, and were in better financial situations two years after the birth.

Taken together, these findings suggest that being a teen mother does not automatically translate into negative outcomes and that some teens purposefully become mothers. The challenge for researchers and practitioners is to design approaches for understanding more about those conditions that foster positive outcomes for the teen and her child, despite age at first birth, and to consider contextual processes that identify ways to dissuade early parenting and ways in which protective factors foster positive outcomes for those who do become parents.

Globally, teenage women are less likely to give birth than their counterparts 20 years ago, but the rates are still high and many of those pregnancies are unwanted. In the United States, despite the decrease in the number of babies born to teenagers, the rate still continues to be more than four times that of many industrialized nations. According to Stephanie Ventura and her colleagues, the United States had 48.7 births per 1,000 women aged fifteen to nineteen, compared to less than 10 births per 1,000 of the same cohort in Denmark, Finland, France, Germany, Italy, Japan, the Netherlands, Spain, Sweden, and Switzerland. Reasons for the difference are unclear. Jacqueline Darroch and colleagues, as well as Douglas Kirby, have suggested that access to effective contraceptives and early exposure to comprehensive sexual health information are lower in the United States than in other developed countries.

See also: **Adolescence and Youth; Teen Pregnancy; Sexuality.**

BIBLIOGRAPHY

Alan Guttmacher Institute. 1981. *Teenage Pregnancy: The Problem That Hasn't Gone Away.* New York: Alan Guttmacher Institute

Brooks-Gunn, Jeanne, and Lindsay Chase-Lansdale. 1995. "Adolescent Parenthood." In *Handbook of Parenting: Vol 3. Status and Social Conditions of Parenting*, ed. Marc H. Bornstein. Mahwah, NJ: Erlbaum.

Darroch, Jacqueline E., Susheela Singh, and Jennifer J. Frost. 2001. "Differences in Teenage Pregnancy Rates among Five Developed Countries: The Roles of Sexual Activity and Contraceptive Use." *Family Planning Perspectives* 33: 6.

East, Patricia L., and Marianne E. Felice. 1996. *Adolescent Pregnancy and Parenting: Findings from a Racially Diverse Sample.* Mahwah, NJ: Erlbaum.

Henshaw, Stanley K. 1998. "Unintended Pregnancy in the United States." *Family Planning Perspectives* 30: 24–29.

Hoffmann, Susie D. 1998. "Teenage Childbearing Is Not So Bad After All . . . or Is It? A Review of the New Literature." *Family Planning Perspectives* 30: 236–243.

Hoyert, Donna L., Mary Anne Freedman, Donna M. Strobino, and Bernard Guyer. 2001. "Annual Summary of Vital Statistics: 2000." *Pediatrics* 6: 1241–1256.

Kirby, Douglas. 2001. *Emerging Answers: Research Findings on Programs to Reduce Teen Pregnancy.* Washington, DC: National Campaign to Prevent Teen Pregnancy.

Lawson, Annette, and Deborah L. Rhode. 1993. "Introduction to Adolescent Pregnancy." In *The Politics of Pregnancy: Adolescent Sexuality and Public Policy*, ed. Annette Lawson and Deborah L. Rhode. New Haven, CT: Yale University Press.

VELMA MCBRIDE MURRY
DIONNE P. STEPHENS

Teenagers

In 1900 teenagers did not exist. There were young people in their teens, but there was no culture or institution that united them or fostered peer group development on a societal scale. While some worked at home, on family farms, or in factories or offices, others attended school. Still more married or prepared for marriage. One hundred years later, in 2000, teenagers were impossible to avoid. There were more teens than ever before and their cultural presence was undeniable. They existed not only as high school students, but as highly sought consumers, carefully watched as trendsetters in FASHION, music, and MOVIES.

In the public imagination teenagers first appeared after World War II, complete with distinctive dress, habits, and culture. The period before 1950, however, proved crucial for the formation of teenagers in the United States. After 1900 reformers, educators, and legislators began to separate teens from adults and children. The legal system created JUVENILE COURTS. State and federal governments legislated minimum age requirements for sexual consent, marriage, school attendance, and work, and later for voting, driving, and drinking alcohol. Often inconsistent, some legislation further divided teens by gender. Girls, for example, could marry younger than boys, but could not legally consent to sexual activity until later.

The dramatic rise in HIGH SCHOOL attendance was the single most important factor in creating teenage culture. High school, based on biological age, reshaped the experiences of thirteen- to eighteen-year-olds. Between 1910 and 1930, enrollment in secondary schools increased almost 400 percent. The proportion of fourteen- to-seventeen-year-olds in high school increased from 10.6 percent in 1901 to 51.1 percent in 1930 and 71.3 percent in 1940. Graduation rates remained low but still rose from 29.0 percent in 1930 to 50.8 percent in 1940. The number of African-American teens in high school was lower, but also rose at a steady rate and by the early 1950s, more than 80 percent of African Americans aged fourteen to seventeen were enrolled in school.

As enrollment grew, the student body changed. No longer an elite institution, students increasingly came from all socioeconomic, ethnic, and racial groups. Educators redesigned rapidly expanding schools to foster responsible citizens, promote social order, and, during the Depression, to keep teens out of the labor market. High schools also promoted unsupervised peer interaction.

During the 1920s, 1930s, and 1940s, some manufacturers, marketers, and retailers also began to recognize high schoolers, especially girls, as consumers with purchasing power and style preferences. Simultaneously, teenagers began to develop a "teenage" identity and recognize their collective strength. Social scientists and parents also engaged in the extensive dialogue over the nature of ADOLESCENCE, high school, and the growing concept *teenager*. Scholarly work, popular advice, and parental strategies emerged alongside the developing high school culture and teen CONSUMER CULTURE. Gendered differences remained—literature on boys emphasized education, work, and rebellion, whereas literature on girls addressed behavior, appearance, and relationships. Media also played an important role, often defining *teenager* as female. Media served to promote teenage trends by offering publicity and a national means for reaching other teens. But by the early 1940s, the BOBBY SOXER stereotype dominated, which negatively portrayed teenage girls as mindless worshipers of celebrities and adolescents fads.

Recognized as separate from the adolescent, the teenager more closely related to high school culture. Use of the words *teen, teener, teen-age*, and even *teenager* first appeared in the 1920s and 1930s. They referred to thirteen- to eighteen-year-olds, increasingly conceptualized as a distinct cohort in media, popular literature, and advertisements. As teenage culture emerged, teens used mass-produced commodities to imitate adults, but they also used them to create fads and to define themselves as teenagers.

See also: **Consumer Culture; Youth Culture.**

BIBLIOGRAPHY

Austin, Joe, and Michael Nevin Willard. 1998. *Generations of Youth: Youth Cultures and History in Twentieth-Century America.* New York: New York University Press.

Inness, Sherrie, ed. 1998. *Delinquents and Debutantes: Twentieth-Century American Girls' Cultures.* New York: New York University Press.

Palladino, Grace. 1996. *Teenagers: An American History.* New York: Basic.

Schrum, Kelly. 2004. *Some Wore Bobby Sox: The Emergence of Teenage Girls' Culture, 1920–1945.* New York: Palgrave Macmillan.

KELLY SCHRUM

Teen Drinking

Teen drinking is not a new phenomenon in the United States, but the practice has received particular attention since the 1970s.

Alcoholic beverages such as cider were a standard part of the diet of American colonists, even for children and sometimes for babies. Taverns welcomed teen boys, whose fathers brought them there as a RITE OF PASSAGE. Local ordinances occasionally limited the drinking of alcohol in public establishments for youths under sixteen years old, but these cases were uncommon and did not affect drinking at home. Alcohol consumption remained high in the early Republic, with adults over fifteen drinking the equivalent of six to seven gallons of absolute alcohol per year. College students, with whom alcohol was always popular, contributed to the high levels of drinking.

During the late nineteenth and early twentieth centuries, child-saving reformers expressed concern at the availability of alcohol to young people in taverns. In 1877, the SOCIETY

FOR THE PREVENTION OF CRUELTY TO CHILDREN helped to enact a law that excluded children from saloons and dance halls; however children selling newspapers and peddling other items frequently gathered outside saloons to hawk their wares, and others hauled buckets of beer from saloons to factories at lunchtime for workingmen. Furthermore, some boys drank in saloons courtesy of bartenders who hoped that those they treated would become loyal customers in adulthood.

Also at this time, members of the Woman's Christian Temperance Union and the Anti-Saloon League spread the message of "scientific temperance" to children through public schools, Sunday schools, and youth temperance clubs, but they did not focus much attention on the drinking habits of youths. Some laws during this period restricted the use of alcohol by young people, but parents could allow them to drink alcohol at home or even in commercial establishments, and sellers of alcohol, not young drinkers themselves, were responsible for violations.

The onset of Prohibition in January 1920 failed to put an end to drinking in the United States. College students, particularly men in fraternities, flouted university regulations and further popularized the drinking of alcohol; many adults worried that high-school fraternities, too, promoted drinking. In 1930, about two-thirds of college students were drinkers, and many adults bemoaned the increase in drinking by young women. Foes of Prohibition argued that the restriction on alcohol would result in increasing automobile accidents as young people sought out places to drink, while supporters of the Eighteenth Amendment claimed that youth drinking was decreasing.

With the end of Prohibition in April 1933, individual states began setting the drinking age, often at twenty-one, though sometimes at eighteen for the purchase of beer. Anti-alcohol education remained standard in the public schools. Nevertheless, young people continued drinking alcohol. A study of drinking habits among college students published through the Yale Center of Alcohol Studies in 1953 found that 79 percent of male drinkers and 65 percent of female drinkers had had their first drink before starting college, and many had already begun drinking regularly. Furthermore, 45 percent of men and 40 percent of women reported having tasted alcohol before they were eleven years old. Studies such as this one failed to raise concerns about teen drinking.

Members of the BABY BOOM GENERATION lobbied for the right to drink alcohol (and to vote) at the age of eighteen rather than twenty-one; by 1975 twenty-eight states had lowered the legal drinking age, most to eighteen. However this new freedom was short-lived, as reports of increased rates of alcohol-related accidents and adolescent alcohol abuse gained publicity, and states quickly raised the drinking age to twenty-one again. A 1984 law made this trend universal by giving federal highway funds only to states that had, by 1986, adopted a legal drinking age of twenty-one.

The drinking age of twenty-one persists in the United States, but people under twenty-one drink between 11 and 25 percent of all alcoholic beverages in the United States. Furthermore, a study by Columbia University's National Center on Addiction and Substance Abuse found that 36 percent of the class of 1999 began drinking by eighth grade, compared to 27 percent of the high school class of 1975. It also appears that young males and females begin drinking at about the same time. Opponents of current laws argue that youths in countries with lower minimum drinking ages learn how to handle alcohol and tend not to abuse it. On the other hand, recent studies in the United States show a connection between teen drinking and sexual activity, high rates of fatalities in drunk driving accidents, possible neurological damage from binge drinking, and increased rates of alcoholism in later life.

Legal drinking ages in Europe vary by country, ranging from sixteen in Spain and the Netherlands, to eighteen in the United Kingdom and Poland, to twenty in Iceland. However, in western Europe, most teens begin drinking at age fifteen or sixteen, often in peer groups, with boys drinking more than girls. Approximately 90 percent of residents of the United Kingdom are drinkers by age seventeen.

See also: **Adolescence and Youth; Drugs; Law, Children and the; Smoking.**

BIBLIOGRAPHY

Mendelson, Jack H., and Nancy K. Mello. 1985. *Alcohol, Use and Abuse in America.* Boston: Little, Brown.

Mosher, James F. 1980. "The History of Youthful-Drinking Laws: Implications for Current Policy." In *Minimum-Drinking-Age Laws: An Evaluation,* ed. Henry Wechsler. Lexington, MA: Lexington Books.

Murdock, Catherine Gilbert. 1998. *Domesticating Drink: Women, Men, and Alcohol in America, 1870–1940.* Baltimore: Johns Hopkins University Press.

National Center on Addiction and Substance Abuse at Columbia University. 1993. *Teen Tipplers: America's Underage Drinking Epidemic.* New York: National Center on Addiction and Substance Abuse at Columbia University.

Straus, Robert, Selden Daskam Bacon, and Yale Center of Alcohol Studies. 1953. *Drinking in College.* New Haven, CT: Yale University Press.

Torr, James D. 2002. *Teens and Alcohol.* San Diego, CA: Greenhaven Press.

ELLEN L. BERG

Teen Magazines

At the turn of the twenty-first century, TEENAGERS could choose from a multitude of magazines that covered the latest teen FASHIONS, music, SPORTS, MOVIES, and advice. Teens, especially teenage girls, were a well-established, lucrative magazine audience—creating and consuming teen-focused products. But this was not always the case. While magazines for children began in the nineteenth century, the first publications to speak to teenagers did not emerge until the twentieth century.

American Girl and *Everygirls*, the official magazines of the GIRL SCOUTS and the Camp Fire Girls, respectively, first addressed girls directly in the 1920s. These magazines, however, only reached organization members. In the late 1920s, *Ladies' Home Journal* introduced "The Sub-Deb, a Page for Girls" with beauty and domestic advice. By 1931, the tone was distinctly "young" and by 1938, teen slang appeared.

Teenage interest in a 1941 PARENTS MAGAZINE column on high school fashion trends, called "Tricks for Teens," inspired *Calling All Girls*, the first general teenage magazine. It offered comics, stories, and advice, but attracted preteen readers rather than the fashion-conscious high school girls of growing interest to advertisers.

Seventeen magazine debuted in September 1944 with broader teen appeal. Circulation exceeded one million copies by February 1947 and two and a half million by July 1949. Despite the predominantly white, middle-class audience, *Seventeen* reached many more teens than *Calling All Girls* or sub-deb columns. *Seventeen* offered a similar recipe of young fashions, beauty, entertainment, and advice, but girls appreciated efforts to make them better teenagers rather than kids or adults, including articles on World War II and the importance of voting.

Boys were also active magazine readers. Editors claimed that boys read girls' magazines and requested advice on fads. Most teenage boys, however, primarily read general interest magazines such as *Life*, and mechanical or sports magazines. By the 1950s, a growing number of boys read automobile magazines such as *Hot Rod*. No such magazine, however, enjoyed *Seventeen*'s enormous success with teenage readers and advertisers.

In the 1950s, gossip magazines, such as *Teen Parade* and *Hep Cats*, sought working-class readers while *Seventeen* emphasized fashion, dating, and early marriage. In the 1960s and 1970s, teen magazines reflected some feminist ideas, but these mostly faded in the 1980s. Newcomers like *Sassy* gained readers in the 1980s, with explicit articles on sex.

Teenage magazines emerged as teens began to rely on commercial popular culture for guidance and entertainment shifted again as teens turned to peers rather than adults. The proliferation of zines, noncommercial girls' magazines, and virtual magazines in the 1990s ensured that many voices speak to and for teenage girls. In addition to commercial teen websites, websites created by girls offered articles, fashion advice, and discussion forums and relied on reader input. As with magazines, sites for teenage boys remained subject specific rather than "teen" centered.

See also: **Adolescence and Youth; Advertising; Consumer Culture; Youth Culture.**

BIBLIOGRAPHY

Duncombe, Stephen. 1998. "Let's All Be Alienated Together: Zines and the Making of Underground Community." In *Generations of Youth: Youth Cultures and History in Twentieth-Century America,* ed. Joe Austin and Michael Nevin Willard. New York: New York University Press.

Palladino, Grace. 1996. *Teenagers: An American History.* New York: Basic Books.

Schrum, Kelly. 1998. "'Teena Means Business': Teenage Girls' Culture and Seventeen Magazine, 1944–1950." In *Delinquents and Debutantes: Twentieth-Century American Girls' Cultures,* ed. Sherrie A. Inness. New York: New York University Press.

Schrum, Kelly. 2004. *Some Wore Bobby Sox: The Emergence of Teenage Girls' Culture, 1920–1945.* New York: Palgrave Macmillan.

KELLY SCHRUM

Teen Pregnancy

Using adolescent birth rates to measure teen pregnancy, adolescent parenthood has been a fairly common experience throughout American history. (It is nearly impossible to gain an accurate measure of teen pregnancy rates over time, because not all pregnancies result in births.) The most recent American teen birth rate of approximately 51.1 births per 1,000 adolescent females is consistent with historical trends and matches the 1920 figure. Nonetheless, since the 1970s, American politicians, policy makers, and social critics have condemned the perceived "epidemic of teenage pregnancy." This label reveals that critics have little knowledge about the incidence of teen pregnancy and parenthood in America's past.

From colonial times through the late nineteenth century, the vast majority of Americans had chosen to marry and have children by their early to mid-twenties. Marriage and parenthood was a rational choice for people living in a society dependent on family production. Race, ethnicity, class, and region could influence individual circumstances, with rural areas experiencing the lowest age at marriage. Few people worried about teen pregnancy as long as the expecting mother married before giving birth. There was strong social pressure to marry before becoming a parent, but the high number of babies born less than nine months after marriage ceremonies shows that many young couples taking their marriage vows were already expecting a child. State codes outlining minimum-age-at-marriage laws followed English common law that permitted girls as young as twelve to marry without parental consent.

The ability to bear children generally established the move from childhood to adulthood for most females. The capacity to do physical labor marked the change for boys from childhood dependence to a state of semi-dependence known as youth. For males, marriage marked full adult independence and its associated responsibilities. Physical capacities and life circumstance set the dividing line between childhood and adulthood, not age. Poor diet and common childhood illnesses delayed physical maturity for many. The majority of girls did not reach menarche (and their ability to have children) until sixteen or seventeen years of age. Many boys assumed strenuous jobs early in their ADOLESCENCE, but few could earn enough to support a family until their early to mid-twenties. This combination of biological, social, and economic factors limited pregnancy and parenthood for most teens.

By 1900, things began to change. The move to an industrial economy had radically changed everyday life for many Americans. Improved health conditions and better economic opportunities for young males in the Progressive Era encouraged a growing number of couples to marry and become parents at younger ages, in their teens and early twenties. Interestingly, this trend toward early marriage and parenthood ran counter to the social definition of adolescence that had become increasingly popular among urban middle-class families. Since the 1820s, a growing number of middle-class parents had been sending their adolescent children to HIGH SCHOOLS. Advocates of the urban-middle-class-family ideal maintained that adolescence was a distinct period of life separate from adult responsibilities. They encouraged parents to leave their teenaged children in school instead of sending them to work or allowing them to marry.

In 1904, G. STANLEY HALL formally defined the broad psychological and physiological parameters of modern adolescence in his two volume work, *Adolescence: Its Psychology and Its Relations to Physiology, Anthropology, Sociology, Sex, Crime, Religion, and Education.* Hall concluded that the teen years were a time of unavoidable physiological and psychological turmoil. While it was normal for teens to think about sex, Hall cautioned that adolescents were too immature, both physically and psychologically, to engage in sexual intercourse or become parents.

Many child welfare reformers agreed. New child labor laws, compulsory education legislation, the establishment of juvenile courts, efforts to control teen sexuality, and a myriad of other age-specific policies reflected new social attitudes defining modern adolescence. A growing number of teens, however, resisted the new restrictions on their autonomy. In 1900, less than 1 percent of males and 11 percent of females fourteen through nineteen years of age were ever married. During the next six decades the age of first marriage and subsequent parenthood continued to fall for both males and females. By 1950, the median age at first marriage was down to 22.8 for males and 20.3 for females. In the 1930s the Great Depression temporarily slowed the trend, but the postwar years saw a dramatic rise in early marriage and teen pregnancy rates. The 1940s, 1950s, and 1960s included the twentieth century's highest teen birth rates (respectively 79.5, 91.0, and 69.7 per thousand). By 1960, nearly one-third of American females had their first child before reaching age twenty.

The 1970s, 1980s, and 1990s reversed this trend. In the face of rising divorce rates, more college graduates, and reliable birth control, growing numbers of young people chose to delay marriage or not to marry at all. At the same time, the average age of menarche dropped to twelve, with some girls as young as eight experiencing menstruation. Many Americans ignored the rising age of marriage, and instead focused on changes in the incidence of unwed motherhood. By the 1990s, almost 25 percent of all babies were born to unmarried women. Teen mothers gave birth to only one-third of these infants, but the fact that black and Hispanic teens were more likely to have children outside of marriage than their white counterparts gained public attention. Furthermore, before 1970 the majority of unwed mothers gave up their babies for adoption. By the 1990s, nine of every ten teen mothers chose to keep their children and, at least for the immediate future, remain unmarried.

After 1970, rising concerns about teen pregnancy and parenthood became mixed with a variety of crucial social, economic, and political shifts. A new wave of immigration spurred by the 1965 Immigration Act increased American diversity. Changes in the nation's racial policies and practices grounded in the civil rights movement became part of federal law. Legal debates over access to abortion often centered on teens. Economic shifts fostered by the move from an industrial to a service- and information-based economy created new social problems. To many critics, unmarried teen mothers became symbols of American immorality and the growing Aid to Families with Dependent Children (AFDC) welfare program. As Hall had theorized decades earlier, teen pregnancy and parenthood, both inside and outside of marriage, seemed unacceptable and a modern social problem.

In 1996, Congress passed the Personal Responsibility and Work Opportunity Reconciliation Act. This new law discontinued AFDC, included incentives for using implanted birth control, and placed restrictions on federal assistance to unwed teen mothers. To supporters, one of the keys to "changing welfare as we know it" was to end federal assistance to unwed teen mothers. Teen birth rates have continued to decline, but the reasons are not clear. It appears that young people, as they have done throughout American history, are making choices about parenthood for themselves.

See also: **Adoption in the United States; Aid to Dependent Children; Dependent Children; Menarche; Parenting; Sexuality; Teenage Mothers in the United States.**

BIBLIOGRAPHY

Gordon, Linda. 1994. *Pitied but Not Entitled: Single Mothers and the History of Welfare.* New York: Free Press.

Growing up with television, c. 1950s. Worries about the effects of television viewing on young children have been around since the birth of television itself. © H. Armstrong Roberts/CORBIS.

Hall, G. Stanley. 1922 [1904]. *Adolescence: Its Psychology and Its Relations to Physiology, Anthropology, Sociology, Sex, Crime, Religion, and Education.* 2 vols. New York: Appleton.

Lindenmeyer, Kriste. 2002. "For Adults Only: The Anti-Child Marriage Campaign and Its Legacy." In *Politics and Progress: American Society and the State since 1865*, ed. Andrew Kersten and Kriste Lindenmeyer. Westport, CT: Praeger.

Luker, Kristin. 1996. *Dubious Conceptions: The Politics of Teen Pregnancy.* Cambridge, MA: Harvard University Press.

Vinovskis, Maris A. 1988. *An "Epidemic" of Adolescent Pregnancy? Some Historical and Policy Considerations.* New York: Oxford University Press.

KRISTE LINDENMEYER

Television

Television was gradually introduced in the United States and Western Europe after World War II, although the medium as such was developed before the war. By the end of the 1950s most countries in the Western hemisphere had access to one or more television channels and in the 1970s the majority of the households were equipped with at least one television set. At the end of the 1990s television was still the most pervasive medium in European households: about 90 percent of children had access to a television in their home. The dissemination of television was also rapid in the Third World and by the end of the twentieth century most people, at least in urban electrified areas, had a set.

Television gradually replaced RADIO as the medium most used by children; primarily attracting children in the younger ages (up to the teenage years). The amount of television viewing is sensitive to the output of children's programs as well as the output of entertainment programs. Thus, children have increased their viewing time as a consequence of more national channels as well as the deregulation of the television market, which have led to an increased output of globally distributed commercial children's programs, such as animated cartoons and action adventure series. Time spent with television varies between different countries, depending on differences in cultural pattern as well as differences in production. By the 2000s, the average child viewer in the United States watched about three to four hours of television a day, whereas the European viewer watched about three hours, with some national variations.

Television in Europe and the United States has changed its function from the early days, when it was a medium gathering the family in the living room, to a more privatized and individual activity, as many children today have their own television set in the bedroom.

Television's Impact

Children's fascination with television has concerned researchers, parents, educators, and other groups dealing with children's well-being ever since the medium was introduced. Much of the public debate has been focused on the effects of media violence, which has resulted in much scrutiny by psychologists and sociologists and has given rise to a massive body of research. But the debate and research has also dealt with whether television viewing in itself is a passive activity, and sometimes television has been compared to a drug, which has a tranquilizing or seducing effect on the viewer. Television has also been blamed for causing negative effects on reading skills and some claim that too much television use makes children stupid. Other worries have concerned children's physical condition, such as too little exercise or that radiation from the screen may affect the brain or eyes. Television viewing has also been linked to obesity in children.

In the history of media effects, a "direct effects era" was dominant for a long period of time. The reception of television was viewed in a linear and one-dimensional manner. Later, researchers realized that children did not react uniformly to the same program, but there were intervening variables such as age, gender, predispositions, perceptions, social environment, past experience, and parental influence. However, even if years of research has stressed that there are a number of so-called intervening variables, the "direct effects model" has been very influential in the public debate about children and television.

When research was done in more realistic settings, rather than in the laboratory, the effects of exposure to television was attenuated and long-term effects were particularly weak or even nonexistent. Long-term research conducted both in the United States and in Europe came to the conclusion that television violence is but one of a number of factors responsible for violent aggressive behavior among young people. Aggressive behavior is mainly related to other factors than exposure to television violence, such as personality or sociocultural variables, for example, family conditions, school, and peers. However, researchers also point to the fact that the frequent occurrence of screen violence reinforces the idea of violence as a solution of problems. The GLOBALIZATION of the television market contributed to increased production of violent programming and to the worldwide dissemination of such programs (e.g., animated cartoons and action adventures).

Learning and the Social Benefits of Television

At the end of the 1960s and the beginning of 1970s there was a belief that television could be used for promoting learning and social behavior. The medium was deliberately used for preschool learning, often called *pro-social learning*, and com-

pensatory education in the United States, in Europe, and in some countries in the Third World, for example, in the Latin American countries of Mexico and Brazil. Producers, educators, and researchers started investigating the possibility of using television to reach out to underprivileged groups in society. In the United States, the educational program *Sesame Street* was developed and became a success also in other countries, where the program sometimes was adjusted to the domestic child audience. For example, Brazil, Germany, Israel, and Spain developed their own versions of *Sesame Street*. In Scandinavia, the domestic public service companies expressed a certain resistance against *Sesame Street*, because of the commercial format. However, in Sweden there was a wave of program series inspired by *Sesame Street*, teaching elementary skills in reading, concept formation as well as promoting pro-social behavior, such as solving conflicts without violence or strengthening children's self-confidence.

Regulation and Public Service

The television market has been more regulated in most European countries than it is in the United States. As a rule, the European broadcasting landscapes are organized as dual systems with public service broadcasters as a central pillar of the broadcasting system, rather than just a supplement to commercial broadcasting. In Northern Europe, children's programs have a particular position and status. Programs for children are offered on a regular basis. For example, in Sweden, about ten percent of the output on public service television was aimed at children and young people by the 2000s. About half of this output was domestic productions, with programs in a variety of genres: fictional dramas, sports, news, documentaries, magazine programs. However, deregulation has been both a challenge and a threat against public service television. The general tendency in Europe is weakened public service television, with fewer investments in domestic children's programs in favor of cheap imports. In recent years public broadcasters have been facing increasing competition by global (American) commercial children's channels like Cartoon Network, The DISNEY Channel, Nickelodeon, and Fox Kids Network. The situation in many countries in the Third World is such that the child audience has no other choice than the output from these channels.

Children's Participation

During the 1950s there was a discussion about whether children should participate in programs or not. In England, it was legislated that children were not allowed to participate or to appear as actors. The legislation originated from the days when CHILD LABOR was a common phenomenon in society. Children's programs were mainly performed by adults, as well as by various kinds of puppets, which acted as children, for example the puppet Andy Pandy from the BBC's *Watch with Mother*, one of the very first children's programs. In Sweden, on the contrary, it was stated from the start of broadcasting that children were welcomed to participate in programs. One of the very first television programs for children exhibited a mother with all her children in the studio. Eventually, children came to be heard and seen in children's programs more generally. But the image of the child is highly related to cultural patterns. For example, there are differences between how children in France are portrayed, where there is a preference for well dressed and proper children, as compared to children in Scandinavia, where the idea of the "natural" child is advocated. However, in the output as a whole, children are underrepresented both in the United States and in Europe. Children are rarely addressed directly, except in advertisements, as children do not have prominent roles in programs aimed for an adult audience. When young people are portrayed, they are often represented as a problem and a threat. Another recurrent picture is the good, innocent and sweet child, which reaches its extreme in advertising.

Media Education

The issue of children and the media (particularly television) has also been a target for the United Nations since the UN CONVENTION ON THE RIGHTS OF THE CHILD, became valid in 1989. One issue of concern has been to increase children's participation in terms of media education. In the United States and in Europe, media education has been inserted into the school curriculum to varying extents. The implementation of media education has been a slow process, often met with resistance from defenders of established school ideals. Wider access to digital video cameras for domestic use as well as computer editing programs makes it easier for children themselves to produce their own programs, which strengthens their positions and makes their voices heard more easily. However, the unequal distribution of technological resources in the world, makes such a scenario realistic only in more economically developed nations.

See also: **Consumer Culture; Media, Childhood and the.**

BIBLIOGRAPHY

Buckingham, David. 2000. *After the Death of Childhood: Growing Up in the Age of Electronic Media.* London: Polity Press.

Lesser, Gerald. 1974. *Children and Television: Lessons from Sesame Street.* New York: Random House.

Livingstone, Sonia, and Moira Bovill, eds. 2001. *Children and Their Changing Media Environment: A European Comparative Study.* London: Lawrence Erlbaum.

Postman, Neil. 1982. *The Disappearance of Childhood.* New York: Delacorte Press.

Rydin, Ingegerd. 2000. "Children's TV Programs on the Global Market." *News from the UNESCO International Clearinghouse on Children and Violence on the Screen.* 1: 17–20.

Von Feilitzen, Cecilia, and Ulla Carlsson, eds. 1998. *Children and Media Violence: Yearbook from the UNESCO International Clearinghouse on Children and Violence on the Screen.* Gothenburg: The UNESCO International Clearinghouse on Children and Violence on the Screen.

Von Feilitzen, Cecilia, and Ulla Carlsson, eds. 1999. *Children and Media: Image, Education, Participation.* Gothenburg: The UNESCO International Clearinghouse on Children and Violence on the Screen.

Wartella, Ellen, and Byron Reeves. 1985. "Historical Trends in Research on Children and the Media: 1900–1960." *Journal of Communication* 35, no. 2: 118–133.

Winn, Marie 1977. *The Plug-in-Drug.* New York: The Viking Press.

INGEGERD RYDIN

Temple, Shirley (b. 1928)

In the annals of movie history, no actor or actress represents the phenomenon of child stardom better than Shirley Temple. "Discovered" by Hollywood at the age of six, Temple achieved extraordinary fame during the 1930s and became, for a decade, the world's most celebrated child. When Temple became a TEENAGER, however, her career declined and by her sixteenth birthday she had fallen out of public favor. Her phenomenal rise and sudden fall, amply documented in the magazines and tabloids of the period, illustrated to Americans both the joys and perils of childhood stardom.

Born in 1928 in Santa Monica, California, Temple began her movie career as a toddler, when she appeared in a series of low budget films called "Baby Burlesks." Trained in singing and tap dancing, in 1933 Temple was hired by Hollywood's Fox studio to appear in the musical *Stand Up and Cheer*, and her performance instantly catapulted her to stardom. Between 1934 and 1940, Temple appeared in over a dozen films for Fox and became not only the studio's biggest asset but, between 1935 and 1938, the most popular film star in America, surpassing such screen giants as Clark Gable and Mae West.

To moviegoers in the 1930s, Temple's appeal was obvious. Perky, talented, and cute—her trademarks were her dimples and ringlets of golden hair—Temple conveyed a message of hope and optimism to Depression-era America. Her on-screen tap dances and renditions of such popular tunes as "The Good Ship Lollipop" won the affections of millions of fans worldwide, who purchased thousands of Shirley Temple dolls, tore at her clothes during her personal appearances, and on her eighth birthday, showered her with over one hundred thousand gifts. Perhaps her most famous admirer was President Franklin Roosevelt, who credited "Little Miss Miracle" with raising the nation's spirits during the economic crisis.

For nearly a decade, Temple enchanted audiences with her appearances in such childhood classics as *Poor Little Rich Girl* (1935), *Wee Willie Winkie* (1937), *Rebecca of Sunnybrook Farm* (1938), and *The Little Princess* (1939). In the early 1940s, Temple left Fox and signed on with producer David Selznick, who cast her in a series of more mature roles, including a part as an adolescent daughter in *Since You Went Away* (1944) and a high school girl with a crush on an older man in the *Bachelor and the Bobbysoxer* (1947). By then, the teenage Temple could no longer attract audiences, and after a role in *Fort Apache* (1948), in which she starred with her husband, John Agar, she retired from the screen.

Unlike many fallen CHILD STARS, however, Temple made a comeback. After a decade hosting television programs, during the 1960s she began a second career, in politics. After an unsuccessful run for Congress in 1967, she was appointed by President Richard Nixon as U.S. ambassador to the United Nations. In 1974, she became U.S. ambassador to Ghana, and in 1976, Chief of Protocol during the Ford administration. Her autobiography, *Child Star*, was published in 1988.

See also: **Media, Childhood and the; Movies.**

BIBLIOGRAPHY

Black, Shirley Temple. 1988. *Child Star*. New York: McGraw-Hill.

SAMANTHA BARBAS

Theme Parks

Children use their imagination extensively when at play. Through the creation of role-play fantasies, children are able to escape their dependent and limited role as children and venture into a world of fantasy to become free-willed, independent persons owning a sense of societal status and importance. Drawing from examples they observe in books, television, and film, children can escape into fantasy roles to become pioneers, heroes, doctors, nurses, royalty, or any inspiring figure of the past, present, or future. As children advance toward adulthood, however, fantasy role-playing is replaced with more passive forms of escapism, such as reading books or watching MOVIES and TELEVISION.

Theme Parks and Amusement Parks

Theme parks are three-dimensional fantasy settings in which both child and adult are actively immersed into fantasy environments inspired by literature, films, and television. They have their roots in the amusement park, which has long been a center of active play where children and adults alike can divert themselves from their typical daily regimes and involve themselves in direct play, thrill, and challenge. Yet even in amusement parks, where adults and children alike can participate in active play, parents are more likely to participate passively as bystanders, observing their children at play.

The theme park differs from the amusement park in that its form and function embrace the childhood activities of role-playing that appeal to children as well as to the inner child of adults. Thus the concept of the theme park is born, in part, from the universal desire of children and the child within adults to escape into their imaginations and pretend to be a part of a nostalgic, exotic, or fantasy setting.

The term *theme park* originated with Disneyland, which opened in Anaheim, California, in 1955. As the first and most widely recognized theme park, Disneyland has long reigned as the model of all modern theme parks. Its unique themed settings and attractions created a shift in the design of parks that followed, many of which placed as much emphasis on their themed environments as on park attractions.

The opening of Disneyland coincided with the transition of North America's demographics toward a predominately middle-class society and with a surge in the population known as the BABY BOOM. With the increasing number of young families came a growing need for family-oriented leisure activities.

As a producer of films and television programs that families could enjoy together, Disneyland's founder, Walt DISNEY, was in close touch with what interested the American middle-class family. He was well aware that children and adults alike enjoyed escaping into his films and television programs. He was also conscious of the need for activities that would appeal equally to young and old, and thus began to conceive a new kind of amusement park that would appeal to patrons of all ages; that would engage the typically inactive parents and promote family participation.

Designing Disneyland

Drawing on his background in film and television production, Disney looked for ways to translate the entertainment that was experienced on a movie or television screen into a physical setting that could be experienced completely by patrons. To do this, he turned to the art directors and animators of his film studio for assistance in designing his park.

The Disney artists came up with the concept of organizing attractions within a series of memorable theatrical settings. All elements of these themed environments would work in harmony, including the architecture, landscaping, attractions, costumes, and even sounds. The intent was that patrons could literally step into the scenes and become a part of the show.

When it opened, Disneyland included five distinct themed settings: Main Street, USA; Adventureland; Frontierland; Fantasyland; and Tomorrowland. Children visiting the park for the first time were already familiar with these settings because they were commonly portrayed on television and in film. For adults, the settings functioned as vivid reminders of their own childhoods. Thus visitors to Disneyland found the park environments instantly familiar and comforting.

Disneyland's designers employed techniques similar to those used in the studio, including the film design ideal of the procession through scenes such as scenic transitions and design tricks with scale and perspective that were commonly used to create convincing environments within the tight confines of a studio sound stage. These immersed the visitor in the theme park experience.

To employ the ideals of scene changes in themed settings, for example, key landmarks were sited at the ends of long vistas to lure guests forward and through park environments. Furthermore, themed settings were organized to carefully transition and unfold as park guests traveled from one themed environment and into another.

For children visiting Disneyland, the smaller-than-life scale promoted a sense of importance, making them feel larger in relation to their surroundings and thus able to experience the scale of space as an adult would. Because of its scale, adults visiting the park experienced an instant sense of nostalgia, as if they were returning to a childhood setting and discovering environments that were smaller and more intimate than they remembered.

Disneyland's Successors

Disney's new theme park was immediately popular among the American public, and it quickly became well known around the world. In fact, Disneyland soon became a stop that many foreign dignitaries requested when visiting the United States.

Disneyland's popularity led to a surge in the opening of theme parks, which drew from Disney's theme ideals in their own designs. The first to prove a strong success since Disneyland's opening was Six Flags over Texas, which opened in 1961 and incorporated themed settings based on the history of Texas. Following this successful example, other theme parks began to open throughout the United States. The formula for the design of these parks typically consisted of six or seven themed areas, each having attractions, shows, and rides that blended with their surroundings.

The success of the Six Flags park also prompted Six Flags to open a park near Atlanta, Georgia, and another one near Saint Louis, Missouri. Following the lead of the three Six Flags parks, chains of theme parks began to appear across the United States. These were largely developed, owned, and operated by global hospitality and beverage companies such as the international hotelier Marriott and the international beverage company Anheuser-Busch.

In the decades following the opening of the Marriott and Anheuser-Busch parks, several of the world's largest entertainment companies began also to design, build, and operate their own theme parks. Today global film companies such as Universal Studios, Fox, Paramount, Warner Brothers, and of course Disney own and operate the majority of chain theme parks in the United States, Europe, and Asia.

The parks produced by these film studios have much in common with the original Disneyland park in that they also employ well-recognized themed designs, often based on popular films. Their patrons, like Disneyland's, are already familiar with the television programs and films upon which the settings and attractions are based and thus feel an immediate sense of familiarity.

Walt Disney World Resort

Today the most notable collection of theme parks within one geographic locale can be found at the Walt Disney World resort in central Florida. As the original Disneyland park revolutionized the future of amusement parks, the Walt Disney World Resort has revolutionized leisure-time destinations.

When the success and profitability of Disneyland far surpassed even his expectations, Walt Disney began to conceive an attraction that would be more than just another theme park. He wanted to create an extensive leisure resort complex that would ultimately contain several other theme parks and a prototype residential community, all within the confines of 27,433 acres of land. Disney referred to this plan as EPCOT, which stood for Experimental Prototype Community of Tomorrow.

Today the Walt Disney World resort is a forty-three-square-mile leisure complex that is home to four theme parks as well as numerous resort hotels; leisure, retail, and entertainment complexes; and a planned residential community. The first park developed for Walt Disney World was the Magic Kingdom, which is similar to Disneyland. This was followed by Epcot, which took its name from Disney's original plan, then by the Disney-MGM Studios theme park, and finally by Disney's Animal Kingdom park. In all, the Walt Disney World resort is one of the world's most popular and most highly attended leisure destinations.

Today, themed environments are commonplace, and themeing is found not only in the realm of amusement and theme parks, but also in retail stores, restaurants, hotels, cruises, high-profile architecture, and in many other types of built environments. Since their conception in the mid-1950s, theme parks have become an international brand of entertainment that continuously leads the amusement park industry in attendance and provides opportunities for play and escapism for children and adults around the world.

See also: **Parades; Vacations; Zoos.**

BIBLIOGRAPHY

Finch, C. 1973. *The Art of Walt Disney: From Mickey Mouse to the Magic Kingdoms.* New York: Abrams.

King, Margaret J. 1981. "Disneyland and Walt Disney World: Traditional Values in Futuristic Form." *Journal of Popular Culture* 15, no. 1 (summer): 116–140.

Kyriazi, G. 1976. *The Great American Amusement Parks: A Pictorial History.* Secaucus, NJ: Citadel.

Roddewig, R. J., et al. January 1986. "Appraising Theme Parks." *Appraisal Journal* 51, no. 1: 85–108.

Thomas, Bob. 1980. *Walt Disney: An American Original.* New York: Pocket Books.

STEPHEN J. REBORI

Theories of Childhood

Childhood is generally considered to be either a natural biological stage of development or a modern idea or invention. Theories of childhood are concerned with what a child is, the nature of childhood, the purpose or function of childhood, and how the notion of the child or childhood is used in society. The concept of childhood, like any invention, was forged from a potent relationship between ideas and technologies within a frame of social, political, and economic needs. Theories of childhood as a concept are often highly colored or emotive, that is to say, they deal with stark contrasts revealing the development over time of the psychological or emotional significance of childhood as viewed from the state of adulthood. Up until the 1990s, theories of childhood tended to be determined in a "top-down" approach which some have described as "imperialistic." This is true of theories about the medieval child as much as the modern child. Children themselves, while the focus of theory, have not generally been considered as having a legitimate voice in influencing its production. However, the UN CONVENTION ON THE RIGHTS OF THE CHILD (1989) created a climate for reconsidering this tendency and a subsequent focus on listening to the views of the child and CHILDREN'S RIGHTS of expression in general. This has led some scholars to explore allowing children themselves to reflect upon their own experience of childhood, resulting in the use of inclusive research methodologies and more democratic frameworks for dissemination.

Ever since JOHANN AMOS COMENIUS (1592–1670) published his *Didactica Magna* (1649) and JOHN LOCKE (1632–1704) produced his treatise *Some Thoughts Concerning Education* (1693), observers of children have been occupied with attempting to understand, document, and comment on what it is and what it means to be a child. The significance of a state of being after the end of infancy, experienced by all humans in all societies, has produced sometimes contradictory theories from philosophical, religious, and scientific schools of thought as well as from the later established disciplines of psychology, anthropology, sociology, and cultural studies. Throughout history, theorists have been fascinated with the distinctive character of human development, unique as compared with other mammals in having evolved a lengthy period of dependency known as childhood.

Theoretical Boundaries of Childhood

The theoretical boundaries drawn between the relative states of childhood and adulthood have historically been highly significant across a range of cultures for social, political, religious, and legal purposes. The status of *child* awarded protection and acknowledged distinct limitations of personal responsibility within a context of parental or community belonging. A child has been defined as any person below a notional age of majority, but this has been variously interpreted and there have been many differences throughout history in the ways that societies have come to recognize the exact beginning and end of childhood. The United Nations Children's Fund (UNICEF) has for its purposes identified childhood as that stage of life experienced by any person between birth and fifteen years. Article 1 of the 1989 United Nations Convention on the Rights of the Child states that a child is any person under the age of eighteen.

Childhood has thus been identified as a stage of life, associated with chronological age, located between infancy and youth, and including ADOLESCENCE. The word *child* has been used in many societies to indicate a kin relationship but also to indicate a state of servitude. But biological determinants have not always been paramount in indicating childhood. Children in the past often lived with and belonged to households rather than their biological parents. The beginning of childhood has been considered variously to occur at birth or at the end of breast-feeding, which lasted sometimes until the age of three in medieval Europe or in preindustrialized societies of modern times. The Qur'an, for example, indicates thirty months as the usual period. Medieval European society considered infancy to end at around seven years, coinciding with the beginning of a young person's competency at performing certain domestic or industrial tasks. At that time, the educational framework which modern societies have come to draw upon in distinguishing stages of infancy and childhood was yet to be invented. The eighteenth-century philosopher JEAN-JACQUES ROUSSEAU (1712–1778), in constructing an ideal childhood, described what he termed the "age of nature" as occurring between birth and twelve years. For the Austrian-born philosopher RUDOLF STEINER (1861–1925), childhood was a state of physical and spiritual being roughly between the ages of seven and fourteen years, indicated initially by certain physiological changes such as the loss of the milk teeth.

Biological-anthropologists, taking a biocultural perspective, regard childhood as a stage in development unique to humans, the function of which is the preparation for adulthood. However, advocates of a new sociology of childhood such as sociologist Alison James have pointed out that chronological age is sometimes of little use when comparing childhood across very different cultures and societies. A ten year old may be a school child in one society, the head of a household in another. As such, the new sociology of childhood prefers to identify a "plurality of childhoods" rather than one structural conditional term. This plurality, it has been argued, is partly reflected through the prism of children's own definition of themselves.

Legal definitions of childhood have emerged gradually over time and during this long evolution the law can be seen to have reflected changing understandings of the meaning, span, and significance of childhood. Medieval English common law indicated, through its recognition of ages of majority, that a child was considered incapable or lacking sufficient

The inherent playfulness of childhood is depicted in Judith Leyster's *Two Children with a Kitten and an Eel* (c. 1630s). © National Gallery Collection; By kind permission of the trustees of the National Gallery, London/CORBIS.

Constructions of the purity and innocence of childhood have often contained colonial and racial subtexts within their apparently universal ideals. The white Anglo-Saxon child, particularly the female child, was considered the embodiment of these ideals, as suggested by Sir Peter Lely's portrait of Lady Charlotte Fitzroy (c. 1674), where the dark-skinned servant merely provides a backdrop to his young mistress. York Museums Trust (York Art Gallery), UK/Bridgeman Art Library.

means of carrying out a range of adult practices. The capacity of the individual to know and reflect upon the moral status of their actions has come to signify the capacity of belonging and contributing to civil society. The age at which a person can be considered capable of moral reflection upon their actions has altered over time according to changes in the understanding of childhood. Thus, for example, according to nineteenth-century English common law, it became established that children should be exempt from criminal liability under the age of seven. This was raised to age eight in 1933 and to ten in 1963.

The necessity of formulating a precise legal definition of childhood grew out of demographic, economic, and related social and attitudinal changes in the industrialized world that together forged a new recognition of the significance of childhood at the end of the nineteenth century and the beginning of the twentieth. Before this time, children had been defined in strict relation to their status as the biological offspring of fathers who also were considered by law to own any of the child's possessions and to whom they were obliged to offer their services. The lowly status of children was reflect-ed in the fact that child theft was not acknowledged by English law before 1814. By the end of the nineteenth century, there was a growing concern among the newly formed middle classes with the moral condition of childhood and the domestic responsibility of parents. Accompanying this was a notion of childhood innocence and vulnerability which was employed to argue for a new definition of childhood—one which associated it less with the world of industry and more with the world of education. Notions of protection and welfare developed strongly in parts of the world which were experiencing for the first time reductions in infant and child mortality.

The social historian Viviana Zelizer has described what she terms a "sacralization" (investing objects with religious or sentimental meaning) of childhood that occurred at this time, creating a transition in the way children were regarded, from a position of economic value to one of emotional pricelessness. Thus, the notion of the economically useful child began to be replaced by the notion of the incalculable emotional value of each child. Such a theoretical development was essential for the generation of a consensus around legally sanctioned compulsory education.

The Significance of Childhood

What was childhood for? Two broad theoretical positions have emerged on this question. One argues that childhood is a characteristic of human evolution designed to ensure the survival and development of the species. The other suggests that the state of childhood or how childhood is viewed is significant in itself as an indicator of the evolution or development of societies and cultures toward notions of civility or modernity. The former, which encompasses the *biosocial* and *evolutionary* approaches, argues that childhood, as a stage of growth and development, has evolved in human society to provide the conditions for optimizing the prospects of maturity. In particular, this perspective has suggested that the distinctively rapid growth of the brain and the immaturity of dentition and digestive tracts characteristic of the early stages of human life have evolved over time to sustain human society. Such a view is consistent with an essentialist or universal view of childhood (that prioritizes biology over environment in explaining childhood) but has also recognized that social conditions and ecology play a part in constructing the social and cultural response to childhood. Somewhat related to bio-social theories, the perspective of evolutionary psychology came to regard childhood as directly linked to the evolution of what has been called a psychology of PARENTING. This theory suggests that certain universal characteristics of infants and young children, such as relatively large heads and eyes in small bodies, act to trigger instinctive emotions and responses in adults, thus securing development toward maturity.

From this perspective, childhood can be seen as a relationship and therefore can be understood in generational terms. The principle relationship of childhood is with adulthood, but more specifically with parenthood. The development or evolution of conscious parenting is the focus of a school of thought known as *psychohistory*, which has developed since the 1970s following the work of Lloyd deMause. DeMause and his associates have developed a distinctive and controversial theory of childhood. This position establishes from empirical evidence that childhood, while seemingly held by society to be a time of freedom and innocence, has been for the majority of children a time of oppression and abuse. DeMause has argued that the parental response to the infant or child has evolved over time from one which was generally abusive and cruel to one which became nurturing and affectionate. Such a development, according to this theory, not only reflected social, technological, and cultural change but indeed generated those changes.

For SIGMUND FREUD (1856–1939) and psychotherapists who have followed Freud, such as Alice Miller, childhood was of key significance in the adjustment of the individual to mature well-being. Freud developed his theories of the subconscious partly through considering the reasons early childhood memory becomes lost. Since childhood was regarded as the key stage in the successful, or unsuccessful, development of ego, psychological well-being in adult life hinged on this period of time and healing might be effected through the recall of repressed childhood experience.

Developmental and Social-Constructionist Models

Before the second half of the twentieth century, physiological, psychological, and cognitive mapping of development was the dominant theoretical model for the study of childhood. However research and theory which emerged from the disciplines of history, anthropology, and sociology came to strongly question the developmental model, shifting the focus from the child itself to the socially and culturally constructed view of childhood specific to time and place. Since the eighteenth century, the dominant paradigm in Western cultures has viewed childhood as a stage of life characterized by dependency, learning, growth, and development. The notion that in the medieval world there was no concept of childhood was first introduced by the French scholar PHILIPPE ARIÈS in his *Centuries of Childhood* (1962), which focused mainly on France. Ariès believed that the evidence drawn from European paintings and texts of the time revealed that children seemed to be viewed as miniature adults. They had no special clothing, food, social space, or time which amounted to a childhood culture. It was only in the seventeenth and eighteenth centuries that the demarcation between the adult world and the world of childhood slowly began to be drawn. In other words, the social and cultural world of childhood was instituted as a key part of the institution of a new kind of adult, the adult of the bourgeoisie. In spite of regional, cultural, and social differences in the experience of being a child and in how childhood is understood, the social-constructionist view of childhood has become the dominant conceptual model.

The late-eighteenth-century conception of children as utterly innocent is exemplified in *The Age of Innocence* (c. 1788), by Sir Joshua Reynolds PRA (1723–1792), from the title of the painting to the young subject's artless expression and pure white clothes. (Oil on canvas). Collection: © Plymouth City Museum and Art Gallery (Plympton Guildhall).

The early twentieth century saw the development of the discipline of psychology and associated with it, within the context of compulsory mass schooling, educational psychology. For the first time, large numbers of children were brought together institutionally with the object of transforming them into literate and numerate citizens. This material fact encouraged the development of learning theory with particular reference to childhood, and a developmental model, drawn from scientific observation and experimentation, came to characterize the understanding of the child as learner. Stage theory, usually associated with the work of JEAN PIAGET (1896–1980), assumes that the child, regardless of social or cultural context, has a certain universal nature which predisposes it to develop in identifiable stages. This understanding had profound effects on the organization of knowledge and pedagogy in the modern school.

During the 1920s anthropologist MARGARET MEAD (1901–1978) challenged Piaget's theory of stages of development. Her research sought to show that children brought up in different cultures did not exhibit a replica of the animistic stage that Piaget thought to be universal. Mead studied important differences in child and adolescent experiences according to environmental factors and while the results were

The Hülsenbeck Children (1805–1806), by Philipp Otto Runge, is one of the most famous Romantic images of childhood. The artist surrounds these robust and healthy children with images of a nature as vital and energetic as they are. Culture, as represented by their house and the neighboring village, recedes in the background. Hamburg Kunsthalle, Hamburg, Germany/Bridgeman Art Library.

controversial, the contextual debate continued throughout the rest of the twentieth century, reflecting a weakening of confidence in the universal view of childhood.

Historians, sociologists, and anthropologists have suggested that there is no single and universal experience or understanding of what childhood is and where it begins and ends but that this has altered according to time and place. Social-constructionist theory seeks to illustrate that there are many possible answers to the questions "What is a child?" or "What is childhood?" While factors such as body weight might be measured scientifically, producing the same answer in any time or place, childhood itself, the social and cultural

expectations of the child, and its roles and responsibilities or stages of legitimacy can be understood very differently according to any contextual worldview. Social-constructionist theory argues that a notion of childhood is generated by successive generations out of a mix of tradition, social intercourse, and technological development. The context is cultural, and the key generating force is *discourse*. A discourse on childhood is the mediation of an interrelated set of ideas which are communicated through predominantly cultural outlets that generate and consolidate a particular worldview.

That children have and actively generate their own cultural worlds is recognized within another social-constructionist approach which has been termed the *tribal child* perspective. IONA AND PETER OPIE's work in the 1950s and 1960s on children's culture as expressed through PLAY and organized games in United Kingdom streets and playgrounds encouraged this understanding of the child operating within and determining its own cultural world. Another variation on the social-constructionist approach is a political theory of childhood, which views children as a minority group. Within this perspective, children are viewed as people who are afforded little status in society but who are capable of becoming the agents of their own destiny. Within this framework, the physical and cognitive characteristics of childhood are subsumed within an approach which questions a key political function of the ideology of childhood, that which denies a voice to the child.

Cultural Theories of Childhood

Considerations of age and physical maturity are not the only factors by which childhood has been characterized. The association of childhood with notions of a spiritual world, or in modern times, a fantasy world, have shaped both the experience and expectation of childhood. In medieval times in Europe and into modern times through much of the rest of the world, childhood has been considered a condition with a special closeness to nature and to things spiritual. Marina Warner has shown how across cultures adult society has universally recognized this attribute by means of its songs, stories, and FAIRY TALES, rituals and iconography. In preliterate or predominantly oral cultures ideas about childhood were and still are transmitted through stories, song, and ritual. Such traditional media carried meanings, communicated moral codes, instructed on the care and protection of the young, and marked the important transition from childhood to adulthood. The end of childhood is a universally recognized stage of transition characterized by physiological changes which indicate sexual maturity. All societies and cultures have variously recognized this important mark of entry into the adult community. In the premodern world, the relative position of the young within the community and the wider cosmos was articulated as clearly to contemporaries through the collective recognition of RITES OF PASSAGE as is the case in the modern world. What came to transform this consideration into what we identify as theory was the development and spread of LITERACY.

Neil Postman has suggested that in western Europe at least, it was the spread of literacy through the invention of the printing press that was the principal force in generating a widely held and understood consensus around the meaning of childhood. In this sense, childhood was recognized as a stage of life essentially separated from the world of adults and adult knowledge by a lack of literacy. Knowledge and skill with the written word became a sign of maturity toward which the young could be trained. Postman has suggested that the information and communications revolution at the turn of the twenty-first century has delivered the end of

Le Gamin de Paris aux Tuileries (1848), Honoré Daumier. Children's penchant for overturning authority is embodied in Daumier's lithograph of a street urchin sitting on the throne of the King of France. Benjamin A. and Julia M. Trustman Collection of Honoré Daumier Lithographs, Robert D. Farber University Archives and Special Collections Department, Brandeis University Libraries.

childhood, since the relational distance between the adult and the child has been terminally altered by the spread and crucial adoption by children of information and communications technologies.

The notion of the disappearance of childhood expresses a sense of loss communicated at an earlier period in history. The Romantic poets of late-eighteenth- and early-nineteenth-century Europe employed the notion of a lost childhood in their responses to an emergent industrial world. As Hugh Cunningham has put it, the child was the "other" for which one yearned (p. 43). From the end of the eighteenth century, particularly through the philosophy of Jean-Jacques Rousseau and the poetry of William Blake and William Wordsworth, childhood began to be associated strongly in the European mind with a state of nature and as a symbol of humanity, a signifier of development, and the root of progress. This was accompanied by a romantic turn against the impact of new forms of industrial organization and production. Blake's *Songs of Innocence and Experience* (1794) deployed the notion of a universal, natural childhood as a symbol of the humanity that Blake and his contemporaries feared would be destroyed through the oppressive effects of industrialization.

The dominant cultural product that emerged from the end of the eighteenth century was the image of the child as

In Hugo Simberg's *The Wounded Angel* (1903), it's not clear whether these children are helping the angel or if they've captured her. Ateneum Art Museum, Helsinki, Finland.

a symbol of innocence and purity, particularly the white Anglo-Saxon child. Within a racial framework, the evolutionary notion of childhood was found to be useful when deployed by the European colonial powers in justifying their "civilizing" domination of Africa. Those to be colonized were, according to the theory of *recapitulation,* likened to children in their behavior and evolutionary stage of development. In cultural and religious terms, the modern theory of childhood came to be identified with notions of innocence and absence of sin or corruption. Innocence was associated more often than not with the female child in the adult mind and it has been argued indicates an awareness of its opposite state. These are essentially adult concerns and not natural attributes, but the inevitable confusion has been exploited, not always in the interests of children themselves. Literary historian James Kincaid has argued that the notion of childhood innocence has been adopted by the adult world in order to imply the potential of violation and as such contains within

it the potential of its opposite meaning. As such, theories of childhood communicate reflections on the state of human nature and the dominating anxieties of adult life at particular historical junctures.

The experience of being a child and the conceptualization of childhood are of course related, but Jens Qvortrup and colleagues have suggested that the idea of childhood developed as a structural form irrespective of children themselves. Theoretical notions of childhood can be seen to reflect adult anxieties, concerns, and needs while at the same time functioning to teach children themselves what it is to be a child and to provide a marker against which any child can be measured and compared. Childhood viewed at a distance, through a historical perspective, is revealing of patterns or what are sometimes called landscapes—general conditions of how children appeared to themselves and to their adult contemporaries at any one time. Historian John Sommerville has adopted the term *standardization* in this context. According to this theory, a consensus is arrived at, usually in accord with a hegemonic ordering of the values and standards of the more prosperous in society, through which a normal or ideal vision of childhood is arrived at. Theorist Henri A. Giroux has argued that the generation of cultural definitions of childhood needs to be understood historically, since the contextual site or framework within which childhood becomes defined alters over time. In modern times this occurs predominantly through commercial or market forces; a dominant site of cultural definition is the media and associated leisure and entertainment industries. For Giroux, the "politics of culture" provide the conceptual space in which childhood is constructed, experienced, and struggled over. For most of the twentieth century the school served as the principal site of cultural production, but in the twenty-first century the media and leisure industries have become at least as significant in the cultural definition of childhood. In a similar vein, childhood has been characterized as *spontaneous desire* by historian of childhood Gary Cross, who has focused on the changing form of children's TOYS over the course of the twentieth century. He traces these changes to the construction of the child as consumer within the context of a view of parenting which emphasizes the importance of fulfilling those desires for healthy cognitive and social development.

Postmodernist Theories of Childhood

The idea of a universal state of childhood was challenged toward the turn of the twenty-first century through an increasingly globalized perspective which accompanied scholarly questioning through ethnographic, cultural, and anthropological studies. The shift toward a recognition and acceptance of children's voices in determining their own worldview brought about a fragmented view which questioned the structural norm of childhood and brought about a theoretical position about pluralities of childhoods. For such theorists as Chris Jenks and Jens Qvortrup, it is more accurate and helpful to talk of many childhoods or a plurality of experience both across cultures and within them. Diversity of experience according to class, ethnicity, gender, culture, place of residence, health, or disability rather than one common childhood is emphasised, in spite of growing recognition of the universalizing effects of GLOBALIZATION.

Popular writing and scholarship on childhood in the last decades of the twentieth century reflected on a changed state of being. The traditional Western notion of childhood, which had held from about the 1850s to the 1950s, was implied in its absence by notions such as "the disappearance of childhood" or David Elkind's "the hurried child." The emerging consensus was that notions of childhood innocence and dependency on adults could no longer be sustained in the context of children's access to and use of new media technologies. The notion of childhood as an apprenticeship period for adulthood was fundamentally challenged by the use of such technologies, particularly in the home.

Such a material change, coupled with an intensification of child-focused popular entertainment (sometimes called *kinderculture*) that began in the second half of the twentieth century, came to place strains on existing contemporary theories of childhood. What has been called by Shirley Steinberg and Joe Kincheloe "the dilemma of postmodern childhood" was characterized by a democratization in family life which placed the expectations of children and the concept of childhood itself in conflict with many of its established institutions such as the traditional family or the authoritarian school. This has also been accompanied by a new vision of CHILDREN'S RIGHTS apart from and even in opposition to their parents.

See also: **Child Development, History of the Concept of; Child Psychology; History of Childhood; Law, Children and the; Sociology and Anthropology of Childhood; Theories of Play.**

BIBLIOGRAPHY

Ariès, Philippe. 1962. *Centuries of Childhood: A Social History of Family Life.* Trans. Robert Baldick. New York: Knopf.

Bogin, Barry. 1999. *Patterns of Human Growth*, 2nd ed. Cambridge, UK: Cambridge University Press.

Cahan, E.; Jay Mechling; B. Sutton-Smith; and S. H. White. 1993. "The Elusive Historical Child: Ways of Knowing the Child of History and Psychology." In *Children in Time and Place: Developmental and Historical Insights*, ed. Glen H. Elder, Jr., John Modell, and Ross D. Parke. Cambridge, UK: Cambridge University Press.

Cross, Gary S. 1997. *Kids' Stuff: Toys and the Changing World of American Childhood.* Cambridge, MA: Harvard University Press.

Cunningham, Hugh. 1991. *The Children of the Poor: Representations of Childhood since the Seventeenth Century.* Oxford, UK: Blackwell.

DeMause, Lloyd, ed. 1974. *The History of Childhood.* New York: Psychohistory Press.

Elkind, David. 1981. *The Hurried Child: Growing Up Too Fast Too Soon.* Reading, MA: Addison-Wesley.

Giroux, Henry A. 2001. *Stealing Innocence: Youth, Corporate Power, and the Politics of Culture.* New York: Palgrave.

James, Allison, and Prout, Alan. 1990. *Constructing and Reconstructing Childhood: Contemporary Issues in the Sociological Study of Childhood.* London: Falmer Press.

Jenks, Chris. 1996. *Childhood.* London: Routledge.

Mead, Margaret. 1928. *Coming of Age in Samoa: A Psychological Study of Primitive Youth for Western Civilisation.* New York: Blue Ribbon Books.

Opie, Iona and Peter. 1959. *The Lore and Language of Schoolchildren.* New York: Oxford University Press.

Panter-Brick, Catherine, ed. 1998. *Biosocial Perspectives on Children.* Cambridge, UK: Cambridge University Press.

Postman, Neil. 1994. *The Disappearance of Childhood.* New York: Vintage Books.

Qvortrup, Jens, ed. 1994. *Childhood Matters: Social Theory, Practice, and Politics.* Aldershot, UK: Avebury.

Sommerville, C. John. 1982. *The Rise and Fall of Childhood.* Beverley Hills, CA: Sage Publications.

Steinberg, Shirley R., and Kincheloe, Joe L., eds. 1997. *Kinderculture: The Corporate Construction of Childhood.* Boulder, CO: Westview Press.

The Wood Children (1789), Joseph Wright of Derby. By the eighteenth century, the Puritan view that play was sinful had largely been abandoned. Play, like childhood itself, was now seen as something to be enjoyed. Used with permission of Derby Museum and Art Gallery.

Warner, Marina. 1999. *No Go the Bogeyman: Scaring, Lulling, and Making Mock.* London: Chatto and Windus.

CATHERINE BURKE

Theories of Play

That children engage in PLAY seems to be a proposition that is universally true. Whatever historical period is examined, evidence can be found of children playing. The same holds across cultures too, although the content of children's play differs across time and space. Play may also transcend species; the young of many other animals also exhibit behaviors that are similar to the play of children. However, while play is apparently universal, a number of necessary conditions need to be present for children's play to occur and be sustained. Among these are time and space, which, in turn, are frequently related to poverty or its absence. If children are engaged in labor, whether in their homes or outside them, the opportunities for play are much curtailed. Space for play has been less of a constraint but as the growth of cities led to a diminution in the availability of space in general and secure or safe space, in particular, space for play became an

issue. A further necessary condition, that by its absence has occasionally disrupted the universality of play, is adult consent. Children's lack of power in relation to adults has led to their play being curtailed when adults have disapproved of it.

These constraints aside, the recognition that play is strongly associated with childhood has given rise to an extensive literature devoted to its definition, explanation, and description. In addition, there is an equally extensive and rather different literature that has focused on how the propensity to play may be harnessed to educational purposes, pedagogy, and forms of schooling. This literature on play is rendered even more extensive by the fact that play has often given rise to controversy. Arguably, this is because whenever play is mentioned, its antithesis, work, is never far away.

Play has been defined in numerous ways but is perhaps best understood by knowing first of all what it is not. In this case the main thing it is not is work. Play and work are powerful binary oppositions that have attached to them a number of signifiers. Work, for example, is valued as a necessity that provides the material basis for life. It is also frequently seen as giving meaning to life. Play, in contrast, is often seen as frivolous and lacking the serious purpose of work. Play takes place in the time not given over to work and in some cultures, such time in school is called *playtime* to distinguish it from time devoted to lessons. These oppositions between play and work are organized not only in the present but also over the time of the life cycle as well. For example, in modern popular perception, childhood is a time for play, whereas adulthood is a time for work. This entry examines the history of these oppositions through a consideration of theories of children's play and methods of education that sought to utilize play. TOYS are central to many kinds of play and attention will be given to their use and the rise of the toy industry and how that has affected play. Finally, theories of play and the practice of play have had to contend with an attitude associated with Puritanism—but found in Christianity in general—that play was at best a distraction and at worst sinful. Any discussion of play needs to take account of this powerful and pervasive belief.

Play in Ancient Civilizations

Play is typically divided into a number of categories. Among them are sociable play, fantasy play, and play with toys. While evidence of the first two kinds are hard to find in the remains of ancient civilizations, artifacts interpreted by archaeologists as toys are widespread. Small clay and stone balls that are thought to have been toys dating back to the Yangshao Culture during the Neolithic Period (4800–4300 B.C.E.) have been found at Banpo village in Xi'an, in present-day China. Small carts, whistles shaped like birds, and toy monkeys have been recovered from Harappa and Mohenjo-Daro, cities that existed in the Indus valley between 3000 to 1500 B.C.E. (There is some debate, however, about whether

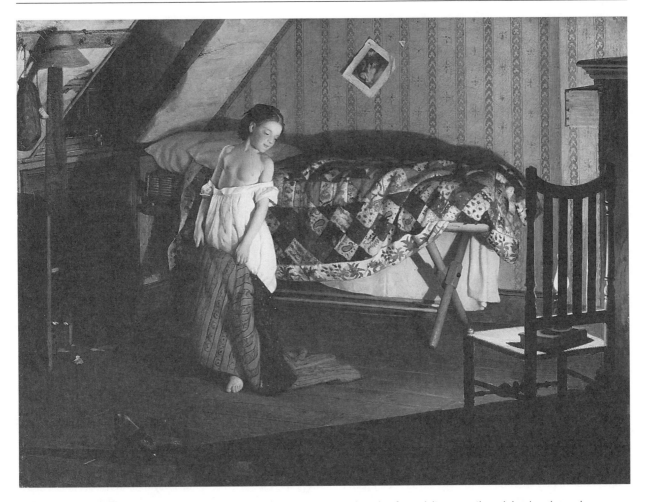

Making a Train (1867), Seymour Guy. A little girl playing dress-up tries on the role of an adult woman through her imaginary play. © Philadelphia Museum of Art/CORBIS.

all these objects were toys or whether they were used in religious rituals.) In later periods, representations of play began to appear. Archaeological finds, such as Egyptian tomb paintings, show abundant evidence of children's games. Images of children playing games or children with toys appear on ancient Greek vases and plates of children playing with toys and playing games and ancient Greek playthings have also been recovered. These include swings, seesaws, kites, hoops with bells, model carts, whipping tops, and wheels that were attached to poles for pulling along. Evidence of toys can also be found among ancient writings. In *The Clouds*, a comedy by the ancient Greek dramatist, Aristophanes, a proud father tells how clever his son is and how, even when quite little he amused himself at home with making boats and chariots and frogs out of pomegranate rinds.

The first known discussions of play and its relation to education also made their appearance in the work of the ancient Greek philosophers PLATO (427–348 B.C.E.) and ARISTOTLE (384–322 B.C.E.). Their references to play are important not so much because of what they said, which in Aristotle's case was not much, but for the use that was made of their ideas in later periods. Encouraging children to play in school was often controversial and the advocates of play methods frequently used the work and prestige of Plato to legitimize their approach. In his *Laws* and the *Republic* Plato provides not a theory of play but a justification for its use in education. In the *Laws*, for example, Plato views play as a form of anticipatory socialization. If children were to become builders, he suggested, they should play at building houses. The teacher's role in this was to try to direct the children's inclinations and pleasures through play towards their final aim in life.

This view of play as best when it is directed by the teacher is a recurrent one and has sometimes been seen as a way of manipulating and controlling children. This was wholly consistent with Plato's concern that education should serve the needs of the state by producing good citizens and with the distinction he drew between play that would lead to that goal and that which would not. Between the ages of three and six, however, this distinction between desirable and undesirable play did not apply; at this stage in their life, Plato wrote in the *Laws*, children had certain natural modes of play, which they discovered for themselves. This idea that children's play was natural is another persistent theme, as is Plato's fear that unless the play of older children was regulated and contained it threatened the stability of the state. His reasoning was not, as might have been expected, that unregulated play would lead to violence but that if children changed the rules of their games, they might, when adults, attempt to change institutions and laws.

This theme of free play leading to serious and detrimental consequences, as Plato put it, was to reappear often in subsequent discussions of play. So too was the philosopher Socrates' notion that children should not be compelled to learn. In Plato's *Republic*, Socrates argues that play, rather than force, should be used in training children. In the *Laws*, Plato described how play could be used as a method in education by noting that in Egypt, arithmetical games had been invented for the use of children so they found learning a pleasure and an amusement.

Play and Education in the Dark and Middle Ages

In the early Christian period, some of the misgivings that Plato expressed about play reappeared in the writings of Saint Augustine of Hippo (354–430 C.E.). In his autobiographical *Confessions*, Augustine related how he had neglected school work when a boy in order to satisfy his love of play and how he was beaten for it. Unlike Plato, he saw no educational value in play whatsoever, noting only its incompatibility with schoolwork. He expressed regret that he had, out of a love of play, not obeyed his teachers and parents and worked harder. Although Augustine goes out of his way to present his early life as sinful, this view of play in childhood as a temptation and a distraction from the work of preparation for adult life is a persistent theme in many variants of Christianity.

While the intellectual histories of play tend to be silent about the Middle Ages, one of the most famous paintings of children playing, Pieter Breughel the Elder's *Children's Games*, in which about eighty-four games are represented, was painted at the end of the Middle Ages in 1559–1560. Why the appearance at this time? The French historian PHILIPPE ARIÈS in his influential book, *Centuries of Childhood*, argued from evidence, including paintings, that a concept of childhood did not exist in the Middle Ages, which is one possible reason for the absence of theories of play during that period. Significantly, Ariès did not argue that children had ceased to play. On the contrary, he argued that children's play, except in infancy, did not become differentiated from that of adults until the eighteenth century. From then on, the growth of schools and changes in the structure of the family led to the modern emergence of childhood as a stage of life marked by its own distinctive characteristics. Perhaps this is why Brueghel's painting appears when it does; it is the

sign of a new image of childhood in which play was newly important, but would soon become suspect. The role of schools was subsequently dominated by moralization and the moralizers who promoted them, like the medieval Church, tended to oppose the playing of games and play in general as a threat to order and authority.

The Enlightenment

This negative attitude was also present among the Puritans of New England among whom the Calvinistic work ethic was deeply rooted. According to the German sociologist Max Weber, such religious groups saw their most urgent task as the destruction of spontaneous, impulsive enjoyment. In pursuit of this, the New England Puritans tried to prevent children playing with toys unless they were related to Biblical stories and adjudged to be morally uplifting. Play was regarded as frivolous if not sinful; work was the road to salvation. But it was an English political philosopher who had been brought up as a Puritan, JOHN LOCKE (1632–1704), who made one of the earliest significant contributions to the modern conception of the place of play in education. Locke discussed play quite extensively in *Thoughts Concerning Education*. Like Plato, Locke thought the chief aim of education ought to be virtue. He was opposed to the use of corporal punishment to motivate children to learn Latin and Greek or any other form of school knowledge. For him, the acquisition of school knowledge was of less importance than producing people who were virtuous and wise. Locke believed that children learned best not by being coerced, but if learning was made a recreation. They then would develop a desire to be taught. As an example of how play could facilitate learning, he proposed that "contrivances" or apparatus might be made to teach children to read. Locke was interested in harnessing play to educational aims, but he also provided clues to a theory of play. By observing how girls spent hours becoming expert at a game called *dibstones*, Locke concluded that this was due to a natural tendency to be active.

Locke's empiricist theory of knowledge, which saw knowledge as being derived through the senses alone, held out the possibility that if the right experiences were presented to children through education then they could be molded by educators to whatever form was desired. In addition to contributing to a growing realization of the importance of childhood in human development, Locke's empiricism appealed to ENLIGHTENMENT radicals seeking to change the society they lived in. Among these, the most prominent was the Genevan-born political philosopher, JEAN-JACQUES ROUSSEAU (1712–1778). In *Émile* (1762), Rousseau's famous treatise on education, Rousseau proposed the rather revolutionary theory that children went through distinct stages in their development and that education should primarily be tailored to those stages. Rousseau's comments on children's play were not in any way systematic but the text reveals that he held, albeit in sketch form, a theory of play. This consisted mainly in the view that play was instinctive and the means provided by nature for growth of the body as well as of the senses that were so important to Locke's empiricism.

Rousseau cited Locke, approvingly for the most part, throughout his book but when he came to consider the relation between play and education he turned only to Plato to support his belief that children should be taught through play. Rousseau thought that in all the games that children played, there could be found material for instruction. He held that what children learned from each other in play was worth far more than what they learned in the classroom. In contrast to the Puritan view, Rousseau did not hold that play was idleness or a waste of time because it contributed to what he believed to be the main object of childhood, that children should be happy.

Rousseau's thoughts on play were set within a position that was hostile to conventional schooling with its emphasis on books and telling pupils what to do. Rousseau believed instead that learning took place best when it was pleasurable and when pupils were hardly aware that they were learning.

Although *Émile* was a text marked by paradox and contradiction and not intended as a guide to practical education, a number of Rousseau's admirers in Europe tried to educate children in the way he outlined. Prominent adherents to Rousseau's advice about play were Maria Edgeworth (1768–1849) and her father Richard Lovell Edgeworth (1744–1817). Their views and those of other members of their Anglo-Irish family appeared in a two-volume book entitled *Practical Education* (1798). In addition to Rousseau, this book drew heavily upon Locke and other sources. It was distinguished from much of the previous literature on play and education by being based upon observation and experience of a domestic education often of an experimental nature. A chapter in *Practical Education* was devoted to a consideration of toys, their nature, their suitability, and how best they might be used for educational purposes. Like Rousseau, the Edgeworths saw play as leading to science through the presence in play of observation, experimentation, and discovery.

The Romantic Movement

Rousseau's emphasis on education following nature and education as self-realization were themes taken up by the Romantic movement which stressed the varieties of experience available to children that were lost with the onset of adulthood. These notions about childhood innocence and the need to protect children from the world of adults were present in the work of the English poets William Blake and William Wordsworth as well as others, and were among those that informed the thinking of the German educationalist and founder of the KINDERGARTEN, FRIEDRICH FROEBEL (1782–1852). Together, Froebel's writing and educational practice constitute a qualitative shift in the conceptualization of children's play and its role in their education. Much of what Froebel advocated, such as the use of play objects or ap-

paratus to provide learning experiences, was not novel. (As was discussed above, Plato had recorded that the ancient Egyptians had used games to teach arithmetic.) However, Froebel went further than any theorist before by placing play at the center of his conception of how young children should be educated. The games he devised and the play apparatus, what he called the *gifts* and *occupations*, were extensively described in his books such as *Mother's Songs, Games and Stories*, a manual for mothers on how to play with their children. In his *Pedagogics of the Kindergarten* Froebel detailed how his play apparatus, the gifts, and occupations should be played with. The persuasiveness of Froebel's theories owes much to the Romantic, sometimes, mystical language he used but his theories were innovative in that his conception of play is free from any warnings that unregulated play might be dangerous. In contrast to earlier traditions Froebel says of play in the early stage of childhood in his *Education of Man* (1826) that "play at this time is not trivial, it is highly serious and of deep significance" (p. 55). However, in Froebel's kindergarten there was no unregulated play as even the free play was planned and constrained. He intimated that play arose from an impulse to activity that in the next stage, a stage he calls *boyhood*, becomes expressed in work.

Evolutionary Theories of Play

Because of the similarities between the play behavior of young children and the behavior of the young of some animal species, the behavior of the latter has also been described as play. Following the publication in 1859 of Charles Darwin's *Origin of Species*, it was almost inevitable that some of his followers would make the connection and attempt adaptive explanations of the play of all species in terms of Darwinian and other evolutionary theories. These theories gave rise to the first attempts to provide explanations for play, rather than observations of play or uses to which play could be put. Although hints as to how play arises are present in earlier texts, it is not until the nineteenth century that theories of play make their first appearance.

One of the most prominent theories arose from the work of the German philosopher J. C. Friedrich von Schiller (1759–1805) in his *Letters on Aesthetic Education* and later the works of English philosopher and sociologist Herbert Spencer (1820–1903). They expounded what was called the *surplus energy theory* to explain animal play. Schiller, writing before Darwin, was principally concerned with the relation between play, art, and aesthetics. He believed that a concern with aesthetic appearance emerged in humans when they acted on an impulse "to extend enjoyment beyond necessity" and thereby stimulate their imagination. Necessity in this context meant the struggle for survival. In support of this argument, he cited the way in nature, a lion sometimes roared, not out of necessity but in order to release its "unemployed energy."

With Herbert Spencer, a break occurs in the history of theories of play as he, like most of the subsequent figures, adopted a scientific approach that was mainly empirical rather than speculative. Spencer, a prominent advocate of an evolutionary theory that preceded Darwin's, wrote, in his *Principles of Psychology* (1855) that once an animal no longer had to expend all its energy on survival, the surplus could be released in play. For Spencer, the release of surplus energy in play took the form of imitation of a "serious" activity.

In his book *Education, Intellectual, Moral and Physical* (1861), Spencer argued that learning should be made as pleasurable as play, although he makes no connection here to his general theories of play. Unusually for the time in which he wrote, Spencer drew attention to the fact that girls were often prevented by schools from engaging in noisy play even though it was thought desirable for the adequate development of boys.

A German contemporary of Spencer named Karl Groos (1861–1946) also presented a biological explanation for play in his books, *The Play of Animals* and *The Play of Man*. Groos argued that play was the expression of an instinct necessary to the survival of the species. The young child, due to its prolonged dependency on adults, did not need the instinct. Hence play is the practice and development of capacities, like sex and fighting, to be used later in life. Thus, for Groos, the purpose of play was a preparation for life. Famously he claimed that, "instead of saying, the animals play because they are young, we must say, the animals have a youth in order that they may play" and thereby they practice skills necessary for their survival. This theory, unlike that of surplus energy, could explain not only why play was most prominent in young animals but also why it occurred in isolated animals that were not able to imitate others. Spencer's theory, which relied on imitation, was unable to explain this.

The American psychologist James Mark Baldwin (1861–1934), who did much to popularize Groos in the United States, concluded that play is a function of high utility. Baldwin subscribed to *race recapitulation*, one of the most pervasive ideas among psychologists, biologists, and educationalists of the late nineteenth century. This view held that the development of the individual (ontogeny) recapitulates, or repeats the principal stages, the development of the human race (phylogeny). Race recapitulation appeared in many different areas of social life. It was present in Froebel's and Spencer's work but the American psychologist G. STANLEY HALL (1844–1924) did most to promote it in education. A variant of race recapitulation was that each individual mind passes through the evolutionary stages that the human race has previously been through. For Hall play was the recapitulation of an earlier evolutionary state. The great American educationalist and pragmatic philosopher JOHN DEWEY (1859–1952) developed a curriculum around the similar idea of cultural epochs that was propounded by the German educator and philosopher, J. F. HERBART (1776–1841) and his followers. In Dewey's scheme, the youngest children were given objects to play with that would have been necessary for survival, for example, in the Stone Age. Throwing sticks at an object was held to recapitulate the hunting of wild animals in the Stone Age and in Hall's view, because it was a reliving of a past evolutionary state it provided more pleasure than throwing sticks at nothing in particular.

John Dewey and Maria Montessori: "Scientific" Education and Play

These often conflicting theories of play encountered many problems, many of which were related to the inadequacy of the definitions of play that had been adopted. For the most part, none of the figures that have been discussed provided anything more than a cursory definition that typically contained the views that play was not a serious activity and that it gave pleasure. It fell to John Dewey to define play on several occasions in the course of his voluminous output. Dewey's attitude to education was scientific in that his views were formed by observation and experimentation. He often presented the world in his writing in terms of binary oppositions and so he defined play in relation to work. Thus, in *How We Think* (1909), Dewey wrote, in a formulation that paralleled Froebel's, that play was an activity not consciously performed for any sake beyond itself whereas work was an activity in which the interest lies in its outcome. In Dewey's conception, play is subordinated to work. He poses this almost as a developmental task. A time comes, he argued in a reversal of Schiller's notion, when children must extend their acquaintance with existing, as opposed to symbolic, things. Dewey did not consider work unpleasant; instead he distinguished it from labor, which was characterized by drudgery. As an antidote to labor, he suggested, adults engaged not in play but in amusement.

The consequences for education, in Dewey's view, were that play and the work into which it grows should give exercise in socially useful occupations. This, as has been seen, was not a novel prescription. Echoes of Rousseau and the Edgeworths may be detected in his contention in *Democracy and Education* (1916) that "[i]t is the business of the school to set up an environment in which play and work shall be conducted with reference to facilitating desirable mental and moral growth. It is not enough just to introduce plays and games, handwork and manual exercises. Everything depends upon the way in which they are employed" (p. 230). There are clear parallels in this statement with Rousseau's advocacy of the manipulation of the child's environment so that it was unaware that its work and play were completely under the control of the teacher. Similarities may also be observed between Dewey's view and that of the Italian educationalist MARIA MONTESSORI (1870–1952). Montessori's system, which blurs the distinction between play and work, was based on sense training by means of didactic apparatus. Montessori was also opposed to FAIRY TALES—the source of much of children's fantasy play before the advent of DISNEY and computer games—favored by Froebel's followers. She wanted children to encounter reality and not have imposed upon them the fantasies of others.

The Growth of the Toy Industry and Organized Play

The context in which the theories of play discussed above were formulated and attempts were made to utilize play in the emerging mass school systems was also one in which certain kinds of play were being exploited commercially on a mass scale by the manufacturers of toys for the first time. It was also a context marked by the codification of games such as football and BASEBALL, which were played by children and adults alike. In a previous era, Locke had recommended that children should make their own toys. The Edgeworths advised that toys be plain and useful and the play materials devised by Froebel and Montessori were just that. The current meanings of the word *toy* did not become widespread until the nineteenth century, when it coincided with an expansion in the mass production of toys.

The expansion of the toy industry during the nineteenth century signified a strengthening of the relation between a newly emergent conception of childhood and forms of play largely outside the direct control of adults. This kind of play was educative in the broadest sense but did not take place in the conditions advocated by Rousseau and Montessori. At the end of the nineteenth century, attempts were made in cities across the United States and Europe to retain or retake control of children's social play through the organized children's PLAYGROUND MOVEMENT. While some have seen these initiatives as an unambiguous attempt to impose adult control over the children of the urban poor, many of the reformers were motivated by another impulse, a Romantic critique of the city as a source of physical and moral degeneration that had violated children's natural right to play. A similar impulse also may be seen in the rise of uniformed youth movements, such as the BOY SCOUTS and GIRL SCOUTS/Girl Guides, during the early years of the twentieth century.

Psychoanalytic Theories

The new concern with children, childhood, and play manifest at the end of the nineteenth century also provided the context for new theories. The revelation of INFANT SEXUALITY by the founder of psychoanalysis, SIGMUND FREUD (1856–1939), produced a view of childhood that conflicted sharply with the view of childhood promoted by Rousseau and the Romantics. The evolutionary biological basis of Freud's general theories meant that his was not an entirely new departure. Strong links may be found between Freud's view of childhood and those of Groos and Hall. Nevertheless, Freud's enormously influential theories countered the Enlightenment optimism visible in the play theories, and the belief that the application of reason to fields such as education would bring about progress towards perfectibility.

Freud's psychoanalytic theory of play was outlined in *Beyond the Pleasure Principle* (1920). In this work, he explicitly conceptualized play as the *repetition compulsion* whereby a child wishes to constantly repeat or re-enact an experience. This he saw as the working out of his pleasure principle; the reduction of tension produced by the life instincts; and, when the experience was unpleasant, of the death instinct. The replacement of the pleasure principle, of which play is part, by the reality principle takes place phylogenetically in Freudian theory as well as ontogenetically within the individual child when its instinctual drives give way to reason.

Psychoanalytic theories of play, which focused on the value of play for emotional development, gave rise to two developments. First, the use of play as psychotherapy was pioneered by the Austrian psychoanalyst MELANIE KLEIN (1882–1960) and described in her book *The Psychoanalysis of Children* (1932). Second, a small number of experimental schools were founded on psychoanalytic principles in the early twentieth century. Among these was the Children's Home opened in Moscow by Vera Schmidt in 1921. The school ran until its closure in 1926. In the United States, Margaret Naumburg (1890–1983) began in 1914 what became known as the Walden School and in England, A. S. NEILL (1883–1973) founded a school named Summerhill. Although different in some respects, the schools were united in a belief that adults should not channel spontaneous, natural play into a learning experience for children. At Summerhill, for example, children were able to play freely without constraint, something Plato feared would lead to dire social and political consequences.

Twentieth-Century Psychological Theories

Discussion of play in the twentieth century tended to be dominated by psychologists, a consequence of psychology having become the dominant discourse of nearly all aspects of childhood and education. Three figures stand out in the debates and discussions around children's play: Swiss psychologist JEAN PIAGET (1896–1980), Russian psychologist LEV VYGOTSKY (1896–1934), and American psychologist Jerome Bruner (b. 1915). Their theories differed from earlier explanatory theories in stressing cognitive rather than biological functions performed by play. Piaget emphasized the importance of play in symbolic representation and its contribution to socialization. Vygotsky described play as a "leading activity" and believed that play allows children opportunities to use language and to learn through role playing, as Plato believed, to "self-regulate" their behavior by following rules. By these means they raise their own learning above the level they had attained previously. Bruner and his associates stressed the role of play in language acquisition and problem solving.

While these psychologists emphasized the cognitive benefits of play, some observers like Neil Postman argued that childhood is under threat and with it the conditions for play. In *The Disappearance of Childhood*, Postman argued that the electronic media, especially TELEVISION, was destroying childhood. Others, like the psychologist ERIK ERIKSON, contributed to the view that as childhood vanishes, so does adulthood as adults become infantilized by a commercialized popular culture.

Conclusion

One of the regularly repeated themes in the history of theories of play and the relation between play and education is the persistence of the binary opposition of play to work. This binary could be rewritten in Freudian terms as the conflict between the pleasure and the reality principles. Those educationalists who advocated the use of play in education generally did so as a means to induct children into the structures of the reality principle. At the start of the twenty-first century, within many education systems (except perhaps in early childhood education), play has lost ground to the perceived demands for a competitive advantage in a global economy.

Paradoxically, since the 1960s, which saw a rise in living standards across the Western world, the boundaries between play and work have become more blurred and the notion that play is the work of the child has been disrupted by the realization, found in the work of the Dutch historian Johan Huizinga (1872–1945), that adults continue to play too. To this is added the growing convergence of children and adults by virtue of both sharing the same mediatized, cultural space. Finally, if the history of theories of children's play illustrates anything, it is that play has far too many social ramifications to be left to children and that the theories are as much about a conception of adulthood—and what the child should become—as they are about childhood.

See also: **Child Development, History of the Concept of; Child Psychology; Media, Childhood and the; Theories of Childhood.**

BIBLIOGRAPHY

Ariès, Philippe. 1962. *Centuries of Childhood: A Social History of Family Life.* Trans. Robert Baldick. New York: Vintage Books.

Augustine, Saint. 2001. *The Confessions of St. Augustine.* Trans. Rex Warner. New York: Signet Classic.

Brehony, Kevin J. 2001. *The Origins of Nursery Education: Friedrich Froebel and the English System.* 6 vols. London: Routledge.

Bruner, Jerome S., Allison Jolly, and Kathy Sylva. 1976. *Play: Its Role in Development and Evolution.* New York: Basic Books.

Curtis, H. S. 1915. *Education through Play.* New York: Macmillan.

Dewey, John. 1910. *How We Think.* London: D.C. Heath.

Dewey, John. 1916. *Democracy and Education.* New York: Macmillan.

Earle, A. M. 1997. *Child Life in Colonial Days.* Bowie, MD: Heritage Classic.

Edgeworth, Maria. 1997 [1798]. *Practical Education,* ed. M. Myers. Brookfield, VT: Pickering and Chatto.

Fagen, R. 1981. *Animal Play Behavior.* Oxford, UK: Oxford University Press.

Freud, Sigmund. 1975 [1920]. *Beyond the Pleasure Principle.* New York, Norton.

Gould, Stephen Jay. 1977. *Ontogeny and Phylogeny.* Cambridge, MA: Belknap Press of Harvard University Press.

Groos, Karl. 1976. *The Play of Animals.* New York: Arno Press.

Groos, Karl. 1976. *The Play of Man.* New York: Arno Press.

Hall, G. Stanley. 1904. *Adolescence.* New York: D. Appleton.

Huizinga, Johan. 1998 [1949]. *Homo Ludens: A Study of the Play-Element in Culture.* London: Routledge.

Johnson, J. E., J. F. Christie, et al. 1999. *Play and Early Childhood Development.* New York: Longman.

Klein, Melanie. 1984 [1932]. *The Psychoanalysis of Children.* New York: Free Press.

Locke, John. 1989 [1693]. *Some Thoughts Concerning Education,* ed. J. W. Yolton. Oxford, UK: Clarendon Press; Oxford University Press.

Montessori, Maria. 1964. *The Advanced Montessori Method.* Cambridge, MA: R. Bentley.

Montessori, Maria. 2002. *The Montessori Method.* Mineola, N.Y.: Dover Publications.

Piaget, Jean. 1999. *Play, Dreams and Imitation in Childhood.* London: Routledge.

Postman, Neil. 1985. *The Disappearance of Childhood.* London: W.H. Allen.

Rousseau, Jean-Jacques. 1993 [1762]. *Émile.* Trans. London: J. M. Dent; C. E. Tuttle.

Schiller, Friedrich. 1992 [1794]. *On the Aesthetic Education of Man, in a Series of Letters.* Ed. Elizabeth M. Wilkinson and L. A. Willoughby. Oxford, UK: Clarendon Press; Oxford University Press.

Spencer, Herbert. 1963 [1861]. *Education: Intellectual, Moral, and Physical.* Paterson, NJ: Littlefield Adams.

Spencer, Herbert. 1977 [1855]. *The Principles of Psychology.* Boston: Longwood Press.

Vygotsky, Lev. 1978. *Mind in Society.* Ed. Michael Cole. Cambridge, MA: Harvard University Press.

Wood, W. d. B. 1915. *Children's Play and its Place in Education.* London: Kegan Paul.

INTERNET RESOURCES

Lyons, T. 2001. "Play and Toys in the Educational Work of Richard Lovell Edgeworth (1744–1817)." Available from <www.socsci.kun.nl/ped/whp/histeduc/edgeworth.html>.

Moog, C. 2002. "Psychological Aspects of Ethnic Doll Play." Available from <www.balchinstitute.org/museum/toys/psych.html>.

Nelson, P. B. 2001. "Toys as History: Ethnic Images and Cultural Change." Available from <www.balchinstitute.org/museum/toys/history.html>.

KEVIN J. BREHONY

Tinker v. Des Moines

In early December 1965, a handful of members of a small Iowa peace group—mainly Quakers and Unitarians—met in a Des Moines home to discuss ways to demonstrate their opposition to America's escalating military activity in Southeast Asia. Without prompting from their parents, several of the young people attending the meeting made the decision to wear black armbands to school in order to express sorrow for casualties in the Vietnam War and to encourage a truce in hostilities. The armband demonstration took place on December 16 and 17, 1965. Only about sixty of the 18,000 students enrolled in the Des Moines public schools participated, and there was no serious disruption of school routine. School administrators, however, suspended a handful of the offending students for violating a hastily enacted school district rule that prohibited the classroom display of symbols of protest.

Represented by the Iowa Civil Liberties Union, three of the armband wearing students—Christopher Eckhardt, John Tinker and Mary Beth Tinker—challenged the school district's position in federal court. At the time, Christopher and John were fifteen-year-old high school sophomores; Mary Beth was thirteen and in the eighth grade. Although not as newsworthy as the raucous political demonstrations of the 1960s in other sections of the country, the Iowa armband protest and the civil liberties issues it raised eventually led to one of the U.S. Supreme Court's most significant decisions on CHILDREN'S RIGHTS.

In his 1969 opinion in *Tinker v. Des Moines* for the seven-member Supreme Court majority, Justice Abe Fortas held that the conduct of the armband wearing Iowa teenagers was "not substantially disruptive" of educational activities and, thus, constituted protected symbolic expression under the First Amendment to the U.S. Constitution. Justice Fortas submitted further that constitutional protections of free expression extend to young people even "inside the schoolhouse gate." Fortas had also written the Court's opinion in IN RE GAULT (1967), which held that full procedural rights should be accorded to youthful offenders appearing before JUVENILE COURTS. The tandem of opinions in *Gault* and *Tinker* made Fortas appear to be the Warren Court's designated spokesperson for children's rights.

In a biting dissent, Justice Hugo Black fulminated that "children should be seen and not heard." At a time when many older Americans were uncomfortable with student political expression, Justice Black's opinion served as a conservative bellwether; he received hundreds of letters praising his stand against classroom protests.

Since the 1960s, the *Tinker* precedent has been significantly qualified. For example, in *Hazelwood School District v. Kuhlmeier* (1988), the U.S. Supreme Court upheld the administrative censorship of a Missouri high school newspaper, concluding that a school principal's decision to excise some student-bylined material was reasonably grounded in the law. *Hazelwood* notwithstanding, however, Justice Fortas's opinions in *Tinker v. Des Moines* and *In re Gault* still remain key starting points for any discussions of children's rights in late twentieth century America.

See also: **Law, Children and the; Youth Activism.**

A French stamp featuring Tintin and his dog Snowy was released during the national *fête du timbre* (stamp fair) in March 2000. © AFP/CORBIS.

BIBLIOGRAPHY

Johnson, John W. 1997. *The Struggle for Student Rights: Tinker v. Des Moines and the 1960s.* Lawrence: University Press of Kansas.

JOHN W. JOHNSON

Tintin and Hergé

The character of Tintin, the courageous boy reporter, was created in 1929 by the Belgian cartoonist Georges Remi (1907–1983). The cast—including Tintin, his dog Snowy, Captain Haddock, Professor Calculus, and Bianca Castafiore, and others—appeared in a series of twenty-three adventures between 1930 and 1976; the final Tintin album, *Tintin et l'Alph-Art* (*Tintin and Alpha-Art* [1990]), was left unfinished at Remi's death and was published in notes form in 1986.

Remi (better known by his *nom de plume* Hergé, the French pronunciation of his initials in reversed order, "R-G") began his career as an illustrator for the conservative, Roman Catholic newspaper *Le vingtième siècle* (The twentieth century). Hergé's earliest picture stories for children, before embarking on Tintin, took the traditional children's form of densely illustrated texts, whereby another author's prose story would be broken down into short units, and each block of text would be placed under a picture that illustrated or glossed it; the pictures were at best decorative and redundant to the text. After seeing imported newspapers from Mexico, which reprinted the then new American comic strip form (in which text was integrated into the pictures as dialogue), Hergé decided to create a new story, introducing this innovative format to his readers.

The first Tintin story, *Tintin au pays des Soviets* (*Tintin in the Land of the Soviets* [1989]), was serialized two pages at a time in the newspaper's children's supplement, *Le petit vingtième* (The little twentieth), and published in a collected version in 1930. Initially a lone artist, Hergé eventually hired a small team of assistants. After the demise of *Le vingtième siècle*, he moved the initial serialization of his Tintin stories to the children's supplement of the newspaper *Le Soir* in 1940, and finally in 1946 to the pages of his own *Tintin* magazine. Unlike American comic book stories for children, which usually comprised either short, stand-alone stories or open-ended serials, Tintin stories were constructed as complete tales, with beginnings, middles, and endings; these stories were then collected and published in a hardcover, or album, format, leading to a complete library of titles that have remained in print, with rare exceptions, since their initial publication.

Tintin in the Land of the Soviets owed a debt to the anticommunist propaganda of the day; Hergé's research was limited to a single anticommunist tract (Joseph Douillet's *Moscou sans voiles* [1928]), in keeping with the newspaper's agenda. This somewhat xenophobic trend continued in books like *Tintin au Congo* (1931; *Tintin in the Congo* [1991]) and *Tintin en Amerique* (1932; *Tintin in America* [1978]), which portrayed nonwhite characters in stereotypical fashion. *Tintin in the Congo* especially suffered from the colonial prejudices of the day, as the Congo was at that time still under Belgian rule.

The fifth volume, *Le lotus bleu* (1936; *The Blue Lotus* [1983]), marked a change in Hergé's conception of the stories; instead of simply crafting escapist adventures based solely on common (mis)conceptions, he would base his stories on more careful research and address, at least indirectly, contemporary concerns. For *Blue Lotus*, Hergé learned about Chinese culture and history from Chang Chong-Chen, a student at Brussels's Académie des Beaux-Arts. The book directly confronts Western misconceptions about China (although Hergé's depictions of Chinese characters still often relied on popular visual stereotypes); the political situation of the time, specifically the Sino-Japanese War, is discussed directly, a rarity for children's fiction in Belgium at the time.

As the years passed, the Tintin volumes were occasionally revised and re-imagined, due both to external pressures such as publishing in foreign markets and to Hergé's own developing realization that his books had an effect on their young readers. The versions available today represent Hergé's final revisions.

Tintin has been marketed with all the fervor of DISNEY's most important characters, with merchandise from children's clothing to fine china. Live-action film versions include *Tintin and the Golden Fleece* (1961) and *Tintin and the Blue Oranges* (1964); animated films consist of *Prisoners of the Sun* (1969) and *Tintin and the Land of Sharks* (1972), and a series of thirty-minute adaptations was produced in 1990.

Hergé has had a wide influence on cartoonists throughout the world. Traces of his *ligne claire* ("clear-line") style of drawing, with simple ink outlines, flat and bold color, and realistic background detail can be seen in the works of various European and other cartoonists, both for children and adults.

See also: **Children's Literature; Comic Books; Series Books.**

BIBLIOGRAPHY

Farr, Michael. 2002. *Tintin: The Complete Companion.* San Francisco, CA: Last Gasp.

Peeters, Benoît. 1992. *Tintin and the World of Hergé: An Illustrated History.* Boston: Little, Brown.

GENE KANNENBERG JR.

Title IX and Girls' Sports

"Title IX," commonly known for its application to athletics, has played an important but controversial role in expanding athletics opportunities for women and girls. Title IX of the Education Amendments of 1972 is a federal statute that prohibits sex discrimination in education programs and activities receiving federal financial assistance. The statute applies to athletics programs at federally funded private and public educational institutions, and is enforced by the U.S. Department of Education's Office for Civil Rights. As outlined in the 1979 Policy Interpretation, Title IX regulation for athletics requires compliance in financial assistance, accommodation of interests and abilities, and other program areas. The Policy Interpretation, though designed for intercollegiate athletics, may also apply to club, intramural, and interscholastic athletics programs.

Since the passage of Title IX, the number of girls participating in athletics has risen dramatically. Fewer than 300,000 girls participated in high school sports in 1971, compared to more than 3.6 million boys; by 2001, the number for girls had reached over 2.7 million, compared to more than 3.9 million boys. The perception of female athletes in society has also undergone change as a result of Title IX. Increased media coverage of women's sports, successes at the

Olympic Games, and the establishment of professional leagues reflect only a few ways in which women are redefined by their image in athletics. Many argued, however, that despite the apparent progress Title IX has made in promoting gender equity, women and girls continued to receive unequal opportunities, benefits, and treatment.

Title IX's meaning for athletics in the United States has been contested since the 1970s, spawning debates in Congress, courts, educational institutions, and various organizations. In particular, the three-part test for assessing Title IX compliance has generated intense disagreement about the intent and purpose of Title IX. Opponents of the test argue that it creates proportionality "quotas" which discriminate against males, leaving schools little choice other than to eliminate, or to reduce budgets for, male sports programs. Others contend that since females are inherently less interested in playing sports than males, the test embodies a misinterpretation of Title IX. Proponents of the three-part test emphasize the correlation between interest levels and a history of discriminatory policies, and argue that female teams and Title IX have been wrongly blamed for the decisions schools make regarding male teams. Stronger enforcement of Title IX regulation, some believe, is necessary to ensure that educational institutions provide nondiscriminatory opportunities for females in all areas of athletics.

Much of the debate surrounding Title IX has centered on the statute's application to intercollegiate programs, but Title IX compliance remains problematic at the younger levels as well. For example, in *Communities for Equity v. Michigan High School Athletic Association* (2001) a U.S. District Court ruled that the scheduling of female high school sports in nontraditional seasons was in violation of Title IX and the Fourteenth Amendment's Equal Protection Clause. Further research that focuses on elementary and secondary school athletics programs is needed to fully examine Title IX's impact on girls' participation in sports. As the controversy over Title IX continues to unfold both on and off the field, this landmark piece of legislation will have far-reaching implications for athletics for both girls and boys.

See also: **Sports.**

BIBLIOGRAPHY

National Coalition for Women and Girls in Education. 2002. *Title IX Athletics Policies: Issues and Data for Education Decision Makers.* Washington, DC: National Coalition for Women and Girls in Education.

"A Policy Interpretation: Title IX and Intercollegiate Athletics." 1979. *Federal Register* 44, no. 239: 71413 et seq. Microfiche.

U.S. Department of Education, Office for Civil Rights. 1997. *Title IX: 25 Years of Progress.* Washington, DC: United States Department of Education.

INTERNET RESOURCE

National Federation of High School Associations. 2002. "2001 High School Participation Survey." Available from <www.nfhs.org/>.

ANDREA KWON

Tobacco. *See* Smoking.

Toilet Training

Although nearly every human learns to control the time and place of urination and defecation, there is considerable historical and cultural variation in this training. The individual's control of these bodily functions carries psychological importance, as the child's body can become the site of a power struggle between the child and the adult caretakers. Children are socialized to surrender to society this particular control over their bodies, and to some anthropologists, such as Mary Douglas (*Natural Symbols*, 1970), the body serves as a powerful symbol of society, including the important cultural categories *clean* and *dirty*. As "dirt" of a special sort, human urine and feces are treated in variable ways that reveal a great deal about the culture. The very phrase *toilet training*, signals the tendency of most Western societies to treat urine and feces as dirty, dangerous materials that must be disposed of safely.

There are few historical references to the training of these bodily functions until the rise of published advice literature, usually written by physicians, in the seventeenth century. In general, the trend over time has been for the advice literature to recommend increasingly permissive approaches to socializing the child, including the early regimes of feeding and toilet training. In the British American colonies, for example, the literature advised parents to make toilet training early and rigorous, a matter of exerting adult will on the willful child. By the eighteenth century and into the nineteenth, the effect of ENLIGHTENMENT thinking was to get parents to see child training as a rational (rather than a necessarily moral) process. Structure and rigid scheduling dominated the child-training regime of the first half of the nineteenth century, but in the latter half the increasing separation in the middle class between the public sphere and the private, domestic sphere, coupled with the increasing responsibility of women for the domestic sphere, led to gentler methods. Still, by modern standards, toilet training well into the early twentieth century stressed structure, regularity, and early onset.

By the early twentieth century, SIGMUND FREUD's ideas about socializing the anal system and about the consequences of events creating anal fixation provided a possible rationale for taking a different approach toward toilet training, though behaviorism, best represented by JOHN B. WATSON, still dominated the advice literature. Behaviorism recognized the child's strong drives and desires and aimed to socialize those desires through consistent, structured training. But by the 1940s, the advice literature assumed a less willful, driven child and advocated a more relaxed, permissive approach to toilet training. Dr. BENJAMIN SPOCK's best-selling book, *Baby and Child Care* (1946), went even further, warning that parental anxiety about toilet training can cause more problems than a relaxed, permissive regime that recognized children's individuality and variability. The advice literature since Spock has remained permissive with regard to toilet training.

While the authors of child-training advice literature did not generally adopt Freudian thinking about the relationships between anal socialization and later adult personality, some psychologists, anthropologists, and sociologists employed psychoanalytic theory in the 1940s and 1950s in trying to understand "group character." One such interdisciplinary project was Whiting and Child's 1953 use of ethnographic reports on seventy-five primitive societies and an American middle-class sample to test specific hypotheses about the relationships between child-training practices (including the socialization of the anal system) and adult customs and traits, and another was Miller and Swanson's 1958 attempts to correlate child-training practices (including toilet training), social class status, and adult personality traits. Interdisciplinary inquiry of this sort disappeared in the 1960s, when group character studies fell into disrepute.

In comparative cultural studies, the researchers found a wide range of practices in anal training. The median age for beginning serious toilet training, for example, was two years of age, with half of the societies beginning as early as age one and a few (e.g., the Bena of Africa) waiting until the child was nearly five. Middle-class American practices tended toward the early extreme in the 1930s through 1950s samples, typically beginning toilet training at six months. Similarly, while there was a wide range of cultural practices regarding the severity of anal training in those studies, the American mothers tended to be quite severe.

Historians have noted the impact of changes in material culture and technology upon toilet training. Gideon's 1948 and Ogle's 1996 histories of household technology recount this revolution and its connections to social history. The invention and wide availability of household washing machines, for example, made the laundering of cloth diapers less onerous, possibly contributing to the relaxation of mothers' distress over dirty diapers, and the invention and inexpensive availability of disposable diapers made the chore that much easier. This is also a factor in explaining why the emphasis on toilet training relaxed faster in the United States than it did in Europe. Similarly, the invention of the zipper,

replacing buttons, and then of Velcro fasteners, replacing zippers, has made it much easier for children to disrobe quickly and to get on the toilet when the urge of urination or a bowel movement comes to them. Toilet training in the late twentieth and early twenty-first centuries has seen the commercial availability of a range of child-sized portable toilets and toilet seats, along with picture and reading books aimed at making toilet training less intimidating and even "fun" for children.

See also: **Child-Rearing Advice Literature; Diapers and Toileting.**

BIBLIOGRAPHY

Giedion, Siegfried. 1948. *Mechanization Takes Command: A Contribution to Anonymous History.* New York: Oxford University Press.

Grant, Julia. 1998. *Raising Baby by the Book: The Education of American Mothers.* New Haven, CT: Yale University Press.

Miller, Daniel R., and Guy E. Swanson. 1958. *The Changing American Parent: A Study in the Detroit Area.* New York: Wiley.

Ogle, Maureen. 1996. *All the Modern Conveniences: American Household Plumbing, 1840–1890.* Baltimore, MD: Johns Hopkins University Press.

Whiting, John, and Irvin L. Child. 1953. *Child Training and Personality: A Cross-Cultural Study.* New Haven, CT: Yale University Press.

JAY MECHLING

Tolkien, J. R. R. *See* Lord of the Rings and J. R. R. Tolkien.

Tolstoy's Childhood in Russia

Childhood in Russia was a literary invention, and it appeared more or less fully formed in the pseudo-autobiographical novel *Childhood* (1852), the debut work by Lev Tolstoy (1828–1910). This is not to assert that before the publication of Tolstoy's work Russians did not experience childhood as a separate phase of life subject to its own laws. However, those who had had such experiences failed to record them in anything more than rudimentary form. The appearance of Tolstoy's novel, and a complementary one by the lesser-known writer Sergei Aksakov in 1858 entitled *The Childhood Years of Bagrov's Grandson*, allowed for the systematization of Russian childhood. Henceforward, autobiographically oriented works by Russians not only tended to include extensive sections devoted to childhood, but autobiographers almost invariably recalled their childhood through a Tolstoyan filter. It should be noted that at least through the early twentieth century we can speak about Russian childhood almost exclusively in connection with the gentry, which made up some 10 percent of the population. Other Russians generally lacked the leisure to reflect on their childhood memories, whatever they might have been.

First and foremost, Russian childhood is distinguished by the fact that it is supposed to have been the happiest stage of life, a time that can never be equaled by adult experience. Chapter 15 of Tolstoy's work begins with what may have been the most influential sentences Tolstoy ever wrote as far as the Russian cultural mind was concerned: "Happy, happy unforgettable time of childhood! How can one not love, not cherish its memories?" Certainly for the next eighty years, practically every first-person description of childhood in Russia, whether in fictional or nonfictional form, was oriented to them. Nineteenth-century autobiographers not only repeated Tolstoy's overall interpretation of childhood, they also borrowed typically Tolstoyan situations, cadences, and turns of phrase. Of course, to say that Tolstoy invented a paradigm that was used for understanding childhood by generations of Russians does not mean that he made this view up out of whole cloth. Rather, it is likely that Tolstoy's vision had such staying power because it coincided with existing Russian views. In any case, it has become quite impossible to separate literary reality from real life, particularly because in a highly bookish country like Russia, no one who sits down to recall his or her childhood or who thinks about the kind of childhood society should provide does so without having Tolstoy's work in mind.

While some autobiographers contented themselves with mere variations on themes of Tolstoy, others strove to develop the myth of childhood as a golden age. Their authors maintained that there was a qualitative difference separating the world in which they grew up from that in which they lived as adults. Eventually, and particularly as the gentry decayed as a class, a happy childhood was seen as their last possession, a synecdoche for traditional Russia itself. Novels and memoirs written in exile after the Soviet revolution, such as Ivan Bunin's *The Life of Arseniev* or Vladimir Nabokov's *Speak, Memory*, continued this tradition, linking a happy childhood to pre-Bolshevik Russian life itself.

The myth of the happy childhood is generally accompanied by some corollaries, including the myth of the perfect mother, the myth of the impotent father, and the equation of the locus of childhood—the country estate—with paradise. As Ekaterina Sabaneeva put it:

> The rivers, the groves, the village paths on which we rode with our parents left such deep impressions on me that my entire moral nature has been woven of them, as if from threads. It is clear to me that my attachment to my homeland, to its people, to the church grew from this foundation: those threads and impressions of childhood gave a direction to the whole contents of my life. (p. 2)

The idealization of the rural paradise in which upper-class autobiographers grew up is often set against the cities in which they spent the latter part of their youth. Constant descriptions of paradise lost lend a nostalgic and elegiac accent to their autobiographies. As a result, instead of viewing life's journey in terms of gradual growth and improvement through the course of one's life, the Russian model is based on a gradual falling away from the perfection of childhood.

One might have expected that the complete destruction of the gentry class in the twentieth century would have led to the appearance of new paradigms of childhood in Russian culture. To be sure, the early twentieth century did witness some new cultural models. One should note, for example, the modernist ideal of childhood as the time in which an observant artistic individual's first impressions are formed, as described in works such as *Kotik Letaev* by Andrei Belyi, *The Noise of Time* by Osip Mandelstam, and *Zhenya Luvers' Childhood* by Boris Pasternak. Such rarified literary work could not, however, provide a general paradigm for Russians. A more potentially influential model was provided by Maxim Gorky in his pseudo-autobiographical novel *Childhood*. In this work, the overall impression is one of childhood as a time of difficulty and hard knocks. In the gentry tradition, recalling childhood leads to nostalgically pleasant reminiscences. By contrast, for Gorky the past must be remembered in order for it to be "exposed to its roots and torn out of grim and shameful life—torn out of the very soul and memory of man" (p. 302). Autobiography is not a nostalgic attempt at eternal return but a means of overcoming the past. Humankind, for whom the child is a synecdoche, is seen growing ever upward toward the sun, which provides the light for the "bright future." Gorky's work thus does not merely express the experience of a writer from a different socioeconomic background; it challenges the Russian notion of childhood as such.

Nevertheless, despite his iconic status for Soviet literature, Gorky and his *Childhood* did not provide the ultimate model for Soviet writers or society. By the 1930s the Soviet government announced that Socialism had been "achieved and won" in the USSR. As a result, a paradigm of childhood which saw it as a period of misery leading to gradual improvement and enlightenment was inappropriate. Instead, the myth of the happy childhood was fated to make a comeback, not precisely in Tolstoyan terms, but in a formula that every Soviet child of the 1930s and 1940s was expected to know by heart: "Thank you for our happy childhood, Comrade Stalin."

See also: **Autobiographies.**

BIBLIOGRAPHY

Aksakov, Sergei. 1984 [1858]. *A Family Chronicle: Childhood Years of Bagrov's Grandson.* Trans. Olga Shartse. Moscow, Raduga Publishers.

Belyi, Andrei. 1999 [1917–1918]. *Kotik Letaev.* Trans. Gerald J. Janecek. Evanston, IL: Northwestern University Press.

Brooks, Jeffrey. 2000. *Thank You, Comrade Stalin! Soviet Public Culture from Revolution to Cold War.* Princeton, NJ: Princeton University Press.

Bunin, Ivan A. 1994 [1930–1939]. *The Life of Arseniev.* Trans. Gleb Struve and Hamish Miles (books 1–4), and Heidi Hillis, Susan

McKean, and Sven A. Wolf (book 5). Evanston, IL: Northwestern University Press.

Creuziger, Clementine G. K. 1996. *Childhood in Russia: Representation and Reality*. Lanham, MD: University Press of America.

Gorky, Maxim. 1961 [1913–1914]. *Childhood*. Trans. Margaret Wettlin. New York: Oxford University Press.

Harris, Jane Gary, ed. 1990. *Autobiographical Statements in Twentieth-Century Russian Literature*. Princeton, NJ: Princeton University Press.

Kirschenbaum, Lisa A. 2001. *Small Comrades: Revolutionizing Childhood in Soviet Russia, 1917–1932*. New York: Garland.

Mandelstam, Osip. 1988 [1925]. *The Noise of Time, And Other Prose Pieces*. Trans. Clarence Brown. London: Quartet.

Nabokov, Vladimir. 1951. *Speak, Memory: A Memoir*. London: Gollancz.

Pasternak, Boris. 1986 [1922]. *Zhenya Luvers' Childhood*. In *Boris Pasternak: The Voice of Prose*, trans. Christopher Barnes. Edinburgh: Polygon.

Roosevelt, Priscilla. 1995. *Life on the Russian Country Estate: A Social and Cultural History*. New Haven, CT: Yale University Press.

Sabaneeva, Ekaterina A. 1914. *Vospominaniia o bylom*. St. Petersburg: M. Stasiulevich.

Tolstoy, Leo. 1930 [1852]. *Childhood, Boyhood, and Youth*. Trans. Louise and Aylmer Maude. New York: Oxford University Press.

Wachtel, Andrew. 1990. *The Battle for Childhood: Creation of a Russian Myth*. Stanford, CA: Stanford University Press.

ANDREW WACHTEL

Toys

While toys today are widely associated with children, historically toys were the province of adults and were only gradually passed on and relegated to the young. Playthings, long rare and slowly changing, became far more varied and transient in modern society, reflecting conflicting cultural and economic influences over the childhood experience.

Origins of Modern Toys

For all but the rich, the preindustrial family's need to work meant PLAY and toys were not encouraged by parents. In ancient and medieval times, adults shared objects of play with children primarily during festivals as occasions for emotional release. Common play objects, such as hoops, tops, balls, and even hobbyhorses, were only gradually abandoned by adults as childish. The passing of toys to children was closely related to the sixteenth-century shift from community spectacle to domestic celebrations (with the miniaturization of crèche, battle, and animal scenes for family amusement and edification). Miniature scenes eventually became children's play sets (e.g., the sixteenth-century wooden Noah's Ark). Only in the late sixteenth century did miniature soldiers shift from being adult to children's toys. In the eighteenth century domestic miniatures, which had formerly been custom-built for luxurious display for adult women, became doll cabinets and houses to instruct girls in the arts of housekeeping and domestic fashion. Domestic automata, mechanical figures or animals that were powered by water and even steam, had amused wealthy men from ancient times, but it was not until the nineteenth century that mass production and cheap clock and winding works let adults pass these novelties down to children as toys.

Poor children, of course, found time to make their own rag- and straw-stuffed DOLLS or balls from animal skins, and created games in unsupervised groups with whittled sticks and castaway bits of cloth. Traditional toys, such as hoops pushed along the street with a stick, or hand-made cup-and-ball toys, let children display skill until the end of the nineteenth century.

The toy industry began in southern Germany (Nuremberg and Groeden Valley especially) in the fourteenth century. At first, seasonal craftspeople specialized in carving wooden animal figures sold regionally through peddlers. But by the end of the eighteenth century, cheap tin toy armies for boys and miniature kitchens for girls were manufactured according to the strict specifications of powerful merchants and distributed across Europe and North America to children in middle-class families. European toy makers also found new, cheaper materials (like sawdust-based "composition" for dolls' heads by 1850 and lithographed paper on wood to simulate domestic interiors or hand painted scenes on play sets by 1890). These innovations not only put more playthings into the hands of less wealthy children, but also made for more variety and more rapid change in toys, thus turning playthings into a fashion industry. Nevertheless, older craft production and distribution through merchants survived in many branches of the toy industry throughout the nineteenth century, delaying mechanization. German toys prevailed until World War I, when Germany still exported 75 percent of its output.

Toys in the United States

Until the mid-nineteenth century, American children had relatively few playthings, especially after the toddler years. Parents seldom thought of toys as tools of learning or character building, but rather as frivolities that interfered with the learning of sex work roles through assisting adults in their daily tasks. Religious strictures against idleness, especially in Puritan New England, made toys suspect, except perhaps on SUNDAYS or holidays. Only after the Civil War, with the spread of factories and the coming of department stores and mail order catalogs, did the American toy industry begin to emerge. Innovative interlocking building blocks and comical windup toys appeared in the 1860s and 1870s. But more common were simple miniatures of adult work tools (toy hammers, saws, and garden tool sets for boys and dolls and miniature houseware sets for girls).

Toys became part of an ideal childhood in the middle-class home. Industrialization removed production from the home and reduced the need for child labor, making playthings essential to preparing the young for adult roles. Parlor board and card games and "scientific" toys (featuring optical illusions) replaced shared domestic work to create family loyalties and to train the child in the values of honesty and competition. Such "educational" playthings served aspiring middle-class parents to isolate their young from often-unruly street gangs while also providing antidotes for loneliness. With greater affluence, the young were increasingly encouraged to enjoy the spontaneity and the pleasures of their freedom from work and responsibility. Playthings were both vehicles to introduce the real world and fantasy objects that shut off the child from that world.

Beginning around 1900 toy manufacturing diversified greatly and began to offer almost annual changes. As boys were withheld longer from the workforce and girls spent less time caring for younger siblings and doing household duties, playthings for older children became more common. Boys up to sixteen years old could look to sophisticated toy construction sets, toy microscopes, chemistry sets, and electric trains as fun, but also as practical preparation for modern careers in engineering, business, and science. Toys became even more sex stereotyped as boys' toys increasingly idealized technology, constant innovation, and the values of competition and teamwork. By contrast, a new generation of playthings for females featured companion and baby dolls, meant to encourage emotional attachments and nurturing "instincts." New interest in early child development created a demand for building blocks, crafts, and other educational playthings. The didactic and often austere character of educational toys (rejecting, for example, any association with popular film or comic book characters) limited their appeal and led to their declining role in children's lives by the 1960s.

Other popular toys encouraged fantasy. They were sometimes drawn from folk literature (like the Scottish elf Brownies figures and play sets of the 1890s) but more often from the ever-changing stories and characters of comics and movies, including Kewpie dolls (1912), Charlie Chaplin dolls (1914), and eventually Mickey Mouse figures (1930). The TEDDY BEAR, based on a story of Teddy Roosevelt sparing a baby bear on a hunt, became an international craze in 1906. This toy, in contrast to the hard wooden or stiff cloth animals of the past, was cuddly (made of upholstering fabric and filled with soft stuffing) and provided children security and protection. Teddies also made children seem innocent and charming and later reminded adults of their own childhoods. Most toys of the early twentieth century were intended to convey adult messages to children either by giving them the adult's image of their future or by presenting adult fantasies or nostalgia about ideal childhood.

Growing Fantasy and Autonomy in Toys

A major shift in playthings began in the 1930s during the Great Depression. In response to reduced sales, toy makers

Boy with Toys on Porch (c. 1909), photographed by Underwood and Underwood. By the early twentieth century, toys had become part of the ideal middle-class childhood. Boys' toys idealized technology and innovation; toy trains were particularly popular. © CORBIS.

offered cheaper toys, often sold by the piece rather than in sets (as they had often been sold in the past). This tended to encourage children to purchase their own toys, bypassing parental control. Toy companies also began to use licensed images of popular radio and movie personalities in their toys to increase sales. Buck Rogers toy guns, Little Orphan Annie decoder rings, Popeye wind-up figures, and SHIRLEY TEMPLE dolls served as props to reenact stories or to identify with heroes. Military figures, science fiction play sets, and cowboy cap guns gained a new prominence in boys' play in the 1930s as war approached and the optimism that had characterized the previous generation of construction and scientific toys declined.

In many ways, toys during the post-1945 BABY BOOM GENERATION returned to the era before 1930. In a period of new scientific and technological advances and perhaps closer bonds between fathers and sons, space toys and miniature cars and trucks were common. Adult fascination with the rugged individualism and moral certainty of the pioneer, cowboy, and Indian fighter led to parents' buying cowboy suits, holster sets, and Lincoln Logs as well as frontier ranch and Fort Apache play sets for their sons. These often featured movie and TV western heroes such as Roy Rogers, Davy Crockett, and the Lone Ranger. By contrast, parents gave their baby boomer daughters miniatures of mother's work, including kitchen sets and replicas of name-brand products like Toni home permanents, presumably to teach girls their future roles as homemakers and consumers. As in the past, baby and companion dolls continued to invite girls to build play around relationships and emotional ties.

While the 1950s seemed to be a throwback to the past, there was one significant innovation in the world of toys during this period—the beginning of mass ADVERTISING of toys directly to children on TV programs. The *Mickey Mouse Club* was not the first children's show to promote toys when it first appeared on TV in 1955, but its advertising was designed to appeal to the child's imagination rather than the parent's values. Mattel toys proved that year-round advertising featuring children actors could create a mass demand for "burp guns" and Barbie dolls even outside of the Christmas gift season. Increasingly children pressured their parents into buying the "must-have" toys seen on TV.

Changes since 1960

In 1959, Mattel's Barbie doll, with her model's body, broke from the friendship and nurturing themes of the companion and baby dolls that had predominated since the 1900s, and put grown-up fashion and spending in its place. To the eight-year-old of 1960, Barbie represented a hoped-for future of teenage freedom from the dependencies of childhood that ignored the likely future responsibilities of her own mother. Barbie certainly did not teach girls to shed female sex stereotypes. Rather, she encouraged girls to associate being grown up with Barbie's "shapely" female body and with her freedom and carefree consumption.

G.I. Joe, introduced in 1964, was at first a boy's military dress-up doll modeled after real soldiers. During the Vietnam War when military toys became controversial, Joe and his friends became a line of adventure figures (who searched for treasure, for example). By 1975 G.I. Joe was again a fighter, but in a science fiction world divorced from the experience of real war. By 1978 boys' toys had become props to reenact the fantastic gadget-filled adventure of the *Star Wars* series, when the producers sold the rights to produce millions of action figures of the movie heroes and villains to Kenner Toys.

Since 1982, toy companies have produced TV cartoons based on their own toy lines. Mattel's series, *He-Man and Masters of the Universe*, featured warring characters from a TV program. However, with these toys, unlike the toy guns of the past, the tiny figures, not the boy, pulled the triggers.

Following on the success of action figures, toy makers introduced little girls to their own world of fantasy figures and play sets. In the early 1980s, greeting card companies developed lines of minidolls (Strawberry Shortcake, Care Bears,

and others) popularized with Saturday morning cartoons and movies. In the 1990s, the periodic release of movies like *Little Mermaid* or *Aladdin* created demand for toy figures associated with movie characters. Each child received her or his own "heroes" based on the media craze of the moment. While the American toy industry grew to sales of over 20 billion by the end of the twentieth century, parents' values and memories had little to do with children's toys even as children experienced more autonomy, albeit in a highly commercialized form of play.

Fate of the Toy Industry Outside the United States

In contrast, toys remained relatively static after 1920 in Europe and elsewhere. American toy innovations penetrated European childhood, especially with Walt DISNEY's aggressive marketing of character licenses to European doll and toy makers in 1935. The Americanization of toys meant a shift of play away from an adult world of training and toward an international culture of childhood created by linking children's movies and other media to toys. Of course, older toys survived after World War II in Europe: British Meccano construction sets returned and the Lesney "Matchbox" cars updated a tradition of play based on realistic miniatures of adult life. The Swedish Brio Company perpetuated a tradition of high-quality wooden toys (simple trains, cars, animals, and blocks) and promoted them as an educational alternative to licensed character toys. In the 1960s, the German Playmobil Company thrived by offering sturdy plastic updates of traditional wooden play sets. German toy makers abandoned war toys and specialized in electric trains, stuffed animals, and fine character dolls.

Where TV advertising was minimal or prohibited (e.g., Sweden), TV toys were somewhat slower to dominate the European market. Traditional craft toys (such as dolls, miniature animals, jumping jacks, and kites), made of common materials and featuring generic humor, still exist in the street markets of Asia and Africa in great regional variation. But even in poor countries, where parents cannot afford American name-brand action figures and dolls, local manufacturers make cheap imitations.

From the 1960s, European toy companies survived by imitating or becoming subsidiaries of aggressive American toy makers (e.g., with imitations of Barbie or European translations of G.I. Joe as Action Man). American control of licensed characters, associated with globally distributed movies like *Star Wars*, assured American dominance of the new type of toy line. The most dramatic exception was the Danish Lego interlocking blocks, which, starting in the mid-1960s, became a global boy's toy. By the late 1980s, however, Lego compromised with the American toy industry by introducing kits or "systems" designed to construct a single model based on exotic science fiction or fantasy themes. While educational toys survived in specialized upscale stores, appealing especially to parents intent on giving their infants and toddlers a head start, the older child has become part of a global consumer culture through satellite TV, movies, COMIC BOOKS, and after 1991 especially video games. Toys are increasingly designed and marketed through American and Japanese companies and manufactured in South China near the international commercial center of Hong Kong for global distribution.

While some toy companies have undertaken research on children's response to new toys (such as Mattel and Lego) and development through toys (e.g., Fisher Price), only recently have children's playthings attracted impartial scholarly research (such as that by the International Toy Research Association). Toy collections are often small and specialized reflecting the particular interests of collectors. But major displays of historic toys are available at the Margaret Strong Museum (Rochester, New York), the Bethnal Green Museum of Childhood (London, England), Legoland (Billund, Denmark), and the Brio Toy Museum (Osby, Sweden).

See also: **Boyhood; Child Development, History of the Concept of; Construction Toys; Early Modern Europe; Economics and Children in Western Societies; European Industrialization; Girlhood; Theories of Play.**

BIBLIOGRAPHY

Chanan, Gabriel, and Hazel Francis. 1984. *Toys and Games of Children of the World.* Paris: UNESCO.

Cross, Gary. 1997. *Kids' Stuff: Toys and the Changing World of American Childhood.* Cambridge, MA: Harvard University Press.

Hewitt, Karen, and Louis Roomet, eds. 1983. *Educational Toys in America: 1800 to the Present.* Burlington, VT: Robert Hull Fleming Museum.

Kline, Stephen. 1993. *Out of the Garden: Toys and Children's Culture in the Age of TV Marketing.* New York: Verso.

McClintock, Inez, and Marshall McClintock. 1961. *Toys in America.* Washington, DC: Public Affairs Press.

GARY CROSS

Toy Soldiers (Tin Soldiers)

Toy soldiers, tin soldiers, or model soldiers are miniature figures representing soldiers from ancient times to the present day. They come in different sizes, usually between 30 millimeters and 75 millimeters measured between the base plate and the eyes to compensate for the height of the headgear. Different types of toy soldiers are the so-called flats, paper-thin castings painted and shaded to look three-dimensional. Semiflats are a few millimeters thicker, and in the case of cavalry, often produced with a semiflat horse and a round rider. The most popular today are the round, solid, or hollow-cast figures.

Toy soldiers are used by children to play with, but can also be used by adults to fight war games as a pastime or for instructive purposes. Toy soldiers—old and new—as well as the expensive and detailed model soldiers that are produced by cottage industries in several countries, are popular collectors' items.

Boys have always been intrigued by war toys. When the Egyptian prince Emsah was buried almost four thousand years ago, he was accompanied in his grave by a unique collection of toy soldiers, which today shoulder by shoulder march steadfastly forward on their wooden bases in the museum in Cairo. Before the modern period, toys were a luxury reserved for the rich and powerful. The French queen Marie de'Medici gave her young son, the future King Louis XIII three hundred silver toy soldiers. The royal collection at Rosenborg Castle in Copenhagen has a collection of silver soldiers made by the silversmith Fabritius for King Frederick IV. French king Louis XIV had a similar army, which however was melted down during the economic crisis of 1715. Catherine the Great of Russia wrote in her autobiography that Tsar Peter III as a young boy had several hundred toy soldiers made of wood, lead, starch, and wax: "They were all paraded on festive occasions, and a special arrangement of springs which could be released by pulling a string, produced a sound as if they fired their guns." It comes as no surprise, then, that the French emperor Napoleon presented his son, the king of Rome, with a large number of toy soldiers. The finest were a set of 117 gold figures made by the goldsmith Claude Odinot.

Toy soldiers as they are known today appeared around the middle of the eighteenth century. Among the first producers of flat figures were the Hilpert family of Nuremberg, Germany. The figures were inspired by the colorful uniforms of Napoleon Bonaparte and the Prussian king Frederick the Great. It is probably figures of this type that inspired the Danish fairytale writer Hans Christian Andersen's tale "The Steadfast Tin Soldier."

The first literary reference to round and solid figures, rather than flat figures, was in the German poet Goethe's *Dichtung und Wahrheit* (Poetry and truth). Goethe describes a boy and a girl who are playing with some tin soldiers that are "round, solid, and meticulously made." The French producer Lucotte started his work before 1789 but no figures made before 1850 were known to still be in existence in the early twenty-first century. One of the greatest collections of these figures are preserved at Blenheim Castle in England, and belonged to the British wartime prime minister Sir Winston Churchill. He describes his army in his biography *My Early Life*: "I had almost 1500 of the same size, all British and organised in an infantry division and a cavalry brigade. I had 15 fieldpieces but lacked a train. My father's old friend, Sir Drummond Wolff, noticed this and created a fund, which to a certain extent remedied this."

The Lucotte Company was bought by the French toy firm Cuperlu, Blondel and Gerbeau, in 1825, which was bought in turn by Mignot in 1876. Mignot continued to exist into the twenty-first century. Besides soldiers, the company produced a number of interesting sets, including a picturesque group of firefighters and vehicles from the Paris Fire Brigade, circa 1900.

The most prolific toy soldier manufacturers were the German manufacturer Georg Heyde and the British toy maker William Britain. Heyde made 4.5 centimeter round, solid figures, with interchangeable heads so that each body could be used to represent the armies of a number of countries. Britain founded his company in 1893 and developed a special metal-saving way of casting hollow figures that became very popular. His first figure represented a British guardsman in red tunic and black bearskin hat, which was quickly followed by a multitude of soldiers from the British Indian army, from the Boer War, World War I, the Abyssinian war, and World War II, complete with guns, vehicles, and airplanes. Britain was still producing toy soldiers into the twenty-first century, but the figures became far too expensive to be used as toys and were mostly directed towards collectors. Toy soldiers today are almost exclusively unpainted plastic figures.

Between the world wars the German companies Elastolin and Lineol produced a large range of 75 millimeter resin figures, representing soldiers from many countries—although the majority of toys represented German soldiers and Nazi party leaders, such as Adolf Hitler and Hermann Goering. Elastolin and Lineol, like Britain and other makers, also made an extensive line of farm people, animals, and equipment.

See also: **Construction Toys; Dolls; Toys; War in the Twentieth Century.**

BIBLIOGRAPHY

Fontana, Dennis. 1991. *The War Toys 2.* London: New Cavendish Books.

Opre, James. 1985. *Britain's Toy Soldiers 1893–1932.* London: Victor Gollancz.

Polaine, Reggie and David Hawkins. 1991 [1976]. *The War Toys 1.* London: New Cavendish Books.

NILS ERIC BOESGAARD

Toy Technology

Production of games and TOYS once involved little in the way of technical sophistication. Early toys were handmade by parents or in limited quantities by artisans. Later, nineteenth-century industrial toy production benefited from technological advances in tool and die, ceramics, and paper, among others, in the same manner as other industries. Doll makers profited from gains in bisque techniques and materials, and doll clothiers used analine dye technology for their miniature couture. But unlike many other industries of the

period, toy manufacturers found it unnecessary to dismantle a new machine in favor of the most recent device. Although it was hardly a craft operation, toy manufacture depended more for success on the creativity of its designers, marketing, and advertising than on technology. Toys, after all, were rather simple objects.

There were in fact only four technological innovations that affected toy manufacture—high-speed color lithography in the nineteenth century and injectable plastics, television, and the microchip in the twentieth. Color lithography enabled toymakers to produce colorful games, brightly illustrated books, and decaled toys. Even then, however, some manufacturers chose to contract their lithographic work to companies specializing in such work. The advent of plastics after World War II created the model-building sector within the toy industry and allowed the major toy manufacturers to market their products with plastic dice, counters, and in some cases, three-dimensional playing boards. At Parker Brothers, for example, plastics technology enabled the company to issue Monopoly with plastic houses and hotels rather than the wooden ones of the earlier editions. Other companies, such as Fisher Price, changed the basic material for their preschool toys from wood to plastic, and doll makers had a new material for sculpting doll bodies and creating realistic hair. TELEVISION altered toy marketing and furnished new toy concepts via licensing of television characters such as Fess Parker as Davy Crockett and program formats such as quiz show games. But it was the microchip that utterly transformed the toy industry.

Advent of Electronic Toys and Games

Beginning in the late 1970s, the largest toy manufacturers confronted difficult business decisions with regard to their participation in the electronic toys and games market. Each company evaluated the new market in light of its corporate personality, its perception of its place within the industry, and its available resources. Board game manufacturers were a case in general and Milton Bradley a case in particular.

For Parker Brothers, maker of Monopoly and other classics, decisions about electronic games spelled short-term profits followed by sharp losses that persuaded its parent company, General Mills, to spin off its toy group as Kenner Parker, which was in turn swallowed by Tonka. For Milton Bradley, entering the electronic games market wrecked havoc with the corporate balance sheet, forcing its sale to a competitor, Hasbro, to avoid a hostile takeover. Mattel's experiment with Intellivision created financial liabilities greater than the assets of the company at one point, compelling the company to restructure entirely. Hasbro and Selchow and Righter, however, found little to attract them to electronic games and toys, and the companies avoided any obligation to microchip technology. Selchow and Righter's minimal commitment to electronic games and introduction of the popular trivia game Trivial Pursuit allowed the company to maintain its position in the industry as well as increase its market share until lack of family management forced its sale to Coleco and ultimately to Hasbro. Hasbro's caution freed the company to capitalize on the consumer's return to basic toys and augmented its bottom line. By 1991 Hasbro had absorbed Tonka, making it the largest toy manufacturer in the world. Microchip technology, in short, rearranged the toy industry, destroying some companies and turning others into titans.

Milton Bradley, a century-old firm and the successful manufacturer of such classic games as Candyland and the Checkered Game of Life, illustrated this transformation. In 1978 Milton Bradley marketed Simon, a fat, Frisbee-shaped device that proved to be the most popular game of the year. *Newsweek* featured the game in a December issue, and the company could not keep pace with the demand. Using the randomizing capabilities of the microprocessor, Simon was a game entirely dependent on the characteristics of the microprocessor and at the same time maintained the traditional mode of play. Players sat around Simon and attempted to repeat the game's pattern of flashing colors. Its success diverted Milton Bradley's energy away from the development of video games, and the company chose not to produce its own video console, believing that such machines and games would shortly be replaced by multiple-use home computers or entertainment centers. Management predicated its rationale on the evolution of a standardized cassette or other electronic medium. When this occurred, Milton Bradley reasoned, the company would develop toys and games to take advantage of the market.

While Milton Bradley executives were traveling to the company's European subsidiaries in the late 1960s and early 1970s, other men were on their way to the moon. Nolan Bushnell, founder of Atari Corporation, had perceived a less scientific application for microchips and, in partnership with another engineer, designed a game called Pong in 1972. Pong in turn spawned a host of imitators, a novel toy producer—the video game company (Nintendo, Sega, and Xbox among the best known), and an entirely different market sector. With Pong's success and the subsequent popularity of the Atari 2600 game console, established game manufacturers saw that there was money—a great deal of money—to be made in video games. Among those watching Atari's mounting profits were the executives at Milton Bradley, and the company entered the video game market with its own game console, Vectrex. By mid-1983 it was clear that Milton Bradley had badly miscalculated; its foray into the video hardware and games market had incurred heavy losses, endangering the financial well-being of the firm. In 1985 Hasbro absorbed Milton Bradley, and Milton Bradley became a division of the larger company, represented only by its "MB" logo on Hasbro's game products.

"I think," said one retailer in 1982 before the toy companies sustained their losses, "it's clear that the video market

scared the daylights out of the board game manufacturers. It was just the shot in the arm they needed to begin promoting their products." Some manufacturers and many consumers returned to familiar, staple products, but for several large, established manufacturers the "shot in the arm" had come too late and had not saved the patient. Milton Bradley discovered that neither adding electronic play features to an already existing game nor buying licenses guaranteed success in the video game scramble. Major game manufacturers, moreover, had failed to exploit the full scope of microchip capabilities; rather, they elected to apply electronic technology to traditional game design—an instance of "add microchips and stir." The mode of play remained generally the same; the board was identical to the nonelectronic board, but the board could do certain tasks for the player. Microchip technology in the 1980s, in short, altered the toy industry—once a group of many small manufacturers—into an oligopoly—a small group of large manufacturers who dominated the industry.

Computer Games

While microchip technology vexed the traditional producers, it created an entirely new breed of toy and game manufacturers. These newcomers, literally the children of the electronic age, were not bound by traditional concepts of toy design. They provided the leadership in the technological revolution in toys and games and also expanded the toy industry by creating a new toy category in much the same way that Edwin Land did with the Polaroid camera and instant pictures. Of those in the forefront of electronic design, Electronic Arts, manufacturer of sports, sci-fi, and fantasy games, and Cyan Worlds, creator of Myst and Riven (marketed by Ubi Soft), illustrated the differences between traditional manufacturers, who adapted microchip technology to existing designs, and ingénue manufacturers, who designed toys and games in a wholly electronic milieu. Electronic Arts and its counterparts capitalized on the intrinsic capabilities of the microchip and computer: randomizing, speed, and mass storage. Because computer game creators operated out of very small shops, as microchip and computer technology grew more sophisticated, they were able to take advantage of the advances almost immediately. Some electronic game firms became marketing firms, advertising and vending products from dozens of small designers in addition to their own wares. The microchip not only underpinned a new genre of toys and games but also altered the nature of play for a stratum of the American population. While microchips allowed toys and games to be more interactive, three-dimensional, and complex, play became more solitary and gender-specific. With a few notable exceptions, adolescent boys, rather than girls, were more likely to play electronic toys and computer games.

For computer game companies, the advent of the Internet and broadband technology promised an entirely new game format, the multiplayer online game—a prospect that in the early twenty-first century is only beginning to be fully realized. In multiplayer games thousands of players from across the globe compete as individuals or in groups in combat or puzzle solving. Several large firms have adapted traditional games as well as successful single-player computer games to the multiplayer format. As broadband reaches more households, however, several "native" Internet multiplayer games have appeared. Probably the most famous of these was a game designed as a marketing tie-in with the film *A.I.* Known informally as The Beast, the game attracted thousands of players, spawned an extensive website, and garnered national press attention.

See also: **Indoor Games; Media, Childhood and the; Theories of Play.**

BIBLIOGRAPHY

Cross, Gary. 1997. *Kids' Stuff: Toys and the Changing World of American Childhood.* Boston: Harvard University Press.

Forman-Brunell, Miriam. *Made to Play House: Dolls and the Commercialization of American Girlhood, 1830–1930.* New Haven, CT: Yale University Press, 1993.

Miller, G. Wayne. 1999. *Toy Wars: The Epic Struggle between G.I. Joe, Barbie, and the Companies that Make Them.* Boston: Adams Media.

Petrik, Paula. 1986. "The House that Parcheesi Built: Selchow and Righter Company." *Business History Review* 60: 410–437.

Walsh, Margaret. 1992. "Plush Endeavors: An Analysis of the Modern American Soft-Toy Industry." *Business History Review* 66, no. 4: 637–670.

INTERNET RESOURCE

Cloudmakers. (Clearinghouse for online gaming.) 2001. Available from <http://www.cloudmakers.org>.

PAULA PETRIK

Toy Trains

The advent of the train in the early nineteenth century had a profound effect on communities throughout the world. Towns grew in vast tracts of previously uninhabited territory and formerly remote villages became accessible. For the first time it was possible to move troops, mail, and freight quickly, and it became much easier for travelers to seek out exciting new areas to explore. The train also had a profound effect on the toy industry. With the arrival of the new technology came the promise of interesting new possibilities in toy design at a time when industrialization and commerce were expanding at a tremendous pace, and research into science and technology was becoming an important educational option for boys.

Very early toy trains were simple TOYS of wood or metal usually consisting of a locomotive with a carriage and wagon that was pushed along the floor. Commercial production of toy trains did not take off until after the opening of the first

German railway between Nuremberg and Furth in 1835. This event was immediately commemorated by makers of metal *flats*, simple flat one-piece models cast in pewter with no working parts. The introduction of mass-produced rolled milled steel around 1850 permitted the production of cheap toys. They were made from thin steel coated with tin to prevent rusting ("tinplate") and stamped and pressed or rolled into a variety of shapes. Key names in the manufacture of tinplate trains and other toys in Germany were Bing, Carette in Nuremberg, Märklin in Göppingen, and Lehmann in Brandenburg. S. Güntermann and J. Issmayer were two important pioneers of the clockwork railway. The model steam train first appeared in the 1860s and grew in popularity over the next two decades. Trains were powerful, "fun" toys, and many children were introduced to physics and engineering through playing with them.

The demand for more realistic trains grew rapidly, and during the period from the 1880s to World War I some of the most authentic and complete systems were produced. Notable manufacturers included George Carette, Issmayer, Fleischmann, Bing, Plank, and Bub. In 1891 Märklin merged with another firm, Lutz, and introduced a gauge system and accessories which for the first time made it possible for children to set up and run a railway system, enabling them to organize and control this miniature mechanized world. Other important names in the toy train industry were JEP and Rossignol in France, and Ives and Lionel in the United States. The Ives product, which had no rails, was unique in the toy trade for being made in cast iron.

In Britain the force behind the toy train market was W. J. Bassett-Lowke, which joined forces with Bing in 1900 to import and sell trains that were adapted for the British market. Bassett-Lowke was determined that the toy trains be accurate copies of the real thing, and the resulting products were hugely popular. F. Hornby, known also for Meccano, started to produce clockwork trains in 1915, followed by the first electric train sets in about 1925. World War II took a heavy toll on the toy train industry. After the war new toys competed for the affections of children and many firms closed in the 1960s, but toy trains continue to be manufactured, including the well-known names of Märklin, Fleischmann, Lehmann, and Hornby. Model railway production today could not exist without the extensive use of high-quality plastics and sophisticated electronic controls, plus some very accomplished miniature engineering.

See also: **Cars as Toys; Collections and Hobbies; Construction Toys; Toy Soldiers.**

BIBLIOGRAPHY

Carlson, Pierce. 1986. *Toy Trains: A History.* London: Gollancz.

Levy, Allen. 1974. *A Century of Model Trains.* London: New Cavendish Books.

Marsh, Hugo, and Pierce Carlson. 2002. *Christie's Toy Railways.* London: Pavilion Books.

Reder, Gustav. 1972. *Clockwork, Steam, and Electric: A History of Model Railways.* Trans. C. Hamilton Ellis. London: Ian Allan.

HALINA PASIERBSKA

Trade Schools. *See* Vocational Education, Industrial Education, and Trade Schools.

Tuberculosis. *See* Contagious Diseases; Vaccination.

Twain, Mark (1835–1910)

The essayist, novelist, and humorist Samuel Langhorne Clemens is better known by the pseudonym Mark Twain. He is most noted for authoring *The Adventures of Tom Sawyer* (1876) and *Adventures of Huckleberry Finn* (1885), the latter often touted as the great American novel.

Soon after Twain's birth in Florida, Missouri, his family moved to Hannibal, Missouri, which he later recast as St. Petersburg, the setting of *Tom Sawyer* and parts of *Huckleberry Finn*. Hannibal, which was important to the slave market on the Mississippi River, had a profound influence on Twain's writing, particularly his views on race, articulated most cynically in *The Tragedy of Pudd'nhead Wilson* (1894). As an adult, Twain became acquainted with Mississippi steamboat life on his abridged journey to South America, where he anticipated establishing himself in the coca trade. Twain received his pilot's license in 1859, working the river until the onset of the Civil War halted river commerce. These years on the Mississippi provided Twain with a diversity of experience that greatly informed his writing, especially his Mississippi River novels, for which he is best known. After serving briefly in the Confederate Army, Twain moved to Nevada, where, as a reporter for the *Territorial Enterprise*, he first signed a piece as Mark Twain, a pseudonym meaning "two fathoms" for riverboat pilots, and "two drinks on credit" for Nevada citizens.

Though renowned for his witty social commentary, Twain's most lasting contribution to literature is, arguably, his children's fiction, which Twain maintained was intended for both children and adults. The somewhat nostalgic depiction of BOYHOOD found in Twain's Tom Sawyer books has come to stand in for boyhood itself, with Tom Sawyer exemplifying the "good bad boy," an important departure from the more didactic children's fiction of the time. This departure is felt most powerfully in *The Adventures of Huckleberry Finn*, Twain's most sensitive rendering of child consciousness. Twain's choice to narrate the novel in Huckleberry's voice was revolutionary. His Tom Sawyer sequels—*Tom Sawyer Abroad* (1894) and *Tom Sawyer, Detective* (1896)—

were neither as intimate nor as complicated, though they were also told in Huck's voice. Twain's other novels associated with child readers, *The Prince and the Pauper* (1882) and *A Connecticut Yankee in King Arthur's Court* (1889) feature adult protagonists.

Theatrical and cinematic versions of Twain's two major books are common; one of the earliest is a dramatization of *Tom Sawyer* authored by Twain in 1884, though never staged. Huckleberry made it to the boards in November 1902, in a production that fared well. Perhaps the most famous of the many film versions of *Huckleberry Finn* is the 1939 Metro-Goldwyn-Mayer production, released the same year as *The Wizard of Oz*. Featuring Mickey Rooney as Huck, this adaptation was the first to focus on the relationship between Huck and Jim, an escaped slave who accompanies Huck down the Mississippi. In 1993 Walt Disney Pictures released their film adaptation, *The Adventures of Huck Finn*, starring Elijah Wood. However, despite these numerous retellings, ubiquitous media representations, and nearly uniform critical acclaim, both *Huckleberry Finn* and *Tom Sawyer* are consistently challenged and banned throughout the United States for addressing so directly issues of race and class.

See also: **Children's Literature.**

BIBLIOGRAPHY

Budd, Louis J. 1983. *Our Mark Twain.* Philadelphia: University of Pennsylvania Press.

Haupt, Clyde V. 1994. *Huckleberry Finn On Film: Film and Television Adaptations of Mark Twain's Novel, 1920–1993.* Jefferson, NC: McFarland.

Hill, Hamlin. 1973. *Mark Twain, God's Fool.* New York: Harper.

Hoffman, Andrew. 1997. *Inventing Mark Twain: The Lives of Samuel Langhorne Clemens.* New York: William Morrow.

JOSEPH T. THOMAS JR.

Twenty-Sixth Amendment

The Twenty-Sixth Amendment to the U.S. Constitution, which was ratified in 1971, lowered the voting age from twenty-one to eighteen years of age. Section One of the Amendment states "the right of citizens of the United States, who are 18 years of age or older, to vote, shall not be denied or abridged by the United States or any state on account of age." At the time the amendment was ratified, significant popular support existed for lowering the voting age from twenty-one to eighteen years of age. However, the process of achieving this modification was not without conflict.

Popular discussion of lowering the voting age from twenty-one years of age to eighteen years of age first appeared in 1942 after Congress amended the Selective Service and Training Act to reflect a draft age of eighteen. From this year forward, on an annual basis, various federal legislators offered proposals to lower the voting age. In addition Presidents Eisenhower, Johnson, and Nixon each advocated lowering the voting age to eighteen. However the voting age remained at twenty-one until 1971. Wendell W. Cultice argues that the pervasive sense of crisis that was present during 1960s and 1970s caused young Americans, who felt unsupported by the political system, to organize and fight for modification of the voting age. The Vietnam War was especially significant in leading young Americans to seek the right to vote. Youth rallied around the slogan "old enough to fight, old enough to vote." Following the 1969 implementation of a lottery-style military draft, popular and political support for lowering the voting age increased.

As popular support grew for lowering the voting age to eighteen, Congress determined that the fastest way to extend the vote to eighteen-year olds would be through an amendment to the Voting Rights Act of 1965. However, many were concerned about whether this would violate the U.S. Constitution. Despite these concerns, President Nixon signed the 1970 Voting Rights Act, which contained a provision lowering the voting age to eighteen years of age, into law on June 22, 1970.

The United States Supreme Court addressed the constitutionality of the act in the 1970 case *Oregon v. Mitchell.* The Court held that although the act could properly lower the voting age for federal elections, the act could not require states to lower the voting age for local elections. As a result of this decision, states would have been faced with the unappealing and costly burden of maintaining separate voting procedures for federal and local elections. In order to eliminate this problem, a constitutional amendment was proposed on January 25, 1971. It was approved by the Senate on March 10, 1971, and by the House on March 23, 1971. It was then ratified by the required thirty-eight states in the fastest ratification process in U.S. history.

The decision to lower the voting age to eighteen was significant for several reasons. First, the decision indicated the belief that eighteen-year olds possessed the requisite emotional and mental maturity to participate in the electoral process. Additionally, passage of the amendment indicated an acceptance of the argument that if eighteen-year olds were old enough to fight in war and were old enough to be held to adult standards for criminal punishment, they should also be considered old enough to cast a vote. Finally, passage of the Twenty-Sixth Amendment caused the age of majority (the age at which one is considered a legal adult) to be lowered to eighteen for many other purposes.

See also: **Baby Boom Generation; Children's Rights; Law, Children and the; Youth Activism.**

BIBLIOGRAPHY

Briffault, Richard. 2002. "Review of *The Right to Vote: The Contested History of Democracy in the United States,* by Alexander Keyssar." *Michigan Law Review* 100 (May): 1506.

Cultice, Wendell W. 1992. *Youth's Battle for the Ballot: A History of Voting Age in America.* New York: Greenwood Press.

Keyssar, Alexander. 2000. *The Right to Vote: The Contested History of Democracy in the United States.* New York: Basic Books.

Rogers, Donald W., ed. 1992. *Voting and the Spirit of American Democracy: Essays on the History of Voting and Voting Rights in America.* Urbana, Illinois: University of Illinois Press.

Scott, Elizabeth S. 2000. "The Legal Construction of Adolescence." *Hofstra Law Review* 29 (winter): 547.

Teitelbaum, Lee E. 1999. "Children's Rights and the Problem of Equal Respect." *Hofstra Law Review* 27 (summer): 799.

AMY L. ELSON

U

Ultrasound. *See* Sonography.

UN Convention on the Rights of the Child

In 1959, the United Nations followed the League of Nations' precedent by adopting a Declaration of the Rights of the Child. However, the declaration's articles advocating the well-being of children in education, health, and protection were nonbinding; states were not legally accountable for their treatment of children. Inspired by the United Nation's International Year of the Child (1979), the Convention on the Rights of the Child (CRC) was adopted by the General Assembly in 1989 and went into effect the following year. The first CHILDREN'S RIGHTS instrument to obligate states to legally comply with its provisions, the Convention became the UN's most ratified treaty, with 191 states becoming party to its provisions. Only two, Somalia and the United States, have not ratified it. To monitor treaty compliance, ratifying states are required to supply scheduled reports to an expert committee, the Committee on the Rights of the Child, which reviews the state's fulfillment of its obligations. Further strengthening international law regarding pressing issues of children's rights, the General Assembly adopted two Protocols to the CRC in 2000: the Protocol on the Involvement of Children in Armed Conflict and the Protocol on the Sale of Children, Child Pornography, and Child Prostitution.

Defining a child as every individual below the age of eighteen, the CRC addresses the child's well-being in forty articles and establishes certain rights, prohibitions, and procedural guidelines. The Convention's fundamental requirement is that the state primarily consider the child's best interests in all its actions concerning children. Among the Convention's provisions are a child's right to life and healthy development without discrimination; to a name and nationality; to free compulsory education; to freedom of expression, thought, conscience, and religion; to the right to enjoy one's own culture, language, and religion; and the general right to receive information. The Convention also confirms the primary rights of parents or guardians concerning their child's care, healthy development, and moral direction; the state is nevertheless obligated to safeguard the child against physical or mental violence, neglect, and exploitation, including sexual abuse.

The Convention expands a state's responsibilities to ensure the health and safety of a child, ranging from improving adoption procedures to encouraging the mass media to disseminate information socially and culturally beneficial to the child. States must also ensure the child's access to the highest attainable standard of health and treatment of illness, including action to reduce infant and child mortality, eradicate certain diseases, guarantee appropriate maternal prenatal and postnatal health care, and provide special protection to children exposed to armed conflict. Under the CRC, states recognize the right of every child to a standard of living adequate for the child's physical, mental, spiritual, moral, and social development. The Convention also establishes rights regarding children accused or convicted of crime, including prohibitions against torture and degrading punishment, the right to due process and the presumption of innocence, and the abolition of capital punishment or life imprisonment without possibility of parole for crimes committed before the age of eighteen.

See also: **Child Abuse; International Organizations; Juvenile Justice: International.**

BIBLIOGRAPHY

Andrews, Arlene Bowers, and Natalie Hevener Kaufman, eds. 1999. *Implementing the UN Convention on the Rights of the Child: A Standard of Living Adequate for Development.* Westport, CT: Praeger.

Harris-Short, Sonia. 2003. "International Human Rights Law: Imperialist, Inept and Ineffective? Cultural Relativism and the UN Convention on the Rights of the Child." *Human Rights Quarterly* 25: 130–181.

Holmström, Lei, ed. 2000. *Concluding Observations of the UN Committee on the Rights of the Child: Third to Seventeenth Session, 1993–1998.* The Raoul Wallenberg Institute Series of Intergovernmental Human Rights Documentation, vol. 1. The Hague; Boston: Martinus Nijhoff Publishers.

Schabas, William A. 1996. "Reservations to the Convention on the Rights of the Child." *Human Rights Quarterly* 18: 472–491.

INTERNET RESOURCES

Defense for Children International. 2003. Available from <http://defence-for-children.org/>.

Human Rights Watch. 2003. Available from <www.hrw.org>.

United Nations. 1989. *Convention on the Rights of the Child.* Available from <www.hri.ca/uninfo/treaties/index.shtml>.

United Nations. 2003. Office of the High Commissioner for Human Rights—Children's Rights. Available from <www.unhchr.ch/html/menu2/isschild.htm>.

DIANE E. HILL

UNICEF

To address the increasing hunger and disease among European children in the wake of World War II, in 1946 the United Nations established a temporary agency, the United Nations International Children's Emergency Fund (UNICEF). In addition to its charge to relieve famine, UNICEF worked with the World Health Organization, founded by the UN in 1950, to reduce INFANT MORTALITY rates, establish mass immunization programs, and organize malaria control demonstration areas in Latin America, Europe, and Africa, as well as tuberculosis testing programs in India, Europe, North Africa, and China.

As a result of its efforts, in 1953 the UN General Assembly established UNICEF as a permanent body under a new name, the United Nations Children's Fund. Its mandate to the world's children remained the provision of safe water, health care, nutrition, sanitation, and education. It also retained its original charge to supply emergency assistance to children affected by crises of war and natural disasters in coordination with other UN and humanitarian agencies. In recognition of its role in uplifting the world's children, the Nobel Peace Prize Committee selected UNICEF as its 1965 recipient. The 1989 UN CONVENTION ON THE RIGHTS OF THE CHILD further guided UNICEF's mission to aid countries in implementing its provisions and to uphold international standards of CHILDREN'S RIGHTS established by the convention and its two protocols adopted in 2000 regarding children engaged in armed conflict and trafficking in children, CHILD PORNOGRAPHY, and CHILD PROSTITUTION.

Under the direction of the General Assembly and the UN's Economic and Social Council, UNICEF is administered by an Executive Board headquartered in New York City. The Executive Board's thirty-six seats are regionally allocated and members serve for a period of three years. The Board is assisted in its work of identifying special program needs and monitoring program effectiveness by the Innocenti Research Centre, located in Florence, Italy, which was created in 1988 to help collect and analyze data on indices of children's well-being for UNICEF.

UNICEF is funded entirely from voluntary sources. Governments and intergovernmental organizations contribute nearly two-thirds of its income. The remainder of its budget is largely funded by private sector groups and individuals as well as nongovernmental organizations, principally the UNICEF National Committees, which exist in thirty-seven countries. These National Committees promote UNICEF's programs within their states and raise funds for its projects through private sector partnerships and selling UNICEF greeting cards and products. In 2001, UNICEF contributions totaled $1.2 billion. From contributions received, UNICEF allocates direct program aid to countries proportionate to need, determined by assessing a state's mortality rate of children under five, the population of its children, and its income level (GNP per capita).

The goals of UNICEF for the first decade of the twenty-first century included the continued promotion of education, especially targeting increased enrollment of girls and child workers, eradication of child trafficking, institution of programs to prevent violence against women and girls, establishment of special programs for children with disabilities, reintegration of child soldiers into their communities, provision of HIV/AIDS information and prevention of mother-to-child transmission of the disease, as well as continued collaboration with the World Health Organization to prevent common childhood diseases and malnutrition. Immunization programs to eliminate vaccine-preventable diseases of childhood remained a major priority; in 2001, UNICEF provided 40 per cent of the vaccines for the world's children and was the main supplier of vaccines to developing countries.

See also: **Child Pornography; Child Prostitution; International Organizations; Juvenile Justice: International; Soldier Children: Gobal Human Rights Issues; Vaccination.**

BIBLIOGRAPHY

Arat, Zehra F. 2002. "Analyzing Child Labor as a Human Rights Issue: Its Causes, Aggravating Policies, and Alternative Proposals." *Human Rights Quarterly* 24: 177–204.

Black, Maggie. 1996. *Children First: The Story of UNICEF, Past and Present.* New York: Oxford University Press.

Hamm, Brigitte I. 2001. "A Human Rights Approach to Development." *Human Rights Quarterly* 23: 1005–1031.

Keeny, Spurgeon Milton. 1957. *Half the World's Children: A Diary of UNICEF at Work in Asia.* New York: Association Press.

Keraka, Margaret Nyanchoka. 2003. "Child Morbidity and Mortality in Slum Environments Along Nairobi River." *Eastern Africa Social Science Research Review* 19: 41–57.

UNICEF. 2003. *The State of the World's Children 2003.* New York: UNICEF.

Watt, Alan S., and Eleanor Roosevelt. 1949. *The Work of the United Nations International Children's Emergency Fund: Its Origin and*

Policies: Statements to the General Assembly of the United Nations. Lake Success, NY: The Fund.

Yamin, Alicia Ely and Maine, Deborah P. 1999. "Maternal Mortality as a Human Rights Issue: Measuring Compliance with International Treaty Obligations." *Human Rights Quarterly* 21: 563–607.

INTERNET RESOURCE

UNICEF. Available from <www.unicef.org>.

DIANE E. HILL

Urban School Systems, The Rise of

Urban schools have dominated historical writing on the rise of modern school systems for several reasons. As sites of wealth and social differentiation, cities spawned the earliest schools. Furthermore, urban schools pioneered many of the institutional innovations that we identify with modern education, including professionalization, district-wide system building, and bureaucratization. Finally, as focal points of nationally publicized struggles, urban schools have had a visibility rural schools could not match. (When it came to school attendance and graduation rates, however, rural schools led the way.) Highly urbanized societies, due to their wealth and demand for formal education, have always been the most extensively schooled. However, the transition to mass schooling (an educational opening that made it possible for the overwhelming majority of children of a region to attend school for a few months per year) has generally begun in rural areas and spread to urban-industrial centers later. Hence, it has been somewhat misleading to place urban schooling at the center of educational history. Still, we know a good deal about the rise of urban school systems.

The Origins of Primary Schooling in Urban Settings

American primary education traces its origins to English settlement. In 1647, the General Court of the Colony of Massachusetts Bay mandated that every town of fifty families or more establish a public elementary school. The law required towns of one hundred families or more to establish public GRAMMAR SCHOOLS with masters "capable of preparing young people for university level study." Called the Old Deluder Satan Act, its purpose was clear: to ensure that the children of Massachusetts would learn to read and understand the scriptures and thereby keep the devil at bay. Within an overwhelmingly rural society, however, most education took place within households—through the family or APPRENTICESHIP—and to a lesser extent, in churches. Moreover, it appears that despite the legal requirement, far from every town directed by law to establish a school actually did so.

By the early 1800s, however, a variety of urban schools had appeared. The most common—independent pay schools—proliferated in the early national period. Essentially, these schools were organized by entrepreneurial tutors who lived on the fees they charged parents. Dame schools, a lower-cost alternative operated by women from their homes, were popular as well. As with later forms of elementary schooling, pay and dame schools served both custodial and educational functions. Since instruction was simple and costs to parents low, many families patronized these kinds of schools, especially in the largest cities. The wealthy and poor, however, did not. Well-heeled merchants and professionals generally opted to employ private tutors at home or send their children to boarding schools. They wanted their offspring to acquire the cultural accoutrements of their class. Inasmuch as social differentiation was the primary object of their training, common pay-school instruction held little appeal. The poorest Americans, in contrast, could not afford even the modest fees of the early pay schools, so their children went unschooled. By the early national period, however, unemployment and crime accompanied the growing socioeconomic inequality in the nation's principal cities, and the emerging urban middle class saw the unschooled children of the lower classes as the cause of the problem. They put great store in the capacity of schools to discipline and guide children and, believing that if left to their own devices poor families reproduced indolence, mischief, and dependence, urban reformers began organizing schools for poor children. It was not so much the welfare of children that concerned them as the long-term impact of educational laissez-faire upon the community.

Several types of schools emerged in response to such concerns. Charity schools were among the first. Like most early schools, they strove to inculcate piety, morality, and self-reliance through instruction in ciphering and the memorization of scripture. Initially organized by individual denominations on behalf of the children of their poorest members, they derived from English models. As they expanded in reach and ambition over the first two decades of the nineteenth century, however, their denominational character receded. As immigration accelerated in the largest seaboard cities from the 1820s, charity schools increasingly targeted the foreign-born populace. Expansion, however, incurred rising costs that voluntary organizations found difficult to bear. The most influential of the efforts to moderate costs was the monitorial system, or Lancaster system, developed in England in the 1790s by Andrew Bell and Richard Lancaster. Designed as an instructional pyramid, it engaged older, more advanced students to teach younger, less skilled ones at little cost. To facilitate this, Lancaster and Bell simplified instruction by dividing their schools into graded classes of varying abilities. This allowed them to separate complex instructional skills into a series of calibrated exercises that their youthful instructors could handle. Monitorial instruction offered several advantages over traditional methods. It allowed one adult teacher to oversee the instruction of hundreds of pupils, keeping costs to a minimum. It enhanced the efficiency of instruction by permitting teachers to address their students all at once, unlike individualized instruction that characterized ungraded classrooms. Finally, it gave teacher-monitors training at a time when the quality of the average teacher was low and training unheard of. By 1830, Lancasterian schools had spread from the Northeast to the urban centers of the South and West.

Sunday and infant schools arose at about the same time as alternatives to charity schooling. Targeting working children, SUNDAY SCHOOLS taught reading, writing, and religion on Sundays. Essentially part-time charity schools, they were nondenominational from the beginning. Infant schools catered to children from two to six years of age. These were informed by the belief that educational intervention worked best on the very young. Known for their relative freedom and encouragement of individual development, they rejected the strict regimentation of monitorial and other philanthropic schools. Still, they sought—as did all charity schooling—to instill in the young Christian morality and a work ethic, primarily through the reading and recitation of scripture. Reformers also sought to foster conservative citizenship that rejected what they considered to be dangerous agitators and demagogues.

The Urban Common Schools

COMMON SCHOOLS, forerunners of the modern public elementary school, built upon this early experience. These publicly financed schools were common in the sense that they brought together groups—boys and girls, Protestants and Catholics, middle-class and poor children—that private and charity schooling had tended to segregate. Far more than autonomous pay schools, charity schooling paved the way for public education by elaborating the organizational know-how and administrative capacity on which it built. While pay schools grew more elite over the early national period, charity schooling became more inclusive. Its contributions to public school systems were several. First, charity organizations bequeathed to the common schools accounting practices designed to limit costs and justify financial subsidies from city and state agencies. Second, this financial coordination often led to the centralization of superintendence, with a single board overseeing the charity schools of the entire city—a model embraced by urban public schools. Finally, Lancasterian graded classes, hierarchical organization, and standardized instruction shaped the pedagogy and curriculum of the emergent common school.

The idea of building a universal public school system, however, came from a group of professional educational leaders, heavily concentrated in New England, who looked to Prussia for inspiration. HORACE MANN of Massachusetts and Henry Barnard of Connecticut were the two most prominent advocates of common schooling. In 1837 Mann took charge of Massachusetts's state board of education and began collecting and publicizing school information throughout the state. Over the next eleven years, he worked on behalf of free, universal, nonsectarian schools staffed by

professional teachers. Barnard did much the same for the public school systems of Connecticut and Rhode Island, before being appointed the first U.S. Commissioner of Education. In particular, he fought to establish normal schools designed to provide for professional teacher training. Due to the efforts of Barnard, Mann, and their allies, combined with a Puritan legacy of religious literacy, New England pioneered public schooling. The Midwest—settled largely by New Englanders—followed closely behind, while the mid-Atlantic region moved more slowly. In contrast, the South did not establish regular and continuous public school systems before the Civil War.

Despite the establishment of centralized departments of education in a few states, locally elected school boards still oversaw and ran virtually every aspect of school activity in 1850. Since costs weighed utmost in the minds of most boards, they hired transient, untrained teachers—increasingly women—more for whom they knew than how much. This was possible because the curriculum was simple—recitation and memorization constituted the predominant instructional methods—and popular expectations were low. Educational system builders felt uncomfortable with such amateurism, however, and sought to upgrade the schools. Unlike local boards, which held down costs by keeping school terms short and staffing schools with footloose, low-cost teachers, reformers sought to extend the school year, professionalize teaching, and introduce standards into American classrooms. This meant transferring control of the schools from boards of cost-conscious amateurs to emergent educational experts. It also meant financing the schools through public taxes, for these reforms required money.

School consolidation became a central goal of reformers since larger schools furthered the cause of administrative centralization, permitted the grading of classes, increased control over teacher hiring, and accelerated the diffusion of "scientific" pedagogy. System builders sought to exclude religion from public institutions because of its divisiveness. They also extolled free public schooling in an effort to ease competition from private schools. Private schooling undercut political support for public education and made large, graded schools harder to build. Suspicious of centralizing outsiders, many urban Democrats, some religious groups, and most rural Americans opposed these reforms. Dissenters wanted their schools to be convenient and near to home, responsive to local beliefs and customs, and as inexpensive as possible. Catholics, pietist Germans, and other religious groups rejected either the Protestant thrust of much of public schooling or the secularizing tendencies of the reformers. Resistance proved especially strong in dispersed rural areas where population densities were low, transportation difficult, and the traditions of local control most ingrained. Consequently, unified common school systems first appeared in the largest urban areas where the reform impulse was strongest, population densities highest, and identification with professionalism strongest. Centralization came only gradually to smaller cities, towns, and rural school districts.

American High Schools

Though often traced to the residential rural academy, American HIGH SCHOOLS owed much to the common school. The common school paved the way for high schools in several ways. It accustomed Americans to the idea of free schooling financed by property taxes. It provided an institutional framework on which the high schools built. Indeed, in some regions, urban high schools literally grew out of common schools through upward extension. Finally, common schools created a public for high schools by preparing the young for entry. ACADEMIES shaped high schools too. Replacing the colonial Latin grammar school in the early nineteenth century, academies were rural, private institutions, largely cultural and preparatory in orientation. The academy bequeathed the academic method to high schools, especially an early emphasis on memorization and deductive learning.

The high school's purpose, however, was quite different from the start. Artisans, shopkeepers, and other urban middle-class parents sought useful, local, affordable education for their children—not costly private boarding schools that stressed the liberal arts. They wanted practical finishing institutions, not preparatory schools that led to further schooling. Consequently, the first school of its type, the Boston English Classical School, established in 1821, aimed to provide middle-class youth with useful skills for vocations in commerce and the mechanical arts. Its curriculum— consisting primarily of mathematics, natural sciences, and modern languages—was academic in approach but practical in purpose. By 1851, eighty cities possessed public high schools, primarily for boys. Americans debated high schooling for girls through the 1850s, when the demand for common school teachers led to the establishment of high and normal schools for young women. Not until the 1880s, however, did high schools begin to find widespread acceptance.

Though it is hard to detail the development of a system as decentralized as the American one, several generalizations emerge from the diversity. Nearly from the beginning, Americans fought over whose interests should dominate the schools. From the 1840s, state governing boards such as the board of regents in New York and Michigan championed an elite, college preparatory curriculum with high standards for public high schools. Local school boards, in contrast, fought for more accessible high schools offering courses in practical subjects with less rigorous standards. Moreover, since only a small percentage of Americans attended high schools initially, and fewer still graduated, opponents contested the schools' right to tax support. In the Kalamazoo case of 1874, however, the supreme court of Michigan ruled that school districts could support high schools with taxes. Thereafter, the fact that they offered free, mostly practical education rendered them an attractive alternative to academies.

Educational Professionalism

Pioneering system builders found much to dislike in American schools. From the 1840s to the end of the century, they decried the incompetence and brutality commonplace in many early American classrooms. When teachers were hired for a season and for their connections to local political machines, their teaching skills were often limited and their discipline sometimes draconian. Educational leaders hoped to develop professional methods of recruitment, training, and development, screening out the most incompetent and brutal. Moreover, they sought to standardize the curriculum to achieve some control over what transpired in classrooms. They understood, however, that so long as local political interests dominated the schools and financial parsimony remained the guiding principal of school policy, professional standards remained beyond their reach. At the same time, like other professionalizing groups, early educational leaders had an agenda of their own. Using the welfare of school children as their justification, they sought better working conditions, higher salaries, and enhanced job status and control. In the 1890s, they began organizing professional associations that lobbied state legislatures to set educational certification standards, which they effectively controlled. Only two states had specialized teaching credentials in 1900. Thirty years later, nearly every state did.

Two developments between 1893 and 1935 dramatically shaped the evolution of the American high school. The first, a two-part shift in the governance structure of American schooling, played out between 1893 and 1930. At the local level, the Panic of 1893 unleashed a series of Progressive-era reforms that insulated the schools from political machines. The financial crisis bankrupted thousands of municipalities and school districts after two decades of heavy borrowing and provoked a transition in local government to professional management practices. These reforms included the emergence of city commissions, city managers, central, consolidated school boards, city-wide, nonpartisan elections, and other measures designed to favor professional administration over political patronage in local and school government. While land acquisition, school construction, school bonds, and the like continued to provide big city machines with ample opportunity for political graft, professionally trained school superintendents gradually took control of areas bearing directly on education, including teacher recruitment, textbook selection, curriculum development, and graduation standards. By legitimizing school expenditures, professional expertise encouraged increased public outlays on the schools.

At the topmost level, a second trend affected American school governance: the growing influence of higher education on the entire educational pyramid. Preoccupied with the flow of high school students into their institutions, colleges and universities banded together to form regional accreditation boards that acquired the capacity to mold high school curricula. These boards prescribed the kinds of academic courses accredited schools had to offer. Since accreditation affected students' capacity to qualify for college, influential parents in virtually every urban district insisted their schools be accredited. This power was reinforced by the emergence of professional schools of education after 1900. Attached to some of America's most prominent universities, these shaped American educational policy in two ways. First, they increasingly monopolized the training of educational leaders, especially state officials, superintendents, and influential teachers. Second, they created a body of "scientific" pedagogy and best practice through educational research that laypeople found difficult to counter. Meanwhile, prominent university presidents assumed leading roles in national debates over the schools, chairing several national commissions that drew up influential guidelines for the secondary schools.

Consequently, just as financial crisis and municipal reform were loosening the hold of the political system over the schools, a professional group of academically trained educators within or allied with higher education moved decisively to govern them. This governance shift favored the college preparatory function of the American high school, an orientation that progressively pushed the grooming of students for workplaces to the periphery of its concerns. After 1900, a rising demand for educational qualifications in the white-collar labor market reinforced this movement. In effect, urban high schools adjusted to the changing occupational and educational aspirations of their predominately middle-class clientele, administration, and staff. Immediately on the heels of this governance shift, however, a second and in many ways countervailing transition occurred. Between 1920 and 1935, American urban high schools metamorphosed from middle-class into mass institutions.

Two events rendered secondary schooling nearly universal throughout the non-Southern United States in these years: the transformation of industrial and commercial workplaces in the 1920s and the GREAT DEPRESSION of the 1930s. Technological innovation marked the decade of the twenties, sharply undercutting the demand for child labor. Consequently, public high schools witnessed a doubling of enrollments over the decade, from 2.2 to 4.4 million. Then, after 1929, the Depression effectively ended full-time juvenile labor in urban America. Working-class kids streamed into the schools, pushing high school enrollments to 6.6 million by 1939–1940. This high school growth spurt proved especially dramatic in the largest, most industrialized cities. Claudia Goldin's data shows that secondary schooling was a function of two factors: the presence of high schools and the demand for juvenile labor. Americans could not attend high schools where none existed. Low property values, restricted school funding, and limited demand for skilled labor discouraged school building in the South—a poor, overwhelmingly agricultural region—until the 1950s. Consequently,

high schooling expanded in two distinct phases: from 1920 to 1935 in the West and North, and from 1950 to 1970 in the South.

Agricultural areas with high average incomes, in contrast, sent their children to high school earlier than their urban counterparts. They built schools because the burdens and rewards of schooling were more fairly distributed in farm areas than in urban areas. Property taxes were more equitable since few farmers had intangible wealth, common in cities, that was easy to hide from assessors. Moreover, farmers had little need for family labor in winter. Consequently, nearly all farm children attended school once school buses guaranteed access, in contrast to cities, where many adolescents worked year-round. Finally, unlike eastern cities, the absence of competition from private institutions encouraged well-heeled citizens to support public schools. Thus, rural states in the Midwest and West built high schools early and sent their children to them. Heavily urbanized, industrial states, in contrast, were far slower to send their children to high school. In 1920, they had the lowest high school attendance and graduation rates outside of the South. Overwhelmingly peopled by immigrants and the children of immigrants, New York, Philadelphia, Boston, Chicago, Detroit, Milwaukee, St. Louis, and other major industrial cities sent the majority of their children to work at the age of fourteen or fifteen, since their families needed the income. This made sense at a time when school diplomas were not required for most jobs and work was one of the best ways to learn a trade.

Thus, urban high schools in 1920 still tended to serve a predominately native-born, middle-class clientele headed for either higher education or white-collar jobs in commerce and industry—just as professional middle-class academics were shoring up their control of the schools. However, as ethnic working-class children flooded the urban high schools after 1920, the social background and life trajectory of the average student changed. This dramatically increased the demands placed upon the schools, both financial and curricular. It led to America's first national teacher shortage, one worsened by a sharp rise in white-collar employment that siphoned off practicing and prospective teachers. It also unleashed a public debate on the character and purpose of schooling.

The Depression hit heavily indebted urban school systems hard by reducing funding in the face of an exploding demand for services. It undercut expensive vocational programs while reinforcing book-based general and college preparatory courses that were much cheaper to deliver. World War II, however, revived the economy, temporarily reduced the demand for secondary schooling as adolescents found work, and led to increased funding for the schools. Thanks to the South's convergence with the educational practices in the rest of the country in the postwar years, secondary schooling became universal though racial segregation rendered school access more difficult for Africa-American children than white children, particularly in the rural South, quite apart from its biased impact on spending per child. However, the middle-class orientation of the schools and their dominance by academics created a system that failed to address the educational needs of all children equally. Savage inequality has characterized America's urban school systems. This is partly due to great variance in the financial, social, and cultural resources available to schools across districts—a legacy of local control and its interaction with housing markets. Less widely recognized has been the impact of a single system of comprehensive schooling that has favored the educational interests of the academically successful over those of everyone else.

America's Urban Schools in Comparative Perspective

Early state building put Europe's urban schools on developmental paths quite different from America's. In Germany, France, and other continental European nations, state bureaucracies preceded the elaboration of public school systems. This gave the state a prominent role in the growth and governance of schools. Whereas the American Constitution severely limited the power of the federal government in school matters, reflecting its anti-centralist origins, continental European governments took an active role in educational policy from the beginning. In particular, they were keen to shape elite higher education, a recruiting ground for state officials. Many economic leaders eventually emerged from elite schools as well. Consequently, as popular free primary schooling appeared in the nineteenth century, it was sharply differentiated from the elite system of secondary education already in place. Whereas American high schools grew out of common schools, the urban German GYMNASIUM and French LYCÉE had little in common with predominately rural *Volksschulen* and *écoles primaires*. Like Americans, however, Europeans initially invested in public schooling to foster social order and instill political allegiance.

The class-based nature of these two-tier systems offended Americans, though for middle-class Europeans they created an opening by substituting achievement for aristocratic, status-based organizing principles. More important still, they encouraged technical and vocational programs governed and financed independently of elite academic tracks. Though backers of the Vocational Education Act of 1917 fought hard to achieve a similar separation of vocational programs from academic schools in the United States, they lost out to a coalition of labor, teacher, superintendent, and women's groups in every state but Wisconsin. Consequently, whereas American educators closely linked to higher education became responsible for all students in comprehensive public schools, European states thought educational policy too important to give over entirely to academics. In an effort to coordinate education and training policy with broader economic and labor market initiatives, Europeans sought to extend a voice in educational policy to nonacademic groups as well. No state went further in this direction than Germany, where organized groups of employers and workers—with state oversight and input from the educational community—govern the entire vocational education and training system. Providing secondary education to a majority of young Germans throughout the twentieth century, the system was specifically designed to limit the role of academics. Its originators in the German southwest had seen how academically trained administrators and staff transformed Prussia's trade schools into elite preparatory institutions, leaving those desirous of affordable, practical education without anywhere to turn. Thus, they built a system governed and staffed by the communities of practice for which it educated and trained. Virtually every European state eventually integrated some form of apprenticeship into its secondary education mix, in contrast to the United States, where school-controlled vocational programs developed such mediocre reputations that many Americans came to think of them as lyceums for losers.

Schooling and modern school systems originated in cities on both sides of the Atlantic. Mass schooling, in contrast, took root in the countryside and diffused to the cities. How this urban-rural divide shaped the development of national educational regimes is still not well understood. Despite considerable variation, European states built educational systems that addressed the different capacities and interests of students. Their greatest challenge has been to render elite education more inclusive, making it accessible to all socioeconomic groups. Americans, in contrast, have focused on equal access and opportunity, but much less on how comprehensive schooling affects the distribution and fairness of educational outcomes. European nations that have tried the American model have found it wanting. Nowhere have its shortcomings been more glaring than in America's cities, the crucible of the events that stamped it in its formative years.

See also: **Compulsory School Attendance; Education, United States; Vocational Education, Industrial Education, and Trade Schools.**

BIBLIOGRAPHY

Beatty, Barbara. 1995. *Preschool Education in America: The Culture of Young Children from the Colonial Era to the Present.* New Haven, CT: Yale University Press.

Boylan, Anne M. 1988. *Sunday School: The Formation of an American Institution, 1790–1880.* New Haven, CT: Yale University Press.

Brown, David K. 1995. *Degrees of Control: A Sociology of Educational Expansion and Occupational Credentialism.* New York: Teachers College Press.

Cremin, Lawrence A. 1988. *American Education: The Metropolitan Experience, 1876–1980.* New York: Harper and Row.

Goldin, Claudia. 1998. "America's Graduation from High School: The Evolution and Spread of Secondary Schooling in the Twentieth Century." *The Journal of Economic History* 58: 345–374.

Goodenow, Ronald K., and Diane Ravitch, eds. 1983. *Schools in Cities: Consensus and Conflict in American Educational History.* New York: Holmes and Meier.

Hawkins, Hugh. 1992. *Banding Together: The Rise of National Associations in American Higher Education, 1877–1950*. Baltimore, MD: Johns Hopkins University Press.

Herbst, Jurgen. 1996. *The Once and Future School: Three Hundred and Fifty Years of American Secondary Education*. New York: Routledge.

Kaestle, Carl. 1983. *Pillars of the Republic: Common Schools and American Society, 1780–1860*. New York: Hill and Wang.

Katz, Michael B. 1971. *Class, Bureaucracy, and Schools: The Illusion of Educational Change in America*. New York: Praeger.

Katznelson, Ira, and Margaret Wier. 1985. *Schooling for All: Class, Race, and the Decline of the Democratic Ideal*. New York: Basic Books.

Kozol, Jonathan. 1992. *Savage Inequalities: Children in America's Schools*. New York: Harper Perennial.

Krug, Edward. 1964. *The Shaping of the American High School*. New York: Harper and Row.

Labaree, David F. 1988. *The Making of an American High School: The Credentials Market and the Central High School of Philadelphia, 1838–1939*. New Haven, CT: Yale University Press.

Leloudis, James L. 1996. *Schooling the New South*. Chapel Hill: University of North Carolina Press.

Maynes, Mary Jo. 1985. *Schooling for the People: Comparative Local Studies of Schooling History in France and Germany, 1750–1850*. New York: Holmes and Meier.

Mirel, Jeffrey. 1993. *The Rise and Fall of an Urban School System*. Ann Arbor: University of Michigan Press.

Peterson, Paul E. 1985. *The Politics of School Reform, 1870–1940*. Chicago: University of Chicago Press.

Prost, Antoine. 1981. *Histoire générale de l'enseignement et de l'éducation en France*. Paris: Armand Colin.

Ravitch, Diane. 1974. *The Great School Wars: New York City, 1805–1973; A History of the Public Schools as Battlefield of Social Change*. New York: Basic Books.

Reese, William J. 1995. *The Origins of the American High School*. New Haven, CT: Yale University Press.

Rury, John L. 1991. *Education and Women's Work: Female Schooling and the Division of Labor in Urban America, 1870–1930*. Albany: State University of New York Press.

Tyack, David. 1974. *The One Best System: A History of American Education*. Cambridge, MA: Harvard University Press.

Tyack, David, Robert Lowe, and Elisabeth Hansot. 1984. *Public Schools in Hard Times: The Great Depression and Recent Years*. Cambridge, MA: Harvard University Press.

Tyack, David, Thomas James, and Aaron Benavot. 1987. *Law and the Shaping of Public Education, 1785–1954*. Madison: University of Wisconsin Press.

HAL HANSEN

U.S. Children's Bureau

Progressive reformers Florence Kelley and Lillian Wald are generally credited with coming up with the idea for a federal children's bureau. The NATIONAL CHILD LABOR COMMITTEE endorsed the idea in 1905 and the 1909 White House Conference on the Care of Dependent Children called for the agency's creation. The Senate passed the Children's Bureau bill by a vote of 54 to 20 and the House passed it by 177 to 17. President William Howard Taft signed legislation on April 8, 1912, establishing the agency within the Department of Commerce and Labor. Taft's signature made the United States the first nation in the world to have a federal agency focused solely on children. The president's naming of Julia C. Lathrop as the bureau's first chief symbolized the important role of female activists in the agency's creation and made Lathrop the first woman to head a federal agency in the United States.

Despite its popularity, the U.S. Children's Bureau faced powerful critics. Some felt that the bureau overstepped federal authority. Manufacturing interests feared that the agency would push for the regulation of CHILD LABOR. Fiscal conservatives contended that the bureau duplicated work already under the jurisdiction of other federal agencies (primarily the U.S. Public Health Service and the Bureau of Education). The Catholic Church warned that the agency might interfere with parochial education or promote birth control. Lathrop sought to quiet criticism by steering clear of partisan politics and focusing on INFANT MORTALITY. Further, under Lathrop's leadership the Children's Bureau embraced the middle-class family ideal: a nuclear family where the father worked as the sole breadwinner, mother served as a full-time housewife, and children attended school, were well-fed and cared for, had a secure future, and labored only at household chores.

With a staff of fifteen and budget of $25,640, the U.S. Children's Bureau relied on data collected by other federal agencies and an army of female volunteers. In 1913 the bureau estimated that the United States' annual infant mortality rate of 132 deaths per 1,000 live births placed it behind New Zealand (83), Norway (94), Ireland (99), Sweden (104), Australia (108), Bulgaria (120), and Scotland (123). Armed with this information, the bureau conducted the nation's first infant mortality study. Staff concluded that poor sanitation, lack of good medical care, and poverty were the major factors contributing to infant deaths. Educating mothers, improving public sanitation, and requiring birth certificates would help save babies' lives. Advice pamphlets published by the bureau became very popular and Congress declared 1918 Children's Year.

In 1921 Congress passed the SHEPPARD-TOWNER MATERNITY AND INFANCY ACT, giving the Children's Bureau administrative authority. Although limited to education, diagnosis, and investigation, by 1926 the Sheppard-Towner Act faced strong opposition from the American Medical Association. The AMA condemned Sheppard-Towner as socialized medicine and disliked the fact that the physician-controlled Public Health Service did not control the program. The Children's Bureau's two physicians, Grace L. Meigs (hired in 1915) and Dorothy Reed Mendenhall (hired in 1917), were not enough to pacify the AMA. Funding ended in 1929, but infant mortality rates had decreased to 67.9 deaths per 1,000 live births.

The Children's Bureau also had an important role in New Deal legislation. Bureau representatives wrote the child welfare sections of the 1935 Social Security Act. Title V provides federal funding for maternal and infant care for poor mothers and children. During World War II Title V expanded to include medical care for the wives and newborns of enlisted men in the military. From 1942 to 1946 one of every seven babies born in the United States benefited from this Emergency Maternity and Infant Health Program. In addition to infant and maternal health care, the 1935 Social Security Act included the AID TO DEPENDENT CHILDREN Program (ADC, later renamed Aid to Families with Dependent Children) and Title VII, which establishes federal funds for handicapped children.

During its first decades of work the Children's Bureau also addressed child labor and those dependent on the state. The 1910 census counted 1,990,225 children under fourteen years of age working for wages (18.4 percent of the total cohort). Beginning in 1915 the bureau lobbied to end the worst abuses of child workers. But the U.S. Supreme Court rejected a 1916 child labor law (the Keating-Owen Act) and a 1922 constitutional amendment was never ratified. The onset of high adult unemployment during the GREAT DEPRESSION led to the first permanent federal restrictions on child labor, included in the 1938 Fair Labor Standards Act. The U.S. Children's Bureau was responsible for enforcing prohibitions on the employment of youngsters less than fourteen years of age and the restrictions on the paid labor of those fourteen through seventeen. Children dependent upon the state or those accused of crimes also drew attention from the Children's Bureau during its early decades of work. By 1920 forty-five of the then forty-eight states had some form of juvenile or family court. Minors charged with delinquency or children whose families could not care for them came before juvenile and family courts.

These victories for children did not end the exploitation or suffering of all American children, nor did they translate to an expanding role for the U.S. Children's Bureau. The Social Security Board (established in 1935) was given authority for administering ADC and the Public Health Service handled Title V's maternal and child health program. Moreover, in 1946 government reorganization lowered the

Children's Bureau status within the federal hierarchy, set the stage for the eventual removal of all bureau administrative and regulatory responsibilities, and removed the "U.S." from the agency's name. The bureau relocated again in 1969, this time to the new Office of Child Development in the Department of Health, Education, and Welfare.

Since 1972 the Children's Bureau's focus has continued to narrow. By the 1990s the agency was one of four bureaus within the Department of Health and Human Services' Administration on Children, Youth, and Families. With an annual budget of over $4 billion, the Children's Bureau works with state and local agencies to prevent CHILD ABUSE; a role much smaller than its original responsibility to investigate and report on the whole child. Overall, everyday life for American children has improved since 1912. However, at the start of the new millennium, children remain the most likely constituency in the United States to experience abuse, poverty, and exploitation.

See also: **Child Guidance; Child Saving; Compulsory School Attendance; Juvenile Justice; Social Welfare; White House Conferences on Children; Work and Poverty.**

BIBLIOGRAPHY

Goodwin, Joanne L. 1997. *Gender and the Politics of Welfare Reform: Mothers' Pensions in Chicago, 1911–1929.* Chicago: University of Chicago Press.

Ladd-Taylor, Molly. 1986. *Raising Baby the Government Way: Mothers' Letters to the Children's Bureau, 1915–1932.* New Brunswick: Rutgers University Press.

Ladd-Taylor, Molly. 1994. *Mother-Work: Women, Child Welfare, and the State, 1890–1930.* Urbana: University of Illinois Press.

Lemons, J. Stanley. 1973. *The Woman Citizen: Social Feminism in the 1920s.* Urbana: University of Illinois Press.

Lindenmeyer, Kriste. 1997. *"A Right to Childhood": The U.S. Children's Bureau and Child Welfare, 1912–1946.* Urbana: University of Illinois Press.

Meckel, Richard. 1989. *Save the Babies: American Public Health Reform and the Prevention of Infant Mortality, 1850–1929.* Baltimore: Johns Hopkins University Press.

Michel, Sonya. 1999. *Children's Interests/Mothers' Rights: The Shaping of America's Child Care Policy.* New Haven: Yale University Press.

Muncy, Robyn. 1991. *Creating a Female Dominion in American Reform, 1890–1935.* New York: Oxford University Press.

Trattner, Walter I. 1970. *Crusade for Children: A History of the National Child Labor Committee and Child Labor Reform in America.* Chicago: Quadrangle Books.

KRISTE LINDENMEYER

V

Vacations

The vacation, understood either as time free from work and other obligations like school and family care, or as time away from home in leisure pursuits, was rare for almost all children until the twentieth century. And yet in the last half of the twentieth century vacations increasingly became associated with the child in affluent societies.

Vacations, in contrast to times of seasonal or trade unemployment or migration away from home for work, were and are largely unknown in agrarian and preindustrial urban societies. Not only were children necessary for daily farming and craft routines, but the idea that the young needed or deserved extended times free from work did not exist in these societies. The childhood vacation was a by-product of changes in work time requirements of households, increased affluence, and new attitudes about children's needs and rights to PLAY and experience.

School Vacations

The expansion of children's access to schooling in the nineteenth century and the creation of annual break periods did not create the modern childhood vacation of rest and nonacademic explorations. Rather, these "vacation" periods were times when child labor, bad weather, or budgetary restraints prevented school from being open. School breaks varied greatly in the nineteenth century: in the United States urban schools had as little as one month's closure, while rural districts could have breaks of up to nine months in total. Often schools were closed not to give children rest, but because roads were poor in winter or because children were needed for spring planting and autumn harvests. Vacation periods depended on the local economy. Wheat farming required little child labor, but corn, tobacco, sugar beets, and cotton placed heavy seasonal demands on children's time. Schools, especially in urban areas, were often open in summer as well as winter. In the 1840s, schools were open in New York City up to 242 days of the year. Gradually, beginning with the common school movement of HORACE MANN in the 1840s, reformers won an increase in the days schools were in session in rural areas. On average, the American school year increased from 132 in 1870 to 162 days by 1920. At the same time, urban areas saw the elimination of summer classes because of poor attendance, inefficient learning on hot days, and parental pressure, especially in the middle classes, to make children available for family vacations. State laws gradually produced the "standard" of the ten week to three month summer vacation in the twentieth century (with 180 days of schooling per year) as differences between rural and urban school terms diminished. To compensate for longer school terms, Mann and subsequent reformers advocated regular holiday periods to provide children with outdoor experience and rest from school routine.

In Europe and elsewhere, the length of children's summer vacations similarly varied by the demands of work and budget in the nineteenth century. By the 2000s, these holiday periods were generally shorter than in the United States, though intermediate vacations (in spring and mid-winter) were often longer. While Japan remains at the extreme end of the spectrum in the 2000s, with a school year of 243 days and a short August vacation, European school children attended classes across a range from 216 to the American standard of 180. Despite the efforts of school reformers in the 1920s and after to extend school time in the United States through July or begin school before Labor Day, parents resisted, claiming a shortened break would interfere with family vacations and other worthy activities like SUMMER CAMPS and SPORTS.

Childless Vacations

The contemporary tendency to identify the child with the vacation is relatively recent. The modern vacation has its roots in the late seventeenth century in the aristocratic pursuit of social and health advantages at wells and mineral springs in places like Tumbridge Wells and Bath in England where the elderly and sickly rich drank or bathed in healing

The Children's Holiday (1864), William Holman Hunt. Family excursions began to become popular in the mid-nineteenth century among the middle classes in Britain. Middle-class fathers, who were usually required to be at work during the week, would join their families on these outings on Sundays and holidays.

waters. Even the seaside resorts that became popular in the early nineteenth century at Brighton, Torquay, and Scarborough in England were not places for child's play in the surf and sands, but rather sites for quiet strolls for health-giving air or drinking salt water. At assembly halls, masters of ceremonies organized formal balls to allow the fashionable to "see and be seen." Colonial and early-nineteenth-century American resorts like Newport, Saratoga Springs, and White Sulphur Springs offered quiet relaxation, status socializing, access to a marriage market, and, in some cases opportunities for gambling at race tracks and card tables. Notably absent were children's activities. Aristocratic youth, but not children, traveled from Britain on the "Grand Tour" of European ruins and cities for edification from as early as 1670 and Northern European youth trekked to Italy in search of adventure and edification in the eighteenth and nineteenth centuries.

This pattern gradually changed as the middle class began to enjoy vacations and travel away from home. From the first decade of the nineteenth century, middle-class sensibilities turned against the adult fashion and social season of the aristocracy and cultivated family leisure. This was expressed both in the creation of family-oriented suburbs and in the family excursion. In the 1840s tour organizers like Thomas Cook in Britain deliberately appealed to family groups, offering them reduced fares that made taking the children, at least, a possibility. Fathers were infrequent participants in this culture. Instead married women with children arranged summer holidays to meet childhood friends at mineral springs or even to share country homes. By the end of the nineteenth century, the bungalow, a small informal, usually one and a half story house with wraparound porch, imported by the British from India, began to dot the southern coast of England as summer homes for families with growing children. In the 1870s, resort town governments attempted to attract this middle-class family vacationer by regulating gypsy beach vendors, encouraging cheap family rail tickets, and building family-oriented entertainment centers like the pleasure piers and Pleasure Gardens of Blackpool in Britain or the Boardwalk of Atlantic City, New Jersey, in the United States. This process was slow in trickling down to the children of wage earners. For most working-class families, couples stopped taking holidays when the children arrived. Through World War II, outside of the middle classes, vacations for children were largely confined to the rare day's excursion to the amusement park, lake, or seashore.

Expansion of the Democratic Family Holiday

Children's vacations depended on their parents' paid leave from work. Paid vacations came first to privileged employees of the courts and gradually spread out to other white collar personnel and foremen during the nineteenth century in the United States and Europe. While annual plant shutdowns (for machine refurbishing) or trade slowdowns brought weeks or months of unemployment to many factory worker parents, few could afford to take themselves or their children on a vacation. In the late nineteenth century, vacation savings clubs emerged in northern England and in some parts of Europe to rectify this problem. In the United States, only ten percent of wage-earners enjoyed a paid vacation as late as 1930, while 85 percent of white collar workers and their children benefited from it. Paid vacation plans emerged in the 1930s and 1940s as part of the explosion of union membership (reaching 93 percent of union contracts by 1949), allowing many union members to at least take their kids to the seashore. Because paid vacations in the United States are tied to employment contracts, instead of being a legal entitlement, there was little expansion of vacation time in the United States with the decline of unions after the 1960s.

In Europe, paid vacations for wage earners appeared first in central Europe in the 1920s and expanded into France and Britain in the 1930s. Even conservatives accepted it as a way of instilling worker loyalty and as a means of strengthening family bonds by uniting children and their parents in leisure

Children investigate the wet sands at Scarborough, England, c. 1913. By the twentieth century the seaside—once a place where aristocratic adults went to see and be seen—had become a popular vacation destination for middle- and working-class families. © Hulton-Deutsch Collection/CORBIS.

to compensate for their separation during work and school. In France, for example, a legal right to a two week paid vacation was won in 1936 and expanded to three weeks in 1956, to four in 1962, and to five in 1982 and six weeks by the 2000s. While holiday leaves varied greatly, European paid vacations remain considerably longer than in the United States.

As children's access to vacation time increased, so did efforts of reformers to shape that time with productive recreation. As early as the 1870s, through the Fresh Air Fund, members of small-town churches opened their homes to slum-dwelling children from New York City. By the end of the nineteenth century, philanthropic groups from large American cities sponsored excursions and weeks at seashore resorts for the children of the poor both to provide healthful fresh air and exercise and to inculcate loyalty to authority. The summer youth camp became a peculiarly American institution where, by 1929, a million children yearly encountered nature in the sheltered moral environment of about 7,000 camps. From the 1880s, British reformers organized summer camps for poor children and their families while French businesses created youth summer camps and recre-

ational programs for young workers and the children of employees in the hopes of easing class tensions.

Groups like the Playground Association (1907) in the United States promoted the construction and staffing of neighborhood playgrounds suitable for supervised children's play and crafts during the summer vacation. Young adult hiking and camping activities were extended to youth and children in the 1930s through groups like the British Youth Hostel Association. At the same time, the Holiday Fellowship, and other labor or local holiday camps in Britain promoted low cost family vacations. A wide range of organizations in France did the same through founding sea or mountain resorts or subsidizing family tourism in the 1930s. Similarly, fascist states and the Soviet Union organized summer vacation tours and youth summer camps to foster political loyalties.

Vacation Designed Around Children

While adults attempted to shape the values and loyalties of children on vacations, a more profound change was occurring. Children's right to time free from the routines of work and school and parents' right to interact with their children in play was becoming a central part of the vacation's meaning. Romantic ideas about children—especially identifying the young with discovery of the delights of nature and associating childhood with nostalgic recollections of carefree times—were well-established in literature and popular images on prints and trading cards by the 1870s. Early manifestations of this sentiment were expressed in seaside rituals like donkey rides, punch and Judy shows, and the building of sand castles. Mechanical amusement rides like the carousel were beginning to pass from adults to children by the end of the nineteenth century. The TEDDY BEAR fad, started at the seaside resorts of New Jersey in the summer of 1906, and the creation of kiddie rides at amusement parks in the 1920s reveal a trend toward the "infantilization" of the vacation site and experience. Instead of the vacation as primarily an opportunity for adults to socialize, gain new experiences, and rest often away from children, it gradually became a "gift" to the child and a chance for adults to relive childhood through their offspring's play.

Older views, however, persisted. In 1888, the famous American child psychologist G. STANLEY HALL praised the father who provided his young sons with a pile of sand for a summer of creative play by themselves. In the 1900s, popular magazines insisted that middle-class parents find "diversions" for their children when they took them on seaside or country vacations. Others sent them on extended absences to summer camp.

By the 1930s, new American child-rearing magazines insisted that family vacations should focus on the child's education. After World War II, the emphasis shifted to the adult's pleasure in the child's delight at seeing for the first time the sea or farm animals. The 1950s saw the widespread use of the station wagon for inexpensive and informal tours of national parks and heritage sites. The increasingly roomy family car was to provide family togetherness on long automobile trips to the Grand Canyon or Old Faithful. The Civil War battlefield of Gettysburg, formerly a place for serious contemplation and memory of war became an obligatory destination for families. From the car, Mom, Dad, and the kids read plaques and later heard taped guided tours about the glorious past after which they drove into the parking lots of motels to swim in the pool and later visit child-oriented amusement parks nearby. Not all embraced this romantic call for the child-oriented vacation. The 1962 movie, *Mr. Hobbes Takes a Vacation*, in which James Stewart played the frustrated family man stuck in a beat-up summer cottage with a son who wanted to do nothing but watch westerns on TV and a teenage daughter unable to get a date, summed up the frustration of many attempting to recreate the wonder of the children's vacation. Still, the holiday increasingly was meant for the family, for bonding, for renewal and celebrations of children's desire.

Today, the classic site for this child-focused celebration is the amusement park, but this was not true in the beginning of these pleasure sites. The first amusement parks were really modern adaptations of the traditional festival where adults were allowed to loosen restraint and enjoy unaccustomed freedoms. The revolutionary amusement parks opened on Coney Island between 1897 and 1904 were certainly more childlike than the surrounding dance/music halls, race tracks, and saloons, but their fare of mechanical rides, freak shows, and spectacles were designed to challenge the male entertainment zone of drink, sex, and gambling with an environment conducive to "respectable" women rather than children. And, the childlike amusements allowed mostly adults to regress, rather than to encourage children to be delighted. As late as the 1920s, even progressive amusement parks like Playland on Long Island still offered playgrounds where parents could drop off their children while the adults rode roller coasters and bumper cars.

Walt DISNEY's Disneyland, opened in 1955, became the template of the child-focused holiday site. Through such architectural features as "Main Street, USA," recalling small town America of 1900, adults were called to share with children memories of their own childhoods (or, at least, the fantasy of an ideal childhood). Disney's buildings, notably constructed at five-eighths the size of "real buildings" make Disneyland child friendly, and the rides provide frequent cues for adults to share with their children in Disney fantasies. The whole of Disneyland could be said to be an evocation to childlike wonder, with or without kids. Disney's achievement was to package, combine, and intensify a half century of movie images that many Americans and families around the world identified with the delights of childhood. He and his company filled a cultural need that the traditional amusement parks, national parks, and museums failed to fill. Disney was so effective at meeting this need that for many American families (as well as Europeans and Pacific Rim Asians at Disney parks in Paris and Tokyo) made a vacation pilgrimage to Disneyland as an essential part of childhood and then, later, the reliving of that childhood.

See also: **Playground Movement; Theme Parks; Zoos.**

BIBLIOGRAPHY

Cross, Gary. 1993. *Time and Money*. London: Routledge.

Dulles, Rhea Foster. 1940. *America Learns to Play: A History of Popular Recreation. 1607–1940*. New York: Appleton-Century.

Huyvaert, Sarah. 1998. *Time Is of the Essence: Learning in Schools*. Boston: Allyn and Bacon.

Pimlott, J. A. R. 1976. *The Englishman's Holiday*. Brighton, UK: Harvester.

Starobinski, Jean. 1966. "The Idea of Nostalgia." *Diogenes* 54 (summer): 81–103.

Walvin, James. 1978. *Beside the Seaside: A Social History of the Popular Seaside Holiday*. London: Allen Lane.

Wasko, Janet. 2001. *Understanding Disney: The Manufacture of Fantasy*. Cambridge: Polity.

GARY CROSS

Vaccination

Chinese physicians discovered about a thousand years ago how to reduce the risk of dying from smallpox by scarifying the skin of susceptible persons with secretions from a healing smallpox bleb, thus inducing a mild attack of smallpox. This procedure, called *variolation*, was not without risk—about one person in a hundred sustained a severe and sometimes fatal attack of smallpox. Nonetheless it was widely used to protect the children of educated well-to-do people in China, and the procedure spread westward along the silk route. Lady Mary Wortley Montagu, wife of the British ambassador in Constantinople, described it in a 1717 letter to a friend in England and introduced it in England when she returned home.

Smallpox Vaccination

Edward Jenner, a naturalist and family doctor in the village of Berkeley, Gloucestershire, knew about variolation, and knew that milkmaids who had been infected with cowpox, a common disease of cattle in that area, never got smallpox. He reasoned that it might be possible to inoculate cowpox serum into the skin in the same way as the more risky smallpox secretions. During an EPIDEMIC of smallpox in 1796, Jenner inoculated a nine-year-old boy, James Phipps, with fluid from a cowpox lesion, and over the following months he inoculated a total of twenty-three people, mostly children, in the same way. All survived unharmed and none got smallpox. Jenner's experiment would not withstand the rigorous ethical scrutiny required for modern human experimentation, but its lasting benefits for humankind have been enormous. Jenner reported his results in *An Inquiry into the Causes and Effects of the Variolae Vaccinae* (1798). *Vaccination* is derived from *vaccinae*, the Latin for the possessive of *vacca*, or cow. Vaccine is the fluid containing weakened or dead pathogens, which stimulate immune responses that protect against CONTAGIOUS DISEASE. First applied to protection from smallpox, *vaccination* and *vaccine* broadened in meaning to include all such immunizing procedures as these developed.

Before vaccination, smallpox epidemics often afflicted virtually all exposed susceptible persons in the population, in other words, all who were not immune because they had survived previous epidemics. Children were the main victims. Depending on the virulence of the strain of smallpox virus, about one child in every eight to twenty would die, and many who survived were left with unsightly scars after the infected blebs on the skin had healed. If the eyes were affected, the result was blindness.

Despite fierce opposition from antivaccination critics, vaccination programs against smallpox began in Europe and the United States in the early nineteenth century, gathering momentum whenever smallpox epidemics occurred, as they continued to do, albeit with declining ferocity, throughout

TABLE 1

Vaccine-preventable diseases of children

Disease	Year Vaccine Developed
Smallpox	c. 1000 (variolation)
	1796 (Jenner)
Rabies	1885 (Pasteur)
Tuberculosis	1924 (BCG)
Diphtheria	1894 (antitoxin after exposure to risk)
	1912 (preventive vaccination)
Tetanus	1890 (antitoxin after exposure to risk)
	1933 (preventive vaccination)
Whooping cough	1931–1939
Poliomyelitis	1954 (Salk)
	1961 (Sabin)
Measles	1960
Mumps	1967
Rubella	1966 (vaccine developed)
	1970 (vaccine licensed)
Hepatitis B	1978

SOURCE: Courtesy of author.

the nineteenth and early twentieth centuries. Vaccination against smallpox was not risk-free. It induced fever, painful swelling, and frequently an unsightly scar at the vaccination site. Adverse effects increased in severity with age, strengthening the case for vaccination in childhood. In an epidemic in 1946, the public health authorities in New York City vaccinated about 5 million people over a six-week period—a considerable logistic feat. The human costs included forty-five cases of vaccine-induced encephalitis (severe brain inflammation) and four deaths, along with many thousands of the milder adverse reactions described above. One of the worst possible adverse reactions was a fatal generalized *vaccinia* infection of the unborn fetus if a pregnant woman was vaccinated.

In 1949 Donald Soper, an American epidemiologist, developed the containment strategy, which consisted of vaccinating all known contacts of every diagnosed case of smallpox rather than indiscriminately vaccinating the entire population. Containment stopped transmission by removing the possibility of the smallpox virus passing from an infected person to others who would have been susceptible in the absence of vaccination, thus reducing the numbers exposed to the risk of adverse reactions. However, in 1965, when the World Health Organization began a vaccination campaign aimed at worldwide eradication of smallpox, total coverage of the entire population in affected countries was the aim. The containment strategy was used later, when the risk of epidemics had declined and the risk of contagion arose mainly from sporadic cases. The last known case of naturally occurring smallpox was a teenage girl in Somalia in 1977. In 1980, the World Health Assembly at its annual meeting de-

TABLE 2

Risks of adverse reactions to vaccinations

Vaccination against	Rate per Million Vaccinations
Smallpox	
Fatal reaction	approx 1
Encephalitis	4
Tuberculosis	
Disseminated TB	1–2
Localized abscess	10–40
Diphtheria/pertussis/tetanus	
Convulsions, brain damage	10–30
Death	1–2
Measles	
Acute brain inflammation	0–1

SOURCE: Courtesy of author.

TABLE 3

Outcomes per million of pertussis (whooping cough) with and without vaccination

	With Vaccination	Without Vaccination
Birth to 6 months		
Hospitalization	1,060	11,098
Death	12	131
Brain inflammation	2	26
Age 6 months to 5 years		
Cases of pertussis	34,048	356,566
Hospitalization	6,529	38,787
Death	44	487
Brain inflammation[a]	162	87

[a]Only brain inflammation is slightly more frequent with than without pertussis vaccination; all other adverse effects including death are a far greater risk without vaccination.

SOURCE: Courtesy of author.

clared that the vaccination campaign had succeeded and that smallpox had been eradicated from the world.

Other Vaccines

Vaccination against smallpox was the only immunological method of preventing any kind of contagious disease until the rise of scientific bacteriology almost a hundred years after Jenner's experiment. In 1885 Louis Pasteur used an attenuated rabies vaccine to protect a teenage boy, Joseph Meister, after the boy had been bitten by a rabid dog. Before Pasteur's anti-rabies vaccine, rabies was always fatal. By applying Pasteur's methods of developing attenuated strains of pathogens to create innocuous cultures suitable for vaccination, vaccines were soon developed to provide protection against several other previously dangerous diseases of children: diphtheria, tetanus, whooping cough, tuberculosis, and then, with advances in virology and immunology in the middle third of the twentieth century, measles, mumps, poliomyelitis, and others. By the end of the twentieth century, vaccines were available to protect against many diseases that were once a danger to the health and life of infants and children (see Table 1). A high priority for public health science is to develop vaccines for contagious diseases against which so far this preventive method has not been available.

The efficacy of vaccines as a way to protect populations depends on factors that influence herd immunity. For example, diphtheria was a terrible and much feared disease that killed by causing inflammation of the windpipe, so that children who got it often choked to death. After about 50 percent of a population has been immunized (vaccinated) against diphtheria, the probability of transmission to susceptible persons declines sharply. This is called the *epidemic threshold*.

The epidemic threshold of vaccine-preventable contagious diseases varies according to the infectivity of the pathogen, its mode of spread, and a very large number of other variables. Measles used to kill from one in ten to one in a thousand children, depending on their prior state of health, nutrition, and resistance to infection. It remains an epidemic risk until over 95 percent of the susceptible population has been vaccinated. Thus it is important to achieve complete coverage of the susceptible population in measles vaccination campaigns, because those who remain vulnerable can be struck down by dangerous complications such as measles encephalitis (which causes permanent brain damage) as well as by bronchopneumonia, a more common and also dangerous complication. Similarly, vaccination against rubella must reach a very high proportion of women in order to protect all against the small risk that a pregnant woman will get rubella and infect a developing fetus with congenital rubella.

Most vaccines are imperfect; although it is rare, they are sometimes contaminated and tragedies occur. Adverse reactions of varying severity can also occur. The frequency of these reactions has been measured in several large-scale campaigns under the auspices of the World Health Organization (WHO) and the United Nations Children's Fund (UNICEF) (see Tables 2 and 3). However, death and serious disease is a far higher risk without than with vaccination against all the common childhood contagious diseases. Despite the fact that the benefits of vaccination far exceed the risks, resistance continues, occasionally jeopardizing the success of communitywide vaccination programs. For example, vaccination against whooping cough was disrupted in Britain in the late twentieth century when a pediatrician made widely publicized but inaccurate statements about the risks of fatal outcome. It is a challenge for public health authorities, pediatricians, and family doctors to allay the understandable anxiety of parents that their children will suffer harm from vaccination against diseases that have been eliminated from affluent modern societies.

See also: **Infant Mortality; Pediatrics.**

BIBLIOGRAPHY

Gruenberg, E. M., ed. 1986. *Vaccinating against Brain Syndromes: The Campaign against Measles and Rubella.* New York: Oxford University Press.

Henderson, D. A. 1980. "The Eradication of Smallpox." In *Public Health and Preventive Medicine*, 11th edition, ed. J. M. Last. New York: Appleton-Century-Crofts.

Wilkinson, Lise. 2001. "Vaccination." In *Oxford Illustrated Companion to Medicine*, 3rd edition, ed. S. P. Lock, J. M. Last, and G. Dunea: New York: Oxford University Press.

JOHN M. LAST

Venereal Disease

Throughout the twentieth century, doctors, educators, social reformers, churches, the government, and the media have warned adolescents about venereal disease (VD), a group of bacterial infections transmitted primarily during sexual contact. Less attention has been paid to children, especially girls, who are presumed not to be sexually active and to be protected within their homes from sexual predators. Medical views about how girls become infected changed dramatically in the nineteenth and twentieth centuries. From the 1890s to the 1940s, doctors did not rely on medical research, but modified their medical views to conform to their assumptions about the type of men they believed capable of sexually abusing children.

A Historical Perspective

Venereal disease has a long history, with major epidemics recorded, for example, in the late fifteenth century in Europe. In popular belief, problems were usually associated with adults, not children, and particularly with the growth of cities and, in the United States, with the arrival of new immigrant groups whose sexual habits seemed suspect. Growing awareness of prostitution and urban red light districts fed concern. Again, actual problems focused primarily on adults, but venereal disease warnings to children amplified nineteenth-century sexual advice, providing yet another reason to urge children to avoid premarital sexual activity. Warnings of this sort continued in the twentieth century, and by the 1960s new patterns of adolescent SEXUALITY, and new venereal diseases, redefined the whole problem both in advice and in actual disease incidence.

Historically, venereal disease has referred primarily to syphilis and gonorrhea, for which no effective cure existed until researchers discovered penicillin in the 1940s. Although antibiotics have nearly eliminated syphilis from the United States, many new infections, which physicians now refer to as sexually transmitted diseases (STDs), have been discovered. The Centers for Disease Control and Prevention (CDC) have identified twenty-five STDs and estimate that each year in the United States more than 15 million people become infected with at least one; 65 million people in the United States are infected with an incurable STD, such as human immunodeficiency virus (HIV) or genital herpes. Most of the children who acquire HIV, which can lead to AIDS, acquire it from their mothers. As of December 2000, more than 9,000 children and 45 adolescents in the United States had died of AIDS.

A Statistical Perspective

Rates of STD infection in the United States may differ by race, ethnicity, class, age, and geographic location, and because of factors such as inadequate health education or access to medical care. But there is no way to know how many people are infected. Statistics are unreliable because only doctors in public health clinics, where most of the patients are poor and people of color, consistently report new infections. In addition, some people never experience any symptoms and others hide infections because they carry a social stigma.

One quarter of the reported infections are among adolescents, who are particularly vulnerable to chlamydia and gonorrhea. The CDC estimate that 3 million people become infected with chlamydia, and over 1 million with gonorrhea, each year; 40 percent of reported chlamydia infections are among adolescent girls, who also have the highest rates of gonorrhea. The CDC has found not only that untreated infections can lead to infertility but that gonorrhea infection, coupled with unprotected sexual contacts, can also facilitate the transmission of HIV, drastically increasing the risk of infection.

As troubling as these numbers are, very little data exist about the numbers of infected children. Most doctors never test children for STDs except as part of a medical investigation for evidence of CHILD ABUSE; when they do, gonorrhea is the single most common diagnosis. Physicians report more than 50,000 gonorrhea infections in children each year. A sexually transmitted disease can spread without penetration, and because genital bruises may disappear quickly, an STD may be the only physical evidence of sexual assault. Gonorrhea is particularly important evidence because the bacteria cause an infection at the point where they enter the body. Boys and girls both suffer from gonorrhea in the rectum and throat, but the vast majority of children diagnosed with an STD, in 1900 as well as 2000, were prepubescent girls with vaginal gonorrhea. What has changed is the medical explanation for how girls become infected.

STDs and Sexual Assault

Although most doctors in the nineteenth century believed that venereal (by which they meant "immoral") diseases originated with prostitutes and spread during sexual intercourse, doctors knew that children also became infected. Doctors expected to find children infected with syphilis or gonorrhea of the eyes, which mothers transmit to their babies. But genital gonorrhea was neither routine nor acquired at birth; most infected children were poor, working-class, or African-American girls who claimed to have been sexually assaulted. Doctors considered these infections important evidence that a girl had been raped, sometimes by her father.

However, when scientific advances at the end of the nineteenth century improved doctors' ability to detect venereal disease, their belief about the link between child sexual assault and infection suddenly changed. Physicians realized not only that venereal disease had spread among Americans from every race, class, and ethnicity, but that genital gonorrhea was so widespread among girls that doctors feared it was epidemic. Most of these girls were between the ages of five and nine and did not claim they had been assaulted. By the time record-keeping systems were in place in the late 1920s, girls under age thirteen accounted for 10 percent of reported infections among females.

Doctors were vexed as to how so many girls had become infected, particularly those from white middle- and upper-class families, which white professionals considered respectable. Many white professionals believed that only foreign or ignorant men abused their daughters and so assumed that IN-CEST occurred only in poor, working-class, immigrant, or African-American families. When the evidence increasingly pointed to men from their own class, doctors, public health officials, social reformers, and educators speculated that girls could become infected from nonsexual contacts with toilet seats, towels, or bedding—modes of transmission doctors had already rejected for adults and boys. Doctors based their speculation on the fact that the epithelial lining of girls' genitals is so thin that it provides little protection against bacteria. They knew it was unlikely that soiled objects could spread gonorrhea because the bacteria dry quickly when exposed to air, yet without proof that even one girl had become infected after using the school toilet, from 1900 to the 1940s, health care professionals ignored the possibility of sexual assault and insisted instead that girls faced the greatest risk of exposure in the school lavatory.

After penicillin was introduced in the 1940s as the first effective cure for gonorrhea, medical interest in the source of girls' infections disappeared. It was not until the 1970s that physicians who specialized in treating abused children began to emphasize the link between gonorrhea infection and child sexual abuse. In 1998 the American Academy of Pediatrics instructed physicians to assume that a child infected with an STD has been assaulted. But many practitioners remain unwilling to believe that white middle- and upper-class fathers abuse their daughters. These doctors and others, whose motivation is to avoid becoming involved in legal proceedings, may simply attribute a child's infection to "source unknown" and send her home.

See also: **Contagious Diseases; Epidemics; Pediatrics.**

BIBLIOGRAPHY

American Academy of Pediatrics. 1998. "Statement." *Pediatrics* 101: 134–35.

Brandt, Allan M. 1987. *No Magic Bullet: A Social History of Venereal Disease in the United States since 1880.* Expanded ed. New York: Oxford University Press.

Division of STD Prevention, National Center for HIV, STD, and TB Prevention. 2001. *Tracking the Hidden Epidemics: Trends in STDs in the United States, 2000.* Rev. ed. Atlanta, GA: Centers for Disease Control and Prevention.

Gutman, Laura T. 1999. "Gonococcal Diseases in Infants and Children." In *Sexually Transmitted Diseases,* 3rd edition, ed. King K. Holmes, et al. New York: McGraw-Hill.

Hamilton, Alice. 1908. "Gonorrheal Vulvo-Vaginitis in Children: With Special Reference to an Epidemic Occurring in Scarlet-Fever Wards." *Journal of Infectious Diseases* 5: (March) 133–57.

Nelson, N.A. 1932. "Gonorrhea Vulvovaginitis: A Statement of the Problem." *New England Journal of Medicine* 207: (21 July) 135–40.

Sgroi, Suzanne M. 1977. "'Kids with Clap': Gonorrhea as an Indicator of Child Sexual Assault." *Victimology* 2: 251–67.

Taylor, Alfred S. 1845. "Rape." In *Medical Jurisprudence,* ed. R. Egglesfield Griffith. Philadelphia: Lea and Blanchard.

Wolbarst, Abraham L. 1901. "Gonorrhea in Boys," *Journal of the American Medical Association* 33: (September 28) 827–30.

LYNN SACCO

Verne, Jules (1828–1905)

Jules Verne, who has been called the "father of science fiction," was born on February 8, 1828, in Nantes, France. As a child, Verne enjoyed exploring the quays on the River Loire near his home. His favorite book was *The Swiss Family Robinson* because of its constant action and because members of the shipwrecked family contribute their different talents to the task of survival. As a young adult, Verne evaded his parents' plans for a career in law. Instead, in 1857, he bought himself a seat on the stock exchange, writing in his spare time. When, in 1862, he sold his first novel (*Cinq Semaines en ballon,* 1863; *Five Weeks in a Balloon,* 1869), he announced to his fellow stockbrokers that he had written a novel in a new genre created by himself. With this, he quit the stock exchange and devoted himself to writing. He was an extraordinarily prolific author, eventually publishing more than sixty novels in the series Les voyages extraordinaires (Fantastic journeys).

In *Jules Verne: Inventor of Science Fiction* (1978) Peter Costello observes that there was nothing new in Verne's concept of "fantastic journeys." Science fiction in this sense can be seen in the writings of the ancient Greeks. However, Costello suggests, Verne was the first to use a well-researched scientific basis for his tales. This makes his work convincing in a way that previous texts are not.

There is some controversy about the extent to which Verne's texts were intended for a child audience. In *Jules*

Verne and His Work (1966) I. O. Evans observes that, although Verne was always mindful of young readers, he rarely wrote especially for them. Moreover, Walter James Miller points out in his foreword to *The Annotated Jules Verne* (1976) that Verne is considered a highly respected writer of adult fiction in much of Europe. It is only in Britain and America that his works are relegated to children—a fact that Miller attributes to the extensive editing and poor translations of the English-language texts.

On the other hand, Verne's novels may have particular appeal to children because of their emphasis on action and suspense. Furthermore, children can easily identify with Verne's protagonists. Just as children are marginalized in an adult-run society, so Verne's protagonists stand apart from society as they travel to the moon or to the center of the earth. In addition, Verne's books suggest ways in which child readers can see themselves as possessing agency. For example, his protagonists often rely upon their wits rather than physical force. In some cases, they also invent alternatives to established social traditions. In *Deux Ans de vacances* (1888; *Two Years' Vacation*, 1889) a group of shipwrecked boys organizes a society based on cooperation and individual development. In many ways, this new society seems superior to the adult-run boarding school from which they came, in which younger boys were expected to act as personal servants for older ones.

Verne's texts have been adapted for film, including *Vingt Mille Lieues sous les mers* (1870; *Twenty Thousand Leagues Under the Sea*, 1873), adapted and released by Walt Disney Productions in 1954, and *Autour de la lune* (1870; *All Around the Moon*, 1876), adapted and released by Jules Verne Films in 1967. His work has also been adapted for theater and television.

See also: **Children's Literature.**

BIBLIOGRAPHY

Costello, Peter. 1978. *Jules Verne: Inventor of Science Fiction.* London: Hodder and Stoughton.

Evans, I. O. 1966. *Jules Verne and His Work.* New York: Twayne.

Miller, Walter James. 1976. "Foreword: A New Look at Jules Verne." In *The Annotated Jules Verne: Twenty Thousand Leagues Under the Sea*, ed. Walter James Miller. New York: Thomas Y. Crowell.

JENNIFER MARCHANT

Victorian Art

The Victorian era (1837–1901) in Great Britain marked the advent of a new kind of childhood, at least for the privileged classes, and when compared with the less child-friendly eighteenth century. The period witnessed a significant increase in the volume of paintings, books, toys, advice manuals, and

John Everett Millais's *Cherry Ripe* (1879), was reproduced as a best-selling print in 1880. The sensual undertones of Millais's image subvert the portrayal of childish innocence the painting purportedly depicts. Private collection/Bridgeman Art Library.

other things designed specifically with children in mind. In the realm of the fine arts, Victorian images appeared mostly as prints, paintings, and illustrations in magazines and books. Countless artists tackled the theme of childhood, which was popular throughout Queen Victoria's long reign and especially during the years 1850–1880. Their range of subjects—from the sentimentalized girl to the young urban worker—was quite vast. Among the most significant painters of the time was the Pre-Raphaelite artist John Everett Millais, who produced numerous landmark images of young protagonists such as *My First Sermon* (1863), a pair titled *Sleeping* and *Waking* (c. 1867), and *Cherry Ripe* (1879). In addition, numerous illustrators—particularly KATE GREENAWAY, BEATRIX POTTER, Arthur Rackham, and Walter Crane—achieved fame for their contributions to a flourishing market in CHILDREN'S LITERATURE.

Demure Girls and Mischievous Boys

Underlying these representations of young protagonists were adult values that clearly demarcated and endorsed gen-

Fairy paintings, such as Joseph Noël Paton's *The Quarrel of Oberon and Titania* (1849), were a popular genre in Victorian England. The fairies in these paintings engaged in a number of illicit behaviors, including nudity, sexual acts, and miscegenation, as well as general misbehavior not allowed to human subjects of the time. National Gallery of Scotland, Edinburgh, Scotland/Bridgeman Art Library.

dered constructions of childhood, whether of demure girls or mischievous boys. Genre paintings capitalized upon themes inspired by contemporary daily life, and many scenes depicted fictionalized domesticity while reinforcing middle-class beliefs. Such didacticism is particularly evident in the paintings by the Irish artist William Mulready, which include *Train Up a Child* (1841) and *A Mother Teaching Her Son* (1859). Their titles alone communicate the signal importance placed on educating a child to exemplify high moral and religious conduct.

Many modern stereotypes of gender owe their origin visually to the separate spheres and expectations produced in Victorian imagery. Due to the inventions of photography and various photomechanical means of reproduction, the Victorian era was flooded with prints, books, and paintings, all of which circulated countless images of decorative, pious, and pretty girls who obediently served the needs of males. There was a darker side to Victorian images of young girls, as evidenced in the photographs and paintings of unclothed girls found in the possession of LEWIS CARROLL, who is perhaps best known as the author of *Alice's Adventures in Wonderland* (1865). Modern viewers often perceive repressed sexuality in these images, with the ideal middle- and upper-class

Victorian girl viewed as womanly and the perfect adult female seen as girlish and innocent. In paintings by William Powell Frith, Sophie Anderson, and James Collinson often girls are cast as mother surrogates, peacemakers, and observers, their passivity in contrast with the stereotyping of boys, who are more typically shown as feisty, independent, and contentious. Schoolrooms and schoolyards are two common sites of male misconduct, aggression, and bravado in works by Collinson, John Faed, and John Morgan, to name a few. In many of these images there are acts of physical violence that remind modern viewers about how accepted corporal punishment was in the Victorian era and how brutality sometimes reached sadistic levels in elite British private schools. More idealized images, by such artists as Edward Ward, Charles Compton, and William Dyce, feature the "boy hero," who preserves highly differentiated masculine modes of behavior; girls in these works appear merely as admiring bystanders in the presence of precocious young male geniuses.

Sexuality

Occasionally images of "calf love," or young courtship, appeared in Victorian art, but SEXUALITY of a more explicit nature was limited to fairy paintings, where prepubescent winged fairies of both sexes (as well as some androgynous ones) cavort, commingle, and pursue one another with a degree of abandonment, aggressiveness, and sensual gratification rare in any pictures on other subjects. This was undoubtedly because many fairies were both nonhuman as well as innocuously childlike in appearance; thus, in works by artists who specialized in this genre—among them John Anster Fitzgerald and Richard Doyle, creator of the popular book *In Fairyland* (1869–1870)—fairies could behave in illicit ways, flaunting their nudity and sometimes performing quite sadistic acts, while retaining an aura of innocence and otherworldliness.

Depictions of the Lower Class

Victorian portrayals of lower- and working-class children in both urban and rural contexts were somewhat different. The lower-class female might be incredibly rosy-cheeked, tidy, and sweet, whether as a farm lass, peasant, or street vendor. All such girls were perceived essentially as objects of pity or amusement, with little sense of the sordid and oppressive social conditions that impoverished children endured. Boy urchins, whether in the pages of *Punch* magazine or in Royal Academy paintings, were sanitized into healthy, scruffy, and unthreatening children.

The dead or dying child appeared frequently in Victorian era paintings as well, reflecting the high mortality rates (compared with modern statistics) among all classes. Many scenarios—by George Hicks, Thomas Faed, and Thomas Brooks—feature parental bedside vigils in which the need for Christian faith and fortitude are endorsed. As in the literary realm, the picturesque appeal of the helpless orphan, especially vulnerable female ones—as in the paintings of Emily Mary Osborn, George Storey, and Philip Calderon—also was favored by Victorian audiences.

Modern audiences have been inculcated with Victorian notions of childhood by a variety of sources, from an endless proliferation of Kate Greenaway-decorated items to contemporary magazines that combine nostalgia for the past with gauzy finery and images of female decorativeness, passivity, leisure, and conspicuous consumerism. The Victorian literary characters Alice, of *Alice's Adventures in Wonderland*, and PETER PAN, of James Barrie's 1904 novel *Peter Pan, or The Boy Who Would Not Grow Up*, have earned permanent places in the public imagination, due to DISNEY films and to the enduring appeal of the girl seeking authority over her fantasies and the boy escaping the responsibilities of adulthood by refusing to grow up.

See also: **ABC Books; Boyhood; Girlhood; Images of Childhood; Madonna, Religious; Madonna, Secular; Photographs of Children; Theories of Childhood.**

BIBLIOGRAPHY

Brown, Marilyn, ed. 2002. *Picturing Innocence*. London: Ashgate Press.

Casteras, Susan P. 1986. *Victorian Childhood*. New York: Harry N. Abrams.

Casteras, Susan P. 1987. *Images of Victorian Womanhood in English Art*. London: Associated University Presses.

Duff, David. 1975. *Punch on Children: A Panorama 1845–1865*. London: Frederick Muller.

Higgonet, Anne. 1998. *Pictures of Innocence: The History and Crisis of Ideal Childhood*. New York: Thames and Hudson.

Holdsworth, Sara, and Joan Crossley. 1992. *Innocence and Experience: Images of Children in British Art from 1600 to the Present*. Manchester: Manchester City Art Galleries.

O'Neil, Richard. 1996. *The Art of Victorian Childhood*. New York: Smithmark Publishers.

Ovenden, Graham, and Robert Melville. 1972. *Victorian Children*. London: Academy Editions.

Schorsch, Anita. 1979. *Images of Childhood: An Illustrated Social History*. New York: Mayflower Books.

Steward, James Christian. 1995. *The New Child: British Art and Origins of Modern Childhood, 1730–1830*. Berkeley: University Art Museum and Pacific Film Archive.

Walvin, James. 1982. *A Child's World: A Social History of English Childhood 1800–1914*. New York: Penguin.

SUSAN P. CASTERAS

Victory Girls

Though she often resists exact definition, the *victory girl* was generally a teenaged girl or young woman who exhibited her patriotism by offering companionship, and often sex, to servicemen during World War II. With fewer opportunities than their male counterparts to partake in the excitement of wartime mobilization, many young women traveled to various encampment or port areas, seeking intimate encounters with men in uniform. The behavior of victory girls was hardly new; so-called patriotic prostitutes and charity girls attracted the concerned attention of Progressive reformers and military officials during World War I. With increased mobilization of the home front during World War II, however, came heightened scrutiny of those girls and women whose apparently misguided patriotism led them onto hazardous moral and social terrain.

Although studies suggest that many victory girls were actually young married women, literature in the 1940s portrayed victory girls—also known as "khaki-wackies," "goodtime charlottes," "free girls," and "grass grabbers"—as single girls and as part of the larger problem of female "sex delinquency." Agencies such as the U.S. CHILDREN'S BUREAU stressed the need to protect local girls from the corrupting influence of servicemen through the provision of social services. Other federal agencies, such as the Social Protection Division (SPD) of the Federal Security Agency, recognized this need but emphasized the importance of stopping victory girls from spreading venereal disease to U.S. troops. Social policy was torn between the ideal of prevention and rehabilitation on the one hand and punitive measures on the other.

At its 1942 conference, the American Social Hygiene Association reported that victory girls were "sexual delinquents of a non-commercial character . . . [seeking] adventure and sociability" and suffering from a misplaced sense of patriotism. Most professionals agreed with this evaluation, stressing the emotional nature of victory girls' behavior. As Karen Anderson explains in *Wartime Women*, the belief that victory girls desired male companionship above other considerations was supported by their high unemployment rates, unwillingness to take well-paid jobs in the war industry, and concentration in the service industry. While wartime authorities viewed men's sexual behaviors as fulfilling inevitable needs, they dismissed or ignored the possibility that physical as well as emotional drives played a part in women's sexual activity. Historians have pointed out that victory girls may have harbored other motivations for their unconventional behavior. Like other groups of Americans at the time—such as African Americans, gays, and lesbians—victory girls may have been "testing the perimeters of social freedom," as Anderson puts it, by rejecting family- and community-based notions of sexual morality in favor of wartime adventure and independent decision making.

For many girls and young women, the consequences of sexual encounters included venereal disease, illegitimate birth, and entrapment in the penal system. Studies by the military and other federal agencies showed that most cases of VENEREAL DISEASE in the Army—perhaps as much as ninety percent, one article in the *Nation* claimed—were traceable to "amateur girls" such as victory girls. Demonstrating a pervasive sexual double standard, the military turned its attention to warning servicemen about the danger of the girl next door and to repressing women's sexual availability. Encouraged by the SPD, cities across the country subjected women and girls arrested on morals charges to mandatory venereal disease testing and detained them for several days or longer while awaiting the results. When the use of detention proved an ineffective deterrent to female sexual behavior, social protection advocates endorsed additional counseling and rehabilitation for unreformed victory girls. Unless they were forced to accept such services by law, however, girls and women tended to reject efforts to influence their behavior, prompting even stronger efforts by policewomen and social workers to thwart unsanctioned sexual practices.

See also: **Delinquency; Sexuality; War in the Twentieth Century.**

BIBLIOGRAPHY

Anderson, Karen. 1981. *Wartime Women: Sex Roles, Family Relations, and the Status of Women during World War II.* Westport, CT: Greenwood Press.

Brandt, Allan M. 1987. *No Magic Bullet: A Social History of Venereal Disease in the United States since 1880.* New York: Oxford University Press.

Hegarty, Marilyn Elizabeth. 1998. "Patriots, Prostitutes, Patriotutes: The Mobilization and Control of Female Sexuality in the United States during World War II." Ph.D. diss., Ohio State University.

AMANDA H. LITTAUER

Violence Against Children

Violence against children went unnoticed for centuries in Western society. Prior to the sixteenth and seventeenth centuries in Europe, as historians have suggested, the age of a child constituted no guarantee and little protection against a variety of now commonly unacceptable actions, including castration, seduction, sodomy, forced sex, battering, physical beating, labor exploitation, CHILD PROSTITUTION, ABANDONMENT, adult bullying, or even infanticide. Prior to the sixteenth and seventeenth centuries, there was no defined concept of childhood vulnerability or childhood innocence. According to historians, a belief in child protection and child nurture were accidental by-products, rather than a central purpose, of family life and child rearing. There was no body of law that defined children as a special class of people and adults as criminally libel when they employed life-threatening forms of DISCIPLINE or punishment against the young. Children and adults were everywhere joined. Children did not attend school for extended periods of time, and as artists and writers portrayed them, children were everywhere visible and underfoot in the full array of social spaces where adult men and women worked, played, slept, bathed, prayed, and consorted. In short, children had few if any protected spaces in which to avoid physical assault and injuries to body, mind, or soul.

Perspectives on Child Violence in the United States

This entry focuses on perspectives on child violence as they evolved in the United States over a three-hundred-year period. Historically, a recognition of violence against children has proceeded simultaneously with other related social discoveries: of children as essentially innocent and vulnerable; of childhood as a distinct and special stage of life; of the family as a protective enclave for the child; of schools as specialized, age-graded, developmentally calibrated institutions for the young; of government as an important vehicle for the protection and elaboration of CHILDREN'S RIGHTS. These new-found notions developed simultaneously with a view of children as a visible class of innocent and vulnerable people in need of LOVE, protection, education, and patient understanding rather than physical battering, sexual assault, or emotional neglect. Each of these evolving social developments catalyzed a continuing series of controversies centered on the relative morality, utility, and legitimacy of corporal punishment and physical restraint; moral persuasion and psychological manipulation; and behavior management, nonviolence, and individual praise as relationship-shaping modes in families, schools, and communities.

Corporal punishment. Among the more persistent controversies were those centering on the appropriate use of physical force and corporal restraint. In the sixteenth and seventeenth centuries, when children typically worked alongside their parents, went to school only on occasion, if at all, and learned a trade through contractual master–apprentice relationships or informally at home and church, controversy centered less on the relative utility of corporal punishment to secure obedience, morality, and good conduct from children than it did on the circumstances which justified its uses and the instruments deemed most appropriate. By statute and by custom, "stubborn and rebellious," physically abusive, disrespectful young people who failed to honor their parents might legally be put to death, but were more likely to become subject to severe beatings for their bad conduct. The concept of "muscular Christianity" was well accepted and so too were applications of the rod, the ferule, the whip, and the belt by parents, churchmen, masters, and school teachers.

Notwithstanding the popularity of severe corporal punishment for disobedient children, reformers such as JOHN LOCKE, Samuel Willard, and Anne Bradstreet viewed childhood as a vulnerable and malleable life stage and enjoined parents, educators, ministers, and masters to attend to the age and condition of the children, to assess the relative gravity of child offenses, and to calculate the potential moral effects of particular forms of discipline before they administered punishment. As one of them suggested, "No parent has a right to put oppression on a child, in the name of authority. . . . Children are not to be treated either as Brutes or Slaves." (quoted in Greven 1990, p. 161). The recognition of inhumane and dangerous forms of child beating in families and in schools led moral and social reformers in the eighteenth and nineteenth centuries to register their distaste for the traditions of muscular Christianity and to identify parents and teachers as major sources of inhumanity and miseducation. Many mounted an all-out assault on any form of corporal punishment as inimical to the well-being of children.

Child labor. In the nineteenth century, massive numbers of poverty-stricken immigrant children lived and worked in the cities and factories. Urban reformers, privy to public displays of children begging, child prostitution, injuries, and ungovernable street children, discovered child neglect and abusive families. They saw children awash in what they believed to be the corrupting influence of dependent, irreligious families and unscrupulous urban entrepreneurs, and identified CHILD LABOR as a form of physical abuse, a symptom of family failure, and an unacceptable violation of children's needs. They articulated a concept of child neglect and condemned the child-rearing practices of families who were unable or unwilling to provide moral oversight or secure the formal education of their children. They invented a legal notion of child abandonment, and condemned the consequences of premature SEXUALITY, sodomy, and sexual exploitation by peers and employers.

In the view of middle-class urban reformers, boarding schools, urban charity schools, and juvenile reformatories were more humane and educative environments for exploited and ungovernable children than the factory, the street, or the laboring household. They could not have known that these institutions would become incubators for the cultivation of new classes of child abusers and sexual exploiters (who would themselves fuel the outrage of a new generation of Progressive reformers in the late nineteenth and early twentieth centuries). Ironically, these nineteenth-century reformers—so passionate in their zeal to eliminate harsh punishments, labor exploitation, premature sexuality, and the like—did not notice the abuse and neglect among enslaved boys and girls in the South or of Native American children in missionary schools, despite the prevalence of rape, harsh beatings, and deadly assaults in these communities.

The Late Nineteenth and Twentieth Centuries

Like their predecessors in the early nineteenth century, a new generation of social reformers grew up in the late nineteenth and early twentieth centuries in a sometimes turbulent, rapidly changing society. They were confronted with ever larger numbers of non-English speaking immigrants and migrant workers who crowded city streets and city schools and, in the view of the reformers, contributed to a series of social practices that were in need of fundamental transformation. Reformers saw a society where juvenile crime was on the rise, where children and youth had slipped the regulatory ties that bound them to their families and churches, and where increasingly large numbers of boys and girls worked as street entrepreneurs, frequented dance halls and movie theaters, and formed juvenile gangs. Within this environment, reformers discovered ADOLESCENCE as a vulnerable and bombastic period of youth development, juvenile DELINQUENCY as a specialized category of curable criminality, and boys as potential perpetrators as well as victims of crime. They identified battered children as a special class in need of shelter and created child and youth advocacy groups. They codified the concept of "the best interest of the child," and established children's rights as a rationale for public investigation. Ultimately, they criminalized child-beating and identified infanticide as a jailable offense.

Over the course of the twentieth century, attempts have emerged to root out violence against children and to expand its meaning to include emotional, social, and psychological abuse as scholars, theologians, journalists, and educators have continued to expose instances of child beating, INCEST, and sexual abuse in families, institutions, and communities across the social spectrum. With the public spotlight on date rape, CHILD PORNOGRAPHY, prostitution, PEDOPHILIA, and homophobia, once silenced realities have become part of the public discussion. The emergence of statistics documenting the existence of forced sex and incest within families, usually by fathers against daughters, has elevated incest to public visibility. Multiple instances of school-based violence: physical beatings, sexual assaults, bullying, and murder by knife, GUN, and bomb, have drawn public attention to the problem of violence by the young against the young. Taken together, these highly visible acts of violence of the young against the young have led society to redefine young men as criminals and perpetrators rather than adolescents and delinquents, and have intensified a new public debate about the relative utility of zero-tolerance laws, incarceration in adult facilities, and capital punishment.

The conception of violence as a form of injury toward children and youth emerged only gradually, after their status as human beings had acquired definition and respect. The definition of children as a specialized class in need of protection and restraint, has altered the nature of acceptable child-rearing practices, family authority, and the legitimacy of particular forms of punishment and discipline. Like all revolutions, the revolution in childhood status has transformed the parameters of what counts as violence against children.

See also: **Child Abuse; Law, Children and the; Theories of Childhood.**

BIBLIOGRAPHY

Ariès, Philippe. 1962. *Centuries of Childhood: A Social History of Family Life.* Trans. Robert. Baldick. New York: Vintage Books.

Beales, Ross W. 1979. "Anne Bradstreet and Her Children." In *Regulated Children/Liberated Children: Education in Psychohistorical Perspective*, ed. Barbara Finkelstein. New York: Psychohistory Press.

Books, Sue, ed. 1998. *Invisible Children in the Society and Its Schools.* Mahwah, NJ: Erlbaum.

Bremner, Robert H. 1970. *Children and Youth in America: A Documentary History.* Cambridge, MA: Harvard University Press.

Clague, Monique Weston. 1983. "*A. Hall v. Tawney*: Corporal Punishment and Judicial Activism." *Education Law Reporter* 2 (March 14): 909–925.

Cobb, Lyman. 1847. *The Evil Tendencies of Corporal Punishment as a Means of Moral Discipline in Families and Schools.* New York: M. H. Newman.

de Mause, Lloyd, ed. 1974. "The Evolution of Childhood." *History of Childhood Quarterly* 1: 503–575.

Fass, Paula. S., and Mary Ann Mason, eds. 2000. *Childhood in America.* New York: New York University Press.

Finkelstein, Barbara. 1985. "Uncle Sam and the Children: A History of Government Involvement in Child Rearing." In *Growing Up in America: Children in Historical Perspective*, ed. N. Ray Hiner and Joseph M. Hawes. Urbana: University of Illinois Press.

Finkelstein, Barbara. 2000. "A Crucible of Contradictions: Historical Roots of Violence against Children in the United States." *History of Education Quarterly* 40, no. 1: 1–22.

Finkelstein, Barbara. 2001. "Is Adolescence Here to Stay? Historical Perspectives on Adolescence and Education." In *Adolescence and Education*, ed. Tim Urdan and Frank Pajares. Greenwich, CT: Information Age Publishing.

Garbarino, James J. 1997. "The Role of Economic Deprivation in the Social Context of Child Maltreatment." In *The Battered Child*, 5th edition, ed. Mary E. Helfer, Ruth. S. Kemp, and Richard D. Krugman. Chicago: University of Chicago Press.

Gordon, Linda. 1988. *Heroes of Their Own Lives: The Politics and History of Family Violence, Boston, 1880–1960.* New York. Viking Press.

Greven, Philip. 1977. *The Protestant Temperament: Patterns of Child Rearing, Religious Experience, and the Self in Early America.* New York: Knopf.

Greven, Philip. 1990. *Spare the Child: The Religious Roots of Punishment and the Psychological Impact of Physical Abuse.* New York: Vintage Books.

Hawes, Joseph M. 1991. *The Children's Rights Movement: A History of Advocacy and Protection.* Boston: Twayne.

Hawes, Joseph M., and N. Ray Hiner. 1985. *American Childhood: A Research Guide and Historical Handbook.* Westport, CT: Greenwood Press.

Hiner, N. Ray. 1979. "Children's Rights, Corporal Punishment, and Child Abuse: Changing American Attitudes, 1870–1920." *Bulletin of the Menninger Clinic* 43, no. 3: 233–248.

Jenkins, Philip. 1998. *Moral Panic: Changing Concepts of the Child Molester in Modern America.* New Haven, CT: Yale University Press.

Kett, Joseph J. 1977. *Rites of Passage: Adolescence in America, 1790–1970.* New York: Basic Books.

Kimmel, Michael. 1995. *Manhood in America: A Cultural History.* New York: Free Press.

Males, M. A. 1996. *The Scapegoat Generation: America's War on Adolescents.* Monroe, ME: Common Courage Press.

Nightingale, Carl Husemoller. 1993. *On the Edge: A History of Poor Black Children and Their American Dreams.* New York: Basic Books.

Plotz, Judith. 1979. "The Perpetual Messiah: Romanticism, Childhood, and the Paradoxes of Human Development." In *Regulated Children/Liberated Children: Education in Psychohistorical Perspective*, ed. Barbara Finkelstein. New York: Psychohistory Press.

Polakow, Valerie, ed. 2001. *The Assault on America's Children: Poverty, Violence, and Juvenile Justice.* New York: Teachers College Press.

Rotundo, E. Anthony. 1993. *American Manhood: Transformations in Masculinity from the Revolution to the Modern Era.* New York: Basic Books.

Schlossman, Steven L. 1977. *Love and the American Delinquent: The Theory and Practice of "Progressive" Juvenile Justice, 1825–1920.* Chicago: University of Chicago Press.

Trennert, Robert A. 1989. "Corporal Punishment and the Politics of Indian Reform." *History of Education Quarterly* 29, no. 4: 595–619.

BARBARA FINKELSTEIN

Vocational Education, Industrial Education, and Trade Schools

The nineteenth century was characterized by the development of many types of vocational schools and programs. These programs had their origins in the movements and philosophies that grew out of the revival of learning during the fifteenth and sixteenth centuries. The humanistic movement at that time placed emphasis on the privileges and responsibilities of the individual. A shift in emphasis occurred during the late-sixteenth and seventeenth centuries when the realism movement took form. This movement was responsible for the introduction of science and practical arts into the curriculum. The eighteenth century, or Age of Reason, was an age of democratic liberalism, benevolence, and tolerance.

Schools of Industry

Schools of industry were developed in Germany and England during the last quarter of the eighteenth century. These schools combined industrial wage work with classroom study. The industrial work was provided to enable students to earn money to pay tuition. Among the different kinds of industrial work done in these schools were flax and wool spinning, knitting, and sewing for girls and braiding, wood joinery, furniture making, and wood carving for boys. Leaders in education during this time stressed self-education, student participation in learning, universal education, and the importance of environmental factors in creating good workers and good citizens, with the result that many new schools and programs were created in the nineteenth century. Increased interest in human welfare was responsible for the development of schools for poor and delinquent children, while increased demands for labor led to school substitutes for the declining APPRENTICESHIP system. The emphasis on mass education and the need for trained workers made necessary the organization of schools and curricula for workers and prospective workers.

Trade School Movement in America

In the early years of the nineteenth century working people battled to obtain equality of education for their children: even their wildest dreams did not include the teaching of trades in free public schools. The idea of "educated labor" as opposed to merely "skilled labor" gradually gained acceptance through the first half of the nineteenth century. But it was not until after the Civil War, during the period of Reconstruction, that the demand grew pressing for a new type of school that could prepare people for employment in the rapidly expanding industrial economy. The trade school movement thus emerged to provide a workable system of industrial education for all Americans.

One of the first private trade schools was Hampton Institute in Virginia, organized by General Samuel Chapman Armstrong in 1868. Hampton Institute was established to provide both liberal and trade training to African Americans to improve character and social status. Students devoted eight hours each day to the study of a trade through organized courses lasting for a three-year period along with academic courses that required four years. If students completed the entire four-year program they earned a diploma. Booker T. Washington was one of Hampton Institute's most famous graduates. He later became principal at Tuskegee Institute in Alabama and had a distinguished educational career until his death in 1915.

The first school to offer specific trade training with supplementary studies related to each trade was the New York Trade School, founded by Colonel Richard Tylden Auchtmuty in 1881. As a result of his study of labor problems, Auchmuty developed a pattern of trade training designed to give pre-employment instruction as well as supplementary instruction for employed workers.

In contrast to the plan of instruction of the New York Trade School, the Hebrew Technical Institute, founded in New York City in November 1883, offered a greater range of general subjects. The need for a school of this nature arose because of the number of Jewish immigrants coming to America in the late nineteenth century.

The Williamson Free School of Mechanical Trades was organized in 1891 in Philadelphia by the merchant and philanthropist Isaiah V. Williamson. The school was designed to take the place of apprenticeship training that was no longer widely practiced. Boys from sixteen to eighteen years of age were bound as indentured apprentices to the school trustees for three years. After preliminary courses were completed, a student was assigned to a trade by the school trustees. Williamson was convinced that the abandonment of apprenticeship resulted in idleness and crime and constituted a threat to society. The school was entirely free—there was no charge for clothing, food, or instruction.

These three different types of schools gave birth to a limited number of trade schools throughout the country in the late 1800s. During this same period, public secondary schools increasingly offered courses in manual training and industrial arts, and a variety of proprietary and endowed vocational schools of less than college grade provided instruction in agriculture, business, home economics, and trades and industry.

As the nation entered the twentieth century, support for the use of state and federal funds to establish and operate a system of vocational education began to grow, even though labor and education groups frequently disagreed about what form vocational education should take. In 1905, Governor William Douglas of Massachusetts appointed a commission composed of representatives of manufacturing, agriculture, labor, and education. The commission was charged with investigating the status of vocational education and making recommendations for any required modifications. The commission's recommendations issued in 1906 included: (1) instruction to acquaint students with industry, agriculture, and homemaking in the elementary schools; (2) incorporation of practical applications into mathematics, science, and drawing at secondary level; and (3) creation of independent vocational schools to provide both day and evening courses in agriculture, domestic occupations, and industrial pursuits.

Smith-Hughes Act

Although the Smith-Hughes Act, which was to provide federal funds for the teaching of agriculture, home economics, and trades in the public schools, was endorsed by many groups, among them the Chamber of Commerce and the Association of American Agricultural Colleges and Experiment Stations, it did not quickly move through Congress. It wasn't until February 17, 1917, largely as a result of appeals from President Woodrow Wilson and pressure from the nation's impending entry into World War I that the bill finally was approved. President Wilson signed the bill, officially titled the Vocational Education Act of 1917, on February 23, thus establishing the federal government's role in shaping the vocational education programs provided by the states.

Provisions of the Smith-Hughes Act established continuing appropriations for the salaries and training costs for teachers in agriculture, trade, and industrial education that were to increase annually until the maximum of $3 million each was reached in 1926. The funds thus provided were intended as seed money to encourage the states to expand programs and increase enrollments, both of which occurred during the period 1917–1926. Grant Venn has noted that within three years, enrollments in federally subsidized programs doubled, and the combination of federal, state, and local expenditures quadrupled.

Over the course of the twentieth century, vocational education became a fixture of public schools, but its appeal as an avenue for advancement and skilled learning declined. Increasingly a part of the curriculum to which the least academically engaged students were directed, vocational education was chronically underfunded, yet at the start of the twenty-first century, the real needs for the development of skills has seen a renewed interest in vocational schooling.

See also: **Delinquency; Progressive Education; Urban School Systems, The Rise of.**

BIBLIOGRAPHY

Barlow, Melvin L. 1967. *History of Industrial Education in the United States.* Peoria, IL: Chas. A. Bennett.

Bennett, Charles A. 1926. *History of Manual and Industrial Education up to 1870.* Peoria, IL: Manual Arts.

Bennett, Charles A. 1937. *History of Manual and Industrial Education 1870 to 1917.* Peoria, IL: Manual Arts.

Gordon, Howard R. D. 2003. *The History and Growth of Vocational Education in America.* Prospect Heights, IL: Waveland Press.

Hawkins, Layton S., Charles A. Prosser, and John C. Wright. 1951. *Development of Vocational Education.* Chicago: Harper and Row.

Roberts, Roy W. 1956. *Vocational and Practical Arts Education.* New York: Harper and Row.

Scott, John L., and Michelle Sarkees-Wircenski. 2001. *Overview of Career and Technical Education.* Homewood, IL: American Technical Publishers.

Venn, Grant. 1964. *Man, Education and Work.* Washington, DC: American Council on Education.

Walter, R. A. 1993. "Development of Vocational Education." In *Vocational Education in the 1990s II: A Sourcebook for Strategies, Methods, and Materials,* ed. Craig Anderson and Larry C. Rampp. Ann Arbor, MI: Prakken.

HOWARD R. D. GORDON

Vygotsky, L. S. (1896–1934)

Lev Semyonovich Vygotsky grew up in a Jewish family in Gomel in Belorussia (now known as Belarus). After a tradi-
tional Jewish education, he was admitted to the law school at Moscow University, but he also took courses in history and philosophy. In 1916 he wrote a master's thesis analyzing Shakespeare's *Hamlet.* In 1917 he returned to Gomel as a teacher and also practiced clinical psychology. Here he wrote *Educational Psychology* and his dissertation, *The Psychology of Art.*

In 1924, at a congress in Leningrad, Vygotsky presented a talk on consciousness. Due to the success of the talk, he gained access to the Kornilov Institute of Experimental Psychology in Moscow. Here, together with Alexander Luria and Alexei Leontiev, he developed the cultural-historical theory as an answer to the crisis in psychology. In *The Historical Meaning of the Crisis in Psychology,* written between 1925 and 1927, Vygotsky argued that there was no unity or consistency in contemporary psychological research. He claimed that it was difficult to see how the psychoanalytic view of human nature and Pavlov's theory on human behavior could be bridged and that Marxist psychology only pieced together quotations from Karl Marx and Friedrich Engels.

In his 1931 work, *The History of the Development of Higher Psychological Functions,* Vygotsky outlined the idea that psychological development can be seen as the transition from natural forms of behavior to higher mental functions that have a mediated structure. Signs, symbols, and languages function as mediators and create this psychological structure. With this cultural-historical approach, changes in psychological processes can be related to changes in the social-cultural type of mediation. Simultaneously, higher mental processes have to be seen as functions of meaningful social activity created through the individual's own activity. He also formulated the concept of the zone of proximal development—that is, the difference between actual achievement (tasks a child can perform on his or her own) and potential achievement (tasks a child can perform with help from another)—which has inspired pedagogues to reflect on the relation between learning and development and between PLAY and teaching.

Vygotsky investigated the development of and the relation between thinking and language, and he described language as a mental tool for thinking. He dictated his manuscript on this topic from his sickbed and it was published in 1934 as *Thought and Language,* which became his most popular book.

He left behind an extensive and still highly regarded body of scientific work. Most of it was not published in his lifetime, and two years after his death in 1936 his few available publications were blacklisted in the Soviet Union. In 1956 Vygotsky was rehabilitated, but almost twenty years passed before his genius was known and his work adopted in the rest of the world. Vygotsky has had an enormous influence on psychological and educational thinking and practice around the world. Thus the American Vygotsky expert Stephen

Toulmin praised Vygotsky for his talents, genius, and sumptuous production and called him the Mozart of psychology.

See also: **Child Development, History of the Concept of; Child Psychology.**

BIBLIOGRAPHY

Toulmin, Stephen. 1978. "The Mozart of Psychology." *New York Review of Books* 28: 51–57.

Van der Veer, René, and Jaan Valsiner. 1991. *Understanding Vygotsky: A Quest for Synthesis.* Oxford, UK: Blackwell.

Vygotsky, Lev S. 1971. *The Psychology of Art.* Cambridge, MA: MIT Press.

Vygotsky, Lev S. 1978. *Mind in Society: The Development of Higher Psychological Processes.* Cambridge, MA: Harvard University Press.

Vygotsky, Lev S. 1986. *Thought and Language.* Cambridge, MA: MIT Press.

Vygotsky, Lev S. 1997. "The Historical Meaning of the Crisis in Psychology: A Methodological Investigation." In *Problems of the Theory and History of Psychology: Vol. 3. The Collected Works of L. S. Vygotsky.* New York: Plenum Press.

Vygotsky, Lev S. 1997. *Educational Psychology.* Boca Raton, FL: St. Lucie Press.

STIG BROSTRÖM

W

War in the Twentieth Century

Children were included in international conventions for the first time in 1949, when the rights and protection of children in war—as part of the civilian population—were mentioned in the fourth Geneva Convention. This was supplemented in 1977 to refer to child soldiers for the first time. The convention provided that children should be protected from military conscription, from the dangers of warfare, from sexual exploitation, and from starvation. In 1989 the UN CONVENTION ON THE RIGHTS OF THE CHILD was introduced. Its articles defined standards for the treatment of children, including a child's right to name and nationality, the need for family reunification, and protection against torture. It prohibited recruitment of children under the age of fifteen as soldiers. These international laws are difficult to enforce, but they set a standard for children in war and for our view of children's legal rights. The fifteen-year-old age limit for military conscription provoked much discussion, and some have suggested it be raised to eighteen. The age issue is interesting because it focuses on the question: When is a child a child, and when does a child became an adolescent or an adult? That in turn brings our understanding of the apolitical child into focus and whom we see as perpetrators and victims in an armed conflict. This is sometimes also an open question in the literature when information about a child's age is unclear or not discussed at all.

Child Soldiers and Activities in Resistance

During World War II, young boys contributed to the war effort on the Allied side as well as in the army units of the Axis powers. There are examples of American boys between thirteen and fifteen years old who lied about their age and succeeded in joining the U.S. Navy, taking part in the battles in Europe. In Germany, meanwhile, during the last period of the German defense in the autumn of 1944 and spring of 1945, many boys between the ages of twelve and sixteen were drafted as German troops on both the Eastern and Western fronts. Many of the boys were recruited from the HITLER YOUTH, and the Führer awarded some the Iron Cross. The boys handled antiaircraft artillery, grenade throwers, and other weapons. Many of the soldiers who refused to surrender when the Americans occupied the Ruhr Valley were boys. They devised roadblocks, ambushes, and other mischief wherever they could until the final German defeat in May 1945.

Technological developments in the last decades of the twentieth century, especially the manufacture of light, easy-to-handle weapons, made it easier to use children as soldiers. UNICEF estimated that in 1988 almost 200,000 children were involved in military actions as soldiers and fighters. In the 1980s many children joined armed groups in Cambodia to get food and protection. In 1990 the situation was the same in Liberia, where boys between six and twenty were gathered in military units. In Myanmar that same year, when guerrillas began to provide clothes and food many parents handed over their children as soldiers for the rebel army.

Girls also were recruited as soldiers, as in the National Resistance Army in Uganda, where approximately 500 girls were among the 3,000 child soldiers there in 1986. Some children fought for political, religious, cultural, or social reasons; others sought revenge for the deaths of family members.

One way to recruit children into military service was to inculcate schoolchildren with propaganda (a tactic used by the Liberation Tigers of Tamil Eelam in Sri Lanka). Others kidnapped and forced children into military activities, for example in Ethiopia in the 1980s and the Renamo in Mozambique in the 1990s. Indoctrination, physical abuse, terror, and execution of children's relatives in front of them were practiced to brutalize children and accustom them to violence and warfare.

One example of children as prisoners of war was during the Boer War of 1901–1902, in which children were among forty-three prisoners who fought on the Boer side. During

Kim Phuc, age nine, runs from a napalm attack on her village in Vietnam by South Vietnamese troops under U.S. command, 1972. In the late twentieth century, civilians, including children, were the chief victims of war. AP/WIDE WORLD PHOTOS.

World War II, about 10,000 underage German boy soldiers were imprisoned in the largest Allied camp for child soldiers, located in the French village of Attichy. In Rwanda, child soldiers were interned and faced trial for genocide.

Children also took part in military conflicts through their activity in resistance movements, for example during World War II in France, Holland, Denmark, and other German-occupied countries. In France boys were trained by the resistance movement. Older children were used as occasional informants or took part in sabotage actions. Others were instructed in how to behave in case of an inspection of the home, keeping quiet about illegal persons living in the house or apartment; others reported to the resistance movement about persons cooperating with the occupation army. The Pioneers Organization of Montenegro, founded in 1942, was for children from ten to fifteen years of age. The children helped the partisans by bringing them food, weapons, clothes, and other necessities. In the war in Uganda (1986) children were used as spies and messengers.

In the long war in Vietnam (1940, 1961–1975) many children grew up with the experience of their mothers and fathers fighting against the French for independence and against the Americans in favor of Ho Chi Minh and the communists. The period of war was so extended that many children were drawn in the military struggle. Both boys and girls distributed leaflets, brought messages, found hiding places for the soldiers, served as liaisons for the resistance fighters, brought them food and equipment, and took part in ambushes. Smaller children, held by their mothers, were among those who stood up or lay down as shields to prevent the enemy from destroying crops. Children were killed in demonstrations, and fifteen- and sixteen-year-old girls became martyrs.

Rape, Torture, and Genocide

Rape of women and young girls was used throughout the twentieth century as a tool of war violence and organized war activity. It has been common in ethnic conflicts. In the genocide carried out against the Tutsi population in Rwanda

(1994), rape was used systematically to destroy community ties by making girls and women pregnant. The mothers often rejected these children; others kept them and the children became integrated into the family. During the war in the ex-Yugoslavia in the mid-1990s there were cases of infanticide as the consequence of forced pregnancy, as well as testimonies about daughters who were raped in front of their fathers and mothers in front of their children. In the Renamo camps in Mozambique, young boys commited sexual violence on young girls.

The dehumanizing effects on a child who has been raped or has witnessed rape are well documented. It is an experience with long-term effects that carry into the child's adult life. Many women and girls have been forced to trade sex for food and shelter in tense conflicts or war situations. In the late twentieth and early twenty-first centuries, sexually transmitted diseases such as AIDS/HIV spread rapidly with sexual violence in wartime, making many children ORPHANS and increasing the number born with HIV.

In several wars and armed conflicts in the twentieth century, children were tortured as a punishment to the parents, as a way to force information about family members, or as part of a collective punishment of a whole community. In large-scale killing of populations and mass executions, children were not spared. In the 1904 uprising of the Hereros of Southwest Africa against the German colonial power, the violence ended with genocide; thousands of Hereros were killed, many of them children. In 1915–1916 the Turks massacred about 1.2 million Armenians, mostly women and children. Under the German military occupation of Poland, and as a part of the HOLOCAUST during World War II, raids on children took place systematically in an attempt to put an end to regeneration of the Jews. The children were killed or sent to concentration camps where they could be used as experimental subjects. Gypsy children and physically disabled children suffered pogroms and murder under the Nazis.

Unaccompanied Children

Large groups of refugees and uprooted peoples were characteristic of the twentieth century. That this was a new phenomenon and a mass movement became clear in the post-1918 period, and it became an increasing problem for the European continent and its children in the following decades. By the late 1990s the refugee problem was seen as a more or less constant global problem, and the greatest number of the world's refugee children were in Africa and Asia.

The general difference between a refugee child and a displaced child is that the former has crossed borders into neighboring countries and the latter has fled and moved elsewhere in the country. But the distinction is not always clear. Characteristic for modern refugee children is the long duration of their status as refugees, often due to the complex question of nationality. They often become isolated from civil society through years of wandering or long periods in camps.

Beginning in 1900 refugee camps sprang up in South Africa as a result of the Boer War. These developed into concentration camps for persons—mainly women and children—whom the British considered supporters of the Boers. Many of the children died as a consequence of poor sanitary conditions and starvation.

After World War I many children became refugees as a consequence of the crumbling of the Ottoman (Turkish), Romanov (Russian), Hapsburg (Austrian-Hungarian), and Wilhelminian (German) empires, and later as a result of civil war in Russia after the Russian Revolution and the persecutions and expulsions carried out by fascist rulers before and during World War II.

The question of citizenship was often a problem for uprooted children. After the breakdown of the Austrian-Hungarian Dual Monarchy in 1918, new states were created in Europe and borders were changed, with the result that the nationality and citizenship of many children remained unclear for years.

In the 1920s large numbers of children in the Soviet Union were without parents or a home as a result of revolution, civil war, famine, and disorder. The Soviet state could not solve the enormous problem of its uprooted children. Some of the orphans were placed in institutions, others in foster families or in labor communes. These children were regarded with suspicion and by the mid-1930s were seen not as victims of the civil war but as criminals.

Just before the end of World War II about 70,000 German refugee children (under the age of fifteen) were sent to Denmark. The children, with few exceptions, received inadequate medical care from Danish authorities. It is estimated that by the autumn of 1946 almost all the refugee children under the age of two had died. In all about 7,000 of the refugee children died in camps in Denmark through poor nutrition and lack of medical care.

Malnutrition and disease were great problems for refugee children throughout the twentieth century. Separation from parents in wartime often meant that children lost their protectors and their economic security and became homeless. If the whole family was dissolved, the children became totally exposed and dependent on others for food and shelter. UNICEF collected pictures and information about unaccompanied children and distributed them throughout refugee camps in an effort to find the children's families. Most of the separations were accidental, but in Haiti and Vietnam parents sometimes sent their children ahead in the hope that the whole family could get asylum in this way. During the civil war in southern Sudan about 20,000 boys between the ages of seven and seventeen fled the country and trekked enormous distances. Many died on the journey. In the last years of the twentieth century unaccompanied children accounted for approximately 5 percent of the refugee population, or about 53 million people.

Outplacing

Sending children away from their parents and home area was used as a solution for different kinds of problems throughout the twentieth century. For example, they were sent abroad or to another part of the country in order to protect them from enemy attacks. During the Munich crisis of 1938–1939, when it was suspected that England could be bombed, children were sent from England to Wales on private initiatives. From the start of World War II there were mass evacuations of British children from cities to the countryside to secure them from German bomb attacks. The evacuees were normally placed with host families in rural areas, and mothers and schoolteachers sometimes accompanied them. Some of the evacuees in Britain were Jewish refugee children from Nazi-controlled countries who now had become refugees for a second time. Children from London and other large cities were also sent abroad to Canada, the United States, South Africa, New Zealand, and Australia. Just as British children were evacuated to protect them from German air attacks, German children in large cities were also evacuated en masse to the southern part of the country or to neighboring occupied countries to escape Allied bombing.

When war between Germany and the Soviet Union broke out in the summer of 1941, more than 264,000 children were evacuated from Leningrad and other areas and sent to other parts of the country to escape the invasion and siege by German forces. About 4,000 Finnish children were sent to Denmark in 1939–1940 and about 65,000 to Sweden in 1941–1945 to protect them from war hostilities and bombings. But this relocation action was also a gesture of solidarity from Sweden and a way for the Finnish government to solve social problems with food supplies. The Finnish government wanted the children back when the war was over, but a number of the children stayed in Sweden and Denmark as foster children, and some became adopted.

Outplacing children was also practiced as part of humanitarian aid actions. Between 1917 and 1925 about half a million German and Austrian children were sent to other countries in Europe, mainly Switzerland and the Netherlands, as a way to give them proper food and recreation. This was intended to last for just a short period, but some of the children stayed several years with host families. These schoolchildren were seen as war victims, but authorities also believed this program would help ensure that the children would not grow up to become a threat to the rebuilding of Europe. After World War II, German children and smaller groups of children from Norway, Belgium, the Netherlands, and Czechoslovakia came to Sweden as part of an aid rescue program for the destitute in Europe. The aim was to give the children medical care, food, and clothes, but the purpose was also to democratize and rebuild Germany through the children.

Outplacing also took place during the Spanish Civil War from 1936 to 1939. Spanish children were sent to England, Norway, Sweden, Denmark, France, and Belgium, both to remove them from the war zone and as part of a humanitarian aid effort. International aid organizations also arranged outplacing of Spanish children in homes and institutions in Spain.

During World War II, the U.S. government, claiming Japanese Americans were a potential threat to national security, forced some 110,000 persons of Japanese descent—most of them children, from infants to adolescents—into camps in the spring of 1942. After being gathered in "assembly centers," these families were then removed to "relocation centers," camps that were protected with armed soldiers and barbed wire, where they were held for the duration of the war.

Schools

When children are evacuated or schools closed or destroyed in war, children fail to get the education that is so important to their futures. They also lose contact with school friends and regularity in their everyday lives. Under the German occupation of the Ukraine in World War II, schools were destroyed and closed down. Partisans and underground resistance movements established secret networks for schooling, in spite of lack of facilities and teachers and problems with enrolling all children of school age.

During World War I, Belgian refugee children in Britain attended ordinary elementary schools until 1915–1916 when separate schools were established for them. Some, not all, of the German and Austrian children who came to Sweden after World War I went to local schools, but only for a short time. Wartime also provided opportunities for progressive elites to carry out educational and pedagogical experiments on refugee children, as Spanish children were subject to in Cambridge, England, in 1937–1938. Schools and education have been used as channels for both political measures and humanitarian aid programs. After the German occupation of Poland in 1939, young German teachers were sent to Poland to educate ethnic German children in German culture and Nazi ideology. Teachers in schools in Vienna after World War I were empowered to suggest which of the pupils should be sent abroad by some of the humanitarian aid organizations operating in the city. French schools were used as distribution centers for food coming from the United States and Switzerland during World War II.

Growing Up in War

The term *home front*, created during World War I, shows the close connection between the military front and the domestic front and the central role children, as part of the civilian population, have played in wars. Children have been prepared for war in different ways: through ideological propaganda in schools and movies and through militarized youth organizations. When World War II broke out, British children were taught how to build air raid shelters, how to use gas masks, and how to cope with fire. Special colored gas

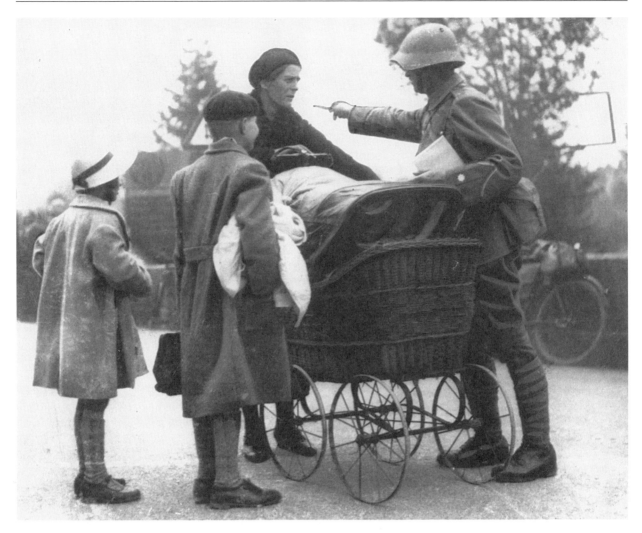

A French woman and her children are directed to a refugee center as they cross the border at Bonfoi, Switzerland, during World War II. Massive displacement of peoples and long-term problems with refugees, including millions of children, were a characteristic of twentieth-century wars. AP/WIDE WORLD PHOTOS.

masks were produced for children under the age of five. German children received similar training when the British army began to bomb German towns. Soviet schoolchildren learned how to take care of wounded soldiers, how to use guns, and how to defend themselves against enemy attacks.

Children saw soldiers on their way to the battlefields and prisoners of war who had been captured. They wrote letters to soldiers. Children met the enemy as soldiers of the occupying army, they saw refugees, and in World War II, non-Jewish children sometimes saw trainloads of Jews on their way to the camps. During this era children got information about the war by listening to RADIO news programs, the official ones or those illegally transmitted from the enemy side. They heard the news of victories and defeats, of invading troops and occupation. In the last decades of the twentieth century children in industrialized countries constantly saw war pictures—often focusing on wounded children—on

TELEVISION screens, pictures that affected their capacity for violence.

The family economy often changes because of war, with the result that children frequently need to contribute to the family's subsistence. In Vienna during World War I, one children's job was to stand in line, sometimes for hours, to buy bread or other necessities for the family. Children also went around railways and warehouses picking up chunks of coal for fuel. During both world wars European children experienced rationing, undernourishment or starvation, cold houses, and lack of clothes and medical care.

Children's family situations changed drastically with fathers, older brothers, or other relatives at the front during World War II. Further, the prisoner of war question was a real problem for many families and had a great impact on the lives of children, who had to live without knowing whether a parent would ever return. If the mothers were active participants in resistance movements or took paid work to support the family, the question of who should take care of the children became urgent. Many children had to cope with news about fathers who were lost, dead, or severely injured. In European and Japanese cities children were eyewitnesses to bombing raids and firestorms caused by both conventional weapons and the atomic bomb. Some survived, others did not.

In war and postwar periods lack of food and water supplies were a great threat against children's health and normal growth; these often killed more children than armaments. Sanctions, blockades, and economic warfare took a heavy toll on children, for example those in Berlin during World War I or in Iraq in the late 1990s and early 2000s. Between 1980 and 1988 approximately 330,000 children died of war-related causes in Angola.

Long-lasting conflicts such as the struggle between Catholics and Protestants in Northern Ireland or the Israeli-Palestinian conflict tend to politicize children to a high degree. The same phenomenon occurred in the wars in Vietnam, where more than one generation in the same family was involved in the struggle. Huge numbers of children never experienced any life but that of war.

After World War II daily life changed once more for children who had to cope with bombed-out houses, the black market, and streams of refugees. American soldiers in occupied Germany offered children sweets, fruits, and chewing gum. Children saw that the enemy could be helpful and kind, and for some German children it was the first time they had ever seen a black man. There were fathers who never returned or came home with psychological or physical wounds. Prewar family life could in many cases not be reestablished. The fall of the Nazi and fascist regimes in Germany and Italy in 1945 gave children new political positions depending on which side their parents had supported. The war had long-term effects on children depending on how traumatized they were by their family situations and experiences of the Holocaust. Because children undergo many changes, they are very vulnerable to war traumas—for example, a sense of hopelessness about the future—as well as malnutrition and war-related diseases.

Increasingly as the century wore on, in areas where landmines were used children continued to be hurt and killed long after the war in their region had ended. Hundreds of thousands of children have been killed and maimed by landmines as they were playing, herding animals, or taking part in agricultural work. If they survive, they live with serious injuries ranging from blindness to loss of arms and legs or chronic pain. In the late twentieth century, Afghanistan, Cambodia, and Angola were probably most devastated by land mines. Many of those children have ended up as beggars or criminals in their struggle to survive.

The War Child Problem

The term *war child* has been used for different types of children: for German orphans outplaced in Germany during World War I, for Viennese children in the 1920s, for children sent from Finland to Sweden and Denmark in 1939–1945, and for children born out of a relation between an occupation soldier or soldier from an allied country and a local woman. The father could also be a part of a peacekeeping force. Children born as a consequence of rape as warfare have also been called war children. A child whose parents are on different sides of the front line often has the same experience of being excluded or stigmatized because of the mother's status as a non-national.

Every country that has experienced war or armed conflict has produced war children. About 10,000 to 12,000 children were born of German soldiers and Norwegian women between 1940 and 1945. The largest group, approximately 100,000, was made up of the children of American soldiers in Vietnam and neighboring countries between 1965 and 1975. Some of the American soldiers in Britain during World War II were black Americans, and children born out of their relations with white Englishwomen were called Brown Babies. Many of those, 1,000 to 2,000 children, were placed in ORPHANAGES. In all there were about 20,000 children born with an American father and an English mother. Children were born out of relations between American soldiers and West German mothers (1945–1956), French soldiers and Algerian women (1954–1962), British soldiers and Soviet women (1941–1945), Japanese soldiers and Chinese women (1945–1950) or Korean women, many of whom were "comfort women" transported to the field (1940–1945). These are but a few examples.

Wars and Humanitarian Aid

During wartime, children have been the victims of medical experiments, such as those performed by the Nazis on twins and other children. They have been neglected medically for political reasons, such as German refugee children in Denmark in 1945. Or in some cases they have been taken care of in order to give doctors medical experience with rare diseases, such as war children in Sweden in the 1920s.

After World War I, children as war victims became an international issue on the American and European agenda, and as a consequence many relief actions came to focus on children. Individuals and organizations throughout the century worked—both legally and illegally—to rescue, protect, and give aid to children affected by wars. The Red Cross movement has been one of the main players on the field. Another is Save the Children, founded after World War I as an international humanitarian organization for child protection. Different religious organizations or groups without an official or unofficial aid program have made great efforts, for example in the rescue of Jewish children during World War II.

In the 1980s the idea of creating a "conflict-free zone" around children emerged in UNICEF's aid work. Negotiations with warring factions worked out corridors of peace for longer or shorter periods, in which children in a war area could get aid and VACCINATIONS, as in El Salvador in 1985 and Uganda in 1986.

In the twentieth century, civilian populations, and therefore children, were participants in war activities in greater numbers than ever before, both as victims and combatants. The century saw an increasing death toll among children, and millions suffered from wars in other ways. We may all believe that children should be above the political divide, but children have taken part in the whole range of military activities. While children are thought to be those who deserve the greatest protection, reality has shown us that they are often the most vulnerable and expendable in war.

See also: **Abduction in Modern Africa; Children's Rights; International Organizations; Latin America: Wars in Central America; Soldier Children.**

BIBLIOGRAPHY

Crosby, Travis L. 1986. *The Impact of Civilian Evacuation in the Second World War.* London: Croom Helm.

Duchen, Claire and Irene Bandhauer-Schoffmann, eds. 2000. *When the War Was Over: Women, War and Peace in Europe, 1940–1956.* London: Leicester University Press.

Eisenberg, Azriel, ed. 1982. *The Lost Generation: Children in the Holocaust.* New York: Pilgrim.

Fishman, Sarah. 1987. "Waiting for the Captive Sons of France: Prisoner of War Wives, 1940–1945." In *Behind the Lines: Gender and the Two World Wars,* ed. Margaret R. Higonnet, Jane Jenson, Sonya Michel, Margaret C. Weitz. New Haven, CT: Yale University Press.

Grieg, Kai. 2001. *The War Children of the World.* Bergen: War and Children Identity Project.

Harvey, Elisabeth. 1998. "Die Deutsche Frau im Osten. Rasse Geschlecht und öffentlicher raum im bebezetzten Polen 1940–1944." *Archiv für Sozialgeschichte* 38: 191–214.

Janfelt, Monika. 1998. *Stormakter i människokärlek. Svensk och dansk krigsbarnshjälp 1917–1924.* Åbo, Sweden: Historical Institution, Åbo Akademi University Press.

Krebs, Paula M. 1992. "The Last of the Gentlemen's Wars: Women in the Boer War Concentration Camp Controversy." *History Workshop Journal* 33: 38–56.

Lindner, Jörg. 1988. *Den svenska Tysklands-hjälpen 1945–1954.* Umeå, Sweden: Acta Universitatis Umensis.

Lylloff, Kirsten. 1999. "Kan laegeløftet gradbøjes? Dødsfald blandt og laegehjaelp til de tyske flygtninge i Danmark 1945." *Historisk Tidsskrift* 1: 33–68.

Marrus, Michael R. 1985. *The Unwanted: European Refugees in the Twentieth Century.* New York: Oxford University Press.

Marten, James, ed. 2002. *Children and War: A Historical Anthology.* New York: New York University Press.

Myers, Kevin. 1999. "National Identity, Citizenship, and Education for Displacement: Spanish Refugee Children in Cambridge, 1937." *History of Education* 3: 313–325.

Myers, Kevin. 2001. "The Hidden History of Refugee Schooling in Britain: The Case of the Belgians, 1914–1918." *History of Education* 2: 153–162.

Raymond, Alan, and Susan Raymond. 2000. *Children in War.* New York: TV Books.

Rosenblatt, Roger. 1983. *Children of War.* Garden City, NY: Anchor Press/Doubleday.

Schwartz, Paula. 1987. "Redefining Resistance: Women's Activism in Wartime France." In *Behind the Lines. Gender and the Two World Wars,* ed. Margaret R. Higonnet, Jane Jenson, Sonya Michel, and Margaret C. Weitz. New Haven, CT: Yale University Press.

Sherrow, Victoria. 2000. *Encyclopedia of Youth and War: Young People as Participants and Victims.* Phoenix, AZ: Oryx Press.

Stevens, Jennie A. 1982. "Children of the Revolution: Soviet Russia's Homeless Children (Besprizorniki) in the 1920s." *Russian History* 9: 242–264.

Taylor, Sandra C. 1999. *Vietnamese Women at War. Fighting for Ho Chi Minh and the Revolution.* Lawrence: University Press of Kansas.

Tuttle, William M. 1993. *Daddy's Gone to War: The Second World War in the Lives of America's Children.* New York: Oxford University Press.

United Nations. 1996. *Promotion and Protection of the Rights of Children: Impact of Armed Conflict on Children.* New York: United Nations.

Weitz, Margaret Collins. 1995. *Sisters in the Resistance: How Women Fought to Free France, 1940–1945.* New York: John Wiley and Sons.

Werner, Emmy. 2000. *Through the Eyes of Innocents: Children Witness World War II.* Boulder, CO: Westview.

INTERNET RESOURCE

UNICEF. 2003. "Children in War." Available from <www.unicef.org/sowc96/>.

MONIKA JANFELT

Watson, John B. (1878–1958)

The details of John B. Watson's contributions to developmental and CHILD PSYCHOLOGY are largely unknown to modern psychologists, who see little of them beyond textbook summaries. Based on an objective, empirical foundation, the best early twentieth-century research in developmental physiology, and his own work with animals, Watson adopted a life-span developmental approach which emphasized combining observational research with laboratory work employing the precision of Pavlovian principles. Watson was one of the first psychologists to argue for the impressive cognitive competence of infants, question the prevailing prejudice of inevitable intellectual decline in old age, and, unlike other pioneering developmentalists such as G. STANLEY HALL, JEAN PIAGET, and ARNOLD GESELL, explicitly reject Ernst Haeckel's discredited recapitulation theory and its questionable behavioral implications.

The origins of Watson's developmental viewpoint can be traced to his earliest work with animals. His dissertation, *Animal Education* (1903), an analysis of the relationship between brain and behavior development in rats, suggested to Watson that infant humans, like infant rats, were not the passive, cognitively limited organisms that some of his contemporaries suggested. His extensive ethological and laboratory studies of seabirds (*The Behavior of Noddy and Sooty Terns,* 1908), monkeys (*Notes on the Development of a Young Monkey,* 1913), and other organisms convinced him of the importance of early experience to the development of adult behavior (a position which paralleled Freud's in some ways) as well as the impossibility of fully understanding learned behavior without also understanding unlearned capabilities.

After 1917, Watson's research shifted from animals to humans. Focusing on unlearned behavior and emotional development, his interests included reflexes, thinking, language acquisition, and handedness. Although he argued that there was little good evidence supporting inherited differences in intelligence and other tendencies based on race and similar factors, Watson never claimed that all behavior was learned. Watson is usually portrayed as a naïve environmentalist who claimed that if given a dozen healthy babies, he could turn them into anything he wanted. But he regarded the study of unlearned behavior in humans as basic to understanding learning and behavior development. A clever debater, his famous "dozen health infants" statement, which seems to assert complete environmentalism, was actually a rhetorical device for revealing the unscientific foundations of early twentieth-century hereditarianism. A Darwinian, Watson believed that the primacy of learning over complex instinctual behavior in humans was an inherited, adaptive characteristic in which complex functional behaviors were conditioned though Pavlovian processes from simple unlearned behaviors.

For Watson, emotional development also consisted of building complex behaviors through conditioning from simpler reactions—in this case, newborns' unlearned reactions of fear, rage, and love. The so-called Little Albert Experiment (where Watson conditioned an eleven-month-old infant to show fear at the sign of a white rat) suggested that new emotional reactions could be conditioned via Pavlovian associations. Research by M. C. Jones (1924a, 1924b), supervised by Watson, showed that emotional responses might be unconditioned using a technique now known as "systematic desensitization." While his theory as a whole was considered an oversimplification, the concept of emotional conditioning was accepted broadly and serves as the basis of modern therapies for anxiety disorders.

A good Progressive, Watson believed in applying scientific findings to social problems. *Psychology from the Standpoint of a Behaviorist* (1919) and *Behaviorism* (1924, revised 1930) contained large sections on developmental topics. Articles on child behavior in *Harpers, McCalls,* and *Cosmopolitan,* as well as advice dispensed by radio, broadened his audience. *Psychological Care of Infant and Child* (1928) is remembered primarily for suggesting that emotional attachment between children and parents breeds overdependency. However, Watson also warned of the negative effects of corporal punishment, allayed unfounded Victorian-era fears about MASTURBATION, and advocated an open approach about sexual issues—a view derived from extensive studies of the effectiveness of SEX EDUCATION in preventing venereal disease.

Watson stopped publishing broadly in 1930. For over thirty years research on conditioning principles dominated behaviorism. Eventually, the successful application of Skinnerian behavioral principles to developmental disabilities in the 1950s reinvigorated a behavioral life-span approach to developmental psychology. The "behavior analysis of child development" has become a major component of modern behavior analysis.

See also: **Child Development, History of the Concept of; Child-Rearing Advice Literature; Spock, Benjamin.**

BIBLIOGRAPHY

Bijou, S. W., and D. M. Baer. 1961. *Child Development I: A Systematic and Empirical Theory.* Englewood Cliffs, NJ: Prentice Hall.

Bijou, S. W., and D. M. Baer. 1965. *Child Development II: The Universal Stage of Infancy.* Englewood Cliffs, NJ: Prentice Hall.

Buckley, K. W. 1989. *Mechanical Man: John Broadus Watson and the Beginnings of Behaviorism.* New York: Guilford Press.

Jones, M. C. 1924a. "The Elimination of Children's Fears." *Journal of Experimental Psychology* 7: 383–390.

Jones, M. C. 1924b. "A Laboratory Study of Fear: The Case of Peter." *Pedagogical Seminary* 31: 308–315.

Todd, James T., and E. K. Morris, eds. 1994. *Modern Perspectives on John B. Watson and Classical Behaviorism.* Westport, CT: Greenwood Press.

Watson, John B. 1914. *Behavior: An Introduction to Comparative Psychology.* New York: Henry Holt.

Watson, John B. 1930. *Behaviorism,* rev. ed. New York: People's Institute.

JAMES T. TODD

Wayland, Francis (1796–1865)

The Reverend Francis Wayland exerted a strong influence over generations of American youth, including not only his own students at Brown University, but also the thousands who relied on his standard textbooks, *The Elements of Moral Philosophy* (1835), and *The Elements of Political Economy* (1837). Wayland was born March 11, 1796 in New York City to English immigrant parents. He graduated from Union College in 1813 and was preparing to become a doctor when he underwent a conversion experience and enrolled at Andover Seminary. After graduating in 1816, Wayland returned as a teacher to Union, then led the First Baptist Church in Boston, before being installed as president of Brown in 1826.

Wayland's legacy is as a reformer. Brown was a troubled institution when he arrived. Wayland embarked on a vigorous program to revivify the school, through a combination of increased student discipline and liberalization of the curriculum. He compelled faculty to live on campus and pay visits to students in their quarters. He insisted that all student infractions be reported to him personally, and he used the threat of expulsion to keep order. Yet Wayland compelled an enormous respect and admiration from many students. In contrast to his restrictive approach to student behavior, Wayland advocated opening Brown's pedagogy. For colleges to be competitive in the market for students, he believed they should offer classes relevant to the new professions of the nineteenth century. Wayland rejected the standard fixed university curriculum of classics, mathematics, and philosophy. He introduced classes in the sciences and engineering. Wayland also advocated for the expansion of the public school system in Rhode Island so that a greater number of youth might be prepared for college. His ideas about education are best expressed in his books *Thoughts on the Present Collegiate System* (1842), and *Report to the Corporation of Brown University on Changes in the System of Collegiate Education* (1850).

Wayland's approach to raising his children mirrored his treatment of students. A personal essay published anonymously in *The American Baptist Magazine* in 1831 testifies to his intensive disciplinary efforts. The piece describes his reaction to the willful refusal of his fifteen-month-old son, Heman, to accept a piece of bread from Wayland's hand. To subdue Heman's temper, Wayland left him alone in a room, without food or drink, for a day and a half. He visited regularly to give Heman a chance to behave compliantly, until the infant finally relented his obstinacy. Wayland's discipline, while strict, was balanced with great openness and love. Heman and his older brother, Francis, Jr., fondly remembered wrestling their imposing father on the living room floor; and both expressed absolute respect and love for him in their personal letters. Historian William G. McLoughlin has suggested that Wayland's disciplinary technique, prompted by religious fears of infantile propensities towards sin, may have been archetypal of evangelical child rearing, and likely to result in "reaction formation."

Wayland retired from Brown in 1855, afterwards devoting himself to reform movements including temperance, antislavery, peace organizing, and prison and hospital reform. He died September 30, 1865, at the age of sixty-nine.

See also: **Child Development, History of the Concept of; Discipline.**

BIBLIOGRAPHY

Cremin, Lawrence. 1980. *American Education: The National Experience, 1783–1876.* New York: Harper and Row Publishers.

McLoughlin, William G. 1975. "Evangelical Child Rearing in the Age of Jackson: Francis Wayland's Views on When and How to Subdue the Willfulness of Children." *Journal of Social History* 9: 20–43.

Smith, Wilson. 1956. *Professors and Public Ethics: Studies of Northern Moral Philosophers before the Civil War.* New York: Cornell University Press.

RACHEL HOPE CLEVES

Welfare Reform Act (1996)

The 1996 Welfare Reform Act, officially the Personal Responsibility and Work Opportunity Reconciliation Act of 1996, fulfilled President William Jefferson Clinton's oft-repeated campaign promise "to end welfare as we know it." It replaced the federal program of Aid to Dependent Children (ADC), founded in 1935 as part of the Social Security Act, and later known as Aid to Families with Dependent Children (AFDC). Between the 1960s and the 1990s, AFDC's rolls increased dramatically, especially in the wealthier Northern industrial states. In accordance with the era's individualistic ideologies, welfare's actual and potential claimants now regarded welfare as a right, not a mere privilege. Conservatives denounced the federal welfare system as a communist plot and a threat to American values.

After 1970, liberals, moderates, and even welfare recipients began to join conservatives in denouncing welfare in general, and AFDC in particular. The discussions tended to accuse AFDC of things such as breaking up the family, fostering a rise in illegitimacy, and stimulating dependency, although the evidence of this was sometimes ambiguous. Some studies showed AFDC promoted the economic, legal, and cultural independence of welfare mothers; some believe that there was a gender as well as a racial basis to the criticism. AFDC permitted impoverished mothers to raise their children at home. As AFDC became increasingly generous in the 1960s and early 1970s, it at last fulfilled the original ADC's promise that mothers be paid to stay at home to raise dependent children.

By the 1990s the political and cultural climate had changed. In the new individualistic and free-market worldview that permeated American political and cultural discourse entitlement programs such as AFDC were vulnerable. As liberals and moderates adopted individualistic perspectives parallel to those of conservatives, AFDC's days were numbered. The turning point was likely the Republican Congressional victories in the 1994 elections, which convinced President Clinton to surrender the program in order to remain re-electable. Congress passed the welfare reform act in summer 1996 and President Clinton signed the bill on August 22, 1996.

The law ended AFDC. It required work in exchange for temporary relief; no more than two years could be used before parents would be working or in job training. No recipient could have more than five years of assistance cumulatively. There were a handful of concessions, such as providing new monies for childcare and medical insurance for mothers in cases in which mothers were shifting to employment. The 1996 act also destroyed the independence mothers enjoyed under AFDC. For example, single mothers could afford to attend school part time, or even full time depending on family resources, to advance themselves and qualify for better jobs than they had before. The new law of 1996 made that very difficult, because states could diminish allocations and also limit the time one was on welfare, a serious problem in a cyclical or depressed local economy. Conservative thinkers won a major victory in politics. Culturally this was also a triumph too for the free market, individualistic worldviews of those who had attacked the rationales for the New Deal and the national welfare state.

See also: **Aid to Dependent Children (AFDC); Great Depression and New Deal; Sheppard-Towner Maternity and Infancy Act; Social Welfare.**

BIBLIOGRAPHY

Grabner, William. 2002. "The End of Liberalism: Narrating Welfare's Decline, from the Moynihan Report (1965) to the Personal Responsibility and Work Opportunity Act (1996)." *Journal of Policy History* 14: 170–190.

HAMILTON CRAVENS

Wet-Nursing

A wet nurse is a woman who breast-feeds a child that is not her biological child. Although specific wet-nursing practices differed among countries from the fifteenth through the early twentieth centuries, diverse customs produced largely identical results. Across space and time, maternal nursing produced the lowest infant death rates while wet-nursing prompted significantly higher INFANT MORTALITY.

Wet-Nursing in France

Wet-nursing was a particularly entrenched cultural phenomenon in France, where the wealthy sent their infants to the countryside to be suckled for several years by peasant women. A high death rate was common among these babies, probably due to neglect. One typical seventeenth-century father reported that only three of his thirteen wet-nursed children survived more than a few years.

By the eighteenth century the custom of sending babies away to be wet-nursed had crossed class lines, as economic conditions forced even the urban working class to place their babies with rural families for up to four years. Workers' wages were so low during this era, and rents so high, that even mothers with infants had to work. Although working women were by no means novel in France, they posed a unique problem in an urban setting. No longer able to keep their infants at their sides as they toiled, working-class urban mothers began to send their babies to the countryside to be cared for by women even poorer than themselves. The custom was so pervasive among all classes that cities like Paris and Lyon literally became cities without babies.

As demand burgeoned, the cost of hiring a wet nurse soared while the quality of care plummeted. Upper-class families responded to ENLIGHTENMENT critiques of the custom and its concomitant dangers not by ending the practice, but by bringing wet nurses into their homes to closely supervise them. Poor working families, on the other hand, could only afford the cheapest wet nurses, who lived at ever-increasing distances. Despite the relatively low cost, working-class families often found themselves in arrears to the wet nurse. Infants paid the price.

Given the ubiquitous demand for the service and the high infant mortality the practice engendered, wet-nursing became a publicly organized venture during the second half of the eighteenth century. As FOUNDLING hospitals, wet-nurse bureaus (employment agencies for wet nurses), and the working poor competed for fewer and more expensive nurses, Parisian police authorities stepped in to combine the four existing wet-nurse bureaus into a municipal Bureau of Wet Nurses, which guaranteed wet nurses a minimum wage. The Bureau served a dual function: it assured parents an adequate supply of wet nurses and it persuaded nurses not to neglect their charges by advancing them their monthly salary. The Bureau, and not the wet nurse, then collected the wet nurses' wages from infants' fathers.

The Bureau of Wet Nurses was one of the few institutions to survive the French Revolution. Bureau records indicate that of the 66,259 nurslings placed between 1770 and 1776, 31 percent died while in wet nurses' care, a considerably lower rate of infant mortality than wet-nursed infants had suffered previously. Until its demise in 1876, the Bureau of Wet Nurses of the City of Paris provided an alternative both to the inferior service offered by private wet-nurse bureaus and the expense of public charities caring for foundlings. With the passage of the Roussel Law in 1874, the supervision of wet-nursed infants became a national, rather than a municipal, responsibility. The Roussel Law mandated that every infant placed with a paid guardian outside the parents' home be registered with the state. In this way the French government was able to monitor how many children were placed with wet nurses (eighty thousand a year between 1874 and World War I) and how many of those infants died (15.1 percent).

The ubiquitous custom of wet-nursing did not wane in France until World War I. The war's tumult disrupted access to wet nurses and demonstrated to urban families, long reluctant to consider any alternative to maternal nursing other than wet-nursing, that safe, inexpensive, and easy artificial infant feeding options now existed. A decline in working mothers after World War I, passage of a law granting a

Farewell to the Wet Nurse (1777), by Etienne Aubry. Wet-nursing was a particularly common practice in France, where, in the eighteenth century, both upper-class and urban working-class parents sent their infants away to be nursed. Pushkin Museum, Moscow, Russia/ Giraudon-Bridgeman Art Library.

monthly bonus of fifteen francs to working women if they breast-fed their babies for twelve months, the routine pasteurization of milk, and the availability of canned milk all contributed to the virtually instantaneous extinction of wet-nursing in France.

Wet-Nursing in England

In other western European countries wet-nursing was not as pervasive as it was in France, but it was a significant cultural practice nonetheless. In England, wealthy married women customarily hired wet nurses while working-class mothers breast-fed their own babies. Historians have gleaned this fact from the stark difference in birth rates between English upper- and working-class women. Parish records show that wealthy women customarily gave birth annually while working-class women gave birth at considerably longer intervals, about every three years. Scholars attribute this dichotomy to the difference in upper- and lower-class infant feeding practices. Breast-feeding—specifically, exclusive, prolonged

breast-feeding—suppresses ovulation and thus is a relatively reliable contraceptive.

Reasons for the class differentiation in infant feeding practice are not clear, although scholars speculate that breast-feeding was linked exclusively with the lower class as early as medieval times. This association made breast-feeding an inappropriate activity for upper-class women. The consequence of this custom for the health of well-to-do women, however, was never acknowledged. In preindustrial England, it was not uncommon for wealthy women to have as many as eighteen children during the first twenty years of their marriages. The near-constant pregnancy experienced by these women was quite debilitating, certainly more incapacitating than breast-feeding would have been. Poor women had far fewer children and were apparently the healthier for it.

Upper-class demand for wet nurses was great enough that wet-nursing constituted the major industry in some rural counties. Two types of wet nurses predominated in England: parish nurses who were on poor relief and rarely able to provide adequate care for their charges, and professional wet nurses who were well paid and well respected. This contrast is evidenced in the dual ramifications of wet-nursing in England. In seventeenth-century England, unlike France, some wet nurses were well known to the well-to-do families who hired them, as they were often former servants who had left the household to marry. In these cases wet nurses were trusted, reliable, well-paid employees and infants were properly cared for. Most wet-nursed infants, however, were raised far from their families for up to three years. In these cases there is evidence that as many as 80 percent of them died during infancy.

Wet-Nursing in Germany

In no other country did infant feeding customs vary more starkly by region then in Germany. In some areas almost all babies—regardless of class, the urban/rural divide, or the availability of animal milk—were breast-fed. In other areas the opposite was equally universal: maternal breast-feeding was nonexistent and all infants were either wet-nursed (if parents could afford that luxury) or fed pap (some combination of meat or rice broth, cows' milk, sugar, and water). One consequence of the homogeneity of infant feeding practices within regions was apparent. Although infant mortality varied between regions in Germany, it did not fluctuate among classes within regions. Demographers have argued that this uniformity in the infant death rate between socioeconomic groups within regions suggests that infant feeding method was a key, if not the key, determinant of infant morbidity and mortality during this era.

Breastfeeding in Germany was least common in the south and southeast—southern and eastern Bavaria and Bohemia—and most common in the northwest—northern and western Bavaria, Baden, and Hessen. Wherever *Nichstillen* (never breast-feeding) was practiced the custom apparently dated back to the fifteenth century, when infants were routinely fed pap instead of human milk and breast-feeding mothers were openly threatened and ridiculed.

Whether wet-nursing or pap was the predominant substitute for maternal feeding likewise depended on region. In seventeenth century Hamburg, for example, wet nurses were common and social critics complained that the possibility of a job as a wet nurse in a comfortable home encouraged immorality among the poor. By the eighteenth century, as it became common knowledge in the medical community that wet-nursed infants died in greater numbers than maternally breast-fed babies, eighteenth-century pediatricians united in their condemnation of the practice. Their disapproval had no discernable impact, however. Hamburg, a city populated by ninety thousand at the time, continued to house almost five thousand wet nurses. Wet nurses lived in the homes of the rich, as well as the homes of merchants and artisans.

Only foundlings were sent to wet nurses in the countryside, where 22 percent of them died their first few weeks there.

By the late nineteenth century, German health officials, alarmed over the country's high infant mortality rate in comparison to other European countries, began to collect data on local infant feeding customs and their effects. All resulting studies showed a strong inverse relationship between maternal breast-feeding and infant mortality. This finding prompted an infant welfare movement whose varied facets all emphasized the benefits of maternal breast-feeding and the risks of feeding infants pap and wet-nursing babies. Infant welfare centers, whose primary purpose was to encourage mothers to breast-feed their own babies, burgeoned. Working mothers not only came to enjoy legal protection so they could stay home and nurse their babies, the state paid allowances to these mothers while they nursed their infants.

By 1937 sharp regional differences in infant feeding had all but disappeared and breast-feeding was becoming the norm in all areas of Germany. In Munich, for example, the percentage of breast-fed infants rose from 14 percent in 1877 to 91 percent in 1933. The resurgence in the initiation of breast-feeding, however, was accompanied by a reduction in the duration of breast-feeding. Women rarely breast-fed their babies beyond the twelve-week nursing allowance provided by the state.

Wet-Nursing in the United States

English colonists brought to colonial North America the practice of PLACING OUT babies to live with wet nurses. Puritans in particular criticized this custom, charging that mothers who did not nurse their children were merely "half-mothers." Yet the well-to-do mothers who customarily hired wet nurses did not seem significantly embarrassed by the accusation, as wet-nursing remained a conspicuous practice in the United States well into the early twentieth century.

By the nineteenth century the practice had changed somewhat—wet nurses now lived in infants' homes rather than vice-versa. While previous living arrangements were directly responsible for a high death rate among wet-nursed infants, the new custom of the wet nurse living in the infant's home engendered a high death rate among wet nurses' own infants, as employers rarely permitted a wet nurse's baby to accompany her. These infants lived instead in foundling homes where caretakers fed them artificially. Their death rate exceeded 90 percent.

It is difficult to ascertain the precise extent of the use of wet nurses in the United States because, unlike Europe, no official records pertaining to wet nurses were ever kept. Instead, their use is evidenced by help-wanted ads in urban newspapers and bitter complaints about the inadequacy of wet nurses in women's and infant-care magazines. Both ads and letters pertaining to wet nurses appeared regularly in newspapers and magazines into the early twentieth century.

There is also evidence in medical journals that urban pediatric societies and medical charities ran employment agencies for wet nurses through the 1910s.

In Gilded Age and Progressive-era America, when employers denigrated all household servants without compunction, wet nurses were among the most maligned of servants. While physicians argued that wet nurses were indispensable when it came to saving the lives of sick, artificially fed infants, including ORPHANS, these same doctors and the women who employed wet nurses were united in their belief that wet nurses were ignorant, uncouth, unclean, unruly, and immoral. Yet the quandaries inherent in wet-nursing in the United States were far more difficult for wet nurses. In addition to being regarded with disdain, they were the ones forced to abandon their babies to institutional living and artificial food in return for unstable jobs. Employers customarily fired wet nurses after a few months of work due to the pervasive belief that the quality of their milk deteriorated over time.

Wet-nursing in the United States waned slowly in proportion to the growing safety of artificial food. The passage of laws governing the production and sale of cow's milk was instrumental in ending the practice by the 1920s.

Maternal and Infant Illness and Death
In all countries where the custom was common, wet-nursing arguably contributed to more ill health and death among mothers and babies than any other practice. Lactation is nature's way of spacing human pregnancies. The mothers who did not breast-feed, and instead hired other women to suckle their children, found themselves perpetually pregnant during their childbearing years, a fact that contributed to their own ill health and premature deaths. Wet-nursed infants who lived in wet nurses' homes died in much higher numbers than those infants who lived with their parents, whether they were maternally breast-fed or wet-nursed. When employers did hire wet nurses to live in their homes so they could supervise them, they customarily (particularly in the United States) forced wet nurses to board their infants elsewhere. As a result, death rates among these wet nurses' infants exceeded 90 percent. In these situations poor babies were effectively sacrificed so rich babies could live. The custom of employing a wet nurse debilitated many more mothers than breast-feeding would have and likely killed many more infants than it saved.

See also: **Baby Farming; Infant Feeding.**

BIBLIOGRAPHY

Campbell, Linda. 1989. "Wet-Nurses in Early Modern England: Some Evidence from the Townshend Archive." *Medical History* 33: 360–370.

Fildes, Valerie. 1988. *Wet Nursing: A History from Antiquity to the Present.* Oxford: Blackwell.

Golden, Janet. 1996. *A Social History of Wet Nursing in America: From Breast to Bottle.* Cambridge, MA: Cambridge University Press.

Kintner, Hallie J. 1985. "Trends and Regional Differences in Breastfeeding in Germany from 1871 to 1937." *Journal of Family History* 10 (summer): 163–182.

Klaus, Alisa. 1993. *Every Child a Lion: The Origins of Maternal and Infant Health Policy in the United States and France, 1890–1920.* Ithaca, NY: Cornell University Press.

Knodel, John, and Etienne Van de Walle. 1967. "Breast Feeding, Fertility, and Infant Mortality: An Analysis of Some Early German Data." *Population Studies* 21: 109–131.

Lehning, James R. 1982. "Family Life and Wetnursing in a French Village." *Journal of Interdisciplinary History* 12: 645–656.

Lindemann, Mary. 1981. "Love for Hire: The Regulation of the Wet-Nursing Business in Eighteenth-Century Hamburg." *Journal of Family History* 5 (winter): 379–395.

McLaren, Dorothy. 1979. "Nature's Contraceptive: Wet-Nursing and Prolonged Lactation: The Case of Chesham, Buckinghamshire, 1578–1601." *Medical History* 23: 426–441.

Sussman, George D. 1982. *Selling Mothers' Milk: The Wet-Nursing Business in France 1715–1915.* Urbana: University of Illinois Press.

Wolf, Jacqueline H. 2001. *Don't Kill Your Baby: Public Health and the Decline of Breastfeeding in the Nineteenth and Twentieth Centuries.* Columbus: Ohio State University Press.

JACQUELINE H. WOLF

White House Conferences on Children

The first White House Conference on Children, called in 1909 by President Theodore Roosevelt, was a watershed event in the history of American child welfare. Roosevelt charged the conference to consider the care of DEPENDENT CHILDREN—that is, children who depended for support on any person or institution other than their parents or other relatives—and to make recommendations regarding them.

In the nineteenth century, dependent children were cared for primarily in ORPHANAGES. Before the U.S. Civil War, orphanages were small, located in towns rather than rural settings, and run almost invariably by women. A typical Protestant orphanage was headed by a board of "lady managers," religiously motivated and usually elite women. A typical Catholic orphanage was run by the Sisters of Charity or a comparable women's religious order, who also ran a school for poor children from the parish (and often paying boarders) as well as the orphans. Heavy Catholic immigration and the formation of many new dioceses led after the war to a reorganization of the Catholic orphanages. The orphanages became larger diocesan institutions, physically dissociated from parish life. Protestant orphanages also increased in size after the war and their lady managers became increasingly distracted by other social and charitable activities.

The major alternative to the women-run orphanages was found in the foster-family movement, begun on a grand scale by the ORPHAN TRAINS of CHARLES LORING BRACE and the NEW YORK CHILDREN'S AID SOCIETY. Late in the century,

CONFERENCE ON THE CARE OF DEPENDENT CHILDREN
CALLED BY PRESIDENT THEODORE ROOSEVELT
JANUARY 25TH AND 26TH, 1909
WASHINGTON, D. C.

After a century in which dependent children were cared for in orphanages, the 1909 White House Conference on the Care of Dependent Children replaced the orphanages with a system of foster care. Courtesy of Marshall B. Jones.

men whose experience lay in corrections, joined by early social workers, also mainly men, adopted Brace's approach, advocating that orphanages be replaced by "home-placing agencies" run by men, and championing women as foster mothers, not lady managers.

A direct challenge to the orphanages came after the turn of the century. In September 1907, the *Delineator*, a women's magazine edited by the novelist Theodore Dreiser, launched a campaign to "rescue" children from orphanages and place them in foster families. In December 1908, Dreiser and others wrote President Roosevelt, asking him to call the first White House Conference. A month later, the conference assembled, hosting 185 men and 30 women. The conference's conclusions would become a foundational text for the then-emerging profession of social work: "Home life is the highest and finest product of civilization. . . . Except in unusual circumstances, the home should not be broken up for reasons of poverty. . . . As to the children who for sufficient reasons must be removed from their own homes or have no homes, if normal in mind and body and not requiring special training, they should be cared for in families whenever practicable" (Hart et al., pp. 9–10).

The second White House Conference, titled "Child Welfare Standards," was called by President Woodrow Wilson in 1919. The standards recommended by the conference were more general but similar to those of a decade earlier. The standard on maternity and infancy was incorporated in the SHEPPARD-TOWNER MATERNITY AND INFANCY ACT of 1921, which authorized grants-in-aid to the states to support child health and prenatal conferences, primarily for poor and rural women.

Sheppard-Towner was administered by the U.S. CHILDREN'S BUREAU, which had been created in 1912 following strong recommendations by the first White House Conference. Sheppard-Towner represented an early step toward a more active role for government in welfare matters and was intensely controversial, as was the Children's Bureau, for the same reason. Congress's refusal to renew Sheppard-Towner in 1929 set the stage for the third White House Conference, "Child Health and Protection," called by President Herbert Hoover in 1930. Controversy over child welfare in the late 1920s turned on not just the role of government but also on which agency within the federal government should administer federal programs. On the one side stood the male-dominated Public Health Service and on the other, the female-dominated Children's Bureau. The issue was debated to a dramatic but inconclusive standstill at the 1930 conference.

Passage of the Social Security Act in 1935 reoriented the White House Conferences for the rest of the century. The 1940 conference was titled "Children in a Democracy," and the next four conferences, 1950, 1960, 1970, and 1980, were equally noncommittal, three of them being called "Children and Youth" and the fourth "Families." The focus on poor children gave way to a general concern with problems and issues that affected all children: how best to rear them for citizenship in a democracy, the role of family, religion, community, and government in children's lives, current research in developmental psychology. Specific problems covered included juvenile DELINQUENCY, school failure, drug use, CHILD ABUSE, daycare centers, racial and religious discrimination, TEEN PREGNANCY, single-parent families—all problems which, while linked with poverty, placed nonpoor as well as poor children at some degree of risk. As conference concerns widened, committees proliferated, recommendations increased in number, and conference proceedings were published in multiple volumes over a period of years. The increase in scope and volume was inversely related to its impact. References in the scholarly literature to any White House Conference after the third are rare.

1990 passed without a presidential call for another White House Conference on Children. When the next conference, on early childhood development and learning, was called in 1997 by President Bill Clinton, it continued the pattern set in 1940 by focusing on issues and problems of possible relevance to all children.

See also: **Child Care: Institutional Forms; Foster Care; Progressive Education; Social Welfare: History.**

BIBLIOGRAPHY

Dreiser, Theodore. 1909. "The Child-Rescue League: The *Delineator* Starts a New and Aggressive Campaign for Doing Away with the Old-Fashioned Orphan Asylum." *Delineator* 73 (January): 102.

Hart, Hastings H., Francis J. Butler, Julian W. Mack, Homer Folks, and James E. West (Committee on Resolutions). 1909. *Proceedings of the Conference on the Care of Dependent Children.* Washington, DC: U.S. Government Printing Office.

McCarthy, Kathleen D. 1982. *Noblesse Oblige: Charity and Cultural Philanthropy in Chicago, 1849–1929.* Chicago: University of Chicago Press.

Muncy, Robyn. 1991. *Creating a Female Dominion in American Reform, 1890–1935.* New York: Oxford University Press.

U.S. Children's Bureau. 1967. *The Story of the White House Conferences on Children and Youth.* Washington, DC: U.S. Department of Health, Education, and Welfare Social and Rehabilitation Service.

MARSHALL B. JONES

Wizard of Oz and L. Frank Baum

Lyman Frank Baum found his stride with just his third major book for children *The Wonderful Wizard of Oz* (1900). His narrative style, direct and unadorned, and the tale of a simple Kansas farm girl whisked by cyclone to a magical country inhabited by small adults, animated mannequins, and talking animals, captured the public's fancy. The whimsical main characters, who longed for qualities they manifestly already possessed, became American classics. William Wallace Denslow's profuse colored illustrations made the book one of the most elaborate of its era. *Oz* proved to be Baum's most enduring work, which he was slow to recognize—perhaps not surprising, for between 1897 and 1903 he produced more than a dozen popular books for children. Baum's books were unusually lavish in design and production. Striking bindings, illustrations by prominent book artists of the era (Denslow, Maxfield Parrish, Frank Ver Beck, Fanny Cory, Frederick Richardson, John R. Neill), novel characters, and magical lands (Oz, Ev, Yew, Ix, Mo) enhanced demand.

Only in 1904 did Baum return to Oz with *The Marvelous Land of Oz.* This sequel offered further adventures of the Scarecrow and the Tin Woodman and introduced a boy protagonist, Tip, who helped provide humor and action. Even so, Baum still did not envision Oz as part of an extended fantasy cycle. His subsequent book-length fantasies, *Queen Zixi of Ix* (1905) and *John Dough and the Cherub* (1906), explored other realms.

Finally in 1907, acknowledging popular demand, Baum began writing an Oz book a year, reintroducing Dorothy and the Wizard as well as other American and fantasy characters to share her adventures inside and outside the borders of Oz. His 1909 Oz book, *The Road to Oz*, incorporated figures from his earlier non-Oz fantasies, suggesting that Oz was part of a larger magical realm and preparing readers for books about new places and characters. In 1910 Baum ended the Oz series with *The Emerald City of Oz*, in which he relocated Dorothy, Aunt Em, and Uncle Henry permanently to the land of Oz.

Baum's next two fantasy novels, *The Sea Fairies* (1911) and *Sky Island* (1912), did not enjoy the success of the Oz books, so Baum resumed the series, expanding his sense of Oz as part of a larger fantasy world. Colorful maps in the 1914 book *Tik-Tok of Oz* showed places not yet described, and some of these appeared in later books, but Baum's death in 1919 cut short his exploration and development of America's first major extended fantasy series. From 1897 to 1919 he had written more than sixty books, fourteen of them about the land of Oz.

The Baum family and the publisher contracted with other authors to continue the Oz series until it totaled forty titles. Authors of the series include Ruth Plumly Thompson, who wrote nineteen books between 1921 and 1939; John R. Neill, who wrote three books between 1940 and 1942; Jack Snow, who wrote two books in 1946 and 1949; Rachel Cosgrove, who wrote one book in 1951; and Eloise Jarvis McGraw and

Lauren Lynn McGraw, who together authored one book in 1963.

Oz on Stage and Screen

In 1902 *The Wizard of Oz*, a musical extravaganza, enjoyed unprecedented success in New York. Baum's efforts from 1905 to 1914 to mount another major Oz hit on stage or screen proved disappointing. However, the Metro-Goldwyn-Mayer movie version in 1939 enjoyed such popularity (especially after 1956 when it was shown regularly on television) that the main characters became worldwide icons. Indeed, several aspects of the book have largely been overshadowed by those of the movie: Dorothy's magical silver shoes became ruby slippers in Technicolor; the book's straightforward fantasy became only a dream; and the final resolution of the book, confirming how Dorothy's companions would employ their special talents, was eliminated when she awoke from her dream.

In 1975 *The Wiz*, a Broadway musical that reinterpreted the story in urban, African-American terms, enjoyed great success. Later Oz-related movies and television shows failed to achieve the popularity of the 1939 classic.

See also: **Children's Literature; Movies; Series Books.**

BIBLIOGRAPHY

Baum, Frank Joslyn, and Russell P. MacFall. 1961. *To Please a Child.* Chicago: Reilly and Lee.

Baum, L. Frank. 1996. *Our Landlady*, ed. Nancy Tystad Koupal. Lincoln: University of Nebraska Press.

Baum, L. Frank. 2000. *The Annotated Wizard of Oz: The Wonderful Wizard of Oz*, ed. Michael Patrick Hearn. New York: Norton.

The Baum Bugle. (1957–). Journal dedicated to L. Frank Baum and *Wizard of Oz* scholarship.

Greene, Douglas G., and Peter E. Hanff. 1988. *Bibliographia Oziana: A Concise Bibliographical Checklist of the Oz Books by L. Frank Baum and His Successors.* Kinderhook, IL: International Wizard of Oz Club.

Riley, Michael O'Neal. 1997. *Oz and Beyond: The Fantasy World of L. Frank Baum.* Lawrence: University Press of Kansas.

Rogers, Katharine M. 2002. *L. Frank Baum: Creator of Oz.* New York: St. Martin's Press.

INTERNET RESOURCE

International Wizard of Oz Club. Available from <www.ozclub.org>.

PETER E. HANFF

Women's Colleges in the United States

In the United States throughout the nineteenth century, a fierce debate raged concerning the wisdom of allowing women access to higher education. Proponents argued that women were the intellectual equals and cultural superiors of men, and that the fulfillment of women's duties as mothers and elementary school teachers necessitated they receive the best and most advanced education available. Those opposed maintained that higher education would "unsex" women, rendering them physically and emotionally unfit for traditional roles.

Despite the controversy, as early as the 1830s and 1840s, women gained access to seminaries, ACADEMIES, and normal schools, some with curricula comparable to those at colleges for men. In the Midwest and West, these institutions tended to be both coeducational and more accessible to middle-class students. Single-sex schools, usually catering to the upper-middle and upper classes, were more common in the South and the Northeast. Not surprisingly, then, the first women's schools to call themselves "colleges" were Georgia Female College (1836), Mary Sharp College in Tennessee (1853), and Elmira College in New York (1855). Indeed, the antebellum South—the nation's most conservative region—was home to the largest number of women's colleges in America, staffed by women teachers from the North. Ironically, the strength of Southern gender norms encouraged wealthier parents to support women's higher education, as their daughters were unlikely to be led astray if they received a college degree. Historians disagree as to the rigor of the education offered at these institutions, however, and the Southern women's colleges did not survive the disruption and devastation caused by the Civil War.

In the post–Civil War era, pressure from tax-paying parents who wanted their daughters to have a means of economic self-support led to the admission of women to the new state universities in the West and the Midwest, created under the terms of the Morrill Land Grant Act (1862). In the South and the East, however, neither well-established prestigious men's colleges nor new state universities accepted women students. In 1870, only one-third of American colleges and universities were coeducational. Thus, between the 1860s and the 1930s, new women's colleges were founded by a variety of individuals and organizations.

The most prominent and prestigious women's colleges were those designated as the "women's Ivy League" or the "Seven Sisters" schools: Vassar, Wellesley, Smith, Bryn Mawr, Barnard, Radcliffe, and Mt. Holyoke. These East Coast colleges were founded between 1865 and 1893 by individual philanthropists or by private organizations of influential women. In the South, individual philanthropy and church support led to the establishment of Goucher (the Woman's College of Baltimore); Sophie Newcomb (the women's college of Tulane University); and Agnes Scott in Decatur, Georgia; among others. Catholic orders of sisters founded nineteen women's colleges between 1900 and 1930, and many more thereafter.

While a few Eastern women's colleges admitted a very small number of African-American students, Southern colleges were exclusively white until the civil rights era. Virtual-

Wellesley College, Class of 1887. Wellesley, as one of the "Seven Sisters," was among the most prominent of women's colleges founded in the late nineteenth century. Early Wellesley students were eager to appear in traditional academic regalia. Courtesy of Wellesley College Archives; photo by Pach Bros.

ly all the historically black colleges were coeducational, however, although white women missionaries established Spelman Seminary for African-American girls and women in 1881; it became a college in 1923. Other black institutions— Bennett, Barber-Scotia, and Houston-Tillotson—were women's colleges at various times in their history.

Other demographic features of women's colleges also remained relatively constant until the 1970s. Some schools, particularly the Catholic institutions, had a more diverse student population, but most restricted admission to those who could pay their own way—usually the Protestant daughters of upper-middle-class families. As college attendance became a less unusual choice for young women, more of the socially elite families sent their daughters as well. The Seven Sisters colleges restricted the admission of Jewish students, and probably Catholics as well, until after World War II. Only in the past few decades have financial aid and affirmative action made it possible for women from a wider range of backgrounds to attend women's colleges.

Women's colleges have always prided themselves on offering an education fully as rigorous as that provided by the best men's colleges. Not content to reproduce the Amherst, Notre Dame, or Morehouse curricula, however, women's colleges pioneered in offering laboratory science and fine arts courses. Some established special opportunities for "returning" older students, and programs designed to encourage women scholars and professionals (e.g., the Bunting Institute at Radcliffe). A few women's colleges offer graduate degrees; Bryn Mawr's program in classics and Smith's in social work are particularly well known. Moreover, women's colleges usually have a large number of women faculty and administrators, who encourage their students to excel and to undertake advanced work. Sometimes criticized for not offering a more vocationally oriented education, such as domestic science courses, the women's colleges have successfully maintained the liberal arts curriculum. Indeed, their historic concern about intellectual separatism led these colleges to be followers of the coeducational universities, rather than leaders, in establishing women's studies programs in the 1970s and 1980s.

In the late nineteenth century, motivated by the need to demonstrate their respectability, women's colleges placed many social restrictions on their students; as a result, ambitious and independent young women often preferred coeducational universities. By the early twentieth century, however, students at women's colleges enjoyed many advantages over their coeducated sisters, including the full attention of the faculty; the opportunity to run their own student governments; control of the publication of the campus newspapers, literary magazines, and yearbooks; and a chance to engage in a wider range of activities, such as debate and competitive athletics. Some women's colleges had sororities; most did not, however, and others eventually abolished them as too socially divisive for small homogeneous campuses. Although administrators often frowned upon official support of the suffrage movement and other controversial causes, many students participated in such movements, albeit sometimes clandestinely. In the 1920s, Calvin Coolidge criticized the Seven Sisters as hotbeds of radicalism. At Southern and Catholic women's colleges, however, strict social regulations remained in place for a much longer period, and students were less likely to become politically engaged. Historians have not yet assessed campus activism at women's colleges between the 1920s and 1970s, but anecdotal evidence indicates that at least some students maintained the tradition of political commitment.

Despite their protestations of social conservatism, women's colleges produced a substantial minority of graduates who adopted nontraditional lifestyles. Many alumnae became career women, participated in politics, remained single, had smaller families, and otherwise modified or defied middle-class gender norms. Recognizing this, the public has periodically attacked the women's colleges for producing spinsters (1890–1920); encouraging lesbian relationships (1920s and 1970–1990); and teaching women to be discontented with domesticity (1930–1960).

Since the advent of the second wave of feminism, women's colleges have seemed anachronistic to many Americans. As the colleges of the men's Ivy League and even the service academies began to admit women, the numbers of women's colleges dropped rapidly—from 233 in 1960 to 90 in 1986. All Catholic men's and women's colleges became coeducational, as did Vassar, Sarah Lawrence, and other prestigious single-sex institutions. In 1960, 10 percent of women college students attended single-sex institutions; by 1986, less than 2 percent did so. And yet recent social science research demonstrates that alumnae of women's colleges, even those from the less prestigious institutions, include a greater percentage of "achievers" than graduates of coeducational schools, especially in nontraditional fields. Scholars argue that superior mentoring and a more supportive envi-

ronment at women's colleges account for this disparity. Thus, while it is unlikely that new women's colleges will be established, it is equally unlikely, and undesirable, that the remaining ones will disappear.

See also: **Coeducation and Same-Sex Schooling; Education, United States; Girls' Schools.**

BIBLIOGRAPHY

Farnham, Christie. 1994. *The Education of the Southern Belle: Higher Education and Student Socialization in the Ante-Bellum South.* New York: New York University Press.

Geiger, Roger L. 2000. "The Superior Instruction of Women, 1836–1890." In *The American College in the Nineteenth Century*, ed. Roger Geiger. Nashville, TN: Vanderbilt University Press.

Gordon, Lynn D. 1989. "Race, Class, and the Bonds of Womanhood at Spelman Seminary, 1881–1923." *History of Higher Education Annual* 9: 7–32.

Horowitz, Helen Lefkowitz. 1984. *Alma Mater: Design and Experience in the Women's Colleges from the Nineteenth Century to the 1930s.* New York: Knopf.

McCandless, Amy Thompson. 1999. *Past in the Present: Women's Higher Education in the Twentieth Century American South.* Tuscaloosa: University of Alabama Press.

Miller-Bernal, Leslie. 2000. *Separate By Degree: Women Students' Experiences in Single Sex and Coeducational Colleges.* New York: Peter Lang.

Nash, Margaret. 2000. "A Salutary Rivalry: The Growth of Higher Education for Women in Oxford, Ohio, 1855–1867." In *The American College in the Nineteenth Century*, ed. Roger Geiger. Nashville, TN: Vanderbilt University Press.

Palmieri, Patricia A. 1988. "Women's Colleges." In *Women in Academe: Progress and Prospects*, ed. Mariam K. Chamberlain. New York: Russell Sage Foundation.

Perkins, Linda M. 1997. "The African American Female Elite: the Early History of African American Women in the Seven Sister Colleges." *Harvard Educational Review* 67, no. 4 (winter): 718–756.

Tidball, M. Elizabeth. 1999. *Taking Women Seriously: Lessons and Legacies for Educating the Majority.* Phoenix, AZ: Oryx Press.

LYNN D. GORDON

Work and Poverty

In the late twentieth century it was estimated that up to 250 million children under fourteen were at work across the world. Such figures aroused deep concern, and numerous international organizations and national governments declared their wish to end child work, or, at the very least, to eliminate the most hazardous and exploitative forms of it. Yet the idea that childhood might be a time without work is relatively recent. For most of history most families have seen nothing unusual in expecting their children to contribute to the family economy as soon as they are able: without that contribution the poverty amid which they lived would be deepened.

Children and Poverty

Children have always made up a disproportionate percentage of those categorized as living in poverty. The reason is

The Old Musician (c. 1861–1862), Édouard Manet. Children who found no financial support at home were sometimes forced to wander the streets, begging and stealing in order to survive. The Art Archive/National Gallery of Art Washington/Album/Joseph Martin.

not hard to find. Children when young cannot be anything other than a cost to a family economy: they need care, shelter, food, and clothing, and cannot begin to make even the smallest contribution until at least age five. And though the eldest child in a family might from that age progressively contribute more and more to a family economy, more children are probably being born. For seventeenth-century England it has been calculated that a family would only begin to get a net gain from having children in the eighteenth year of a marriage; by then there would be a sufficient number of older children who would be contributing positively to the family economy, and the wife's child-bearing years would be over. These elementary facts, well-known through hard experience to the poor, were publicized by B. Seebohm Rowntree in 1901 in a famous study entitled *Poverty: A Study of Town Life*. In it he argued that there was a family life cycle. A married couple might start off in relative prosperity, but once the children started arriving the family would enter a trough of poverty, emerging from it only when a sufficient number of the children were earning. Then, when the children left home and the parents' earning potential was re-

duced, there would be another trough of poverty lasting through old age to death. The good times came when you were a teenager and again when your children were teenagers.

In premodern societies, and in developing societies in the contemporary world, children constitute a much higher proportion of the population than they do in twenty-first-century Western society, but the proportion of them among the poor is even higher. In the sixteenth and seventeenth centuries in England about half of those listed as poor were children, a figure identical to Rowntree's findings at the turn of the nineteenth and twentieth centuries. The extent of child poverty is brought home to us by the responses to it by parents, children themselves, and public authorities. In the Western world and in China parents frequently abandoned children—from the medieval period onward, normally in FOUNDLING hospitals—where their chances of survival were not very great. The illegitimate were much more likely to be abandoned than the legitimate, but especially in hard times, legitimate children were also abandoned in huge numbers.

Overall, in mid-nineteenth-century Europe about one hundred thousand babies were abandoned every year, probably about half of them legitimate, by families who felt that their resources could not stretch to take in another dependent member.

Children themselves, finding no sustenance at home, or perhaps orphaned or half-orphaned, sometimes formed gangs. In southern France in the eighteenth century gangs of children roamed the roads, begging and pillaging. In Prussia one-third of all beggars were said to be children. As to the authorities, they were aware, as JOHN LOCKE put it at the end of the seventeenth century, that a man and his wife could not "by their ordinary labor" support more than two children, and as a result many families were impoverished simply because they were "overburdened with children." What could be done for them? Locke thought that parishes ought to set up workhouses where children from three or four years of age could begin to engage in productive labor, normally spinning. The solution, that is, seemed to be to provide work opportunities for children, or, perhaps more accurately, to put children to work with a greater or lesser degree of compulsion. Schemes proliferated to provide employment for children in Schools of Industry, in lace making, and in straw plaiting, all with the aim of structuring the time of children, preventing idleness, inuring children to a life of labor, and increasing family income.

The perception of authorities in the eighteenth century, on the eve of the Industrial Revolution, was that the problem of child poverty was primarily a problem of lack of employment for them. Where children were in the care of philanthropic organizations or of the state it was axiomatic that they should be put to work; they were imported into Leiden in the Netherlands to work in the cloth industry in the seventeenth century; from Germany it was reported that manufacturers in eighteenth-century Potsdam and Berlin relied on children from the orphanage. That children should work as soon as age permitted was taken for granted. Their earnings were crucial to family survival, and perhaps to national economies.

Such a perception of the desirability of child work was not confined to the authorities: it would have been shared by parents and probably by children. Ideally the family itself would constitute a work unit. Where there was land to be worked, the prevailing situation for the vast majority of families in premodern times and in the developing world today, children could be gradually initiated to work for the family: scaring crows off the crops, collecting firewood, helping around the home (which itself might be a productive unit), looking after younger siblings. In sixteenth-century Castile, for example, both boys and girls helped collect firewood, herd livestock, assist with ploughing, collect or destroy aphids or worms on the vines, and rear silkworms. Work of this kind can seem rooted in nature and not far from idyllic,

but from a parental point of view there was a set amount of labor which needed to be carried out, and the number and gender of children might match those needs less than perfectly. Extra labor might need to be brought in from outside the family, or conversely, family (i.e., child) labor might be exported to other families. Where, as in England, an economy of peasant holdings had been replaced by one where agricultural laborers were hired by farmers, children might well be surplus to family requirements; in parts of England boys left home at the age of nine and were apprenticed out to farmers until the age of twenty-one. In the pre–Industrial Revolution economy of Europe child work within the family might be the desired norm, but it was not always available.

Early Industrial Society

Household industrial production, commonly known as cottage industry, increased rapidly in the seventeenth and eighteenth centuries, and provided an alternative to work in the agricultural economy. There was nothing new about child work in industry. Archaeological evidence from Bonn in Germany, dating back to the early thirteenth century, shows children's fingerprints on pots, indicating children's role in carrying freshly turned pots to drying areas in a business which was exporting to England, Scandinavia, and Poland; there is also evidence from a number of sources of children working in coal mines. What was new in the early modern era was the increase in the number of opportunities for household industrial production where children's usefulness was undeniable. Most of the work was in textiles, with production serving international as well as national and regional markets. In the early eighteenth century in parts of England Daniel Defoe was delighted to find occasional examples of children as young as four apparently earning their keep. Household production of this kind was frequently combined with agricultural work, sometimes on a seasonal basis, sometimes with some family members working on the land while others concentrated on industry. These essentially rural industries provided a much wider range of employment opportunities for children than were available in purely agricultural areas. Indeed, it was an assumption in England as late as the 1830s that where there was local cottage industry children were likely to be employed, whereas in purely agricultural areas child unemployment was to be expected.

In rural industries production might be based on the household, but the labor employed was not always confined to family members. Children might be surplus to the labor requirements of their own family, but could find work in someone else's household. The coming of the Industrial Revolution in the late eighteenth and early nineteenth centuries furthered this process of separating children at work from family and household. Now the new work opportunities were in textile factories, the early ones driven by water-power and so necessarily sited near fast-flowing streams, and perhaps far from any locally available labor. In Britain, the pioneer of this new form of work organization, the child labor came from "pauper apprentices," children who had been left in the care of the Poor Law and were dispatched from London to work in the factories of the Midlands and north of England, where they were often very cruelly treated. By the early nineteenth century steam power began to replace water power, and textile towns grew up in the vicinity of coal supplies. The wages on offer in these factories, higher than those available in agricultural work, attracted families to them, and women and children came to constitute a high proportion of the factory workforces. In Alsace in France in the 1820s one-third or more of the workforce in mills were under sixteen; in Glasgow at much the same time 35.6 percent were under fourteen and 48.3 percent under sixteen. The extent of the use of child labor was dependent much more on the labor strategies of employers than on technology. In mills in northern Massachusetts and in New Hampshire, young women rather than children were preferred, and child labor was rare. Sometimes, but by no means always, family members might work together within a factory. A frequent complaint was that the work opportunities for women and children were at the expense of those offered to adult men who might find themselves, against all tradition, as homemakers.

Child Labor in Industrial Society

The child labor practices of the early Industrial Revolution, both at the time and since, have been widely condemned. Children were taken out of their homes, starting full-time work often before they were ten years of age, and subjected to long hours and unremitting DISCIPLINE; it was hardly surprising that their health was jeopardized. Those who defended the system made three main points: first, children were better able than adults to carry out some of the more delicate work necessary in textile factories or to work their way along narrow seams in coal mines. Second, in a system of national and international competition, cheap child labor was a crucial ingredient for success. Third, factory work had the benefit of preventing children from being idle and protecting them from all the evils that followed from idleness. Advocates of child labor also cast doubt on the statistics about the ill-health of child factory workers and child miners that those who opposed the system so frequently produced. The defenders of child labor were, however, outgunned by those who drew attention to the cruelties inflicted on children and who for the first time in human history began to question whether childhood should be a time for work. Under the influence of a view of childhood proposed by the Romantic poets, in particular William Wordsworth, opponents of child labor in factories and mines argued that childhood should be a time of self-discovery and happiness, in communion with the natural world. Childhood should be extended, and work delayed, for "when labor begins," as an American put it, ". . . the child ceases to be" (Zelizer, p. 55). The work of children from this perspective was, in a word frequently invoked, "slavery."

Although child work in factories and mines attracted an immense amount of attention it was not, even at the height of the Industrial Revolution, the most common form of child employment. In England and Wales in 1851, for boys aged five to nine, agricultural workers were more than two and a half times as numerous as cotton workers, and for those aged ten to fourteen the disproportion was even greater. For girls aged ten to fourteen the twenty-nine thousand cotton workers were far outnumbered by the fifty thousand domestic servants. In other words, well-entrenched forms of gendered child work—agriculture for boys, domestic service for girls—remained the dominant forms of child work even after half a century and more of industrialization. The same is true in the developing world today: in India in 1981 over 80 percent of child workers were engaged in agriculture.

In the second half of the nineteenth century the industrializing countries passed laws to restrict the employment of children in what had been the cutting-edge industries of the Industrial Revolution. Textiles and coal mining were normally the first to become subject to regulation, followed by many others, such as pottery work and brick making. The legislation raised the permissible age of entry, restricted hours, laid down safety regulations, and sometimes insisted on evidence of schooling. It was a response to the outcry about conditions, combined with a realization by some leading manufacturers that productivity might be impeded rather than enhanced by the use of child workers. At the same time governments sought to strengthen and upgrade legislation compelling children to attend school (in some countries such legislation dated back to the eighteenth century). Both labor legislation and, to a lesser extent, schooling legislation was difficult to enforce, but by the early twentieth century in most industrializing countries, children's work was distinctly part-time up to the time they left school somewhere between the ages of twelve and fourteen. And when they did leave school, except in some distinctive local economies, they were much more likely to find work as messengers, shop assistants, or domestic servants than as factory or mine workers. In effect, the labor market had become segregated by marking out certain types of work as belonging to children, and these were now on the margin of the economy, rather than at its center. The typical child worker would be delivering newspapers or milk, or cleaning, not tending a machine.

Family Economies

In the nineteenth and first half of the twentieth centuries a distinctive family economy linked together urban working-class families in Europe and North America. Adult males were ideally, and normally in practice, the main wage earners; their wives, particularly once children started to be born, rarely worked for wages on a regular basis outside the home; children found waged work as soon as they were able, or as soon as the law allowed, and turned over most of their earnings to their mothers for family use. In Belgium, for example, children were contributing 22 percent of family income in

1853, and 31 percent in 1891. In the United States toward the end of the nineteenth century, by the time the adult male in a family was in his fifties, children were contributing about one-third of the family's income; in Europe, it was rather more: 41 percent. The deep-rooted assumption, inherited from an agricultural economy, was that children should contribute to the family economy as soon as possible. Factory laws and laws enforcing schooling raised the starting age over time, but there is much evidence that children themselves felt proud to be able to start making a contribution to family welfare. Their mothers, the only alternative wage earner in the family, were fully engaged in child rearing, housekeeping, and sometimes bringing in further income through casual work or taking in lodgers. No one could be in any doubt that children's earnings improved a family's economic position, and children who might have continued at school often did not take up the opportunity, aware of the family's need for income.

The majority of working-class children in Western society lived in families whose economies were structured in this way. There were, of course, many differences from country to country and within them; they were most visible in the United States where immigrant and ethnic communities had different traditions and different responses to the changing economic situation. Italian immigrant families in New York, for example, made much more use of child labor than did Jewish immigrants, in part because of traditions in the countries they came from, but perhaps mainly because the earning power of Italian adult males was less than that of Jewish ones: extra income was needed, and children were the obvious source of it. The same argument holds true for Philadelphia in the late nineteenth century: the children of Irish and German immigrant families were more likely than those of native whites to be in the workforce, but this was mainly because the fathers in these families earned less than those of native whites. As the income levels of immigrant families rose the dependence on child labor declined. By the early twentieth century a common white American response to the economic situation was becoming apparent: an increasing emphasis on the desirability that the adult male should be the sole wage earner and that children should be in school. In hard times, for example in the depression of the 1930s, there would be a return to the use of child labor, but legal restrictions on its use meshed with values and norms that made child labor undesirable. The situation for black families was rather different. In Philadelphia, for example, black children were less likely to be employed than immigrant Irish or German children, not because their families were better off, but because of ethnic structuring in the labor market which denied access to blacks. Partly for this reason, partly because black families seem to have placed a higher value on the education of their children than immigrant families, black married women were, in a range of U.S. cities, between four and fifteen times more likely to be employed than immigrant wives. Unlike white communities, whether native or immigrant, black families put the emphasis on mothers rather than children as the key supplementary wage earners.

Street Children

Children in families headed by two adults were the lucky ones. For others—in one-parent families (some 20 percent of English children born in the mid-eighteenth century would lose one parent to death by the age of fifteen), or where one or both parents were economic failures, or where the local economy offered few jobs either to adults or to children—other solutions to earning a living had to be sought, and they were likely to involve leaving home. From Savoy since the sixteenth century children had traveled through France and England as chimney sweeps. In the nineteenth century in poor villages in the Apennines in Italy, families apprenticed their children to padrones who put the children to work on the streets of Paris, London, New York, Moscow, and many other cities to perform with animals or with musical instruments; the children, perhaps as many as six thousand of them at the height of the business in the late 1860s, were expected to earn a set sum for the padrone each day. In the cities in which these Italian children performed, there were already many street children, both those who sought a living from the street, selling goods, performing as acrobats, offering services such as cleaning crossings, and those whose sleeping quarters were under some rough shelter. The former were often from migrant families, and were working to support their families. The same thing could be found in the late twentieth century: in Istanbul the forced migration of Kurds from southeast Turkey led to many children of these families working on the streets selling tissue papers.

Philanthropists and governments were keen to rescue street children for what was seen as a better life, and to remove the scourge of mendicancy from the public gaze. Many such children were sent to institutions. In the United States the 77 private ORPHANAGES of 1851 had increased to 613 by 1880 and to over a thousand by 1900; and if there is one generalization one can confidently make about the inmates of "orphanages" it is that the majority of them were not orphans, but children perceived to be in need of care. Institutionalization was not always the preferred way of "saving" these children; ideally they might be transported to some better environment away from what were seen as corrupting cities. In the late nineteenth and early twentieth centuries eighty thousand British children were "emigrated" to Canada, where they were mostly allocated work on farms. In New York CHARLES LORING BRACE's Children's Aid Society in the second half of the nineteenth century sent out sixty thousand children to farms in New York State and to midwestern states. In the existence of all these schemes to rescue children we can see evidence of the failure of the ideal that all children should be raised in well-functioning families and that local economies should provide suitable work opportunities so that children could contribute to the family economy. Families themselves failed, and local economies did not always provide the kind of work opportunities which were thought suitable: children, in consequence, became mobile, some traveling thousands of miles in search of work, and, whether under the control of a padrone or in the care of a philanthropic society, often had minimal control over their own destinations and destinies.

The Mid- to Late Twentieth Century

Around the middle of the twentieth century in Western society the assumption that children's prime responsibility was to contribute to the family economy as soon as they were able began to be questioned. This was probably largely due to rising living standards which made the child's contribution less crucial. For the good of the family as a whole, investment in a child's education beyond a minimum required level began to make sense. At much the same time married women began to play an increasing role in the workforces of the Western world, thereby providing an income stream which had simply not been available or not tapped until then. But it would be wrong to see this as simply the substitution of adult female wages for children's wages. Within the home itself children were expected to do less and less in terms of chores; their status and ranking within the family rose. The goal of many parents came to be an improvement in the life-chances of their children; the "slaves" now seemed to be the parents, in particular mothers, who catered to their children's needs.

There were indications, however, that this child-centered phase in the history of Western white families was coming to an end by the late twentieth century. Within it the dominant thrust was the segregation of children from the adult world, which was defined, among other criteria, as the world of work. From the 1980s, however, there was accumulating evidence that child labor in the developed as well as in the undeveloped world was on the increase, an outcome of the meshing of the needs of rapidly changing family forms and of the international global economy. Children were working, largely on the margins of the economy and in service industries, in a context where the deregulation of controls on labor was paramount. They were also contributing to the functioning of the household, in part because mothers were now much less likely to see their sole or main function as homemaking. Mothers continued, in addition to paid labor, to contribute the most to homemaking, but, as a Norwegian study showed, girls in particular, but also boys, were more likely than adult men to contribute to housework in the course of a day. Children supported mothers in the functioning of the home.

International Perspectives

In the first half of the twentieth century it was widely hoped and assumed that the Western pattern of a diminution, and perhaps elimination, of children's work would spread to the rest of the world. The International Labor Office (ILO), established in the aftermath of World War I, had assigned to it as one of its tasks "the abolition of child labor," and countries signed conventions which laid down minimum ages for participation in a variety of industries. Colonial powers were under pressure to apply these limitations to their colonies, and appropriate laws appeared on their statute books. There was, it is true, a certain amount of bending of what might be thought desirable within the ILO to local conditions—in Indonesia, for example, restrictions on night work were evaded by redefining night to encompass fewer hours. It is also true that the will to enforce these laws was often lacking. But at an international level, as late as 1973 the ILO set down a norm of fifteen as the minimum age for entry to the labor force, with fourteen for developing countries, and with a recommended target age of sixteen.

The experience of the last quarter of the twentieth century made this look quite unobtainable—and perhaps not even desirable that it should be attained. The GLOBALIZATION of the world economy enabled employers to seek out the cheapest labor markets—and no labor is cheaper than that of children—and the impoverishment of many families in so-called developing countries increased the pressure to make use of all potential family labor. Observers in the 1980s were reporting an increase in child work in countries such as Ghana, the Philippines, Sri Lanka, and Peru. Concurrent with these international trends, though more muted, was a questioning of the deeply entrenched Western reflex that there is something morally wrong with child work. The focus of international organizations became the control or elimination of the manifestly exploitative forms of child work, whether in terms of the age of the child, the type of work, the contract involved (the bonded labor of children to pay off adult debts received much attention), or the amount of pay, rather than an attempt to stop all child work, and to enforce a segregation of children from the world of production. Advocates began to listen to what child workers themselves said, rather than assuming that all child work was wrong.

These reassessments were accompanied by an ongoing discussion about the cost of children. In a situation where the world population had doubled within a generation, but where the means to control it were available, it was natural to ask why people had children—or did not have them. As we saw at the outset, children are unquestionably a cost to families in their early years, and it may be many years before they can, in economic terms, become a net benefit. Considered as an "investment good," children are a very long-term form of saving. In many developing countries many of them did not survive long enough to become assets, and this might encourage families to have large numbers of children on the assumption that not all of them would live. Other economic factors could encourage people to have children, in particular the assumption in countries where welfare was negligible or nonexistent that children would look after parents in their old age. There might well be a gender preference, normally for boys rather than girls, since boys would be less of a cost (no dowry on marriage) and more of an economic benefit. But the idea that parents had children for economic reasons, in the sense that children would be an economic asset to them, though often expressed, rarely looked plausible. On the contrary, the assumption in nearly all societies, developed and undeveloped, was that the income stream would be from parents to children rather than vice versa. In the better-off sections of developed countries so much was this so that the selfish act was not to have children at all or to keep their numbers low, since at no time would they contribute to the family economy, and at all ages through to their early or mid-twenties they were likely to be a cost. Although taxation systems could help meet some of those costs, it remained the case that in developed countries children were disproportionately numbered among the poor. The same was true in developing countries, and there family survival dictated an early recourse to the child employment market.

In both undeveloped and developed parts of the world children worked, at least in part, through a desire to have the means to purchase goods for themselves; that appeared to be true for Indonesia as well as for the United States. The existence of a global market producing goods aimed at children and young people was both testimony to that and a reinforcement of it. This fact needs to be seen alongside the profound reassessment of attitudes to child work in the late twentieth century. In these circumstances it became possible to imagine a future in which children who so desired worked for money which would enable them to purchase the goods they wanted or to improve their sense of well-being in other ways. This may be one form the future will take. But anyone who surveyed, on a global scale, the circumstances in which children worked in the late twentieth and early twenty-first centuries was forced to admit the profound and enduring relationship between poverty and child work: It took different forms in different cultural traditions, but family poverty remained by far the biggest inducement toward child work. Most child workers in the developing world saw as an ideal some combination of work and school, rather than either one or the other, and they accepted the necessity of a contribution to the family economy. That was also the case in most of the centuries of recorded history. Only since the Industrial Revolution encouraged reflection on the experience of children at work in the early nineteenth century has it been possible to envisage a world in which children do not work at all. That legacy left people confused about the morality of child work. What it did not do was to break the relationship between child work and poverty.

See also: **Apprenticeship; Child Labor in Developing Countries; Child Labor in the West; Compulsory School Attendance; Economics and Children in Western Societies: From Agriculture to Industry; European Industrialization; Placing Out.**

BIBLIOGRAPHY

Bolin-Hort, Per. 1989. *Work, Family, and the State: Child Labour and the Organization of Production in the British Cotton Industry, 1780–1920.* Lund, Sweden: Lund University Press.

Cohen, Miriam. 1981–1982. "Changing Education Strategies Among Immigrant Generations: New York Italians in Comparative Perspective." *Journal of Social History* 15: 443–466.

Cornia, Giovanni Andrea, Richard Jolly, and Frances Stewart. 1987–1988. *Adjustment with a Human Face.* 2 vols. Oxford, UK: Clarendon Press.

Cunningham, Hugh. 1990. "The Employment and Unemployment of Children in England c. 1680–1851." *Past and Present* 126: 115–150.

Cunningham, Hugh. 1995. *Children and Childhood in Western Society since 1500.* London: Longman.

Cunningham, Hugh. 2000. "The Decline of Child Labour: Labour Markets and Family Economies in Europe and North America since 1830." *Economic History Review* 53: 409–428.

Cunningham, Hugh, and Pier Paolo Viazzo, eds. 1996. *Child Labour in Historical Perspective, 1800–1985: Case Studies from Europe, Japan, and Colombia.* Florence, Italy: UNICEF.

de Coninck-Smith, Ning, Bengt Sandin, and Ellen Schrumpf, eds. 1997. *Industrious Children: Work and Childhood in the Nordic Countries, 1850–1990.* Odense, Denmark: Odense University Press.

Goldin, Claudia. 1981. "Family Strategies and the Family Economy in the Late Nineteenth Century: The Role of Secondary Workers." In *Philadelphia: Work, Space, Family, and Group Experience in the Nineteenth Century,* ed. Thomas Hershberg. New York: Oxford University Press.

Heywood, Colin. 1988. *Childhood in Nineteenth-Century France: Work, Health, and Education among the "Classes Populaires."* Cambridge, UK: Cambridge University Press.

Lansky, Michael. 1997. "Child Labour: How the Challenge Is Being Met." *International Labour Review* 136: 233–257.

Lavalette, Michael, ed. 1999. *A Thing of the Past? Child Labour in Britain in the Nineteenth and Twentieth Centuries.* Liverpool, UK: Liverpool University Press.

Lieten, Kristoffel, and Ben White. 2001. *Child Labour: Policy Options.* Amsterdam, the Netherlands: Aksant.

Nardinelli, Clark. 1990. *Child Labor and the Industrial Revolution.* Bloomington: Indiana University Press.

Parr, Joy. 1980. *Labouring Children: British Immigrant Apprentices to Canada, 1869–1924.* London: Croom Helm.

Pleck, Elizabeth H. 1978. "A Mother's Wages: Income Earning among Married Italian and Black Women, 1896–1911." In *The American Family in Social-Historical Perspective,* ed. Michael Gordon. New York: St. Martin's Press.

Slack, Paul. 1988. *Poverty and Policy in Tudor and Stuart England.* London: Longman.

Smith, Richard M., ed. 1984. *Land, Kinship, and Life-Cycle.* Cambridge, UK: Cambridge University Press.

UNICEF. 1994. *The State of the World's Children, 1994.* Oxford: Oxford University Press.

UNICEF. 1997. *The State of the World's Children, 1997.* Oxford: Oxford University Press.

Weiner, Myron. 1991. *The Child and the State in India: Child Labour and Education Policy in Comparative Perspective.* Princeton: Princeton University Press.

White, Ben. 1994. "Children, Work, and 'Child Labour': Changing Responses to the Employment of Children." *Development and Change* 25: 848–878.

Yilmaz, Bediz. 2001. "Street-Vendor Children in Istanbul: The Visible Facet of Urban Poverty." In *Childhood in South East Europe: Historical Perspectives on Growing Up in the 19th and 20th Century*, ed. Slobodan Naumovic and Miroslav Jovanovic. Belgrade, Serbia and Yugoslavia: Graz.

Zelizer, Viviana A. 1985. *Pricing the Priceless Child: The Changing Social Value of Children*. New York: Basic Books.

Zucchi, John E. 1992. *The Little Slaves of the Harp: Italian Child Street Musicians in Nineteenth-Century Paris, London, and New York*. Montreal: McGill-Queen's University Press.

HUGH CUNNINGHAM

Working Papers

When societies decide to curb or abolish CHILD LABOR, they confront a number of problems. In addition to the lack of available alternatives, especially schooling, and the cultural and economic incentives that make child labor attractive to employers and parents, a number of more practical issues must be addressed. If age limits are to be imposed, or if hours are to be limited for those under a certain age, there must be some method to document a worker's age. Many methods have been attempted and some have been more effective than others. While age documentation provides one vehicle for enforcing child labor restrictions, it cannot, by itself, solve the child labor problem. Documents attesting that the child is of legal age for employment are referred to as working papers.

A requirement for legal working papers presupposes an adequate system of birth records. Before birth records became important, many parents had only a general recollection of the actual age of their children. Some parents kept birth records in family Bibles and other records; parents of modest means might have records in insurance policies; but many parents did not know the precise age of their children. Further, a private system of birth records was vulnerable to abuse. Many parents, often under the coercive influence of their employers, were willing to deliberately misstate the age of their children in order to get them work. Requiring working papers for children could only become fully effective when public birth records had been kept long enough to cover the current cohort of working children.

In America, where, until 1938, "states' rights" precluded a federal role in regulating who should work, each state experimented with age documentation regimes to find a preferred approach. While each state had to find its own way, a more or less orderly evolution took place. Some of the first age limits adopted by northern states required no documentation whatsoever. For example, Pennsylvania had a long-standing minimum age of fourteen for work in mining (sixteen for underground work), but did not require documentation until 1905. Thus, when the Anthracite Coal Strike Commission began holding hearings on the great strike of 1902, the nation was stunned to learn that 10,000 or more children under fourteen were working in the mines and breakers of eastern Pennsylvania. The first laws requiring age documentation typically required only the parent's oath taken by a notary public. Many mines, mills, and factories had their own notaries on staff to handle the paperwork. Some early laws provided for "hardship" exceptions, so that in 1907 there were at least five hundred children under twelve working legally in the cotton mills of South Carolina. The system was fraught with problems and proved an utter failure in eliminating child labor.

Parents had numerous incentives to commit perjury, and many who spoke no English did not even realize they were committing perjury. Employers had little interest in effective enforcement—so long as the children provided papers "that lets us out." Notaries themselves confronted numerous conflicts of interest, for some it was petty corruption in selling work papers, for others they were simply too closely related to the employers who hired children. Eventually laws began to require independent "proof" of age. Various records could suffice including insurance records or statements from ministers, rabbis, and priests, but until reliable systems of public birth records came into use, these methods were not fully effective. For example, in 1916 a priest in eastern Pennsylvania reported he was losing parishioners because he would not issue false birth certificates. In the United States, state and local birth registration laws were adopted on a piecemeal basis, typically lagging enactment of the first child labor laws by several years. Even where the laws were adopted, their application to rural areas and immigrant children remained problematic.

Ultimately, responsibility for issuing and tracking work permits shifted to the schools. When coupled with systems of reliable birth records, this provided a more effective documentation regime. By the end of the twentieth century local schools and health departments bore primary responsibility for administering programs of working papers for youth workers. Beginning in the mid-twentieth century, working papers became a common means for young people to find summer and part-time employment.

See also: **Age and Development; Economics and Children in Western Societies; Law, Children and the; Work and Poverty.**

BIBLIOGRAPHY

Abbott, Grace. 1938. *The Child and the State, Vol. I: Legal Status in the Family, Apprenticeship and Child Labor*. Chicago: University of Chicago Press.

Anthracite Coal Strike Commission. 1903. *Report to the President on the Anthracite Coal Strike of May–October, 1902*. Washington: Government Printing Office.

Hindman, Hugh D. 2002. *Child Labor: An American History*. Armonk, NY: M. E. Sharpe.

Kelley, Florence. 1905. *Some Ethical Gains Through Legislation*. New York: Macmillan.

Kohn, August. 1907. *The Cotton Mills of South Carolina.* Columbia: South Carolina Department of Agriculture, Commerce and Immigration.

HUGH D. HINDMAN

Wright, Henry Clarke (1797–1870)

Henry Clarke Wright devoted his life to overturning structures of domination, including those within the family. His support for the rights of children challenged parental power at a time when American law and society still recognized the complete authority of parents within the domestic sphere. He had no children of his own, having married a wealthy older widow in 1823, but he had a wonderful rapport with the many youths to whom he ministered during his decades of reform work.

Wright was born in Connecticut to a farming family. When he was four, his parents moved the family to western New York, a region swept so often by religious revivals that it was known as the Burnt-Over District. His mother died a couple of years after the move, a loss he always felt. In his teens he trained briefly as a hat maker, before British imports crippled the American trade. Afterwards Wright decided to become a minister. He attended Andover Seminary from 1819 to 1823, then served as minister to the Congregationalist church in West Newbury, Massachusetts. In 1833 Wright left his ministry to become an itinerant reformer, representing a series of causes over the next forty years.

An interest in education first led Wright to become involved in the network of antebellum reform groups known collectively as the Benevolent Empire. Initially he expressed the standard conservative support for schools as an instrument of social order. But his experiences as a reformer soon radicalized him, and he began to question the justice of the order he had hoped to ensure. In a few years, Wright progressed from raising money for Amherst College (1833), to serving as an agent for the American Sunday School Union (1833 to 1834), to ministering to the poor children of Boston (1834 to 1835), and finally to organizing juvenile antislavery societies for the American Anti-Slavery Society (1836 to 1837). He was dismissed from the AASS for endangering the cause with his radical social views after he published a series of "domestic scenes" that challenged parental dominion over children. Later Wright would extend his critique of force within the family to the conjugal relationship, depicting sexual intercourse itself as a form of violence. He advocated that married couples limit their conjugal relations to procreative instances, directing their energies into loving sentiment instead of passion.

In 1837 Wright helped William Lloyd Garrison establish the New England Non-Resistance Society, a radical pacifist organization that opposed any use of force. As an official agent for the society, and later under his own auspices, Wright traveled in the United States and Europe lecturing for his many causes. These included the antislavery movement, Christian anarchism, marriage reform, temperance, and healthy living. However, childhood remained his core concern. In 1842 he published *A Kiss for a Blow*, a collection of anecdotes intended to teach children not to quarrel. He instructed children to suppress their anger, and to answer aggression with love. In Wright's later books including *Marriage and Parentage* (1854), *The Unwanted Child* (1858), and *The Empire of the Mother* (1863), he revised his views to stress the importance of the uterine environment in shaping children's personalities. If fetuses were subjected to passions, resentments, or other negative influences in the womb, then no amount of behavioral training might later be able to reform them.

See also: **Anger and Aggression; Child Development, History of the Concept of; Child-Rearing Advice Literature; Children's Rights; Discipline.**

BIBLIOGRAPHY

Perry, Lewis. 1980. *Childhood, Marriage, and Reform: Henry Clarke Wright 1797–1870.* Chicago: University of Chicago Press.

Walker, Peter. 1978. *Moral Choices: Memory, Desire, and Imagination in Nineteenth-Century American Abolitionism.* Baton Rouge: Louisiana State University Press.

RACHEL HOPE CLEVES

Y

YMCA. *See* YWCA and YMCA.

Youth Activism

The desire of some university students to emphasize recreational pursuits over academics has been a constant over the centuries. Another historical constant has been the tension between students and those they interact with off the campus. Moreover, it has usually required extraordinary events outside the university to move youths to act in a political manner. For example, with the isolated exception of antislavery organizing before the Civil War (1861–1865), it took until the twentieth century for political activism to become a rite of passage for a small portion of American students.

Premodern Europe

In the twelfth and thirteenth centuries universities such as Bologna, Oxford, and Paris took the lead in reviving higher education in Europe. At Bologna foreign students enjoyed no civil rights and often found themselves at the mercy of price-gouging landlords and merchants. In spite of their apparent powerlessness, however, Bologna students could easily migrate to other universities.

The lack of residential campus accommodations and classroom buildings gave students enormous mobility, as well as economic leverage over their schools. Bologna students, for instance, could withhold payment if faculty failed to show up for lectures. Once medieval universities began to construct housing and lecture halls, however, students became more rooted and fell under the authority of campus administrators.

Student discipline was a major issue at medieval universities. Bologna's rectors prohibited students from patronizing gambling establishments and conducting business with moneylenders. Oxford banned students from keeping bears and falcons in their campus quarters and prohibited them from consorting with prostitutes. In addition, Oxford punished students for assaulting faculty and entering townspeople's homes to commit violent acts. Since students representing a variety of nationalities attended Oxford in the 1300s, the university also enacted speech codes to prohibit anyone from making disparaging ethnic remarks.

Sanctions against student offenders could range from expulsion to being required to purchase rounds of wine for the aggrieved parties. When student offenders came from the aristocracy, offers of financial restitution from their fathers served as substitutes for expulsion and flogging.

Relations between students who were engaged in scholarly pursuits and townspeople who toiled for little reward could turn sour in medieval Europe. On Saint Scholastica's Day, February 10, 1354, Oxford students instigated a tavern brawl. This brawl turned into a riot as townspeople armed with bows and arrows battled sword-wielding students and faculty. As the second day of the riot commenced, townspeople invaded the Oxford campus, killing scores of students and faculty.

Although the lethal combat ensuing from the Saint Scholastica Day riot was disproportionate to the immediate provocation, the seeds of discord had deep roots. Isolated incidents of assaults between students and locals had occurred for years. Indeed, between the years 1297 and 1322 nearly half the murders in the community had been committed by Oxford students.

Noting that in 1200 King Philip Augustus had given the University of Paris jurisdiction over its students and faculty, the English crown—following the Saint Scholastica Day riot—went a step further. Oxford received legal jurisdiction over the townspeople. The universities of Paris and Oxford established a precedent whereby campuses were regarded by governing authorities as intellectual sanctuaries whose territory was nearly inviolate.

Students throw stones at the police, May 1968. Protests by students at the University of Paris in May 1968 coincided with strikes being held by French workers, leading to massive unrest that quickly spread to other French cities. © Hulton-Deutsch Collection/CORBIS.

Colonial and Early America

In light of Harvard's founding mission to train Congregational ministers, it is not surprising that 130 years passed before the school experienced a student riot. Harvard's 1766 riot, however, was decidedly apolitical. At a time when large numbers of Bostonians were criticizing Great Britain's colonial policies, Harvard students protested the quality of the campus food service.

In contrast, by the eve of the American Revolution (1775–1783), students at the College of Rhode Island (later Brown), the College of New Jersey (later Princeton), Dartmouth, Harvard, William and Mary, and Yale had become caught up in colonial politics. In 1772 Princeton students hung in effigy politicians whom they viewed as allies of the Crown. For the most part, however, as historian Steven Novak concluded, students played little role in the events leading up to the Revolution.

Following the Revolution, American colleges faced economic hard times, which were accompanied by an expansion of the number of institutions of higher education. Between 1782 and 1802 nineteen new colleges came into existence, and the resulting competition for a limited pool of students forced a lowering of academic standards. In order to remain viable, and confronted by threats from students who insisted they would take their tuition money elsewhere, Dickinson College (in Pennsylvania), the University of Pennsylvania (Penn), and Princeton awarded a bachelor's degree after two years of attendance instead of four. Dickinson students went so far in 1798 as to go on strike until a bachelor's degree was granted after just one year of classroom instruction. Dickinson administrators gave in to student demands.

Issues of student discipline and violence in early America seemed reminiscent of medieval Europe. In 1799, students at the University of North Carolina (Chapel Hill), angered over the expulsion of two disruptive students, horsewhipped the president and stoned two professors. Three years later, William and Mary students, upset over college regulations forbidding duels to the death, instigated a riot in which they

College students in the United States strongly supported Eugene McCarthy's bid for the Democratic presidential nomination in 1968, leading some to call it McCarthy's "Children's Crusade." © Bettmann/CORBIS.

broke windows on campus, tore up Bibles, and vandalized the homes of professors.

At Princeton in 1807, students occupied a university building in protest over the expulsion of three students. At that point, Princeton and Harvard administrators created a blacklist among the nation's colleges to prevent habitual troublemakers from enrolling elsewhere. While North Carolina, Dartmouth, and other colleges embraced the blacklist, Penn undermined its effectiveness by admitting that it could not afford to turn away students, regardless of their disciplinary records.

Along with mounting disciplinary problems and declining academic standards, universities were finding somewhat larger numbers of politically active students. At William and Mary in 1798, students observed Independence Day by burning Federalist President John Adams in effigy. They believed Adams was trying to provoke war with revolutionary France. Most college students in the North who took an interest in politics staged protest rallies against Thomas Jefferson and his Republican followers. Williams College student (and future poet) William Cullen Bryant penned a Federalist screed in 1808 that depicted President Jefferson as an incompetent leader as well as a sexual predator.

The Era of the Civil War

Although in the decades preceding the Civil War the four-year bachelor's degree made a comeback, discipline remained problematic. In 1842 Harvard students and working-class Bostonians stoked longstanding "town-gown" tensions into a full-blown riot. The proximate cause of the 1842 riot was apolitical. Harvard students resented locals who mocked their English-inspired apparel choices. Seeing lower-class townspeople wearing cheap imitations of the coveted Oxford cap, Harvard students assaulted the offenders. Enraged, a mob of three hundred attempted to invade the Harvard campus, where they were met by fifty students armed with pistols, clubs, and knives. Faculty and police intervened but neither could quell the random beatings and property destruction that ensued off-campus for the next nine days.

Even as Harvard students and townies traded insults during the 1830s and 1840s, the antislavery movement sank its roots on a few northern campuses. At Lane Theological Seminary in Cincinnati, Ohio, antislavery students and faculty in 1834 confronted trustees who did not want to antagonize community residents sympathetic to the South. Ordered to disband their abolitionist group, a number of Lane students and faculty migrated to Oberlin College. Established in 1834 and located in the northern region of Ohio that had been settled by New Englanders, Oberlin College became a hotbed of antislavery activism.

In 1835 Oberlin College announced its intention to admit women and African Americans, creating the only gender and racially integrated campus in the United States. (Five percent of Oberlin's student body in the years before the Civil War was black.) Students and faculty established the Oberlin Anti-Slavery Society and became members of the abolitionist Liberty Party and, ultimately, of the Republican Party. The spirit of Oberlin's antislavery zeal spread to the University of Michigan, as well as to Dartmouth and Williams.

With the passage of the 1850 Fugitive Slave Act, requiring citizens not to interfere with the capture of runaway slaves, Oberlin became a literal battlefield. In the summer of 1858, on three separate occasions southern slave hunters were warned away by Oberlin students, faculty, and community residents. In the fall of 1858, after slave hunters captured a fugitive slave near Oberlin, abolitionists stormed the building where he was being held and rescued him. The federal government subsequently indicted thirty-seven members of the Oberlin community under the Fugitive Slave Act. Their trials captured national news media attention—the first time student and faculty political activists at an American college had ever done anything to merit such coverage.

While Americans debated the morality of slavery, western European reformers—including some students and professors—contested the political and economic future of their homelands. In 1848 the German manufacturing and university town of Cologne became the epicenter of social discontent. Some professors-turned-radical-journalists—notably Karl Marx—looked for a socialist workers' revolution. Skilled craftsmen, fearful that industrialization was eroding their economic standing, looked backward toward an era without machinery. Still others called for a unified German nation built around free trade or protectionism, capitalism or socialism, and democracy or a constitutional monarchy. Ultimately the kingdom of Prussia ended the debate with grapeshot. (By 1871 a unified Germany became an army with a nation built around it.)

Early-Twentieth-Century America

Between 1869 and 1900 the number of students enrolled in American universities increased from 52,000 to 237,000. That figure rose to 1.1 million by 1929. In 1900, 4 percent of the college-age cohort (18 to 22) was enrolled as students, compared to 12.5 percent thirty years later. The universities of Chicago, Johns Hopkins, and Stanford had come into existence even as land-grant colleges such as Ohio State—which were originally geared more toward instruction in agricultural and engineering than toward instruction in the liberal arts—expanded their student bodies.

At the same time, more women entered higher education. In 1870 women had represented one fifth of those enrolled in college. By 1900, one-third of college students were female. In 1900 women earned 60 percent of the nation's HIGH SCHOOL diplomas but accounted for just 19 percent of students granted college degrees. Overall, the greater likelihood that female students would drop out—whether to find employment or to get married—helped depress the pool of college graduates.

Setting aside the somewhat greater proportion of women enrolled in higher education by 1900, the profile of the typical American college student had changed little since the Revolution. Most students came from middle- and upper-middle-class white Anglo-Saxon Protestant families. What had changed, however, was the desire among larger numbers of students to grapple with social issues. Where mere handfuls of students had protested against slavery in the 1850s, in 1911 over ten thousand volunteered to work in settlement houses in an effort to improve education and health care among the urban poor. Such student volunteers included the future socialist activist Norman Thomas.

In 1905, according to historian Philip Altbach (1974), the Intercollegiate Socialist Society (ISS) became the first nationally organized vehicle for student activism. With the encouragement of novelists Upton Sinclair and Jack London, the ISS established chapters at Chicago, Columbia, Michigan, the University of California-Berkeley, Wisconsin, and Yale. In 1904 at Berkeley, a year before the founding of its ISS chapter, some students had violently protested the presence of the Reserve Officers' Training Corps program (ROTC) on campus. Altbach identifies this incident as Berkeley's first student riot.

By 1912 Harvard claimed one of the largest campus ISS chapters, with fifty members. In 1917, on the eve of America's entry into World War I, the ISS nationally had nine hundred undergraduate members. The ISS, like its close relative the Young Peoples' Socialist League (YPSL), which had been created in 1907 and had the backing of the Socialist Party, opposed U.S. involvement in World War I. Both the ISS and YPSL, which had few college-student members, experienced schisms over the 1917 Russian Revolution. ISS leaders were suspicious of communist revolutionaries and sought to salvage the fortunes of socialism. Toward those ends they created the League for Industrial Democracy (LID). Disaffected radicals in 1922 created the Young Communist League (YCL).

Both the YCL and LID, along with the crippled YPSL, competed for student followers at Chicago, the City College of New York, Hunter (in New York), Temple (in Philadelphia), and Wisconsin. Student activists in the 1920s managed to organize the disruption of ROTC drills at forty universities. The objective of such protests was to abolish compulsory ROTC for male students. How much of this antiwar activism was motivated by the desire to create a peaceful new world order and how much was the expression of deeply rooted American isolationism—as well as a desire among young men to avoid physical exercise—is, as Altbach notes, unclear.

The decade of the 1920s was not an era of student activism. For every Columbia student such as Whittaker Chambers who joined the Communist Party—and later achieved fame before the House Committee on Un-American Activities—tens of thousands of students remained apolitical. However, as historian Paula Fass observed, male and female students in the 1920s were more likely to embrace new hair and clothing styles, and openly consume alcohol and smoke cigarettes, than had previous generations.

Although female students retained a strong dose of traditionalism, as evidenced by a 1923 poll of Vassar women which revealed that 90 percent preferred marriage over a professional career, they were far more likely to endorse BIRTH CONTROL than the general population. It was in reaction to a perceived loosening of morals among students in the 1920s that the dean of women at Ohio State lamented that youths selfishly valued their individual rights over their obligations to society.

If college administrators could not change how students balanced individual freedom and societal duty, they could attempt to regulate moral behavior on campus through the strict enforcement of *in loco parentis*. University leaders, regarding themselves as acting in the absence of parents, segregated the sexes in campus dormitories after nightfall and banned alcohol. While *in loco parentis* worked well at small, somewhat isolated residential colleges, administrators discovered that rapidly expanding urban campuses and large commuter institutions such as City College were more challenging.

The Era of the Great Depression

The GREAT DEPRESSION (1929–1941) proved to be the best of times and the worst of times for American education and college students. As a result of a high national unemployment rate (e.g., 25 percent in 1932), many youths were forced out of the job market and back into the classroom. By 1936 the greatest proportion of TEENAGERS in American history, 65 percent, were attending HIGH SCHOOL. The proportion of Americans with college degrees went from 3.9 percent in 1930 to 4.6 percent in 1940 while enrollment increased from 1.2 million to 1.5 million. At the same time the share of bachelor's degrees awarded to women topped 40 percent.

On the other hand, the unemployment rate among college graduates in the early years of the Depression was at least two times higher than the national average; providing incentive to remain sheltered on the campus if possible. Thanks to creation of the National Youth Administration (NYA) in 1935, the federal government for the first time subsidized part-time jobs for 600,000 students who might have otherwise left college without their degrees. Another 1.5 million high school students and 2.6 million unemployed youths who were no longer in the education system also received NYA assistance.

Although the 1930s became known as the Red Decade on the college campus and in society at large, radicalism was not the dominant political strain at most universities. A 1932 survey of 56,000 university students revealed that less than a third had voted for the victorious Democratic presidential candidate, Franklin Roosevelt. (Eighteen percent did, however, vote for the Socialist Party nominee, Norman Thomas.) Upon the occasion of Harvard's three hundredth anniversary in 1936, students turned their backs on Roosevelt when he began to speak.

In 1932 the LID opted to step up its campus organizing, establishing a youth affiliate which it called the Student League for Industrial Democracy (SLID). Within a year SLID claimed fifty campus chapters, moving beyond the activist footholds of City College, Harvard, and Swarthmore to include Wayne State University in Detroit. Both Victor and Walter Reuther—the future organizers of the United Automobile Workers union—belonged to the Wayne State chapter. At Swarthmore, SLID activist Molly Yard helped organize a series of protests that culminated in the banning of sororities that practiced racial and religious discrimination. Decades later, Yard served as president of the National Organization for Women.

Hoping to raise its campus profile, the Communist Party USA (CPUSA) created the National Student League (NSL) in 1931. In 1935, as the Soviet Union became more concerned with the military threat posed by Nazi Germany, Communists were ordered to form a Popular Front with socialists and "progressive" Democrats. Toward that end, the NSL, the NCL, and SLID forged the American Student Union (ASU), whose leaders included Molly Yard and Joseph Lash—later an admiring biographer of First Lady Eleanor Roosevelt. The CPUSA also kept an active interest in youth organizing off campus through the American Youth Congress (AYC). YPSL, while willing to cooperate with the ASU, focused the bulk of its efforts on organizing young workers rather than college students.

While comprehensive data on the demographics of the 1930s student movement is not available, Altbach and other historians (e.g., Brax and Cohen) have been able to reconstruct a general profile of collegiate activists. Most student activists came from middle- and upper-middle-class households. The exceptions to this were second-generation Jewish-Americans, who tended to cluster at City College, which was free and which did not have discriminatory religious admissions quotas in place, as the Ivy League schools and some major state universities did.

Most student activists of the 1930s pursued study in the social sciences and the humanities, not in business, the sciences, and technical fields. It may be that students who sought employment in the public sector were more liberally inclined than those hoping to land jobs in the private sector. Thus a 1934 poll of 700 students at Kansas State teachers College (in Manhattan) showed that 65 percent regarded themselves as antibusiness New Dealers. Though located in the heartland of American conservatism, students intending to become public school teachers perhaps had a vested interest in the expansion of government, as well as a suspicion of Republican politicians who often appeared to seek budget cuts in education first.

Public sentiment, either in spite or because of increasing Nazi and Japanese military aggression, remained markedly isolationist. A 1937 Gallup Public Opinion Poll reported that 70 percent of Americans thought that becoming involved in World War I had been a mistake. Campus attitudes were, if anything, even more intensely hostile toward war as an instrument of U.S. foreign policy. Cornell activists in 1933 distributed anti-ROTC pins that bore the inscription, "Duck the Goose Step," equating student cadets with Nazis.

After the Oxford University Student Union in 1933 adopted a pledge not to defend Britain in the event of war, both SLID and the NSL encouraged students to adopt an equivalent American oath. In 1934 SLID and the NSL organized a national peace strike in support of the Oxford Pledge. Campus activists claimed that twenty-five thousand students—of whom fifteen thousand resided in New York City—had participated in the strike.

In 1935 the ASU and the AYC, along with the pacifist National Council of Methodist Youth, mounted a second, and purportedly larger, peace strike. Organizers claimed that anywhere from 150,000 to 500,000 students supported the Oxford Pledge. Berkeley, Chicago, City College, Columbia, Smith, Stanford, and the University of Virginia witnessed student rallies of varying size and militancy. At Penn, Vassar, and the universities of Idaho, North Dakota, and Oklahoma, sympathetic administrators worked with the ASU to sponsor antiwar events.

By 1936 the ASU, responding to the competing agendas of its socialist, communist, and religious pacifist constituencies, ended up reaffirming the Oxford Pledge and simultaneously championing U.S. military intervention in Europe if Germany attacked the Soviet Union. That meant the ASU would not have supported war in the event that Germany declared war on the United States. This position was untenable and by 1938 the ASU repudiated the Oxford Pledge and called upon students to defend the Soviet Union and the western democracies from fascism. The pacifist and SLID factions were irate. Then after the 1939 Stalin-Hitler Pact, which paved the way for the invasion of Poland and the outbreak of World War II in Europe, New Deal liberals and communists clashed within the ASU. As communists defended the Stalin-Hitler Pact and called upon Americans to stay out of the war, the ASU fell apart.

After Japan bombed the American Pacific Fleet at Pearl Harbor on December 7, 1941, only 49,000 draftees out of 10 million men registered for the draft claimed conscientious objector status. American students, regardless of class, ethnic, racial, and regional origins, marched off to war. With the exception of a clash between Hispanic teenagers and sailors in Los Angeles—the ZOOT SUIT RIOT of 1943—American youths focused on the task at hand.

The 1960s

As the United States entered the post–World War II era, its universities grew in number, ultimately topping out at 3,535. The number of students enrolled in college reached 10 million by 1970, with the proportion of women increasing until they became a majority in 1979. In spite of the rapid growth of higher education in the 1960s, however, the class profile of students remained little changed from the 1930s. Just 17 percent of all college students in the 1960s came from working- and lower-middle-class backgrounds. Given such demographics, and the generous provision of student deferments from Selective Service, 80 percent of the men who went to fight in the Vietnam War (1965–1973) were working class. Antiwar protest on the campus in the 1960s inevitably provoked resentment in many blue-collar communities.

Four key issues confronted college students after the relative calm of the 1940s and 1950s, helping to spark the largest campus protests in American history. First there was the insistence of university administrators on maintaining *in loco parentis* and, in deference to conservative state legislatures, upholding bans on political activities on the campus. (This ban sparked the 1964 Berkeley Free Speech Movement, which historians have credited for inspiring student activism at other campuses.)

Second, the civil rights movement in the 1950s South drew northern students into the struggle for racial justice by the early 1960s. White activists played a supporting role in the civil rights movement. In 1964 students at Berkeley, for example, staged sit-ins at local business branches whose main offices did not challenge segregation in the South; they also went to Mississippi to register blacks to vote.

Third and fourth, the specter of military service in Vietnam after graduation—or after flunking out—fed the ranks of campus peace protestors, as well as contributed to youthful alienation from a Democratic Party committed to the policy of communist containment. For youths who were not prepared to support a radical critique of U.S. foreign policy, Minnesota senator Eugene McCarthy's 1968 campaign to capture the Democratic presidential nomination was a veritable children's crusade.

The year 1962 witnessed the birth of a campus-based New Left and New Right. SLID officially became the Students for a Democratic Society (SDS) at its Port Huron, Michigan, convention. SDS carried on much of the ASU's opposition to an interventionist U.S. foreign policy as well as its hostility to corporations and ROTC. This was perhaps not surprising given that at least a third of the approximately 100,000 students who joined SDS or participated in other leftist organizations in the 1960s were "red diaper babies," the children of 1930s socialist and communist activists.

SDS, which grew out of elite institutions such as Chicago, Harvard, Michigan, Oberlin, and Swarthmore, was an organization mainly of middle and upper-middle-class youths. Their parents were most frequently lawyers, doctors, and academics. In terms of religion, 60 percent of SDSers hailed from secular Jewish households, 35 percent from white Protestant families, and 5 percent from Catholic homes. Although the proportion of Jewish students in SDS varied according to the academic quality of the institutions they attended—a majority at Chicago, a minority at Kent State University in Ohio—residential origins held constant. Many leftist student activists who attended universities such as Michigan and Wisconsin came from out of state. A sizeable proportion of student activists in general hailed from metropolitan areas. Nearly all were liberal arts and social science majors.

As universities abandoned *in loco parentis* and the Student Nonviolent Coordinating Committee, which had been established in 1960 by black and white southern students, embraced racial separatism, activists and growing numbers of students turned their attention to the escalating Vietnam War. Antiwar protest, even at its height in the late 1960s, seldom mobilized more than a third of any particular student body—and those high proportions were true only at the Berkeleys, Columbias, and Harvards. The greatest student uprising only took place in response to the slaying of four Kent State students by the Ohio National Guard on May 4, 1970, when 4 million students across the country went on strike.

Once it became clear that the April 1970 U.S. incursion into Cambodia—which had triggered antiwar protests at Kent State and had led to the Ohio National Guard occupying the campus—was not going to lead to escalation of the Indochina war, student protest evaporated. President Richard Nixon in 1969 had already instituted the draft lottery, which, by eliminating college deferments and assigning young males a draft number, significantly reduced student anxiety. With reduced troop levels in Vietnam, most college students knew that they were not going to be drafted if they had a high enough lottery number. Student support for antiwar protest melted away, leaving such organizations as SDS, which in 1969 had split into a Maoist faction (the Progressive Labor Party) and a terrorist sect (the Weather Underground), adrift.

It is often overlooked that the 1960s witnessed the first large conservative student movement on American college campuses. Meeting in 1962 at the Sharon, Connecticut, estate of *National Review* editor William F. Buckley Jr., the Young Americans for Freedom (YAF) was born. YAF's membership included anticommunists who wanted a more muscular response to the Soviet Union and China than the one provided by President John F. Kennedy, as well as religious conservatives and free-market libertarians.

Although YAF grew to over 60,000 members, like SDS it tore itself apart in 1969 as libertarians demanded an end to the draft, condemned the Vietnam War, and argued for the legalization of narcotics and abortion. Libertarians, who often attended elite universities and hailed from professional families, clashed with religious conservatives, many of whom were lower-middle-class Catholic students at less prestigious state universities.

In the long haul, the one advantage YAF had over SDS was its greater commitment to entering the institutional political process—ideological schisms and all. This meant, as sociologist Rebecca Klatch and historian Gregory Schneider have argued, that by the 1980s YAF's alumni played a growing role in the national Republican Party—whether serving in local, state, or federal elective office or working as advisors in the administration of President Ronald Reagan. In contrast, many SDSers remained on the college campus, moving from graduate liberal arts programs into (if they were lucky) tenure-track faculty positions.

The disruptions being played out on some of America's campuses in the 1960s had their counterparts in the United Kingdom, West Germany, and France. Western European students—whose overall numbers were less than their American counterparts given the smaller and more academically selective university systems in which they were enrolled—also protested the Vietnam war and the administrative regulation of their sexual conduct. Most famously in May 1968, at the newly constructed Nanterre campus of the University of Paris—which was located in an impoverished, segregated Arab neighborhood—thousands of students took to the streets.

Following the lead of Nanterre sociology major Daniel Cohn-Bendit—himself an admirer of the German Socialist Students' League (known by its German initials, SDS)—students threw cobblestones at police as they protested the American war in Vietnam and university restrictions on their sexual behavior. This coincided, but was not coordinated, with a strike by workers protesting the managerial reorganization of their economically uncompetitive industries. In this turbulent milieu, revolution appeared inevitable. French leader Charles DeGaulle, however, persuaded workers and students to return to their jobs and desks with the promise of reform.

Since the 1960s

The collapse of large-scale student protest after 1970 coincided with declining public confidence in higher education. In 1966, 61 percent of the public expressed approval of higher education, as compared to 25 percent by 1994. Beyond a public backlash against higher education, Philip Altbach has argued that one of the most important legacies the protest movements of the 1960s gave to the American university was the "politicization of the campus" (1997, p. 32).

Most campus activism after the Vietnam era centered around U.S. foreign policy and identity politics, as organizations based upon gender, sexual preference, and race competed for influence over the curriculum. Outward appearances to the contrary, however, the people who drove the debates over such issues as affirmative action and military disarmament were not students but faculty members who had experienced the 1960s as graduate students and junior instructors.

By the 1980s newly created campus organizations in opposition to America's foreign policy often centered upon a single nation—for instance, the Committee In Solidarity with the People of El Salvador and the Students for a Free South Africa. There were, however, efforts to create a multi-issue and transnational clearinghouse for the campus left through the Progressive Student Network.

Campus activism in the 1980s was nonviolent and mainly low-key, involving no more than several thousand students on a consistent basis. Youths who were opposed to U.S. support for the white apartheid (segregationist) regime in South Africa gained some national media attention in 1987 by erecting shanties on their campuses. (The shanties were to symbolize the conditions black South Africans endured as a result of apartheid.) College Republican chapters sometimes responded by constructing Berlin Walls around the shanties and posting "communist" border guards.

In 1997 the United Students Against Sweatshops (USAS) came into existence. Liza Featherstone, a journalist and supporter of the USAS, reported in 2002 that a number of the student activists at Berkeley, Columbia, Duke, and Wisconsin had parents who belonged to SDS and grandparents who had joined the ASU and NCL in the 1930s.

While ostensibly opposed to the labor conditions of people working in U.S.- and multinational-owned garment factories overseas, the USAS joined other groups to disrupt meetings of the World Trade Organization. Protest moved off the campus and became more violently confrontational. After the September 11, 2001, attacks on the United States, which killed 3,000 people, campus activists linked their opposition to GLOBALIZATION and capitalism to President George W. Bush's Afghanistan phase of the War on Terrorism.

While antiwar organizations rallied tens of thousands of people in Washington, D.C., few campuses outside Berkeley and Michigan experienced demonstrations involving more than two hundred students. Although protests in spring 2003 against the war in Iraq attracted larger numbers of participants, demonstrators were largely faculty and community residents who had marched against the war in Vietnam thirty years earlier. Few American students oppose the war on terror, unlike their western European counterparts. Explanations as to why this is so include: Americans were attacked on their own soil; the absence of a draft to move apathetic students to antiwar action; and finally, Jewish students and faculty, who were disproportionately represented within the ranks of the Vietnam protestors, were divided over what many perceived to be the anti-Semitic and anti-Israeli stances of antiwar organizations. Historical lessons from earlier student movements are of some analytical value for understanding political dynamics on the campus of the early twenty-first century, but the inescapable reality is that American youths are venturing into an uncertain future.

See also: **Campus Revolts in the 1960s; Communist Youth; Fascist Youth; Hitler Youth; School Shootings and School Violence; Youth Culture.**

BIBLIOGRAPHY

Altbach, Philip G. 1974. *Student Politics in America: A Historical Analysis.* New York: McGraw-Hill.

Altbach, Philip G. 1997. *The Academic Profession: The Professoriate in Crisis.* New York: Garland.

Brandt, Nat. 1990. *The Town That Started the Civil War.* Syracuse, NY: Syracuse University Press.

Brax, Ralph S. 1981. *The First Student Movement: Student Activism in the United States During the 1930s.* Port Washington, NY: Kennikat Press.

Cohen, Robert. 1993. *When the Old Left Was Young: Student Radicals and America's First Mass Student Movement.* New York: Oxford University Press.

DeConde, Alexander, ed. 1971. *Student Activism: Town and Gown in Historical Perspective.* New York: Scribner.

Fass, Paula S. 1977. *The Damned and the Beautiful: American Youth in the 1920s.* New York: Oxford University Press.

Featherstone, Liza. 2002. *Students Against Sweatshops.* New York: Verso.

Heineman, Kenneth J. 1993. *Campus Wars: The Peace Movement at American State Universities in the Vietnam Era.* New York: New York University Press.

Heineman, Kenneth J. 2001. *Put Your Bodies upon the Wheels: Student Revolt in the 1960s.* Chicago: Ivan R. Dee.

Klatch, Rebecca E. 1999. *A Generation Divided: The New Left, the New Right, and the 1960s.* Berkeley: University of California Press.

Leff, Gordon. 1968. *Paris and Oxford Universities in the Thirteenth and Fourteenth Centuries: An Institutional and Intellectual History.* New York: Wiley.

Marsden, George M. 1994. *The Soul of the American University: From Protestant Establishment to Established Nonbelief.* New York: Oxford University Press.

Novak, Steven J. 1977. *The Rights of Youth: American Colleges and Student Revolt, 1798–1815.* Cambridge, MA: Harvard University Press.

Palladino, Grace. 1996. *Teenagers: An American History.* New York: Basic Books.

Rait, Robert S. 1912. *Life in the Medieval University.* Cambridge, UK: Cambridge University Press.

Schneider, Gregory L. 1998. *Cadres for Conservatism: Young Americans for Freedom and the Rise of the Contemporary Right.* New York: New York University Press.

Sperber, Jonathan. 1991. *Rhineland Radicals: The Democratic Movement and the Revolution of 1848–1849.* Princeton: Princeton University Press.

Touraine, Alain. 1971. *The May Movement: Revolt and Reform.* New York: Random House.

INTERNET RESOURCES

Jensen, Richard. 2003. "American Political History On-Line." Available from <http://tigger.uic.edu/~rjensen/pol-gl.htm>.

U.S. Department of Education, National Center for Education Statistics. 2001. "Digest of Education Statistics." Available from <http://nces.ed.gov/pubs200s/digest2001/>.

KENNETH J. HEINEMAN

Youth Agencies of the New Deal

The GREAT DEPRESSION threatened the futures of tens of millions of Americans, but perhaps none so enduringly as the young. In keeping with the cultural pluralism of the times and the response of the federal government to World War I, Franklin D. Roosevelt's administration attacked the Depression with a host of "alphabet agencies" targeting the group identities of the unemployed. But whether the nature of what was called "the youth problem" lay in the changes wrought by the Industrial Revolution, by the Depression, or by a world careening toward fascism was a source of dispute. Hence, the youth problem was a catch-all phrase encompassing a variety of concerns. Writers spoke of "boy and girl tramps," the millions of youth doomed to idleness in an industrial world where job prospects required more job training, not less. But many also feared that youth as a whole might lose their faith that the democratic way of life could meet people's basic needs.

The New Deal (1933–1939) wove a tapestry of programs to deal with this danger. Since the late nineteenth century, reformers were certain that charities and government both had to provide the out-of-doors physical activity that nature alone had once provided the young. As the nation aged, so did the youth group that social experts considered endangered, centering first on children and then moving to young people aged eighteen to twenty-five. During the 1930s, when the percentage of female college students rose from 33 percent to 39 percent, the youth problem focused less on physical and more on emotional health, less on athleticism and more on the alienation and lack of purpose felt by the young. Increasingly physical conditioning and exposure to nature seemed a pointless answer to a problem that appeared more psychological than physical, a matter of morale more than morals. The concern for youth, spurred by the fear of

the wild and unsupervised youth of the "Roaring Twenties," was redirected as the Depression politicized the attitudes of many young people. With the crisis of capitalism and the popularity of radical ideologies, New Dealers sought ways to preserve the political morale of youth by demonstrating the practical efficacy of an organized and compassionate democracy.

Those federal programs that aided youth before 1935 (the Federal Emergency Relief Administration, or FERA, and the Civilian Conservation Corps, or CCC) did so incidentally, in the course of helping such causes as college budgets and conservation. While the CCC, for example, aided 250,000 young (eighteen to twenty-five), mostly urban men in 1933, the men worked mostly at bucolic tasks that were noncompetitive with adult labor and ill suited to prepare them for industrialized work. Young men received little from the CCC that was formative, but the nation secured the removal of an incendiary element from the city streets without worsening the adult unemployment problem. In addition, critics wondered why the CCC did not aid women and why the New Deal, in their words, had no "she-she-she." Meanwhile, the National Recovery Administration's efforts to prohibit child labor ran headlong into the unwillingness of children to accept schools that offered no job training as alternatives to work. With state cuts pressuring college budgets, the New Deal responded with ideas for addressing multiple problems in inexpensive ways. By February 1934, the New Deal authorized the FERA to provide one hundred thousand college students the part-time jobs they needed to remain in school. The youth programs of 1933 and 1934 were cobbled together largely to plug the holes in the adult unemployment problem created by other New Deal ventures.

While some officials in the Office of Education favored the use of emergency programs to fund the ideas and aims of traditional educators, relief officials won the struggle in 1935 for the soul of the New Deal youth policy. The resulting National Youth Administration (NYA) was curious. Viewed one way, it appears decentralist; viewed another, it seemed to transform Uncle Sam into a schoolmaster himself. Half of the program extended the FERA student-aid program to high school students as well as college students, aiding 390,000 in the first year. The NYA's innovation was an out-of-school training program that served, in the initial year, 210,000 youth's need for job training. Yet, even here, decentralization was the watchword as all jobs were noncompetitive with private labor and selected and supervised by local leaders. The NYA was signed into law by executive order in 1935 and received $50 million its first year (compared to the CCC's almost $300 million in the same year). The NYA was, until the war, a poor relation of the CCC, receiving a pittance of what Congress earmarked for the "tree army." Not until 1941 did the NYA's funding approach the amount received by the CCC ($119 million and $155 million, respectively).

Yet because of its timing and administrative provenance, the NYA would be far more progressive, reformist, and "youth-centered" than either the CCC or FERA. Led by the liberal Aubrey Williams, the NYA gave charge of a Division of Negro Affairs to Mary McLeod Bethune, head of the New Deal's unofficial "black cabinet," making her then the highest-ranking black American ever to serve in an official government post. Unlike the segregated CCC camps, NYA work projects were frequently integrated. State administrators, in part because of their own relatively young ages, often possessed an energy that endeared them to their charges and served their own future careers well (one was Texas State Director Lyndon B. Johnson).

But the rise of another youth movement, Nazism, also lent urgency and focus to the NYA's work. When FDR gave the agency an extension in 1936, he declared tellingly, "no greater obligation faces the government than to justify the faith of its young people in the fundamental rightness of our democratic institutions." In its later years, many of the NYA programs, from aid to a scattering of Jewish refugee youths to training for national defense work, would be designed to quietly support the cause of democracy in an increasingly dangerous world.

Ironically, the war effort that it served so well from 1939 to 1942 rendered the NYA seemingly obsolete, as jobs and industrial training opportunities mushroomed following Pearl Harbor. The NYA was helpless before Congressional budget-cutters, who saw to it that its funding lapsed in 1943. By then, nearly five million youths (nearly twice as many as were aided through the CCC) had received jobs without which they could not have remained in school or received valuable job training. Although the connection was indirect, the NYA was the first national agency to possess the same federalized approach to *both* funding and administration that would later characterize the G.I. Bill and the student aid programs of the Great Society and the present. In a sense, it was historically fitting that the New Deal's most lasting service to young people would be largely forgotten by the generation that had received so much from it, and by their children. Although the Roosevelt administration eventually came to respond to the plight of the young, it did so quietly, after first subsuming it within the vast, amorphous problem of "unemployment."

See also: **Social Welfare; Work and Poverty.**

BIBLIOGRAPHY

Reiman, Richard A. 1992. *The New Deal and American Youth: Ideas and Ideals in a Depression Decade.* Athens: University of Georgia Press.

Salmond, John A. 1983. *A Southern Rebel: The Life and Times of Aubrey Willis Williams.* Chapel Hill: University of North Carolina Press.

RICHARD A. REIMAN

Youth Culture

Culture is among the most complicated words in the English language. It refers to the processes by which the symbolic systems (e.g., common sense, "usual way of doing things"; traditions and rituals, frameworks for understanding experience, etc.) characteristically shared by a group of people are maintained and transformed across time. Despite the appearance of stability, culture is a dynamic, historical process. Youth culture refers to those processes and symbolic systems that young people share that are, to some degree, distinctive from those of their parents and the other adults in their community.

Youth cultures have not been part of all societies throughout history; they appear most frequently where significant realms of social autonomy for young people become regularized and expected features of the socialization process. Most scholars would agree that the conditions necessary for the mass youth cultures recognizable today appeared after the formation of modern nation-states and the routinization of the human life course in the industrializing nations of the nineteenth century. The mass institutions of the nation-state, which separate young people from adults and gather them in large numbers for education, religious instruction, training, work, or punishment have been consistent locations in which youth cultures have developed. There is some evidence suggesting that youth cultures may have existed in certain circumstances during the medieval period. Also, it is important to recognize that there are significant gaps in our historical understanding, particularly for populations outside of Europe and the United States. Youth cultures have been clearly evident in the twentieth century, particularly since the end of World War II. The history of this period is notably marked by significant social and cultural influences of youth cultures on society at large, a trend that continues in the contemporary period.

Research into youth cultures has been most prolific in the disciplines of sociology, psychology, and anthropology; it is readily apparent in criminology of juveniles, demographic analyses, studies of the family and adolescent social development, and the study of ritual. The analytic frameworks and debates about youth cultures that have emerged from the three major disciplines have been taken up in other areas of study, including history. Like most fields in the humanities and social sciences, youth studies is marked less by the certainty of its knowledge than by a series of long-running debates. To what extent are youth cultures functional for a liberal capitalist society? To what extent is the formation of youth cultures an unintended disruption in social systems? How is the range between contributory and resistive youth cultures socially negotiated and contained? To what extent are youth cultures separate and different from the cultures of their parents? What role do other social identities (race, ethnicity, and social class) play in the formation of youth cultures? Are the youth cultures of young men different from those of young women? To what extent are young people willing agents of social, cultural, and political change? What are the effects of consumer goods and the consumer marketplace on youth cultures? How do the major institutions of socialization (e.g., family, religion, and schools) shape and reflect youth cultures? Although there are numerous earlier studies, these questions are the products of research from the late twentieth century; the discipline of history has entered these debates most significantly during years since then. There is some question, therefore, about whether descriptions and theories of contemporary youth cultures are adequate for historical studies that reach back as far as five hundred years.

Youth Culture before the Modern Period

Evidence of youth cultures before the early modern period is piecemeal and suggestive at best, and it is usually found in the public records describing young men's misbehaviors. There are innumerable complaints of rowdy young men disturbing the peace at night in villages and towns throughout the medieval period. Young men having conflicts with adult authorities is no clear indication that a distinctive male youth culture was in place, of course. Many premodern societies regularly allowed young people who were nearing the age of marriage to congregate separately after the workday or during community celebrations and festivals. Local youth peer groups formed, and in some circumstances, some aspects of a youth culture emerged. On the other hand, these accounts often include mention of roguish adults, and the incidents and offenses may be nothing more than youthful boisterousness, overindulgence, impatience with social strictures, or the cultural disorientation caused by the progressive loss of established outlets for young men's energies (for instance, knighthood).

Most societies of this period integrated young people into the labors of everyday family and community life on a more or less continuous basis, including community-sanctioned events and associations for young people. Still, the repeated complaints over long periods during the medieval period in Europe suggest that young men were "claiming the night" as a realm of their own in a new way, and their elders were deeply concerned about it. During this period, young men replaced women (of all ages) as the audiences that the clergy perceived to be most in need of moral and religious instruction. Scholars of medieval Italy have argued that self-initiated elite youth associations, with their own rituals and cultural rules, did form and sustain themselves for a significant time in some Italian cities. Young men in some areas

In the early modern period, young men were often the chief participants in charivaries, rowdy gatherings held to punish or otherwise call attention to those who trangressed community standards. The participants in William Hogarth's early-eighteenth-century engraving beat sticks together in a mocking allusion to the tailor's supposed beating by his wife. Archives Charmet/ Bridgeman Art Library.

were given the task of organizing festivals, which again allowed a significant realm of freedom both in planning and in presentation. European CHARIVARIES—informal, rowdy evening parades in which cuckolded husbands, scolding wives, or other offenders of community standards were mocked or sanctioned (sometimes physically)—were initiated and lead by village youths with the tacit approval of (and sometimes participation from) local adults. There is also some evidence that youth cultures may have formed in institutions such as monasteries and ACADEMIES, where large numbers of young people were separated from most other adults for purposes of extended training and instruction. For instance, aspects of a youth culture are evident in the reports

Cars revolutionized youth culture, giving teenagers not only mobility, but a space in which they could do as they pleased. This photograph appeared in a 1953 *McCall's Magazine* article depicting a day in the life of the American teenager. © Genevieve Naylor/CORBIS.

of academy students collectively tossing unpopular teachers and professors from classroom windows.

Youth Cultures in the Eighteenth and Nineteenth Centuries

As the institutions and practices of civil life within modern capitalist nation-states began to take their characteristic shape in the eighteenth and nineteenth centuries, several cultural, social, and economic trends emerged that formed the material basis for modern notions of mass youth culture.

Protestantism came to understand the period in the life course that would later be categorized as ADOLESCENCE as a particularly vulnerable time in moral development and thus open to collective supervision by trusted adult authorities. SUNDAY SCHOOLS served this purpose. As industrialization proceeded and expanded, rural populations migrated and concentrated in urban areas. No longer connected to long-standing, stable communities in which the responsibilities for the socialization and oversight of the young were collectively shared, the youth peer group often became a substi-

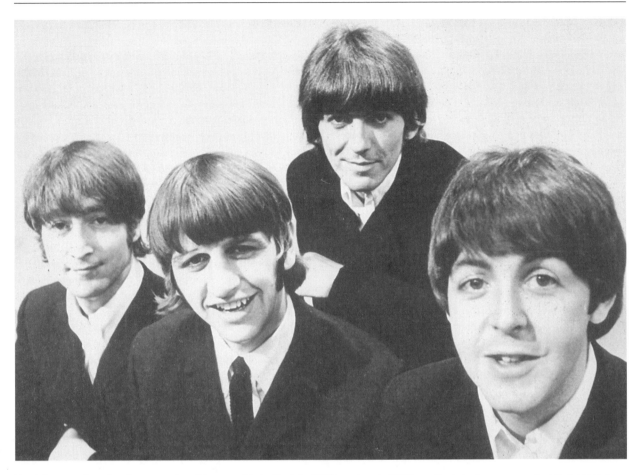

The influence of youth culture was almost inescapable by the late 1950s and early 1960s as the baby boomers reached their teenage years, making groups popular among young people, such as the Beatles, household icons. Archive Photos, Inc.

tute, particularly for ORPHANS, youths of marrying age, and runaways. Cities offered employment for wages for young people and a more or less open marketplace in necessities and leisure to people of any age. What many criminologists now recognize as YOUTH GANGS had appeared in major European cities as early as the Middle Ages; they appeared in New York City before the mid-nineteenth century, along with non-violent working-class youth cultures centered around volunteer fire departments. As these examples indicate, a distinction between a cultural realm created for youth and monitored by adults on the one hand (an "approved" youth culture), and a cultural realm sustained primarily by young people themselves on the other (a "rogue" youth culture) is useful, although it must be recognized that the boundary separating the two is fluid and permeable.

The emerging social stratum of middle-class professionals (e.g., doctors, lawyers, engineers, and teachers) whose legitimacy was dependent upon formal education grew and expanded as the scientific and industrial revolutions placed secular experts alongside those from religious institutions. Reflecting the professional classes' power base in education, their children were sent to school rather than to APPREN-

TICESHIPS in the trades. In the schools, large numbers of young people were segmented by age and placed under the supervision of adults that exercised very different relationships with these youths than those of their parents and community elders. The professional middle classes increasingly became the cultural and social standard bearers in many of the leading democratic capitalist countries during the eighteenth and nineteenth centuries. As this group moved to assume responsibility for the unintended and unattended consequences of urbanization and industrialization, it took up an advocacy role for those young people who had been socially and economically displaced by the transition from agriculture to industrialization. In taking this advocacy role (through charitable and religious organizations and later through governmental agencies), their views of children and adolescence became the dominant and institutionalized view.

These developments began to coalesce to form a new understanding of the "place" of young people in leading industrial societies after the mid-nineteenth century. A period of public education was made mandatory for young people in many parts of Europe and the United States; increasingly, schooling became an expected and routine part of the life course. At roughly the same time, the field of medicine and the emerging discipline of psychology began to differentiate the stages of the human life course more precisely, determining a "normal" standard for biological and social development based on chronological age. The influx of migrants and immigrants to industrializing cities relieved some of the demand for the labor of young people, pushing young people to assume new roles outside the workplace. As concerns for the integration of immigrant children became a public issue, the schools took up this task as well. In 1904 American psychologist G. STANLEY HALL attempted to synthesize and codify the contradictory biological, psychological, and social understandings of youth that had emerged during the nineteenth century in a two-volume work entitled *Adolescence: Its Psychology and Its Relations to Anthropology, Sociology, Sex, Crime, Religion and Education*. This work laid a "scientific" basis for the collective socialization of the young in large institutions, justifying the social segregation of young people by age. With progressive shift in the identity of young people from workers to students in the late nineteenth century, the process for the creation of mass youth cultures was in place.

The uneven rate and extent of this shift both within and across national boundaries is important to bear in mind. Slaves, indigenous peoples, and colonial subjects did not proceed along this timeline. For instance, young African-American slaves were chattel property in the United States until emancipation in 1865, a clear divergence from the experiences of even the most destitute of white youths. Despite these limits, however, elements of a youth culture in the form of games, rituals, and stories did develop among young slaves, particularly during the period of their lives (sometimes as late as fifteen years old) before they entered the regulated agricultural work of adulthood. Indigenous Inuit youth in north-central Canada did not pass through a period of adolescence before contact with Europeans, instead experiencing a swift transition between childhood and adulthood. Parents arranged marriages for their children, sometimes at birth, leaving scant space for a youth culture to emerge. Even the homogeneity of the shifts within Europe and the United States in the eighteenth and nineteenth centuries can be overemphasized. As many contemporary scholars note, there have been many "pathways" from childhood to adulthood.

The institutional structures and practices of mass socialization in place at the end of the nineteenth century created a new place (both figuratively and literally) for young people to emphasize their common bonds over other mediating differences. Identities connected to parent communities—class, ethnicity, gender, religion, and later, SEXUALITY and race—were often partially (but rarely completely) subsumed under the common experiences of youth and the rituals of the new mass socialization. The autonomous realms in which youth cultures developed in these institutions were not always in-

tentionally granted to them by adults. Adults have only limited abilities to constrain the activities of their youthful subordinates, and young people across history have demonstrated great resourcefulness in collectively exploiting those limitations to gain some self-directed social space. Drawing on that shared experience, the peer group became an (unintended) mass social institution in its own right, at times creating alternatives that were visibly opposed to adult cultural and social norms. Schools took young people away from the daily activities of most adults, opening the possibility for a youth social system, even if that social system was limited and constrained.

Youth Cultures, 1900–1940

New distinctions are needed to understand the development of youth cultures in the twentieth century. First, while the conditions for mass youth cultures to emerge were in place, young people did not become a homogenous social group; there has never been a singular youth culture in complex societies, but rather a wide variety of youth (sub)cultures. Second, a distinction needs to be made between the wide variety of commercial products (including forms of entertainment) marketed to youth and the unique ways in which young people took up the opportunities of these activities and products to produce a separate sphere of cultural processes and practices. It has become commonplace to refer to youth-marketed products as "youth culture," but this tells us little about the cultural lives of young people themselves. While the development of national markets did offer new connections between youth people across great distances, the youth market did not lead to a homogenization of youth cultures. Third, the definition of youth itself changes, as more young people extend their period of semi-dependence on family to attend colleges and universities.

Scholars have argued that the first authentically independent mass youth culture in the twentieth century emerged among these college students, who fashioned new rituals and customs that have since marked memories of that period in American history. While these new rituals and customs often were (and still are) seen as a more radical departure from the parent culture than they really were, the college youth of this period did set the example for other developments. Youth clubs and youth cultures appeared in HIGH SCHOOLS, as education beyond the elementary level became more common, and many of the new customs were borrowed from college youth and adapted to the high schools. With the loss of employment during the Great Depression of the 1930s, even more young people entered high school. Since its appearance in the late nineteenth century, commercial popular culture had accepted youths' money, but many of the new forms of urban popular culture, particularly film, explicitly catered to young people. The consumption of MOVIES, novels, and music (and later, COMIC BOOKS and TELEVISION) became an expected part of youth. While the majority of research has focused on the effects of commercial popular culture on youth, popular culture's role as a shared and identity-generated commodity among youth has been investigated to a much lesser degree. Youth cultures do not consume popular culture commodities in a vacuum; their consumption forms the basis of affiliations (e.g., fans and collectors), a wide variety of social rituals (e.g., FRIENDSHIP and DATING), and the everyday stuff of common conversations.

Youth Cultures, 1940–1970

Although the commercialization of youth as a consumer market did not end with the 1920s, college youth's role as the avant-garde of consumerism diminished significantly during the Depression. That role was passed on to another group of consumers, high school students, during the early 1940s, when the word TEENAGER came into common usage among marketers. This trend coincided with America's entrance into World War II. During the war, youth cultures in high schools became a national social problem, initiated through a series of moral panics about their sexual activities (especially between high school girls and GIs), DELINQUENCY, and the influence of mass popular culture, particularly COMIC BOOKS, films, and ROCK-AND-ROLL music. By the late 1950s and early 1960s, the existence of a mass youth culture itself was widely recognized, although mostly ridiculed. Youth cultures adopting unusual and spectacular clothing and hair styles appeared in the United States (the Beats) and Great Britain (the Teds). Fears of urban youth gangs and their potential influence on the less-threatening teenager initiated some of the first studies of youth culture. Besides the expansion of popular culture and the commonality of high school, the automobile had a dramatic effect on youth culture, particularly in the United States. The car not only provided a means for suburban and rural youth to travel to central cities, but it also created a kind of portable "private space" that enhanced other customs, including courtship, sex, drinking, and listening to the RADIO.

The number of youth cultures proliferated in the 1960s. College-age youth once again took the public (and world) stage as "hippies" and as organized radical groups, which often spread to the high schools. Spectacular subcultures continued to appear in Great Britain as well, notably mods, rockers, and near the end of the decade, skinheads. These subcultures, along with the participation of young people in mass protests and radical politics, signaled some realization of the cultural, social, and economic influence of young people. That this had been true for almost forty years is not a coincidence, since most young people had participated in those formations that seemed the least threatening to adults. The mass mobilization of youth against military service and restrictions on their speech, among other issues, signaled a mass refusal of the social terms accepted by their parents. This mobilization did not only apply to white middle-class youths, but also was apparent in a wide variety of social groups. For instance, young African Americans were key players in the dramatic civil rights demonstrations of this era; young central-city residents of all races and ethnicities took part in the urban riots that followed later in the decade.

While youthful drug use and sexual experimentation had been cause for hysteria among adults for at least fifty years, these practices became much more widespread during this period. Drug use was associated with rock music and visual culture (films, posters, and art of all sorts), both their consumption by youth and their production by popular musicians and artists. "Hippies" (including high-school students) took hallucinogenics and smoked marijuana in public. Drug use, like drinking rituals, became an expected part of youth, although the majority of young people did not participate. Sexual experimentation appears to have been rising steadily throughout the century, but the public emphasis on "free love" and recreational sex broke new boundaries, particularly after the development of oral contraceptives.

Youth Cultures since 1970

In the aftermath of the 1960s' youth rebellion, youth culture became a normalized feature of life in many developed nations, and the youth cultures in those countries often set the terms for emulation by other nations. Parents and adults continued to try to control their wards, but if they found a son or daughter dressed in strange clothing (often self-fashioned) or with a strange haircut, they no longer panicked. Recognizing that the most rebellious of youth cultures of the 1960s had been commodified by entrepreneurs and later by mundane retail outlets, some youth cultures searched for identities that could either not be quickly co-opted or that embraced CONSUMER CULTURE for its own ends. Punk, with its trash-heap, "do-it-yourself" aesthetics and its claim that anyone could be a musician was an open attack on the hippie subculture of the previous generation. Despite its best efforts to resist mass marketing, punk too became a style available in shopping centers around the world. Glam rockers and disco dancers moved in the other direction, openly embracing some aspects of popular culture, particularly fashions borrowed from marginalized social groups. Most young people did not formally "join" a subculture, although they may have bought the records and adopted some of the clothing styles when they became available in stores.

Three trends developed in youth cultures formed after the 1970s. First, as marketers moved more definitively to segment pre-adolescents as a separate market, a mass "kid" culture has begun to emerge. Because of the limits on this group's mobility and autonomy, new analytical tools are needed for investigations. However, it is important to note that this group is segmented from adult and adolescent culture at an early age, often within the context of institutions such as day care and school, and the preconditions necessary for many aspects of youth culture to emerge are in place. At the very least, the shared experience of consumer goods (TOYS, foods, movies, radio stations, clothing), adult authority in socializing institutions, and common activities (skateboarding, scooters) strengthen the cultural connections between young people at an earlier age while further distancing them from the experiences of their parents and older siblings. Youth culture has gotten younger. At the same time, youth culture has taken on new meanings and gotten older: In particular, there is strong evidence that some people are continuing their youth culture affiliations into adulthood, so that youth cultures become "lifestyles." This raises some interesting questions. What are we to make of a forty-year-old punk? A sixty-year-old hippie? Finally, new communication and media technologies, particularly the Internet, create spaces for new youth cultures to emerge. Teenage computer hackers and phone "phreaks" had already appeared during the 1980s, but the Internet allows for a much more expanded notion of cyber-cultures detached from everyday off-line identities. The Internet, like "lovers' lane," is a more or less unpatrolled wilderness that has allowed new cultural affiliations (e.g., netGoths) to be formed.

See also: **Adolescence and Youth; Bobby Soxers; Campus Revolts in the 1960s; Charivari; Drugs; Flappers; Teen Drinking; Teen Magazines; Victory Girls; Youth Activism.**

BIBLIOGRAPHY

Amit-Talai, Vered, and Helena Wulff, eds. 1995. *Youth Cultures: A Cross-Cultural Perspective.* London: Routledge.

Austin, Joe, and Michael Willard, eds. 1998. *Generations of Youth: Youth Cultures and History in Twentieth-Century America.* New York: New York University Press.

Brake, Michael. 1985. *Comparative Youth Culture.* London: Routledge and Kegan Paul.

Fass, Paula S. 1977. *The Damned and the Beautiful: American Youth in the 1920s.* New York: Oxford University Press.

Gelder, Ken, and Sarah Thornton, eds. 1997. *The Subcultures Reader.* London: Routledge.

Inness, Sherrie, ed. 1998. *Delinquents and Debutantes: Twentieth Century American Girls' Culture.* New York: New York University Press.

Kett, Joseph. 1977. *Rites of Passage: Adolescence in America 1790 to the Present.* New York: Basic Books.

Levi, Giovanni, and Jean-Claude Schmitt, eds. 1997. *A History of Young People in the West, Vol. 1.* Cambridge, MA: Harvard University Press.

JOE AUSTIN

Youth Gangs

Youth gangs are self-identified, organized groups of adolescents, banded together under common interests and a common leader in activities that typically are regarded as menacing to society or illegal. Gangs, or their prototypes, have existed for hundreds of years in a number of cultures, however many scholars locate the emergence of the modern youth gang in the nineteenth century, during the shift from agrarian to industrial society. Most youth gangs arise among the urban poor, though not always. Although gangs participate in unlawful activities associated with controlling a territory or illegal enterprise, most of their pursuits remain purely social and within the law.

Gangs and youth groups have existed since at least the Middle Ages. Accounts from England in the fourteenth and fifteenth centuries describe criminal gangs that robbed, extorted, and raped. In France, England, and Germany, medieval juvenile groups known as *abbeys of misrule* participated in violent sports and fights against rival groups in honor of the abbeys from which they were recruited. Other youth groups rioted and intimidated deviant villagers, and were sanctioned by adults for enforcing the social order. In the seventeenth and eighteenth centuries, English gangs wore colored ribbons to mark their allegiances, battled rivals, and terrorized communities. In the American colonies, people complained about troublesome groups who caroused, fought, and stole, as well.

Although these earlier prototypical gangs possessed characteristics associated with the modern youth gang, quintessential urban street gangs only emerged in the nineteenth century. In the United States, the social and economic pressures associated with rapid industrialization, urbanization, and immigration gave rise to organized criminal gangs that thrived under these conditions. Gangs like the "Pug Uglies" and the "Dead Rabbits" conducted illegal activities in slums and recruited youths and adults. They were linked with the criminal underworld, saloons, and political machines. As new immigrants arrived and ethnic conflicts increased in the late 1800s, ethnic youth gangs battling for turf and status became more prevalent.

Urban reformers interpreted the gang phenomena as part of the depravity and degradation of city life. Alarmed by the tenacity and success of some of these organizations, they began to study the causes of gangs. Significantly, researchers focused on the role of juvenile DELINQUENCY in the development of adult criminal gangs. Partly as a result of these studies, many reformers throughout the late nineteenth and early twentieth centuries promoted child welfare services and education as a means of stemming gang activity and reestablishing social order.

Frederic M. Thrasher's work *The Gang* (1927) epitomized this new trend in the study of gangs. Thrasher located the roots of criminal groups not only in the miserable living conditions and economic disadvantages of the poor, but also in adolescent development. He proposed that gangs were a normal adaptation to slums and an extension of natural adolescent bonding. Young gang members entered into adult organizations only when social conditions remained inadequate and social mobility was unattainable. Influenced by Thrasher's study, public officials and experts throughout the 1920s and 1930s largely either dismissed juvenile gangs as adolescent play or elevated them to the level of adult organized crime, rather than recognizing them as menacing, independent entities of their own.

Youth gangs received heightened attention during World War II. In Europe, the disastrous upheaval of war caused a significant rise in delinquency. Acting out of necessity, juvenile gangs participated in the black market, prostitution, and theft. In the United States, the increase in youth gang activity was as much a product of Americans' new awareness of the problem as it was of true increases in numbers. Public officials and the press blamed wartime conditions, like disruptions in family life, for contributing to juvenile delinquency. At the same time, people became concerned with ethnic youth subcultures and fads, like the zoot-suit fashion. The style, and its connection to a series of race riots in 1943, created a situation in which minority youths began to band together into ethnic gangs for protection, and which also crystallized the public's conception of youth gang violence. By the end of the war, the combined awareness of the juvenile delinquency problem and of interethnic clashes solidified American's fears about youth gangs.

In the postwar period, American youth gangs were a major social dilemma on the streets and in the public consciousness. In the 1950s gangs were characterized by their ethnic and racial affiliations, their control of territory, and their greater use of violence against rivals. Law enforcement and social services targeted gangs for research, surveillance, and interventions, and the popular media portrayed youth gangs in movies like *The Wild Ones*. However, by the mid-1960s, adolescent gang activities slowed. Gang intervention programs and public policy did much to disrupt gangs. Scholars also suggest that political involvement in civil rights issues and the anti-war movement drew many youths away from gang participation, or redirected gang activities into militant groups like the Black Panthers. Moreover, the increased use of DRUGS such as heroin by gang members destroyed gang cohesion and created loose drug subcultures in its place.

Youth gangs resurfaced in the 1970s in response to the economic downturn in inner cities and to the growing drug culture. A number of returning veterans from Vietnam reorganized gangs and provided new leadership and experience. Though youth gangs actually fought against the prevailing drug culture at first, many juvenile gangs increasingly turned to drug trafficking for profit. By the 1980s, gangs were involved in more predatory crimes, and battled for control of illegal markets as well as turf. Gang activity was marked by brutal violence as gang members began to carry and use guns.

Modern juvenile gangs have been a problem around the world. Various youth gangs in Great Britain and Germany have emerged in response to ongoing class rivalries and rising immigrant populations, including rowdy and nationalist soccer hooligans and racist, violent skinheads. Studies in African youth gangs have also turned up groups like the skollie gangs of South Africa, who provide protection, support, and economic survival for their members. In Jamaica, posses recruit members living in extreme poverty, and commonly use violence and torture in their drug trafficking operations, and in Colombia, adolescent gangs protect territory and carry out murders for drug cartels.

See also: **Juvenile Court; Law, Children and the; Soldier Children; Zoot Suit Riots.**

BIBLIOGRAPHY

Asbury, Herbert. 1970 [1927]. *The Gangs of New York: An Informal History of the Underworld.* New York: Capricorn Books.

Covey, Herbert C., Scott Menard, and Robert J. Franzese, eds. 1997. *Juvenile Gangs,* 2nd edition. Springfield, IL: Charles C. Thomas.

Jankowski, Martín Sánchez. 1991. *Islands in the Street: Gangs and American Urban Society.* Berkeley: University of California Press.

Schneider, Eric C. 1999. *Vampires, Dragons, and Egyptian Kings: Youth Gangs in Postwar New York.* Princeton, NJ: Princeton University Press.

Thrasher, Frederic M. 1947 [1927]. *The Gang: A Study of 1,313 Gangs in Chicago.* Chicago: The University of Chicago Press.

LAURA MIHAILOFF

Youth Ministries

Youth ministries—or religious programs and organizations for adolescents—are among the most notable institutional innovations in the modern history of religion. They have involved millions of young people as members, especially from among Protestant Christianity in Europe and the United States, but also from other Christian denominations around the globe as well as JUDAISM, ISLAM, Buddhism, and Hinduism. Of course, religious leaders have always tried to communicate their beliefs and practices across generations. RITES OF PASSAGE and coming-of-age rituals are ancient. But focused religious attention to a group of young people located in age between childhood and adulthood developed along with the notion of ADOLESCENCE, and shortly after SUNDAY SCHOOLS, in the late nineteenth and early twentieth centuries.

The earliest religious youth societies appeared in Europe, but youth ministries grew most dramatically in contexts of religious voluntarism and pluralism, such as existed in the United States. Observers had long noted the predominance of young people among converts at American religious revivals. As some American religious leaders began to note an absence of young people among active members in the late nineteenth century, the revivalist strategy of targeting youth for conversion became a pattern for more enduring programs and organizations. The most notable organizations to develop this strategy were the Young Men's Christian Association (YMCA), founded by George Williams in 1844 in London, and the Young Women's Christian Association (YWCA), founded in Boston and New York in the 1850s by women such as Mrs. Marshall Roberts and Lucretia Boyd. Both youth movements were connected in sometimes general, sometimes quite specific, ways to local Protestant churches. They also established numerous links with business and industry, and occasionally with labor. Both movements also sought to engage youth in wholesome activities such as recreation, missionary endeavor, and education, and to protect young people from what experts considered unsavory elements in cities. Over the course of the twentieth century, the Ys developed a tripartite focus on programs for "body, mind, and spirit," and offered a wide range of social services for young people, including several radical initiatives in the 1960s. In the last decades of the twentieth century, both the YMCA and YWCA largely transformed themselves into family-serving recreational centers with services for individuals of all ages, regardless of religious affiliation.

As their organizational structure suggests, the YMCA and YWCA movements were initially committed to a rigid separation of the genders. The same was true of ethnicity. African-American young people were segregated by the Ys into separate but not equal facilities until the 1940s, and much longer in some settings. This rigid gender and racial separation was characteristic of the early years of many youth ministries, and often provided occasions for women and minorities to lead organizations in ways that, ironically, overturned the assumptions of white male superiority that had led to the segregation. Consequently, segregation softened considerably over the decades, as did the evangelical zeal and Protestant dominance of the Ys. The YWCA especially eventually embraced an ideology of ethnic and cultural pluralism as part of a "global women's movement," as Judith Weisenfeld and Nancy Boyd have documented. The Ys also spawned, beginning in the 1920s, a number of other significant Christian youth movements and agencies that were very influential in the global ecumenical movement, such as the World Christian Student Federation, the Student Volunteer Movement, and the youth bureau of the World Council of Churches (see Ans van der Bent's *From Generation to Generation*). These movements often linked missionary activity with political activism of a "progressive" stripe, as young people began to confront the global consequences of European and American colonialism.

Along with the emergence of the YMCA and YWCA in the late nineteenth century came many other Protestant youth ministries. Some of them welcomed African Americans, although most traditionally black denominations also developed their own youth boards and bureaus. The nondenominational Christian Endeavor was the largest of the numerous Protestant youth ministries. Christian Endeavor began at Williston Congregational Church in Portland, Maine, under the direction of Dr. Francis E. Clark, on Feb-

ruary 2, 1881. By 1887 the organization boasted seven thousand societies with five hundred thousand members, mostly from Presbyterian and Congregationalist Protestant churches (the so-called mainline churches) around the globe, although members were also drawn from other denominations. The structure of Christian Endeavor established a much imitated pattern: weekly meetings for prayer, devotions, education, and recreation in local societies (usually a congregation), a publication, *The Christian Endeavor World*, annual conventions or gatherings, and a board of directors. Christian Endeavor was also distinguished by its pledge, which committed young people to daily bible reading and prayer, active membership in a local congregation, and missionary activism. Christian Endeavor continued to operate into the twenty-first century, although membership declined dramatically as particular denominations developed their own in-house youth boards, publications, and offices.

If Christian youth ministries began as ventures among mainline Protestant groups, evangelical and fundamentalist Protestants after World War II founded many enduring nondenominational youth ministries. Youth for Christ adapted the well-known revival format into radio broadcast rallies for young people at sporting arenas around the country in the 1940s, featuring up-tempo white gospel music and testimony by war heroes and sport stars. Billy Graham was the first traveling evangelist for Youth for Christ. Young Life was another enduring evangelical youth ministry begun in the 1940s, but it was quickly followed by Campus Crusade for Christ, Inter-Varsity Christian Fellowship, Fellowship of Christian Athletes, Youth Specialties, Group Publishing, and many others.

These Protestant youth ministries in the United States shared many features and a common historical trajectory. They generally began in urban settings, triggered by the migrations of young people to cities for industrial and other specialized work. They were organized in conjunction with local congregations, and established networks through national conferences, publications, and SUMMER CAMPS. They originated to meet needs among young people for employment assistance, housing, education, recreation, and spiritual fellowship, but were quickly tailored by religious leaders to specific agendas. They were generally middle class in mentality and morality, proved strongest in the Midwest, and increasingly took on the trappings of a profession as trained and certified youth ministers began to be placed in congregations in the 1950s and after.

By the twenty-first century, youth ministries and ministers were conventional features of religious traditions in the United States, with institutional presence in buildings, denominational offices, publications, congregations, web pages, and campgrounds. Through their missionary activity, some youth ministries have spun off or collaborated with international organizations committed to social justice and environmental causes, akin to the Peace Corps. Among the most notable to engage youth in this way are the youth and campus chapters of Habitat for Humanity, the Jesuit Volunteer Corps, the Lutheran Volunteer Corps, and the youth internships and other programs of the Mennonite Central Committee. All in all, GLOBALIZATION has become a contested topic among the leaders of Christian youth ministries in the early twenty-first century. Of course, conversion-oriented missions also continue among some Protestant youth ministries and among Mormons, whose two-year mission requirements for college-aged young people and daily "seminary" programs for youths aged fourteen to eighteen continue to be supported by broad social pressures among Mormons.

Among Roman Catholics, youth ministry has often been connected to parish-based catechesis, or education to prepare for the sacraments of confirmation, communion, and marriage. Nevertheless, specific organizations and programs, such as World Youth Day, have also developed among Catholics to target particular groups of young people. In the United States these organizations and programs grew slowly and sporadically in local venues, due in part to the competing ethnic enclaves into which Catholics tended to cluster after immigration. The Catholic Youth Organization (CYO) was the first movement to bridge some of these groups into a pan-ethnic youth-serving organization. CYO began in the 1930s under the leadership of Bishop Bernard Sheil of Chicago, initially as youth BOXING leagues, but eventually spinning off into a range of ministries, and continuing in some locales into the twenty-first century under Archdiocesan auspices. The Young Christian Workers (YCW) and the Young Christian Students (YCS) were part of the international Catholic Action movement that revitalized mid-twentieth-century Catholicism, and drew thousands of lay Catholic youth into particularly formative programs until the energy behind that movement was absorbed in the reforms of the second Vatican Council (1962–1965).

Outside of the United States, church–state unity or religious and ethnic homogeneity lent youth ministries a different political dynamic. German youth movements, and especially the relationships between both Protestant and Catholic youth groups and the rise of National Socialism, have been closely studied, as have the connections between YMCA missionaries and traditional religious and political practices in Japan (see Mark Roseman and Jon Davidann, respectively). Elsewhere, relationships forged between the international missionary activity of youth ministries and cultural developments were complex and variable. One recurring phenomenon is the appearance of young people in new religious movements, such as the flourishing Pentecostalism across the Southern Hemisphere. Religious youth have also often been implicated in religious extremism and violence, although historical causality is anything but clear in these cases. What is clear is that some malleable but durable myths or cultural conventions about the life stage known as youth, with young people represented as both problems (devils) and with potential (angels), have become cross-cultural currency, and that the international presence of Christian youth ministries played a role in the construction and dissemination of these conventions.

It is therefore not surprising that what began as an innovation within Christian traditions has also spread to other religious groups. For instance, Jewish youth have organized throughout the nineteenth and twentieth centuries, most notably in the B'nai B'rith Youth Organization and B'nai B'rith Girls, but also in Hillel, a campus-based organization, the Federation of Zionist Youth, and others. Muslim youth have founded the World Assembly of Muslim Youth, the Muslim Youth of North America (affiliated with the Islamic Society of North America), and the Muslim Student Association, among others. Buddhist youth could by the late twentieth century participate in a range of activities through the Dharma Realm Buddhist Youth organization and the World Federation of Buddhist Youth, and Hindu high schoolers could join the Hindu Students Council. Many local synagogues, temples, and mosques also ran programs tailored specifically to adolescents.

The significance of these youth ministries for the history of childhood cannot be measured singly, but some broad generalities may pertain. Throughout the twentieth century, youth ministries clearly extended the span of childhood and solidified middle-class desires and status across traditions. They often had links to business. Connections with labor were less frequent. Youth ministries have also tended to be bastions of conservative gender and racial ideologies, although they often unwittingly provided space for experimentation in gender roles, and sometimes explicitly encouraged leadership among women and racial minorities. Usually intended to preserve religious traditions, youth ministries have also been marked by fuzzy ideological boundaries, and have been located on the social margins of official traditions, thus allowing ecumenical and interfaith experimentation on the part of young members. Generally nationalist in politics, if not colonialist or imperialist, youth ministries have also multiplied opportunities for young people to gain international experience, and thus have indirectly (especially in the late twentieth century) promoted multicultural awareness, when they have not motivated religious extremism.

All in all, little evidence remains to support the judgments of Joseph Kett that youth ministries vanished in America during the late twentieth century, or were only banal and culturally confirming. In fact, the significance of these movements deserves careful historical investigation in both local and international contexts, in discrete periods. Recent studies have clarified that the organizations nurtured future leaders for religious groups throughout the twentieth century, and that they sometimes radically reshaped traditions and cultures through visionary leadership and through the agency of the young people who joined them.

See also: **Organized Recreation and Youth Groups; YWCA and YMCA.**

BIBLIOGRAPHY

Bergler, Thomas E. 2001. "Winning America: Christian Youth Groups and the Middle-Class Culture of Crisis, 1930–1965." Ph.D. diss., University of Notre Dame.

Boyd, Nancy. 1986. *Emissaries: The Overseas Work of the American YWCA, 1895–1970.* New York: Woman's Press.

Coble, Christopher Lee. 2001. "Where Have All the Young People Gone? The Christian Endeavor Movement and the Training of Protestant Youth, 1881–1918." Ph.D. diss., Harvard University.

Davidann, Jon Thares. 1998. *A World of Crisis and Progress: The American YMCA in Japan, 1890–1930.* Bethlehem, PA: Lehigh University Press.

Kett, Joseph. 1977. *Rites of Passage: Adolescence in America, 1790 to the Present.* New York: Basic Books.

Mjagkij, Nina, and Margaret Spratt, eds. 1997. *Men and Women Adrift: The YMCA and the YWCA in the City.* New York: New York University Press.

Myers, William R. 1991. *Black and White Styles of Youth Ministry: Two Congregations in America.* New York: Pilgrim Press.

Pahl, Jon. 1993. *Hopes and Dreams of All: The International Walther League and Lutheran Youth in American Culture, 1893–1993.* Chicago: Wheat Ridge.

Pahl, Jon. 2000. *Youth Ministry in Modern America: 1930 to the Present.* Peabody, MA: Hendrickson Publishers.

Roseman, Mark, ed. 1995. *Generations in Conflict: Youth Revolt and Generation Formation in Germany, 1770–1968.* Cambridge, UK: Cambridge University Press.

Senter, Mark H., III. 1992. *The Coming Revolution in Youth Ministry.* Wheaton, IL: Victor Books.

Van der Bent, Ans J. 1986. *From Generation to Generation: The Story of Youth in the World Council of Churches.* Geneva: World Council of Churches.

Weisenfeld, Judith. 1997. *African American Women and Christian Activism: New York's Black YWCA, 1905–1945.* Cambridge, MA: Harvard University Press.

Zotti, Mary Irene. 1991. *A Time of Awakening: The Young Christian Worker Story in the United States, 1938–1970.* Chicago: Loyola University Press.

JON PAHL

YWCA and YMCA

The Young Women's Christian Association (YWCA) and the Young Men's Christian Association (YMCA) both began in London, England in the mid-nineteenth century as prayer unions aimed at saving the souls of young men and women who had gone to the city in search of employment. Concerned with the immoral influences of urban life, both organizations expanded to provide new migrants with wholesome recreation, religious instruction, and, eventually, supervised housing. The movement came to the United States in 1852 when the first YMCAs were established in New York City and Boston. Six years later a group of women formed a prayer union in New York City that would lead to the formation of the first American YWCA. Although the two organizations shared similar ideological roots, their structures, funding, and leadership remained separate on the national level.

Initially, the YMCA concentrated on recruiting its membership from the ranks of young middle-class businessmen, but realizing that the future depended on a new generation, work among boys began in the 1880s. By this time, the YMCA had moved from its earlier revivalist phase of the prayer union and evangelical meetings to one that stressed character building. The gymnasium was the centerpiece of this new approach. By 1900, 77 percent of YMCAs had gyms, and many also added libraries, meeting rooms, and classrooms. Young boys were attracted to the new facilities and the recreational activities they provided. YMCA leaders grasped the opportunities to entice boys into their facility where they could instill Christian middle-class values through Bible classes and team sports. Beginning in the 1880s the YMCA sponsored SUMMER CAMPS for boys. By 1930, the YMCA boasted of a youth membership of over 300,000 boys, many of who belonged to Hi-Y or county wide boys clubs. Recruitment among grade school boys was most successful in the twentieth century as the YMCA formed groups of Friendly Indians (boys under twelve) in America's elementary schools. However, the YMCA's reliance on large urban facilities, a reputation of Protestant conservatism, and relatively expensive membership and camping fees limited its ability to attract a wide diversity of boys.

Individual YWCAs engaged in work with various groups of girls beginning in 1881 with the Little Girls' Christian Association, but the national association did not regulate this work until the Girl Reserve movement was organized in 1918. Members voted to change their name from Girl Reserves to Y-Teens in 1946, and membership was open to any girl between the ages of twelve and eighteen. The YWCA stressed group work and opened its doors to various youth groups, providing space for dances, clubs, and athletic activities. Just as the YMCA had done, the YWCA constructed gymnasiums and swimming pools. The YWCA also had a camping program for youth that stressed wholesome outdoor recreation and survival skills. During World War II, the YWCA sponsored youth canteens, attracting high school boys and girls. In 1949, Y-Teens took part in the YWCA's national convention for the first time, sitting on various committees and voting on association proposals. For both associations, youth work was vital to the future of the movement.

See also: **Organized Recreation and Youth Groups; Youth Ministries.**

BIBLIOGRAPHY

Hopkins, C. Howard. 1951. *History of the Y.M.C.A. in North America*. New York: Association Press.

Macleod, David I. 1983. *Building Character in the American Boy: The Boy Scouts, YMCA, and Their Forerunners, 1870–1920.* Madison: University of Wisconsin Press.

Mjagkij, Nina, and Spratt, Margaret, eds. 1997. *Men and Women Adrift: The YMCA and the YWCA in the City.* New York: New York University Press

Sims, Mary S. 1950. *The YWCA: An Unfolding Purpose.* New York: Woman's Press.

Margaret A. Spratt

Z

Zoos

The word *zoo* first appeared in the 1867 music hall hit *Walking in the Zoo on Sunday*, which includes the observation: "the OK thing to do / On Sunday afternoon is to toddle in the Zoo." An abbreviation of zoological garden, "zoo" sounds cute and childlike. From the start the zoological garden had a special appeal to children. In 1828 the Zoological Society of London opened the zoological garden in Regent's Park, and its very first guidebook, *Henry and Emma's Visit to the Zoological Gardens*, addressed children as the main guests.

For centuries, various societies have established collections of wild and exotic animals. Ancient Egyptian, Greek, Roman, and Chinese civilizations all had magnificent collections of animals. Aristotle based his zoological studies on menageries in ancient Greece, and in ancient Rome enormous menageries were established to furnish the sanguine spectacles with exotic animals. Medieval princes marked their symbolic power by having various types of animals in their castles and surrounding grounds. The great discoveries of the sixteenth century incited a new interest in exotic animals, and the princes of the Renaissance and the Baroque gathered these animals in well-defined spaces, buildings, or gardens, thus establishing the forerunners of the modern, public zoological garden. But at this time any notion of a special relationship between children and animals seems to have been absent.

The menagerie was a symbol of power, and the king would define himself as the center of the world by having the animals gathered around his feet. The seventeenth- and eighteenth-century menageries of Austria and France were based on radiating plans with a pavilion in the center and paddocks radiating from there. In 1765 the menagerie at Schönbrunn opened to the public as the oldest continuous animal collection. At Versailles the menagerie also was constructed to appeal to the royal gaze. The French Revolution in 1789 changed the royal menagerie to a public institution.

The animals were moved from the court to Paris's Jardin des Plantes. At first the revolutionaries wanted this zoological garden to represent bourgeois values such as utility and reason, but the Napoleonic Wars reintroduced the need for power display. On July 27, 1798, French troops entered Paris in a triumphal march with exotic animals among the war booty.

The first director of the Jardin des Plantes organized the facility according to the principles of the picturesque English landscape garden: no fixed center, sinuous paths, nature as a symbol of freedom. The landscape garden became the dominant model for the exhibition of animals in the nineteenth century, and the term *zoological garden* was coined when the Zoological Society of London in 1828 opened its collections.

After the founding of the London Zoo hardly a year passed without a new zoo being established in the major European and American cities. In Copenhagen the zoological garden opened 1859, at the same time when the ramparts around the medieval city were demolished. The zoological garden was a symbol of modernity—but was also "an ark in the park," where nature could be protected in the midst of the ongoing process of urbanization.

These collections of animals were established for different purposes, and the specific character of a collection may be used as a key to the understanding of the culture within which the animals were collected. The ancient and medieval menageries were sites of worship and power-display, whereas the main purposes of the modern zoological garden are research, education, and entertainment. In the modern era, the process of rationalization has taken away the spell animals once had. In earlier times they entered the imagination as magic beings, messengers with supernatural powers. In the zoological garden any children would understand that they were the masters of the universe.

From their very beginning, zoological gardens, or zoos, have been considered to have a special appeal for children. Jim McElhom.

By the nineteenth century animals had become objectified as meat, fur, or exotic spectacles. However, animals maintained traces of their traditional significance as humanity's partner in nature as PETS, and the brutal expansion of civilization's dominance over nature was accompanied by a growing sentimentalism. Animals became "worthy" of human feelings; the loyalty of dogs became a popular motive in the arts. A market for pets came about, and the growing distaste for cruelty against animals led to legal measures against such behavior.

Zoos also promoted a more tender view of animals. One famous animal attraction was Jumbo the elephant. He was captured in the African jungle in 1861, sold to a Paris zoo and after that to the London Zoo, where he was given the name Jumbo after an African word for elephant. In 1881 the London Zoo decided to sell Jumbo to the American showman P. T. Barnum, and this caused a Jumbo-mania on both sides of the Atlantic. Jumbo's keeper in the London Zoo declared: "He has been engaged in carrying around the children of the human family almost daily for twenty years."

If animals were treated as a kind of human beings, it was only natural that they should live like human beings. In the nineteenth century zoos excelled in exotic architecture for

animals: Indian pagodas for the elephants, Moorish temples for the monkeys, Gothic towers for the owls. This environment offered entertaining information on the geographical origin of the animals, and it also witnessed the new fraternity between man and beast. The publication of Charles Darwin's *On the Origins of Species* in 1859 only enhanced such sentiments.

The call for a return to nature had been answered by early romantic landscape gardeners who invented the sunken, and therefore invisible, fence called the "ha-ha." The "ha-ha" made possible the revolutionary innovations in zoo design patented by the great German zoo director Carl Hagenbeck. In 1907, near Hamburg, he opened a zoo where the bars between man and beast were replaced by concealed moats, and where the animal houses were replaced by theatrical scenery. These "panoramas" with animals roaming "freely" in African or Arctic landscapes paved the way for later efforts to show the animals in their natural surroundings.

The tendency to remove the barriers between nature and culture had a great impact on efforts to make the zoo relate to children. Three strategies were adopted: the farm strategy where children could look at and play with cows, pigs, goats, and the like; the fairy tale strategy where the children could identify with fairy tales about animals behaving like man (or kids); and the pedagogical strategy which attempted to make it possible for children to experience the world from the perspective of different animals.

The farm strategy was introduced by the Philadelphia Zoo, which in 1938 was the first zoo to introduce a petting zoo for children, with small cages built like farm stables, where children could see and sometimes play with ducks, pigs, calves, turtles, mice and even baby lions.

The fairy tale strategy has been used by a number of zoos. In 1958 the San Francisco Zoo opened Storyland with twenty-six animated action and audio sets in two and three dimensions depicting scenes from Little Red Riding Hood, Snow White, and other fairy tales and nursery rhymes. This was the first "fairy tale" zoo. In Catskill Game Farm Inc., New York, the children's zoo was built as a kindergarten with fairy tale houses where the young animals could live with their mothers.

Pedagogical considerations have been a part of the zoo history since its beginning. The farm strategy may be considered a pedagogical method offering urban children an opportunity to see cows, goats, horses, and other animals. When the Children's Zoo of London Zoo was founded in 1938, the idea was to give urban children a chance to come into close contact with young and domesticated animals. A more explicit pedagogical strategy could be found in San Diego Zoological Garden. Here education was the aim of the children's zoo, and it even had its own school with teachers, several school buses, and other similar features. An extreme version of the efforts to make children understand the world of animals may be found in zoos where children can romp on giant spider webs or crawl through a meerkat tunnel (such as at the San Francisco Zoo), spend a night in an animal house (the Lincoln Park Zoo), or see the world through the eyes of a prairie dog by peering through a fiberglass prairie dog burrow (the Bronx Zoo).

In the first zoos bars made the difference between children and animals visible, and the zoo experience was primarily one of wonder, fear, and pride of man's dominance over nature. In the modern zoo the bars have been removed or concealed, thus stressing the connections between all living things and emphasizing education and identification. Now most zoos offer schools an extension of their classrooms and define their mission as that of fostering curiosity, empathy, and learning about animals in order to stimulate a sense of responsibility for the natural environment.

See also: **Vacations.**

BIBLIOGRAPHY

Baratay, Éric, and Élisabeth Hardouin-Fugier. 1998. *Zoos. Histoire des jardins zoologiques en Occident (XVIe–XXe siècle).* Paris: Éditions La Dècouverte.

Kirchshofer, Rosl, ed. 1966. *Zoologische Gärten der Welt. Die Welt des Zoo.* Frankfurt am Main: Umschau Verlag.

MARTIN ZERLANG

Zoot Suit Riots

The "zoot suit riots" occurred in Los Angeles, California, between June 3 and June 10, 1943, and were the largest upheavals in that city's history up to that time. During the riots American soldiers, sailors, and civilians stationed around Los Angeles attacked Mexican-American boys and young men. Attackers roamed the streets and entered bars, theaters, and restaurants in search of victims wearing distinctive zoot suits (very baggy pants and oversized, almost knee-length coats with wide lapels and heavy shoulder pads), and when they found them, beat them and tore off their suits. By the end of the riots, the servicemen were assaulting Mexican-American youths between their teens and early twenties indiscriminately, whether or not they wore zoot suits. The Los Angeles Police Department (LAPD) did little to stop the upheaval, instead arresting over six hundred Mexican-American youths during the riots. The riots subsided only after the U.S. War Department declared the city off-limits to military personnel.

The zoot suit riots resulted from intense bias against the growing Mexican-American community, exacerbated by anxieties generated by World War II. Sensationalized press coverage of alleged crimes by Mexican-American TEEN-AGERS helped generate public hysteria over a perceived crime wave. The LAPD also contributed to ethnic tensions by both blaming Mexican Americans for the apparent outbreak of crime and mistreating Mexican-American youth. During the war years, the LAPD routinely pulled over cars driven by Mexican Americans to conduct "field interrogations." In 1942 they began making mass arrests, blockading streets in the barrios and detaining teenagers and young adults on vague charges, such as vagrancy or unlawful assembly.

The precipitating cause of the riots was the placement of a Navy training facility in a Mexican-American neighborhood. As thousands of military personnel came and went from the facility, they inevitably transgressed the mores of the surrounding immigrant communities. Local men and boys responded to perceived disrespect and violations of neighborhood standards by physically challenging and verbally threatening the servicemen. While no specific incident sparking the riots is known, these confrontations between military personnel and civilian youth accelerated in the wartime crisis atmosphere of the spring of 1943. In early June, sailors who had apparently been accosted by Mexican-American youths decided to search for zoot suiters, initiating the ensuing violence.

For Mexican-American youth, wearing zoot suits could highlight their resistance to a discriminatory culture. Jazz musicians such as Cab Calloway had popularized the fashion among African-American hipsters in East Coast cities in the early 1940s before West Coast youth adopted it. During the war years, when Americans prized the neat look of service-men and were urged to conserve cloth, the outlandish zoot suits rejected conventional values. For Mexican-American youth, wearing zoot suits and indulging in the associated wild life of dancing and drinking helped to construct their own subculture and rejected assimilation into mainstream America. At the same time, white Los Angeles identified zoot suits as signs of inherent criminality.

See also: **Fashion; Youth Culture.**

BIBLIOGRAPHY

Escobar, Edward J. 1999. *Race, Police, and the Making of a Political Identity: Mexican Americans and the Los Angeles Police Department, 1900–1945.* Berkeley: University of California Press.

Mazon, Mauricio. 1984. *The Zoot-Suit Riots: The Psychology of Symbolic Annihilation.* Austin: University of Texas Press.

McWilliams, Carey. 1948. *North from Mexico: The Spanish-Speaking People of the United States.* Philadelphia: J. B. Lippincott.

Pagan, Eduardo Obregon. 2000. "Los Angeles Geopolitics and the Zoot Suit Riots, 1943." *Social Science History* 24: 223–256.

DAVID WOLCOTT

Primary Sources

Primary Sources

Table of Contents

Advice through Sermons and Letters

A Letter from Theodore Roosevelt to His Son Ted, Advice and News, 1901

SOURCE: Roosevelt, Theodore. 1919. *Theodore Roosevelt's Letters to His Children*. New York: Charles Scribner's Sons.

Introduction

President Theodore Roosevelt (1858–1919) wrote prolifically throughout his lifetime, publishing books on nature, history, hunting, American politics, the family, and society. In the year of his death, a collection of his letters to his children was published, offering American readers insight into the personal life of this famous father to six children. In the following excerpt, Roosevelt advises his son Ted on his performance at school, and offers him glimpses into life at home. The letter reveals both the purposeful effort that Roosevelt put into shaping his son's character and his simple pleasure in his children's antics. To Roosevelt, children were both a joy and a heavy responsibility.

Oyster Bay, May 7th, 1901

BLESSED TED:

It was the greatest fun seeing you, and I really had a satisfactory time with you, and came away feeling that you were doing well. I am entirely satisfied with your standing, both in your studies and in athletics. I want you to do well in your sports, and I want even more to have you do well with your books; but I do not expect you to stand first in either, if so to stand could cause you overwork and hurt your health. I always believe in going hard at everything, whether it is Latin or mathematics, boxing or football, but at the same time I want to keep the sense of proportion. It is never worth while to absolutely exhaust one's self or to take big chances unless for an adequate object. I want you to keep in training the faculties which would make you, if the need arose, able to put your last ounce of pluck and strength into a contest. But I do not want you to squander these qualities. To have you play football as well as you do, and make a good name in boxing and wrestling, and be cox of your second crew, and stand second or third in your class in the studies, is all right.

I should be rather sorry to see you drop too near the middle of your class, because, as you cannot enter college until you are nineteen, and will therefore be a year later in entering life, I want you to be prepared in the best possible way, so as to make up for the delay. But I know that all you can do you will do to keep substantially the position in the class that you have so far kept, and I have entire trust in you, for you have always deserved it.

The weather has been lovely here. The cherry trees are in full bloom, the peach trees just opening, while the apples will not be out for ten days. The May flowers and bloodroot have gone, the anemonies and bellwort have come and the violets are coming. All the birds are here, pretty much, and the warblers troop through the woods.

To my delight, yesterday Kermit, when I tried him on Diamond, did excellently. He has evidently turned the corner in his riding, and was just as much at home as possible, although he was on my saddle with his feet thrust in the leathers above the stirrup. Poor mother has had a hard time with Yagenka, for she rubbed her back, and as she sadly needs exercise and I could not have a saddle put upon her, I took her out bareback yesterday. Her gaits are so easy that it is really more comfortable to ride her without a saddle than to ride Texas with one, and I gave her three miles sharp cantering and trotting.

Dewey Jr. is a very cunning white guinea pig. I wish you could see Kermit taking out Dewey Sr. and Bob Evans to spend the day on the grass. Archie is the sweetest little fellow imaginable. He is always thinking of you. He has now struck up a great friendship with Nicholas, rather to Mame's (the nurse's) regret, as Mame would like to keep him purely for Quentin. The last-named small boisterous person was in fearful disgrace this morning, having flung a block at his mother's head. It was done in sheer playfulness, but of course could not be passed over lightly, and after the enormity of the crime had been brought fully home to him, he fled with howls of anguish to me and lay in an abandon of yellow-headed grief in my arms. Ethel is earning money for the purchase of the Art Magazine by industriously hoeing up the weeds in the walk. Alice is going to ride Yagenka bareback this afternoon, while I try to teach Ethel on Diamond, after Kermit has had his ride.

Yesterday at dinner we were talking of how badly poor Mrs. Blank looked, and Kermit suddenly observed in an aside to Ethel, entirely unconscious that we were listening: "Oh, Effel, I'll tell you what Mrs. Blank looks like: Like Davis' hen dat died—you know, de one dat couldn't hop up on de perch." Naturally, this is purely a private anecdote.

Excerpt from *Christian Nurture* by Horace Bushnell, 1847

SOURCE: Bushnell, Horace. 1847. *Christian Nurture.* New York: Scribner, Armstrong and Co.

Introduction

In the nineteenth century ministers, not doctors, were seen as the experts in child rearing. The American liberal evangelical minister Horace Bushnell (1802–1876) broke with two centuries of American Christian thought when, in his 1847 book *Christian Nurture,* he refuted the accepted doctrine of infant damnation. The American Protestant tradition, until then, had emphasized the centrality of the conversion experience in Christian faith. Born into a state of sin, man had to receive grace before he was saved. Bushnell rejected this tenet. He argued that children were born innocent and that if they were raised Christian (a responsibility that fell primarily on their mothers), there would never be a need for conversion. Bushnell's program of Christian Nurture represents a larger change in attitudes regarding childhood during the nineteenth century, toward viewing children as innocents and mothers as nurturers.

What then is the true idea of Christian or divine nurture, as distinguished from that which is not Christian? What is its aim? What its method of working? What its powers and instruments? What its contemplated results? Few questions have greater moment; and it is one of the pleasant signs of the times, that the subject involved is beginning to attract new interest, and excite a spirit of inquiry which heretofore has not prevailed in our churches.

In ordinary cases, the better and more instructive way of handling this subject, would be to go directly into the practical methods of parental discipline, and show by what modes of government and instruction we may hope to realize the best results. But unhappily the public mind is preoccupied extensively by a view of the whole subject, which I must regard as a theoretical mistake, and one which will involve, as long as it continues, practical results systematically injurious. This mistaken view it is necessary, if possible, to remove. And accordingly what I have to say will take the form of an argument on the question thus put in issue; though I design to gather round the subject, as I proceed, as much of practical instruction as the mode of the argument will suffer. Assuming then the question above stated, What is the true idea of Christian education?—I answer in the following proposition, which it will be the aim of my argument to establish,

viz:

That the child is to grow up a Christian, and never know himself as being otherwise.

In other words, the aim, effort, and expectation should be, not, as is commonly assumed, that the child is to grow up in sin, to be converted after he comes to a mature age; but that he is to open on the world as one that is spiritually renewed, not remembering the time when he went through a technical experience, but seeming rather to have loved what is good from his earliest years. I do not affirm that every child may, in fact and without exception, be so trained that he certainly will grow up a Christian. The qualifications it may be necessary to add will be given in another place, where they can be stated more intelligibly.

This doctrine is not a novelty, now rashly and for the first time propounded, as some of you may be tempted to suppose. I shall show you, before I have done with the argument, that it is as old as the Christian church, and prevails extensively at the present day in other parts of the world. Neither let your own experience raise a prejudice against it. If you have endeavored to realize the very truth I here affirm, but find that your children do not exhibit the character you have looked for; if they seem to be intractable to religious influences, and sometimes to display an apparent aversion to the very subject of religion itself, you are not of course to conclude that the doctrine I here maintain is untrue or impracticable. You may be unreasonable in your expectations of your children.

Possibly, there may be seeds of holy principle in them, which you do not discover. A child acts out his present feelings, the feelings of the moment, without qualification or disguise. And how, many times, would all you appear, if you were to do the same? Will you expect of them to be better, and more constant and consistent, than yourselves; or will you rather expect them to be children, human children still, living a mixed life, trying out the good and evil of the world, and preparing, as older Christians do, when they have taken a lesson of sorrow and emptiness, to turn again to the true good?

Perhaps they will go through a rough mental struggle, at some future day, and seem, to others and to themselves, there to have entered on a Christian life. And yet it may be true that there was still some root of right principle established in their childhood, which is here only quickened and developed, as when Christians of a mature age are revived in their piety, after a period of spiritual lethargy; for it is conceivable that regenerate character may exist, long before it is fully and formally developed.

But suppose there is really no trace or seed of holy principle in your children, has there been no fault of piety and constancy in your church? no want of Christian sensibility and love to God? no carnal spirit visible to them and to all, and imparting its noxious and poisonous quality to the Christian atmosphere in which they have had their nurture? For it is not for you alone to realize all that is included in the idea of Christian education. It belongs to the church of God, according to the degree of its social power over you and in you and around your children, to bear a part of the responsibility with you.

A Letter from Rufus W. Bailey to His Daughters at School, 1857

SOURCE: Bailey, Rufus William. 1857. *Daughters at School Instructed in a Series of Letters.* Philadelphia, PA: Presbyterian Board of Publication.

Introduction

Published collections of letters from parents to children were a very popular form of advice literature during the eighteenth and nineteenth centuries. Lord Chesterfield's letters to his illegitimate son, first published in the 1770s, defined the genre and attracted many readers in Europe and America. While Chesterfield's letters were concerned with the social graces required to succeed in aristocratic society, many of his imitators geared their advice to less elevated social spheres. In a series of letters to his daughters published in 1857, the American Presbyterian minister and educator Rufus W. Bailey (1793–1863) gave instruction on how to meet the challenges of ordinary life by practicing the American virtues of pragmatism, temperance, honesty, and independence. In the letter excerpted below, Bailey addresses behaviors that were perceived at the time as typically female—for example, his injunction not to gossip—but the basic values he promotes were prescribed to both men and women of the middle class in nineteenth-century America.

LETTER XL.

PRACTICAL ADVICE.

MY DEAR CHILDREN,— AS you are advancing to maturity, and now begin to mingle with mixed society, allow me to throw into a narrow compass some practical rules and maxims which you may find of great use, and the importance of which you will begin immediately to feel.

In the first place, I will say then, endeavour always to look at things as they are. Avoid visionary views. You will always have to do with the realities of life. All, therefore, which magnifies or diminishes things beyond reality, unfits the mind for safe and efficient action. Avoid, therefore, all prejudice, passion, strong party feeling, personal hatred, a spirit of envy, malice, or revenge, which always unfit the mind to judge soberly and truly. Every unnatural excitement produces this effect, and this may not only come of intemperance, but from any one of the sources just enumerated. In a state of excitement, things are made to appear different from what they really are, and if, under the illusion, you are not urged on to high crimes, you may do some indiscreet act, which will embitter life, and require to be repented of.

Never permit yourselves to be out of humour, especially with a dumb animal, or inanimate object. The brute acts from impulse or instinct, and when you act from passion, you put yourself on a level with him. Consider, too, that when you permit yourselves to be displeased with an inanimate object, you take a still bolder stand to act a more depraved part. You fight against Providence. Did you ever figure to yourselves Xerxes chastising the waves of the Hellespont? I have sometimes wondered that scene has never, among other objects, employed the pencil of the painter. How pigmy-like Xerxes would appear in the picture, giving, with feeble voice, command to the elements, amid the roar of the angry Bosphorus, lashing the shore and rolling its surges mountain high! How puny his uplifted arm applying the whip to chastise their insolence! How contemptible, throwing the chains, which are immediately swallowed up by the element that bids defiance to his threats and rage! Then to see him contending with the Almighty who rides on the whirlwind, and directs the storm, daring heaven to single combat! It is a subject which language imperfectly reaches, but I think it might be put upon canvass, and made to speak expressively. Now what Xerxes was, in his rage against the sea, you may consider a young lady to be, on a smaller scale, when she loses her temper, or frets against Providence.

Realities are what we have to meet. To know them is truth. To perform our duties under the government of God in every relation to that truth is religion. Avoid high wrought and extravagant feelings on every subject, even on religious subjects, except as truth leads the way, and that will ever make you sober, deliberate, concerned with things as they are.

Speak always with candour and consideration. Indiscreet speech makes more work for repentance, with most persons, than overt and flagrant acts of error. It creates more wars than all other causes. It originates, probably, nine-tenths of all the personal conflicts which occur. I have sometimes thought that if I could regulate my speech to exact propriety, I could easily regulate every other part of conduct. It is very easy to say a thing. But once said, it can never be recalled, and we usually feel that it must be maintained. Most persons talk too much. How rare a virtue is silence! Still more rare, the man or woman who never speaks inopportunely, and always speaks what ought to be spoken. You know how it is in experience. "Miss B said so," and that starts the ball. Lazy as many may be in ordinary duties, here is all activity. There are enough volunteers to keep it in motion. It flies with accelerated velocity. And like a stone which the delicate touch of a single hand started from the top of a mountain, it soon acquires a force which no human power can resist. It bears down all in its way, and spreads desolation in its track. Be careful how you start these stones. While on the poise, they are in your power. Once moved, they soon become beyond control. So are words—little words. So may be a touch, a gentle touch, a pointing of the finger, or a cast of the eye. Such is the tongue among our members; such is our conversation in society. If you learn to govern the tongue, and regulate your speech, you gain a victory, and may avoid many conflicts.

Be especially careful not to report in one family what you have heard said in another; nor to one friend what may have been imprudently whispered to her disadvantage, except when truth and vital interests demand it. The tale bearer and informer is a mischief-maker, and although he may be listened to with earnestness, he cannot but be despised. In your social relations, avoid a suspicious temper; yet presume on the friendship of no one. Be always ready to grant all the favours you can, consistently with your duties to yourselves and others; but never do favours on the supposition that others are equally ready to reciprocate them. If you commence otherwise, you will be painfully taught that a warm heart bestows its charities on a cold world.

Be not too confiding. There is one inference which has done much injury. Because a man is regarded as a good man, it is therefore presumed that he will always do what is right. Let your own view of what is right be always higher authority than that of any mortal, whose opinion conflicts with your principles.

If a particular friend offers you special favours, use them not too liberally. If he puts a favourite article at your disposal, the strength of his friendship may prove to be weak should you practise too freely on his indulgence. When a friend that you wish to retain offers special favours, it is well for you if you are not obliged to use them.

Be indulgent toward the faults of others, severe towards your own. We are often impatient of the infirmities of others, forgetting that what in them offends us, may pertain, in a great degree, to ourselves. The same weak, and offensive, and erring natures pertain to all, and we are frail, feeble and offensive to others, wherein we often congratulate or excuse ourselves.

A Letter from Jeanette Hulme Platt to Samuel C. Damon, 1861

SOURCE: Platt, Cyrus. 1882. *Life and Letters of Mrs. Jeanette H. Platt*. Philadelphia, PA: E. Claxton and Co.

Introduction

This personal letter from a married woman to an old friend eloquently captures a portrait of family life in mid-nineteenth-century America. Jeanette Hulme Platt (1816–1877) describes her hopes and aspirations for each of her six children and offers reflections on her own passage from light-hearted youth to mature adulthood. Platt includes her beloved aunt, who shares their home, in her letter, thus completing the vision of multigenerational domestic harmony. Her letter also suggests the central role that religion played in nineteenth-century domesticity. Platt's most important maternal responsibility is to guide her children along the path to salvation. This letter is collected along with many more in the 1882 volume *Life and Letters of Mrs. Jeanette H. Platt*.

Delaware, Ohio, January 14, 1861

Rev. S. C. Damon [Honolulu.]

My Dear Old Friend:—"There is a Providence that shapes our ends." Does not the same guide the pen?—prompt it? Or why should I write to you to-day? My heart is not a bit warmer, truer, or more full of interest for you and yours, than it has been these twenty-two years. The desire and intention to write is no stronger than for five years, since when your last has been looking me in the face every time my portfolio opened. Here are the "second causes." Delaware, Ohio, a half-country, half-village home; dinner time; a pattering rain, with January sleet, all over the lawn and old oak trees; a bright wood fire in the little back bedroom—aunty's room. A dear old aunt in the great rocking-chair, with knitting and newspaper on the stand at her elbow. A plate, with knife and half-pared great apple, is brought in from the dinner-table by a little "mother," who fills the small rocking-chair, coaxing "father" to sit down and eat his apple, too. "No, must get back to business."

The door closes, and the apple-paring goes on for one minute; put down to open the door for a three-year old curly head, leading in baby F——, fourteen months old to-day. The latter, after pulling about the tongs, and trying to get the shovel, was sent off to the dining-room to get dinner with his nurse, Mary. The former, never still, climbed up into the rocking-chair, and made piano of mother's back. Then the apple was finished, divided, and handed round with the remark, "Only think, Aunt Clara, that young lady I met the other evening, just from Connecticut, never heard of Holden, Mass., or Oxford! I was hunting up something to say to the Quaker stranger, and spoke of dear old friends coming from these places. Martha's old school friend, Celia Campbell, came from Oxford, and my Honolulu friend, Mr. Damon, from Holden. Do you know anything about Holden? Why, I have a book on the shelves that will tell about it! Jump down, H——; let me get it,—'History of Holden.' 'Jeanette and Martha, with the author's kind regards, 1841.' You must see the letter he wrote me, June 24, 1846, so very kind and brotherly. It is in my portfolio. I have been *always* going to answer it." With moistened eyes the letter was read, and then the pen came on this sheet, and would turn words to say, "Just as warm and true is the regard (why not say affection?) 'Jeanette' retains for her friend, 'S. C. D.,' this day, as when they rambled over the lanes and fields of old Burlington, or knelt together in the little Presbyterian prayer-meeting: just the same."

The form, the features, and heart of my old friend are before me, fresh as in daily intercourse. It seems as if he could step in this very afternoon and take that vacant chair. How pleased and interested in this old aunt he would be, to hear her say, as she did to me just now, "Tell him I am just as much interested in his Holden history as if I was a Massachusetts woman." Ah, there are hearts that never grow old! and this aunty is one of them. Old age is beautiful in her. In the hushed evening hour He spares her to us to show us how full of comfort and support He can make life's close, when from the days of youth the Creator has been remembered. (Here she comes to my table, looking for a pencil to make some extracts from your book.) Twenty years taken down, dusted, and put back, has this little book passed through my hands, scarcely opened; now it comes fresh with interest, almost hallowed with never-dying associations of the past. Yes, never-dying! My precious sister! it seems but yesterday that we three were together.

You want to take a peep at my children? I wish you could after they are all asleep for the night; that is the time I most enjoy looking at them. Come up into the boys' room, and see if they are not two fine-looking fellows. No need to step lightly; school all day, with skating and sliding, and home chores, give sound slumber. Is not that shaggy head big enough for a Webster? Sound-looking enough for a President? I hope not. Their mother's only prayerful wish is, that God will accept her boys; call and fit them for ambassadors for Christ. This is quiet, thoughtful H. See mirthful, laughter-loving F.! His face is hardly at rest even when asleep; arm over his brother's neck, promptings of a heart full of affection. His hair is soft and light, with blue eyes. H—— has soft, brown eyes,—the gentle expression, some think, of his Aunt Martha. His hair is as brown as his mother's *used* to be.

But come across the hall and see our girls. Take them to your heart as your own, too, if God has not lent you any. E., my eldest, first born! words can never tell how dear is this child to me. I have from the first hour of taking her to my bosom tried to hold her lightly, as loaned a little while only to be trained for the Master's service, here or there, as He will. Should her life be prolonged you may have her as a fellow-worker for Christ in the Sandwich Islands. Shall she be educated for a teacher? or what post will you assign her? I could not let her go to any other foreign field without much grace being given; but your Islands have seemed very near and very inviting ever since you made home there. And the little fingers have traced out their bearings ever since the geography came into her hands. "O mother, do write that letter to your friend Mr. Damon!" she has said a thousand times.

This little sister by her side, J. we call her, but she has not a bit of mother about her; very beautiful as a baby, but now baby loveliness has given place to a strong-willed, determined, quiet, self-reliant look. "Our oaken twig," I often call her, and wonder what are the storms and tempests that little heart is to brave. With religious principle she will be fully able to bear all that the providence of God lays upon her. Will you have her, too?

But here in the nursery come. Here is your old friend herself, with curly head, nestled among the pillows—I cannot describe *her*. In her I see myself as others see me. God sparing her life there will be another Jeanette Hulme. Will you like her?

And now the *crib*. Ah, this is the child among them all! Months of ill health and tedious confinement to the house and couch preceded the birth of this precious baby boy. His mother looks upon him as coming for some special mercy and comfort, and regards him as all the Lord's. I wish you could see him—see us all! Now, my children are just like all other children, doubtless, only in their mothers' eyes. Remember this, and when you come to see them don't expect too much. You know well just what an impulsive, undisciplined mother they have.

Twenty-two years!—the changes, "sundry and manifold changes of the world," as one of our collects beautifully says—what record shall this page bear? "Whoso offereth thanks he honoreth me;" with thanksgiving must begin and end all my testimony of "all the way which the Lord God hath led me these forty years," to humble and prove me. Ah, dear friend, I am the same; I have only all this time been learning more and more of His long-suffering patience. Oh, the power, the fulness, the preciousness of a Saviour's love! The thirteen years of married life have been full of blessings, though chequered with care and disappointment in regard to outward prosperity. My husband is not rich; a golden portion is not to be our lot, I often assure him. But that does not belong to *happiness*. Discipline, trial, must come in some form; and want of riches is the very least ill earth can know.

What of the outward changes in your old friend Jeanette? She often gives a look, not a sigh, saying, "This is Mrs. Platt, I suppose." Jeanette Hulme has gone, I told you; you may find her hereafter in her daughter H. I do not know that the mother is *sobered* a whit; and if the eye is dimmed, so that I hear talk of "spectacles coming," not a sunbeam can stray into her apartment, or flower open at her feet with tint unseen or unfelt. The chestnut curls are gone, turned into thin bands that are marbled over with silver threads. Never mind; in half an hour's time you would get used to all changes, and have just as pleasant times with her as twenty-two years ago. Come, try it. Is it not time to visit the States again? Does not friend Julia want to see her friend again? Is it not time to bring the boys for school to prepare for college? Their college is in Ohio, Gambier, Knox County, good for sound learning, better for healthy moral influences, best for the quickening graces of the Holy Spirit that year after year are showered upon that institution. There is a good grammar school connected with it. May I not have your boys to go to school, and spend vacations with me? I will make them Episcopalians? Certainly. Their father ought to have been one.(?) I have learned to value our church more and more, year by year; not others less, but her more. What has become of your prayer-book? Don't you want a new one? Is the "Daily Food" worn out? Mine is now open before me, the daily companion since childhood. This little collection from the "exceeding great and precious promises," how enriched and hallowed by associations of the past! What helpers in time of need! The Psalms for the day, as appointed in the prayer-book, have made my daily Bible reading now for the last few years. Meet me here with fervent prayer for each other's soul's welfare, and for the families committed to our care.

I say nothing on the state of our beloved country, so torn with dissensions; the newspapers can better show you this. God reigneth. I am, though no longer a Quaker, nor a "peace" woman, yet for peace, and tell my husband we will run away to Canada or the Sandwich Islands.

But I must stop; my pen has run freely as if you were at my side. Can you read these outpourings of an old friend's heart?

Excerpt from *Gentle Measures in the Management and Training of the Young* by Jacob Abbott, 1871

SOURCE: Abbott, Jacob. 1871. *Gentle Measures in the Management and Training of the Young.* New York: Harper and Brothers.

Introduction

> In *Gentle Measures in the Management and Training of the Young* (1871), Jacob Abbott instructs parents how to manage their children with love and discipline. Abbott (1803–1879) was a Congregational clergyman and well-known author of children's books. His Rollo series, beginning with *The Little Scholar Learning to Talk* (1834), featured a young boy named Rollo who learned moral lessons with the guidance of love and discipline. Abbott's emphasis on gentleness distinguished him from earlier religious authorities, who instructed parents to break their children's wills. Abbott did not endorse the orthodox doctrine of infant depravity, but thought that children were morally neutral. He discouraged frequent or harsh punishment. Yet Abbott's child-rearing advice is far stricter than the permissive attitudes common in the late twentieth and early twenty-first centuries. He always maintained the

primacy of authority and obedience in the parent-child relationship.

CHAPTER I.

THE THREE MODES OF MANAGEMENT.

IT is not impossible that in the minds of some persons the idea of employing gentle measures in the management and training of children may seem to imply the abandonment of the principle of authority, as the basis of the parental government, and the substitution of some weak and inefficient system of artifice and manoeuvring in its place. To suppose that the object of this work is to aid in effecting such a substitution as that, is entirely to mistake its nature and design. The only government of the parent over the child that is worthy of the name is one of authority complete, absolute, unquestioned authority. The object of this work is, accordingly, not to show how the gentle methods which will be brought to view can be employed as a substitute for such authority, but how they can be made to aid in establishing and maintaining it.

Three Methods.

There are three different modes of management customarily employed by parents as means of inducing their children to comply with their requirements. They are,

1. Government by Manoeuvring and Artifice.
2. By Reason and Affection.
3. By Authority.

Manoeuvring and Artifice. 1. Many mothers manage their children by means of tricks and contrivances, more or less adroit, designed to avoid direct issues with them, and to beguile them, as it were, into compliance with their wishes. As, for example, where a mother, recovering from sickness, is going out to take the air with her husband for the first time, and—as she is still feeble—wishes for a very quiet drive, and so concludes not to take little Mary with her, as she usually does on such occasions; but knowing that if Mary sees the chaise at the door, and discovers that her father and mother are going in it, she will be very eager to go too, she adopts a system of maneuvres to conceal her design. She brings down her bonnet and shawl by stealth, and before the chaise comes to the door she sends Mary out into the garden with her sister, under pretense of showing her a bird's nest which is not there, trusting to her sister's skill in diverting the child's mind, and amusing her with something else in the garden, until the chaise has gone. And if, either from hearing the sound of the wheels, or from any other cause, Mary's suspicions are awakened—and children habitually managed on these principles soon learn to be extremely distrustful and suspicious—and she insists on going into the house, and thus discovers the stratagem, then, perhaps, her mother tells her that they are only going to the doctor's, and that if Mary goes with them, the doctor will give her some dreadful medicine, and compel her to take it, thinking thus to deter her from insisting on going with them to ride.

As the chaise drives away, Mary stands bewildered and perplexed on the door-step, her mind in a tumult of excitement, in which hatred of the doctor, distrust and suspicion of her mother, disappointment, vexation, and ill humor, surge and swell among those delicate organizations on which the structure and development of the soul so closely depend—doing perhaps an irreparable injury. The mother, as soon as the chaise is so far turned that Mary can no longer watch the expression of her countenance, goes away from the door with a smile of complacency and satisfaction upon her face at the ingenuity and success of her little artifice.

In respect to her statement that she was going to the doctor's, it may, or may not, have been true. Most likely not; for mothers who manage their children on this system find the line of demarkation between deceit and falsehood so vague and ill defined that they soon fall into the habit of disregarding it altogether, and of saying, without hesitation, any thing which will serve the purpose in view.

Governing by Reason and Affection.

2. The theory of many mothers is that they must govern their children by the influence of reason and affection. Their method may be exemplified by supposing that, under circumstances similar to those described under the preceding head, the mother calls Mary to her side, and, smoothing her hair caressingly with her hand while she speaks, says to her,

"Mary, your father and I are going out to ride this afternoon, and I am going to explain it all to you why you can not go too. You see, I have been sick, and am getting well, and I am going out to ride, so that I may get well faster. You love mamma, I am sure, and wish to have her get well soon. So you will be a good girl, I know, and not make any trouble, but will stay at home contentedly won't you? Then I shall love you, and your papa will love you, and after I get well we will take you to ride with us some day."

The mother, in managing the case in this way, relies partly on convincing the reason of the child, and partly on an appeal to her affection.

Governing by Authority.

3. By the third method the mother secures the compliance of the child by a direct exercise of authority. She says to her—the circumstances of the case being still supposed to be the same—

"Mary, your father and I are going out to ride this afternoon, and I am sorry, for your sake, that we can not take you with us."

"Why can't you take me?" asks Mary.

"I can not tell you why, now," replies the mother, "but perhaps I will explain it to you after I come home. I think there is a good reason, and, at any rate, I have decided that you are not to go. If you are a good girl, and do not make any difficulty, you can have your little chair out upon the front door-step, and can see the chaise come to the door, and see your father and me get in and drive away; and you can wave your handkerchief to us for a good-bye."

Then, if she observes any expression of discontent or insubmission in Mary's countenance, the mother would add,

"If you should not be a good girl, but should show signs of making us any trouble, I shall have to send you out somewhere to the back part of the house until we are gone."

But this last supposition is almost always unnecessary; for if Mary has been habitually managed on this principle she will not make any trouble. She will perceive at once that the question is settled—settled irrevocably—and especially that it is entirely beyond the power of any demonstrations of insubmission or rebellion that she can make to change it. She will acquiesce at once. She may be sorry that she can not go, but she will make no resistance. Those children only attempt to carry their points by noisy and violent demonstrations who find, by experience, that such measures are usually successful. A child, even, who has become once accustomed to them, will soon drop them if she finds, owing to a change in the system of management, that they now never succeed. And a child who never, from the beginning, finds any efficiency in them, never learns to employ them at all.

Conclusion.

Of the three methods of managing children exemplified in this chapter, the last is the only one which can be followed either with comfort to the parent or safety to the child; and to show how this method can be brought effectually into operation by gentle measures is the object of this book. It is, indeed, true that the importance of tact and skill in the training of the young, and of cultivating their reason, and securing their affection, can not be overrated. But the influences secured by these means form, at the best, but a sandy foundation for filial obedience to rest upon. The child is not to be made to comply with the requirements of his parents by being artfully inveigled into compliance, nor is his obedience to rest on his love for father and mother, and his unwillingness to displease them, nor on his conviction of the rightfulness and reasonableness of their commands, but on simple submission to authority—that absolute and almost unlimited authority which all parents are commissioned by God and nature to exercise over their offspring during the period while the offspring remain dependent upon their care.

Poetry and Memoir

"Before the Birth of One of Her Children" by Anne Bradstreet, c. 1645

SOURCE: Bradstreet, Anne. 1678. *Several Poems Compiled with Great Variety of Wit and Learning.* Boston: Printed by John Foster.

Introduction

Historically, one of the greatest dangers facing children has been the death of a parent. Before mortality rates declined in the nineteenth century, it was not uncommon for a child to be orphaned before he or she reached adulthood. The death of a father could bring impoverishment to a family; the death of a mother could leave the child without nurturance, and if the father remarried, subject the child to a potentially hostile stepparent. The Puritan poet Anne Bradstreet (1612–1672) expresses these fears for her children in the following poem, probably composed in 1645 while she was nine months pregnant. In its verses she begs her husband to protect their children should she die in labor and not allow them to suffer abuse.

Before the Birth of One of Her Children

All things within this fading world hath end,
Adversity doth still our joys attend;
No ties so strong, no friends so dear and sweet,
But with death's parting blow is sure to meet.
The sentence past is most irrevocable,
A common thing, yet oh, inevitable.
How soon, my Dear, death may my steps attend.
How soon't may be thy lot to lose thy friend,
We both are ignorant, yet love bids me
These farewell lines to recommend to thee,
That when that knot's untied that made us one,
I may seem thine, who in effect am none.
And if I see not half my days that's due,
What nature would, God grant to yours and you;
The many faults that well you know
I have Let be interred in my oblivious grave;
If any worth or virtue were in me,
Let that live freshly in thy memory
And when thou feel'st no grief, as I no harms,
Yet love thy dead, who long lay in thine arms.
And when thy loss shall be repaid with gains
Look to my little babes, my dear remains.
And if thou love thyself, or loved'st me,
These O protect from step-dame's injury.
And if chance to thine eyes shall bring this verse,
With some sad sighs honour my absent hearse;
And kiss this paper for thy love's dear sake,
Who with salt tears this last farewell did take.

Excerpt from *Incidents in the Life of a Slave Girl* by Harriet Jacobs, 1861

SOURCE: Jacobs, Harriet. 1861. *Incidents in the Life of a Slave Girl, Written by Herself.* Ed. L. Maria Child. Boston: Published for the Author.

Introduction

In the opening pages of her memoir, *Incidents in the Life of a Slave Girl* (1861), Harriet Jacobs indelibly renders the slave child's utter vulnerability to the interests of her white masters. As a young girl, Jacobs is lucky and does not experience the brutality of slavery, but her family is powerless to protect her from eventual exploitation. After the death of her mother and then of her first "kind" mistress, Jacobs learns the meaning of her status as chattel. Her welfare has no weight in her owner's decisions concerning her future. In the following chapters, Harriet is sent to live with the cruel Dr. Flint, who torments her with sexual advances while she is still a child. Eventually she flees, spending seven years concealed in a crawlspace above a shed attached to her grandmother's house, before she escapes north.

I.

CHILDHOOD.

I WAS born a slave; but I never knew it till six years of happy childhood had passed away. My father was a carpenter, and considered so intelligent and skilful in his trade, that, when buildings out of the common line were to be erected, he was sent for from long distances, to be head workman. On condition of paying his mistress two hundred dollars a year, and supporting himself, he was allowed to work at his trade, and manage his own affairs. His strongest wish was to purchase his children; but, though he several times offered his hard earnings for that purpose, he never succeeded. In complexion my parents were a light shade of brownish yellow, and were termed mulattoes. They lived together in a comfortable home; and, though we were all slaves, I was so fondly shielded that I never dreamed I was a piece of merchandise, trusted to them for safe keeping, and liable to be demanded of them at any moment. I had one brother, William, who was two years younger than myself—a bright, affectionate child. I had also a great treasure in my maternal grandmother, who was a remarkable woman in many respects. She was the daughter of a planter in South Carolina, who, at his death, left her mother and his three children free, with money to go to St. Augustine, where they had relatives. It was during the Revolutionary War; and they were captured on their passage, carried back, and sold to different purchasers. Such was the story my grandmother used to tell me; but I do not remember all the particulars. She was a little girl when she was captured and sold to the keeper of a large hotel. I have often heard her tell how hard she fared during childhood. But as she grew older she evinced so much intelligence, and was so faithful, that her master and mistress could not help seeing it was for their interest to take care of such a valuable piece of property. She became an indispensable personage in the household, officiating in all capacities, from cook and wet nurse to seamstress. She was much praised for her cooking; and her nice crackers became so famous in the neighborhood that many people were desirous of obtaining them. In consequence of numerous requests of this kind, she asked permission of her mistress to bake crackers at night, after all the household work was done; and she obtained leave to do it, provided she would clothe herself and her children from the profits. Upon these terms, after working hard all day for her mistress, she began her midnight bakings, assisted by her two oldest children. The business proved profitable; and each year she laid by a little, which was saved for a fund to purchase her children. Her master died, and the property was divided among his heirs. The widow had her dower in the hotel, which she continued to keep open. My grandmother remained in her service as a slave; but her children were divided among her master's children. As she had five, Benjamin, the youngest one, was sold, in order that each heir might have an equal portion of dollars and cents. There was so little difference in our ages that he seemed more like my brother than my uncle. He was a bright, handsome lad, nearly white; for he inherited the complexion my grandmother had derived from Anglo-Saxon ancestors. Though only ten years old, seven hundred and twenty dollars were paid for him. His sale was a terrible blow to my grandmother; but she was naturally hopeful, and she went to work with renewed energy, trusting in time to be able to purchase some of her children. She had laid up three hundred dollars, which her mistress one day begged as a loan, promising to pay her soon. The reader probably knows that no promise or writing given to a slave is legally binding; for, according to Southern laws, a slave, *being* property, can *hold* no property. When my grandmother lent her hard earnings to her mistress, she trusted solely to her honor. The honor of a slaveholder to a slave!

To this good grandmother I was indebted for many comforts. My brother Willie and I often received portions of the crackers, cakes, and preserves, she made to sell; and after we ceased to be children we were indebted to her for many more important services.

Such were the unusually fortunate circumstances of my early childhood. When I was six years old, my mother died; and then, for the first time, I learned, by the talk around me, that I was a slave. My mother's mistress was the daughter of my grandmother's mistress. She was the foster sister of my mother; they were both nourished at my grandmother's breast. In fact, my mother had been weaned at three months old, that the babe of the mistress might obtain sufficient food. They played together as children; and, when they became women, my mother was a most faithful servant to her whiter foster sister. On her death-bed her mistress promised that her children should never suffer for any thing; and during her lifetime she kept her word. They all spoke kindly of my dead mother, who had been a slave merely in name, but in nature was noble and womanly. I grieved for her, and my young mind was troubled with the thought who would now take care of me and my little brother. I was told that my home was now to be with her mistress; and I found it a happy one. No toilsome or disagreeable duties were imposed upon me. My mistress was so kind to me that I was always glad to do her bidding, and proud to labor for her as much as my young years would permit. I would sit by her side for hours, sewing diligently, with a heart as free from care as that of any free-born white child. When she thought I was tired, she would send me out to run and jump; and away I bounded, to gather berries or flowers to decorate her room. Those were happy days—too happy to last. The slave child had no thought for the morrow; but there came that blight, which too surely waits on every human being born to be a chattel.

When I was nearly twelve years old, my kind mistress sickened and died. As I saw the cheek grow paler, and the eye more glassy, how earnestly I prayed in my heart that she might live! I loved her; for she had been almost like a mother to me. My prayers were not answered. She died, and they buried her in the little churchyard, where, day after day, my tears fell upon her grave.

I was sent to spend a week with my grandmother. I was now old enough to begin to think of the future; and again and again I asked myself what they would do with me. I felt sure I should never find another mistress so kind as the one who was gone. She had promised my dying mother that her children should never suffer for any thing; and when I remembered that, and recalled her many proofs of attachment to me, I could not help having some hopes that she had left me free. My friends were almost certain it would be so. They thought she would be sure to do it, on account of my mother's love and faithful service. But, alas! we all know that the memory of a faithful slave does not avail much to save her children from the auction block.

After a brief period of suspense, the will of my mistress was read, and we learned that she had bequeathed me to her sister's daughter, a child of five years old. So vanished our hopes. My mistress had taught me the precepts of God's Word: "Thou shalt love thy neighbor as thyself." "Whatsoever ye would that men should do unto you, do ye even so unto them." But I was her slave, and I suppose she did not recognize me as her neighbor. I would give much to blot out from my memory that one great wrong. As a child, I loved my mistress; and, looking back on the happy days I spent with her, I try to think with less bitterness of this act of injustice. While I was with her, she taught me to read and spell; and for this privilege, which so rarely falls to the lot of a slave, I bless her memory.

She possessed but few slaves; and at her death those were all distributed among her relatives. Five of them were my grandmother's children, and had shared the same milk that nourished her mother's children. Notwithstanding my grandmother's long and faithful service to her owners, not one of her children escaped the auction block. These God-breathing machines are no more, in the sight of their masters, than the cotton they plant, or the horses they tend.

Excerpt from a Letter from William Penn to His Wife and Children, 1682

Source: The American Colonist's Library, a Treasury of Primary Documents. Available from <http://personal.pitnet.net/primarysources/pennletter.html>.

Introduction

William Penn (1644–1718), the founder and proprietor of the colony of Pennsylvania, wrote this letter to his wife and children before he sailed for America in 1682. In the excerpt below, Penn offers his children advice on how to behave in his absence. He acknowledges the possibility that he might not survive the journey and return to England, so he writes in a tone of deep seriousness. As a committed Quaker, Penn's first concern was for his children's salvation. He reminds his children of their duties to obey the Lord and their mother. These stern injunctions are followed by practical rules to live by and finally by affectionate sentiments revealing his great love for the children, and his hope that they will treat each other, and their own children, with equal love. William Penn's letters to his children have been used to support claims that a more affectionate and less authoritarian mode of child rearing emerged within Quaker families during the late seventeenth and eighteenth centuries, presaging broader child-rearing changes within Anglo-American society during the nineteenth century.

And now, my dear children that are the gifts and mercies of the God of your tender father, hear my counsel and lay it up in your hearts. Love it more than treasure and follow it, and you shall be blessed here and happy hereafter.

In the first place, remember your Creator in the days of your youth. It was the glory of Israel in the 2d of Jeremiah: and how did God bless Josiah, because he feared him in his youth! And so He did Jacob, Joseph, and Moses. Oh! my dear children, remember and fear and serve Him who made you, and gave you to me and your dear mother, that you may live to Him and glorify Him in your generations. To do this, in your youthful days seek after the Lord, that you may find Him, remembering His great love in creating you; that you are not beasts, plants, or stones, but that He has kept you and given you His grace within, and substance without, and provided plentifully for you. This remember in your youth, that you may be kept from the evil of the world; for, in age, it will be harder to overcome the temptations of it.

Wherefore, my dear children, eschew the appearance of evil, and love and cleave to that in your hearts that shows you evil from good, and tells you when you do amiss, and reproves you for it. It is the light of Christ, that He has given you for your salvation. If you do this, and follow my counsel, God will bless you in this world and give you an inheritance in that which shall never have an end. For the light of Jesus is of a purifying nature; it seasons those who love it and take heed to it, and never leaves such till it has brought them to the city of God that has foundations. Oh! that ye may be seasoned with the gracious nature of it; hide it in your hearts, and flee, my dear children, from all youthful lusts, the vain sports, pastimes and pleasures of the world, redeeming the time, because the days are evil. You are now beginning to live—what would some give for your time? Oh! I could have lived better, were I as you, in the flower of youth. Therefore, love and fear the Lord, keep close to meetings; and delight to wait upon the Lord God of your father and mother, among his despised people, as we have done. And count it your honor to be members of that society, and heirs of that living fellowship, which is enjoyed among them—for the experience of which your father's soul blesses the Lord forever.

Next, be obedient to your dear mother, a woman whose virtue and good name is an honor to you; for she has been exceeded by none in her time for her plainness, integrity, industry, humanity, virtue, and good understanding, qualities not usual among women of her worldly condition and quality. Therefore, honor and obey her, my dear children, as your mother, and your father's love and delight; nay, love her too, for she loved your father with a deep and upright love, choosing him before all her many suitors. And though she be of a delicate constitution and noble spirit, yet she descended to the utmost tenderness and care for you, performing in painfulness acts of service to you in your infancy, as a mother and a nurse too. I charge you before the Lord, honor and obey, love and cherish, your dear mother.

Next betake yourselves to some honest, industrious course of life; and that not of sordid covetousness, but for example and to avoid idleness. And if you change your condition and marry, choose with the knowledge and consent of your mother, if living, guardians, or those that have the charge of you. Mind neither beauty nor riches, but the fear of the Lord and a sweet and amiable disposition, such as you can love above all this world and that may make your habitations pleasant and desirable to you. And being married, be tender, affectionate, and patient, and meek. Live in the fear of the Lord, and He will bless you and your offspring. Be sure to live within compass; borrow not, neither be beholden to any. Ruin not yourselves by kindness to others, for that exceeds the due bounds of friendship; neither will a true friend expect it. Small matters I heed not.

Let your industry and parsimony go no farther than for a sufficiency for life, and to make a provision for your children (and that in moderation, if the Lord gives you any). I charge you to help the poor and needy. Let the Lord have a voluntary share of your income, for the good of the poor, both in our Society and others; for we are all His creatures, remembering that he that gives to the poor, lends to the Lord. Know well your incomings, and your outgoings may be the better regulated. Love not money, nor the world. Use them only and they will serve you; but if you love them, you serve them, which will debase your spirits as well as offend the Lord. Pity the distressed, and hold out a hand of help to them; it may be your case, and as you mete to others, God will mete to you again.

Be humble and gentle in your conversation; of few words, I charge you; but always pertinent when you speak, hearing out before you attempt to answer, and then speaking as if you would persuade, not impose.

Affront none, neither revenge the affronts that are done to you; but forgive, and you shall be forgiven of your Heavenly Father.

In making friends, consider well, first; and when you are fixed, be true, not wavering by reports nor deserting in affliction, for that becomes not the good and virtuous.

Watch against anger; neither speak nor act in it, for like drunkenness, it makes a man a beast and throws people into desperate inconveniences.

Avoid flatterers; for they are thieves in disguise. Their praise is costly, designing to get by those they bespeak. They are the worst of creatures; they lie to flatter and flatter to cheat, and, which is worse, if you believe them, you cheat yourselves most dangerously. But the virtuous—though poor—love, cherish, and prefer. Remember David, who asking the Lord, "Who shall abide in Thy tabernacle; who shall dwell in Thy holy hill?" answers, "He that walks uprightly, works righteousness, and speaks the truth in his heart; in whose eyes the vile person is condemned, but honors them who fears the Lord."

Next, my children, be temperate in all things: in your diet, for that is physic by prevention; it keeps, nay, it makes people healthy and their generation sound. This is exclusive of the spiritual advantage it brings. Be also plain in your apparel; keep out that lust which reigns too much over some. Let your virtues be your ornaments; remembering, life is more than food, and the body than raiment. Let your furniture be simple and cheap. Avoid pride, avarice, and luxury. Read my *No Cross, No Crown*; there is instruction. Make your conversation with the most eminent for wisdom and piety; and shun all wicked men, as you hope for the blessing of God, and the comfort of your father's living and dying prayers. Be sure you speak no evil of any; no, not of the meanest, much less of your superiors, as magistrates, guardians, tutors, teachers, and elders in Christ.

Be no busybodies; meddle not with other folks' matters but when in conscience and duly pressed, for it procures trouble, and is ill-mannered, and very unseemly to wise men.

In your families, remember Abraham, Moses, and Joshua, their integrity to the Lord; and do as [if] you have them for your examples. Let the fear and service of the living God be encouraged in your houses, and that plainness, sobriety, and moderation in all things, as becomes God's chosen people. And, as I advise you, my beloved children, do you counsel yours, if God should give you any. Yea, I counsel and command them, as my posterity, that they love and serve the Lord God with an upright heart, that He may bless you and yours, from generation to generation.

And as for you who are likely to be concerned in the government of Pennsylvania and my parts of East Jersey, especially the first, I do charge you before the Lord God and his only angels that—you be lowly, diligent, and tender; fearing God, loving the people, and hating covetousness. Let justice have its impartial course, and the law free passage. Though to your loss, protect no man against it, for you are not above the law, but the law above you. Live therefore the lives yourselves you would have the people live; and then you have right and boldness to punish the transgressor. Keep upon the square, for God sees you; therefore do your duty; and be sure you see with your own eyes, and hear with your own ears. Entertain no lurchers; cherish no informers for gain or revenge; use no tricks, fly to no devices to support or cover injustice, but let your hearts be upright before the Lord, trusting in Him above the contrivances of men, and none shall be able to hurt or supplant.

Oh! the Lord is a strong God; and He can do whatsoever He pleases. And though men consider it not, it is the Lord that rules and overrules in the kingdoms of men; and He builds up and pulls down. I, your father, am the man that can say, he that trusts in the Lord shall not be confounded. But God, in due time, will make His enemies be at peace with Him.

If you thus behave yourselves, and so become a terror to evildoers and a praise to them that do well, God, my God, will be with you, in wisdom and a sound mind, and make you blessed instruments in His hand for the settlement of some of those desolate parts of the world—which my soul desires above all worldly honors and riches, both for you that go and you that stay, you that govern and you that are governed— that in the end you may be gathered with me to the rest of God.

Finally, my children, love one another with a true and endeared love, and your dear relations on both sides; and take care to preserve tender affection in your children to each other, often marrying within themselves, so [long] as it be without the bounds forbidden in God's law. That so they may not, like the forgetting and unnatural world, grow out of kindred and as cold as strangers; but, as becomes a truly natural and Christian stock, you and yours after you may live in the pure and fervent love of God toward one another, as becomes brethren in the spiritual and natural relation.

So my God, that has blessed me with His abundant mercies, both of this and the other and better life, be with you all, guide you by His counsel, bless you, and bring you to His eternal glory, that you may shine, my dear children, in the firmament of God's power, with the blessed spirits of the just, that celestial family, praising and admiring Him, the God and Father of it, forever and ever. For there is no God like unto Him: the God of Abraham, of Isaac, and of Jacob; the God of the Prophets, the Apostles, and Martyrs of Jesus; in whom I live forever.

So farewell to my thrice dearly beloved wife and children. Yours, as God pleases, in that which no waters can quench, no time forget, nor distance wear away, but remains forever.

Worminghurst, 4th August, 1682. William Penn

"The Barefoot Boy" by John Greenleaf Whittier, 1855

SOURCE: Stedman, Edmund Clarence, ed. 1900. *An American Anthology, 1787–1900.* Boston: Houghton Mifflin.

Introduction

The poet John Greenleaf Whittier (1807–1892) wrote frequently on the theme of childhood. In "The Barefoot Boy" (1855), one of his most famous poems, Whittier rhapsodizes over the pleasures of his boyhood in rural New England. Whittier's vision of childhood is romantic; no hints of the fears or vulnerabilities associated with youth penetrate his poem. Childhood is represented as a time of innocence, before man is corrupted by knowledge, money, responsibility, or work. The optimistic tone and simple rhymes of Whittier's poems made them popular within classrooms throughout the nineteenth and twentieth centuries. Whittier is also well remembered for his abolitionist poetry and his political work in support of antislavery. He ran for Congress in 1842 on the Liberty Party ticket, edited the Liberty Party newspaper, and participated in the founding of the Republican Party.

Blessings on thee, little man,
Barefoot boy, with cheek of tan!
With thy turned-up pantaloons,
And thy merry whistled tunes;
With thy red lip, redder still
Kissed by strawberries on the hill;
With the sunshine on thy face,
Through thy torn brim's jaunty grace;
From my heart I give thee joy,—
I was once a barefoot boy!

Prince thou art,—the grown-up man
Only is republican.
Let the million-dollared ride!
Barefoot, trudging at his side,
Thou hast more than he can buy
In the reach of ear and eye,—
Outward sunshine, inward joy:
Blessings on thee, barefoot boy!
Oh for boyhood's painless play,
Sleep that wakes in laughing day,
Health that mocks the doctor's rules,
Knowledge never learned of schools,
Of the wild bee's morning chase,
Of the wild flower's time and place,
Flight of fowl and habitude
Of the tenants of the wood;
How the tortoise bears his shell,
How the woodchuck digs his cell,
And the ground-mole sinks his well;
How the robin feeds her young,
How the oriole's nest is hung;
Where the whitest lilies blow,
Where the freshest berries grow,
Where the ground-nut trails its vine,
Where the wood-grape's clusters shine;
Of the black wasp's cunning way,
Mason of his walls of clay,
And the architectural plans
Of gray hornet artisans!
For, eschewing books and tasks,
Nature answers all he asks;
Hand in hand with her he walks,
Face to face with her he talks,
Part and parcel of her joy,—
Blessings on the barefoot boy!
Oh for boyhood's time of June,
Crowding years in one brief moon,
When all things I heard or saw,
Me, their master, waited for.
I was rich in flowers and trees,
Humming-birds and honey-bees;
For my sport the squirrel played,
Plied the snouted mole his spade;
For my taste the blackberry cone
Purpled over hedge and stone;
Laughed the brook for my delight
Through the day and through the night,—
Whispering at the garden wall,
Talked with me from fall to fall;
Mine the sand-rimmed pickerel pond,
Mine the walnut slopes beyond,
Mine, on bending orchard trees,
Apples of Hesperides!
Still as my horizon grew,
Larger grew my riches too;

All the world I saw or knew
Seemed a complex Chinese toy,
Fashioned for a barefoot boy!
Oh for festal dainties spread,
Like my bowl of milk and bread;
Pewter spoon and bowl of wood,
On the door-stone, gray and rude!
O'er me, like a regal tent,
Cloudy-ribbed, the sunset bent,
Purple-curtained, fringed with gold,
Looped in many a wind-swung fold;
While for music came the play
Of the pied frogs' orchestra;
And, to light the noisy choir,
Lit the fly his lamp of fire.
I was monarch: pomp and joy
Waited on the barefoot boy!
Cheerily, then, my little man,
Live and laugh, as boyhood can!
Though the flinty slopes be hard,
Stubble-speared the new-mown sward,
Every morn shall lead thee through
Fresh baptisms of the dew;
Every evening from thy feet
Shall the cool wind kiss the heat:
All too soon these feet must hide
In the prison cells of pride,
Lose the freedom of the sod,
Like a colt's for work be shod,
Made to tread the mills of toil,
Up and down in ceaseless moil:
Happy if their track be found
Never on forbidden ground;
Happy if they sink not in
Quick and treacherous sands of sin.
Ah! that thou couldst know thy joy,
Ere it passes, barefoot boy!

"Sleep, Sleep, Happy One" by Christina Rossetti, c. late nineteenth century

SOURCE: Unpublished.

Introduction

In previous centuries, when childhood mortality rates were much higher, the deaths of children inspired many poetic elegies. Christina Rossetti (1830–1894) wrote numerous poems about dying infants (none inspired by her own loss, Rossetti had no children herself). In "Sleep, Sleep, Happy One," Rossetti writes sentimentally about the child's death as a release from the pains and hardships of mortal life. Her poems are still frequently read today at funeral services for children. Her strong religious faith and her promise of a better life in heaven have provided comfort to countless bereaved parents.

Sleep, Sleep, Happy One

Sleep, sleep, happy one;
Thy night is but just begun.
Sleep in peace; still angels keep
Holy watches o'er thy sleep.
Softest breasts are pillowing,
Softest wings are shadowing
Thy calm slumber; little child,
Sleep in thy white robes undefiled.
There is no more aching now
In thy heart or in thy brow.
The red blood upon thy breast
Cannot scare away thy rest.
Though thy hands are clasped as when
A man thou prayedst among men,
Thy pains are lulled, thy tears are dried,
And thy wants are satisfied.
Sleep, sleep; what quietness
After the world's noise is this!
Sleep on, where the hush and shade
Like a veil are round thee laid.
At thy head a cross is hewn
Whereon shines the Advent moon:
Through all the hours of the night
Its shadow rests on thee aright.
In temptation thou wert firm;
Now have patience with the worm.
Yet a little while, and he
And death and sin shall bow to thee.
Yet a little while, and thou
Shalt have a crown upon thy brow,
And a palm branch in thy hand
Where the holy angels stand.
Sleep, sleep, till the chime
Sound of the last matin prime:
Sleep on until the morn
Of another Advent dawn.

Excerpt from *The Souls of Black Folk* by W. E. B. DuBois, 1903

SOURCE: Du Bois, W. E. B. 1903. *The Souls of Black Folk.* Chicago: A.C. McClurg and Co.; Cambridge, MA: University Press John Wilson and Son.

Introduction

In this heartrending chapter from *The Souls of Black Folk* (1903), W. E. B. DuBois's seminal volume on the impact of race on the lives of African Americans, the author describes how the veil of the color line falls over black children at the moment of their birth. DuBois, himself a light-skinned man, recalls his emotional distress at the visual evidence of his son's mixed heritage, as well as his anger that his son's future must be constrained by classifications of race. When, at the age of eighteen months, his son dies from a childhood illness, DuBois and his wife are swallowed by grief, yet DuBois also recognizes death as a liberation from the tyranny of the color line. That ending note illuminates how indelibly the lives of African-American children are marked by race.

Chapter XI.

Of the Passing of the First-Born
O sister, sister, thy first-begotten,
The hands that cling and the feet that follow,
The voice of the child's blood crying yet,
Who hath remembered me? who hath forgotten?
Thou hast forgotten, O summer swallow,
But the world shall end when I forget.
SWINBURNE.

"UNTO you a child is born," sang the bit of yellow paper that fluttered into my room one brown October morning. Then the fear of fatherhood mingled wildly with the joy of creation; I wondered how it looked and how it felt,—what were its eyes, and how its hair curled and crumpled itself. And I thought in awe of her,—she who had slept with Death to tear a man-child from underneath her heart, while I was unconsciously wandering. I fled to my wife and child, repeating the while to myself half wonderingly, "Wife and child? Wife and child?"—fled fast and faster than boat and steam-car, and yet must ever impatiently await them; away from the hard-voiced city, away from the flickering sea into my own Berkshire Hills that sit all sadly guarding the gates of Massachusetts.

Up the stairs I ran to the wan mother and whimpering babe, to the sanctuary on whose altar a life at my bidding had offered itself to win a life, and won. What is this tiny formless thing, this new-born wail from an unknown world,—all head and voice? I handle it curiously, and watch perplexed its winking, breathing, and sneezing. I did not love it then; it seemed a ludicrous thing to love; but her I loved, my girl-mother, she whom now I saw unfolding like the glory of the morning—the transfigured woman.

Through her I came to love the wee thing, as it grew and waxed strong; as its little soul unfolded itself in twitter and cry and half-formed word, and as its eyes caught the gleam and flash of life. How beautiful he was, with his olive-tinted flesh and dark gold ringlets, his eyes of mingled blue and brown, his perfect little limbs, and the soft voluptuous roll which the blood of Africa had moulded into his features! I held him in my arms, after we had sped far away to our Southern home,—held him, and glanced at the hot red soil of Georgia and the breathless city of a hundred hills, and felt a vague unrest. Why was his hair tinted with gold? An evil omen was golden hair in my life. Why had not the brown of his eyes crushed out and killed the blue?—for brown were his father's eyes, and his father's father's. And thus in the Land of the Color-line I saw, as it fell across my baby, the shadow of the Veil.

Within the Veil was he born, said I; and there within shall he live,—a Negro and a Negro's son. Holding in that little head—ah, bitterly!—the unbowed pride of a hunted race, clinging with that tiny dimpled hand—ah, wearily!—to a hope not hopeless but unhopeful, and seeing with those bright wondering eyes that peer into my soul a land whose freedom is to us a mockery and whose liberty a lie. I saw the shadow of the Veil as it passed over my baby, I saw the cold city towering above the blood-red land. I held my face beside his little cheek, showed him the star-children and the twinkling lights as they began to flash, and stilled with an even-song the unvoiced terror of my life.

So sturdy and masterful he grew, so filled with bubbling life so tremulous with the unspoken wisdom of a life but eighteen months distant from the All-life,—we were not far from worshipping this revelation of the divine, my wife and I. Her own life builded and moulded itself upon the child; he tinged her every dream and idealized her every effort. No hands but hers must touch and garnish those little limbs; no dress or frill must touch them that had not wearied her fingers; no voice but hers could coax him off to Dreamland, and she and he together spoke some soft and unknown tongue and in it held communion. I too mused above his little white bed; saw the strength of my own arm stretched onward through the ages through the newer strength of his; saw the dream of my black fathers stagger a step onward in the wild phantasm of the world; heard in his baby voice the voice of the Prophet that was to rise within the Veil.

And so we dreamed and loved and planned by fall and winter, and the full flush of the long Southern spring, till the hot winds rolled from the fetid Gulf, till the roses shivered and the still stern sun quivered its awful light over the hills of Atlanta. And then one night the little feet pattered wearily to the wee white bed, and the tiny hands trembled; and a warm flushed face tossed on the pillow, and we knew baby was sick. Ten days he lay there,—a swift week and three endless days, wasting, wasting away. Cheerily the mother nursed him the first days, and laughed into the little eyes that smiled again. Tenderly then she hovered round him, till the smile fled away and Fear crouched beside the little bed.

Then the day ended not, and night was a dreamless terror, and joy and sleep slipped away. I hear now that Voice at midnight calling me from dull and dreamless trance,—crying, "The Shadow of Death! The Shadow of Death!" Out into the starlight I crept, to rouse the gray physician,—the Shadow of Death, the Shadow of Death. The hours trembled on; the night listened; the ghastly dawn glided like a tired thing across the lamplight. Then we two alone looked upon the child as he turned toward us with great eyes, and stretched his string-like hands,—the Shadow of Death! And we spoke no word, and turned away.

He died at eventide, when the sun lay like a brooding sorrow above the western hills, veiling its face; when the winds spoke not, and the trees, the great green trees he loved, stood motionless. I saw his breath beat quicker and quicker, pause, and then his little soul leapt like a star that travels in the night and left a world of darkness in its train. The day changed not; the same tall trees peeped in at the windows, the same green grass glinted in the setting sun. Only in the chamber of death writhed the world's most piteous thing—a childless mother.

I shirk not. I long for work. I pant for a life full of striving. I am no coward, to shrink before the rugged rush of the storm, nor even quail before the awful shadow of the Veil. But hearken, O Death! Is not this my life hard enough,—is not that dull land that stretches its sneering web about me cold enough,—is not all the world beyond these four little walls pitiless enough, but that thou must needs enter here,—thou, O Death? About my head the thundering storm beat like a heartless voice, and the crazy forest pulsed with the curses of the weak; but what cared I, within my home beside my wife and baby boy? Wast thou so jealous of one little coign of happiness that thou must needs enter there,—thou, O Death?

A perfect life was his, all joy and love, with tears to make it brighter,—sweet as a summer's day beside the Housatonic. The world loved him; the women kissed his curls, the men looked gravely into his wonderful eyes, and the children hovered and fluttered about him. I can see him now, changing like the sky from sparkling laughter to darkening frowns, and then to wondering thoughtfulness as he watched the world. He knew no color-line, poor dear,—and the Veil, though it shadowed him, had not yet darkened half his sun. He loved the white matron, he loved his black nurse; and in his little world walked souls alone, uncolored and unclothed. I—yea, all men—are larger and purer by the infinite breadth of that one little life. She who in simple clearness of vision sees beyond the stars said when he had flown, "He will be happy There; he ever loved beautiful things." And I, far more ignorant, and blind by the web of mine own weaving, sit alone winding words and muttering, "If still he be, and he be There, and there be a There, let him be happy, O Fate!"

Blithe was the morning of his burial, with bird and song and sweet-smelling flowers. The trees whispered to the grass, but the children sat with hushed faces. And yet it seemed a ghostly unreal day,—the wraith of Life. We seemed to rumble down an unknown street behind a little white bundle of posies, with the shadow of a song in our ears. The busy city dinned about us; they did not say much, those pale-faced hurrying men and women; they did not say much,—they only glanced and said, "Niggers!"

We could not lay him in the ground there in Georgia, for the earth there is strangely red; so we bore him away to the northward, with his flowers and his little folded hands. In vain, in vain!—for where, O God! beneath thy broad blue sky shall my dark baby rest in peace,—where Reverence dwells, and Goodness, and a Freedom that is free?

All that day and all that night there sat an awful gladness in my heart,—nay, blame me not if I see the world thus darkly through the Veil,—and my soul whispers ever to me, saying, "Not dead, not dead, but escaped; not bond, but free." No bitter meanness now shall sicken his baby heart till it die a living death, no taunt shall madden his happy boyhood. Fool that I was to think or wish that this little soul should grow choked and deformed within the Veil! I might have known that yonder deep unworldly look that ever and anon floated past his eyes was peering far beyond this narrow Now. In the poise of his little curl-crowned head did there not sit all that wild pride of being which his father had hardly crushed in his own heart? For what, forsooth, shall a Negro want with pride amid the studied humiliations of fifty million fellows? Well sped, my boy, before the world had dubbed your ambition insolence, had held your ideals unattainable, and taught you to cringe and bow. Better far this nameless void that stops my life than a sea of sorrow for you.

Idle words; he might have borne his burden more bravely than we,—aye, and found it lighter too, some day; for surely, surely this is not the end. Surely there shall yet dawn some mighty morning to lift the Veil and set the prisoned free. Not for me,—I shall die in my bonds,—but for fresh young souls who have not known the night and waken to the morning; a morning when men ask of the workman, not "Is he white?" but "Can he work?" When men ask artists, not "Are they black?" but "Do they know?" Some morning this may be, long, long years to come. But now there wails, on that dark shore within the Veil, the same deep voice, Thou shalt forego! And all have I foregone at that command, and with small complaint,—all save that fair young form that lies so coldly wed with death in the nest I had builded.

If one must have gone, why not I? Why may I not rest me from this restlessness and sleep from this wide waking? Was not the world's alembic, Time, in his young hands, and is not my time waning? Are there so many workers in the vineyard that the fair promise of this little body could lightly be tossed away? The wretched of my race that line the alleys of the nation sit fatherless and unmothered; but Love sat beside his cradle, and in his ear Wisdom waited to speak. Perhaps now he knows the All-love, and needs not to be wise. Sleep, then, child,—sleep till I sleep and waken to a baby voice and the ceaseless patter of little feet—above the Veil.

"Stormy Nights" by Robert Louis Stevenson, 1922

SOURCE: Osbourne, Lloyd, and Fanny Van de Grift Stevenson. 1922–1923. *The Works of Robert Louis Stevenson*, Vailima Edition. New York: Scribners.

Introduction

In the poem "Stormy Nights," Robert Louis Stevenson (1850–1894) captures the fears of childhood. He challenges the romanticized and nostalgic view of childhood proffered by his poetic contemporaries, such as William Wordsworth, recalling instead how terrifying the world appeared through his youthful eyes. Stevenson had been a sickly child and spent many weeks in bed both fantasizing about adventure and fearing the stormy nights. He recalled this experience frequently. His poem "Windy Nights" is a better known variation on the theme. The imagery also appeared in his novels; for example, in the opening chapter of *Treasure Island* the narrator recalls his childhood terror during stormy nights.

Stormy Nights

I cry out war to those who spend their utmost,
Trying to substitute a vain regret
For childhood's vanished moods,
Instead of a full manly satisfaction
In new development.
Their words are vain as the lost shouts,
The wasted breath of solitary hunters
That are far buried in primeval woods—
Clamour that dies in silence,
Cries that bring back no answer
But the great voice of the wind-shaken forest,
Mocking despair.
No—they will get no answer;
For I too recollect,
I recollect and love my perished childhood,
Perfectly love and keenly recollect;
I too remember; and if it could be
Would not recall it.
Do I not know, how, nightly, on my bed
The palpable close darkness shutting round me,
How my small heart went forth to evil things,
How all the possibilities of sin
That were yet present to my innocence
Bound me too narrowly,
And how my spirit beat
The cage of its compulsive purity:
How—my eyes fixed,
My shot lip tremulous between my fingers
I fashioned for myself new modes of crime,
Created for myself with pain and labour
The evil that the cobwebs of society,
The comely secrecies of education,
Had made an itching mystery to meward.
Do I not know again,
When the great winds broke loose and went abroad

At night in the lighted town—
Ah! then it was different—
Then, when I seemed to hear
The storm go by me like a cloak-wrapt horseman
Stooping over the saddle—
Go by, and come again and yet again,
Like some one riding with a pardon,
And ever baffled, ever shut from passage:—
Then when the house shook and a horde of noises
Came out and clattered over me all night,—
Then, would my heart stand still,
My hair creep fearfully upon my head
And, with my tear-wet face
Buried among the bed-clothes,
Long and bitterly would I pray and wrestle
Till gentle sleep
Threw her great mantle over me,
And my hard breathing gradually ceased.
I was then the Indian,
Well and happy and full of glee and pleasure,
Both hands full of life.
And not without divine impulses
Shot into me by the untried non-ego;
But, like the Indian, too,
Not yet exempt from feverish questionings
And on my bed of leaves,
Writhing terribly in grasp of terror,
As when the still stars and the great white moon
Watch me athwart black foliage,
Trembling before the interminable vista,
The widening wells of space
In which my thought flags like a wearied bird
In the mid ocean of his autumn flight—
Prostrate before the indefinite great spirit
That the external warder
Plunged like a dagger
Into my bosom.
Now, I am a Greek
White-robed among the sunshine and the statues
And the fair porticos of carven marble—
Fond of olives and dry sherry,
Good tobacco and clever talk with my fellows,
Free from inordinate cravings.
Why would you hurry me, O evangelist,
You with the bands and the shilling packet of tracts
Greatly reduced when taken for distribution?
Why do you taunt my progress,
O green-spectacled Wordsworth! in beautiful verses,
You, the elderly poet?
So I shall travel forward
Step by step with the rest of my race,
In time, if death should spare me,
I shall come on to a farther stage.
And show you St. Francis of Assisi.

Children's Literature

"Rosalie and Hetty" from *Little Ferns for Fanny's Little Friends* by Fanny Fern (Sara Willis), 1853

SOURCE: Willis Parton, Sara Payson. 1853. *Little Ferns for Fanny's Little Friends.* Auburn: Derby and Miller.

Introduction

The following story appeared in *Little Ferns for Fanny's Little Friends* (1853), a collection of children's stories written by the enormously popular antebellum American newspaper columnist, Sara Willis (1811–1872), known to her readers as Fanny Fern. Willis was born in Maine and was educated at Catharine Beecher's seminary in Connecticut. However, her views on the circumscribed role of women in American society diverged from the traditionalist attitudes of her teacher. Willis criticized male dominance, supported the women's suffrage movement, and advocated less housework for women as well as smaller family size. She expressed great love for children, and her stories are filled with sympathy for their needs. Readers will recognize a resemblance between these stories and *Little Women* by Louisa May Alcott. In "Rosalie and Hetty," Willis teaches young girls the importance of cultivating their intellects, rather than their appearances. Willis, who was not an attractive woman, had a successful career and married three times.

Rosalie and Hetty

Everybody called Rosalie a beauty. Everybody was right. Her cheeks looked like a ripe peach; her hair waved over as fair a forehead as ever a zephyr kissed; her eyes and mouth were as perfect as eyes and mouth could be; no violet was softer or bluer than the one, no rose-bud sweeter than the other. All colors became Rosalie, and whatever she did was gracefully done.

Yes, everybody thought Rosalie was "a beauty." Rosalie thought so herself: So, she took no pains to be good, or amiable, or obliging. She never cared about learning anything, for she said to herself, I can afford to have my own way; I can afford to be a dunce if I like; I shall be always sought and admired for my pretty face.

So, Rosalie dressed as tastefully as she and the dressmaker knew how, and looked *up* to show her fine eyes, and *down* to show her long eye-lashes, and held up her dress and hopped over little imaginary puddles, to show her pretty feet; and smiled to show her white teeth; and danced to show her fine form and was as brilliant and as brainless as a butterfly.

Now, I suppose you think that Rosalie was very happy. Not at all! She was in a perfect fidget lest she should not get all the admiration she wanted. She was torturing herself all the while, for fear some prettier face would come along, and eclipse hers. If she went to a party and every person in the room (but one) admired her, she would fret herself sick, because *that one* didn't bow down and worship her.

Never having studied or read anything, Rosalie could talk nothing but nonsense; so, everybody who conversed with her, talked nonsense, too, and paid her silly compliments, and made her believe that all she needed to make her *quite* an angel was a pair of wings; and then she would hold her pretty head on one side, and simper; and they would go away laughing in their sleeves, and saying, "What a vain little fool Rosalie is!"

Now, Rosalie's cousin Hetty was as plain as a chestnut-bur. She had not a single pretty feature in her face. Nobody ever thought of calling Hetty a beauty, and *she knew it!* She was used to being overlooked; but she didn't go whining round and making herself unhappy about it,—not she. She just put her mind on something else. She studied, and read books, and learned a great many useful things; so, she had a great deal in her mind to think of, and went singing about as happy as could be, without minding whether anybody noticed her or not.

So she grew up sweet-tempered, amiable, generous and happy. When she went into company, strangers would say, "What a plain little body Hetty is." If they could not find anybody else to talk to, they'd go speak to her. Then Hetty would look up at them with one of her quiet smiles, and commence talking. She would say a great many very sensible things, and some queer ones, and they would listen—and listen—and listen—and by and by look at their watch and wonder what *had* made time fly so; and then go home, wondering to themselves *how they could ever call such an agreeable girl as Hetty "homely."*

So you see, everybody learned to love her when they found out what a *beautiful soul* she had; and while Rosalie was pining and fretting herself sick because her beauty was fading, and her admirers were dropping off one by one, to flatter prettier faces, Hetty went quietly on her way, winning hearts and—*keeping them, too.*

Excerpt from *Ragged Dick* by Horatio Alger, 1868

SOURCE: Alger, Horatio. 1868. *Ragged Dick; or, Street Life in New York With the Boot-Blacks.* Boston: Loring.

Introduction

Horatio Alger's *Ragged Dick* stories were published between 1867 and 1870. They are all sentimental tales of poor young heroes who, through a combination of good character and good luck, rise from their depressed circumstances and become successful.

Alger's stories were based on the lives of the New York City street children whom he met at the charitable Newsboys' Lodging House. The books were enormously popular among American boys, who learned from Dick and his companions the importance of virtue and perseverance. The *Ragged Dick* stories conveyed many of the same messages popular in children's advice literature from the period. In the following opening scene from the original *Ragged Dick,* the reader is introduced to the character of Dick and learns that some types of behavioral transgressions are acceptable, but there are certain values that a good boy can never compromise.

"WAKE up there, youngster," said a rough voice.

Ragged Dick opened his eyes slowly, and stared stupidly in the face of the speaker, but did not offer to get up.

"Wake up, you young vagabond!" said the man a little impatiently; "I suppose you'd lay there all day, if I hadn't called you."

"What time is it?" asked Dick.

"Seven o'clock."

"Seven o'clock! I oughter've been up an hour ago. I know what 'twas made me so precious sleepy. I went to the Old Bowery last night, and didn't turn in till past twelve."

"You went to the Old Bowery? Where'd you get your money?" asked the man, who was a porter in the employ of a firm doing business on Spruce Street. "Made it by shines, in course. My guardian don't allow me no money for theatres, so I have to earn it."

"Some boys get it easier than that," said the porter significantly.

"You don't catch me stealin', if that's what you mean," said Dick.

"Don't you ever steal, then?"

"No, and I wouldn't. Lots of boys does it, but I wouldn't."

"Well, I'm glad to hear you say that. I believe there's some good in you, Dick, after all."

"Oh, I'm a rough customer!" said Dick. "But I wouldn't steal. It's mean."

"I'm glad you think so, Dick," and the rough voice sounded gentler than at first. "Have you got any money to buy your breakfast?"

"No, but I'll soon get some."

While this conversation had been going on, Dick had got up. His bedchamber had been a wooden box half full of straw, on which the young bootblack had reposed his weary limbs, and slept as soundly as if it had been a bed of down. He dumped down into the straw without taking the trouble of undressing.

Getting up too was an equally short process. He jumped out of the box, shook himself, picked out one or two straws that had found their way into rents in his clothes, and, drawing a well-worn cap over his uncombed locks, he was all ready for the business of the day.

Dick's appearance as he stood beside the box was rather peculiar. His pants were torn in several places, and had apparently belonged in the first instance to a boy two sizes larger than himself. He wore a vest, all the buttons of which were gone except two, out of which peeped a shirt which looked as if it had been worn a month. To complete his costume he wore a coat too long for him, dating back, if one might judge from its general appearance, to a remote antiquity.

Washing the face and hands is usually considered proper in commencing the day, but Dick was above such refinement. He had no particular dislike to dirt, and did not think it necessary to remove several dark streaks on his face and hands. But in spite of his dirt and rags there was something about Dick that was attractive. It was easy to see that if he had been clean and well dressed he would have been decidedly good-looking. Some of his companions were sly, and their faces inspired distrust; but Dick had a frank, straightforward manner that made him a favorite.

Dick's business hours had commenced. He had no office to open. His little blacking-box was ready for use, and he looked sharply in the faces of all who passed, addressing each with, "Shine yer boots, sir?"

"How much?" asked a gentleman on his way to his office.

"Ten cents," said Dick, dropping his box, and sinking upon his knees on the sidewalk, flourishing his brush with the air of one skilled in his profession.

"Ten cents! Isn't that a little steep?"

"Well, you know 'taint all clear profit," said Dick, who had already set to work. "There's the *blacking* costs something, and I have to get a new brush pretty often."

"And you have a large rent too," said the gentleman quizzically, with a glance at a large hole in Dick's coat.

"Yes, sir," said Dick, always ready to joke; "I have to pay such a big rent for my manshun up on Fifth Avenoo, that I can't afford to take less than ten cents a shine. I'll give you a bully shine, sir."

"Be quick about it, for I am in a hurry. So your house is on Fifth Avenue, is it?"

"It isn't anywhere else," said Dick, and Dick spoke the truth there.

"What tailor do you patronize?" asked the gentleman, surveying Dick's attire.

"Would you like to go to the same one?" asked Dick, shrewdly.

"Well, no; it strikes me that he didn't give you a very good fit."

"This coat once belonged to General Washington," said Dick, comically. "He wore it all through the Revolution, and it got torn some, 'cause he fit so hard. When he died he told his widder to give it to some smart young feller that hadn't got none of his own; so she gave it to me. But if you'd like it, sir, to remember General Washington by, I'll let you have it reasonable."

"Thank you, but I wouldn't want to deprive you of it. And did your pants come from General Washington too?"

"No, they was a gift from Lewis Napoleon. Lewis had outgrown 'em and sent 'em to me, — he's bigger than me, and that's why they don't fit."

"It seems you have distinguished friends. Now, my lad, I suppose you would like your money."

"I shouldn't have any objection," said Dick.

"I believe," said the gentleman, examining his pocket-book, "I haven't got anything short of twenty-five cents. Have you got any change?"

"Not a cent," said Dick. "All my money's invested in the Erie Railroad."

"That's unfortunate."

"Shall I get the money changed, sir?"

"I can't wait; I've got to meet an appointment immediately. I'll hand you twenty-five cents, and you can leave the change at my office any time during the day."

"All right, sir. Where is it?"

"No. 125 Fulton Street. Shall you remember?"

"Yes, sir. What name?"

"Greyson,—office on second floor."

"All right, sir; I'll bring it."

"I wonder whether the little scamp will prove honest," said Mr. Greyson to himself, as he walked away. "If he does, I'll give him my custom regularly. If he don't as is most likely, I shan't mind the loss of fifteen cents."

Mr. Greyson didn't understand Dick. Our ragged hero wasn't a model boy in all respects. I am afraid he swore sometimes, and now and then he played tricks upon unso-phisticated boys from the country, or gave a wrong direction to honest old gentlemen unused to the city. A clergyman in search of the Cooper Institute he once directed to the Tombs Prison, and, following him unobserved, was highly delighted when the unsuspicious stranger walked up the front steps of the great stone building on Centre Street, and tried to obtain admission.

"I guess he wouldn't want to stay long if he did get in," thought Ragged Dick, hitching up his pants. "Leastways I shouldn't. They're so precious glad to see you that they won't let you go, but board you gratooitous, and never send in no bills."

Another of Dick's faults was his extravagance. Being always wide-awake and ready for business, he earned enough to have supported him comfortably and respectably. There were not a few young clerks who employed Dick from time to time in his professional capacity, who scarcely earned as much as he, greatly as their style and dress exceeded his. But Dick was careless of his earnings. Where they went he could hardly have told himself. However much he managed to earn during the day, all was generally spent before morning. He was fond of going to the Old Bowery Theatre, and to Tony Pastor's, and if he had any money left afterwards, he would invite some of his friends in somewhere to have an oyster stew; so it seldom happened that he commenced the day with a penny.

Then I am sorry to add that Dick had formed the habit of smoking. This cost him considerable, for Dick was rather fastidious about his cigars, and wouldn't smoke the cheapest. Besides, having a liberal nature, he was generally ready to treat his companions. But of course the expense was the smallest objection. No boy of fourteen can smoke without being affected injuriously. Men are frequently injured by smoking, and boys always. But large numbers of the news-boys and boot-blacks form the habit. Exposed to the cold and wet they find that it warms them up, and the self-indulgence grows upon them. It is not uncommon to see a little boy, too young to be out of his mother's sight, smoking with all the apparent satisfaction of a veteran smoker.

There was another way in which Dick sometimes lost money. There was a noted gambling-house on Baxter Street, which in the evening was sometimes crowded with these juvenile gamesters, who staked their hard earnings, generally losing of course, and refreshing themselves from time to time with a vile mixture of liquor at two cents a glass. Sometimes Dick strayed in here, and played with the rest.

I have mentioned Dick's faults and defects, because I want it understood, to begin with, that I don't consider him a model boy. But there were some good points about him nevertheless. He was above doing anything mean or dishonorable. He would not steal, or cheat, or impose upon younger boys, but was frank and straight-forward, manly and self-reliant. His nature was a noble one, and had saved him from all mean faults. I hope my young readers will like him as I do, without being blind to his faults. Perhaps, although he was only a boot-black, they may find something in him to imitate.

And now, having fairly introduced Ragged Dick to my young readers, I must refer them to the next chapter for his further adventures.

Lesson Eight from *McGuffey's Fifth Eclectic Reader* by William Holmes McGuffey, 1879

SOURCE: McGuffey, William Holmes. 1879. *McGuffey's Fifth Eclectic Reader.* New York: American Book Co.

Introduction

The McGuffey Readers, prepared by William Holmes McGuffey (1800–1873), were the second most popular American books of the nineteenth century, after the King James Bible. The readers, composed of previously published selections and organized by six different reading levels, were especially popular in the Midwest and sold over 122 million copies between 1836 and 1920. They were used to teach American children how to read as well as how to think. The following excerpt from *McGuffey's Fifth Eclectic Reader,* published in 1879, inculcates in students the ethic of hard work, a central moral value of American Victorian culture. Other values promoted by McGuffey readers included Christianity, personal responsibility, sobriety, and female domesticity. While some look back on McGuffey's readers with nostalgia, many recent historians have criticized the texts' moral lessons for serving the interests of late-nineteenth-century industrialism rather than the self-realization of individual students.

VIII WORK

Eliza Cook (1817–1889) was born in London. In 1837 she commenced contributing to periodicals. In 1840 the first collection of her poems was made. In 1849 she became editor of "Eliza Cook's Journal."

Work, work, my boy, be not afraid;
Look labor boldly in the face;
Take up the hammer or the spade,
And blush not for your humble place.
There's glory in the shuttle's song;
There's triumph in the anvil's stroke;
There's merit in the brave and strong
Who dig the mine or fell the oak.
The wind disturbs the sleeping lake,
And bids it ripple pure and fresh;
It moves the green boughs till they make
Grand music in their leafy mesh.
And so the active breath of life
Should stir our dull and sluggard wills;

For are we not created rife
With health, that stagnant torpor'kills?
I doubt if he who lolls his head
Where idleness and plenty meet,
Enjoys his pillow or his bread
As those who earn the meals they eat.
And man is never half so blest
As when the busy day is spent
So as to make his evening rest
A holiday of glad content.

DEFINITIONS.—3. Mesh, *network.* 4. Rife, *abounding.* Stagnant, *inactive.* Torpor, *laziness, stupidity.* 5. Lolls, *reclines, leans.*

Excerpt from *Tarzan of the Apes* by Edgar Rice Burroughs, 1914

SOURCE: Burroughs, Edgar Rice. 1914. *Tarzan of the Apes.* Chicago: McClurg.

Introduction

In the first half of the twentieth century a new genre of popular writing, known as pulp fiction, became popular. Printed on inexpensive paper, "pulp" magazines serialized tales of adventure, crime, and romance. *Tarzan of the Apes,* first published in *All-Story* magazine in 1912, is one of the genre's greatest successes. Its enormous popularity inspired two dozen Tarzan novels, as well as radio programs, movies, television shows, and branded products. In the following chapter from the original novel, Tarzan the infant is taken by the female ape Kala after the ferocious ape Kerchak has killed his father. *Tarzan* attracted young readers because unlike many Victorian-era children's books, it aimed at entertainment and not moral instruction. However, modern critics point out that the Tarzan stories are heavily weighted with ideological messages about masculinity, imperialism, and whiteness.

Chapter 4

The Apes

In the forest of the table-land a mile back from the ocean old Kerchak the Ape was on a rampage of rage among his people.

The younger and lighter members of his tribe scampered to the higher branches of the great trees to escape his wrath; risking their lives upon branches that scarce supported their weight rather than face old Kerchak in one of his fits of uncontrolled anger.

The other males scattered in all directions, but not before the infuriated brute had felt the vertebra of one snap between his great, foaming jaws.

A luckless young female slipped from an insecure hold upon a high branch and came crashing to the ground almost at Kerchak's feet.

With a wild scream he was upon her, tearing a great piece from her side with his mighty teeth, and striking her viciously upon her head and shoulders with a broken tree limb until her skull was crushed to a jelly.

And then he spied Kala, who, returning from a search for food with her young babe, was ignorant of the state of the mighty male's temper until suddenly the shrill warnings of her fellows caused her to scamper madly for safety.

But Kerchak was close upon her, so close that he had almost grasped her ankle had she not made a furious leap far into space from one tree to another—a perilous chance which apes seldom if ever take, unless so closely pursued by danger that there is no alternative.

She made the leap successfully, but as she grasped the limb of the further tree the sudden jar loosened the hold of the tiny babe where it clung frantically to her neck, and she saw the little thing hurled, turning and twisting, to the ground thirty feet below.

With a low cry of dismay Kala rushed headlong to its side, thoughtless now of the danger from Kerchak; but when she gathered the wee, mangled form to her bosom life had left it.

With low moans, she sat cuddling the body to her; nor did Kerchak attempt to molest her. With the death of the babe his fit of demoniacal rage passed as suddenly as it had seized him.

Kerchak was a huge king ape, weighing perhaps three hundred and fifty pounds. His forehead was extremely low and receding, his eyes bloodshot, small and close set to his coarse, flat nose; his ears large and thin, but smaller than most of his kind.

His awful temper and his mighty strength made him supreme among the little tribe into which he had been born some twenty years before.

Now that he was in his prime, there was no simian in all the mighty forest through which he roved that dared contest his right to rule, nor did the other and larger animals molest him.

Old Tantor, the elephant, alone of all the wild savage life, feared him not—and he alone did Kerchak fear. When Tantor trumpeted, the great ape scurried with his fellows high among the trees of the second terrace.

The tribe of anthropoids over which Kerchak ruled with an iron hand and bared fangs, numbered some six or eight families, each family consisting of an adult male with his females and their young, numbering in all some sixty or seventy apes.

Kala was the youngest mate of a male called Tublat, meaning broken nose, and the child she had seen dashed to death was her first; for she was but nine or ten years old.

Notwithstanding her youth, she was large and powerful—a splendid, clean-limbed animal, with a round, high forehead, which denoted more intelligence than most of her kind possessed. So, also, she had a great capacity for mother love and mother sorrow.

But she was still an ape, a huge, fierce, terrible beast of a species closely allied to the gorilla, yet more intelligent; which, with the strength of their cousin, made her kind the most fearsome of those awe-inspiring progenitors of man.

When the tribe saw that Kerchak's rage had ceased they came slowly down from their arboreal retreats and pursued again the various occupations which he had interrupted.

The young played and frolicked about among the trees and bushes. Some of the adults lay prone upon the soft mat of dead and decaying vegetation which covered the ground, while others turned over pieces of fallen branches and clods of earth in search of the small bugs and reptiles which formed a part of their food.

Others, again, searched the surrounding trees for fruit, nuts, small birds, and eggs.

They had passed an hour or so thus when Kerchak called them together, and, with a word of command to them to follow him, set off toward the sea.

They traveled for the most part upon the ground, where it was open, following the path of the great elephants whose comings and goings break the only roads through those tangled mazes of bush, vine, creeper, and tree. When they walked it was with a rolling, awkward motion, placing the knuckles of their closed hands upon the ground and swinging their ungainly bodies forward.

But when the way was through the lower trees they moved more swiftly, swinging from branch to branch with the agility of their smaller cousins, the monkeys. And all the way Kala carried her little dead baby hugged closely to her breast.

It was shortly after noon when they reached a ridge overlooking the beach where below them lay the tiny cottage which was Kerchak's goal.

He had seen many of his kind go to their deaths before the loud noise made by the little black stick in the hands of the strange white ape who lived in that wonderful lair, and Kerchak had made up his brute mind to own that death-dealing contrivance, and to explore the interior of the mysterious den.

He wanted, very, very much, to feel his teeth sink into the neck of the queer animal that he had learned to hate and fear, and because of this, he came often with his tribe to reconnoiter, waiting for a time when the white ape should be off his guard.

Of late they had quit attacking, or even showing themselves; for every time they had done so in the past the little stick had roared out its terrible message of death to some member of the tribe.

Today there was no sign of the man about, and from where they watched they could see that the cabin door was open. Slowly, cautiously, and noiselessly they crept through the jungle toward the little cabin.

There were no growls, no fierce screams of rage—the little black stick had taught them to come quietly lest they awaken it.

On, on they came until Kerchak himself slunk stealthily to the very door and peered within. Behind him were two males, and then Kala, closely straining the little dead form to her breast.

Inside the den they saw the strange white ape lying half across a table, his head buried in his arms; and on the bed lay a figure covered by a sailcloth, while from a tiny rustic cradle came the plaintive wailing of a babe.

Noiselessly Kerchak entered, crouching for the charge; and then John Clayton rose with a sudden start and faced them.

The sight that met his eyes must have frozen him with horror, for there, within the door, stood three great bull apes, while behind them crowded many more; how many he never knew, for his revolvers were hanging on the far wall beside his rifle, and Kerchak was charging.

When the king ape released the limp form which had been John Clayton, Lord Greystoke, he turned his attention toward the little cradle; but Kala was there before him, and when he would have grasped the child she snatched it herself, and before he could intercept her she had bolted through the door and taken refuge in a high tree.

As she took up the little live baby of Alice Clayton she dropped the dead body of her own into the empty cradle; for the wail of the living had answered the call of universal motherhood within her wild breast which the dead could not still.

High up among the branches of a mighty tree she hugged the shrieking infant to her bosom, and soon the instinct that was as dominant in this fierce female as it had been in the breast of his tender and beautiful mother—the instinct of mother love—reached out to the tiny man-child's half-formed understanding, and he became quiet.

Then hunger closed the gap between them, and the son of an English lord and an English lady nursed at the breast of Kala, the great ape.

In the meantime the beasts within the cabin were warily examining the contents of this strange lair.

Once satisfied that Clayton was dead, Kerchak turned his attention to the thing which lay upon the bed, covered by a piece of sailcloth.

Gingerly he lifted one corner of the shroud, but when he saw the body of the woman beneath he tore the cloth roughly from her form and seized the still, white throat in his huge, hairy hands.

A moment he let his fingers sink deep into the cold flesh, and then, realizing that she was already dead, he turned from her, to examine the contents of the room; nor did he again molest the body of either Lady Alice or Sir John.

The rifle hanging upon the wall caught his first attention; it was for this strange, death-dealing thunder-stick that he had yearned for months; but now that it was within his grasp he scarcely had the temerity to seize it.

Cautiously he approached the thing, ready to flee precipitately should it speak in its deep roaring tones, as he had heard it speak before, the last words to those of his kind who, through ignorance or rashness, had attacked the wonderful white ape that had borne it.

Deep in the beast's intelligence was something which assured him that the thunder-stick was only dangerous when in the hands of one who could manipulate it, but yet it was several minutes ere he could bring himself to touch it.

Instead, he walked back and forth along the floor before it, turning his head so that never once did his eyes leave the object of his desire.

Using his long arms as a man uses crutches, and rolling his huge carcass from side to side with each stride, the great king ape paced to and fro, uttering deep growls, occasionally punctuated with the ear-piercing scream, than which there is no more terrifying noise in all the jungle.

Presently he halted before the rifle. Slowly he raised a huge hand until it almost touched the shining barrel, only to withdraw it once more and continue his hurried pacing.

It was as though the great brute by this show of fearlessness, and through the medium of his wild voice, was endeavoring to bolster up his courage to the point which would permit him to take the rifle in his hand.

Again he stopped, and this time succeeded in forcing his reluctant hand to the cold steel, only to snatch it away almost immediately and resume his restless beat.

Time after time this strange ceremony was repeated, but on each occasion with increased confidence, until, finally, the rifle was torn from its hook and lay in the grasp of the great brute.

Finding that it harmed him not, Kerchak began to examine it closely. He felt of it from end to end, peered down the black depths of the muzzle, fingered the sights, the breech, the stock, and finally the trigger.

During all these operations the apes who had entered sat huddled near the door watching their chief, while those outside strained and crowded to catch a glimpse of what transpired within.

Suddenly Kerchak's finger closed upon the trigger. There was a deafening roar in the little room and the apes at and beyond the door fell over one another in their wild anxiety to escape.

Kerchak was equally frightened, so frightened, in fact, that he quite forgot to throw aside the author of that fearful noise, but bolted for the door with it tightly clutched in one hand.

As he passed through the opening, the front sight of the rifle caught upon the edge of the inswung door with sufficient force to close it tightly after the fleeing ape.

When Kerchak came to a halt a short distance from the cabin and discovered that he still held the rifle, he dropped it as he might have dropped a red hot iron, nor did he again attempt to recover it—the noise was too much for his brute nerves; but he was now quite convinced that the terrible stick was quite harmless by itself if left alone.

It was an hour before the apes could again bring themselves to approach the cabin to continue their investigations, and when they finally did so, they found to their chagrin that the door was closed and so securely fastened that they could not force it.

The cleverly constructed latch which Clayton had made for the door had sprung as Kerchak passed out; nor could the apes find means of ingress through the heavily barred windows.

After roaming about the vicinity for a short time, they started back for the deeper forests and the higher land from whence they had come.

Kala had not once come to earth with her little adopted babe, but now Kerchak called to her to descend with the rest, and as there was no note of anger in his voice she dropped lightly from branch to branch and joined the others on their homeward march.

Those of the apes who attempted to examine Kala's strange baby were repulsed with bared fangs and low menacing growls, accompanied by words of warning from Kala.

When they assured her that they meant the child no harm she permitted them to come close, but would not allow them to touch her charge.

It was as though she knew that her baby was frail and delicate and feared lest the rough hands of her fellows might injure the little thing.

Another thing she did, and which made traveling an onerous trial for her. Remembering the death of her own little one, she clung desperately to the new babe, with one hand, whenever they were upon the march.

The other young rode upon their mothers' backs; their little arms tightly clasping the hairy necks before them, while their legs were locked beneath their mothers' armpits.

Not so with Kala; she held the small form of the little Lord Greystoke tightly to her breast, where the dainty hands clutched the long black hair which covered that portion of her body. She had seen one child fall from her back to a terrible death, and she would take no further chances with this.

Child Protection: Government and the Courts

Ex parte Crouse, 1839

SOURCE: Supreme Court of Pennsylvania, Eastern District. 1839. 4 Whart. 9; 1839 Pa. Decided January 5, 1839.

Introduction

The Pennsylvania Supreme Court's decision in the case of *Ex parte Crouse* (1839), asserted the right of the state to intervene in the private sphere of family by assuming custody of a child. The court affirmed the right of the county of Philadelphia to detain Mary Ann Crouse, a child, in the reformatory "by reason of her vicious conduct." Her father filed a habeas corpus petition to release Mary Ann because there was no evidence that she had committed any crime. The court rejected the petition citing the state's right as *parens patriae*—or political parent—to protect Mary Ann from continuing along a depraved course in life. Because Mary had been impounded for her protection, rather than as punishment, she was not entitled to the same due process that guided criminal lawsuits. The *Ex parte Crouse* decision initiated the development of a separate more informal justice system for child offenders, which was nominally designed for their protection yet often trampled their rights.

Ex parte Crouse
SUPREME COURT OF PENNSYLVANIA, EASTERN DISTRICT, PHILADELPHIA
4 Whart. 9; 1839 Pa.

January 5, 1839, Decided

PRIOR HISTORY: [**1] HABEAS CORPUS.

THIS was a habeas corpus directed to the keeper and managers of the "House of Refuge," in the county of Philadelphia, requiring them to produce before the court one Mary Ann Crouse, an infant, detained in that institution. The petition for the habeas corpus was in the name of her father.

By the return to the writ it appeared, that the girl had been committed to the custody of the managers by virtue of a warrant under the hand and seal of Morton McMichael, Esq., a justice of the peace of the county of Philadelphia, which recited that complaint and due proof had been made before him by Mary Crouse, the mother of the said Mary Ann Crouse, "that the said infant by reason of vicious conduct, has rendered her control beyond the power of the said complainant, and made it manifestly requisite that from regard to the moral and future welfare of the said infant she should be placed under the guardianship of the managers of the House of Refuge;" and the said alderman certified that in his opinion the said infant was "a proper subject for the said House of Refuge." Appended to the warrant of commitment were the names and places of residence of the witnesses examined, [**2] and the substance of the testimony given by them respectively, upon which the adjudication of the magistrate was founded.

The House of Refuge was established in pursuance of an Act of Assembly passed on the 23d day of March 1826. The sixth section of that act declared that the managers should, "at their discretion, receive into the said House of Refuge, such children who shall be taken up or committed as vagrants, or upon any criminal charge, or duly convicted of criminal offences, as may be in the judgment of the Court of Oyer and Terminer, or of the Court of Quarter Sessions of the peace of the county, or of the Mayor's Court of the city of Philadelphia, or of any alderman or justice of the peace, or of the managers of the almshouse and house of employment, be deemed proper objects." By a supplement to the act passed on the 10th day of April 1835, it was declared, that in lieu of the provisions of the act of 1826, it should be lawful for the managers of the House of Refuge "at their discretion, to receive into their care and guardianship, infants, males under the age of twenty-one years, and females under the age of eighteen years committed to their custody in either of the [**3] following modes, viz First: Infants committed by an alderman or justice of the peace on the complaint and due proof made to him by the parent, guardian or next friend of such infant, that by reason of incorrigible or vicious conduct such infant has rendered his or her control beyond the power of such parent, guardian or next friend, and made it manifestly requisite that from regard for the morals and future welfare of such infant, he or she should be placed under the guardianship of the managers of the House of Ref-uge. Second: Infants committed by the authority aforesaid, where complaint and due proof have been made that such infant is a proper subject for the guardianship of the managers of the House of Refuge, in consequence of vagrancy, or of incorrigible or vicious conduct, and that from the moral depravity or otherwise of the parent or next friend in whose custody such infant may be, such parent or next friend is incapable or unwilling to exercise the proper care and discipline over such incorrigible or vicious infant. Third: Infants committed by the courts of this Commonwealth in the mode provided by the act to which this is a supplement."

DISPOSITION: Remanded.

HEADNOTES: The provisions of the acts of 23d of March 1826, and 10th of April 1835, which authorize the committal of infants to the House of Refuge, under certain circumstances, and their detention there, without a previous trial by jury, are not unconstitutional.

COUNSEL: Mr. W. L. Hirst, for [**4] the petitioner, now contended, that these provisions, so far as they authorized the committal and detention of an infant without a trial by jury, were unconstitutional. He referred to the sixth and ninth sections of the Bill of Rights; and cited the Commonwealth v. Addicks, 5 Binn. 520; S. C. 2 S. & R. 174; Commonwealth v. Murray, 4 Binn. 492, 494.

Mr. Barclay and Mr. J. R. Ingersoll, for the managers of the House of Refuge.

OPINION: [*11] PER CURIAM.—The House of Refuge is not a prison, but a school. Where reformation, and not punishment, is the end, it may indeed be used as a prison for juvenile convicts who would else be committed to a common gaol; and in respect to these, the constitutionality of the act which incorporated it, stands clear of controversy. It is only in respect of the application of its discipline to subjects admitted on the order of the court, a magistrate or the managers of the Almshouse, that a doubt is entertained. The object of the charity is reformation, by training its inmates to industry; by imbuing their minds with principles of morality and religion; by furnishing them with means to earn a living; and, above all, by separating them from the corrupting [**5] influence of improper associates. To this end may not the natural parents, when unequal to the task of education, or unworthy of it, be superseded by the *parens patriae*, or common guardian of the community? It is to be remembered that the public has a paramount interest in the virtue and knowledge of its members, and that of strict right, the business of education belongs to it. That parents are ordinarily intrusted with it is because it can seldom be put into better hands; but where they are incompetent or corrupt, what is there to prevent the public from withdrawing their faculties, held, as they obviously are, at its sufferance? The right of parental control is a natural, but not an unalienable one. It is not excepted by the declaration of rights out of the subjects of ordinary legislation; and it consequently remains subject to the ordinary legislative power which, if wantonly or inconveniently used, would soon be constitutionally restricted, but the competency of which, as the government is constituted, cannot be doubted. As to abridgment of indefeasible rights by confinement of the person, it is no more than what is borne, to a greater or less extent, in every school; and [**6] we know of no natural right to exemption from restraints which conduce to an infant's welfare. Nor is there a doubt of the propriety of their application in the particular instance. The infant has been snatched from a course which must have ended in confirmed depravity; and, [*12] not only is the restraint of her person lawful, but it would be an act of extreme cruelty to release her from it.

Remanded.

Excerpt from "The Maiden Tribute of Modern Babylon" by W. T. Stead, 1885

SOURCE: Stead, W. T. 1885. "The Maiden Tribute of Modern Babylon I: The Report of Our Secret Commission." *The Pall Mall Gazette*, Monday, July 6.

Introduction

In 1885 the *Pall Mall Gazette* published a series of articles, collectively titled "The Maiden Tribute of Modern Babylon," that exposed the existence of a busy trade in child prostitutes in the city of London. Their author, W. T. Stead, was a deeply religious journalist who had written many previous exposés of the evils afflicting poor Britons. But none shocked his middle-class readership as thoroughly as the "Maiden Tribute." The articles garnered public support for the passage of the Criminal Law Amendment Act, which raised the age of consent to sixteen, and led to the conviction of W. T. Stead himself, who had "purchased" a young girl to substantiate the claims in his articles. In the following excerpt from his first essay Stead expresses outrage not only over the events he describes, but at the tacit acceptance of their existence that he finds among the police and parliamentary authorities with whom he speaks.

In ancient times, if we may believe the myths of Hellas, Athens, after a disastrous campaign, was compelled by her conqueror to send once every nine years a tribute to Crete of seven youths and seven maidens. The doomed fourteen, who were selected by lot amid the lamentations of the citizens, returned no more. . . .

The fact that the Athenians should have taken so bitterly to heart the paltry maiden tribute that once in nine years they had to pay to the Minotaur seems incredible, almost inconceivable. This very night in London, and every night, year in and year out, not seven maidens only, but many times

seven, selected almost as much by chance as those who in the Athenian market-place drew lots as to which should be flung into the Cretan labyrinth, will be offered up as the Maiden Tribute of Modern Babylon. Maidens they were when this morning dawned, but to-night their ruin will be accomplished, and to-morrow they will find themselves within the portals of the maze of London brotheldom. Within that labyrinth wander, like lost souls, the vast host of London prostitutes, whose numbers no man can compute, but who are probably not much below 50,000 strong. Many, no doubt, who venture but a little way within the maze make their escape. But multitudes are swept irresistibly on and on to be destroyed in due season, to give place to others, who also will share their doom. The maw of the London Minotaur is insatiable, and none that go into the secret recesses of his lair return again. . . .

Before beginning this inquiry I had a confidential interview with one of the most experienced officers who for many years was in a position to possess an intimate acquaintance with all phases of London crime. I asked him, "Is it or is it not a fact that, at this moment, if I were to go to the proper houses, well introduced, the keeper would, in return for money down, supply me in due time with a maid—a genuine article, I mean, not a mere prostitute tricked out as a virgin, but a girl who had never been seduced?" "Certainly," he replied without a moment's hesitation. "At what price?" I continued. "That is a difficult question," he said. "I remember one case which came under my official cognizance in Scotland-yard in which the price agreed upon was stated to be £20. Some parties in Lambeth undertook to deliver a maid for that sum—to a house of ill fame, and I have no doubt it is frequently done all over London." "But," I continued, "are these maids willing or unwilling parties to the transaction—that is, are they really maiden, not merely in being each a virgo intacta in the physical sense, but as being chaste girls who are not consenting parties to their seduction?" He looked surprised at my question, and then replied emphatically: "Of course they are rarely willing, and as a rule they do not know what they are coming for." "But," I said in amazement, "then do you mean to tell me that in very truth actual rapes, in the legal sense of the word, are constantly being perpetrated in London on unwilling virgins, purveyed and procured to rich men at so much a head by keepers of brothels?" "Certainly," said he, "there is not a doubt of it." "Why," I exclaimed, "the very thought is enough to raise hell." "It is true," he said; "and although it ought to raise hell, it does not even raise the neighbours." "But do the girls cry out?" "Of course they do. But what avails screaming in a quiet bedroom? Remember, the utmost limit of howling or excessively violent screaming, such as a man or woman would make if actual murder was being attempted, is only two minutes, and the limit of screaming of any kind is only five. Suppose a girl is being outraged in a room next to your house. You hear her screaming, just as you are dozing to sleep. Do you get up, dress, rush downstairs, and insist on admittance? Hardly. But suppose the screams continue and you get uneasy, you begin to think whether you should not do something? Before you have made up your mind and got dressed the screams cease, and you think you were a fool for your pains." "But the policeman on the beat?" "He has no right to interfere, even if he heard anything. Suppose that a constable had a right to force his way into any house where a woman screamed fearfully, policemen would be almost as regular attendants at childbed as doctors. Once a girl gets into such a house she is almost helpless, and may be ravished with comparative safety." "But surely rape is a felony punishable with penal servitude. Can she not prosecute?" "Whom is she to prosecute? She does not know her assailant's name. She might not even be able to recognize him if she met him outside. Even if she did, who would believe her? A woman who has lost her chastity is always a discredited witness. The fact of her being in a house of ill fame would possibly be held to be evidence of her consent. The keeper of the house and all the servants would swear she was a consenting party; they would swear that she had never screamed, and the woman would be condemned as an adventuress who wished to levy black mail." "And this is going on to-day?" "Certainly it is, and it will go on, and you cannot help it, as long as men have money, procuresses are skilful, and women are weak and inexperienced."

VIRGINS WILLING AND UNWILLING.

So startling a declaration by so eminent an authority led me to turn my investigations in this direction. On discussing the matter with a well-known member of Parliament, he laughed and said: "I doubt the unwillingness of these virgins. That you can contract for maids at so much a head is true enough. I myself am quite ready to supply you with 100 maids at £25 each, but they will all know very well what they are about. There are plenty of people among us entirely devoid of moral scruples on the score of chastity, whose daughters are kept straight until they are sixteen or seventeen, not because they love virtue, but solely because their virginity is a realizable asset, with which they are taught they should never part except for value received. These are the girls who can be had at so much a head; but it is nonsense to say it is rape; it is merely the delivery as per contract of the asset virginity in return for cash down. Of course there may be some cases in which the girl is really unwilling, but the regular supply comes from those who take a strictly businesslike view of the saleable value of their maidenhead." My interlocutor referred me to a friend whom he described as the first expert on the subject, an evergreen old gentleman to whom the brothels of Europe were as familiar as Notre Dame and St. Paul's. This specialist, however, entirely denied that there was such a thing as the procuring of virgins, willing or unwilling, either here or on the Continent. Maidenheads, he maintained, were not assets that could be realized in the market, but he admitted that there were some few men whose taste led them to buy little girls from their mothers

in order to abuse them. My respect for this "eminent authority" diminished, however, on receiving his assurance that all Parisian and Belgian brothels were managed so admirably that no minors could be harboured, and that no English girls were ever sent to the Continent for immoral purposes. Still even he admitted that little girls were bought and sold for vicious purposes, and this unnatural combination of slave trade, rape, and unnatural crime seemed to justify further inquiry.

I then put myself into direct and confidential communication with brothel-keepers in the West and East of London and in the provinces. . . .

THE CONFESSIONS OF A BROTHEL-KEEPER.

Here, for instance, is a statement made to me by a brothel keeper, who formerly kept a noted House in the Mile-end road, but who is now endeavouring to start life afresh as an honest man. I saw both him and his wife, herself a notorious prostitute whom he had married off the streets, where she had earned her living since she was fourteen:—

"Maids, as you call them—fresh girls as we know them in the trade—are constantly in request, and a keeper who knows his business has his eyes open in all directions, his stock of girls is constantly getting used up, and needs replenishing, and he has to be on the alert for likely "marks" to keep up the reputation of his house. I have been in my time a good deal about the country on these errands. The getting of fresh girls takes time, but it is simple and easy enough when, once you are in it. I have gone and courted girls in the country under all kinds of disguises, occasionally assuming the dress of a parson, and made them believe that I intended to marry them, and so got them in my power to please a good customer. How is it done? Why, after courting my girl for a time, I propose to bring her to London to see the sights. I bring her up, take her here and there, giving her plenty to eat and drink—especially drink. I take her to the theatre, and then I contrive it so that she loses her last train. By this time she is very tired, a little dazed with the drink and excitement, and very frightened at being left in town with no friends. I offer her nice lodgings for the night: she goes to bed in my house, and then the affair is managed. My client gets his maid, I get my £10 or £20 commission, and in the morning the girl, who has lost her character, and dare not go home, in all probability will do as the others do, and become one of my "marks"—that is, she will make her living in the streets, to the advantage of my house. The brothel keeper's profit is, first, the commission down for the price of a maid, and secondly, the continuous profit of the addition of a newly seduced, attractive girl to his establishment. That is a fair sample case of the way in which we recruit. Another very simple mode of supplying maids is by breeding them. Many women who are on the streets have female children. They are worth keeping. When they get to be twelve or thirteen they become merchantable. For a very likely "mark" of this kind you may get as much as £20 or £40. I sent my own daughter out on the streets from my own brothel. I know a couple of very fine little girls now who will be sold before very long. They are bred and trained for the life. They must take the first step some time, and it is bad business not to make as much out of that as possible. Drunken parents often sell their children to brothel keepers. In the East-end, you can always pick up as many fresh girls as you want. In one street in Dalston you might buy a dozen. Sometimes the supply is in excess of the demand, and you have to seduce your maid yourself, or to employ some one else to do it, which is bad business in a double sense. There is a man called S—— whom a famous house used to employ to seduce young girls and make them fit for service when there was no demand for maids and there was a demand for girls who had been seduced. But as a rule the number seduced ready to hand is ample, especially among very young children. Did I ever do anything else in the way of recruiting? Yes. I remember one case very well. The girl, a likely "mark," was a simple country lass living at Horsham. I had heard of her, and I went down to Horsham to see what I could do. Her parents believed that I was in regular business in London, and they were very glad when I proposed to engage their daughter. I brought her to town and made her a servant in our house. We petted her and made a good deal of her, gradually initiated her into the kind of life it was; and then I sold her to a young gentleman for £15. When I say that I sold her, I mean that he gave me the gold and I gave him the girl, to do what he liked with. He took her away and seduced her. I believe he treated her rather well afterwards, but that was not my affair. She was his after he paid for her and took her away. If her parents had inquired, I would have said that she had been a bad girl and run away with a young man. How could I help that? I once sold a girl twelve years old for £20 to a clergyman, who used to come to my house professedly to distribute tracts. The East is the great market for the children who are imported into West-end houses, or taken abroad wholesale when trade is brisk. I know of no West-end houses, having always lived at Dalston or thereabouts, but agents pass to and fro in the course of business. They receive the goods, depart, and no questions are asked. Mrs. S., a famous procuress, has a mansion at ————, which is one of the worst centres of the trade, with four other houses in other districts, one at St. John's-wood. This lady, when she discovers ability, cultivates it—that is, if a comely young girl of fifteen falls into her net, with some intelligence, she is taught to read and write, and to play the piano."

Excerpt from Report Issued by the First White House Conference on the Care of Dependent Children, 1909

SOURCE: Conference on the Care of Dependent Children. 1909. *Proceedings of the Conference on the Care of Dependent Children Held at Washington, D.C., January 25, 26, 1909.* Washington, DC: GPO.

Introduction

Throughout the twentieth century, a series of national conferences on the subject of children and youth were held at the White House. The first conference convened in 1909, at the invitation of President Theodore Roosevelt. Its instigators were two early leaders in the field of social work, Lillian Wald from the Henry Street Settlement and Florence Kelly of the National Consumers League. They proposed the establishment of a federal children's bureau to watch over the nation's youth. This became the U.S. Children's Bureau, which was established in 1912. Attendees of the first White House Conference included Theodore Dreiser, Jacob Riis, Jane Addams, and Booker T. Washington. The following excerpt from a report issued by the conference declares that children are deserving of special measures to ensure their protection and well being. The conference is an important landmark in the modern era's shift in attitude toward the relationship between children and the state. While urging the importance of the home and the preservation of the family, it provides official recognition of the government's responsibility for the welfare of the child and upholds the state's right to intervene in the private sphere of family on their behalf.

First White House Conference on the Care of Dependent Children
January 25, 1909
Hon. Theodore Roosevelt, President

Sir: Having been invited by you to participate in a conference on the care of dependent children . . . we desire to express the very great satisfaction felt by each member of this conference in the deep interest you have taken in the well-being of dependent children. The proper care of destitute children has indeed an important bearing upon the welfare of the nation. We now know so little about them as not even to know their number, but we know that there are in institutions about 93,000, and that many additional thousands are in foster or boarding homes. As a step, therefore, in the conservation of the productive capacity of the people, and the preservation of high standards of citizenship, and also because each of these children is entitled to receive humane treatment, adequate care, and proper education, your action . . . will have, we believe, a profound effect upon the well-being of many thousands of children, and upon the nation as a whole. . . .

Our conclusions are as follows:

HOME CARE

1. Home life is the highest and finest product of civilization. . . . It is the great molding force of mind and of character. Children should not be deprived of it except for urgent and compelling reasons. Children of parents of worthy char-

acter, suffering from temporary misfortune and children of reasonably efficient and deserving mothers who are without the support of the normal breadwinner, should, as a rule, be kept with their parents, such aid being given as may be necessary to maintain suitable homes for the rearing of the children. This aid should be given by such methods and from such sources as may be determined by the general relief policy of each community, preferably in the form of private charity, rather than of public relief. Except in unusual circumstances, the home should not be broken up for reasons of poverty, but only for considerations of inefficiency or immorality.

PREVENTIVE WORK

2. The most important and valuable philanthropic work is not the curative, but the preventive. . . . We urge upon all friends of children the promotion of effective measures, including legislation to prevent blindness; to check tuberculosis and other diseases in dwellings and work places, and injuries in hazardous occupations; to secure compensation or insurance so as to provide a family income in case of sickness, accident, death, or invalidism of the breadwinner; to promote child-labor reforms, and, generally, to improve the conditions surrounding child life. To secure these ends we urge efficient cooperation with all other agencies for social betterment.

HOME FINDING

3. As to the children who for sufficient reasons must be removed from their own homes, or who have no homes, it is desirable that, if normal in mind and body and not requiring special training, they should be cared for in families whenever practicable. . . . Such homes should be selected by a most careful process of investigation, carried on by skilled agents through personal investigation and with due regard to the religious faith of the child. After children are placed in homes, adequate visitation, with careful consideration of the physical, mental, moral, and spiritual training and development of each child on the part of the responsible home-finding agency is essential.

It is recognized that for many children foster homes without payment for board are not practicable immediately after the children become dependent and that for children requiring temporary care only the free home is not available. . . . Contact with family life is preferable for these children, as well as for other normal children. It is necessary, however, that a large number of carefully selected boarding homes be found if these children are to be cared for in families. . . .Unless and until such homes are found, the use of institutions is necessary.

4. So far as it may be found necessary temporarily or permanently to care for certain classes of children in institutions, these institutions should be conducted on the cottage plan, in order that routine and impersonal care may not unduly suppress individuality and initiative. . . . It secures for the children a larger degree of association with adults and a nearer approach to the conditions of family life, which are required for the proper molding of childhood. These results more than justify the increased outlay and are truly economical. . . . Cheap care of children is ultimately enormously expensive, and is unworthy of a strong community. Existing congregate institutions should so classify their inmates and segregate them into groups as to secure as many of the benefits of the cottage system as possible, and should look forward to the adoption of the cottage type when new buildings are constructed.

The sending of children of any age or class to almshouses is an unqualified evil, and should be forbidden everywhere by law, with suitable penalty for its violation.

INCORPORATION

5. To engage in the work of caring for needy children is to assume a most serious responsibility, and should, therefore, be permitted only to those who are definitely organized for the purpose, who are of suitable character, and possess, or have reasonable assurance of securing, the funds needed for their support. The only practicable plan of securing this end is to require the approval, by a state board of charities or other body exercising similar powers, of the incorporation of all child-caring agencies. . . .

STATE INSPECTION

6. The proper training of destitute children being essential to the well-being of the State, it is a sound public policy that the State, through its duly authorized representative, should inspect the work of all agencies which care for dependent children. . . .

INSPECTION OF EDUCATIONAL WORK

7. Destitute children at best labor under many disadvantages. . . . It is desirable that the education of children in orphan asylums and other similar institutions or placed in families should be under the supervision of the educational authorities of the State. . . .

PHYSICAL CARE

8. . . . Each child . . . should be carefully examined by a competent physician, especially for the purpose of ascertaining whether such peculiarities, if any, as the child presents may be due to any defect of the sense organs or other physical defect. Both institutions and placing-out agencies should take every precaution to secure proper medical and surgical care of their children and should see that suitable instruction is given them in matters of health and hygiene.

COOPERATION

9. Great benefit can be derived from a close cooperation between the various child-caring agencies, institutional and otherwise, in each locality. . . . The establishment of a joint bureau of investigation and information by all the child-caring agencies of each locality is highly commended, in the absence of any other suitable central agency through which they may cooperate.

UNDESIRABLE LEGISLATION

10. We greatly deprecate the tendency of legislation in some States to place unnecessary obstacles in the way of placing children in family homes in such States by agencies whose headquarters are elsewhere, in view of the fact that we favor the care of destitute children, normal in mind and body, in families, whenever practicable. . . .

The people of the more prosperous and less congested districts owe a debt of hospitality to the older communities from which many of them came. . . .

PERMANENT ORGANIZATION

11. The care of dependent children is a subject about which nearly every session of the legislature of every State in the Union concerns itself; it is a work in which State and local authorities in many States are engaged, and in which private agencies are active in every State. Important decisions are being made constantly. . . . Each of these decisions should be made with full knowledge of the experience of other States and agencies, and of the trend of opinion among those . . . able to speak from wide experience and careful observation. One effective means of securing this result would be the establishment of a permanent organization to undertake, in this field, work comparable to that carried on by . . . similar organizations in their respective fields. It is our judgment that the establishment of such a permanent voluntary organization, under auspices which would insure a careful consideration of all points of view, broad mindedness and tolerance, would be desirable and helpful, if reasonably assured of adequate financial support.

FEDERAL CHILDREN'S BUREAU

12. A bill is pending in Congress for the establishment of a federal children's bureau to collect and disseminate information affecting the welfare of children. In our judgment the establishment of such a bureau is desirable, and we earnestly recommend the enactment of the pending measure . . .

Hammer v. Dagenhart, 1918

SOURCE: Supreme Court of the United States. *Hammer v. Dagenhart,* 247 U.S. 251. 1918. Argued April 15, 16, 1918. Decided June 3, 1918.

Introduction

The U.S. Supreme Court's 1918 decision in the case of *Hammer v. Dagenhart* overturned the federal government's Keating-Owen Act, a Progressive-era law that limited the exploitation of child labor. The Keating-Owen Act—in order to impose limits on the age of child laborers and on the number of hours they were permitted to work—had called upon the federal government's power to regulate interstate commerce by preventing the passage of goods manufactured under unacceptable conditions. In *Hammer v. Dagenhart,* the five-person majority opinion, written by Justice William Day, maintained that the government had the power to limit only the means by which such goods were transported, not their movement—if the goods themselves were harmless. Justice Oliver Wendell Holmes wrote the dissenting opinion, arguing that "it does not matter whether the supposed evil precedes or follows the transportation. It is enough that, in the opinion of Congress, that transportation encourages the evil."

Hammer v. Dagenhart, 247 U.S. 251 (1918) No. 704
Argued April 15, 16, 1918; Decided June 3, 1918
APPEAL FROM THE DISTRICT COURT OF THE UNITED STATES FOR THE WESTERN DISTRICT OF NORTH CAROLINA

MR. JUSTICE DAY delivered the opinion of the court.

A bill was filed in the United States District Court for the Western District of North Carolina by a father in his own behalf and as next friend of his two minor sons, one under the age of fourteen years and the other between the ages of fourteen and sixteen years, employees in a cotton mill at Charlotte, North Carolina, to enjoin the enforcement of the act of Congress intended to prevent interstate commerce in the products of child labor. Act of Sept. 1, 1916, c. 432, 39 Stat. 675.

The District Court held the act unconstitutional and entered a decree enjoining its enforcement. This appeal brings the case here. The first section of the act is in the margin.

Other sections of the act contain provisions for its enforcement and prescribe penalties for its violation.

The attack upon the act rests upon three propositions: first: it is not a regulation of interstate and foreign commerce; second: it contravenes the Tenth Amendment to the Constitution; third: it conflicts with the Fifth Amendment to the Constitution.

The controlling question for decision is: is it within the authority of Congress in regulating commerce among the States to prohibit the transportation in interstate commerce of manufactured goods, the product of a factory in which, within thirty days prior to their removal therefrom, children under the age of fourteen have been employed or permitted to work, or children between the ages of fourteen and sixteen years have been employed or permitted to work more than eight hours in any day, or more than six days in any week, or after the hour of seven o'clock P.M. or before the hour of 6 o'clock A.M.?

The power essential to the passage of this act, the Government contends, is found in the commerce clause of the Constitution, which authorizes Congress to regulate commerce with foreign nations and among the States. In Gibbons v. Ogden, Chief Justice Marshall, speaking for this court and defining the extent and nature of the commerce power, said, "It is the power to regulate; that is, to prescribe the rule by which commerce is to be governed." In other words, the power is one to control the means by which commerce is carried on, which is directly the contrary of the assumed right to forbid commerce from moving, and thus destroy it as to particular commodities. But it is insisted that adjudged cases in this court establish the doctrine that the power to regulate given to Congress incidentally includes the authority to prohibit the movement of ordinary commodities, and therefore that the subject is not open for discussion. The cases demonstrate the contrary. They rest upon the character of the particular subjects dealt with, and the fact that the scope of governmental authority, state or national, possessed over them is such that the authority to prohibit is as to them but the exertion of the power to regulate.

. . .

It is further contended that the authority of Congress may be exerted to control interstate commerce in the shipment of child-made goods because of the effect of the circulation of such goods in other States where the evil of this class of labor has been recognized by local legislation, and the right to thus employ child labor has been more rigorously restrained than in the State of production. In other words, that the unfair competition thus engendered may be controlled by closing the channels of interstate commerce to manufacturers in those States where the local laws do not meet what Congress deems to be the more just standard of other States.

There is no power vested in Congress to require the States to exercise their police power so as to prevent possible unfair competition. Many causes may cooperate to give one State, by reason of local laws or conditions, an economic advantage over others. The Commerce Clause was not intended to give to Congress a general authority to equalize such conditions. In some of the States, laws have been passed fixing minimum wages for women, in others, the local law regulates the hours of labor of women in various employments. Business done in such States may be at an economic disadvantage when compared with States which have no such regulations; surely, this fact does not give Congress the power to deny transportation in interstate commerce to those who

carry on business where the hours of labor and the rate of compensation for women have not been fixed by a standard in use in other States and approved by Congress. The grant of power to Congress over the subject of interstate commerce was to enable it to regulate such commerce, and not to give it authority to control the States in their exercise of the police power over local trade and manufacture.

The grant of authority over a purely federal matter was not intended to destroy the local power always existing and carefully reserved to the States in the Tenth Amendment to the Constitution.

. . .

That there should be limitations upon the right to employ children in mines and factories in the interest of their own and the public welfare, all will admit. That such employment is generally deemed to require regulation is shown by the fact that the brief of counsel states that every State in the Union has a law upon the subject, limiting the right to thus employ children. In North Carolina, the State wherein is located the factory in which the employment was had in the present case, no child under twelve years of age is permitted to work.

It may be desirable that such laws be uniform, but our Federal Government is one of enumerated powers; "this principle," declared Chief Justice Marshall in McCulloch v. Maryland, "is universally admitted."

A statute must be judged by its natural and reasonable effect. Collins v. New Hampshire. The control by Congress over interstate commerce cannot authorize the exercise of authority not entrusted to it by the Constitution. Pipe Line Cases, 560. The maintenance of the authority of the States over matters purely local is as essential to the preservation of our institutions, as is the conservation of the supremacy of the federal power in all matters entrusted to the Nation by the Federal Constitution.

. . .

HOLMES, Dissenting Opinion

MR. JUSTICE HOLMES, dissenting.

The single question in this case is whether Congress has power to prohibit the shipment in interstate or foreign commerce of any product of a cotton mill situated in the United States in which, within thirty days before the removal of the product, children under fourteen have been employed or children between fourteen and sixteen have been employed more than eight hours in a day, or more than six days in any week, or between seven in the evening and six in the morning. The objection urged against the power is that the States have exclusive control over their methods of production, and that Congress cannot meddle with them, and, taking the proposition in the sense of direct intermeddling, I agree to it, and suppose that no one denies it. But if an act is within the powers specifically conferred upon Congress, it seems to me that it is not made any less constitutional because of the indirect effects that it may have, however obvious it may be that it will have those effects, and that we are not at liberty upon such grounds to hold it void.

. . .

The Pure Food and Drug Act which was sustained in Hipolite Egg Co. v. United States, with the intimation that "no trade can be carried on between the States to which it [the power of Congress to regulate commerce] does not extend," applies not merely to articles that the changing opinions of the time condemn as intrinsically harmful, but to others innocent in themselves, simply on the ground that the order for them was induced by a preliminary fraud. Weeks v. United States. It does not matter whether the supposed evil precedes or follows the transportation. It is enough that, in the opinion of Congress, the transportation encourages the evil. I may add that, in the cases on the so-called White Slave Act, it was established that the means adopted by Congress as convenient to the exercise of its power might have the character of police regulations. Hoke v. United States, Caminetti v. United States. In Clark Distilling Co. v. Western Maryland R. Co., Leisy v. Hardin, is quoted with seeming approval to the effect that a subject matter which has been confided exclusively to Congress by the Constitution is not within the jurisdiction of the police power of the State unless placed there by congressional action. I see no reason for that proposition not applying here.

The notion that prohibition is any less prohibition when applied to things now thought evil I do not understand. But if there is any matter upon which civilized countries have agreed—far more unanimously than they have with regard to intoxicants and some other matters over which this country is now emotionally aroused—it is the evil of premature and excessive child labor. I should have thought that, if we were to introduce our own moral conceptions where in my opinion they do not belong, this was preeminently a case for upholding the exercise of all its powers by the United States.

But I had thought that the propriety of the exercise of a power admitted to exist in some cases was for the consideration of Congress alone, and that this Court always had disavowed the right to intrude its judgment upon questions of policy or morals. It is not for this Court to pronounce when prohibition is necessary to regulation—if it ever may be necessary—to say that it is permissible as against strong drink, but not as against the product of ruined lives.

The act does not meddle with anything belonging to the States. They may regulate their internal affairs and their domestic commerce as they like. But when they seek to send their products across the state line, they are no longer within their rights. If there were no Constitution and no Congress, their power to cross the line would depend upon their neighbors. Under the Constitution, such commerce belongs not to the States, but to Congress to regulate. It may carry out its views of public policy whatever indirect effect they may have upon the activities of the States. Instead of being encountered by a prohibitive tariff at her boundaries, the State encounters the public policy of the United States, which it is for Congress to express. The public policy of the United States is shaped with a view to the benefit of the nation as a whole. If, as has been the case within the memory of men still living, a State should take a different view of the propriety of sustaining a lottery from that which generally prevails, I cannot believe that the fact would require a different decision from that reached in Champion v. Ames. Yet, in that case, it would be said with quite as much force as in this that Congress was attempting to intermeddle with the State's domestic affairs. The national welfare, as understood by Congress, may require a different attitude within its sphere from that of some self-seeking State. It seems to me entirely constitutional for Congress to enforce its understanding by all the means at its command.

MR. JUSTICE McKENNA, MR. JUSTICE BRANDEIS and MR. JUSTICE CLARKE concur in this opinion.

Meyer v. State of Nebraska, 1923

SOURCE: Supreme Court of the United States. *Meyer v. State of Nebraska*, 262 U.S. 390. 1923. Argued Feb. 23, 1923. Decided June 4, 1923.

Introduction

The U.S. Supreme Court decision in the 1923 case of *Meyer v. the State of Nebraska* overturned a state law that prohibited teachers from using modern foreign languages in the classroom or from teaching those languages to children in grades one through eight. Nebraskan legislators passed the "Foreign Language Statute" to force the state's German-speaking population to teach their children English. The Supreme Court did not reject the state's interest in Americanizing the children of immigrants, but it found that the state law violated teachers' individual liberties as protected in the Fourteenth Amendment. The decision limited the power of states to control the curriculums of private schools. *Meyer v. Nebraska* helped to establish the individual's right to privacy in the United States and would later be cited in *Griswold v. Connecticut* (1965) and *Roe v. Wade* (1973), two cases that secured Americans' rights to access contraceptives and abortions respectively. The case also strengthened the cause of academic freedom.

U.S. Supreme Court
Meyer v. State of Nebraska, 262 U.S. 390 (1923) No. 325
Argued Feb. 23, 1923. Decided June 4, 1923.

[262 U.S. 390, 391] Messrs. A. F. Mullen, of Omaha, Neb., C. E. Sandall, of York, Neb., and I. L. Albert, of Columbus, Neb., for plaintiff in error.

[262 U.S. 390, 393] Messrs. Mason Wheeler, of Lincoln, Neb., and O. S. Spillman, of Pierce, Neb., for the State of Nebraska.

[262 U.S. 390, 396]

Mr. Justice McREYNOLDS delivered the opinion of the Court.

Plaintiff in error was tried and convicted in the district court for Hamilton county, Nebraska, under an information which charged that on May 25, 1920, while an instructor in Zion Parochial School he unlawfully taught the subject of reading in the German language to Raymond Parpart, a child of 10 years, who had not attained [262 U.S. 390, 397] and successfully passed the eighth grade. The information is based upon 'An act relating to the teaching of foreign languages in the state of Nebraska,' approved April 9, 1919 (Laws 1919, c. 249), which follows:

'Section 1. No person, individually or as a teacher, shall, in any private, denominational, parochial or public school, teach any subject to any person in any language than the English language.

'Sec. 2. Languages, other than the English language, may be taught as languages only after a pupil shall have attained and successfully passed the eighth grade as evidenced by a certificate of graduation issued by the county superintendent of the county in which the child resides.

'Sec. 3. Any person who violates any of the provisions of this act shall be deemed guilty of a misdemeanor and upon conviction, shall be subject to a fine of not less than twenty-five dollars ($25), nor more than one hundred dollars ($100), or be confined in the county jail for any period not exceeding thirty days for each offense.

'Sec. 4. Whereas, an emergency exists, this act shall be in force from and after its passage and approval.'

The Supreme Court of the state affirmed the judgment of conviction. 107 Neb. 657, 187 N. W. 100. It declared the offense charged and established was 'the direct and intentional teaching of the German language as a distinct subject to a child who had not passed the eighth grade,' in the parochial school maintained by Zion Evangelical Lutheran Congregation, a collection of Biblical stories being used therefore. And it held that the statute forbidding this did not conflict with the Fourteenth Amendment, but was a valid exercise of the police power. The following excerpts from the opinion sufficiently indicate the reasons advanced to support the conclusion:

'The salutary purpose of the statute is clear. The Legislature had seen the baneful effects of permitting for [262 U.S. 390, 398] foreigners, who had taken residence in this country, to rear and educate their children in the language of their native land. The result of that condition was found to be inimical to our own safety. To allow the children of foreigners, who had emigrated here, to be taught from early childhood the language of the country of their parents was to rear them with that language as their mother tongue. It was to educate them so that they must always think in that language, and, as a consequence, naturally inculcate in them the ideas and sentiments foreign to the best interests of this country. The statute, therefore, was intended not only to require that the education of all children be conducted in the English language, but that, until they had grown into that language and until it had become a part of them, they should not in the schools be taught any other language. The obvious purpose of this statute was that the English language should be and become the mother tongue of all children reared in this state. The enactment of such a statute comes reasonably within the police power of the state. Pohl v. State, 102 Ohio St. 474, 132 N. E. 20; State v. Bartels, 191 Iowa, 1060, 181 N. W. 508.

'It is suggested that the law is an unwarranted restriction, in that it applies to all citizens of the state and arbitrarily interferes with the rights of citizens who are not of foreign ancestry, and prevents them, without reason, from having their children taught foreign languages in school. That argument is not well taken, for it assumes that every citizen finds himself restrained by the statute. The hours which a child is able to devote to study in the confinement of school are limited. It must have ample time for exercise or play. Its daily capacity for learning is comparatively small. A selection of subjects for its education, therefore, from among the many that might be taught, is obviously necessary. The Legislature no doubt had in mind the practical operation of the law. The law affects few citizens, except those of foreign lineage. [262 U.S. 390, 399] Other citizens, in their selection of studies, except perhaps in rare instances, have never deemed it of importance to teach their children foreign languages before such children have reached the eighth grade. In the legislative mind, the salutary effect of the statute no doubt outweighed the restriction upon the citizens generally, which, it appears, was a restriction of no real consequence.'

The problem for our determination is whether the statute as construed and applied unreasonably infringes the liberty guaranteed to the plaintiff in error by the Fourteenth Amendment:

'No state . . . shall deprive any person of life, liberty or property without due process of law.'

While this court has not attempted to define with exactness the liberty thus guaranteed, the term has received much consideration and some of the included things have been definitely stated. Without doubt, it denotes not merely freedom from bodily restraint but also the right of the individual to contract, to engage in any of the common occupations of life, to acquire useful knowledge, to marry, establish a home and bring up children, to worship God according to the dictates of his own conscience, and generally to enjoy those privileges long recognized at common law as essential to the orderly pursuit of happiness by free men. Slaughter-House Cases, 16 Wall. 36; Butchers' Union Co. v. Crescent City Co., 111 U.S. 746, 4 Sup. Ct. 652; Yick Wo v. Hopkins, 118 U.S. 356, 6 Sup. Ct. 1064; Minnesota v. Bar er, 136 U.S. 313, 10 Sup. Ct. 862; Allegeyer v. Louisiana, 165 U.S. 578, 17 Sup. Ct. 427; Lochner v. New York, 198 U.S. 45, 25 Sup. Ct. 539, 3 Ann. Cas. 1133; Twining v. New Jersey 211 U.S. 78, 29 Sup. Ct. 14; Chicago, B. & Q. R. R. v. McGuire, 219 U.S. 549, 31 Sup. Ct. 259; Truax v. Raich, 239 U.S. 33, 36 Sup. Ct. 7, L. R. A. 1916D, 545, Ann. Cas. 1917B, 283; Adams v. Tanner, 224 U.S. 590, 37 Sup. Ct. 662, L. R. A. 1917F, 1163, Ann. Cas. 1917D, 973; New York Life Ins. Co. v. Dodge, 246 U.S. 357, 38 Sup. Ct. 337, Ann. Cas. 1918E, 593; Truax v. Corrigan, 257 U.S. 312, 42 Sup. Ct. 124; Adkins v. Children's Hospital (April 9, 1923), 261 U.S. 525, 43 Sup. Ct. 394, 67 L. Ed. —; Wyeth v. Cambridge Board of Health, 200 Mass. 474, 86 N. E. 925, 128 Am. St. Rep. 439, 23 L. R. A. (N. S.) 147. The established doctrine is that this liberty may not be interfered [262 U.S. 390, 400] with, under the guise of protecting the public interest, by legislative action which is arbitrary or without reasonable relation to some purpose within the competency of the state to effect. Determination by the Legislature of what constitutes proper exercise of police power is not final or conclusive but is subject to supervision by the courts. Lawton v. Steele, 152 U.S. 133, 137, 14 S. Sup. Ct. 499.

The American people have always regarded education and acquisition of knowledge as matters of supreme importance which should be diligently promoted. The Ordinance of 1787 declares:

'Religion, morality and knowledge being necessary to good government and the happiness of mankind, schools and the means of education shall forever be encouraged.'

Corresponding to the right of control, it is the natural duty of the parent to give his children education suitable to their station in life; and nearly all the states, including Nebraska, enforce this obligation by compulsory laws.

Practically, education of the young is only possible in schools conducted by especially qualified persons who de-

vote themselves thereto. The calling always has been regarded as useful and honorable, essential, indeed, to the public welfare. Mere knowledge of the German language cannot reasonably be regarded as harmful. Heretofore it has been commonly looked upon as helpful and desirable. Plaintiff in error taught this language in school as part of his occupation. His right thus to teach and the right of parents to engage him so to instruct their children, we think, are within the liberty of the amendment.

The challenged statute forbids the teaching in school of any subject except in English; also the teaching of any other language until the pupil has attained and successfully passed the eighth grade, which is not usually accomplished before the age of twelve. The Supreme Court of the state has held that 'the so-called ancient or dead languages' are not 'within the spirit or the purpose of [262 U.S. 390, 401] the act.' Nebraska District of Evangelical Lutheran Synod, etc., v. McKelvie et al. (Neb.) 187 N. W. 927 (April 19, 1922). Latin, Greek, Hebrew are not proscribed; but German, French, Spanish, Italian, and every other alien speech are within the ban. Evidently the Legislature has attempted materially to interfere with the calling of modern language teachers, with the opportunities of pupils to acquire knowledge, and with the power of parents to control the education of their own.

It is said the purpose of the legislation was to promote civic development by inhibiting training and education of the immature in foreign tongues and ideals before they could learn English and acquire American ideals, and 'that the English language should be and become the mother tongue of all children reared in this state.' It is also affirmed that the foreign born population is very large, that certain communities commonly use foreign words, follow foreign leaders, move in a foreign atmosphere, and that the children are thereby hindered from becoming citizens of the most useful type and the public safety is imperiled.

That the state may do much, go very far, indeed, in order to improve the quality of its citizens, physically, mentally and morally, is clear; but the individual has certain fundamental rights which must be respected. The protection of the Constitution extends to all, to those who speak other languages as well as to those born with English on the tongue. Perhaps it would be highly advantageous if all had ready understanding of our ordinary speech, but this cannot be coerced by methods which conflict with the Constitution—a desirable end cannot be promoted by prohibited means.

For the welfare of his Ideal Commonwealth, Plato suggested a law which should provide:

'That the wives of our guardians are to be common, and their children are to be common, and no parent is to know his own child, [262 U.S. 390, 402] nor any child his parent. . . . The proper officers will take the offspring of the good parents to the pen or fold, and there they will deposit them with certain nurses who dwell in a separate quarter; but the offspring of the inferior, or of the better when they chance to be deformed, will be put away in some mysterious, unknown place, as they should be.'

In order to submerge the individual and develop ideal citizens, Sparta assembled the males at seven into barracks and intrusted their subsequent education and training to official guardians. Although such measures have been deliberately approved by men of great genius their ideas touching the relation between individual and state were wholly different from those upon which our institutions rest; and it hardly will be affirmed that any Legislature could impose such restrictions upon the people of a state without doing violence to both letter and spirit of the Constitution.

The desire of the Legislature to foster a homogeneous people with American ideals prepared readily to understand current discussions of civic matters is easy to appreciate. Unfortunate experiences during the late war and aversion toward every character of truculent adversaries were certainly enough to quicken that aspiration. But the means adopted, we think, exceed the limitations upon the power of the state and conflict with rights assured to plaintiff in error. The interference is plain enough and no adequate reason therefor in time of peace and domestic tranquility has been shown.

The power of the state to compel attendance at some school and to make reasonable regulations for all schools, including a requirement that they shall give instructions in English, is not questioned. Nor has challenge been made of the state's power to prescribe a curriculum for institutions which it supports. Those matters are not within the present controversy. Our concern is with the prohibition approved by the Supreme Court. Adams v. [262 U.S. 390, 403] Tanner, 244 U.S. 594, 37 Sup. Ct. 662, L. R. A. 1917F, 1163, Ann. Cas. 1917D, 973, pointed out that mere abuse incident to an occupation ordinarily useful is not enough to justify its abolition, although regulation may be entirely proper. No emergency has arisen which renders knowledge by a child of some language other than English so clearly harmful as to justify its inhibition with the consequent infringement of rights long freely enjoyed. We are constrained to conclude that the statute as applied is arbitrary and without reasonable relation to any end within the competency of the state.

As the statute undertakes to interfere only with teaching which involves a modern language, leaving complete freedom as to other matters, there seems no adequate foundation for the suggestion that the purpose was to protect the child's health by limiting his mental activities. It is well known that proficiency in a foreign language seldom comes to one not instructed at an early age, and experience shows that this is not injurious to the health, morals or understanding of the ordinary child.

The judgment of the court below must be reversed and the cause remanded for further proceedings not inconsistent with this opinion.

REVERSED.

Mr. Justice Holmes and Mr. Justice Sutherland, dissent.

Children's Bureau Pamphlet #189, *Public Dance Halls,* 1929

SOURCE: Gardner, Ella. 1929. *Public Dance Halls, Their Regulation and Place in the Recreation of Adolescents.* Washington, DC: United States Department of Labor, U.S. Children's Bureau.

Introduction

The U.S. Children's Bureau, established by the federal government in 1912, promoted the health and welfare of American children by administering programs, researching problems, publishing pamphlets, and promoting legislation. The following excerpts are from a Children's Bureau pamphlet published in 1929, which reported on the danger that public dance halls posed to adolescents. As in many of its publications, the Children's Bureau emphasized parental responsibility and advocated increased parental supervision. The report also offers an example of the tension underlying many Children's Bureau's programs; its initiatives to protect vulnerable young people often prompted reforms to restrict their behaviors. In the case of dance halls, the Bureau advocated tightening supervision, educating parents about the dangers, and providing more wholesome recreational activities for young people.

Inquiries received by the Children's Bureau as to methods of supervision of commercialized amusements, especially public dance halls, and public provision of recreational opportunities for boys and girls of adolescent age have increased during recent years. At the request of agencies in several cities the Children's Bureau, therefore, undertook to assemble information as to the legal machinery with which communities are endeavoring to protect young people from the evils of the unregulated commercial dance hall. An effort was also made to discover what features of their community recreation programs are successful in meeting the demands of young people of this age.

Until recent years the public dance hall was unregulated and regarded by many persons as impossible of successful regulation. In small towns as well as in large industrial centers it had a bad reputation. The stories of crime and debauchery which newspapers reported from time to time as having their origin in one of these "parks" or "academies" or "halls" revealed the fact that they were frequently connected with saloons and so-called hotels which encouraged immorality on the part of the dance-hall patrons and tolerated the presence of criminals. Police attended these dances not as inspectors or supervisors but in order to be at hand to interfere in case of brawls or too flagrant disorder of any kind.

With the development of the community recreation movement studies were made of commercialized recreation, and with the facts as to the conditions in the dance halls made public, attempts were made at public control or regulation. The investigations revealed that the public dance halls offered almost the only opportunity for this form of social recreation to many farm boys and girls who came to the towns for their amusements, to large numbers of young people who were working in industrial centers away from their parents and childhood friends, and to many city boys and girls whose parents through poverty or ignorance made no provision for the social needs of their children. The movement for the regulation of commercialized recreation and the provision of community dance halls and other forms of recreation for young people developed almost simultaneously as a result.

The investigations did not reveal uniformly bad conditions in the public dance halls, and this fact furnished the best argument for successful regulation. Some dance-hall managers had demonstrated that it was profitable to offer well-conducted dances in attractive halls with good music; more, probably men with less business ability as well as with less character, sought to increase their earnings by tolerating excesses of one sort or another; and some exploited the innocent desire of young people for gayety and a good time by exposing them, through the dance hall, to the worst elements in the community.

The problem presented by the dance hall has two special phases in its relation to and effect upon young people. The first is its value or danger to very young boys and girls, those between 14 and 18. Should these children be admitted to the dance hall? If so, what safeguards should be thrown around them; and if not, how should they be excluded, and what counter attractions, if any, should be offered by parents, school, municipality, and other agencies? The second is the dancing of the older group of adolescents, those who are in school or employed but whose chief form of recreation it seems to be. For them the question has been how to keep the dance hall from becoming a demoralizing influence and how to make it a real recreational opportunity rather than a brighter form of boredom. This report describes some of the attempts that have been made to accomplish these purposes.

Regulation of public dances and methods of enforcement rather than dance-hall conditions were made the subject of the study. Officials in all cities of 15,000 population or more (approximately 500) were requested to send copies of their ordinances and regulations concerning public dances, reports on the administration of the ordinances, and on the recreation provided by the community. Replies were received from 416 cities. Copies of State laws pertaining to the control of public dances were obtained from the 25 States that have passed such legislation, and these together with the city ordinances have been analyzed and summarized for this report.

Fifteen cities in different parts of the country which offer examples of different types of control of commercial dances and of provision for community recreation were visited by bureau agents in 1925 and 1926—Butte, Mont.; Chicago, Ill.; Dayton, Ohio; Detroit, Mich.; Duluth, Minn.; Houston, Tex.; Los Angeles, Calif.; New Bedford, Mass.; Ottumwa, Iowa; Paterson N. J.; Portland Oreg.; Rochester, N.Y.; San Francisco, Calif.; Seattle, Wash.; and Wichita, Kans. Two other cities (Gary, Ind., and Oakland, Calif.) were studied from the standpoint of community provision for recreation only.

In these cities officials in control of public-amusement inspection and those in charge of community recreation were interviewed, and dances were visited in the regular dance academies, in rented halls, in outdoor pavilions, in amusement parks, in cafés, in cabarets, in closed halls, in schools, armories, and other public buildings and in halls outside the city limits. The opinions and experience of persons closely in touch with the boys and girls—teachers, juvenile-court officials, and other social workers—were sought as to the success of the existing program and as to needs which had not been adequately considered.

. . .

In 9 of the 15 selected cities the ordinances set an age limit under which young people might not attend public dances unless accompanied by a parent or legal guardian. This age limit was 18 years in all the cities, and in all but one, where girls only were excluded, it applied to both boys and girls. In Los Angeles no one under 18 was permitted even when properly chaperoned. In Wichita, instead of the requirement that each minor be accompanied by a parent or guardian, a group of young people could be accompanied by the parent of one member of the group. This arrangement had been found very satisfactory, it was reported.

The ordinances of 6 cities contained no age regulations. In one of them the inspector took home any girl under 15. In another the policewoman tried without the backing of a law to keep out girls under this age. The department of recreation in Detroit and the police department of New Bedford made special rules supplementing their ordinances. In both these cities 17 was set as the lowest age limit for entrance to dance halls. Of the two remaining cities Houston had made no ruling on the subject and in Chicago the association of ballroom managers had agreed to exclude anyone under 16 years of age.

The enforcement of these regulations depended in the majority of the cities upon the individual managers and their employees, although the inspectors in several cities sent home those under the age limit and in some cases did follow-up work with them.

In Wichita each doorman was required to keep a register of the name, address, and age claimed, by any person who seemed under age. If the person insisted he was over 18 he was admitted and the supervisor checked up on it. If the supervisor found upon visiting the home that the boy or girl was under 18 the management had to see to it that he did not gain admission again.

Through an arrangement with the Portland juvenile court, the dance-hall inspector turned over young girls found in the dance halls to the night matron of the detention home, who took them home if they were first offenders or to the detention home if they were repeaters. The dance-hall inspector in Butte said that when she found very young girls in the dance halls she "just let them stay and dance for awhile—until 10.30. I think it's better for them to be there where we know what they're doing than to send them out on the streets." She felt that often the girls did not go home when they were sent and sometimes visited out-of-town places with "pick-ups." Her theory apparently was that having danced until 10.30 they would be ready to go home.

The hostesses in the Los Angeles halls, according to a regulation of the Dance Hall Managers' Association, were supposed to register anyone who seemed to be a minor. Registration blanks were used which required the patron's name, last school attended, teacher's name, and similar facts. When the hostess suspected that a patron was under 18 years of age he had to fill out one of these blanks. If the hostess was still in doubt after the blank was filled out as to whether the patron was 18, she sent a form letter of inquiry with a return stamped envelope to the school. If the reply showed that the person under investigation was 18 an admission card was issued to him, but if it showed that he was under 18 his description and name were given all the other halls. In the opinion of one of the police officials this method of enforcement was successful. One hall was reported to have filled out blanks for 7,000 young people during a year.

Some of the hostesses questioned closely a girl who seemed very young, and, if they believed she was under 16, sent her home at 10 o'clock, calling her parents to let them know she was on her way. Others telephoned the parents at once to ask if they wished their daughter sent home. One hostess permitted the girls to do the calling, listening to be certain that they told a straight tale. In one city the hostesses urged mothers to take their daughters to the better halls after they had been found at the dances. Although many of the mothers had been persuaded to take their daughters to the Saturday afternoon dances at one of the best halls, it was difficult to make them understand the basis of the child's demand for this kind of recreation.

The inspectors quite generally agreed that it was difficult to interest parents in their children's attendance at dance halls. Some parents were unable to control their children, others could see no harm in permitting them to attend the dances, although they were under the legal age. An inspector who had difficulty in gaining the cooperation of the mothers of girls said: "About 50 per cent of the mothers knew they were going to public dance halls and wanted to 'trust' them, etc.; the other 50 per cent were ignorant of their daughters' whereabouts." The chief inspector in one city said that the parents of the children with whom she worked were the greatest handicap that she had encountered.

Nearly all the officials responsible for dance-hall inspection felt that the exclusion of young persons was an extremely difficult regulation to enforce; a number of the authorities considered it the most difficult. "The short dresses and hair make it almost impossible to guess a girl's age," they said. Moreover, it is the boys and girls between 16 and 18 years old who are most eager for dancing, feel very confident of their ability to take care of themselves, and resent any parental or public control. Many officials had themselves little sympathy with the age provisions of the ordinance they were supposed to enforce. Some made the excuse that if these youngsters were sent out of the dance hall they might go to worse places, and many made it a practice not to enforce too drastically the age regulations, but endeavored to supervise the dancing carefully and to safeguard the trip between the hall and the home. Several officials in one city stressed the value of the requirement of a chaperone in safeguarding the boys and girls. As one of them explained the value of the chaperone, "It's not the dancing; it's the going and coming and the meeting up with bad characters in the halls, who will take advantage of the unaccompanied girl when they won't the girl who has a father, or mother, or brother with her."

When the ordinance of one city was amended to raise the age limit to 18, the problem was presented of excluding from the halls they had previously frequented a large number of girls, many of whom had been going to public dances since they were 14. Like many others, this city had made inadequate provision for boys and girls between 14 and 18 who wanted social activities, especially dancing. The city officials admitted that they excluded from the dance halls but added. "We can't make that an excuse for not ending what we know is a bad condition."

The real solution of the problem of minors in the dance halls lies in the education of parents and in the training of the children, according to several city officials. What they were doing was in the nature of a palliative rather than a cure. As young people can not be protected from contact with all sorts of people they should be taught by their parents how to meet them. Even so, the training given by parents would need to be reinforced by supervision of the halls, in the opinion of these officials.

Brown v. Board of Education, 1954

SOURCE: Supreme Court of the United States. *Brown v. Board of Education.* 347 U.S. 483. 1954. Argued December 9, 1952. Reargued December 8, 1953. Decided May 17, 1954.

Introduction

In the case of *Brown v. Board of Education* (1954), the U.S. Supreme Court, led by Chief Justice Earl Warren, ruled that the segregation of public schools was unconstitutional. The court unanimously agreed that segregation deprived black school children of their right to equal protection guaranteed by the Fourteenth Amendment. The case dismantled the justification of segregation as "separate but equal," which had been established in the case of *Plessy v. Ferguson* (1896), by arguing that segregated institutions were inherently unequal. The decision in *Brown v. Board* inspired many more legal attacks on segregation, based on the same constitutional reasoning, in public accommodations, including motels, lunch counters, public libraries, and beaches. *Brown v. Board* demonstrates the central role children have occupied both in the definition of the American racial caste system and in the ongoing effort to dismantle it.

SUPREME COURT OF THE UNITED STATES
Brown v. Board of Education, 347 U.S. 483 (1954)
(USSC+)
Argued December 9, 1952
Reargued December 8, 1953
Decided May 17, 1954
APPEAL FROM THE UNITED STATES DISTRICT
COURT FOR THE DISTRICT OF KANSAS*

Syllabus

Segregation of white and Negro children in the public schools of a State solely on the basis of race, pursuant to state laws permitting or requiring such segregation, denies to Negro children the equal protection of the laws guaranteed by the Fourteenth Amendment—even though the physical facilities and other "tangible" factors of white and Negro schools may be equal.

(a) The history of the Fourteenth Amendment is inconclusive as to its intended effect on public education.

(b) The question presented in these cases must be determined not on the basis of conditions existing when the Fourteenth Amendment was adopted, but in the light of the full development of public education and its present place in American life throughout the Nation.

(c) Where a State has undertaken to provide an opportunity for an education in its public schools, such an opportunity is a right which must be made available to all on equal terms.

(d) Segregation of children in public schools solely on the basis of race deprives children of the minority group of equal educational opportunities, even though the physical facilities and other "tangible" factors may be equal.

(e) The "separate but equal" doctrine adopted in **Plessy v. Ferguson, 163 U.S. 537,** has no place in the field of public education.

(f) The cases are restored to the docket for further argument on specified questions relating to the forms of the decrees.

Opinion

WARREN

MR. CHIEF JUSTICE WARREN delivered the opinion of the Court.

These cases come to us from the States of Kansas, South Carolina, Virginia, and Delaware. They are premised on different facts and different local conditions, but a common legal question justifies their consideration together in this consolidated opinion.

In each of the cases, minors of the Negro race, through their legal representatives, seek the aid of the courts in obtaining admission to the public schools of their community on a nonsegregated basis. In each instance, they had been denied admission to schools attended by white children under laws requiring or permitting segregation according to race. This segregation was alleged to deprive the plaintiffs of the equal protection of the laws under the Fourteenth Amendment. In each of the cases other than the Delaware case, a three-judge federal district court denied relief to the plaintiffs on the so-called "separate but equal" doctrine announced by this Court in **Plessy v. Ferguson, 163 U.S. 537.** Under that doctrine, equality of treatment is accorded when the races are provided substantially equal facilities, even though these facilities be separate. In the Delaware case, the Supreme Court of Delaware adhered to that doctrine, but ordered that the plaintiffs be admitted to the white schools because of their superiority to the Negro schools.

The plaintiffs contend that segregated public schools are not "equal" and cannot be made "equal," and that hence they are deprived of the equal protection of the laws. Because of the obvious importance of the question presented, the Court took jurisdiction. Argument was heard in the 1952 Term, and reargument was heard this Term on certain questions propounded by the Court.

Reargument was largely devoted to the circumstances surrounding the adoption of the Fourteenth Amendment in 1868. It covered exhaustively consideration of the Amendment in Congress, ratification by the states, then-existing practices in racial segregation, and the views of proponents and opponents of the Amendment. This discussion and our own investigation convince us that, although these sources cast some light, it is not enough to resolve the problem with which we are faced. At best, they are inconclusive. The most avid proponents of the post-War Amendments undoubtedly intended them to remove all legal distinctions among "all persons born or naturalized in the United States." Their opponents, just as certainly, were antagonistic to both the letter and the spirit of the Amendments and wished them to have the most limited effect. What others in Congress and the state legislatures had in mind cannot be determined with any degree of certainty.

An additional reason for the inconclusive nature of the Amendment's history with respect to segregated schools is the status of public education at that time. In the South, the movement toward free common schools, supported by general taxation, had not yet taken hold. Education of white children was largely in the hands of private groups. Education of Negroes was almost nonexistent, and practically all of the race were illiterate. In fact, any education of Negroes was forbidden by law in some states. Today, in contrast, many Negroes have achieved outstanding success in the arts and sciences, as well as in the business and professional world. It is true that public school education at the time of the Amendment had advanced further in the North, but the effect of the Amendment on Northern States was generally ignored in the congressional debates. Even in the North, the conditions of public education did not approximate those existing today. The curriculum was usually rudimentary; ungraded schools were common in rural areas; the school term was but three months a year in many states, and compulsory school attendance was virtually unknown. As a consequence, it is not surprising that there should be so little in the history of the Fourteenth Amendment relating to its intended effect on public education.

In the first cases in this Court construing the Fourteenth Amendment, decided shortly after its adoption, the Court interpreted it as proscribing all state-imposed discriminations against the Negro race. The doctrine of "separate but equal" did not make its appearance in this Court until 1896 in the case of **Plessy v. Ferguson,** supra, involving not education but transportation. American courts have since labored with the doctrine for over half a century. In this Court, there have been six cases involving the "separate but equal" doctrine in the field of public education. In **Cumming v. County Board of Education, 175 U.S. 528,** and **Gong Lum v. Rice, 275 U.S. 78,** the validity of the doctrine itself was not challenged. In more recent cases, all on the graduate school level, inequality was found in that specific benefits enjoyed by white students were denied to Negro students of the same educational qualifications. **Missouri ex rel. Gaines v. Canada, 305 U.S. 337; Sipuel v. Oklahoma, 332 U.S. 631; Sweatt v. Painter, 339 U.S. 629; McLaurin v. Oklahoma State Regents, 339 U.S. 637.** In none of these cases

was it necessary to reexamine the doctrine to grant relief to the Negro plaintiff. And in **Sweatt v. Painter,** supra, the Court expressly reserved decision on the question whether **Plessy v. Ferguson** should be held inapplicable to public education.

In the instant cases, that question is directly presented. Here, unlike **Sweatt v. Painter,** there are findings below that the Negro and white schools involved have been equalized, or are being equalized, with respect to buildings, curricula, qualifications and salaries of teachers, and other "tangible" factors. Our decision, therefore, cannot turn on merely a comparison of these tangible factors in the Negro and white schools involved in each of the cases. We must look instead to the effect of segregation itself on public education.

In approaching this problem, we cannot turn the clock back to 1868, when the Amendment was adopted, or even to 1896, when **Plessy v. Ferguson** was written. We must consider public education in the light of its full development and its present place in American life throughout the Nation. Only in this way can it be determined if segregation in public schools deprives these plaintiffs of the equal protection of the laws.

Today, education is perhaps the most important function of state and local governments. Compulsory school attendance laws and the great expenditures for education both demonstrate our recognition of the importance of education to our democratic society. It is required in the performance of our most basic public responsibilities, even service in the armed forces. It is the very foundation of good citizenship. Today it is a principal instrument in awakening the child to cultural values, in preparing him for later professional training, and in helping him to adjust normally to his environment. In these days, it is doubtful that any child may reasonably be expected to succeed in life if he is denied the opportunity of an education. Such an opportunity, where the state has undertaken to provide it, is a right which must be made available to all on equal terms.

We come then to the question presented: Does segregation of children in public schools solely on the basis of race, even though the physical facilities and other "tangible" factors may be equal, deprive the children of the minority group of equal educational opportunities? We believe that it does.

In **Sweatt v. Painter,** supra, in finding that a segregated law school for Negroes could not provide them equal educational opportunities, this Court relied in large part on "those qualities which are incapable of objective measurement but which make for greatness in a law school." In **McLaurin v. Oklahoma State Regents,** supra, the Court, in requiring that a Negro admitted to a white graduate school be treated like all other students, again resorted to intangible considerations: " . . . his ability to study, to engage in discussions and exchange views with other students, and, in general, to learn his profession." Such considerations apply with added force to children in grade and high schools. To separate them from others of similar age and qualifications solely because of their race generates a feeling of inferiority as to their status in the community that may affect their hearts and minds in a way unlikely ever to be undone. The effect of this separation on their educational opportunities was well stated by a finding in the Kansas case by a court which nevertheless felt compelled to rule against the Negro plaintiffs:

Segregation of white and colored children in public schools has a detrimental effect upon the colored children. The impact is greater when it has the sanction of the law, for the policy of separating the races is usually interpreted as denoting the inferiority of the negro group. A sense of inferiority affects the motivation of a child to learn. Segregation with the sanction of law, therefore, has a tendency to [retard] the educational and mental development of negro children and to deprive them of some of the benefits they would receive in a racial[ly] integrated school system.

Whatever may have been the extent of psychological knowledge at the time of **Plessy v. Ferguson,** this finding is amply supported by modern authority. Any language in **Plessy v. Ferguson** contrary to this finding is rejected.

We conclude that, in the field of public education, the doctrine of "separate but equal" has no place. Separate educational facilities are inherently unequal. Therefore, we hold that the plaintiffs and others similarly situated for whom the actions have been brought are, by reason of the segregation complained of, deprived of the equal protection of the laws guaranteed by the Fourteenth Amendment. This disposition makes unnecessary any discussion whether such segregation also violates the Due Process Clause of the Fourteenth Amendment.

Because these are class actions, because of the wide applicability of this decision, and because of the great variety of local conditions, the formulation of decrees in these cases presents problems of considerable complexity. On reargument, the consideration of appropriate relief was necessarily subordinated to the primary question—the constitutionality of segregation in public education. We have now announced that such segregation is a denial of the equal protection of the laws. In order that we may have the full assistance of the parties in formulating decrees, the cases will be restored to the docket, and the parties are requested to present further argument on Questions 4 and 5 previously propounded by the Court for the reargument this Term The Attorney General of the United States is again invited to participate. The Attorneys General of the states requiring or permitting segregation in public education will also be permitted to appear as amici curiae upon request to do so by September 15, 1954, and submission of briefs by October 1, 1954.

It is so ordered.

*Together with **No. 2, Briggs et al. v. Elliott et al.,** on appeal from the United States District Court for the Eastern District of South Carolina, argued December 9–10, 1952, reargued December 7–8, 1953; **No. 4, Davis et al. v. County School Board of Prince Edward County, Virginia, et al.,** on appeal from the United States District Court for the Eastern District of Virginia, argued December 10, 1952, reargued December 7–8, 1953, and **No. 10, Gebhart et al. v. Belton et al.,** on certiorari to the Supreme Court of Delaware, argued December 11, 1952, reargued December 9, 1953.

Excerpt from *In re Gault,* 1967

SOURCE: U.S. Supreme Court. *In re Gault*, 387 U.S. 1. 1967. Argued December 6, 1966. Decided May 15, 1967.

Introduction

In the case of *In re Gault* (1967) the U.S. Supreme Court extended to American children the rights guaranteed to adult criminal defendants. The decision was based on the due process clause of the Fourteenth Amendment. During the twentieth century, as a result of the introduction of the juvenile court in most states in the early twentieth century, a separate legal system for children had developed based on the premise that children deserved special protection by the state. However, in practice this more informal legal system often victimized disorderly youths, including fifteen-year-old Gerald Gault, who was sentenced to six years at an Arizona state industrial school for allegedly making an obscene phone call. Gault had been arrested without the notification of his parents, tried without the benefit of attorney, and sentenced without possibility for appeal. The Gault case is basic to a new modern emphasis on the rights of children. In the following excerpt from the decision, Justice Abe Fortas, writing for the majority, explains the court's opinion.

From the inception of the juvenile court system, wide differences have been tolerated—indeed insisted upon—between the procedural rights accorded to adults and those of juveniles. In practically all jurisdictions, there are rights granted to adults which are withheld from juveniles. In addition to the specific problems involved in the present case, for example, it has been held that the juvenile is not entitled to bail, to indictment by grand jury, to a public trial or to trial by jury. It is frequent practice that rules governing the arrest and interrogation of adults by the police are not observed in the case of juveniles.

The history and theory underlying this development are well-known, but a recapitulation is necessary for purposes of this opinion. The Juvenile Court movement began in this country at the end of the last century. From the juvenile court statute adopted in Illinois in 1899, the system has spread to every State in the Union, the District of Columbia, and Puerto Rico. The constitutionality of Juvenile Court laws has been sustained in over 40 jurisdictions against a variety of attacks.

The early reformers were appalled by adult procedures and penalties, and by the fact that children could be given long prison sentences and mixed in jails with hardened criminals. They were profoundly convinced that society's duty to the child could not be confined by the concept of justice alone. They believed that society's role was not to ascertain whether the child was "guilty" or "innocent," but "What is he, how has he become what he is, and what had best be done in his interest and in the interest of the state to save him from a downward career." The child—essentially good, as they saw it—was to be made "to feel that he is the object of [the state's] care and solicitude," not that he was under arrest or on trial. The rules of criminal procedure were therefore altogether inapplicable. The apparent rigidities, technicalities, and harshness which they observed in both substantive and procedural criminal law were therefore to be discarded. The idea of crime and punishment was to be abandoned. The child was to be "treated" and "rehabilitated" and the procedures, from apprehension through institutionalization, were to be "clinical" rather than punitive.

These results were to be achieved, without coming to conceptual and constitutional grief, by insisting that the proceedings were not adversary, but that the state was proceeding as parens patriae. The Latin phrase proved to be a great help to those who sought to rationalize the exclusion of juveniles from the constitutional scheme; but its meaning is murky and its historic credentials are of dubious relevance. The phrase was taken from chancery practice, where, however, it was used to describe the power of the state to act in loco parentis for the purpose of protecting the property interests and the person of the child. But there is no trace of the doctrine in the history of criminal jurisprudence. At common law, children under seven were considered incapable of possessing criminal intent. Beyond that age, they were subjected to arrest, trial, and in theory to punishment like adult offenders. In these old days, the state was not deemed to have authority to accord them fewer procedural rights than adults.

The right of the state, as parens patriae, to deny to the child procedural rights available to his elders was elaborated by the assertion that a child, unlike an adult, has a right "not to liberty but to custody." He can be made to attorn to his parents, to go to school, etc. If his parents default in effectively performing their custodial functions—that is, if the child is "delinquent"—the state may intervene. In doing so, it does not deprive the child of any rights, because he has none. It merely provides the "custody" to which the child is entitled. On this basis, proceedings involving juveniles were described as "civil" not "criminal" and therefore not subject to the requirements which restrict the state when it seeks to deprive a person of his liberty.

Accordingly, the highest motives and most enlightened impulses led to a peculiar system for juveniles, unknown to our law in any comparable context. The constitutional and theoretical basis for this peculiar system is—to say the least—debatable. And in practice, as we remarked in the Kent case, supra, the results have not been entirely satisfactory. Juvenile Court history has again demonstrated that unbridled discretion, however benevolently motivated, is frequently a poor substitute for principle and procedure. In 1937, Dean Pound wrote: "The powers of the Star Chamber were a trifle in comparison with those of our juvenile courts. . . ." The absence of substantive standards has not necessarily meant that children receive careful, compassionate, individualized treatment. The absence of procedural rules based upon constitutional principle has not always produced fair, efficient, and effective procedures. Departures from established principles of due process have frequently resulted not in enlightened procedure, but in arbitrariness. The Chairman of the Pennsylvania Council of Juvenile Court Judges has recently observed: "Unfortunately, loose procedures, high-handed methods and crowded court calendars, either singly or in combination, all too often, have resulted in depriving some juveniles of fundamental rights that have resulted in a denial of due process."

Failure to observe the fundamental requirements of due process has resulted in instances, which might have been avoided, of unfairness to individuals and inadequate or inaccurate findings of fact and unfortunate prescriptions of remedy. Due process of law is the primary and indispensable foundation of individual freedom. It is the basic and essential term in the social compact which defines the rights of the individual and delimits the powers which the state may exercise. As Mr. Justice Frankfurter has said: "The history of American freedom is, in no small measure, the history of procedure." But in addition, the procedural rules which have been fashioned from the generality of due process are our best instruments for the distillation and evaluation of essential facts from the conflicting welter of data that life and our adversary methods present. It is these instruments of due process which enhance the possibility that truth will emerge from the confrontation of opposing versions and conflicting data. "Procedure is to law what 'scientific method' is to science."

It is claimed that juveniles obtain benefits from the special procedures applicable to them which more than offset the disadvantages of denial of the substance of normal due process. As we shall discuss, the observance of due process standards, intelligently and not ruthlessly administered, will not compel the States to abandon or displace any of the substantive benefits of the juvenile process. But it is important, we think, that the claimed benefits of the juvenile process should be candidly appraised. Neither sentiment nor folklore should cause us to shut our eyes, for example, to such startling findings as that reported in an exceptionally reliable study of repeaters or recidivism conducted by the Stanford Research Institute for the President's Commission on Crime in the District of Columbia. This Commission's Report states:

"In fiscal 1966 approximately 66 percent of the 16- and 17-year-old juveniles referred to the court by the Youth Aid Division had been before the court previously. In 1965, 56 percent of those in the Receiving Home were repeaters. The SRI study revealed that 61 percent of the sample Juvenile Court referrals in 1965 had been previously referred at least once and that 42 percent had been referred at least twice before." Id., at 773.

Certainly, these figures and the high crime rates among juveniles to which we have referred (supra, n. 26), could not lead us to conclude that the absence of constitutional protections reduces crime, or that the juvenile system, functioning free of constitutional inhibitions as it has largely done, is effective to reduce crime or rehabilitate offenders. We do not mean by this to denigrate the juvenile court process or to suggest that there are not aspects of the juvenile system relating to offenders which are valuable. But the features of the juvenile system which its proponents have asserted are of unique benefit will not be impaired by constitutional domestication. For example, the commendable principles relating to the processing and treatment of juveniles separately from adults are in no way involved or affected by the procedural issues under discussion. Further, we are told that one of the important benefits of the special juvenile court procedures is that they avoid classifying the juvenile as a "criminal." The juvenile offender is now classed as a "delinquent." There is, of course, no reason why this should not continue. It is disconcerting, however, that this term has come to involve only slightly less stigma than the term "criminal" applied to adults. It is also emphasized that in practically all jurisdictions, statutes provide that an adjudication of the child as a delinquent shall not operate as a civil disability or disqualify him for civil service appointment. There is no reason why the application of due process requirements should interfere with such provisions.

Beyond this, it is frequently said that juveniles are protected by the process from disclosure of their deviational behavior. As the Supreme Court of Arizona phrased it in the present case, the summary procedures of Juvenile Courts are sometimes defended by a statement that it is the law's policy "to hide youthful errors from the full gaze of the public and bury them in the graveyard of the forgotten past." This claim of secrecy, however, is more rhetoric than reality. Disclosure of court records is discretionary with the judge in most jurisdictions. Statutory restrictions almost invariably apply only to the court records, and even as to those the evidence is that many courts routinely furnish information to the FBI and the military, and on request to government agencies and

even to private employers. Of more importance are police records. In most States the police keep a complete file of juvenile "police contacts" and have complete discretion as to disclosure of juvenile records. Police departments receive requests for information from the FBI and other law-enforcement agencies, the Armed Forces, and social service agencies, and most of them generally comply. Private employers word their application forms to produce information concerning juvenile arrests and court proceedings, and in some jurisdictions information concerning juvenile police contacts is furnished private employers as well as government agencies.

In any event, there is no reason why, consistently with due process, a State cannot continue, if it deems it appropriate, to provide and to improve provision for the confidentiality of records of police contacts and court action relating to juveniles. It is interesting to note, however, that the Arizona Supreme Court used the confidentiality argument as a justification for the type of notice which is here attacked as inadequate for due process purposes. The parents were given merely general notice that their child was charged with "delinquency." No facts were specified. The Arizona court held, however, as we shall discuss, that in addition to this general "notice," the child and his parents must be advised "of the facts involved in the case" no later than the initial hearing by the judge. Obviously, this does not "bury" the word about the child's transgressions. It merely defers the time of disclosure to a point when it is of limited use to the child or his parents in preparing his defense or explanation.

Further, it is urged that the juvenile benefits from informal proceedings in the court. The early conception of the Juvenile Court proceeding was one in which a fatherly judge touched the heart and conscience of the erring youth by talking over his problems, by paternal advice and admonition, and in which, in extreme situations, benevolent and wise institutions of the State provided guidance and help "to save him from a downward career." Then, as now, goodwill and compassion were admirably prevalent. But recent studies have, with surprising unanimity, entered sharp dissent as to the validity of this gentle conception. They suggest that the appearance as well as the actuality of fairness, impartiality and orderliness—in short, the essentials of due process—may be a more impressive and more therapeutic attitude so far as the juvenile is concerned. For example, in a recent study, the sociologists Wheeler and Cottrell observe that when the procedural laxness of the "parens patriae" attitude is followed by stern disciplining, the contrast may have an adverse effect upon the child, who feels that he has been deceived or enticed. They conclude as follows: "Unless appropriate due process of law is followed, even the juvenile who has violated the law may not feel that he is being fairly treated and may therefore resist the rehabilitative efforts of court personnel." Of course, it is not suggested that juvenile court judges should fail appropriately to take account, in their demeanor and conduct, of the emotional and psychological attitude of the juveniles with whom they are confronted. While due process requirements will, in some instances, introduce a degree of order and regularity to Juvenile Court proceedings to determine delinquency, and in contested cases will introduce some elements of the adversary system, nothing will require that the conception of the kindly juvenile judge be replaced by its opposite, nor do we here rule upon the question whether ordinary due process requirements must be observed with respect to hearings to determine the disposition of the delinquent child.

Ultimately, however, we confront the reality of that portion of the Juvenile Court process with which we deal in this case. A boy is charged with misconduct. The boy is committed to an institution where he may be restrained of liberty for years. It is of no constitutional consequence—and of limited practical meaning—that the institution to which he is committed is called an Industrial School. The fact of the matter is that, however euphemistic the title, a "receiving home" or an "industrial school" for juveniles is an institution of confinement in which the child is incarcerated for a greater or lesser time. His world becomes "a building with white-washed walls, regimented routine and institutional hours. . . ." Instead of mother and father and sisters and brothers and friends and classmates, his world is peopled by guards, custodians, state employees, and "delinquents" confined with him for anything from waywardness to rape and homicide.

In view of this, it would be extraordinary if our Constitution did not require the procedural regularity and the exercise of care implied in the phrase "due process." Under our Constitution, the condition of being a boy does not justify a kangaroo court. The traditional ideas of Juvenile Court procedure, indeed, contemplated that time would be available and care would be used to establish precisely what the juvenile did and why he did it—was it a prank of adolescence or a brutal act threatening serious consequences to himself or society unless corrected? Under traditional notions, one would assume that in a case like that of Gerald Gault, where the juvenile appears to have a home, a working mother and father, and an older brother, the Juvenile Judge would have made a careful inquiry and judgment as to the possibility that the boy could be disciplined and dealt with at home, despite his previous transgressions. Indeed, so far as appears in the record before us, except for some conversation with Gerald about his school work and his "wanting to go to . . . Grand Canyon with his father," the points to which the judge directed his attention were little different from those that would be involved in determining any charge of violation of a penal statute. The essential difference between Gerald's case and a normal criminal case is that safeguards available to adults were discarded in Gerald's case. The summary procedure as well as the long commitment was possible because Gerald was 15 years of age instead of over 18.

If Gerald had been over 18, he would not have been subject to Juvenile Court proceedings. For the particular offense immediately involved, the maximum punishment would have been a fine of $5 to $50, or imprisonment in jail for not more than two months. Instead, he was committed to custody for a maximum of six years. If he had been over 18 and had committed an offense to which such a sentence might apply, he would have been entitled to substantial rights under the Constitution of the United States as well as under Arizona's laws and constitution. The United States Constitution would guarantee him rights and protections with respect to arrest, search and seizure, and pretrial interrogation. It would assure him of specific notice of the charges and adequate time to decide his course of action and to prepare his defense. He would be entitled to clear advice that he could be represented by counsel, and, at least if a felony were involved, the State would be required to provide counsel if his parents were unable to afford it. If the court acted on the basis of his confession, careful procedures would be required to assure its voluntariness. If the case went to trial, confrontation and opportunity for cross-examination would be guaranteed. So wide a gulf between the State's treatment of the adult and of the child requires a bridge sturdier than mere verbiage, and reasons more persuasive than cliche can provide. As Wheeler and Cottrell have put it, "The rhetoric of the juvenile court movement has developed without any necessarily close correspondence to the realities of court and institutional routines."

Excerpt from California Megan's Law, 1996

SOURCE: California Department of Justice. California Penal Code, Section 290.

Introduction

Many Americans grew concerned during the late twentieth century about the dangers that sex offenders posed to children. National and state governments attempted to respond to that concern through legislation. After seven-year-old Megan Kanka was raped and murdered in 1994 by a neighbor who was known to the police as a dangerous sex offender, grass-roots advocacy groups pushed New Jersey (Megan's home state) and then every other state in the union to pass laws permitting residents to gain access to information about the presence of sex offenders in their neighborhoods. In May 1996 President Bill Clinton signed the federal Megan's Law which encouraged states to register sex offenders and disseminate information about such offenders to the general public. The following excerpt from California's Megan's Law, passed in 1996, indicates the detailed level of information collected and published by authorities. While the main trend in American jurisprudence during the second half of the twentieth century was toward the protection of personal privacy, the public stake in children's welfare produced an opposite dynamic in laws concerning their protection.

California Penal Code
Section 290

290. (a) (1) (A) Every person described in paragraph (2), for the rest of his or her life while residing in, or, if he or she has no residence, while located within California, or while attending school or working in California, as described in subparagraph (G), shall be required to register with the chief of police of the city in which he or she is residing, or if he or she has no residence, is located, or the sheriff of the county if he or she is residing, or if he or she has no residence, is located, in an unincorporated area or city that has no police department, and, additionally, with the chief of police of a campus of the University of California, the California State University, or community college if he or she is residing, or if he or she has no residence, is located upon the campus or in any of its facilities, within five working days of coming into, or changing his or her residence or location within, any city, county, or city and county, or campus in which he or she temporarily resides, or, if he or she has no residence, is located.

. . .

(2) The following persons shall be required to register pursuant to paragraph (1):

(A) Any person who, since July 1, 1944, has been or is hereafter convicted in any court in this state or in any federal or military court of a violation of Section 207 or 209 committed with intent to violate Section 261, 286, 288, 288a, or 289, Section 220, except assault to commit mayhem, Section 243.4, paragraph (1), (2), (3), (4), or (6) of subdivision (a) of Section 261, or paragraph (1) of subdivision (a) of Section 262 involving the use of force or violence for which the person is sentenced to the state prison, Section 264.1, 266, 266c, subdivision (b) of Section 266h, subdivision (b) of Section 266i, 266j, 267, 269, 285, 286, 288, 288a, 288.5, or 289, subdivision (b), (c), or (d) of Section 311.2, Section 311.3, 311.4, 311.10, 311.11, or 647.6, former Section 647a, subdivision (c) of Section 653f, subdivision 1 or 2 of Section 314, any offense involving lewd or lascivious conduct under Section 272, or any felony violation of Section 288.2; or any person who since that date has been or is hereafter convicted of the attempt to commit any of the abovementioned offenses.

(B) Any person who, since July 1, 1944, has been or hereafter is released, discharged, or paroled from a penal institution where he or she was confined because of the commission or attempted commission of one of the offenses described in subparagraph (A).

(C) Any person who, since July 1, 1944, has been or hereafter is determined to be a mentally disordered sex offender under Article 1 (commencing with Section 6300) of Chapter 2 of Part 2 of Division 6 of the Welfare and Institutions Code or any person who has been found guilty in the guilt phase of a trial for an offense for which registration is required by this section but who has been found not guilty by reason of insanity in the sanity phase of the trial.

(D) Any person who, since July 1, 1944, has been, or is hereafter convicted in any other court, including any state, federal, or military court, of any offense which, if committed or attempted in this state, would have been punishable as one or more of the offenses described in subparagraph (A) or any person ordered by any other court, including any state, federal, or military court, to register as a sex offender for any offense, if the court found at the time of conviction or sentencing that the person committed the offense as a result of sexual compulsion or for purposes of sexual gratification.

(E) Any person ordered by any court to register pursuant to this section for any offense not included specifically in this section if the court finds at the time of conviction or sentencing that the person committed the offense as a result of sexual compulsion or for purposes of sexual gratification. The court shall state on the record the reasons for its findings and the reasons for requiring registration.

. . .

(m) (1) When a peace officer reasonably suspects, based on information that has come to his or her attention through information provided by any peace officer or member of the public, that a child or other person may be at risk from a sex offender convicted of a crime listed in paragraph (1) of subdivision (a) of Section 290.4, a law enforcement agency may, notwithstanding any other provision of law, provide any of the information specified in paragraph (4) of this subdivision about that registered sex offender that the agency deems relevant and necessary to protect the public, to the following persons, agencies, or organizations the offender is likely to encounter, including, but not limited to, the following:

(A) Public and private educational institutions, day care establishments, and establishments and organizations that primarily serve individuals likely to be victimized by the offender.

(B) Other community members at risk.

(2) The law enforcement agency may authorize persons and entities who receive the information pursuant to paragraph (1) to disclose information to additional persons only if the agency does the following:

(A) Determines that all conditions set forth in paragraph (1) have been satisfied regarding disclosure to the additional persons.

(B) Identifies the appropriate scope of further disclosure.

(3) Persons notified pursuant to paragraph (1) may disclose the information provided by the law enforcement

agency in the manner and to the extent authorized by the law enforcement agency.

(4) The information that may be disclosed pursuant to this section includes the following:

(A) The offender's full name.

(B) The offender's known aliases.

(C) The offender's gender.

(D) The offender's race.

(E) The offender's physical description.

(F) The offender's photograph.

(G) The offender's date of birth.

(H) Crimes resulting in registration under this section.

(I) The offender's address, which must be verified prior to publication.

(J) Description and license plate number of offender's vehicles or vehicles the offender is known to drive.

(K) Type of victim targeted by the offender.

(L) Relevant parole or probation conditions, such as one prohibiting contact with children.

(M) Dates of crimes resulting in classification under this section.

(N) Date of release from confinement.

However, information disclosed pursuant to this subdivision shall not include information that would identify the victim.

English Language Education for Immigrant Children, California Education Code, Proposition 227, 1998

SOURCE: California Education Code. 1998. Education Code Sections 300–340, and California Code of Regulations, Title 5, Sections 4301–4320.

Introduction

Debate over the best way to acculturate immigrant children into American society has been ongoing for two hundred years. During the late nineteenth and early twentieth centuries, when rates of immigration were very high, public schools were the primary tool in the Americanization of non-native children. In the 1960s and 1970s immigration again grew following the repeal of tight controls and quotas that had been set in the 1920s, but models of enforced assimilation were disavowed. Starting in the 1970s, federal legislation and federal courts began to require that school districts provide bilingual instruction to those who needed it. In many schools in California, a popular destination for immigrant families, bilingual classrooms offered instruction in both English and a second language. While many immigrants supported bilingual education because it nurtured their children's attachment to their cultures of origin, critics of bilingual edu-

cation have lambasted the system for failing to teach children fluency in English. In 1998, California voters passed an "English for Children" initiative, or Proposition 227, which sought to end bilingual education in the state.

SECTION 1. Chapter 3 (commencing with Section 300) is added to Part 1 of the Educational Code, to read:

CHAPTER 3. ENGLISH LANGUAGE EDUCATION FOR IMMIGRANT CHILDREN

ARTICLE 1. Findings and Declarations

300. The People of California find and declare as follows:

(a) WHEREAS the English language is the national public language of the United States of America and of the state of California, is spoken by the vast majority of California residents, and is also the leading world language for science, technology, and international business, thereby being the language of economic opportunity; and

(b) WHEREAS immigrant parents are eager to have their children acquire a good knowledge of English, thereby allowing them to fully participate in the American Dream of economic and social advancement; and

(c) WHEREAS the government and the public schools of California have a moral obligation and a constitutional duty to provide all of California's children, regardless of their ethnicity or national origins, with the skills necessary to become productive members of our society, and of these skills, literacy in the English language is among the most important; and

(d) WHEREAS the public schools of California currently do a poor job of educating immigrant children, wasting financial resources on costly experimental language programs whose failure over the past two decades is demonstrated by the current high drop-out rates and low English literacy levels of many immigrant children; and

(e) WHEREAS young immigrant children can easily acquire full fluency in a new language, such as English, if they are heavily exposed to that language in the classroom at an early age.

(f) THEREFORE it is resolved that: all children in California public schools shall be taught English as rapidly and effectively as possible.

ARTICLE 2. English Language Education

305. Subject to the exceptions provided in Article 3 (commencing with Section 310), all children in California public schools shall be taught English by being taught in English. In particular, this shall require that all children be placed in English language classrooms. Children who are English

learners shall be educated through sheltered English immersion during a temporary transition period not normally intended to exceed one year. Local schools shall be permitted to place in the same classroom English learners of different ages but whose degree of English proficiency is similar. Local schools shall be encouraged to mix together in the same classroom English learners from different native-language groups but with the same degree of English fluency. Once English learners have acquired a good working knowledge of English, they shall be transferred to English language mainstream classrooms. As much as possible, current supplemental funding for English learners shall be maintained, subject to possible modification under Article 8 (commencing with Section 335) below.

306. The definitions of the terms used in this article and in Article 3 (commencing with Section 310) are as follows:

(a) "English learner" means a child who does not speak English or whose native language is not English and who is not currently able to perform ordinary classroom work in English, also known as a Limited English Proficiency or LEP child.

(b) "English language classroom" means a classroom in which the language of instruction used by the teaching personnel is overwhelmingly the English language, and in which such teaching personnel possess a good knowledge of the English language.

(c) "English language mainstream classroom" means a classroom in which the students either are native English language speakers or already have acquired reasonable fluency in English.

(d) "Sheltered English immersion" or "structured English immersion" means an English language acquisition process for young children in which nearly all classroom instruction is in English but with the curriculum and presentation designed for children who are learning the language.

(e) "Bilingual education/native language instruction" means a language acquisition process for students in which much or all instruction, textbooks, and teaching materials are in the child's native language.

ARTICLE 3. Parental Exceptions

310. The requirements of Section 305 may be waived with the prior written informed consent, to be provided annually, of the child's parents or legal guardian under the circumstances specified below and in Section 311. Such informed consent shall require that said parents or legal guardian personally visit the school to apply for the waiver and that they there be provided a full description of the educational materials to be used in the different educational program choices and all the educational opportunities available to the child. Under such parental waiver conditions, children may be transferred to classes where they are taught English and other subjects through bilingual education techniques or other generally recognized educational methodologies permitted by law. Individual schools in which 20 students or more of a given grade level receive a waiver shall be required to offer such a class; otherwise, they must allow the students to transfer to a public school in which such a class is offered.

311. The circumstances in which a parental exception waiver may be granted under Section 310 are as follows:

(a) Children who already know English: the child already possesses good English language skills, as measured by standardized tests of English vocabulary comprehension, reading, and writing, in which the child scores at or above the state average for his grade level or at or above the 5th grade average, whichever is lower; or

(b) Older children: the child is age 10 years or older, and it is the informed belief of the school principal and educational staff that an alternate course of educational study would be better suited to the child's rapid acquisition of basic English language skills; or

(c) Children with special needs: the child already has been placed for a period of not less than thirty days during that school year in an English language classroom and it is subsequently the informed belief of the school principal and educational staff that the child has such special physical, emotional, psychological, or educational needs that an alternate course of educational study would be better suited to the child's overall educational development. A written description of these special needs must be provided and any such decision is to be made subject to the examination and approval of the local school superintendent, under guidelines established by and subject to the review of the local Board of Education and ultimately the State Board of Education. The existence of such special needs shall not compel issuance of a waiver, and the parents shall be fully informed of their right to refuse to agree to a waiver.

ARTICLE 4. Community-Based English Tutoring

315. In furtherance of its constitutional and legal requirement to offer special language assistance to children coming from backgrounds of limited English proficiency, the state shall encourage family members and others to provide personal English language tutoring to such children, and support these efforts by raising the general level of English language knowledge in the community. Commencing with the fiscal year in which this initiative is enacted and for each of the nine fiscal years following thereafter, a sum of fifty million dollars ($50,000,000) per year is hereby appropriated from the General Fund for the purpose of providing additional funding for free or subsidized programs of adult English language instruction to parents or other members of the community who pledge to provide personal English language tutoring to California school children with limited English proficiency.

316. Programs funded pursuant to this section shall be provided through schools or community organizations. Funding for these programs shall be administered by the Office of the Superintendent of Public Instruction, and shall be disbursed at the discretion of the local school boards, under reasonable guidelines established by, and subject to the review of, the State Board of Education.

ARTICLE 5. Legal Standing and Parental Enforcement

320. As detailed in Article 2 (commencing with Section 305) and Article 3 (commencing with Section 310), all California school children have the right to be provided with an English language public education. If a California school child has been denied the option of an English language instructional curriculum in public school, the child's parent or legal guardian shall have legal standing to sue for enforcement of the provisions of this statute, and if successful shall be awarded normal and customary attorney's fees and actual damages, but not punitive or consequential damages. Any school board member or other elected official or public school teacher or administrator who willfully and repeatedly refuses to implement the terms of this statute by providing such an English language educational option at an available public school to a California school child may be held personally liable for fees and actual damages by the child's parents or legal guardian.

ARTICLE 6. Severability

325. If any part or parts of this statute are found to be in conflict with federal law or the United States or the California State Constitution, the statute shall be implemented to the maximum extent that federal law, and the United States and the California State Constitution permit. Any provision held invalid shall be severed from the remaining portions of this statute.

ARTICLE 7. Operative Date

330. This initiative shall become operative for all school terms which begin more than sixty days following the date at which it becomes effective.

ARTICLE 8. Amendment

335. The provisions of this act may be amended by a statute that becomes effective upon approval by the electorate or by a statute to further the act's purpose passed by a two-thirds vote of each house of the Legislature and signed by the Governor.

ARTICLE 9. Interpretation

340. Under circumstances in which portions of this statute are subject to conflicting interpretations, Section 300 shall be assumed to contain the governing intent of the statute.

Classics

Excerpt from *The Republic* by Plato, 370–375 B.C.E.

SOURCE: Plato. 1910 [370–375 B.C.E.]. *The Republic.* Trans. Benjamin Jowett. New York: P. F. Collier and Sons.

Introduction

Plato's classic text, *The Republic,* written around 370–375 B.C.E., is an investigation into the nature of justice, and an effort to discover the moral truths that must guide men's actions. Plato used the form of Socratic dialogues to raise his questions about man and the state. In *The Republic,* he proposes establishing an authoritarian state led by guardians who have undergone special philosophical training. In Book III, the character of Socrates engages in a discussion with Glaucon and Adeimantus—brothers of Plato—regarding the proper childhood education for the guardians. In the following passage, Plato makes a strong argument for the strict censorship of literature to protect the morality of the republic's future leaders. In *The Republic,* the purpose of education is to secure the state, not to further the self-discovery of youth.

Then he who is to be a really good and noble guardian of the State will require to unite in himself philosophy and spirit and swiftness and strength?

Undoubtedly.

Then we have found the desired natures; and now that we have found them, how are they to be reared and educated? Is not this enquiry which may be expected to throw light on the greater enquiry which is our final end—How do justice and injustice grow up in States? for we do not want either to omit what is to the point or to draw out the argument to an inconvenient length.

SOCRATES–ADEIMANTUS

Adeimantus thought that the enquiry would be of great service to us.

Then, I said, my dear friend, the task must not be given up, even if somewhat long.

Certainly not.

Come then, and let us pass a leisure hour in story-telling, and our story shall be the education of our heroes.

By all means.

And what shall be their education? Can we find a better than the traditional sort?—and this has two divisions, gymnastic for the body, and music for the soul.

True.

Shall we begin education with music, and go on to gymnastic afterwards?

By all means.

And when you speak of music, do you include literature or not?

I do.

And literature may be either true or false?

Yes.

And the young should be trained in both kinds, and we begin with the false?

I do not understand your meaning, he said.

You know, I said, that we begin by telling children stories which, though not wholly destitute of truth, are in the main fictitious; and these stories are told them when they are not of an age to learn gymnastics.

Very true.

That was my meaning when I said that we must teach music before gymnastics.

Quite right, he said.

You know also that the beginning is the most important part of any work, especially in the case of a young and tender thing; for that is the time at which the character is being formed and the desired impression is more readily taken.

Quite true.

And shall we just carelessly allow children to hear any casual tales which may be devised by casual persons, and to receive into their minds ideas for the most part the very opposite of those which we should wish them to have when they are grown up?

We cannot.

Then the first thing will be to establish a censorship of the writers of fiction, and let the censors receive any tale of fiction which is good, and reject the bad; and we will desire mothers and nurses to tell their children the authorised ones only. Let them fashion the mind with such tales, even more fondly than they mould the body with their hands; but most of those which are now in use must be discarded.

Of what tales are you speaking? he said.

You may find a model of the lesser in the greater, I said; for they are necessarily of the same type, and there is the same spirit in both of them.

Very likely, he replied; but I do not as yet know what you would term the greater.

Those, I said, which are narrated by Homer and Hesiod, and the rest of the poets, who have ever been the great story-tellers of mankind.

But which stories do you mean, he said; and what fault do you find with them?

A fault which is most serious, I said; the fault of telling a lie, and, what is more, a bad lie.

But when is this fault committed?

Whenever an erroneous representation is made of the nature of gods and heroes,—as when a painter paints a portrait not having the shadow of a likeness to the original.

Yes, he said, that sort of thing is certainly very blamable; but what are the stories which you mean?

First of all, I said, there was that greatest of all lies in high places, which the poet told about Uranus, and which was a bad lie too,—I mean what Hesiod says that Uranus did, and how Cronus retaliated on him. The doings of Cronus, and the sufferings which in turn his son inflicted upon him, even if they were true, ought certainly not to be lightly told to young and thoughtless persons; if possible, they had better be buried in silence. But if there is an absolute necessity for their mention, a chosen few might hear them in a mystery, and they should sacrifice not a common [Eleusinian] pig, but some huge and unprocurable victim; and then the number of the hearers will be very few indeed.

Why, yes, said he, those stories are extremely objectionable.

Yes, Adeimantus, they are stories not to be repeated in our State; the young man should not be told that in committing the worst of crimes he is far from doing anything outrageous; and that even if he chastises his father when does wrong, in whatever manner, he will only be following the example of the first and greatest among the gods.

I entirely agree with you, he said; in my opinion those stories are quite unfit to be repeated.

Neither, if we mean our future guardians to regard the habit of quarrelling among themselves as of all things the basest, should any word be said to them of the wars in heaven, and of the plots and fightings of the gods against one another, for they are not true. No, we shall never mention the battles of the giants, or let them be embroidered on garments; and we shall be silent about the innumerable other quarrels of gods and heroes with their friends and relatives. If they would only believe us we would tell them that quarrelling is unholy, and that never up to this time has there been any, quarrel between citizens; this is what old men and old women should begin by telling children; and when they grow up, the poets also should be told to compose for them in a similar spirit. But the narrative of Hephaestus binding

Here his mother, or how on another occasion Zeus sent him flying for taking her part when she was being beaten, and all the battles of the gods in Homer—these tales must not be admitted into our State, whether they are supposed to have an allegorical meaning or not. For a young person cannot judge what is allegorical and what is literal; anything that he receives into his mind at that age is likely to become indelible and unalterable; and therefore it is most important that the tales which the young first hear should be models of virtuous thoughts.

There you are right, he replied; but if any one asks where are such models to be found and of what tales are you speaking—how shall we answer him?

I said to him, You and I, Adeimantus, at this moment are not poets, but founders of a State: now the founders of a State ought to know the general forms in which poets should cast their tales, and the limits which must be observed by them, but to make the tales is not their business.

Excerpt from *A Brief Account of the Destruction of the Indies* by Bartolomé de Las Casas, 1552

SOURCE: Las Casas, Bartolomé de. 1552. *A Brief Account of the Destruction of the Indies.* Available from <www.american-journey.psmedia.com/>.

Introduction

In his *Brief Account of the Destruction of the Indies, or The Tears of the Indians* (written 1542 and published in 1552), the Spanish missionary Bartolomé de Las Casas recorded the atrocities committed by his compatriots in the New World. The sadistic murders of infants and children are the most horrifying aspect of his narrative. According to Las Casas, Spanish soldiers killed Indian children for sport. The missionary also argues that enslavement caused enormous infant mortality and hampered the Indians' ability to have children. *Tears of the Indians* reveals that conquest is enacted not only on the battlefield, but in the family. The destruction of the next generation is perhaps the most effective way to defeat a people. Las Casas wrote *Tears of the Indians* to persuade the Spanish government to treat the natives of the New World with greater justice; but perhaps its most effective legacy was upon its English audience, who used its horrors to justify competing with the Spanish for control of the Western Hemisphere.

Of Hispaniola.

In the Island of Hispaniola, to which the Spaniards came first, these slaughters and ruines of mankinde took their beginning. They took away their women and children to serve them, though the reward which they gave them was a sad and fatal one. Their food got with great pain and dropping sweat, the Spaniards still consumed, not content with what the poor Indians gave them gratis out of their own want; One Spaniard consuming in one day as much as would suffice three families, every one containing ten persons. Being thus broken with so many evils, afflicted with so many torments, and handled so ignominiously, they began at length to believe that the Spaniards were not sent from Heaven. And therefore some of them hid their Children, others their Wives, others their Victuals in obscure and secret places; Others not being able to endure a Nation that conversed among them with such a boysterous impiety sought for shelter in the most abrupt and inaccessible mountains. For the Spaniards while they were among them did not only entertain them with cruel beating them with their fists, and with their slaves, but presumed also to lay violent hands upon the Rulers and Magistrates of their Cities: and they arriv'd at that height of impudence and unheard of boldnesse, that a certain private Captain scrupled not to force the Wife of the most potent King among them. From which time forward they began to think what way they might take to expell the Spaniards out of their Countrey. But good God! what fort of Armes had they? such as were as available to offend or defend as bulrushes might be. Which when the Spaniards saw, they came with their Horsemen well armed with Sword and Launce, making most cruel havocks and slaughters among them. Overrunning Cities and Villages, where they spared nos fex nor age; neither would their cruelty pity Women with childe, whose bellies they would rip up, taking out the Infant to hew it in pieces. They would often lay wagers who should with most dexterity either cleave or cut a man in the middle, or who could at one blow footnest cut off his head. The children they would take by the feet and dash their innocent heads against the rocks, and when they were fallen into the water, with a strange and cruel derision they would call upon them to swim. Sometimes they would run both Mother and Infant, being in her belly quite through at one thrust. They erected certain Gallowses, that were broad but so low, that the tormented creatures might touch the ground with their feet, upon every one of which they would hang thirteen persons, blasphemously affirming that they did it in honour of our Redeemer and his Apostles, and then putting fire under them, they burnt the poor wretches alive. Those whom their pity did think fit to spare, they would send away with their hands half cut off, and so hanging by the skin. Thus upbraiding their flight, Go carry letters to those who lye bid in the mountains and are fled from us.

This Death they found out also for the Lords and Nobles of the Land; they stuck up forked sticks in the ground, and then laid certain perches upon them, and so laying them upon those perches, they put a gentle fire under, causing the fire to melt them away by degrees, to their unspeakable torment.

One time above the rest I saw four of the Nobles laid upon these perches, and two or three other of these kinde of hurdles furnished after the same manner; the clamours and cries of which persons being troublesome to the Captain, he gave order that they should be hang'd, but the Executioner whose name I know, and whose parents are not obscure, hindred their Calamity from so quick a conclusion, stopping their mouthes, that they should not disturb the Captain, and still laying on more wood, till being roasted according to his pleasure, they yeelded up the ghost. Of these and other things innumerable I have been an eye-witnesse; Now because there were some that shun'd like so many rocks the cruelty of a Nation so inhumane, so void of piety and love to mankinde, and therefore fled from them to the mountains; therefore they hunted them with their Hounds, whom they bred up and taught to pull down and tear the Indians like beasts: by these Dogs much humane bloud was shed; and because the Indians did now and then kill a Spaniard, taking him at an advantage, as justly they might; therefore the Spaniards made a Law among themselves, that for one Spaniard so slaine, they should kill a hundred Indians.

. . .

The wars begin now at an end, and the inhabitants all killed up, the women and children being only reserved, they divided them among themselves, giving to one thirty, to another forty, to one a hundred, to another two hundred, and those that had most, received them on this condition, that they should instruct them in the Catholick Faith, though commonly their Masters were a company of stupid, ignorant, and covetous fellowes, and defiled with all manner of vices. But the main care was to send the men to work in the Gold Mines, which is an intolerable labour, and to send the women to manure and till the ground; an exercise fit only for the sloutest men. These they fed with nothing but roots and hearbs, so that the milk of women with childe being dried up, by that reason the poor little infants died. And the men being separated from the women, there was no more issue to be expected from them. The men perished in the Gold Mines with hunger and labour, the women perished in the fields, being tired out with the same calamities: and thus was a vast number of the inhabitants of this Island wholly extirpated. Besides all this they caused them to carry great burdens of a hundred and fourscore pound, and to travell with it a hundred or two hundred miles. They were also forc'd to carry the Spaniards up and down in their Hamechs, using them in manner of beasts to carry their burthens and the necessaries of their journeys. And as for the blows which they gave them with whips, cudgels and their fists, wherewith they continually tormented them in their labour, I could be hardly able to finde either time or paper to make a narration large enough of those things.

Matthew 2, King James Bible, 1611

SOURCE: *The King James Bible,* 1611.

Introduction

The following verses from Chapter 2 of the Gospel of Matthew in the New Testament tell the story of King Herod's hunt to kill Christ when he is born. Herod learns that Christ is in Bethlehem, so he orders the slaughter of all the male children in the city and its villages who are under two years of age. Jesus escapes with Mary and Joseph to Egypt. This is not the only passage in the Bible to describe the murder of infants. Matthew's story parallels the passages from Exodus that describe Pharaoh's order to slaughter all male Jewish children during the time of the Jews' enslavement in Egypt. Moses also escaped his fate, then led his people to freedom. Many critics have questioned the historical truth of Herod's "slaughter of the innocents" and instead have read these verses as Matthew's effort to legitimize Jesus using the Old Testament.

1: Now when Jesus was born in Bethlehem of Judaea in the days of Herod the king, behold, there came wise men from the east to Jerusalem,

2: Saying, Where is he that is born King of the Jews? for we have seen his star in the east, and are come to worship him.

3: When Herod the king had heard these things, he was troubled, and all Jerusalem with him.

4: And when he had gathered all the chief priests and scribes of the people together, he demanded of them where Christ should be born.

5: And they said unto him, In Bethlehem of Judaea: for thus it is written by the prophet,

6: And thou Bethlehem, in the land of Juda, art not the least among the princes of Juda: for out of thee shall come a Governor, that shall rule my people Israel.

7: Then Herod, when he had privily called the wise men, inquired of them diligently what time the star appeared.

8: And he sent them to Bethlehem, and said, Go and search diligently for the young child; and when ye have found him, bring me word again, that I may come and worship him also.

9: When they had heard the king, they departed; and, lo, the star, which they saw in the east, went before them, till it came and stood over where the young child was.

10: When they saw the star, they rejoiced with exceeding great joy.

11: And when they were come into the house, they saw the young child with Mary his mother, and fell down, and worshipped him: and when they had opened their treasures, they presented unto him gifts; gold, and frankincense, and myrrh.

12: And being warned of God in a dream that they should not return to Herod, they departed into their own country another way.

13: And when they were departed, behold, the angel of the Lord appeareth to Joseph in a dream, saying, Arise, and take the young child and his mother, and flee into Egypt, and be thou there until I bring thee word: for Herod will seek the young child to destroy him.

14: When he arose, he took the young child and his mother by night, and departed into Egypt:

15: And was there until the death of Herod: that it might be fulfilled which was spoken of the Lord by the prophet, saying, Out of Egypt have I called my son.

16: Then Herod, when he saw that he was mocked of the wise men, was exceeding wroth, and sent forth, and slew all the children that were in Bethlehem, and in all the coasts thereof, from two years old and under, according to the time which he had diligently inquired of the wise men.

17: Then was fulfilled that which was spoken by Jeremy the prophet, saying,

18: In Rama was there a voice heard, lamentation, and weeping, and great mourning, Rachel weeping for her children, and would not be comforted, because they are not.

19: But when Herod was dead, behold, an angel of the Lord appeareth in a dream to Joseph in Egypt,

20: Saying, Arise, and take the young child and his mother, and go into the land of Israel: for they are dead which sought the young child's life.

21: And he arose, and took the young child and his mother, and came into the land of Israel.

22: But when he heard that Archelaus did reign in Judaea in the room of his father Herod, he was afraid to go thither: notwithstanding, being warned of God in a dream, he turned aside into the parts of Galilee:

23: And he came and dwelt in a city called Nazareth: that it might be fulfilled which was spoken by the prophets, He shall be called a Nazarene.

Kings 1:3, 15–28, King James Bible, 1611

SOURCE: *The King James Bible*, 1611.

Introduction

Many famous Bible stories involve children. In Kings 1, Chapter 3, King Solomon proves his wisdom by discovering the true parent of a contested child. When two women come before him each laying claim to the same infant, Solomon threatens to divide the baby by the sword. His wisdom is revealed when the true mother renounces her claim on the child in order to preserve his life. The story suggests that parents should protect their children's safety over their own interests. In the Book of Proverbs, King Solomon offers more wisdom concerning children, including many injunctions for parents to discipline their sons and for sons to treat their parents with respect.

15: And Solomon awoke; and, behold, it was a dream. And he came to Jerusalem, and stood before the ark of the covenant of the LORD, and offered up burnt offerings, and offered peace offerings, and made a feast to all his servants.

16: Then came there two women, that were harlots, unto the king, and stood before him.

17: And the one woman said, O my lord, I and this woman dwell in one house; and I was delivered of a child with her in the house.

18: And it came to pass the third day after that I was delivered, that this woman was delivered also: and we were together; there was no stranger with us in the house, save we two in the house.

19: And this woman's child died in the night; because she overlaid it.

20: And she arose at midnight, and took my son from beside me, while thine handmaid slept, and laid it in her bosom, and laid her dead child in my bosom.

21: And when I rose in the morning to give my child suck, behold, it was dead: but when I had considered it in the morning, behold, it was not my son, which I did bear.

22: And the other woman said, Nay; but the living is my son, and the dead is thy son. And this said, No; but the dead is thy son, and the living is my son. Thus they spake before the king.

23: Then said the king, The one saith, This is my son that liveth, and thy son is the dead: and the other saith, Nay; but thy son is the dead, and my son is the living.

24: And the king said, Bring me a sword. And they brought a sword before the king.

25: And the king said, Divide the living child in two, and give half to the one, and half to the other.

26: Then spake the woman whose the living child was unto the king, for her bowels yearned upon her son, and she said, O my lord, give her the living child, and in no wise slay it. But the other said, Let it be neither mine nor thine, but divide it.

27: Then the king answered and said, Give her the living child, and in no wise slay it: she is the mother thereof.

28: And all Israel heard of the judgment which the king had judged; and they feared the king: for they saw that the wisdom of God was in him, to do judgment.

The Qur'an, 2:233, 4:11, Pickthall translation, 1930

SOURCE: Pickthall, Muhammad Marmaduke William. 1930. *The Meaning of the Glorious Qur'an.* New York: Knopf.

Introduction

In the Qur'an, the sacred scripture of Islam, verses revealed by God to the prophet Muhammed are arranged in sequence from the longest to the shortest. The verses take the form of stories, commands, spiritual teachings, and guides to practical behavior. In the following verses the Qur'an instructs parents in how to raise their children, specifying the length of time required for breast-feeding and the proper distribution of inheritances. The passages emphasize the parental obligation to provide for children. Other verses from the Qur'an emphasize children's duty to be obedient and to respect their parents. Muslim wisdom concerning the raising of children is also to be found in the Hadith, a collection of the Prophet Muhammed's sayings.

AL-BAQARA (THE COW) 002.233. Mothers shall suckle their children for two whole years; (that is) for those who wish to complete the suckling. The duty of feeding and clothing nursing mothers in a seemly manner is upon the father of the child. No-one should be charged beyond his capacity. A mother should not be made to suffer because of her child, nor should he to whom the child is born (be made to suffer) because of his child. And on the (father's) heir is incumbent the like of that (which was incumbent on the father). If they desire to wean the child by mutual consent and (after) consultation, it is no sin for them; and if ye wish to give your children out to nurse, it is no sin for you, provide that ye pay what is due from you in kindness. Observe your duty to Allah, and know that Allah is Seer of what ye do.

AN-NISA (WOMEN) 004.11. Allah chargeth you concerning (the provision for) your children: to the male the equivalent of the portion of two females, and if there be women more than two, then theirs is two-thirds of the inheritance, and if there be one (only) then the half. And to each of his parents a sixth of the inheritance, if he have a son; and if he have no son and his parents are his heirs, then to his mother appertaineth the third; and if he have brethren, then to his mother appertaineth the sixth, after any legacy he may have bequeathed, or debt (hath been paid). Your parents and your children: Ye know not which of them is nearer unto you in usefulness. It is an injunction from Allah. Lo! Allah is Knower, Wise.

Educators

Excerpt from *Some Thoughts Concerning Education* by John Locke, 1693

SOURCE: Locke, John. 1909–1914 [1693]. *Some Thoughts Concerning Education.* The Harvard Classics 37 (1). New York: P.F. Collier and Son.

Introduction

The seventeenth-century political philosopher John Locke is famous for his claim that human beings are born as *tabulae rasae,* or blank slates. Knowledge and moral sense, he argued, arose solely from experience. He therefore placed enormous importance on the process of education, which he discussed at length in his book *Some Thoughts Concerning Education* (1693). Locke's concern in this text is the proper education of gentlemen's sons but his reformist ideas had extensive influence beyond the sphere of the elite. In his *Thoughts* Locke rejected the tedious inculcation of scholastic knowledge that had defined his own education and instead emphasized students' moral instruction. Among the most notable reforms of traditional pedagogy that he advocated for in his treatise was a new style of discipline that substituted moral pressure for traditional corporal punishment. Although he limited use of the rod, Locke's disciplinary style should not be mistaken for soft—instilling moral sense was a rigorous process. In the following passage, Locke criticizes the old style of discipline.

§ 43. This being laid down in general, as the course that ought to be taken, 'tis fit we now come to consider the parts of the discipline to be us'd, a little more particularly. I have spoken so much of carrying a strict hand over children, that perhaps I shall be suspected of not considering enough, what is due to their tender age and constitutions. But that opinion will vanish, when you have heard me a little farther: for I am very apt to think, that great severity of punishment does but very little good, nay, great harm in education; and I believe it will be found, that, caeteris paribus, those children who have been most chastis'd, seldom make the best men. All that I have hitherto contended for, is, that whatsoever rigor is necessary, it is more to be us'd, the younger children are; and having by a due application wrought its effect, it is to be relax'd, and chang'd into a milder sort of government.

§ 44. A compliance and suppleness of their wills, being by a steady hand introduc'd by parents, before children have memories to retain the beginnings of it, will seem natural to them, and work afterwards in them as if it were so, preventing all occasions of struggling or repining. The only care is, that it be begun early, and inflexibly kept to 'till awe and respect be grown familiar, and there appears not the least reluctancy in the submission, and ready obedience of their minds. When this reverence is once thus established, (which it must be early, or else it will cost pains and blows to recover it, and the more the longer it is deferr'd) 'tis by it, still mix'd with as much indulgence as they make not an ill use of, and not by beating, chiding, or other servile punishments, they are for the future to be govern'd as they grow up to more understanding.

§ 45. That this is so, will be easily allow'd, when it is but consider'd, what is to be aim'd at in an ingenuous education; and upon what it turns.

1. He that has not a mastery over his inclinations, he that knows not how to resist the importunity of present pleasure or pain, for the sake of what reason tells him is fit to be done, wants the true principle of virtue and industry, and is in danger never to be good for anything. This temper therefore, so contrary to unguided nature, is to be got betimes; and this habit, as the true foundation of future ability and happiness, is to be wrought into the mind as early as may be, even from the first dawnings of knowledge or apprehension in children, and so to be confirm'd in them, by all the care and ways imaginable, by those who have the oversight of their education.

§ 46. 2. On the other side, if the mind be curb'd, and humbled too much in children; if their spirits be abas'd and broken much, by too strict an hand over them, they lose all their vigour and industry, and are in a worse state than the former. For extravagant young fellows, that have liveliness and spirit, come sometimes to be set right, and so make able and great men; but dejected minds, timorous and tame, and low spirits, are hardly ever to be rais'd, and very seldom attain to any thing. To avoid the danger that is on either hand, is the great art; and he that has found a way how to keep up a child's spirit easy, active, and free, and yet at the same time to restrain him from many things he has a mind to, and to draw him to things that are uneasy to him; he, I say, that knows how to reconcile these seeming contradictions, has, in my opinion, got the true secret of education.

§ 47. The usual lazy and short way by chastisement and the rod, which is the only instrument of government that tutors generally know, or ever think of, is the most unfit of any to be us'd in education, because it tends to both those mischiefs; which, as we have shewn, are the Scylla and Charybdis, which on the one hand or the other ruin all that miscarry.

§ 48. 1. This kind of punishment contributes not at all to the mastery of our natural propensity to indulge corporal and present pleasure, and to avoid pain at any rate, but rather encourages it, and thereby strengthens that in us, which is the root from whence spring all vicious actions, and the irregularities of life. For what other motive, but of sensual pleasure and pain, does a child act by, who drudges at his book against his inclination, or abstains from eating unwholesome fruit, that he takes pleasure in, only out of fear of whipping? He in this only prefers the greater corporal pleasure, or avoids the greater corporal pain. And what is it, to govern his actions, and direct his conduct by such motives as these? What is it, I say, but to cherish that principle in him, which it is our business to root out and destroy? And therefore I cannot think any correction useful to a child, where the shame of suffering for having done amiss, does not work more upon him than the pain.

§ 49. 2. This sort of correction naturally breeds an aversion to that which 'tis the tutor's business to create a liking to. How obvious is it to observe, that children come to hate things which were at first acceptable to them, when they find themselves whipp'd, and chid, and teas'd about them? And it is not to be wonder'd at in them, when grown men would not be able to be reconcil'd to any thing by such ways. Who is there that would not be disgusted with any innocent recreation, in itself indifferent to him, if he should with blows or ill language be haled to it, when he had no mind? Or be constantly so treated, for some circumstances in his application to it? This is natural to be so. Offensive circumstances ordinarily infect innocent things which they are join'd with; and the very sight of a cup wherein any one uses to take nauseous physick, turns his stomach, so that nothing will relish well out of it, tho' the cup be never so clean and well-shap'd, and of the richest materials.

§ 50. 3. Such a sort of slavish discipline makes a slavish temper. The child submits, and dissembles obedience, whilst the fear of the rod hangs over him; but when that is remov'd, and by being out of sight, he can promise himself impunity, he gives the greater scope to his natural inclination; which by this way is not at all alter'd, but, on the contrary, heighten'd and increas'd in him; and after such restraint, breaks out usually with the more violence; or,

§ 51. 4. If severity carry'd to the highest pitch does prevail, and works a cure upon the present unruly distemper, it often brings in the room of it a worse and more dangerous disease, by breaking the mind; and then, in the place of a disorderly young fellow, you have a low spirited moap'd creature, who, however with his unnatural sobriety he may please silly people, who commend tame unactive children, because they make no noise, nor give them any trouble; yet at last, will probably prove as uncomfortable a thing to his friends, as he will be all his life an useless thing to himself and others.

§ 52. Beating them, and all other sorts of slavish and corporal punishments, are not the discipline fit to be used in the education of those we would have wise, good, and ingenuous men; and therefore very rarely to be apply'd, and that only in great occasions, and cases of extremity. On the other side, to flatter children by rewards of things that are pleasant to them, is as carefully to be avoided. He that will give to his son apples or sugar-plumbs, or what else of this kind he is most delighted with, to make him learn his book, does but authorize his love of pleasure, and cocker up that dangerous propensity, which he ought by all means to subdue and stifle in him. You can never hope to teach him to master it, whilst you compound for the check you gave his inclination in one place, by the satisfaction you propose to it in another. To make a good, a wise, and a virtuous man, 'tis fit he should learn to cross his appetite, and deny his inclination to riches, finery, or pleasing his palate, &c. whenever his reason advises the contrary, and his duty requires it. But when you draw him to do any thing that is fit by the offer of money, or reward the pains of learning his book by the pleasure of a luscious morsel; when you promise him a lace-cravat or a fine new suit, upon performance of some of his little tasks; what do you by proposing these as rewards, but allow them to be the good things he should aim at, and thereby encourage his longing for 'em, and accustom him to place his happiness in them? Thus people, to prevail with children to be industrious about their grammar, dancing, or some other such matter, of no great moment to the happiness or usefulness of their lives, by misapply'd rewards and punishments, sacrifice their virtue, invert the order of their education, and teach them luxury, pride, or covetousness, &c. For in this way, flattering those wrong inclinations which they should restrain and suppress, they lay the foundations of those future vices, which cannot be avoided but by curbing our desires and accustoming them early to submit to reason.

Excerpt from *Émile, or, On Education* by Jean-Jacques Rousseau, 1762

SOURCE: Rousseau, Jean-Jacques. 1911 [1762]. *Émile, or, On Education.* Trans. Barbara Foxley. New York: E. P. Dutton and Co.

Introduction

Jean-Jacques Rousseau's *Émile, or, On Education* (1762) has been perhaps the most influential educational text of the modern age. Written in the form of a novel, *Émile* traces the development of a fictional young man and provides Rousseau a platform to deliver his theories on the proper training of children. Rousseau abjured the pedagogical methods of his day, which relied on bribery and coercion to impose a body of knowledge upon the student. Instead, he proposed a child-centered education, where the student's curiosity and growing knowledge was encouraged through carefully contrived experiences that would allow learning to originate internally. Rousseau's pedagogy was founded on the then-radical assumption that human beings are innately good before they are corrupted by society; a good education fostered and protected the child's goodness. Since *Émile,* child-centered learning has become the standard of progressive education. In the following passage, Rousseau stresses the importance of treating children as children, not forcing them to be adults.

Nature wants children to be children before they are men. If we try to pervert this order we shall produce a forced fruit that will have neither ripeness nor flavor and that will soon spoil. We will have young doctors and old children. Childhood has its ways of seeing, thinking, and feeling that are proper to it. Nothing is less sensible than to try and substitute our ways. I would like no more to require a young child be five feet tall than that he have judgment at the age of ten. Indeed, what use would reason be to him at that age? It is the curb of strength, and the child does not need this curb.

In trying to persuade your pupils of the duty of obedience you add to this so-called persuasion force and threats, or still worse, flattery and bribes. Thus attracted by self-interest or constrained by force, they pretend to be convinced by reason. They see very well that obedience is to their advantage and disobedience to their disadvantage as soon as you perceive one or the other. But since you only demand disagreeable things of them, and since it is always painful to do another's will, they hide themselves so that they may do as they please, persuaded that they are doing well if no one knows of their disobedience, but ready, if found out, to admit they are in the wrong for fear of worse evils. Since the rationale for duty is beyond their age, there is not a man in the world who could make them really aware of it. But the fear of punishment, the hope of forgiveness, importunity, the difficulty of answering, wrings from them as many confessions as you want; and you think you have convinced them when you have only wearied or frightened them.

What is the result of all this? In the first place, by imposing on them a duty which they do not feel, you make them disinclined to submit to your tyranny and turn them away from loving you. You teach them to become deceitful, false, liars in order to extort rewards or escape punishment. Finally, by accustoming them to conceal a secret motive under an apparent one, you yourself give them the means of ceaselessly abusing you, of depriving you of the means of knowing their real character, and of answering you and others with empty words whenever they have the chance. Laws, you say, though binding on conscience, exercise the same constraint over grown men. I agree, but what are these men if not children spoiled by education? This is exactly what one must avoid. Use force with children and reason with men; this is the natural order. The wise man needs no laws.

Treat your pupil according to his age. Put him in his place from the first, and keep him there so well that he does not try to leave it. Then before he knows what wisdom is, he will be practicing its most important lesson. Never command him to do anything, whatever in the world it may be. Do not let him even imagine that you claim to have any authority over him. He must know only that he is weak and you are strong, that his condition and yours put him at your mercy. Let him know this, let him learn it, let him feel it. At an early age let his haughty head feel the heavy yoke which nature imposes upon man, the heavy yoke of necessity under which every finite being must bow. Let him see this necessity in things, not in the whims of man. Let the curb that restrains him be force, not authority. If there is something he should not do, do not forbid him, but prevent him without explanation or reasoning. What you grant him, grant it at his first word without solicitations or pleading, above all without conditions. Grant with pleasure, refuse only with repugnance; but let your refusal be irrevocable so that no entreaties move you. Let your "No," once uttered, be a wall of bronze against which the child may have to exhaust his strength five or six times in order not to be tempted again to overthrow it.

It is thus that you will make him patient, equable, resigned, peaceful, even when he does not get all he wants. For it is in man's nature to bear patiently with the necessity of things but not with the ill-will of others. A child never rebels against "There is none left," unless he thinks the reply is false. Moreover, there is no middle course; you must either make no demands on him at all, or else you must fashion him to perfect obedience. The worst education of all is to leave him hesitating between his own will and yours, constantly disputing whether you or he is master. I would rather a hundred times that he were master.

It is very strange that ever since people began to think about raising children they should have imagined no other way of guiding them other than emulation, jealousy, envy, vanity, greediness, cowardice—all the most dangerous passions, the quickest to ferment, and the most likely to corrupt the soul even before the body is formed. With each precocious instruction which you try to force into children's minds you plant a vice in the depths of their hearts. Senseless teachers think they are doing wonders when they are making their pupils evil in order to teach them what goodness is. And then they tell us gravely, "Such is man." Yes, such is the man that you have made.

Every means has been tried except one, the one precisely that could succeed—well-regulated freedom. One should not undertake to raise a child unless one knows how to guide him where one wants by the laws of the possible and the impossible alone. The limits of both being equally unknown, they can be extended or contracted around him at will. Without a murmur the child is restrained, urged on, held back, only by the bands of necessity. One can make him supple and docile solely by the force of things, without any chance for vice to spring up in him. For passions never become aroused so long as they have no effect.

Do not give your pupil any kind of verbal lessons; he should receive them only through experience. Do not inflict on him any kind of punishment, for he does not know what it is to do wrong. Never make him beg your pardon, for he does not know how to offend you. Deprived of all morality

in his actions, he can do nothing that is morally wrong, and he deserves neither punishment nor reprimand.

Already I see the frightened reader comparing this child with those of our time. He is mistaken. The perpetual annoyance imposed upon your pupils irritates their vivacity; the more constrained they are under your eyes, the more stormy they are the moment they escape. Whenever they can they must make up for the harsh constraint that you that you hold them in. Two schoolboys from the city will do more damage in the country than all the children of the village. Shut up a young gentleman and a young peasant in a room; the former will have upset and smashed everything before the latter has stirred from his place. Why is this, unless that the one hastens to abuse a moment's license, while the other, always sure of freedom, does not use it rashly? And yet the village children, often flattered or constrained, are still very far from the state in which I would have them kept.

Let us lay it down as an incontestable maxim that the first movements of nature are always right. There is no original perversity in the human heart. There is not a single vice about which one cannot say how and whence it came. The only passion natural to man is amour de soi or amour-propre taken in an extended sense. This amour-propre in itself or relative to ourselves is good and useful, and since it has no necessary rapport to others it is in this regard naturally indifferent: it only becomes good or evil by what it is applied to and by the relations it is given. Until the appearance of reason, which is the guide of amour-propre, the main thing is that the child should do nothing because you are watching him or listening to him; in a word, nothing because of other people, but only what nature asks of him. Then he will only do good.

Excerpt from *How Gertrude Teaches Her Children* by Johann Heinrich Pestalozzi, 1801

SOURCE: Pestalozzi, Johann Heinrich. 1894 [1801]. *How Gertrude Teaches Her Children*. Trans. Lucy E. Holland and Frances C. Turner. New York: Gordon Press.

Introduction

The Swiss educator Johann Heinrich Pestalozzi (1746–1827) attempted to reform pedagogical practice by applying the lessons of Rousseau's *Émile* to the classroom. The Pestalozzi method, which has had great influence both in Europe and America, encourages children to learn from experience and emphasizes physical activities over reading. Pestalozzi's 1801 text, *How Gertrude Teaches Her Children*, describes his philosophy in a series of simple lectures. In the following excerpt, "Education According to Nature," Pestalozzi explains why one should teach children "sense-impressions" prior to reading. He offers a romantic vision of children's innate potential, as well as a scathing indictment of the traditional classroom. Pestalozzi is also remembered for his dedication to social justice. Unlike many educational philosophers who preceded him, Pestalozzi strongly advocated the education of poor children and criticized traditional education for failing these students.

Education According to Nature

All instruction of man is then only the Art of helping Nature to develop in her own way; and this Art rests essentially on the relation and harmony between the impressions received by the child and the exact degree of his developed powers. It is also necessary in the impressions that are brought to the child by instruction that there should be a sequence, so that beginning and progress should keep pace with the beginning and progress of the powers to be developed in the child. I soon saw that an inquiry into this sequence throughout the whole range of human knowledge, particularly those fundamental points from which the development of the human mind originates, must be the simple and only way ever to attain and to keep satisfactory school and instruction books, of every grade, suitable for our nature and our wants. I saw just as soon that in making these books the constituents of instruction must be separated according to the degree of the growing power of the child; and that in all matters of instruction, it is necessary to determine with the greatest accuracy which of these constituents is fit for each age of the child, in order on the one hand not to hold him back if he is ready; and on the other, not to load him and confuse him with anything for which he is not quite ready.

This was clear to me. The child must be brought to a high degree of knowledge both of things seen and of words before it is reasonable to teach him to spell or read. I was quite convinced that at their earliest age children need psychological training in gaining intelligent sense-impressions of all things. But since such training, without the help of art, is not to be thought of or expected of men as they are, the need of picture-books struck me perforce. These should precede the A-B-C books, in order to make those ideas that men express by words clear to the children (by means of well-chosen real objects, that either in reality, or in the form of well-made models and drawings, can be brought before their minds).

A happy experiment confirmed my then unripe opinion in a striking way (in spite of all the limitations of my means, and the error and one-sidedness in my experiments). An anxious mother entrusted her hardly three-year-old child to my private teaching. I saw him for a time every day for an hour; and for a time felt the pulse of a method with him. I tried to teach him by letters, figures, and anything handy; that is, I aimed at giving him clear ideas and expressions by these means. I made him name correctly what he knew of anything—color, limbs, place, form, and number. I was obliged to put aside that first plague of youth, the miserable letters; he would have nothing but pictures and things.

He soon expressed himself clearly about the objects that lay within the limits of his knowledge. He found common illustrations in the street, the garden, and the room; and soon learned to pronounce the hardest names of plants and animals, and to compare objects quite unknown to him with those known, and to produce a clear sense-impression of them in himself. Although this experiment led to byeways, and worked for the strange and distant to the disadvantage of the present, it threw a many-sided light on the means of quickening the child to his surroundings, and showing him the charm of self-activity in the extension of his powers.

But yet the experiment was not satisfactory for that which I was particularly seeking, because the boy had already three unused years behind him. I am convinced that nature brings the children even at this age to a definite consciousness of innumerable objects. It only needs that we should with psychological art unite speech with this knowledge in order to bring it to a high degree of clearness; and so enable us to connect the foundations of many-sided arts and truths with that which nature herself teaches, and also to use what nature teaches as a means of explaining all the fundamentals of art and truth that can be connected with them. Their power and their experience both are great at this age; but our unpsychological schools are essentially only artificial stifling-machines for destroying all the results of the power and experience that nature herself brings to life in them.

You know it, my friend. But for a moment picture to yourself the horror of this murder. We leave children up to their fifth year in the full enjoyment of nature; we let every impression of nature work upon them; they feel their power; they already know full well the joy of unrestrained liberty and all its charms. The free natural bent which the sensuous happy wild thing takes in his development, has in them already taken its most decided direction. And after they have enjoyed this happiness of sensuous life for five whole years, we make all nature round them vanish from before their eyes; tyrannically stop the delightful course of their unrestrained freedom; pen them up like sheep, whole flocks huddled together, in stinking rooms; pitilessly chain them for hours, days, weeks, months, years, to the contemplation of unattractive and monotonous letters, and (contrasted with their former condition) to a maddening course of life.

I cease describing; else I shall come to the picture of the greater number of schoolmasters, thousands of whom in our days merely on account of their unfitness for any means of finding a respectable livelihood have subjected themselves to the toilsomeness of this position, which they in accordance with their unfitness for anything better look upon as a way that leads little further than to keep them from starvation. How infinitely must the children suffer under these circumstances, or, at least, be spoiled!

Excerpt from "A Treatise on Domestic Economy for the Use of Young Ladies at Home and at School" by Catharine E. Beecher, 1841

SOURCE: Beecher, Catharine E. 1841. "A Treatise on Domestic Economy for the Use of Young Ladies at Home and at School." *The United States Democratic Review* 9, no. 42: 605.

Introduction

Catharine Beecher (1800–1878) was an influential nineteenth-century advocate for the education of American girls. Beecher belonged to a large family notable for its commitment to social reform. Her father Lyman Beecher was a renowned evangelical preacher; her sister Harriet Beecher Stowe was a famous novelist; and her brother Henry Ward Beecher was an influential antislavery minister. In the following excerpt from her "Treatise on Domestic Economy" (1841), Catharine Beecher describes her program for female learning. Beecher argues that girls should learn proficiency in domestic skills; as future mothers they were responsible for nurturing the moral character of the American people. Although her vision is essentially conservative, situating girls in the private sphere of home and family, Beecher's agenda should not be underestimated. Her advocacy for female education extended beyond prescriptive writings to the founding of numerous schools and educational organizations, including the Hartford Female Seminary in 1823, the Board of National Popular Education in 1847, and the American Women's Educational Association in 1852. Curiously, Beecher herself never married, instead devoting her prodigious energies to public service.

Parents are little aware of the immense waste incurred by the present mode of conducting female education. In the wealthy classes, young girls are sent to school, as a matter of course, year after year, confined, for six hours a day, to the schoolhouse, and required to add some time out of school to learning their lessons. Thus, during the most critical period of life, they are for a long time immured in a room, filled with an atmosphere vitiated by many breaths, and are constantly kept under some sort of responsibility in regard to mental effort. Their studies are pursued at random, often changed with changing schools, while book after book (heavily taxing the parent's purse) is conned awhile, and then supplanted by others. Teachers have usually so many pupils, and such a variety of branches to teach, that little time can be afforded to each pupil; while scholars, at this thoughtless period of life, feeling sure of going to school as long as they please, manifest little interest in their pursuits.

The writer believes that the actual amount of education, permanently secured by most young ladies from the age of ten to fourteen, could all be acquired in one year, at the Institution described, by a young lady at the age of fifteen or sixteen.

Instead of such a course as the common one, if mothers would keep their daughters as their domestic assistants, until they are fourteen, requiring them to study one lesson, and go out, once a day, to recite it to a teacher, it would abundantly prepare them, after their constitutions are firmly established to enter such an institution, where, in three years, they could secure more, than almost any young lady in the Country now gains by giving the whole of her youth to school pursuits.

In the early years of female life, reading, writing, needlework, drawing, and music, should alternate with domestic duties; and one hour a day, devoted to some study, in addition to the above pursuits, would be all that is needful to prepare them for a thorough education after growth is attained, and the constitution established. This is the time when young women would feel the value of an education, and pursue their studies with that maturity of mind, and vividness of interest, which would double the perpetuity and value of all their acquisitions.

The great difficulty, which opposes such a plan, is, the want of institutions that would enable a young lady to complete, in three years, the liberal course of study, here described. But if American mothers become convinced of the importance of such advantages for their daughters, and will use their influence appropriately and efficiently, they will certainly be furnished. There are other men of liberality and wealth, besides the individual referred to, who can be made to feel that a fortune, expended in securing an appropriate education to American women, is as wisely bestowed, as in founding colleges for the other sex, who are already so abundantly supplied. We ought to have institutions, similar to the one described, in every part of this Nation; and funds should be provided, for educating young women destitute of means: and if American women think and feel, that, by such a method, their own trials will be lightened, and their daughters will secure a healthful constitution and a thorough domestic and intellectual education, the appropriate expression of their wishes will secure the necessary funds. The tide of charity, which has been so long flowing from the female hand to provide a liberal education for young men, will flow back with abundant remuneration.

The last method suggested for lessening the evils peculiar to American women, is, a decided effort to oppose the aristocratic feeling, that labor is degrading; and to bring about the impression, that it is refined and lady-like to engage in domestic pursuits. In past ages, and in aristocratic countries, leisure and indolence and frivolous pursuits have been deemed lady-like and refined, because those classes, which were most refined, countenanced such an opinion. But whenever ladies of refinement, as a general custom, patronise domestic pursuits, then these employments will be deemed lady-like. It may be urged, however, that it is impossible for a woman who cooks, washes, and sweeps, to appear in the dress, or acquire the habits and manners, of a lady; that the drudgery of the kitchen is dirty work, and that no one can appear delicate and refined, while engaged in it. Now all this depends on circumstances. If a woman has a house, destitute of neat and convenient facilities; if she has no habits of order and system; if she is remiss and careless in person and dress;—then all this may be true. But, if a woman will make some sacrifices of costly ornaments in her parlor, in order to make her kitchen neat and tasteful; if she will sacrifice expensive dishes, in order to secure such conveniences for labor as protect from exposures; if she will take pains to have the dresses, in which she works, made of suitable materials, and in good taste; if she will rise early, and systematize and oversee the work of her family, so as to have it done thoroughly, neatly, and in the early part of the day; she will find no necessity for any such apprehensions. It is because such work has generally been done by vulgar people, and in a vulgar way, that we have such associations; and when ladies manage such things, as ladies should, then such associations will be removed. There are pursuits, deemed very refined and genteel, which involve quite as much exposure as kitchen employments. For example, to draw a large landscape, in colored crayons, would be deemed very lady-like; but the writer can testify, from sad experience, that no cooking, washing, sweeping, or any other domestic duty, ever left such deplorable traces on hands, face, and dress, as this same lady-like pursuit. Such things depend entirely on custom and associations; and every American woman, who values the institutions of her Country, and wishes to lend her influence in extending and perpetuating such blessings, may feel that she is doing this, whenever, by her example and influence, she destroys the aristocratic association, which would render domestic labor degrading.

Excerpt from *Schools of To-Morrow* by John Dewey, 1915

SOURCE: Dewey, John. 1915. *Schools of To-Morrow*. New York: E. P. Dutton and Company.

Introduction

The philosopher John Dewey (1859–1952) is regarded as the father of the American school of Progressive education but his influence has extended far beyond the United States. Dewey argued that education should encourage the self-realization of each child as an individual, thus enabling him or her to become an effective member of the democratic community. Dewey framed his pedagogy as a reaction against traditional attitudes toward education, which promoted conformity and taught children to be obedient citizens, rather than critical participants. Dewey implemented his educational ideas at the Laboratory School, which he founded at the University of Chicago in 1896, and later at Teachers College, Columbia University. Dewey also promoted his thought through his prolific writings. In the following excerpt from his book *Schools of To-Morrow* (1915), co-written with his daughter Evelyn, Dewey acknowledges the influence of an earlier educational authority, Jean-Jacques Rousseau, upon his own pedagogical beliefs.

EDUCATION AS NATURAL DEVELOPMENT

"We know nothing of childhood, and with our mistaken notions of it the further we go in education the more we go astray. The wisest writers devote themselves to what a man ought to know without asking what a child is capable of learning." These sentences are typical of the "Emile" of Rousseau. He insists that existing education is bad because parents and teachers are always thinking of the accomplishments of adults, and that all reform defends upon centering attention upon the powers and weaknesses of children. Rousseau said, as well as did, many foolish things. But his insistence that education be based upon the native capacities of those to be taught and upon the need of studying children in order to discover what these native powers are, sounded the key-note of all modern efforts for educational progress. It meant that education is not something to be forced upon children and youth from without, but is the growth of capacities with which human beings are endowed at birth. From this conception flow the various considerations which educational reformers since his day have most emphasized.

It calls attention, in the first place, to a fact which professional educators are always forgetting: What is learned in school is at the best only a small part of education, a relatively superficial part; and yet what is learned in school makes artificial distinctions in society and marks persons off from one another. Consequently we exaggerate school learning compared with what is gained in the ordinary course of living. We are, however, to correct this exaggeration, not by despising school learning, but by looking into that extensive and more efficient training given by the ordinary course of events for light upon the best ways of teaching within school walls. The first years of learning proceed rapidly and securely before children go to school, because that learning is so closely related with the motives that are furnished by their own powers and the needs that are dictated by their own conditions. Rousseau was almost the first to see that learning is a matter of necessity; it is a part of the process of self-preservation and of growth. If we want, then, to find out how education takes place most successfully, let us go to the experiences of children where learning is a necessity, and not to the practices of the schools where it is largely an adornment, a superfluity and even an unwelcome imposition.

But schools are always proceeding in a direction opposed to this principle. They take the accumulated learning of adults, material that is quite unrelated to the exigencies of growth, and try to force it upon children, instead of finding out what these children need as they go along. "A man must indeed know many things which seem useless to a child.

Must the child learn, can he learn, all that the man must know? Try to teach a child what is of use to him as a child, and you will find that it takes all his time. Why urge him to the studies of an age he may never reach, to the neglect of those studies which meet his present needs? But, you ask, will it not be too late to learn what he ought to know when the time comes to use it? I cannot tell. But this I know; it is impossible to teach it sooner, for our real teachers are experience and emotion, and adult man will never learn what befits *him* except under his own conditions. A child knows he must become a man; all the ideas he may have as to man's estate are so many opportunities for his instruction, but he should remain in complete ignorance of those ideas that are beyond his grasp. My whole book is one continued argument in support of this fundamental principle of education."

Probably the greatest and commonest mistake that we all make is to forget that learning is a necessary incident of dealing with real situations. We even go so far as to assume that the mind is naturally averse to learning—which is like assuming that the digestive organs are averse to food and have either to be coaxed or bullied into having anything to do with it. Existing methods of instruction give plenty of evidence in support of a belief that minds are opposed to learning—to their own exercise. We fail to see that such aversion is in reality a condemnation of our methods; a sign that we are presenting material for which the mind in its existing state of growth has no need, or else presenting it in such ways as to cover up the real need. Let us go further. We say only an adult can really learn the things needed by the adult. Surely the adult is much more likely to learn the things befitting him when his hunger for learning has been kept alive continuously than after a premature diet of adult nutriment has deadened desire to know. We are of little faith and slow to believe. We are continually uneasy about the things we adults know, and are afraid the child will never learn them unless they are drilled into him by instruction before he has any intellectual or practical use for them. If we could really believe that attending to the needs of present growth would keep the child and teacher alike busy, and would also provide the best possible guarantee of the learning needed in the future, transformation of educational ideals might soon be accomplished, and other desirable changes would largely take care of themselves.

It is no wonder, then, that Rousseau preaches the necessity of being willing to lose time. "The greatest, the most important, the most useful rule of education is: Do not save time, but lose it. If the infant sprang at one bound from its mother's breast to the age of reason, the present education would be quite suitable; but its natural growth calls for quite a different training." And he says, again, "The whole of our present method is cruel, for it consists in sacrificing the present to the remote and uncertain future. I hear from afar the shouts of the false wisdom that is ever dragging us on, counting the present as nothing, and breathlessly pursuing a future

that flies as we pursue; a false wisdom that takes us away from the only place we ever have and never takes us anywhere else."

In short, if education is the proper growth of tendencies and powers, attention to the process of growing *in the particular form in which it goes on from day to day* is the only way of making secure the accomplishments of adult life. Maturity is the result of the slow growth of powers. Ripening takes time; it cannot be hurried without harm. The very meaning of childhood is that it is the time of growth, of developing. To despise the powers and needs of childhood, in behalf of the attainments of adult life, is therefore suicidal. Hence "Hold childhood in reverence, and do not be in any hurry to judge it for good or ill. Give nature time to work before you take upon yourself her business, lest you interfere with her dealings. You assert that you know the value of time and are afraid to waste it. You fail to perceive that it is a greater waste of time to use it ill than to do nothing, and that a child ill taught is further from excellence than a child who has learned nothing at all. You are afraid to see him spending his early years doing nothing. What! Is it nothing to be happy, nothing to jump and run all day! He will never be so busy again all his life long. . . . What would you think of a man who refused to sleep lest he should waste part of his life!" Reverence for childhood is identical with reverence for the needs and opportunities of growth. Our tragic error is that we are so anxious for the results of growth that we neglect the process of growing. "Nature would have children be children before they are men. If we try to invert this order we shall produce a forced fruit, immature and flavorless, fruit that rots before it can ripen. . . . Childhood has its own ways of thinking, seeing, and feeling."

Human Rights of Children

Excerpt from *Report on the Physical Welfare of Infants and Mothers, 1917*

SOURCE: Hope, E.W. 1917. *Carnegie United Kingdom Trust Report on the Physical Welfare of Mothers and Children.* Liverpool: C. Tinling and Co., Ltd.

Introduction

During the early twentieth century, European countries became concerned about the threat that declining rates of fertility posed to national health. Particularly during World War I, every "unnecessary" death in the population was seen as a threat to the country's future. In 1917 the Carnegie United Kingdom Trust published a report on the physical welfare of children and mothers that stated the need for better health care. In the following passages from the report, researchers describe the problem of infant mortality in the United Kingdom. Diarrhea, premature birth, and problems during labor, among other causes, killed ninety thousand infants every year. The report had a strong impact on policymakers in the United Kingdom, leading to the establishment of maternity and child-care clinics that became building blocks of the welfare state.

Causes of Infantile Mortality.

The chief causes of the deaths of infants may be arranged into groups, as follows, each being distinctly marked off as to its characteristics from the others, viz.:—

- 1. Developmental, wasting diseases, and convulsions.
- 2. Diarrhoea and enteritis.
- 3. Measles and whooping cough, bronchitis and pneumonia.

Under the first group of causes are classed prematurity, atrophy, debility and other associated conditions, due to developmental and other causes which constitute the largest proportion (30 to 50 per cent.) of the deaths of infants under the first year of age. An examination of Chart H following page 72, compiled from returns from various parts of the country, reveals this aspect of affairs very strikingly.

Recent statistics show that one-third of the deaths during the first year, occur in the first month of life. Further, it has been shown that seven-eighths of these deaths occur in the first two weeks. During the first month the diagnosis of disease is very difficult and the records of vital statistics for this period are, on the whole, unreliable.

Some accurate observations have, however, been made by Holt and Babbitt concerning the mortality of newly-born children in the Sloane Hospital for Women, New York. This is a modern lying-in hospital, and is established only to deal with emergencies. Here diagnosis has been made more accurate by the help afforded by autopsies when the occasion arose. These observers confirm the view that *prematurity* is the largest single factor in infantile mortality during the first fourteen days of life. Half the total deaths under fourteen days investigated by them were from this cause, and 66 per cent. of these deaths occurred on the first day.

The *causes* assigned are as follows:—

Congenital weakness: In half the total deaths under fourteen days, the cause is to be sought in the physical weakness of the mother during pregnancy.

Accidents of Labour: Difficult labour, persistent malpresentation and prolonged labour, causing intracranial haemorrhage, injuries to head, etc.

Malformations and Congenital Disease: Cardiac, intestinal and nervous malformation, status lymphaticus, etc.

Atelectasis: 8 per cent of all deaths due to undetermined causes.

Asphyxia: Laryngeal obstruction, knot in cord, cord round neck, etc.

Congenital Syphilis contributes only to a trifling extent; recognised cases of this disease are not admitted to hospital.

Haemorrhage of New-born:

Sepsis—Infection, phlebitis, etc.

Pneumonia—Caused nine per cent. of deaths in first fortnight, and ranks next to congenital weakness.

Stillbirths.—In 10,000 confinements there were 429 stillbirths, equalling 4 per cent. of the confinements, and the causes assigned were as follows:—

Prolonged, difficult or complicated labour 45%

Toxaemia of pregnancy 14%

Syphilis 9%

Prematurity 4%

Malformation 2%

Unknown 26%

Summary: Congenital Weakness and Atelectasis, together make up 58 per cent. of the total deaths during the first fourteen days. The number from conditions associated with delivery made up 20 per cent. of deaths during the first fourteen days. Malformations and congenital disease other than syphilis equalled 4 per cent. The only important disease developing after birth was pneumonia.

Regarding prematurity (or congenital weakness) there can be no doubt that the social condition of the parent has much to do with its production. The struggle for existence amongst the poor reacts on the foetus.

There seems to be very little doubt that there is a high proportion of still-births amongst those births recorded as illegitimate, as well as an excessive mortality amongst these children during the first year of life.

Much of this mortality in the first month of life is preventable; appropriate action might be taken to ascertain the number of stillbirths, and to trace the causes associated with them, and also the causes of the deaths of infants in the first month of life. A close application of all the powers under the Midwives Act and Notification of Births Acts, will be of especial service in revealing conditions directly causing or affecting this mortality, for example:—

- 1. The presence of some ante-natal condition in the mother, which requires treatment;
- 2. The need for emergency medical assistance before, during, and after confinement;
- 3. The prevalence of syphilis in the stillborn, or in the parents;

- 4. Skilled midwifery attendance;
- 5. Improvement and care in the feeding and management of infants; breast-feeding is best and artificial feeding should be undertaken only under medical advice.

The second group of causative factors, leading to deaths from diarrhoea and enteritis are those directly associated with the feeding of infants.

Formidable ailments arise from disease organisms gaining an entrance into the digestive tract by means of the infants' food. These germs are found in filth and dirt in neighbourhoods where there is defective sanitation and bad housing, and give rise to an extremely fatal choleraic diarrhoea.

It has been found, for example, that in towns where an out of date conservancy system is employed, or the pail closet system used, the infant mortality is excessive; conversely the lowest incidence of diarrhoeal disease occurs where the districts are supplied with a water-carriage system. In the case of several towns the conversion of a conservancy system into a water-carriage system has been associated with a great reduction of mortality from diarrhoeal diseases.

The importance of municipal cleanliness in street washing, supply of baths, etc., cannot be over estimated. In addition, the necessity for the regular and frequent removal of stable manure should be emphasised in order to prevent the breeding of the domestic fly, which has such a potent influence in carrying disease germs from filthy middens, etc., to milk and other infant foods.

The absence of personal and domestic hygiene and cleanliness are potent contributing factors in the spread of the intestinal diseases of infancy.

Amongst these contributing factors may also be included inadequate water supply, choked closets and drains, over-full dustbins, filthy courts and alleys, neglected sanitary defects, and the absence of proper facilities for the storage of food.

The campaign for the reduction of infantile mortality has had a marked effect in lowering the death rate, but especially in the case of deaths due to diarrhoeal diseases. The third group of causative agents in infantile mortality includes the infectious complaints, measles and whooping cough, with the associated complications of bronchitis and pneumonia. The majority of cases make a good recovery if adequate treatment and care be exercised; unfortunately, however, in many the after effects are bronchitis and pneumonia, often ending fatally; under better conditions these could have been avoided. By far the largest number of deaths from measles occur below two years of age; 21,000 deaths occurred at or below this age out of a total of approximately 36,000 in England and Wales during the three years (1913–15). Measles frequently causes permanent injury to the growing infant,

even if it survives the attack, and it will be seen therefore, why so many efforts are made to postpone measles to a later period of life when the child will have more strength.

Whooping cough is almost equally destructive of infant life, and is always a most painful and distressing disease.

Associated with the primary causes of death mentioned are certain contributory circumstances which have an important influence on or connection with them. The relative importance of these many factors is difficult to determine; they may be classified as :—

- (a) *Seasonal and climatic.* Epidemic diarrhoea, which, as already mentioned, is one of the most potent of all causes of infant deaths, only exerts its influence (always greatest where general sanitation is neglected) during the late summer and autumn months, and then only when the temperature of the air is high and the rainfall low: a wet and cool third quarter of the year is always associated with a low infant death rate from diarrhoea and enteritis. Measles and whooping-cough prevail to a varying extent in different years and in different districts in the same year. The associated bronchitis and pneumonia are most fatal in the first and last quarters of the year, and are influenced by temperature.

- (b) *Topographical and local conditions* are well illustrated by the variations in different districts of the same town. The question of good and bad housing conditions, industrial conditions, size of families, poverty and social conditions, municipal cleanliness, the extent of carelessness and lack of elementary knowledge among sections of the people, all these have their bearing.

- (c) *Domestic and personal hygiene* include personal and domestic cleanliness, disposal of house refuse, proper use of suitable food, individual care of the infant, and temperance. The extreme care of infancy, and the attention to maternal hygiene to be found amongst the Jewish race, find their reward in a low infant mortality.

United Nations Declaration of the Rights of the Child, 1959

SOURCE: Office of the United Nations High Commissioner for Human Rights. 1959. Available from <http://193.194.138.190>. Reprinted by permission.

Introduction

The United Nations Declaration of the Rights of the Child establishes the international principle that all children possess the rights to physical, mental, and spiritual development; to a name and nationality; to social security; to loving care; to education and play; and to protection from abuse or neglect. Child advocates pushed the League of Nations into passing an earlier and more limited statement of children's rights in 1923, in response to concerns over the exploitation of child labor and the suffering of children during war. The horrors of World War II further impressed upon human rights advocates the need for the special protection of children. After many years of political pressure and negotiation, the United Nations passed the declaration unanimously in 1959, with only two abstentions. Its principles were not enforceable. However, thirty years later, the United Nations approved a Convention on the Rights of the Child, which outlined mechanisms of enforcement.

Declaration of the Rights of the Child
Proclaimed by General Assembly resolution 1386(XIV) of 20 November 1959

Whereas the peoples of the United Nations have, in the Charter, reaffirmed their faith in fundamental human rights and in the dignity and worth of the human person, and have determined to promote social progress and better standards of life in larger freedom,

Whereas the United Nations has, in the Universal Declaration of Human Rights, proclaimed that everyone is entitled to all the rights and freedoms set forth therein, without distinction of any kind, such as race, colour, sex, language, religion, political or other opinion, national or social origin, property, birth or other status,

Whereas the child, by reason of his physical and mental immaturity, needs special safeguards and care, including appropriate legal protection, before as well as after birth,

Whereas the need for such special safeguards has been stated in the Geneva Declaration of the Rights of the Child of 1924, and recognized in the Universal Declaration of Human Rights and in the statutes of specialized agencies and international organizations concerned with the welfare of children,

Whereas mankind owes to the child the best it has to give,

Now therefore,

The General Assembly

Proclaims this Declaration of the Rights of the Child to the end that he may have a happy childhood and enjoy for his own good and for the good of society the rights and freedoms herein set forth, and calls upon parents, upon men and women as individuals, and upon voluntary organizations, local authorities and national Governments to recognize these rights and strive for their observance by legislative and other measures progressively taken in accordance with the following principles:

Principle 1

The child shall enjoy all the rights set forth in this Declaration. Every child, without any exception whatsoever, shall be entitled to these rights, without distinction or discrimination on account of race, colour, sex, language, religion, political or other opinion, national or social origin, property, birth or other status, whether of himself or of his family.

Principle 2

The child shall enjoy special protection, and shall be given opportunities and facilities, by law and by other means, to enable him to develop physically, mentally, morally, spiritually and socially in a healthy and normal manner and in conditions of freedom and dignity. In the enactment of laws for this purpose, the best interests of the child shall be the paramount consideration.

Principle 3

The child shall be entitled from his birth to a name and a nationality.

Principle 4

The child shall enjoy the benefits of social security. He shall be entitled to grow and develop in health; to this end, special care and protection shall be provided both to him and to his mother, including adequate pre-natal and post-natal care. The child shall have the right to adequate nutrition, housing, recreation and medical services.

Principle 5

The child who is physically, mentally or socially handicapped shall be given the special treatment, education and care required by his particular condition.

Principle 6

The child, for the full and harmonious development of his personality, needs love and understanding. He shall, wherever possible, grow up in the care and under the responsibility of his parents, and, in any case, in an atmosphere of affection and of moral and material security; a child of tender years shall not, save in exceptional circumstances, be separated from his mother. Society and the public authorities shall have the duty to extend particular care to children without a family and to those without adequate means of support. Payment of State and other assistance towards the maintenance of children of large families is desirable.

Principle 7

The child is entitled to receive education, which shall be free and compulsory, at least in the elementary stages. He shall be given an education which will promote his general culture and enable him, on a basis of equal opportunity, to develop his abilities, his individual judgement, and his sense of moral and social responsibility, and to become a useful member of society.

The best interests of the child shall be the guiding principle of those responsible for his education and guidance; that responsibility lies in the first place with his parents.

The child shall have full opportunity for play and recreation, which should be directed to the same purposes as education; society and the public authorities shall endeavour to promote the enjoyment of this right.

Principle 8

The child shall in all circumstances be among the first to receive protection and relief.

Principle 9

The child shall be protected against all forms of neglect, cruelty and exploitation. He shall not be the subject of traffic, in any form.

The child shall not be admitted to employment before an appropriate minimum age; he shall in no case be caused or permitted to engage in any occupation or employment which would prejudice his health or education, or interfere with his physical, mental or moral development.

Principle 10

The child shall be protected from practices which may foster racial, religious and any other form of discrimination. He shall be brought up in a spirit of understanding, tolerance, friendship among peoples, peace and universal brotherhood, and in full consciousness that his energy and talents should be devoted to the service of his fellow men.

United Nations Convention on the Rights of the Child, 1989

SOURCE: UNICEF. 1989. *Convention on the Rights of the Child.* United Nations General Assembly Resolution 44/25. Available from <www.unicef.org>. Reprinted by permission.

Introduction

In 1989, thirty years after the passage of its groundbreaking Declaration of the Rights of the Child, the United Nations restated its commitment to the protection of children in even stronger terms in the international human rights treaty title the Convention on the Rights of the Child. The Convention emphasizes the entitlement of all people under age eighteen everywhere, without discrimination, to the rights that it enumerates, including survival, protection, self-development, cultural heritage, family, education,

health, rest, and play. The Convention is also notable for including enforcement mechanisms intended to monitor its observance. In 2002 the UN agreed upon two optional Protocols to the Convention, which strengthened the treaty's statements against the use of children as soldiers, or in the prostitution trade. The parties to the 1989 Convention include all the member nations with the exception of the United States and Somalia, which have stated their intention to ratify the treaty, and Timor-Leste, a new nation.

Convention on the Rights of the Child

Adopted and opened for signature, ratification and accession by General Assembly resolution 44/25 of 20 November 1989

entry into force 2 September 1990, in accordance with article 49

Preamble

The States Parties to the present Convention,

Considering that, in accordance with the principles proclaimed in the Charter of the United Nations, recognition of the inherent dignity and of the equal and inalienable rights of all members of the human family is the foundation of freedom, justice and peace in the world,

Bearing in mind that the peoples of the United Nations have, in the Charter, reaffirmed their faith in fundamental human rights and in the dignity and worth of the human person, and have determined to promote social progress and better standards of life in larger freedom,

Recognizing that the United Nations has, in the Universal Declaration of Human Rights and in the International Covenants on Human Rights, proclaimed and agreed that everyone is entitled to all the rights and freedoms set forth therein, without distinction of any kind, such as race, colour, sex, language, religion, political or other opinion, national or social origin, property, birth or other status,

Recalling that, in the Universal Declaration of Human Rights, the United Nations has proclaimed that childhood is entitled to special care and assistance,

Convinced that the family, as the fundamental group of society and the natural environment for the growth and well-being of all its members and particularly children, should be afforded the necessary protection and assistance so that it can fully assume its responsibilities within the community,

Recognizing that the child, for the full and harmonious development of his or her personality, should grow up in a family environment, in an atmosphere of happiness, love and understanding,

Considering that the child should be fully prepared to live an individual life in society, and brought up in the spirit of the ideals proclaimed in the Charter of the United Nations, and in particular in the spirit of peace, dignity, tolerance, freedom, equality and solidarity,

Bearing in mind that the need to extend particular care to the child has been stated in the Geneva Declaration of the Rights of the Child of 1924 and in the Declaration of the Rights of the Child adopted by the General Assembly on 20 November 1959 and recognized in the Universal Declaration of Human Rights, in the International Covenant on Civil and Political Rights (in particular in articles 23 and 24), in the International Covenant on Economic, Social and Cultural Rights (in particular in article 10) and in the statutes and relevant instruments of specialized agencies and international organizations concerned with the welfare of children,

Bearing in mind that, as indicated in the Declaration of the Rights of the Child, "the child, by reason of his physical and mental immaturity, needs special safeguards and care, including appropriate legal protection, before as well as after birth,"

Recalling the provisions of the Declaration on Social and Legal Principles relating to the Protection and Welfare of Children, with Special Reference to Foster Placement and Adoption Nationally and Internationally; the United Nations Standard Minimum Rules for the Administration of Juvenile Justice (The Beijing Rules); and the Declaration on the Protection of Women and Children in Emergency and Armed Conflict,

Recognizing that, in all countries in the world, there are children living in exceptionally difficult conditions, and that such children need special consideration,

Taking due account of the importance of the traditions and cultural values of each people for the protection and harmonious development of the child,

Recognizing the importance of international co-operation for improving the living conditions of children in every country, in particular in the developing countries,

Have agreed as follows:

PART I

Article 1

For the purposes of the present Convention, a child means every human being below the age of eighteen years unless under the law applicable to the child, majority is attained earlier.

Article 2

1. States Parties shall respect and ensure the rights set forth in the present Convention to each child within their jurisdiction without discrimination of any kind, irrespective of the child's or his or her parent's or legal guardian's race, colour, sex, language, religion, political or other opinion, national, ethnic or social origin, property, disability, birth or other status.

2. States Parties shall take all appropriate measures to ensure that the child is protected against all forms of discrimination or punishment on the basis of the status, activities, expressed opinions, or beliefs of the child's parents, legal guardians, or family members.

Article 3

1. In all actions concerning children, whether undertaken by public or private social welfare institutions, courts of law, administrative authorities or legislative bodies, the best interests of the child shall be a primary consideration.

2. States Parties undertake to ensure the child such protection and care as is necessary for his or her well-being, taking into account the rights and duties of his or her parents, legal guardians, or other individuals legally responsible for him or her, and, to this end, shall take all appropriate legislative and administrative measures.

3. States Parties shall ensure that the institutions, services and facilities responsible for the care or protection of children shall conform with the standards established by competent authorities, particularly in the areas of safety, health, in the number and suitability of their staff, as well as competent supervision.

Article 4

States Parties shall undertake all appropriate legislative, administrative, and other measures for the implementation of the rights recognized in the present Convention. With regard to economic, social and cultural rights, States Parties shall undertake such measures to the maximum extent of their available resources and, where needed, within the framework of international co-operation.

Article 5

States Parties shall respect the responsibilities, rights and duties of parents or, where applicable, the members of the extended family or community as provided for by local custom, legal guardians or other persons legally responsible for the child, to provide, in a manner consistent with the evolving capacities of the child, appropriate direction and guidance in the exercise by the child of the rights recognized in the present Convention.

Article 6

1. States Parties recognize that every child has the inherent right to life.

2. States Parties shall ensure to the maximum extent possible the survival and development of the child.

Article 7

1. The child shall be registered immediately after birth and shall have the right from birth to a name, the right to acquire a nationality and. as far as possible, the right to know and be cared for by his or her parents.

2. States Parties shall ensure the implementation of these rights in accordance with their national law and their obligations under the relevant international instruments in this field, in particular where the child would otherwise be stateless.

Article 8

1. States Parties undertake to respect the right of the child to preserve his or her identity, including nationality, name and family relations as recognized by law without unlawful interference.

2. Where a child is illegally deprived of some or all of the elements of his or her identity, States Parties shall provide appropriate assistance and protection, with a view to re-establishing speedily his or her identity.

Article 9

1. States Parties shall ensure that a child shall not be separated from his or her parents against their will, except when competent authorities subject to judicial review determine, in accordance with applicable law and procedures, that such separation is necessary for the best interests of the child. Such determination may be necessary in a particular case such as one involving abuse or neglect of the child by the parents, or one where the parents are living separately and a decision must be made as to the child's place of residence.

2. In any proceedings pursuant to paragraph 1 of the present article, all interested parties shall be given an opportunity to participate in the proceedings and make their views known.

3. States Parties shall respect the right of the child who is separated from one or both parents to maintain personal relations and direct contact with both parents on a regular basis, except if it is contrary to the child's best interests.

4. Where such separation results from any action initiated by a State Party, such as the detention, imprisonment, exile, deportation or death (including death arising from any cause while the person is in the custody of the State) of one or both parents or of the child, that State Party shall, upon request, provide the parents, the child or, if appropriate, another member of the family with the essential information concerning the whereabouts of the absent member(s) of the family unless the provision of the information would be detrimental to the well-being of the child. States Parties shall further ensure that the submission of such a request shall of itself entail no adverse consequences for the person(s) concerned.

Article 10

1. In accordance with the obligation of States Parties under article 9, paragraph 1, applications by a child or his or her parents to enter or leave a State Party for the purpose of family reunification shall be dealt with by States Parties in a positive, humane and expeditious manner. States Parties shall further ensure that the submission of such a request shall entail no adverse consequences for the applicants and for the members of their family.

2. A child whose parents reside in different States shall have the right to maintain on a regular basis, save in exceptional circumstances personal relations and direct contacts with both parents. Towards that end and in accordance with the obligation of States Parties under article 9, paragraph 1, States Parties shall respect the right of the child and his or her parents to leave any country, including their own, and to enter their own country. The right to leave any country shall be subject only to such restrictions as are prescribed by law and which are necessary to protect the national security, public order (ordre public), public health or morals or the rights and freedoms of others and are consistent with the other rights recognized in the present Convention.

Article 11

1. States Parties shall take measures to combat the illicit transfer and non-return of children abroad.

2. To this end, States Parties shall promote the conclusion of bilateral or multilateral agreements or accession to existing agreements.

Article 12

1. States Parties shall assure to the child who is capable of forming his or her own views the right to express those views freely in all matters affecting the child, the views of the child being given due weight in accordance with the age and maturity of the child.

2. For this purpose, the child shall in particular be provided the opportunity to be heard in any judicial and administrative proceedings affecting the child, either directly, or through a representative or an appropriate body, in a manner consistent with the procedural rules of national law.

Article 13

1. The child shall have the right to freedom of expression; this right shall include freedom to seek, receive and impart information and ideas of all kinds, regardless of frontiers, either orally, in writing or in print, in the form of art, or through any other media of the child's choice.

2. The exercise of this right may be subject to certain restrictions, but these shall only be such as are provided by law and are necessary:

(a) For respect of the rights or reputations of others; or

(b) For the protection of national security or of public order (ordre public), or of public health or morals.

Article 14

1. States Parties shall respect the right of the child to freedom of thought, conscience and religion.

2. States Parties shall respect the rights and duties of the parents and, when applicable, legal guardians, to provide direction to the child in the exercise of his or her right in a manner consistent with the evolving capacities of the child.

3. Freedom to manifest one's religion or beliefs may be subject only to such limitations as are prescribed by law and are necessary to protect public safety, order, health or morals, or the fundamental rights and freedoms of others.

Article 15

1. States Parties recognize the rights of the child to freedom of association and to freedom of peaceful assembly.

2. No restrictions may be placed on the exercise of these rights other than those imposed in conformity with the law and which are necessary in a democratic society in the interests of national security or public safety, public order (ordre public), the protection of public health or morals or the protection of the rights and freedoms of others.

Article 16

1. No child shall be subjected to arbitrary or unlawful interference with his or her privacy, family, home or correspondence, nor to unlawful attacks on his or her honour and reputation.

2. The child has the right to the protection of the law against such interference or attacks.

Article 17

States Parties recognize the important function performed by the mass media and shall ensure that the child has access to information and material from a diversity of national and international sources, especially those aimed at the promotion of his or her social, spiritual and moral well-being and physical and mental health. To this end, States Parties shall:

(a) Encourage the mass media to disseminate information and material of social and cultural benefit to the child and in accordance with the spirit of article 29;

(b) Encourage international co-operation in the production, exchange and dissemination of such information and material from a diversity of cultural, national and international sources;

(c) Encourage the production and dissemination of children's books;

(d) Encourage the mass media to have particular regard to the linguistic needs of the child who belongs to a minority group or who is indigenous;

(e) Encourage the development of appropriate guidelines for the protection of the child from information and material injurious to his or her well-being, bearing in mind the provisions of articles 13 and 18.

Article 18

1. States Parties shall use their best efforts to ensure recognition of the principle that both parents have common responsibilities for the upbringing and development of the child. Parents or, as the case may be, legal guardians, have the primary responsibility for the upbringing and development of the child. The best interests of the child will be their basic concern.

2. For the purpose of guaranteeing and promoting the rights set forth in the present Convention, States Parties shall render appropriate assistance to parents and legal guardians in the performance of their child-rearing responsibilities and shall ensure the development of institutions, facilities and services for the care of children.

3. States Parties shall take all appropriate measures to ensure that children of working parents have the right to benefit from child-care services and facilities for which they are eligible.

Article 19

1. States Parties shall take all appropriate legislative, administrative, social and educational measures to protect the child from all forms of physical or mental violence, injury or abuse, neglect or negligent treatment, maltreatment or exploitation, including sexual abuse, while in the care of parent(s), legal guardian(s) or any other person who has the care of the child.

2. Such protective measures should, as appropriate, include effective procedures for the establishment of social programmes to provide necessary support for the child and for those who have the care of the child, as well as for other forms of prevention and for identification, reporting, referral, investigation, treatment and follow-up of instances of child maltreatment described heretofore, and, as appropriate, for judicial involvement.

Article 20

1. A child temporarily or permanently deprived of his or her family environment, or in whose own best interests cannot be allowed to remain in that environment, shall be entitled to special protection and assistance provided by the State.

2. States Parties shall in accordance with their national laws ensure alternative care for such a child.

3. Such care could include, inter alia, foster placement, kafalah of Islamic law, adoption or if necessary placement in suitable institutions for the care of children. When considering solutions, due regard shall be paid to the desirability of continuity in a child's upbringing and to the child's ethnic, religious, cultural and linguistic background.

Article 21

States Parties that recognize and/or permit the system of adoption shall ensure that the best interests of the child shall be the paramount consideration and they shall:

(a) Ensure that the adoption of a child is authorized only by competent authorities who determine, in accordance with applicable law and procedures and on the basis of all pertinent and reliable information, that the adoption is permissible in view of the child's status concerning parents, relatives and legal guardians and that, if required, the persons concerned have given their informed consent to the adoption on the basis of such counselling as may be necessary;

(b) Recognize that inter-country adoption may be considered as an alternative means of child's care, if the child cannot be placed in a foster or an adoptive family or cannot in any suitable manner be cared for in the child's country of origin;

(c) Ensure that the child concerned by inter-country adoption enjoys safeguards and standards equivalent to those existing in the case of national adoption;

(d) Take all appropriate measures to ensure that, in inter-country adoption, the placement does not result in improper financial gain for those involved in it;

(e) Promote, where appropriate, the objectives of the present article by concluding bilateral or multilateral arrangements or agreements, and endeavour, within this framework, to ensure that the placement of the child in another country is carried out by competent authorities or organs.

Article 22

1. States Parties shall take appropriate measures to ensure that a child who is seeking refugee status or who is considered a refugee in accordance with applicable international or domestic law and procedures shall, whether unaccompanied or accompanied by his or her parents or by any other person, receive appropriate protection and humanitarian assistance in the enjoyment of applicable rights set forth in the present Convention and in other international human rights or humanitarian instruments to which the said States are Parties.

2. For this purpose, States Parties shall provide, as they consider appropriate, co-operation in any efforts by the United Nations and other competent intergovernmental organizations or non-governmental organizations co-operating with the United Nations to protect and assist such a child and to trace the parents or other members of the family of any refugee child in order to obtain information necessary for reunification with his or her family. In cases where no parents or other members of the family can be found, the child shall be accorded the same protection as any other child permanently or temporarily deprived of his or her family environment for any reason, as set forth in the present Convention.

Article 23

1. States Parties recognize that a mentally or physically disabled child should enjoy a full and decent life, in conditions which ensure dignity, promote self-reliance and facilitate the child's active participation in the community.

2. States Parties recognize the right of the disabled child to special care and shall encourage and ensure the extension, subject to available resources, to the eligible child and those responsible for his or her care, of assistance for which application is made and which is appropriate to the child's condition and to the circumstances of the parents or others caring for the child.

3. Recognizing the special needs of a disabled child, assistance extended in accordance with paragraph 2 of the present article shall be provided free of charge, whenever possible, taking into account the financial resources of the parents or others caring for the child, and shall be designed to ensure that the disabled child has effective access to and receives education, training, health care services, rehabilitation services, preparation for employment and recreation opportunities in a manner conducive to the child's achieving the fullest possible social integration and individual development, including his or her cultural and spiritual development.

4. States Parties shall promote, in the spirit of international cooperation, the exchange of appropriate information in the field of preventive health care and of medical, psychological and functional treatment of disabled children, including dissemination of and access to information concerning methods of rehabilitation, education and vocational services, with the aim of enabling States Parties to improve their capabilities and skills and to widen their experience in these areas. In this regard, particular account shall be taken of the needs of developing countries.

Article 24

1. States Parties recognize the right of the child to the enjoyment of the highest attainable standard of health and to facilities for the treatment of illness and rehabilitation of health. States Parties shall strive to ensure that no child is deprived of his or her right of access to such health care services.

2. States Parties shall pursue full implementation of this right and, in particular, shall take appropriate measures:

(a) To diminish infant and child mortality;

(b) To ensure the provision of necessary medical assistance and health care to all children with emphasis on the development of primary health care;

(c) To combat disease and malnutrition, including within the framework of primary health care, through, inter alia, the application of readily available technology and through the provision of adequate nutritious foods and clean drinking-water, taking into consideration the dangers and risks of environmental pollution;

(d) To ensure appropriate pre-natal and post-natal health care for mothers;

(e) To ensure that all segments of society, in particular parents and children, are informed, have access to education and are supported in the use of basic knowledge of child health and nutrition, the advantages of breastfeeding, hygiene and environmental sanitation and the prevention of accidents;

(f) To develop preventive health care, guidance for parents and family planning education and services.

3. States Parties shall take all effective and appropriate measures with a view to abolishing traditional practices prejudicial to the health of children.

4. States Parties undertake to promote and encourage international co-operation with a view to achieving progressively the full realization of the right recognized in the present article. In this regard, particular account shall be taken of the needs of developing countries.

Article 25

States Parties recognize the right of a child who has been placed by the competent authorities for the purposes of care, protection or treatment of his or her physical or mental health, to a periodic review of the treatment provided to the child and all other circumstances relevant to his or her placement.

Article 26

1. States Parties shall recognize for every child the right to benefit from social security, including social insurance, and shall take the necessary measures to achieve the full realization of this right in accordance with their national law.

2. The benefits should, where appropriate, be granted, taking into account the resources and the circumstances of the child and persons having responsibility for the maintenance of the child, as well as any other consideration relevant to an application for benefits made by or on behalf of the child.

Article 27

1. States Parties recognize the right of every child to a standard of living adequate for the child's physical, mental, spiritual, moral and social development.

2. The parent(s) or others responsible for the child have the primary responsibility to secure, within their abilities and financial capacities, the conditions of living necessary for the child's development.

3. States Parties, in accordance with national conditions and within their means, shall take appropriate measures to assist parents and others responsible for the child to implement this right and shall in case of need provide material assistance and support programmes, particularly with regard to nutrition, clothing and housing.

4. States Parties shall take all appropriate measures to secure the recovery of maintenance for the child from the parents or other persons having financial responsibility for the child, both within the State Party and from abroad. In particular, where the person having financial responsibility for the child lives in a State different from that of the child, States Parties shall promote the accession to international agreements or the conclusion of such agreements, as well as the making of other appropriate arrangements.

Article 28

1. States Parties recognize the right of the child to education, and with a view to achieving this right progressively and on the basis of equal opportunity, they shall, in particular:

(a) Make primary education compulsory and available free to all;

(b) Encourage the development of different forms of secondary education, including general and vocational education, make them available and accessible to every child, and take appropriate measures such as the introduction of free education and offering financial assistance in case of need;

(c) Make higher education accessible to all on the basis of capacity by every appropriate means;

(d) Make educational and vocational information and guidance available and accessible to all children;

(e) Take measures to encourage regular attendance at schools and the reduction of drop-out rates.

2. States Parties shall take all appropriate measures to ensure that school discipline is administered in a manner consistent with the child's human dignity and in conformity with the present Convention.

3. States Parties shall promote and encourage international cooperation in matters relating to education, in particular with a view to contributing to the elimination of ignorance and illiteracy throughout the world and facilitating access to scientific and technical knowledge and modern teaching methods. In this regard, particular account shall be taken of the needs of developing countries.

Article 29

1. States Parties agree that the education of the child shall be directed to:

(a) The development of the child's personality, talents and mental and physical abilities to their fullest potential;

(b) The development of respect for human rights and fundamental freedoms, and for the principles enshrined in the Charter of the United Nations;

(c) The development of respect for the child's parents, his or her own cultural identity, language and values, for the national values of the country in which the child is living, the country from which he or she may originate, and for civilizations different from his or her own;

(d) The preparation of the child for responsible life in a free society, in the spirit of understanding, peace, tolerance, equality of sexes, and friendship among all peoples, ethnic, national and religious groups and persons of indigenous origin;

(e) The development of respect for the natural environment.

2. No part of the present article or article 28 shall be construed so as to interfere with the liberty of individuals and bodies to establish and direct educational institutions, subject always to the observance of the principle set forth in paragraph 1 of the present article and to the requirements that the education given in such institutions shall conform to such minimum standards as may be laid down by the State.

Article 30

In those States in which ethnic, religious or linguistic minorities or persons of indigenous origin exist, a child belonging to such a minority or who is indigenous shall not be denied the right, in community with other members of his or her group, to enjoy his or her own culture, to profess and practise his or her own religion, or to use his or her own language.

Article 31

1. States Parties recognize the right of the child to rest and leisure, to engage in play and recreational activities appropriate to the age of the child and to participate freely in cultural life and the arts.

2. States Parties shall respect and promote the right of the child to participate fully in cultural and artistic life and shall encourage the provision of appropriate and equal opportunities for cultural, artistic, recreational and leisure activity.

Article 32

States Parties recognize the right of the child to be protected from economic exploitation and from performing any work that is likely to be hazardous or to interfere with the child's education, or to be harmful to the child's health or physical, mental, spiritual, moral or social development.

States Parties shall take legislative, administrative, social and educational measures to ensure the implementation of the present article. To this end, and having regard to the relevant provisions of other international instruments, States Parties shall in particular:

(a) Provide for a minimum age or minimum ages for admission to employment;

(b) Provide for appropriate regulation of the hours and conditions of employment;

(c) Provide for appropriate penalties or other sanctions to ensure the effective enforcement of the present article.

Article 33

States Parties shall take all appropriate measures, including legislative, administrative, social and educational measures, to protect children from the illicit use of narcotic drugs and psychotropic substances as defined in the relevant international treaties, and to prevent the use of children in the illicit production and trafficking of such substances.

Article 34

States Parties undertake to protect the child from all forms of sexual exploitation and sexual abuse. For these purposes, States Parties shall in particular take all appropriate national, bilateral and multilateral measures to prevent:

(a) The inducement or coercion of a child to engage in any unlawful sexual activity;

(b) The exploitative use of children in prostitution or other unlawful sexual practices;

(c) The exploitative use of children in pornographic performances and materials.

Article 35

States Parties shall take all appropriate national, bilateral and multilateral measures to prevent the abduction of, the sale of or traffic in children for any purpose or in any form.

Article 36

States Parties shall protect the child against all other forms of exploitation prejudicial to any aspects of the child's welfare.

Article 37

States Parties shall ensure that:

(a) No child shall be subjected to torture or other cruel, inhuman or degrading treatment or punishment. Neither capital punishment nor life imprisonment without possibility of release shall be imposed for offences committed by persons below eighteen years of age;

(b) No child shall be deprived of his or her liberty unlawfully or arbitrarily. The arrest, detention or imprisonment of a child shall be in conformity with the law and shall be used only as a measure of last resort and for the shortest appropriate period of time;

(c) Every child deprived of liberty shall be treated with humanity and respect for the inherent dignity of the human person, and in a manner which takes into account the needs of persons of his or her age. In particular, every child deprived of liberty shall be separated from adults unless it is considered in the child's best interest not to do so and shall have the right to maintain contact with his or her family through correspondence and visits, save in exceptional circumstances;

(d) Every child deprived of his or her liberty shall have the right to prompt access to legal and other appropriate assistance, as well as the right to challenge the legality of the deprivation of his or her liberty before a court or other competent, independent and impartial authority, and to a prompt decision on any such action.

Article 38

1. States Parties undertake to respect and to ensure respect for rules of international humanitarian law applicable to them in armed conflicts which are relevant to the child.

2. States Parties shall take all feasible measures to ensure that persons who have not attained the age of fifteen years do not take a direct part in hostilities.

3. States Parties shall refrain from recruiting any person who has not attained the age of fifteen years into their armed forces. In recruiting among those persons who have attained the age of fifteen years but who have not attained the age of eighteen years, States Parties shall endeavour to give priority to those who are oldest.

4. In accordance with their obligations under international humanitarian law to protect the civilian population in armed conflicts, States Parties shall take all feasible measures to ensure protection and care of children who are affected by an armed conflict.

Article 39

States Parties shall take all appropriate measures to promote physical and psychological recovery and social reintegration of a child victim of: any form of neglect, exploitation, or abuse; torture or any other form of cruel, inhuman or degrading treatment or punishment; or armed conflicts. Such recovery and reintegration shall take place in an environment which fosters the health, self-respect and dignity of the child.

Article 40

1. States Parties recognize the right of every child alleged as, accused of, or recognized as having infringed the penal law to be treated in a manner consistent with the promotion of the child's sense of dignity and worth, which reinforces the child's respect for the human rights and fundamental freedoms of others and which takes into account the child's age and the desirability of promoting the child's reintegration and the child's assuming a constructive role in society.

2. To this end, and having regard to the relevant provisions of international instruments, States Parties shall, in particular, ensure that:

(a) No child shall be alleged as, be accused of, or recognized as having infringed the penal law by reason of acts or omissions that were not prohibited by national or international law at the time they were committed;

(b) Every child alleged as or accused of having infringed the penal law has at least the following guarantees:

(i) To be presumed innocent until proven guilty according to law;

(ii) To be informed promptly and directly of the charges against him or her, and, if appropriate, through his or her parents or legal guardians, and to have legal or other appropriate assistance in the preparation and presentation of his or her defence;

(iii) To have the matter determined without delay by a competent, independent and impartial authority or judicial body in a fair hearing according to law, in the presence of legal or other appropriate assistance and, unless it is considered not to be in the best interest of the child, in particular, taking into account his or her age or situation, his or her parents or legal guardians;

(iv) Not to be compelled to give testimony or to confess guilt; to examine or have examined adverse witnesses and to obtain the participation and examination of witnesses on his or her behalf under conditions of equality;

(v) If considered to have infringed the penal law, to have this decision and any measures imposed in consequence thereof reviewed by a higher competent, independent and impartial authority or judicial body according to law;

(vi) To have the free assistance of an interpreter if the child cannot understand or speak the language used;

(vii) To have his or her privacy fully respected at all stages of the proceedings.

3. States Parties shall seek to promote the establishment of laws, procedures, authorities and institutions specifically applicable to children alleged as, accused of, or recognized as having infringed the penal law, and, in particular:

(a) The establishment of a minimum age below which children shall be presumed not to have the capacity to infringe the penal law;

(b) Whenever appropriate and desirable, measures for dealing with such children without resorting to judicial proceedings, providing that human rights and legal safeguards are fully respected.

(c) A variety of dispositions, such as care, guidance and supervision orders; counselling; probation; foster care; education and vocational training programmes and other alternatives to institutional care shall be available to ensure that children are dealt with in a manner appropriate to their well-being and proportionate both to their circumstances and the offence.

Article 41

Nothing in the present Convention shall affect any provisions which are more conducive to the realization of the rights of the child and which may be contained in:

(a) The law of a State party; or

(b) International law in force for that State.

PART II

Article 42

States Parties undertake to make the principles and provisions of the Convention widely known, by appropriate and active means, to adults and children alike.

Article 43

1. For the purpose of examining the progress made by States Parties in achieving the realization of the obligations undertaken in the present Convention, there shall be established a Committee on the Rights of the Child, which shall carry out the functions hereinafter provided.

2. The Committee shall consist of ten experts of high moral standing and recognized competence in the field covered by this Convention. The members of the Committee shall be elected by States Parties from among their nationals and shall serve in their personal capacity, consideration being given to equitable geographical distribution, as well as to the principal legal systems.

3. The members of the Committee shall be elected by secret ballot from a list of persons nominated by States Parties. Each State Party may nominate one person from among its own nationals.

4. The initial election to the Committee shall be held no later than six months after the date of the entry into force of the present Convention and thereafter every second year. At least four months before the date of each election, the Secretary-General of the United Nations shall address a letter to States Parties inviting them to submit their nominations within two months. The Secretary-General shall subsequently prepare a list in alphabetical order of all persons thus nominated, indicating States Parties which have nominated them, and shall submit it to the States Parties to the present Convention.

5. The elections shall be held at meetings of States Parties convened by the Secretary-General at United Nations Headquarters. At those meetings, for which two thirds of States Parties shall constitute a quorum, the persons elected to the Committee shall be those who obtain the largest number of votes and an absolute majority of the votes of the representatives of States Parties present and voting.

6. The members of the Committee shall be elected for a term of four years. They shall be eligible for re-election if renominated. The term of five of the members elected at the first election shall expire at the end of two years; immediately after the first election, the names of these five members shall be chosen by lot by the Chairman of the meeting.

7. If a member of the Committee dies or resigns or declares that for any other cause he or she can no longer perform the duties of the Committee, the State Party which nominated the member shall appoint another expert from among its nationals to serve for the remainder of the term, subject to the approval of the Committee.

8. The Committee shall establish its own rules of procedure.

9. The Committee shall elect its officers for a period of two years.

10. The meetings of the Committee shall normally be held at United Nations Headquarters or at any other convenient place as determined by the Committee. The Committee shall normally meet annually. The duration of the meetings of the Committee shall be determined, and reviewed, if necessary, by a meeting of the States Parties to the present Convention, subject to the approval of the General Assembly.

11. The Secretary-General of the United Nations shall provide the necessary staff and facilities for the effective performance of the functions of the Committee under the present Convention.

12. With the approval of the General Assembly, the members of the Committee established under the present Convention shall receive emoluments from United Nations resources on such terms and conditions as the Assembly may decide.

Article 44

1. States Parties undertake to submit to the Committee, through the Secretary-General of the United Nations, reports on the measures they have adopted which give effect to the rights recognized herein and on the progress made on the enjoyment of those rights:

(a) Within two years of the entry into force of the Convention for the State Party concerned;

(b) Thereafter every five years.

2. Reports made under the present article shall indicate factors and difficulties, if any, affecting the degree of fulfil-

ment of the obligations under the present Convention. Reports shall also contain sufficient information to provide the Committee with a comprehensive understanding of the implementation of the Convention in the country concerned.

3. A State Party which has submitted a comprehensive initial report to the Committee need not, in its subsequent reports submitted in accordance with paragraph 1 (b) of the present article, repeat basic information previously provided.

4. The Committee may request from States Parties further information relevant to the implementation of the Convention.

5. The Committee shall submit to the General Assembly, through the Economic and Social Council, every two years, reports on its activities.

6. States Parties shall make their reports widely available to the public in their own countries.

Article 45

In order to foster the effective implementation of the Convention and to encourage international co-operation in the field covered by the Convention:

(a) The specialized agencies, the United Nations Children's Fund, and other United Nations organs shall be entitled to be represented at the consideration of the implementation of such provisions of the present Convention as fall within the scope of their mandate. The Committee may invite the specialized agencies, the United Nations Children's Fund and other competent bodies as it may consider appropriate to provide expert advice on the implementation of the Convention in areas falling within the scope of their respective mandates. The Committee may invite the specialized agencies, the United Nations Children's Fund, and other United Nations organs to submit reports on the implementation of the Convention in areas falling within the scope of their activities;

(b) The Committee shall transmit, as it may consider appropriate, to the specialized agencies, the United Nations Children's Fund and other competent bodies, any reports from States Parties that contain a request, or indicate a need, for technical advice or assistance, along with the Committee's observations and suggestions, if any, on these requests or indications;

(c) The Committee may recommend to the General Assembly to request the Secretary-General to undertake on its behalf studies on specific issues relating to the rights of the child;

(d) The Committee may make suggestions and general recommendations based on information received pursuant to articles 44 and 45 of the present Convention. Such suggestions and general recommendations shall be transmitted to any State Party concerned and reported to the General Assembly, together with comments, if any, from States Parties.

PART III

Article 46

The present Convention shall be open for signature by all States.

Article 47

The present Convention is subject to ratification. Instruments of ratification shall be deposited with the Secretary-General of the United Nations.

Article 48

The present Convention shall remain open for accession by any State. The instruments of accession shall be deposited with the Secretary-General of the United Nations.

Article 49

1. The present Convention shall enter into force on the thirtieth day following the date of deposit with the Secretary-General of the United Nations of the twentieth instrument of ratification or accession.

2. For each State ratifying or acceding to the Convention after the deposit of the twentieth instrument of ratification or accession, the Convention shall enter into force on the thirtieth day after the deposit by such State of its instrument of ratification or accession.

Article 50

1. Any State Party may propose an amendment and file it with the Secretary-General of the United Nations. The Secretary-General shall thereupon communicate the proposed amendment to States Parties, with a request that they indicate whether they favour a conference of States Parties for the purpose of considering and voting upon the proposals. In the event that, within four months from the date of such communication, at least one third of the States Parties favour such a conference, the Secretary-General shall convene the conference under the auspices of the United Nations. Any amendment adopted by a majority of States Parties present and voting at the conference shall be submitted to the General Assembly for approval.

2. An amendment adopted in accordance with paragraph 1 of the present article shall enter into force when it has been approved by the General Assembly of the United Nations and accepted by a two-thirds majority of States Parties.

3. When an amendment enters into force, it shall be binding on those States Parties which have accepted it, other States Parties still being bound by the provisions of the present Convention and any earlier amendments which they have accepted.

Article 51

1. The Secretary-General of the United Nations shall receive and circulate to all States the text of reservations made by States at the time of ratification or accession.

2. A reservation incompatible with the object and purpose of the present Convention shall not be permitted.

3. Reservations may be withdrawn at any time by notification to that effect addressed to the Secretary-General of the United Nations, who shall then inform all States. Such notification shall take effect on the date on which it is received by the Secretary-General.

Article 52

A State Party may denounce the present Convention by written notification to the Secretary-General of the United Nations. Denunciation becomes effective one year after the date of receipt of the notification by the Secretary-General.

Article 53

The Secretary-General of the United Nations is designated as the depositary of the present Convention.

Article 54

The original of the present Convention, of which the Arabic, Chinese, English, French, Russian and Spanish texts are equally authentic, shall be deposited with the Secretary-General of the United Nations.

IN WITNESS THEREOF the undersigned plenipotentiaries, being duly authorized thereto by their respective governments, have signed the present Convention.

Excerpt from *The Child Soldiers Global Report,* 2001

SOURCE: Coalition to Stop the Use of Child Soldiers. 2001. Available from <www.child-soldiers.org>. Reprinted by permission.

Introduction

In 2001 six international humanitarian organizations (Amnesty International, Human Rights Watch, the International Save the Children Alliance, Jesuit Refugee Service, the Quaker UN Office—Geneva, and International Federation Terre des Hommes) released a jointly authored report on the global problem of child soldiers. The report points both to the continuing vulnerability of the world's children, and to the growing humanitarian recognition of their need to be protected. The UN High Commissioner for Human Rights, Mary Robinson, welcomed the report and called for the world's nations to ratify the protocol to the Convention on the Rights of the Child, adopted by the UN General Assembly on May 25, 2000, that prohibits the use of soldiers under age eighteen. The following ex-

cerpt from the introduction of the *Child Soldiers Global Report* gives a detailed account of the abuses suffered by child soldiers in many nations.

At any one time, more than 300,000 children under 18—girls and boys—are fighting as soldiers with government armed forces and armed opposition groups in more than 30 countries worldwide. In more than 85 countries, hundreds of thousands more under-18s have been recruited into government armed forces, paramilitaries, civil militia and a wide variety of non-state armed groups. Millions of children worldwide receive military training and indoctrination in youth movements and schools. While most child soldiers are aged between 15 and 18, the youngest age recorded in this report is seven.

These statistics represent only a 'snapshot' of the problem, as children are recruited, captured, demobilised, wounded or even killed every day. Many of today's adult soldiers started out as children, growing up in military ranks; in many countries, with inadequate systems of birth registration, age can be difficult to determine.

Conflicts come and go as well; the more protracted the armed conflict, the more likely children will participate. In recent years, large numbers of children fighting in Latin America and the Middle East region have been replaced as conflicts recede by new generations of child soldiers in Africa and Asia. In the industrialised world, there is general trend away from conscription and towards volunteer, professional armies; combined with economic and social change this has made enlistment levels more difficult to sustain and placed downward pressures on recruitment age.

While many children fight in the frontline, others are used as spies, messengers, sentries, porters, servants and sexual slaves; children are often used to lay and clear landmines or conditioned to commit atrocities even against their own families and communities. Most child soldiers suffer physical abuse and other privations within the armed forces; in extreme cases, child soldiers are driven to suicide or murder when they cannot bear the mistreatment any longer. When children are used as soldiers, all children in a conflict zone are often suspected and targeted by the warring parties.

While some children are recruited forcibly, others are driven into armed forces by poverty, alienation and discrimination. Many children join armed groups after having experienced or witnessed abuse at the hands of state authorities. The widespread availability of modern lightweight weapons has also contributed to the child soldiers problem, enabling even the smallest children to become efficient killers in combat. International political and military support for armed forces and armed groups using children, sometimes linked to the exploitation of natural resources like diamonds or oil, has in many cases deepened conflicts and the involvement of children.

Many governments and armed groups claim to use children because of a shortage of adult recruits. But often children are recruited because of their very qualities as children—they can be cheap, expendable and easier to condition into fearless killing and unthinking obedience. Sometimes, children are supplied with drugs and alcohol to achieve these aims.

Often child soldiers are recruited from second countries, among refugee communities or ethnic disasporas, and trafficked across borders. Children from Angola, Burundi, Kenya, Rwanda and Uganda have fought alongside their adult sponsors in the civil war in the Democratic Republic of Congo. Children have been recruited from various countries of western Europe by Kurdish and Kosovar armed groups.

In many countries, military training and indoctrination is provided through schools and youth movements, often as a means of bolstering defence preparedness or recruitment levels. In Iraq, thousands of children aged 10 to 15 participate in the Ashbal Saddam (Saddam Lion Cubs) youth movement formed after the 1991 Gulf War; training reportedly includes small-arms use, hand-to-hand combat, and infantry tactics. In the United States of America, military-run programmes exist for children as young as eight. In the Young Marines, boys and girls from age 8–18 wear uniforms, are assigned military ranks, and participate in "boot camp" and rifle drills; the programme has over 200 units nation-wide, with 14,865 participants in early 2001.

THE IMPACT OF SOLDIERING ON CHILDREN

Child soldiers do not only lose their childhood and opportunities for education and development—they risk physical injury, psychological trauma and even death. Children are often at an added disadvantage as combatants in relation to adults.

Widely perceived to be a cheap and expendable commodity, child soldiers tend to receive little or no training before being thrust into the front line. In the early 1980s, during the Iran-Iraq war, thousands of Iranian children, many straight from school, were sent with popular militias to the frontline, often given a symbolic key to the paradise promised them as martyrs. More recently, during the border war with Eritrea in 1999–2000, Ethiopian government forces reportedly press-ganged thousands of secondary schools students from marketplaces and villages, some of whom were used in human wave attacks across minefields. Children's immaturity may lead them to take excessive risks—according to one armed group commander in the Democratic Republic of Congo, "[children] make good fighters because they're young and want to show off. They think it's all a game, so they're fearless."

Children may begin participating in conflict from as young as seven. Some serve as porters (carrying food or ammunition) or messengers, others as spies. In Myanmar, for instance civilians, including children as young as 10, are forced to porter for the military and even used as human shields and minesweepers: the International Labour Organisation reported in 1999 that children had been forced to sweep roads with tree branches or brooms to detect or detonate mines. As soon as children are strong enough to handle an assault rifle or a semi-automatic weapon (normally at 10 years of age), they may be used in frontline roles. One former child soldier from Burundi stated that: "We spent sleepless nights watching for the enemy. My first role was to carry a torch for grown-up rebels. Later I was shown how to use hand grenades. Barely within a month or so, I was carrying an AK-47 rifle or even a G3."

When not actively engaged in combat, children can often be seen manning checkpoints. In Afghanistan, young students from religious schools in Pakistan perform military service with the Taleban, policing urban centres and checkpoints to free more experienced fighters for the front line. Others, such as 15-year-old Stevica in the Former Republic of Yugoslavia, perform domestic tasks: "I prepare the weapons, I write reports from the field and I cook. I work for the Serb Tigers. There are 100 of us from Macedonia but we are all Serbs."

In many countries, girls too are used as soldiers, though generally in much smaller numbers than boys. Many governments and armed groups around the world are increasing the recruitment and functions performed by females in their armed forces, in many cases including girls under the age of 18. In Sri Lanka, for instance, young Tamil girls, often orphans, have been systematically recruited by the opposition Liberation Tigers of Tamil Eelam (LTTE) since the mid-1980s. Dubbed "Birds of Freedom", many are reportedly trained as suicide bombers as they may better evade government security. In October 1999, 49 children, including 32 girls aged between 11 and 15 years of age were among the 140 LTTE cadres killed in a battle with the security forces at Ampakamam in the north.

Girls are at particular risk of rape, sexual slavery and abuse, although the exploitation of boys for these purposes is also reported. Concy A., a 14-year old girl abducted from Kitgum in Uganda by the Lord's Resistance Army (LRA) and taken to camps in Sudan told how "we were distributed to men and I was given to a man who had just killed his woman. I was not given a gun, but I helped in the abductions and grabbing of food from villagers. Girls who refused to become LRA wives were killed in front of us to serve as a warning to the rest of us." Grace A. gave birth on open ground to a girl fathered by one of her [LRA] abductors: "I picked up a gun and strapped the baby on my back" and continued to fight the government forces. In Colombia, girls fighting with armed groups are frequently subjected to sexual abuse. The Revolutionary Armed Forces of Colombia (FARC) operates a "sexual freedom" policy and there are reports of young girls being fitted with inter-uterine devices; one 15-year-old girl soldier who was killed was found to be pregnant.

Even in the supposedly sophisticated armed forces of industrialised countries, young recruits—especially girls—are subject to 'hazing', harassment and abuse. In recent years, cases of bullying and humiliation of under-18 recruits in the British Army have included mock execution, forced simulation of sexual acts, 'regimental baths' in vomit and urine and the forced ingestion of mud. In August 1997, a 17-year-old recruit to the British Army was forced to perform a sex act and raped by a drunken instructor while she was on manoeuvres. She told the judge that she "didn't shout out because he is a sergeant and a higher rank. You don't disrespect your boss". (The instructor was jailed for seven years in November 1998.) In 1999, one school district in the US state of Washington banned recruiters from schools after several Army recruiters from a local recruiting station were investigated for sexual harassment of high school girls.

Besides the risk of death or injury in combat, child soldiers suffer disproportionately from the rigours of military life. Younger children collapse under heavy loads; malnutrition, respiratory and skin infections and other ailments are frequent. Child soldiers may also be at additional risk of drug and alcohol abuse (often used to recruit children or desensitise them for violence), sexually transmitted disease, including HIV/AIDS, and unwanted pregnancies. Auditory and visual problems are common, along with landmine injuries.

Harsh training regimes and other forms of ill-treatment often lead to casualties and even deaths among young recruits. In Paraguay, 56 under-18s died during their military service, six of them in 2000 alone. On 3 April 2001, 17-year-old Héctor Adon Maciel was shot by a fellow conscript after he refused to give him cigarettes. He died due to inadequate medical care as the Armed Forces argued that intensive care would be too expensive. Maciel was recruited at 16 after the armed forces reportedly falsified his mother's signature on documents giving her consent. Between 1982 and 1999, 92 recruits aged 16 and 17 died during service with the British Army, including four deaths as result of battle wounds or injuries. In 1998 one 16-year-old Royal Marine recruit drowned wearing full kit during a river-crossing exercise during a 30-week commando training course; he was the fourth to die during training in two and a half years.

Children are often treated brutally and punishments for mistakes or desertion are severe. In May 2001 four children in the Democratic Republic of Congo, aged between 14 and 16, were sentenced to death by a military court under a special law designed to crack down on looting and robberies by gangs of child soldiers. In Ethiopia, young conscripts claimed that comrades who tried to escape during attacks were shot; others who returned alive after battles were reportedly ill-treated, charged with desertion and even imprisoned in pits in the ground. In September 2000, the UN Committee on the Rights of the Child raised a general concern about the application of military laws to under-18 recruits, in possible contradiction with the Convention on the Rights of the Child and international standards on juvenile justice.

In many countries, child soldiers who are captured, escape or surrender often face ill-treatment, torture and even death. On 26 May 2000 in Nepal, one girl aged 17 was killed with five other Maoist suspects in Urma village, allegedly after being wounded and captured. In Burundi, the government has imprisoned and tortured children, many accused of collaborating with armed opposition groups, for long periods without charge or trial. Others face retaliation from the community and are given little protection. On 25 October 2000 in Sri Lanka, a mob from nearby villages attacked Bindunuwewa rehabilitation camp killing 26 inmates between the ages of 14 and 23; an inquiry is underway into the circumstances. In Sierra Leone, many demobilised children have been re-recruited by armed groups, sometimes from rehabilitation camps themselves.

Whenever even a few children are involved as soldiers in a conflict, all children in that particular community or area—civilian or combatant—come under suspicion. For instance, the UN Committee on the Rights of the Child and UN Special Rapporteurs have expressed concern about cases of extra-judicial execution, torture and 'disappearance' of juveniles suspected of involvement with armed groups in the northeast states of India. On 15 August 2000 in Colombia, an army unit near Pueblo Rico, Antioquia, mistook a party of schoolchildren for a guerrilla unit and opened fire, killing six children aged between 6 and 10 and wounding six others.

The full psychological impact on children of participation in armed conflict, especially for those who have witnessed or committed atrocities, is only beginning to be understood. According to one 14-year-old girl abducted by the Revolutionary United Front in Sierra Leone in January 1999, "I've seen people get their hands cut off, a ten-year-old girl raped and then die, and so many men and women burned alive . . . So many times I just cried inside my heart because I didn't dare cry out loud." From Algeria, one report cites boys who appeared to be around the age of 12 decapitating a 15-year-old girl and then playing 'catch' with her head.

However there is growing experience today in many parts of the world with the physical and psycho-social rehabilitation of child soldiers and their successful reintegration into society, some of which is documented in this report. Often these programs combine the latest developments in psychology and child development with traditional custom and ritual. The adjustment from highly-militarised environments to civilian life can be extremely difficult, particularly for those who have lost or are rejected by their families or in societies where social infrastructure has been shattered by years of war. Special attention needs to be paid in such programs to the experience and needs of girls, who have often been overlooked in assistance programs and disadvantaged by traditional patriarchal social values.

These programs are vitally important to peacebuilding efforts and the long term stability and development of postconflict societies. The United Nations, including in Security Council Resolution 1314 of August 2000, has recognised the importance of incorporating the disarmament, demobilisation and reintegration of former child soldiers into peace negotiations and agreements, and donors are committing more resources to this critical area. But a more consistent and long-term commitment is desperately needed if this problem is to be squarely addressed.

Excerpt from *Children on the Brink 2002: A Joint USAID/UNICEF/UNAIDS Report on Orphan Estimates and Program Strategies*, 2002

SOURCE: Joint United Nations Program on HIV/AIDS. (2002). Available from <www.unaids.org>. Reprinted by permission.

Introduction

Perhaps the most pressing issue facing the world's children at the beginning of the third millennium is AIDS. In 2002, UNAIDS, USAIDS, and UNICEF jointly issued a report entitled *Children on the Brink 2002*, that detailed the impact of the epidemic on youth. The introduction, excerpted below, offers readers a sense of the enormity of the crisis. The report calls for unified action to combat the epidemic and outlines ways to help its youngest victims. The report is also an example of the humanitarian imperative to protect children that became powerful during the twentieth century.

No other infectious disease of the modern era has had such a devastating impact on the world's youngest and most vulnerable citizens as HIV/AIDS. Since researchers first identified HIV/AIDS nearly a generation ago, more than 20 million people around the world have died from the disease. An estimated 40 million are living with HIV today, including almost 3 million children under age 15.

One of the most telling and troubling consequences of the epidemic's growing reach is the number of children it has orphaned or seriously impacted. Today more than 13 million children currently under age 15 have lost one or both parents to AIDS, most of them in sub-Saharan Africa. By 2010, this number is expected to jump to more than 25 million.

While the impact of this loss of life differs across families, communities and societies, one thing is clear: a child's life often falls apart when he or she loses a parent. With infection rates still rising and adults continuing to succumb to the disease, HIV/AIDS will continue to cause large-scale suffering among children for at least the next two decades.

Children on the Brink 2002 contains statistics on children orphaned by HIV/AIDS from 88 countries, analysis of the trends found in those statistics, and strategies and principles for helping the children. The third in a series (earlier editions were published in 1997 and 2000), this document covers 1990 to 2010 and provides the broadest and most comprehensive statistics yet on the historical, current, and projected number of children orphaned by HIV/AIDS. The report is a collaboration by the U.S. Agency for International Development (USAID), the United Nations Children's Fund (UNICEF), and the Joint United Nations Programme on HIV/AIDS (UNAIDS).

Estimates of orphans from all causes are included to give a more realistic picture of the scale at which responses must be developed. By 2010, an estimated 106 million children are projected to lose one or both parents, with 25 million of this group orphaned due to HIV/AIDS. The report also stresses that the growing needs of other children made vulnerable by HIV/AIDS must be met.

Turning the tide of this emergency requires immediate and sustained action at all levels. This report hopes to convey a few critical points that can help develop well-coordinated and compassionate responses from families, communities, governments and others. They are:

HIV/AIDS has created an orphan crisis. This unprecedented orphan crisis will require radically scaled-up national, regional, and community responses for at least two decades—especially in sub-Saharan Africa, where children have been hardest hit.

Orphans due to other causes also demand attention. Increases in the number of orphans due to AIDS should be considered as part of a much larger problem of orphaning due to all causes. In 12 African countries, projections show that orphans will comprise at least 15% of all children under 15 years of age by 2010.

Other children are also vulnerable. The safety, health, and survival of all children in affected countries are increasingly jeopardized due to the effects of AIDS on families and communities. Increasing numbers of children are living with sick or dying parents or in households that have taken in orphans. Moreover, the pandemic is deepening poverty in entire communities, with children usually the first to suffer from the deprivation.

AIDS threatens children's lives. The impacts of AIDS on children are both complex and multifaceted. Children suffer psychosocial distress and increasing material hardship due to AIDS. They may be pressed into service to care for ill and dying parents, required to drop out of school to help with farm or household work, or experience declining access to food and health services. Many are at risk of exclusion, abuse, discrimination, and stigma.

Communities with a high proportion of orphans require urgent assistance. Responses need to be focused and scaled up in communities with high proportions of orphans and children affected by HIV/AIDS. Because they are at the center of the crisis, these communities are the most overstretched.

Collaboration is key. The estimates on orphans due to AIDS presented here are the result of the first unified effort to provide a consistent set of numbers. This effort demonstrates the importance of strengthened collaboration and provides a springboard for expanded responses. No one can tackle this crisis alone.

Growing Global Commitment

Earlier editions of *Children on the Brink* helped break the silence about the effects of HIV/AIDS on children worldwide. With the pandemic's impact on children continuing unabated, contributors hope this year's edition will draw an even stronger response. The strategies and principles outlined in this report are designed to bolster national, regional, and local efforts by providing practical recommendations for action by policymakers, donors, nongovernmental organizations (NGOs), religious leaders, and others who have a stake in securing the future of these children.

This report and its recommendations for action will add momentum to an international effort to confront HIV/AIDS that has taken root in the last couple years and is growing rapidly. A pivotal event was the June 2001 United Nations General Assembly Special Session on HIV/AIDS, where member nations issued a Declaration of Commitment on HIV/AIDS. It calls for new commitments to strong leadership at all levels of society, and specifies benchmarks for prevention, care, support, and treatment of HIV/AIDS. The Declaration established two goals specific to children affected by HIV/AIDS:

- Member countries will develop national policies and strategies that build and strengthen the ability of government, community, and family to support orphans and children infected with and affected by HIV/AIDS by 2003; and
- Member countries will implement these policies and strategies by 2005.

Reaching these goals will be difficult, but efforts are under way. For example, delegates from 21 West and Central African countries met for the first time in April 2002 to coordinate and strengthen their action to confront the crisis. And prominent African religious leaders met in Nairobi in June 2002 to commit themselves to concerted efforts on behalf of orphans and children made vulnerable by HIV/AIDS.

Modern Studies of the Child

Excerpt from *Adolescence* by G. Stanley Hall, 1904

SOURCE: Hall, G. Stanley. 1904. "Adolescent Girls and their Education." In *Adolescence: Its Psychology and its Relations to Physiology, Anthropology, Sociology, Sex, Crime, Religion, and Education*, vol. 2. New York: Appleton.

Introduction

G. Stanley Hall (1844–1924) earned the first American Ph.D. in psychology and founded the field of child study. Influenced by the evolutionary theories of Charles Darwin, Hall theorized that children's maturation progressed through three distinct stages: early childhood, late childhood, and adolescence. He further claimed that "ontogeny recapitulates phylogeny," or in other words, that the child's development recreated the path of human societies from savagery to barbarism to civilization. Hall emphasized the significance of the adolescent period to the health of the greater society. Like most Victorian thinkers, Hall strongly distinguished the development of boys and girls. Adolescent boys, he believed, should be encouraged to be manly and strong-willed. Adolescent girls, he worried, were endangering their feminine vitality through overly rigorous study and other masculine pursuits. In the following excerpt from Chapter 17 of his seminal text *Adolescence* (1904), Hall encourages girls to study motherhood and domesticity, rather than risk their fecundity on more intellectual subjects.

CHAPTER XVII
ADOLESCENT GIRLS AND THEIR EDUCATION

. . .

From the available data it seems, however, that the more scholastic the education of women, the fewer children and the harder, more dangerous, and more dreaded is parturition, and the less the ability to nurse children. Not intelligence but education by present man-made ways is inversely as fecundity. The sooner and the more clearly this is recognized as a universal rule, not, of course, without many notable and much vaunted exceptions, the better for our civilization. For one, I plead with no whit less earnestness and conviction than any of the feminists, and indeed with more fervor because on nearly all their grounds and also on others, for the higher education of women, and would welcome them to every opportunity available to men if they can not do better; but I would open to their election another education, which every competent judge would pronounce more favorable to motherhood, under the influence of female principals who do not publicly say that it is "not desirable" that women students should study motherhood, because they do not know whether they will marry; who encourage them to elect "no special subjects because they are women," and who think infant psychology "foolish." Various interesting experiments in coeducation are now being made in England. Some are whole-hearted and encourage the girls to do almost everything that the boys do in both study and play. There are girl prefects, cricket teams are formed sometimes of both sexes, but often the sexes matched against each other, one play-yard, a dual staff of teachers, and friendships between the boys and girls are not tabooed, etc. In other schools the sexes meet perhaps in recitation only, have separate rooms for study, entrances, playgrounds, and their relations are otherwise restricted. The opinion of English writers generally favors coeducation up to about the beginning of the teens, and from there on views are more divided. It is admitted that, if there is a very great preponderance of either sex over the other, the latter is likely to lose its characteristic qualities, and something of this occurs where the average age of one sex is distinctly greater than that of the other. On the other hand, several urge that, where age and numbers are equal, each sex is more inclined to develop the best qualities peculiar to itself in the presence of the other.

Some girls are no doubt far fitter for boys' studies and men's careers than others. Coeducation, too, generally means far more assimilation of girls' to boys' ways and work than conversely. Many people believe that girls either gain or are more affected by coeducation, especially in the upper grades, than boys. It is interesting, however, to observe the differences that still persist. Certain games, like football and boxing, girls can not play; they do not fight; they are not flogged or caned as English boys are when their bad marks foot up beyond a certain aggregate; girls are more prone to cliques; their punishments must be in appeals to school sentiment, to which they are exceedingly sensitive; it is hard for them to bear defeat in games with the same dignity and unruffled temper as boys; it is harder for them to accept the school standards of honor that condemn the tell-tale as a sneak, although they soon learn this. They may be a little in danger of being roughened by boyish ways and especially by the crude and unique language, almost a dialect in itself, prevalent among schoolboys. Girls are far more prone to overdo; boys are persistingly lazy and idle. Girls are content to sit and have the subject-matter pumped into them by recitations, etc., and to merely accept, while boys are more inspired by being told to do things and make tests and experiments. In this, girls are often quite at sea. One writer speaks of a certain feminine obliquity, but hastens to say that girls in these schools soon accept its code of honor. It is urged, too, that in singing classes the voices of each sex are better in quality for the presence of the other. In many topics of all kinds boys and girls are interested in different aspects of the same theme, and therefore the work is broadened. In manual training girls excel in all artistic work; boys, in carpentry.

Girls can be made not only less noxiously sentimental and impulsive, but their conduct tends to become more thoughtful; they can be made to feel responsibility for bestowing their praise aright and thus influencing the tone of the school. Calamitous as it would be for the education of boys beyond a certain age to be entrusted entirely or chiefly to women, it would be less so for that of girls to be given entirely to men. Perhaps the great women teachers, whose life and work have made them a power with girls comparable to that of Arnold and Thring with boys, are dying out. Very likely economic motives are too dominant for this problem to be settled on its merits only. Finally, several writers mention the increased healthfulness of moral tone. The vices that infest boys' schools, which Arnold thought a quantity constantly changing with every class, are diminished. Healthful thoughts of sex, less subterranean and base imaginings on the one hand, and less gushy sentimentality on the other, are favored. Foe either sex to be a copy of the other is to be weakened, and each comes normally to respect more and to prefer their own sex.

Not to pursue this subject further here, it is probable that many of the causes for the facts set forth are very different and some of them almost diametrically opposite in the two sexes. Hard as it is *per se*, it is after all a comparatively easy matter to educate boys. They are less peculiarly responsive in mental tone to the physical and psychic environment, tend more strongly and early to special interests, and react more vigorously against the obnoxious elements of their surroundings. This is truest of the higher education, and more so in proportion as the tendencies of the age are toward special and vocational training. Woman, as we saw, in every fiber of her soul and body is a more generic creature than man, nearer to the race, and demands more and more with advancing age an education that is essentially liberal and humanistic. This is progressively hard when the sexes differentiate in the higher grades. Moreover, nature decrees that with advancing civilization the sexes shall not approximate, but differentiate, and we shall probably be obliged to carry sex distinctions, at least of method, into many if not most of the topics of the higher education. Now that woman has by general consent attained the right to the best that man has, she must seek a training that fits her own nature as well or better. So long as she strives to be manlike she will be inferior and a pinchbeck imitation, but she must develop a new sphere that shall be like the rich field of the cloth of gold for the best instincts of her nature.

Divergence is most marked and sudden in the pubescent period—in the early teens. At this age, by almost worldwide consent, boys and girls separate for a time, and lead their lives during this most critical period more or less apart, at least for a few years, until the ferment of mind and body which results in maturity of functions then born and culminating in nubility, has done its work. The family and the home abundantly recognize this tendency. At twelve or fourteen, brothers and sisters develop a life more independent of each other than before. Their home occupations differ as do their plays, games, tastes. History, anthropology, and sociology, as well as home life, abundantly illustrate this. This is normal and biological. What our schools and other institutions should do, is not to obliterate these differences to make boys more manly and girls more womanly. We should respect the law of sexual differences, and not forget that motherhood is a very different thing from fatherhood. Neither sex should copy nor set patterns to the other, but all parts should be played harmoniously and clearly in the great sex symphony.

I have here less to say against coeducation in college, still less in university grades after the maturity which comes at eighteen or twenty has been achieved, but it is high time to ask ourselves whether the theory and practise of identical coeducation, especially in the high school, which has lately been carried to a greater extreme in this country than the rest of the world recognizes, has not brought certain grave dangers, and whether it does not interfere with the natural differentiations seen everywhere else. I recognize, of course, the great argument of economy. Indeed, we should save money and effort could we unite churches of not too diverse creeds. We could thus give better preaching, music, improve the edifice, etc. I am by no means ready to advocate the radical abolition of coeducation, but we can already sum up in a rough, brief way our account of profit and loss with it. On the one hand, no doubt each sex develops some of its own best qualities best in the presence of the other, but the question still remains, how much, when, and in what way, identical coeducation secures this end?

. . .

Again, while I sympathize profoundly with the claim of woman for every opportunity which she can fill, and yield to none in appreciation of her ability, I insist that the cardinal defect in the woman's college is that it is based upon the assumption, implied and often expressed, if not almost universally acknowledged, that girls should primarily be trained to independence and self-support, and that matrimony and motherhood, if it come, will take care of itself, or, as some even urge, is thus best provided for. If these colleges are as the above statistics indicate, chiefly devoted to the training of those who do not marry, or if they are to educate for celibacy, this is right. These institutions may perhaps come to be training stations of a new-old type, the agamic or even agenic woman, be she aunt, maid—old or young—nun, school-teacher, or bachelor woman. I recognize the very great debt the world owes to members of this very diverse class in the past. Some of them have illustrated the very highest ideals of self-sacrifice, service, and devotion in giving to mankind what was meant for husband and children. Some of them belong to the class of superfluous women, and others illustrate the noblest type of altruism and have impoverished the heredity of the world to its loss, as did the monks, who

Leslie Stephens thinks contributed to bring about the Dark Ages, because they were [p. 633] the best and most highly selected men of their age and, by withdrawing from the function of heredity and leaving no posterity, caused Europe to degenerate. Modern ideas and training are now doing this, whether for racial weal or woe can not yet be determined, for many whom nature designed for model mothers.

The bachelor woman is an interesting illustration of Spencer's law of the inverse relation of individuation and genesis. The completely developed individual is always a terminal representative in her line of descent. She has taken up and utilized in her own life all that was meant for her descendants, and has so overdrawn her account with heredity that, like every perfectly and completely developed individual, she is also completely sterile. This is the very apotheosis of selfishness from the standpoint of every biological ethics. While the complete man can do and sometimes does this, woman has a far greater and very peculiar power of overdrawing her reserves. First she loses mammary function, so that should she undertake maternity its functions are incompletely performed because she can not nurse, and this implies defective motherhood and leaves love of the child itself defective and maimed, for the mother who has never nursed can not love or be loved aright by her child. It crops out again in the abnormal or especially incomplete development of her offspring, in the critical years of adolescence, although they may have been healthful before, and a less degree of it perhaps is seen in the diminishing families of cultivated mothers in the one-child system. These women are the intellectual equals and often the superiors of the men they meet; they are very attractive as companions, like Miss Mehr, the university student, in Hauptmann's Lonely Lives, who alienated the young husband from his noble wife; they enjoy all the keen pleasures of intellectual activity; their very look, step, and bearing is free; their mentality makes them good fellows and companionable in all the broad intellectual spheres; to converse with them is as charming and attractive for the best men as was Socrates's discourse with the accomplished hetaera; they are at home with the racket and on the golf links; they are splendid friends; their minds, in all their widening areas of contact, are as attractive as their bodies; and the world owes much and is likely to owe far more to high Platonic friendships of this kind. These women are often in every way magnificent, only they are not mothers, and sometimes have very little wifehood in them, and to attempt to marry them to develop these functions is one of the unique and too frequent tragedies of modern life and literature. Some, though by no means all, of them are functionally castrated; some actively deplore the necessity of child-bearing, and perhaps are parturition phobiacs, and abhor the limitations of married life; they are incensed whenever attention is called to the functions peculiar to their sex, and the careful consideration of problems of the monthly rest are thought "not fit for cultivated women."

Excerpt from *The Spirit of Youth and the City Streets* by Jane Addams, 1909

SOURCE: Addams, Jane. 1909. *The Spirit of Youth and the City Streets.* New York: Macmillan.

Introduction

Jane Addams (1860–1935) was a founder of the American settlement house movement and an influential social reformer, feminist, peace activist, moral leader and Nobel laureate. At Hull-House, the settlement in Chicago where Addams lived for forty-six years, she worked with countless poor children and families to better their lives. In essays and books, Addams advanced her social vision at the national level. In Chapter One of *The Spirit of Youth and the City Streets* (1909), Addams describes the particular difficulties experienced by America's urban youth. While they were eagerly courted by industrial employers, these young men and women had few structured opportunities for healthy recreation or practical education. Addams writes from a sympathetic perspective, demanding social change to benefit these disaffected youth.

A further difficulty lies in the fact that this industrialism has gathered together multitudes of eager young creatures from all quarters of the earth as a labor supply for the countless factories and workshops, upon which the present industrial city is based. Never before in civilization have such numbers of young girls been suddenly released from the protection of the home and permitted to walk unattended upon city streets and to work under alien roofs; for the first time they are being prized more for their labor power than for their innocence, their tender beauty, their ephemeral gaiety. Society cares more for the products they manufacture than for their immemorial ability to reaffirm the charm of existence. Never before have such numbers of young boys earned money independently of the family life, and felt themselves free to spend it as they choose in the midst of vice deliberately disguised as pleasure.

This stupid experiment of organizing work and failing to organize play has, of course, brought about a fine revenge. The love of pleasure will not be denied, and when it has turned into all sorts of malignant and vicious appetites, then we, the middle aged, grow quite distracted and resort to all sorts of restrictive measures. We even try to dam up the sweet fountain itself because we are affrighted by these neglected streams; but almost worse than the restrictive measures is our apparent belief that the city itself has no obligation in the matter, an assumption upon which the modern city turns over to commercialism practically all the provisions for public recreation.

Quite as one set of men has organized the young people into industrial enterprises in order to profit from their toil, so another set of men and also of women, I am sorry to say, have entered the neglected field of recreation and have organized enterprises which make profit out of this invincible love of pleasure.

In every city arise so-called "places"—"gin-palaces," they are called in fiction; in Chicago we euphemistically say merely "places,"—in which alcohol is dispensed, not to allay thirst, but, ostensibly to stimulate gaiety, it is sold really in order to empty pockets. Huge dance halls are opened to which hundreds of young people are attracted, many of whom stand wistfully outside a roped circle, for it requires five cents to procure within it for five minutes the sense of allurement and intoxication which is sold in lieu of innocent pleasure. These coarse and illicit merrymakings remind one of the unrestrained jollities of Restoration London, and they are indeed their direct descendants, properly commercialized, still confusing joy with lust, and gaiety with debauchery. Since the soldiers of Cromwell shut up the people's playhouses and destroyed their pleasure fields, the Anglo-Saxon city has turned over the provision for public recreation to the most evil-minded and the most unscrupulous members of the community. We see thousands of girls walking up and down the streets on a pleasant evening with no chance to catch a sight of pleasure even through a lighted window, save as these lurid places provide it. Apparently the modern city sees in these girls only two possibilities, both of them commercial: first, a chance to utilize by day their new and tender labor power in its factories and shops, and then another chance in the evening to extract from them their petty wages by pandering to their love of pleasure.

As these overworked girls stream along the street, the rest of us see only the self-conscious walk, the giggling speech, the preposterous clothing. And yet through the huge hat, with its wilderness of bedraggled feathers, the girl announces to the world that she is here. She demands attention to the fact of her existence, she states that she is ready to live, to take her place in the world. The most precious moment in human development is the young creature's assertion that he is unlike any other human being, and has an individual contribution to make to the world. The variation from the established type is at the root of all change, the only possible basis for progress, all that keeps life from growing unprofitably stale and repetitious.

Is it only the artists who really see these young creatures as they are—the artists who are themselves endowed with immortal youth? Is it our disregard of the artist's message which makes us so blind and so stupid, or are we so under the influence of our *Zeitgeist* that we can detect only commercial values in the young as well as in the old? It is as if our eyes were holden to the mystic beauty, the redemptive joy, the civic pride which these multitudes of young people might supply to our dingy towns.

The young creatures themselves piteously look all about them in order to find an adequate means of expression for their most precious message: One day a serious young man came to Hull-House with his pretty young sister who, he explained, wanted to go somewhere every single evening, "although she could only give the flimsy excuse that the flat was too little and too stuffy to stay in." In the difficult role of elder brother, he had done his best, stating that he had taken her "to all the missions in the neighborhood, that she had had a chance to listen to some awful good sermons and to some elegant hymns, but that some way she did not seem to care for the society of the best Christian people." The little sister reddened painfully under this cruel indictment and could offer no word of excuse, but a curious thing happened to me. Perhaps it was the phrase "the best Christian people," perhaps it was the delicate color of her flushing cheeks and her swimming eyes, but certain it is, that instantly and vividly there appeared to my mind the delicately tinted piece of wall in a Roman catacomb where the early Christians, through a dozen devices of spring flowers, skipping lambs and a shepherd tenderly guiding the young, had indelibly written down that the Christian message is one of inexpressible joy. Who is responsible for forgetting this message delivered by the "best Christian people" two thousand years ago? Who is to blame that the lambs, the little ewe lambs, have been so caught upon the brambles?

Excerpt from "The Origin and Development of Psychoanalysis" by Sigmund Freud, 1910

SOURCE: Freud, Sigmund. 1910. "The Origin and Development of Psychoanalysis." *American Journal of Psychology* 21 (April): 181–218.

Introduction

Sigmund Freud (1856–1939) argued that childhood experiences determined adult behaviors, thus revolutionizing the modern understanding of human personality. Freud was a medical doctor who lived in Vienna, where he specialized in the treatment of patients suffering mental disturbances. To help them, he developed the practice of psychotherapy, or the "talking cure," in which patients talked through their childhood memories in order to resolve present traumas. The perspective on childhood that Freud gained through talking with his patients diverged radically from the predominant assumptions of the late Victorian period. Most importantly, he believed that children were sexual beings, and that issues concerning childhood sexuality were at the root of most adult mental problems. In the following passage from "The Origin and Development of Psychoanalysis" (1910), Freud explains his theory of infantile sexuality. Freud expects his audience to receive his theories with disbelief; a century later, many people still have problems accepting the concept of infantile sexuality.

The work of analysis which is necessary for the thorough explanation and complete cure of a case of sickness does not stop in any case with the experience of the time of onset of the disease, but in every case it goes back to the adolescence and the early childhood of the patient. Here only do we hit upon the impressions and circumstances which determine the later sickness. Only the childhood experiences can give the explanation for the sensitivity to later traumata and only when these memory traces, which almost always are forgotten, are discovered and made conscious, is the power developed to banish the symptoms. We arrive here at the same conclusion as in the investigation of dreams—that it is the incompatible, repressed wishes of childhood which lend their power to the creation of symptoms. Without these the reactions upon later traumata discharge normally. But we must consider these mighty wishes of childhood very generally as sexual in nature.

Now I can at any rate be sure of your astonishment. Is there an infantile sexuality? you will ask. Is childhood not rather that period of life which is distinguished by the lack of the sexual impulse? No, gentlemen, it is not at all true that the sexual impulse enters into the child at puberty, as the devils in the gospel entered into the swine. The child has his sexual impulses and activities from the beginning, he brings them with him into the world, and from these the so-called normal sexuality of adults emerges by a significant development through manifold stages. It is not very difficult to observe the expressions of this childish sexual activity; it needs rather a certain art to overlook them or to fail to interpret them.

. . .

Lay aside your doubts and let us evaluate the infantile sexuality of the earliest years. The sexual impulse of the child manifests itself as a very complex one, it permits of an analysis into many components, which spring from different sources. It is entirely disconnected from the function of reproduction which it is later to serve. It permits the child to gain different sorts of pleasure sensations, which we include, by the analogues and connections which they show, under the term sexual pleasures. The great source of infantile sexual pleasure is the auto-excitation of certain particularly sensitive parts of the body; besides the genitals are included the rectum and the opening of the urinary canal, and also the skin and other sensory surfaces. Since in this first phase of child sexual life the satisfaction is found on the child's own body and has nothing to do with any other object, we call this phase after a word coined by Havelock Ellis, that of "auto-erotism." The parts of the body significant in giving sexual pleasure we call "erogenous zones." The thumb-sucking (*Ludeln*) or passionate sucking (*Wonnesaugen*) of very young children is a good example of such an auto-erotic satisfaction of an erogenous zone. The first scientific observer of this phenomenon, a specialist in children's diseases in Budapest by the name of Lindner, interpreted these rightly as sexual satisfaction and described exhaustively their transformation into other and higher forms of sexual gratification. Another sexual satisfaction of this time of life is the excitation of the genitals by masturbation, which has such a great significance for later life and, in the case of many individuals, is never fully overcome. Besides this and other auto-erotic manifestations we see very early in the child the impulse-components of *sexual pleasure*, or, as we may say, of the *libido*, which presupposes a second person as its object. These impulses appear in opposed pairs, as active and passive. The most important representatives of this group are the pleasure in inflicting pain (sadism) with its passive opposite (masochism) and active and passive exhibition pleasure (*Schaulust*). From the first of these later pairs splits off the curiosity for knowledge, as from the latter the impulse toward artistic and theatrical representation. Other sexual manifestations of the child can already be regarded from the view-point of object-choice, in which the second person plays the prominent part. The significance of this was primarily based upon motives of the impulse of self-preservation. The difference between the sexes plays, however, in the child no very great rôle. One may attribute to every child, without wronging him, a bit of the homosexual disposition.

The sexual life of the child, rich, but dissociated, in which each single impulse goes about the business of arousing pleasure independently of every other, is later correlated and organized in two general directions, so that by the close of puberty the definite sexual character of the individual is practically finally determined. The single impulses subordinate themselves to the overlordship of the genital zone, so that the whole sexual life is taken over into the service of procreation, and their gratification is now significant only so far as they help to prepare and promote the true sexual act. On the other hand, object-choice prevails over auto-erotism, so that now in the sexual life all components of the sexual impulse are satisfied in the loved person. But not all the original impulse components are given a share in the final shaping of the sexual life. Even before the advent of puberty certain impulses have undergone the most energetic repression under the impulse of education, and mental forces like shame, disgust and morality are developed, which, like sentinels, keep the repressed wishes in subjection. When there comes, in puberty, the high tide of sexual desire it finds dams in this creation of reactions and resistances. These guide the outflow into the so-called normal channels, and make it impossible to revivify the impulses which have undergone repression.

The most important of these repressed impulses are koprophilism, that is, the pleasure in children connected with the excrements; and, further, the tendencies attaching themselves to the persons of the primitive object-choice.

Gentlemen, a sentence of general pathology says that every process of development brings with it the germ of pathological dispositions in so far as it may be inhibited, delayed, or incompletely carried out. This holds for the development of the sexual function, with its many complications. It is not smoothly completed in all individuals, and may leave behind either abnormalities or disposition to later diseases by the way of later falling back or *regression*. It may happen that not all the partial impulses subordinate themselves to the rule of the genital zone. Such an impulse which has remained disconnected brings about what we call a perversion, which may replace the normal sexual goal by one of its own. It may happen, as has been said before, that the auto-erotism is not fully overcome, as many sorts of disturbances testify. The originally equal value of both sexes as sexual objects may be maintained and an inclination to homosexual activities in adult life result from this, which, under suitable conditions, rises to the level of exclusive homosexuality. This series of disturbances corresponds to the direct inhibition of development of the sexual function, it includes the perversions and the general *infantilism* of the sex life that are not seldom met with.

The disposition to neuroses is to be derived in another way from an injury to the development of the sex life. The neuroses are related to the perversions as the negative to the positive; in them we find the same impulse-components as in perversions, as bearers of the complexes and as creators of the symptoms; but here they work from out the unconscious. They have undergone a repression, but in spite of this they maintain themselves in the unconscious. Psychoanalysis teaches us that overstrong expression of the impulse in very early life leads to a sort of fixation (*Fixirung*), which then offers a weak point in the articulation of the sexual function. If the exercise of the normal sexual function meets with hindrances in later life, this repression, dating from the time of development, is broken through at just that point at which the infantile fixation took place.

You will now perhaps make the objection: "But all that is not sexuality." I have used the word in a very much wider sense than you are accustomed to understand it. This I willingly concede. But it is a question whether you do not rather use the word in much too narrow a sense when you restrict it to the realm of procreation. You sacrifice by that the understanding of perversions; of the connection between perversion, neurosis and normal sexual life; and have no means of recognizing, in its true significance, the easily observable beginning of the somatic and mental sexual life of the child. But however you decide about the use of the word, remember that the psychoanalyst understands sexuality in that full sense to which he is led by the evaluation of infantile sexuality.

Now we turn again to the sexual development of the child. We still have much to say here, since we have given more attention to the somatic than to the mental expressions of the sexual life. The primitive object-choice of the child, which is derived from his need of help, demands our further interest. It first attaches to all persons to whom he is accustomed, but soon these give way in favor of his parents. The relation of the child to his parents is, as both direct observation of the child and later analytic investigation of adults agree, not at all free from elements of sexual accessory-excitation (*Miterregung*). The child takes both parents, and especially one, as an object of his erotic wishes. Usually he follows in this the stimulus given by his parents, whose tenderness has very clearly the character of a sex manifestation, though inhibited so far as its goal is concerned. As a rule, the father prefers the daughter, the mother the son; the child reacts to this situation, since, as son, he wishes himself in the place of his father, as daughter, in the place of the mother. The feelings awakened in these relations between parents and children, and, as a resultant of them, those among the children in relation to each other, are not only positively of a tender, but negatively of an inimical sort. The complex built up in this way is destined to quick repression, but it still exerts a great and lasting effect from the unconscious. We must express the opinion that this with its ramifications presents the *nuclear complex* of every neurosis, and so we are prepared to meet with it in a not less effectual way in the other fields of mental life. The myth of King Oedipus, who kills his father and wins his mother as a wife is only the slightly altered presentation of the infantile wish, rejected later by the opposing barriers of incest. Shakespeare's tale of Hamlet rests on the same basis of an incest complex, though better concealed. At the time when the child is still ruled by the still unrepressed nuclear complex, there begins a very significant part of his mental activity which serves sexual interest. He begins to investigate the question of where children come from and guesses more than adults imagine of the true relations by deduction from the signs which be sees. Usually his interest in this investigation is awakened by the threat to his welfare through the birth of another child in the family, in whom at first he sees only a rival. Under the influence of the partial impulses which are active in him be arrives at a number of "infantile sexual theories," as that the same male genitals belong to both sexes, that children are conceived by eating and born through the opening of the intestine, and that sexual intercourse is to be regarded as an inimical act, a sort of overpowering.

But just the unfinished nature of his sexual constitution and the gaps in his knowledge brought about by the hidden condition of the feminine sexual canal, cause the infant investigator to discontinue his work as a failure. The facts of this childish investigation itself as well as the infant sex theories created by it are of determinative significance in the building of the child's character, and in the content of his later neuroses.

It is unavoidable and quite normal that the child should make his parents the objects of his first object-choice. But his *libido* must not remain fixed on these first chosen objects, but must take them merely as a prototype and transfer from these to other persons in the time of definite object-choice. The breaking loose (*Ablösung*) of the child from his parents is thus a problem impossible to escape if the social virtue of the young individual is not to be impaired. During the time that the repressive activity is making its choice among the partial sexual impulses and later, when the influence of the parents, which in the most essential way has furnished the material for these repressions, is lessened, great problems fall to the work of education, which at present certainly does not always solve them in the most intelligent and economic way.

Gentlemen, do not think that with these explanations of the sexual life and the sexual development of the child we have too far departed from psychoanalysis and the cure of neurotic disturbances. If you like, you may regard the psychoanalytic treatment only as a continued education for the overcoming of childhood-remnants (*Kindheitsresten*).

Excerpt from "Conditioned Emotional Reactions" by John B. Watson and Rosalie Rayner, 1920

SOURCE: Watson, John, and Rosalie Raynor. 1920. "Conditioned Emotional Reactions." *Journal of Experimental Psychology* 3, no. 1: 1–14.

Introduction

The behavioral psychologist John Broadus Watson (1878–1958) is notorious for the child-rearing advice he offered parents in the 1920s, including the injunction never to cuddle their infants. Watson instructed parents to treat their children as little adults, in order to prepare them psychologically to become independent adults. His lack of sympathy or affection for children extended into the design of his experiments in behaviorism. In the following excerpt from an article first published in the *Journal of Experimental Psychology* in 1920, Watson and his co-author describe a series of experiments performed on an infant to develop his fear reaction. Watson describes in clinical detail his efforts to make the child cry. His plans for more extensive experimentation on babies were fortunately interrupted by an embarrassing divorce and public revelations of adultery. Within Watson's own family, his cold child-rearing style had a very damaging impact. One of Watson's sons committed suicide; the other suffered a nervous breakdown.

In recent literature various speculations have been entered into concerning the possibility of conditioning various types of emotional response, but direct experimental evidence in support of such a view has been lacking. If the theory advanced by Watson and Morgan to the effect that in infancy the original emotional reaction patterns are few, consisting so far as observed of fear, rage and love, then there must be some simple method by means of which the range of stimuli which can call out these emotions and their compounds is greatly increased. Otherwise, complexity in adult response could not be accounted for. These authors without adequate experimental evidence advanced the view that this range was increased by means of conditioned reflex factors. It was suggested there that the early home life of the child furnishes a laboratory situation for establishing conditioned emotional responses. The present authors have recently put the whole matter to an experimental test.

Experimental work had been done so far on only one child, Albert B. This infant was reared almost from birth in a hospital environment; his mother was a wet nurse in the Harriet Lane Home for Invalid Children. Albert's life was normal: he was healthy from birth and one of the best developed youngsters ever brought to the hospital, weighing twenty-one pounds at nine months of age. He was on the whole stolid and unemotional. His stability was one of the principal reasons for using him as a subject in this test. We felt that we could do him relatively little harm by carrying out such experiments as those outlined below.

At approximately nine months of age we ran him through the emotional tests that have become a part of our regular routine in determining whether fear reactions can be called out by other stimuli than sharp noises and the sudden removal of support. Tests of this type have been described by the senior author in another place. In brief, the infant was confronted suddenly and for the first time successively with a white rat, a rabbit, a dog, a monkey, with masks with and without hair, cotton wool, burning newspapers, etc. A permanent record of Albert's reactions to these objects and situations has been preserved in a motion picture study. Manipulation was the most usual reaction called out. *At no time did this infant ever show fear in any situation.* These experimental records were confirmed by the casual observations of the mother and hospital attendants. No one had ever seen him in a state of fear and rage. The infant practically never cried.

Up to approximately nine months of age we had not tested him with loud sounds. The test to determine whether a fear reaction could be called out by a loud sound was made when he was eight months, twenty-six days of age. The sound was that made by striking a hammer upon a suspended steel bar four feet in length and three-fourths of an inch in diameter. The laboratory notes are as follows:

One of the two experimenters caused the child to turn its head and fixate her moving hand; the other stationed back of the child, struck the steel bar a sharp blow. The child started violently, his breathing was checked and the arms were raised in a characteristic manner. On the second stimulation the same thing occurred, and in addition the lips began to pucker and tremble. On the third stimulation the child broke into a sudden crying fit. This is the first time an emotional situation in the laboratory has produced any fear or even crying in Albert.

We had expected just these results on account of our work with other infants brought up under similar conditions. It is worth while to call attention to the fact that removal of support (dropping and jerking the blanket upon which the infant was lying) was tried exhaustively upon this infant on the same occasion. It was not effective in producing the fear response. This stimulus is effective in younger children. At what age such stimuli lose their potency in producing fear is not known. Nor is it known whether less placid children ever lose their fear of them. This probably depends upon the training the child gets. It is well known that children eagerly run to be tossed into the air and caught. On the other hand it is equally well known that in the adult fear responses are called out quite clearly by the sudden removal of support, if the individual is walking across a bridge, walking out upon a beam, etc. There is a wide field of study here which is aside from our present point.

The sound stimulus, thus, at nine months of age, gives us the means of testing several important factors. I. Can we condition fear of an animal, *e.g.*, a white rat, by visually presenting it and simultaneously striking a steel bar? II. If such a conditioned emotional response can be established, will there be a transfer to other animals or other objects? III. What is the effect of time upon such conditioned emotional responses? IV. If after a reasonable period such emotional responses have not died out, what laboratory methods can be devised for their removal?

I. The establishment of conditioned emotional responses.

At first there was considerable hesitation upon our part in making the attempt to set up fear reactions experimentally. A certain responsibility attaches to such a procedure. We decided finally to make the attempt, comforting ourselves by the reflection that such attachments would arise anyway as soon as the child left the sheltered environment of the nursery for the rough and tumble of the home. We did not begin this work until Albert was eleven months, three days of age. Before attempting to set up a conditioned response we, as before, put him through all of the regular emotional tests. *Not the slightest sign of a fear response was obtained in any situation.*

The steps taken to condition emotional responses are shown in our laboratory notes.

11 Months 3 Days

1. White rat suddenly taken from the basket and presented to Albert. He began to reach for rat with left hand. Just as his hand touched the animal the bar was struck immediately behind his head. The infant jumped violently and fell forward, burying his face in the mattress. He did not cry, however.

2. Just as the right hand touched the rat the bar was again struck. Again the infant jumped violently, fell forward and began to whimper.

In order not to disturb the child too seriously no further tests were given for one week.

11 Months 10 Days

1. Rat presented suddenly without sound. There was steady fixation but no tendency at first to reach for it. The rat was then placed nearer, whereupon tentative reaching movements began with the right hand. When the rat nosed the infant's left hand, the hand was immediately withdrawn. He started to reach for the head of the animal with the forefinger of the left hand, but withdrew it suddenly before contact. It is thus seen that the two joint stimulations given the previous week were not without effect. He was tested with his blocks immediately afterwards to see if they shared in the process of conditioning. He began immediately to pick them up, dropping them, pounding them, etc. In the remainder of the tests the blocks were given frequently to quiet him and to test his general emotional state. They were always removed from sight when the process of conditioning was under way.

2. Joint stimulation with rat and sound. Started, then fell over immediately to right side. No crying.

3. Joint stimulation. Fell to right side and rested upon hands, with head turned away from rat. No crying.

4. Joint stimulation. Same reaction.

5. Rat suddenly presented alone. Puckered face, whimpered and withdrew body sharply to the left.

6. Joint stimulation. Fell over immediately to right side and began to whimper.

7. Joint stimulation. Started violently and cried, but did not fall over.

8. Rat alone. *The instant the rat was shown the baby began to cry. Almost instantly he turned sharply to the left, fell over on left side, raised himself on all fours and began to crawl away so rapidly that he was caught with difficulty before reaching the edge of the table.*

This was as convincing a case of a completely conditioned fear response as could have been theoretically pictured. In all seven joint stimulations were given to bring about the complete reaction. It is not unlikely had the sound been of greater intensity or of a more complex clang character that the number of joint stimulations might have been materially reduced. Experiments designed to define the nature of the sounds that will serve best as emotional stimuli are under way.

The Working Child

Isaiah Thomas's Indenture Papers, 1756

SOURCE: Thomas, Isaiah. 1756. Papers. American Antiquarian Society, Worcester, Massachusetts.

Introduction

Throughout the seventeenth and eighteenth centuries, American children were often "indentured" by their parents or guardians to potential employers. The indenture was a paper contract that was literally indented at one side and then torn in half through the notch, thus allowing each party to keep "matching" evidence of the agreement. Many immigrants signed indentures of servitude to pay for passage to the United States. Native-born children were more frequently indentured as apprentices, an agreement that guaranteed the child's services, for a set number of years, in return for room, board, basic education, and training in a craft. The following indenture, made for eleven-year-old Isaiah Thomas, offers a typical example. Printing was a difficult trade that relied on the forced contributions of dependent children like Thomas. Despite his inauspicious beginning, Thomas rose to become a very important publisher of the Revolutionary and early National eras. During this period, indentures fell out of practice because they were perceived as contrary to the newly enshrined rights of white men to liberty.

This Indenture Witnesseth,

That Jacob Wendell Andrew Oliver Esq. Isaac Walker Ebenezer Storer John Barratt Nathanael Greenwood Royall Tyler Thomas Flucker John Tudor and William Phillips Gentlemen

Overseers of the Poor of the Town of Boston in the County of Suffolk in New England, by and with the Consent of two of his Majesty's Justices of the Peace for said County, Have placed and by these Presents do place and bind out Isaiah Thomas a poor Child belonging to said Boston unto Zerhariah Fowle of Boston aforcs.

Printer and to his Wife and heirs and with them after the Manner of an Apprentice to Dwell and Serve, from the Day of the Date of these Presents, until the Eighth day of January which will be in the year of Our Lord One thousand Seven hundred and Sixty Nine hundred Nineth said Apprentice if Living will Arrive to the Age of Twenty One Years

During all which said Time or Term, the said Apprentice his said Master & Mistress well and faithfully shall Serve, their Secrets he shall keep close, their Commandments lawful and honest every where he shall gladly obey: he shall do no Damage to his—said Master VP nor suffer it to be done by others, without letting or giving seasonable Notice thereof to his—said Master VP he shall not waste the Goods of his said Master VP nor lend them unlawfully to any: At Cards, Dice, or any other unlawful Game or Games he shall not play: Fornication he shall not commit: Matrimony during the E. Term he shall not contract: Taverns, Ale-Houses, or Places of Gaming he shall not haunt or frequent: From the Service of his said Master VP by Day or Night he shall not absent him self; but in all Things and at all Times, he shall carry and behave him self towards his said Master VP and all theirs as a good and faithful Apprentice ought to do to his utmost Ability during all the Time or Term aforesaid. And the said Master doth hereby Covenant and Agree, for himself his Wife and heirs to teach or Gauge the said Apprentice to be taught by the best way and means he can the Art and Mistery of a Printer also to Read write & Cypher. And also shall and will, well and truly find, allow unto, and provide for the said Apprentice, sufficient and wholsome Meat and Drink, with Washing, Lodging, and Apparrell and other Necessaries meet and convenient for such an Apprentice, during all the Time or Term aforesaid: And at the End and Expiration thereof shall dismiss the said Apprentice with two good suits of Apparrell for all parts of his Body One for the Lords days the other for working days suitable to his Degree.

In Testimony Whereof the said Parties have to these Indentures interchangeably set their Hands and Seals, the Fourth Day of June In the 29th Year of the Reign of Our Sovereign Lord George the Second King Over Great Britain VO Annoque Domini, One Thousand Seven Hundred and Fifty Six.

Signed Sealed and Delivered in Presence of us

Samuel Edely William Seymour

Suffolk is Boston July 7th 1756

Assented to by John Phillips John Hill

Justices of the Peace

Jacob Wendell

Isaac Walker El: Storer

John Barrett

Nath Greenwood

Royall Tyler

Tho. Flucker

Wm. Phillips

Two Interviews with English Workhouse Children from the *Ashton Chronicle*, 1849

SOURCE: Stephens, James Raynor. 1849. Interview with Sarah Carpenter. *Ashton Chronicle*, June 23; Interview with John Birley. *Ashton Chronicle*, May 19.

Introduction

In 1849 the *Ashton Chronicle,* a newspaper that advocated radical social reform, published a series of interviews with adults who had been child laborers. In nineteenth-century England, many factories and mills relied upon the labor of poor children who were "apprenticed" to company owners by workhouses and orphanages under terms that closely resembled sale. Sarah Carpenter and John Birley explain the conditions under which they worked and make it clear that working in the country was no better than in the city, although city life was more notorious at the time. In both mills, overseers forced the children to labor ceaselessly for long hours, under threat of severe bodily punishment. For meals the children ate oat cakes and little else. The children received neither pay, skills, nor assets, for their years spent as apprentices. As both witnesses testify, all that the children took with them when their contracts ended was physical and emotional damage. Joseph Rayner Stephens, the publisher of the *Ashton Chronicle,* hoped the former apprentices' testimony would influence the government to outlaw child labor.

Sarah Carpenter, interviewed in The Ashton Chronicle (23rd June, 1849)

My father was a glass blower. When I was eight years old my father died and our family had to go to the Bristol Workhouse. My brother was sent from Bristol workhouse in the same way as many other children were—cart-loads at a time. My mother did not know where he was for two years. He was taken off in the dead of night without her knowledge, and the parish officers would never tell her where he was.

It was the mother of Joseph Russell who first found out where the children were, and told my mother. We set off together, my mother and I, we walked the whole way from Bristol to Cressbrook Mill in Derbyshire. We were many days on the road.

Mrs. Newton fondled over my mother when we arrived. My mother had brought her a present of little glass ornaments. She got these ornaments from some of the workmen, thinking they would be a very nice present to carry to the mistress at Cressbrook, for her kindness to my brother. My brother told me that Mrs. Newton's fondling was all a blind; but I was so young and foolish, and so glad to see him again; that I did not heed what he said, and could not be persuaded to leave him. They would not let me stay unless I would take the shilling binding money. I took the shilling and I was very proud of it.

They took me into the counting house and showed me a piece of paper with a red sealed horse on which they told me to touch, and then to make a cross, which I did. This meant I had to stay at Cressbrook Mill till I was twenty one.

Our common food was oatcake. It was thick and coarse. This oatcake was put into cans. Boiled milk and water was poured into it. This was our breakfast and supper. Our dinner was potato pie with boiled bacon it, a bit here and a bit there, so thick with fat we could scarce eat it, though we were hungry enough to eat anything. Tea we never saw, nor butter. We had cheese and brown bread once a year. We were only allowed three meals a day though we got up at five in the morning and worked till nine at night.

We had eightpence a year given us to spend: fourpence at the fair, and fourpence at the wakes. We had three miles to go to spend it. Very proud we were of it, for it seemed such a sight of money, we did not know how to spend it.

The master carder's name was Thomas Birks; but he never went by any other name than Tom the Devil. He was a very bad man—he was encouraged by the master in ill-treating all the hands, but particularly the children. I have often seen him pull up the clothes of big girls, seventeen or eighteen years of age, and throw them across his knee, and then flog them with his hand in the sight of both men and boys. Everybody was frightened of him. He would not even let us speak. He once fell poorly, and very glad we were. We wished he might die.

There was an overlooker called William Hughes, who was put in his place whilst he was ill. He came up to me and asked me what my drawing frame was stopped for. I said I did not know because it was not me who had stopped it. A little boy that was on the other side had stopped it, but he was too frightened to say it was him. Hughes starting beating me with a stick, and when he had done I told him I would let my mother know. He then went out and fetched the master in to me. The master started beating me with a stick over the head till it was full of lumps and bled. My head was so bad that I could not sleep for a long time, and I never been a sound sleeper since.

There was a young woman, Sarah Goodling, who was poorly and so she stopped her machine. James Birch, the overlooker knocked her to the floor. She got up as well as she could. He knocked her down again. Then she was carried to the apprentice house. Her bed-fellow found her dead in bed. There was another called Mary. She knocked her food can down on the floor. The master, Mr. Newton, kicked her where he should not do, and it caused her to wear away till she died. There was another, Caroline Thompson. They beat her till she went out of her mind.

We were always locked up out of mill hours, for fear any of us should run away. One day the door was left open. Charlotte Smith, said she would be ringleader, if the rest would follow. She went out but no one followed her. The master found out about this and sent for her. There was a carving knife which he took and grasping her hair he cut if off close to the head. They were in the habit of cutting off the hair of all who were caught speaking to any of the lads. This head shaving was a dreadful punishment. We were more afraid of it than of any other, for girls are proud of their hair.

I was there ten years and saw a great deal more than I can think of. My brother, after he was free, came to Cressbrook and stole me away. But I was so frightened and dateless with the punishment I had received, that for a long time I was like a person with no wits. I could hardly find my way from one street into another. They said at Wright's Factory where I worked that they were sure that I was "none right".

John Birley interviewed in The Ashton Chronicle (19th May, 1849)

I was born in Hare Street, Bethnal Green, London, in the year 1805. My father died when I was two years old, leaving two children, myself and Sarah my sister. My mother kept us both till I was about five years old, and then she took badly and was taken to the London Hospital. My sister and I were taken to the Bethnal Green Workhouse. My mother died and we stayed in the workhouse. We had good food, good beds and given liberty two or three times a week. We were taught to read and in every respect were treated kindly.

The same year my mother died, I being between six and seven years of age, there came a man looking for a number of parish apprentices. We were all ordered to come into the board room, about forty of us. There were, I dare say, about twenty gentlemen seated at a table, with pens and paper before them. Our names were called out one by one. We were all standing before them in a row. My name was called and I stepped out in the middle of the room. They said, "Well John, you are a fine lad, would you like to go into the country?" I said "Yes sir".

We had often talked over amongst ourselves how we should like to be taken into the country, Mr. Nicholls the old master, used to tell us what fine sport we should have amongst the hills, what time we should have for play and pleasure. He said we should have plenty of roast beef and get plenty of money, and come back gentlemen to see our friends.

The committee picked out about twenty of us, all boys. In a day or two after this, two coaches came up to the workhouse door. We were got ready. They gave us a shilling piece to take our attention, and we set off. I can remember a crowd of women standing by the coaches, at the workhouse door, crying "shame on them, to send poor little children away from home in that fashion." Some of them were weeping. I heard one say, "I would run away if I was them." They drove us to the Paddington Canal, where there was a boat provided to take us.

We got to Buxton at four o'clock on Saturday afternoon. A covered cart was waiting for us there. We all got in, and drove off to the apprentice house at Litton Mill, about six miles from Buxton. The cart stopped, and we marched up to the house, where we saw the master, who came to examine us and gave orders where we were put. They brought us some supper. We were very hungry, but could not eat it. It was Derbyshire oatcake, which we had never seen before. It tasted as sour as vinegar.

Our regular time was from five in the morning till nine or ten at night; and on Saturday, till eleven, and often twelve o'clock at night, and then we were sent to clean the machinery on the Sunday. No time was allowed for breakfast and no sitting for dinner and no time for tea. We went to the mill at five o'clock and worked till about eight or nine when they brought us our breakfast, which consisted of water-porridge, with oatcake in it and onions to flavour it. Dinner consisted of Derbyshire oatcakes cut into four pieces, and ranged into two stacks. One was buttered and the other treacled. By the side of the oatcake were cans of milk. We drank the milk and with the oatcake in our hand, we went back to work without sitting down.

We then worked till nine or ten at night when the water-wheel stopped. We stopped working, and went to the apprentice house, about three hundred yards from the mill. It was a large stone house, surrounded by a wall, two to three yards high, with one door, which was kept locked. It was capable of lodging about one hundred and fifty apprentices. Supper was the same as breakfast—onion porridge and dry oatcake. We all ate in the same room and all went up a common staircase to our bed-chamber; all the boys slept in one chamber, all the girls in another. We slept three in one bed. The girls' bedroom was of the same sort as ours. There were no fastenings to the two rooms; and no one to watch over us in the night, or to see what we did.

Mr. Needham, the master, had five sons: Frank, Charles, Samuel, Robert and John. The sons and a man named Swann, the overlooker, used to go up and down the mill with hazzle sticks. Frank once beat me till he frightened himself. He thought he had killed me. He had struck me on the temples and knocked me dateless. He once knocked me down and threatened me with a stick. To save my head I raised my arm, which he then hit with all his might. My elbow was broken. I bear the marks, and suffer pain from it to this day, and always shall as long as I live.

I was determined to let the gentleman of the Bethnal Green parish know the treatment we had, and I wrote a letter with John Oats and put it into the Tydeswell Post Office. It was broken open and given to old Needham. He beat us with a knob-stick till we could scarcely crawl. Sometime after this three gentlemen came down from London. But before we were examined we were washed and cleaned up and ordered to tell them we liked working at the mill and were well treated. Needham and his sons were in the room at the time. They asked us questions about our treatment, which we answered as we had been told, not daring to do any other, knowing what would happen if we told them the truth.

Excerpt from *Germinal* by Émile Zola, 1885

SOURCE: Zola, Émile. 1894. *Germinal.* Trans. Havelock Ellis. Available from <http://209.11.144.65/eldritchpress/ez/germinal.html>.

Introduction

In the novel *Germinal* (1885), Émile Zola applied his naturalistic writing style to the lives of coal miners in northern France. Zola depicts his characters' experiences as unremittingly bleak. Low pay forced entire families, including children as young as eight, into the mines, where they confronted unsafe conditions and hard, tedious, labor. In the following passage, from Book Three, Chapter Four, Zola describes the horrors that could befall children in the mines. Jeanlin, age eleven, is trapped in a land slide. His sisters, brothers, and father, are also working in the mine, and they all rush to the scene of the landslide. Eventually Jeanlin is rescued, but his legs have been crushed. Physical injury is not the only damage suffered by children in *Germinal*. They are also psychologically brutalized by their deprived upbringing. Jeanlin himself is a brutal young man, an abuser, and a murderer.

Jeanlin, who closed the door, had remained behind. He bent down and looked at the mud through which he was paddling, then, raising his lamp, he saw that the wood had given way beneath the continual bleeding of a spring. Just then a pikeman, one Berloque, who was called Chicot, had arrived from his cutting, in a hurry to go to his wife who had just been confined. He also stopped and examined the planking. And suddenly, as the boy was starting to rejoin his train, a tremendous cracking sound was heard, and a landslip engulfed the man and the child.

There was deep silence. A thick dust raised by the wind of the fall passed through the passages. Blinded and choked, the miners came from every part, even from the farthest stalls, with their dancing lamps which feebly lighted up this gallop of black men at the bottom of these molehills. When the first men tumbled against the landslip, they shouted out and called their mates. A second band, come from the cutting below, found themselves on the other side of the mass of earth which stopped up the gallery. It was at once seen that the roof had fallen in for a dozen metres at most. The damage was not serious. But all hearts were contracted when a death-rattle was heard from the ruins.

Bébert, leaving his train, ran up, repeating:

"Jeanlin is underneath! Jeanlin is underneath!"

Maheu, at this very moment, had come out of the passage with Zacharie and Étienne. He was seized with the fury of despair, and could only utter oaths:

"My God! my God! my God!"

Catherine, Lydie, and Mouquette, who had also rushed up, began to sob and shriek with terror in the midst of the fearful disorder, which was increased by the darkness. The men tried to make them be silent, but they shrieked louder as each groan was heard.

The captain, Richomme, had come up running, in despair that neither Négrel, the engineer, nor Dansaert was at the pit. With his ear pressed against the rocks he listened; and, at last, said those sounds could not come from a child. A man must certainly be there. Maheu had already called Jeanlin twenty times over. Not a breath was heard. The little one must have been smashed up.

And still the groans continued monotonously. They spoke to the agonized man, asking him his name. The groaning alone replied.

"Look sharp!" repeated Richomme, who had already organized a rescue, "we can talk afterwards."

From each end the miners attacked the landslip with pick and shovel. Chaval worked without a word beside Maheu and Étienne, while Zacharie superintended the removal of the earth. The hour for ascent had come, and no one had touched food; but they could not go up for their soup while their mates were in peril. They realized, however, that the settlement would be disturbed if no one came back, and it was proposed to send off the women. But neither Catherine nor Mouquette, nor even Lydie, would move, nailed to the spot with a desire to know what had happened, and to help. Levaque then accepted the commission of announcing the landslip up above—a simple accident, which was being repaired. It was nearly four o'clock; in less than an hour the men had done a day's work; half the earth would have already been removed if more rocks had not slid from the roof. Maheu persisted with such energy that he refused, with a furious gesture, when another man approached to relieve him for a moment.

"Gently! said Richomme at last, "we are getting near. We must not finish them off."

In fact the groaning was becoming more and more distinct. It was a continuous rattling which guided the workers; and now it seemed to be beneath their very picks. Suddenly it stopped.

In silence they all looked at one another, and shuddered as they felt the coldness of death pass in the darkness. They dug on, soaked in sweat, their muscles tense to breaking. They came upon a foot, and then began to remove the earth with their hands, freeing the limbs one by one. The head was not hurt. They turned their lamps on it, and Chicot's name went round. He was quite warm, with his spinal column broken by a rock.

"Wrap him up in a covering, and put him in a tram," ordered the captain. "Now for the lad; look sharp."

Maheu gave a last blow, and an opening was made, communicating with the men who were clearing away the soil from the other side. They shouted out that they had just found Jeanlin, unconscious, with both legs broken, still breathing. It was the father who took up the little one in his arms, with clenched jaws constantly uttering "My God!" to express his grief, while Catherine and the other women again began to shriek.

A procession was quickly formed. Bébert had brought back Bataille, who was harnessed to the trams. In the first lay Chicot's corpse, supported by Étienne; in the second, Maheu was seated with Jeanlin, still unconscious, on his knees, covered by a strip of wool torn from the ventilation door. They started at a walking pace. On each tram was a lamp like a red star. Then behind followed the row of miners, some fifty shadows in single file. Now that they were overcome by fatigue, they trailed their feet, slipping in the mud, with the mournful melancholy of a flock stricken by an epidemic. It took them nearly half an hour to reach the pit-eye. This procession beneath the earth, in the midst of deep darkness, seemed never to end through galleries which bifurcated and turned and unrolled.

At the pit-eye Richomme, who had gone on before, had ordered an empty cage to be reserved. Pierron immediately loaded the two trams. In the first Maheu remained with his wounded little one on his knees, while in the other Étienne kept Chicot's corpse between his arms to hold it up. When the men had piled themselves up in the other decks the cage rose. It took two minutes. The rain from the tubbing fell very cold, and the men looked up towards the air impatient to see daylight.

Fortunately a trammer sent to Dr. Vanderhaghen's had found him and brought him back. Jeanlin and the dead man were placed in the captains' room, where, from year's end to year's end, a large fire burnt. A row of buckets with warm water was ready for washing feet; and, two mattresses having been spread on the floor, the man and the child were placed on them. Maheu and Étienne alone entered. Outside, putters, miners, and boys were running about, forming groups and talking in a low voice.

As soon as the doctor had glanced at Chicot:

"Done for! You can wash him."

Two overseers undressed and then washed with a sponge this corpse blackened with coal and still dirty with the sweat of work.

"Nothing wrong with the head," said the doctor again, kneeling on Jeanlin's mattress. "Nor the chest either. Ah! it's the legs which have given."

He himself undressed the child, unfastening the cap, taking off the jacket, drawing off the breeches and shirt with the skill of a nurse. And the poor little body appeared, as lean as an insect, stained with black dust and yellow earth, marbled by bloody patches. Nothing could be made out, and they had to wash him also. He seemed to grow leaner beneath the sponge, the flesh so pallid and transparent that one could see the bones. It was a pity to look on this last degeneration of a wretched race, this mere nothing that was suffering and half crushed by the falling of the rocks. When he was clean they perceived the bruises on the thighs, two red patches on the white skin.

Jeanlin, awaking from his faint, moaned. Standing up at the foot of the mattress with hands hanging down, Maheu was looking at him and large tears rolled from his eyes.

"Eh, are you the father?" said the doctor, raising his eyes; "no need to cry then, you can see he is not dead. Help me instead."

He found two simple fractures. But the right leg gave him some anxiety, it would probably have to be cut off.

At this moment the engineer, Négrel, and Dansaert, who had been informed, came up with Richomme. The first listened to the captain's narrative with an exasperated air. He broke out: Always this cursed timbering! Had he not repeated a hundred times that they would leave their men down there! and those brutes who talked about going out on strike if they were forced to timber more solidly. The worst was that now the Company would have to pay for the broken pots. M. Hennebeau would be pleased!

"Who is it?" he asked of Dansaert, who was standing in silence before the corpse which was being wrapped up in a sheet.

"Chicot! one of our good workers," replied the chief captain. "He has three children. Poor chap!"

Dr. Vanderhaghen ordered Jeanlin's immediate removal to his parents'. Six o'clock struck, twilight was already coming on, and they would do well to remove the corpse also; the engineer gave orders to harness the van and to bring a stretcher. The wounded child was placed on the stretcher while the mattress and the dead body were put into the van.

Some putters were still standing at the door talking with some miners who were waiting about to look on. When the door reopened there was silence in the group. A new procession was then formed, the van in front, then the stretcher, and then the train of people. They left the mine square and went slowly up the road to the settlement. The first November cold had denuded the immense plain; the night was now slowly burying it like a shroud fallen from the livid sky.

Excerpt from *A New England Girlhood, Outlined from Memory* by Lucy Larcom, 1889

SOURCE: Larcom, Lucy. 1889. *A New England Girlhood, Outlined from Memory.* Boston and New York: Houghton, Mifflin and Company.

Introduction

In this excerpt from her memoir, *A New England Girlhood, Outlined from Memory* (1889), Lucy Larcom describes how she began working at a mill in Lowell, Massachusetts, in 1836, after her father died. Larcom was only twelve when she became a bobbin girl. At first she appreciated her escape from the classroom. But soon the tedium of industrial labor prompted Larcom to reevaluate her feelings about education. After working at the mill for ten years, Larcom became a schoolteacher and successful poet. Her poems often celebrated the outdoors, a subject of her daydreams during her hours in the mill. She also edited a magazine for children entitled *Our Young Folks*.

For the first time in our lives, my little sister and I became pupils in a grammar school for both girls and boys, taught by a man. I was put with her into the sixth class, but was sent the very next day into the first. I did not belong in either, but somewhere between. And I was very uncomfortable in my promotion, for though the reading and spelling and grammar and geography were perfectly easy, I had never studied anything but mental arithmetic, and did not know how to "do a sum." We had to show, when called up to recite, a slateful of sums, "done" and "proved." No explanations were ever asked of us.

The girl who sat next to me saw my distress, and offered to do my sums for me. I accepted her proposal, feeling, however, that I was a miserable cheat. But I was afraid of the master, who was tall and gaunt, and used to stalk across the school-room, right over the desk-tops, to find out if there was any mischief going on. Once, having caught a boy annoying a seat-mate with a pin, he punished the offender by pursuing him around the school-room, sticking a pin into his shoulder whenever he could overtake him. And he had a fearful leather strap, which was sometimes used even upon the shrinking palm of a little girl. If he should find out that I was a pretender and deceiver, as I knew that I was, I could not guess what might happen to me. He never did, however. I was left unmolested in the ignorance which I deserved. But

I never liked the girl who did my sums, and I fancied she had a decided contempt for me.

There was a friendly looking boy always sitting at the master's desk; they called him "the monitor." It was his place to assist scholars who were in trouble about their lessons, but I was too bashful to speak to him, or to ask assistance of anybody. I think that nobody learned much under that regime, and the whole school system was soon after entirely reorganized.

Our house was quickly filled with a large feminine family. As a child, the gulf between little girlhood and young womanhood had always looked to me very wide. I supposed we should get across it by some sudden jump, by and by. But among these new companions of all ages, from fifteen to thirty years, we slipped into womanhood without knowing when or how.

Most of my mother's boarders were from New Hampshire and Vermont, and there was a fresh, breezy sociability about them which made them seem almost like a different race of beings from any we children had hitherto known.

We helped a little about the housework, before and after school, making beds, trimming lamps, and washing dishes. The heaviest work was done by a strong Irish girl, my mother always attending to the cooking herself. She was, however, a better caterer than the circumstances required or permitted. She liked to make nice things for the table, and, having been accustomed to an abundant supply, could never learn to economize. At a dollar and a quarter a week for board, (the price allowed for mill-girls by the corporations) great care in expenditure was necessary. It was not in my mother's nature closely to calculate costs, and in this way there came to be a continually increasing leak in the family purse. The older members of the family did everything they could, but it was not enough. I heard it said one day, in a distressed tone, "The children will have to leave school and go into the mill."

There were many pros and cons between my mother and sisters before this was positively decided. The mill-agent did not want to take us two little girls, but consented on condition we should be sure to attend school the full number of months prescribed each year. I, the younger one, was then between eleven and twelve years old.

I listened to all that was said about it, very much fearing that I should not be permitted to do the coveted work. For the feeling had already frequently come to me, that I was the one too many in the overcrowded family nest. Once, before we left our old home, I had heard a neighbor condoling with my mother because there were so many of us, and her emphatic reply had been a great relief to my mind:—

"There isn't one more than I want. I could not spare a single one of my children."

But her difficulties were increasing, and I thought it would be a pleasure to feel that I was not a trouble or burden or expense to anybody. So I went to my first day's work in the mill with a light heart. The novelty of it made it seem easy, and it really was not hard, just to change the bobbins on the spinning-frames every three quarters of an hour or so, with half a dozen other little girls who were doing the same thing. When I came back at night, the family began to pity me for my long, tiresome day's work, but I laughed and said,—

"Why, it is nothing but fun. It is just like play."

And for a little while it was only a new amusement; I liked it better than going to school and "making believe" I was learning when I was not. And there was a great deal of play mixed with it. We were not occupied more than half the time. The intervals were spent frolicking around among the spinning-frames, teasing and talking to the older girls, or entertaining ourselves with games and stories in a corner, or exploring, with the overseer's permission, the mysteries of the carding-room, the dressing-room, and the weaving-room.

I never cared much for machinery. The buzzing and hissing and whizzing of pulleys and rollers and spindles and flyers around me often grew tiresome. I could not see into their complications, or feel interested in them. But in a room below us we were sometimes allowed to peer in through a sort of blind door at the great waterwheel that carried the works of the whole mill. It was so huge that we could only watch a few of its spokes at a time, and part of its dripping rim, moving with a slow, measured strength through the darkness that shut it in. It impressed me with something of the awe which comes to us in thinking of the great Power which keeps the mechanism of the universe in motion. Even now, the remembrance of its large, mysterious movement, in which every little motion of every noisy little wheel was involved, brings back to me a verse from one of my favorite hymns:—

"Our lives through various scenes are drawn, And vexed by trifling cares, While Thine eternal thought moves on Thy undisturbed affairs."

There were compensations for being shut in to daily toil so early. The mill itself had its lessons for us. But it was not, and could not be, the right sort of life for a child, and we were happy in the knowledge that, at the longest, our employment was only to be temporary.

When I took my next three months at the grammar school, everything there was changed, and I too was changed. The teachers were kind, and thorough in their instruction; and my mind seemed to have been ploughed up during that year of work, so that knowledge took root in it easily. It was a great delight to me to study, and at the end of the three months the master told me that I was prepared for the high school.

But alas! I could not go. The little money I could earn—one dollar a week, besides the price of my board—was needed in the family, and I must return to the mill. It was a severe disappointment to me, though I did not say so at home. I did not at all accept the conclusion of a neighbor whom I heard talking about it with my mother. His daughter was going to the high school, and my mother was telling him how sorry she was that I could not.

"Oh," he said, in a soothing tone, "my girl hasn't got any such head-piece as yours has. Your girl doesn't need to go."

Of course I knew that whatever sort of a "head-piece" I had, I did need and want just that very opportunity to study. I think the resolution was then formed, inwardly, that I would go to school again, some time, whatever happened. I went back to my work, but now without enthusiasm. I had looked through an open door that I was not willing to see shut upon me.

I began to reflect upon life rather seriously for a girl of twelve or thirteen. What was I here for? What could I make of myself? Must I submit to be carried along with the current, and do just what everybody else did? No: I knew I should not do that, for there was a certain Myself who was always starting up with her own original plan or aspiration before me, and who was quite indifferent as to what people generally thought.

Well, I would find out what this Myself was good for, and what she should be!

Excerpt from a Report on Child Labor in New York City Tenements by Mary Van Kleeck, 1908

SOURCE: Van Kleeck, Mary. 1908. *Charities and the Commons*, January 18. U.S. Department of Labor, Wirtz Labor Library.

Introduction

The following excerpt is from a report on child labor in New York City prepared by Mary Van Kleeck in January, 1908. Van Kleeck, a member of the settlement house movement, studied women factory workers and child laborers in order to gather evidence to support state legislative reforms. In New York City during the early twentieth century, children were protected by law from working in factories. However, employers evaded this regulation by giving children piecework to do at home. In her report, Van Kleeck attempts to persuade readers that the exploitation of child labor in urban tenements is as harmful as their exploitation in more traditional workplaces such as factories, mills, and mines. For the next three decades, both from within government and without, Van Kleeck tried to improve laws for the protection of children and women. Eventually she turned to socialism for answers, criticizing even New Deal measures for weakening workers and unions.

The following brief report gives the results of a joint investigation made during the months from October, 1906, to April, 1907, into the labor of children in manufacture in tenement houses in New York City. The National Consumers' League and the Consumers' League of New York City, the National and New York Child Labor Committees, and the College Settlements Association co-operated in the undertaking.

In the most thickly populated districts of New York City, especially south of Fourteenth street, little children are often seen on the streets carrying large bundles of unfinished garments, or boxes containing materials for making artificial flowers. This work is given out by manufacturers or contractors to be finished in tenement homes, where the labor of children of any age may be utilized. For the laws of New York state, prohibiting the employment of children under fourteen years of age in factories, stores, or other specified work-places, have never been extended to home workrooms. In this fact is presented a child labor problem,—as yet scarcely touched,—namely: How to prevent employment of young children in home work in manufacture?

So difficult has been the problem of regulating by law the conditions of employment in home workrooms, that advance in measures to protect children against premature toil in factories has had no parallel in provisions designed to regulate manufacture in tenement homes. Between these two systems of manufacture,—one carried on in factories and the other in the homes of the workers,—there are, therefore, some striking contrasts in the law. No maker of artificial flowers can employ in his factory any child under fourteen years of age, but he may give out work to an Italian family, in whose tenement rooms flowers are made by six children, aged two and one-half, five, eight, ten, fourteen and sixteen years. In another family Angelo, aged fourteen years, cannot work legally in a factory until he reaches a higher grade in school, nor can he work at home during hours when school is in session, but his little sister Maria, aged three years, because she is not old enough to go to school and because the home work law contains no prohibition of child labor, may help her mother pull bastings and sew on buttons. A public school teacher notices that Eva and Mary R., aged eleven and ten years, are pale and under-nourished, but although the compulsory education law supports her in requiring their attendance in school during school hours, she cannot prevent their making flowers at home from three o'clock until nine or ten at night. Many good citizens would demand the prosecution of a manufacturer who employed in his factory Tony aged four years, Maria aged nine, Rose aged ten, Lousia aged eleven, and Josephine aged thirteen years. For such an offense the employer might be fined $100 for each child under fourteen years of age found at work in his factory. Yet public has not raised an effective protest against the same employer when he turns these children's home into a branch of his factory and gives them work in which event the smallest child in the family joins through long hours under a necessity as imperious in its demand for the constant work and attention of the child as would be the commands of a foreman in a factory.

In brief, the law which regulates home work manufacture in New York City, contains no provisions to prevent the employment of children nor to restrict the working hours of minors or women. It provides merely that work on certain specified articles (forty-one in number) given out by manufacturers or contractors, may not be carried on in a tenement living room, unless the owner of the house has first obtained a license from the New York State Department of Labor. Any articles not named in the law may legally be manufactured in unlicensed houses.

That the law in New York state does not protect more effectively these child workers in tenement homes, is due not to a lack of opposition to premature employment of children, but to the impossibility of dealing with the problem merely as a child labor question apart from deep-rooted evils essential to the "sweating system," of which home work is an important part. The evils of the system,—intense competition among unskilled workers in a crowded district, low wages, unrestricted hours of work, irregularity of employment, and utilization of child labor,—are the very conditions which make the system possible and profitable to the employer. Any effective attempt to improve conditions must therefore be an attack upon the sweating system. The manufacturer or contractor, whose employees work in their home, escapes responsibility entailed by the presence of workers in his factory. He saves costs of rent, heat, and light; avoids the necessity of keeping the force together and giving them regular employment when work is slack. And by turning the workers' homes into branches of the factory, he escapes in them the necessity of observing the factory laws. Instead of the manifold restrictions which apply to employees working in the factory, he is here responsible only for keeping a list of his home workers and he may not send any goods, which are named in the home work law into a tenement which has not been licensed.

SOME TYPICAL CASES

The salient features of child labor in home work in New York City may best be illustrated by describing conditions of work of a few of the children so employed, indicating the baffling nature of the problem and at the same time disclosing the serious defect in the present law already described,— its failure to prevent child labor.

If fifty of these children could be gathered together to tell their stories, they would be found to illustrate very distinct conditions under which work is carried on in tenement homes. There is the child of the very poor family who, for various reasons, has fallen below the level of economic independence, and is receiving partial support from a relief society. Another child belongs to a family whose earnings from employment outside the home are entirely adequate for support, but who because of the custom of the neighborhood and a desire to earn a little extra money, take work from a factory to be done at home by members who would otherwise be non-wage earners, the mother and the younger children. In other cases supplementary income derived from home work enables wage earners in outside employments to work with less regularity or to underbid their competitors.

Aside from differences in family circumstances, the children's employment varies greatly in regularity. One child goes every day to school and works only when school is not in session. Another, although of school age, has been kept at home more or less regularly throughout the day, to make flowers or pull bastings. Others, ever since their arrival in the United States, have succeeded in escaping the truant officer, to add their daily earnings to the family income. And although living in the most crowded districts of New York City have never learned to speak or write the English language. Finally there are those who, although they take little part in work brought from the factories, nevertheless bear the burden of the home work system by being compelled to care for younger children or do house work while the mother sews or makes flowers or engages in some other of the numerous varieties of work carried on in tenement homes.

The children are found to illustrate also various phases of the law's application, according to their relation to compulsory education on the one hand and the attempted regulation of home work on the other. This relation of the child to the law demands especial emphasis as illustrating concretely the scope of present regulation.

Index

*Page numbers in **boldface** indicate main article on subject. Those in italics indicate illustrations, figures, and tables.*

Burt, Sir Cyril, **125**

Business curriculum. *See* Commercial curriculum

Busing, school desegregation and, 730

Byzantium, 592

C

Caldwell, J. C., 361–362

Calling All Girls, 811

Calvin, John, 700, 701

Calvinist Christianity, emotional life and, 315
    See also Christianity

Calvin Klein (company), *163*, 163–164

Calyo, Nicolino, *346*

Cameron, Julia Margaret, *453*, 460, 672

Camp Fire Girls, 385, 386, 406–407

Camps, summer. *See* Summer camps

Campus revolts in the 1960s, **127–129**
    See also Youth activism

Canada, **129–131**
    child labor, 160
    colonial period: New France, 130
    fertility rates, 362
    First Nations: Kwakiutl and Huron, 129–130
    placing out, 680
    schooling in the nineteenth century, 130–131
    See also Native American children

Canons Regular of Saint Augustine, 266

Capital punishment for youth, 515, 517

Capparomi, Jennie, *296*

Captain America (comic book hero), 219, 220

Care, child. *See* Child care

The Care and Feeding of Children (Holt), 651

Caries, dental, 258–260

Carnegie, Andrew, 192

Carnegie Foundation for the Advancement of Teaching, 724

Carnegie units, 511

Carroll, Lewis, **131–132**
    children's literature, *179*, 182
    images of childhood, 460
    photographs of children, 162, *672*, *675*
    Victorian art, 866
    See also Children's literature

Cars
    and accidents, 12, 14
    as toys, **132–133**
    in youth culture, *912*, 915

Carstens, C. C., 771

Cartoons, 273, 274, *274*, *275*

CAS. *See* New York Children's Aid Society (CAS)

Casa dei Bambini (Children's House), 602

Cassatt, Mary, **133–134**, 458, *575*
    See also Images of childhood; Mothering and motherhood

Castle Waiting series, 221

Catacomb of Priscilla, 566

Cathedral schools. *See* Convent schools (cathedral schools)

Catherine of Siena, Saint, 63

Catholicism, **134–138**, *135*
    American Catholicism and childhood, 136–137
    artificial insemination, 71
    baptism, 80, 134, 135
    bastardy, 86
    birth control, 97–99
    Brazil, 114, 115
    coeducation and same-sex schooling, 214
    communion, first, 223–224
    confirmation, 240
    early Church, 134–136
    education, Europe, 302, 303–304
    fathering and fatherhood, 350
    girls' schools, 387–388
    Helene, 414
    literacy, 553–554
    Madonna, religious, 568
    Mortara abduction, **603**
    naming, 614, 615
    New York Children's Aid Society, 622–623
    orphanages, 638, 887
    orphan trains, 643
    Reformation, 250, 288, 350, 614
    self-starvation, 63
    sexual abuse, 143–144
    Sunday, 800
    youth ministries, 919
    See also Parochial schools; Protestant Reformation

Catholic Youth Organization (CYO), 85, 107, 785, 919

The Cat in the Hat (Seuss), *182*, 282

Cavities, 258–260

CCA (Comics Code Authority), 220–221

CCC (Civilian Conservation Corps) (U.S.), 909, 910

CDC (Centers for Disease Control and Prevention) (U.S.), 863

Cele, Joan, 536

Cells and bells schools, 727

Centers for Disease Control and Prevention (CDC) (U.S.), 863

Central America. *See* Latin America

Centuries of Childhood (Ariès), 66–67
    age and development, 38
    boyhood, 108
    history of childhood, 422–423, 426
    medieval and Renaissance Europe, 590
    play, 683, 828
    theories of childhood, 821

Century of the Child (Key), **138**, 523
    See also Children's rights; Key, Ellen

Cesarean section, 234, 235–236, 237, 631

Chadwick, Edwin, 764–765

Chairs, high and low, 375

Challenge Program (California), 737

Chambers, Robert, 153

Chapbooks, 4, 338

Charcot, Jean-Martin, 96

Charity schools, 849, 850

Charivari, **138–140**, 911, *911*

Charter schools, **140–141**, 729
    See also Education, United States; School choice

Cherry Ripe (Millais), 460, *865*

Cherubs as images of childhood, 450

Chess, child prodigies in, 165

Chickamy (game), 792, 793

Child, L. Maria, 468

Child abuse, **141–144**
    child saving, 195
    defining, 141–142
    foster care, 364
    Freud, Sigmund, 370, 371
    incest, 463–464
    innocence and abuse, 142–143
    juvenile justice, 514
    law, 544–545
    preventing and prosecuting, 143–144
    See also Sexual abuse; Sexual abuse; Violence against children

Child Abuse Prevention and Treatment Act (1972) (U.S.), 364

Child analysis, 369, 526–527, 595–596

The Child and the Curriculum (Dewey), 268

Childbirth. *See* Conception and birth

Child Bitten by a Crayfish (Anguissola), *314*, 450

Child care, **144–152**
    in-home, **144–146**, 604–605
    institutional forms, **146–149**, 190

Gustavus Adolphus (king of Sweden), 479

Gutmann, Bessie Pease, **409**

  See also Images of childhood

Gutmann, Lucille, 409

GutsMuths, J. C. F., **409–410**

Guy, Seymour, 458, *827*

Guy Fawkes Day, 414

Gymnasium schooling, 306, **410–411**

  See also Education, Europe; Latin school; Lycée

Gymnastics, 409–410, **411–412**

  See also Physical education; Sports

Gymnastik für die Jugend (Gymnastics for youth) (GutsMuths), 410, 411

H

Haas, Louis, 424

Hadrian (emperor of Rome), 745

Haiselden, Harry, 329

Hall, Granville Stanley, **413**

  adolescence and youth, 16, 812

  adolescent medicine, 20

  Boy Scouts, 79

  child care, 150

  child study, 200–201

  junior high school, 511–512

  puberty, 703

  sandbox, 723

  scientific child rearing, 734

  theories of play, 830

  youth culture, 914

  See also Child development, history of the concept of

Hall, Joseph, 788

Hallesches Waisenhaus (Halle Orphanage), 366–367

Halloween, **414**

Halvini, David Weiss, 435

Hammer v. Dagenhart (1918), **414–415**, 957–959

  See also Child labor in the West

Hampstead War Nurseries, 369

Hampton Institute (Virginia), 871

Hanawalt, Barbara, 683–684

"Hands to mouths" ratio, 295, 297

Harding, Warren G., 751, 752

The Hardy Boys series, 521

Harmon v. Harmon (1922), 278

Harris, Benjamin, 4, 179

Harry Potter and J. K. Rowling, **415–416**, *416*

  See also Children's literature

Hart, John, 3

Harvard College, 902, 903

Hasbro, 842, 843

Haskell Boarding School (Lawrence, Kansas), 53–54

Hathaway, Mary, 46

Hauptmann, Bruno Richard, 553

Hauptschule (secondary schools), 306

Hausa, 772

Hawes, Joseph M., 206, 427–428

Hays, William Harrison, 587, 608

Hays Code, 587, 608

Headmasters' Conference (Britain), 704

Head Start, **416–417**

  See also Education, United States

Healy, William, **417–418**, 596

  See also Delinquency

Hearnshaw, L. S., 125

Hearst, Patricia, 7

Hebrew Technical Institute (New York City), 871

Hecht, George J., 654

Hecht, Tobias, 530

Heckel, Erich, *280*, 460

He-Man and Masters of the Universe, 840

Henry IV (king of France), 471, 472

Hepatitis, 246, 247

  See also Contagious diseases

Herbart, J. F., **418–419**

  See also Education, Europe

Heredity, 328–329, 490

Hergé. *See* Tintin and Hergé

Héroard, Jean, 471, 472

Herod I (king of Judea), 9

L'Heure Joyeuse libraries, 192

Heyde, Georg, 842

Hiding the Switch game, 685

Higgonet, Anne, 453, 461

High school, **419–421**

  dating, 253, 254

  as mass institution, 310–311

  student government, 794–795

  teenagers, 809

  urban school systems, 851–853

  See also Junior high school

Hilda of Whitby, Saint, 249

Hillel, Rabbi, 501

Hilpert family, 841

Himmelweit, Hilde, 588

Himmler, Heinrich, 432, 433

Hinduism, 227, 465, 466

Hine, Lewis, *160*, 161, *296*, **421–422**

  See also Photographs of children

Hiner, N. Ray, 206, 427–428

Hints and Directions for Building, Fitting Up, and Arranging School Rooms (Lancaster), 725

Hippies, 915

Hippocrates, 56, 63, 657, 712

Hispanic children and youth, 690, 730–731

Histoire des populations françaises (Ariès), 67

Historia scholastica (Comestor), 90, 91

The Historical Meaning of the Crisis in Psychology (Vygotsky), 872

Histories, ou countes du temps passé, avec des Moralitez (Perrault), 181

Historiography. *See* Comparative history of childhood; History of childhood

History of childhood, **422–430**

  Europe, **422–426**

  United States, **426–430**

  See also Comparative history of childhood

History of Childhood (deMause), 423, 426

The History of Little Goody Two-Shoes, 180

The History of the Development of Higher Psychological Functions (Vygotsky), 872

The History of the Fairchild Family (Sherwood), 181

Hitler, Adolf, 430, 431, 432

Hitler Youth, *343*, 344, **430–431**, *431*

  See also Communist Youth; Fascist youth

HIV. *See* AIDS

Hobbes, Sir Thomas, 539

Hobbies. *See* Collections and hobbies

The Hobbitt (Tolkien), 559

Hobsbawm, Eric, 425

Hoffman, Heinrich, 182

Hoff Sommers, Christine, 108

Hogarth, William, *330*, 452, *670*, *671*, 911

Holbein, Hans (the Younger), 450, *451*

Holidays, commercialization of, 243

Holmes, Lowell, 583

Holocaust, 367–368, **431–434**, 446, 877

  Jewish ghetto education and the, **434–435**

Holt, Luther Emmett, 651

Homeless children and runaways in the United States, **436–438**

  See also Street arabs and street urchins

Homer, Winslow, **438–439**

  See also Images of childhood

Homeschooling, **439–440**

The Home Treasury (Cole), 181

Homework, **440–441**

Megan's laws, **594**, 664, 970–972

    See also Pedophilia

Meillassoux, Claude, 30

Mein Kampf (Hitler), 430

Menarche, **594–595**, 748, 812

    See also Girlhood; Puberty

Mengele, Josef, 433

Men I Have Fished With (Mather), 407

Mental hygiene, 156, **595–596**

Mental illness, **597–599**

Mental retardation. *See* Retardation

Metaphors, familial, 315–316

A methode, or comfortable beginning for all unlearned (Hart), 3

Metsu, Gabriel, *245*

Mexican American children and youth

    school desegregation, 730–731

    zoot suit riots, 925–926

Mexico, photographs of children, *401*, 546

    See also Latin America

Meyer, Adolf, 595

Meyer v. State of Nebraska, 959–962

Michtom, Morris, 807

Michtom, Rose, 807

Mickey Mouse, 273, 274, *274*

Microchip technology in toys, 842–843

Middle Ages. *See* Medieval and Renaissance Europe

Middle East, **599–601**, 776

Middle school literature, 184

    See also Children's literature

Midwifery. *See* Obstetrics and midwifery

Mifepristone, 239

Mignot (company), 841–842

Milicevic, Milan Ðuro, 293

Military service, child. *See* Soldier children

Millais, John Everett, *443*, 460, *571*, 865, *865*

Miller, Walter James, 865

Milliken v. Bradley (1974), 730

Milne, A. A., *181*

    See also Children's literature

Milton Bradley (company), 842, 843

A Mind That Found Itself (Beers), 595

Miner, Horace, 446

Mines and Collieries Act (1842) (Britain), 765

Ministries, youth. *See* Youth ministries

Les Misérables (Hugo), 457

Miss Anna Ward with Her Dog (Reynolds), *669*

Missbrukad kvinnokraft (Misused womanpower) (Key), 523

Mitchell, Mary, 578–579

Modell, John, 420

Model soldiers. *See* Toy soldiers (tin soldiers)

Modern Adolescence and Youth (Krausman Ben-Amos), 425

Monastic schools. *See* Convent schools (cathedral schools)

Monitorial system, 727, 849–850

"Monitoring the Future" surveys, 284

Montagu, Lady Mary Wortley, 658, 861

Montessori, Maria, 79, 241, **601–602**, 830–831

    See also Education, Europe

The Montessori Method (Montessori), 602

Moody, Eleazar, 575–576, 577, 578

Morgenstern, Naomi, 434

Morisot, Berthe, *349*, 458

Morozov, Pavel, 230

Mortality

    Brazil, 117

    children's exposure to death, 401

    economics and children in Western societies, 296, 297

    Europe, 360

    history of childhood, 423

    images of childhood, 451, 452

    medieval and Renaissance Europe, 593

    neonatal, 475, 477

    post-neonatal, 475

    slavery, United States, 757

    See also Grief, death, funerals; Infant mortality; Life expectancy; Maternal mortality

Mortara, Edgardo, 603

Mortara abduction, **603**

Moses (Biblical figure), 91, 92

Mosquitoes, contagious diseases and, 245, 248

Mother Goose rhymes, 182

Mother Goose's Tales (Perrault), 181

Mothering and motherhood, **603–608**, *604*

    agricultural societies, 605–606

    care-giving, 603, 604

    child psychology, 168

    children's rights, 186

    China, 606

    dependent children, 261, 262–263

    drugs, 283

    Dutch Republic, 424

    France, 606, 607

    importance of, 650

    industrial societies, 606–607

    Japan, 604, 605

    Latin America, 531

    law, children and the, 540

    love, 561, 562

    motherhood, 603–604, *604*

    mothering, 604–605

    post-World War II, 652

    republican motherhood, 650

    Russia, 605, 606

    scientific child rearing, 735

    United States, 605, 607

    See also Fathering and fatherhood; Madonna, secular; Working mothers

Mothers' pensions, 262–263

Mother's Songs, Games and Stories (Froebel), 374–375

A Mother Teaching Her Son (Mulready), 866

Motion Picture Producers and Distributors of America, 587, 608

Motion Picture Research Council, 587

Mouly, Françoise, 221

Movies, **608–610**

    childhood and the media, 586–587

    child stars, 198–199

    comic book adaptations, 221

    consumer culture, 243, 244

    Disney, 274, 275, *275*

    fear, 356

Mozart, Wolfgang Amadeus, 211

Muhammad, Prophet, 497

Mulready, William, 866

Multiculturalism, children's literature and, 184

Multiple births, 234, 358, 494, **610**, 753

    See also Fertility drugs

Munch, Edvard, 460, *702*

Muscular Christianity, 784, 869

Music, child prodigies in, 165

Music education, **610–611**

Music Television (MTV), 805

Mussolini, Benito, 343, 344, 602

Mutual education, 725

My Early Life (Churchill), 841

Myerhoff, Barbara, 714

The Myth of Motherhood (Badinter), 423–424

N

Nabokov, Vladimir, 558–559

Nag factor in advertising, 27, 28, 302, 428, 840

Naismith, James, 784

Naked Breton Boy (Gauguin), 460

Naming, **613–616**

    African-American children and youth, 36

OECD (Organisation for Economic Cooperation and Development), 306–307

Oedipus complex, 370–371, 481

Office of Indian Affairs (U.S.), 51, 52

Old Deluder Satan Act (1647) (Massachusetts), 393, 849

The Old Musician (Manet), 457, *893*

Old Testament, imagery of children and childhood in, 92, 93
    See also Bible

Oliver Twist (Dickens), **633–634**

Olympic games, 412

Onania, 581

L'Onanisme (Tissott), 581

Oneida Community, 149

Onesimus (slave), 325

"On Good Manners for Boys" *(De civilitate morum puerorum)* (Desiderius Erasmus of Rotterdam), 267

"On Infants' Early Deaths" (Gregory of Nyssa), 210

On the Origin of Species (Darwin), 153

"On Vainglory and the Right Way for Parents to Bring Up Their Children" (Chrysostom), 210

Open air school movement, 191, **634–635**, 726, 727–728
    See also Children's spaces; School buildings and architecture

Open plan schools, 191–192

Opie, Iona, 483, **635–636**, *684*, 685, 792
    See also Fairy tales and fables

Opie, Peter, **635–636**, *684*, 685, 792

Opie, Robert, 483

"Optional Protocol to the Convention on the Rights of the Child on Involvement of Children in Armed Conflict," 778

Oral phase of infant sexuality, 481

Orbis sensualism pictus (Visible World) (Comenius), 3, 179, *218*

Order of World Scouts, 111, 112

Ordo Baptismi Parvulorum, 80

Oregon, compulsory school attendance in, 678–679

Oregon v. Mitchell (1970), 846

Orff, Carl, 611

Organic selection, 154

Organisation for Economic Cooperation and Development (OECD), 306–307

Organized recreation and youth groups, 196, **636–638**
    See also specific groups by name

Original sin, 209–210, 227–228

"The Origin and Development of Psychoanalysis" (Freud), 1008–1010

Orme, Nicholas, 669

Orphanages, **638–640**
    Catholicism, 638, 887
    children's spaces, 192
    Latin America, 531, 534
    United States, 150, 261, 638–640
    See also Baby farming; Orphans

Orphans, **640–643**
    Africa, 327
    early modern Europe, 290
    family patterns, 340
    inheritance and property, 487
    Judaism, 641
    in literature, 633–634
    in series books, 739
    Venice (Italy), 641, 642
    See also Abandonment; Foundlings

Orphan trains, 113–114, 150, 623, **643–644**, 680
    See also Foster care; New York Children's Aid Society (CAS)

Osgood, Rev. David, 407

Our Gang films, 198, 199

Our Lady of Guadalupe, *568*, 569

Ovarian cancer, fertility drugs and, 358–359

Ovarian hyperstimulation syndrome, 358

Ovulation induction medications. *See* Fertility drugs

Owen, Robert, 191

The Oxford Dictionary of Nursery Rhymes (Opie and Opie), 635

Oxford Pledge, 906

Oxford University, 901, 906

P

Pacifier, **645–646**

Paideia, 58

Paidology. *See* Child study

Pall Mall Gazette, 166

Pampers, 270

Panchatantra (Five Books or Five Teachings) (Johannes of Capua), 337

Pap in infant feeding, 886

Parades, **646–648**, *647*

Parens patriae, 335, 336, 539, 541, 542, 543
    See also Law, children and the

Parental love. *See* Love

Parenting, **648–654**
    Catholicism, 135, 136, 137
    children's rights, 186–187
    education for, 538–539
    Islam, 499

styles, 87–88
    and welfare state, 768–769
    See also Fathering and fatherhood; Mothering and motherhood; Same-sex parenting

Parents Magazine, **654–655**
    See also Child-rearing advice literature

Parent-teacher associations, **655**
    See also Education, United States

Parham v. J. R. (1979), 187

Parisian-style collegiate system, 537

Parks, Gordon, *122*, 461

Parks as children's spaces, 193

Parley, Peter, 181

Parochial schools, 136, 214, **655–657**
    See also Catholicism; Private and independent schools

Parsons, Talcott, 772

Partners in Transition, 21

Passions in emotional life, 315, 316

Pasteur, Louis, 659, 862

Pathogens, 244–245, 249

Patmore, Coventry, 571

Paton, Joseph Noël, *866*

Patria potestas, 348–349, 531

Patterson, Charlotte, 722

Patterson, Haywood, 736

Pavilion schools, 726

Pavlovians, 881, 882

Payne Study and Experiment Fund, 587

Pay schools, 849, 850

Pears' Soap, *443*, 457

Pease, Louis, 113

Pedagogical Anthropology (Montessori), 601–602

Pedagogical strategy of zoos, 925

Pedal cars, 133

Pediatrics, 175, *657*, **657–661**, *658*, 734
    See also Children's hospitals; Contagious diseases; Epidemics

Pedophilia, **661–665**, *662*, *663*
    See also *Lolita* (Nabokov)

Penelope Boothby (Reynolds), *382*, 452

Penn, William, letter to wife and children, 938–940

Pennsylvania, working papers in, 899

Pennsylvania House of Refuge, 336

Pennsylvania Supreme Court, 543

People ex rel. Sinclair v. Sinclair, 277

Perkins, Lawrence Bradford, 728

Permissiveness in child-rearing advice literature, 172, 173, 781